WOMEN IN AMERICAN POLITICS
HISTORY AND MILESTONES

WOMEN IN AMERICAN POLITICS
HISTORY AND MILESTONES

DORIS WEATHERFORD

Los Angeles | London | New Delhi
Singapore | Washington DC

Los Angeles | London | New Delhi
Singapore | Washington DC

FOR INFORMATION:

CQ Press
An Imprint of SAGE Publications, Inc.
2455 Teller Road
Thousand Oaks, California 91320
E-mail: order@sagepub.com

SAGE Publications Ltd.
1 Oliver's Yard
55 City Road
London, EC1Y 1SP
United Kingdom

SAGE Publications India Pvt. Ltd.
B 1/I 1 Mohan Cooperative Industrial Area
Mathura Road, New Delhi 110 044
India

SAGE Publications Asia-Pacific Pte. Ltd.
33 Pekin Street #02-01
Far East Square
Singapore 048763

Development Editor: Linda Dziobek
Production Editor: Laura Stewart
Typesetter: C&M Digitals (P) Ltd.
Proofreader: Stefanie Storholt
Indexer: Enid Zafran
Cover Designer: Rose Storey
Marketing Manager: Kathryn Brummitt

Printed in the United States of America

Library of Congress Cataloging-in-Publication Data

Weatherford, Doris.

Women in American politics: history and milestones / Doris Weatherford.

v. cm.
Includes bibliographical references and indexes.

Contents: Preface — Battle for the vote — Female officeholders prior to the Nineteenth Amendment — Statewide elective officeholders — State representatives — State senators — United States representatives — United States Senators — Governors and lieutenant governors — Mayors — Presidential and vice-presidential candidates — Cabinet and subcabinet — Ambassadors — Pioneers in the judiciary — State courts — Federal courts — Political parties and conventions — Interest groups — Political action committees.

ISBN 978-1-60871-007-2

1. Women—Political activity—United States—History. I. Title.

HQ1236.5.U6W43 2012
324.0820973—dc23   2011044100

Editorial and Book Development Services by MTM Publishing, Inc.
New York City; www.mtmpublishing.com
Publisher/President: Valerie Tomaselli
VP, Book Development: Hilary Poole
Editorial Assistants: Zach Gajewski, Meghan McHugh, Abby Rugg

SFI Certified Sourcing
www.sfiprogram.org
SFI-00453

This book is printed on acid-free paper.

11 12 13 14 15 10 9 8 7 6 5 4 3 2 1

CONTENTS

FOREWORD

When I was a child, my parents taught me that I could grow up and become anything I wanted. I believed them. After all, I was born in 1966, in the era of women's empowerment. I never knew a time when there were no women in public office. My parents also taught me to reach for the stars and to follow my dreams. Just a few years later America witnessed Sally Ride literally prove them right. But it wasn't always that easy.

Ever since Abigail Adams told her husband to "remember the ladies," American women have been fighting to be included in our nation's collective memory. For years, women were told to wait their turn, to busy themselves with more important work, to let men do the talking.

Unable to remain quiet, unwilling to stand down, they resisted. They spoke up. They fought not with violence but with their voices, their pens, and their vote. This chorus started many years ago and continues today. Women are no longer barred from voting or owning property, but they still earn only 78 cents to every dollar a man earns. And though they make up more than half of the nation's population, they comprise only 17 percent of Congress.

Many firsts are cited in the pages of this reference: Jeannette Rankin, the first woman to serve in Congress, who is perhaps most famous for sticking to her principles and being the only member to vote against the United States entering World War I and World War II; Shirley Chisholm, the first African American woman to serve in Congress, who passionately spoke out on behalf of underserved and under-acknowledged members of society; and Bella Abzug, the first Jewish woman to be elected in her own right, whose words are a reminder to this day that a woman's place is in the House … and the Senate too.

But, even after the election of Nancy Pelosi as Speaker of the House, one first remains elusive. Former first lady, sitting U.S. senator, and eventual secretary of state Hillary Rodham Clinton in 2008 came closer than any woman

before her to being elected president. When she announced the end of her candidacy on June 7, 2008, to a capacity crowd at the National Building Museum in Washington, D.C., she left behind not only eighteen million cracks in the glass ceiling but also a path to the White House—rocky, hard-fought, and paved—for the women coming up behind her.

A woman's work is never done, and it is never easy. But the firsts—and the seconds, the thirds, and even the tenths—in this book illustrate that our work is not only valuable, it is vital.

Women bring an undeniably unique perspective to politics, and American democracy suffers when women's voices are excluded from the dialogue. Women have a different way of looking at policy and of approaching the obstacles before them. In my experience, women are especially effective at working across party lines, building consensus, and coming up with creative solutions to problems. That's why it was so devastating that in 2010, for only the second time in history, the number of women elected to serve in Congress declined. Women are already 50 percent less likely than men to consider running for office. In the tradition of Hillary Clinton and all the way back to Elizabeth Cady Stanton, they must work to increase the number of women who seek public office and remember that when they achieve something great—whether it is elected office or the corner office—they must reach behind and extend a hand to the next generation of women.

As a mother of two young girls, this concept is paramount to me. My daughters don't think twice about their mom being a member of Congress, as I've been in public office since before they were born. I have made it a priority not only to encourage them as young women in their own right but also to share the stories of the women who came before them, women who made it possible for their mom to run for office and serve as the first Jewish woman to represent Florida in the U.S. Congress.

And even that had its challenges. During my first election for state representative at the age of twenty-five, the fact that I was a woman did not give the good ol' boys club pause so much as my youth. The men didn't take me seriously because they thought I didn't stand a chance without a massive war chest and key connections. But what I lacked in resources I made up in shoe leather—knocking on twenty-five thousand doors that summer—and I won the six-way Democratic primary with 53 percent of the vote.

Thanks to my parents, it never occurred to me that my opportunities in life would be limited because I was a woman. It's important to me that I pass on this belief to my own children, and future generations, that women can achieve anything with hard work. At the very beginning of my career, I made a promise to myself that I would never be unsuccessful or lose an opportunity, a floor vote, or an election because I was outworked. And I owe a huge debt of gratitude to the women who spent years struggling to have their say, and be given their due, all with the hope that one day the tide would turn.

This important reference work documents a rising tide. But there is more work to do. And it is up to us—to the next generation of women—to set the example. Just as we look to Abigail Adams, Eleanor Roosevelt, and Hillary Clinton, the next generation is looking to us to ensure that women continue to rise and thrive in politics and in every other segment of our society.

Representative Debbie Wasserman Schultz (FL-20)
December 2011

PREFACE

Much like the old saw that those who do not know history are doomed to repeat it, an unfortunate lack of awareness of their history has caused political women to continue to invent wheels that have been invented earlier. Over and over again, individuals and the media announce something as a first that is not. Experience matters in politics, as in every other aspect of life, but women have repeatedly failed to avail themselves of the leadership skills and organizational strategies that have worked (or failed to work) in the past—because the past is not known or understood. This book aspires to begin correcting that mistake.

BRIEF OVERVIEW OF WOMEN'S POLITICAL HISTORY

While women's political activism for other causes predated the fight for their own right to vote, the suffrage movement that began in the mid-nineteenth century was the first robust engagement of women in political life. After men refused to allow their participation at the World Anti-Slavery Convention in London in 1840, Lucretia Mott and Elizabeth Cady Stanton launched the women's rights movement by organizing the first gathering in Seneca Falls, New York, in 1848. The 1850s were a time of great energy for both political and social change, and women's rights became a permanent part of the political landscape during that decade, as national conventions with representation from many states became annual occurrences. This momentum got lost during the Civil War, however, as women subjugated their own cause to that of others.

In the years following the war's end, women's political engagement and activity increased again. Women in at least a dozen political jurisdictions, from South Carolina to California tested the Fourteenth and Fifteenth Amendments to the U.S. Constitution by attempting to vote. The amendments were intended to give civil rights to black men, but not to women of any race. When the U.S. Supreme Court ruled in *Minor v. Happensett* (1875) that the gender-neutral language of the Fifteenth Amendment did not imply that women were granted any rights, women were forced to set out on a long political process. Overturning the decision meant either winning enfranchisement on a state-by-state basis or mounting the high hurdles of amending the U.S. Constitution.

Not surprisingly, the decades that followed were frustrating, especially as Susan B. Anthony and other leaders aged and died around the turn of the century. The West led the way, with Colorado and Idaho granting full voting rights in the 1890s. The movement truly revitalized with California's victory in 1911. In the East, younger and more polemically radical women, such as Alice Paul and Lucy Burns of the National Woman's Party, brought new attention. Brilliant strategist Carrie Chapman Catt led the mainstream organization when victory finally was achieved in 1920. It is useful for modern leaders to know that more than two million people paid dues to her organization, constituting a much greater proportion of the population than today's political groups.

In the first election in which all women could vote, 1922, many dozens were the first elected to offices in their state, but the Roaring Twenties developed as socially liberal and politically conservative. In terms of the election of women, that political conservatism continued in the 1930s, when the Great Depression meant that women gave up all sorts of jobs, including political ones, to men. World War II in the next decade again brought much social change, but little political achievement. The era nonetheless produced significant women who have been largely forgotten, including women who chaired the House Labor Committee and the House Veterans Committee.

Not until the 1960s did a movement revive the level of feminism that had won the vote in 1920. ("Revive," actually, is an exaggeration, as most 1960s activists thought they were inventing the proverbial wheel. Most had little to no awareness that they could have benefited from understanding their grandmothers' experience in politics.) This time period, commonly referred to as second-wave feminism, was fueled by Betty Friedan's 1963 groundbreaking analysis, *The Feminine Mystique*. Other hallmarks of the period included the 1964 presidential candidacy of Sen. Margaret Chase Smith, the 1965 Supreme Court ruling in *Griswold v. Connecticut* against the state's ban on contraceptive sales (even to married people), and the 1966 formation of the National Organization for Women, with Friedan as president.

The 1970s continued with more milestones. As measured by feminist legislation and women elected to new offices, another dip occurred in the 1980s. With 1992, the Year of the Woman, new precedents again were set, especially in the election of women to Congress. The 2000s, however, went measurably backward, and the periodic waves of feminism threaten extant sandcastles, which lack a sufficiently firm foundation grounded in knowledge of past dips and eddies. I trust that readers will find this book filled with inspiration that can reverse this negative trend. By learning and using the lessons of experience, perhaps another crash can be avoided akin to that which followed the victorious year of 1922, when women made a brilliant beginning at elective office but failed to follow through.

STRUCTURE AND FEATURES

Women in American Politics: History and Milestones is organized in a framework both logical and useful to readers and researchers. Chapter 1 begins with the campaign to win the vote, from 1840 to 1920, and the second chapter follows with the numerous women who were elected to office prior to 1920, both in places where they could vote and in places where men elected voteless women to office.

It continues with women in state legislatures. The first representatives were in Colorado in 1894; the first state senator, in the very next election, was in Utah. Other chapters focus on women in both houses of Congress, from the first elected in 1916 up through 2010, as well as state executive officers, governors, mayors, cabinet members, presidential candidates, and ambassadors. Chapters on the judiciary and on partisan policies are next. At the end is a brief essay on each of the fifty states. Much of the research is original, gathering material that will help students, scholars, teachers, speechwriters, lobbyists, and especially politicians to understand the complicities of American women and politics.

Dozens of tables cover everything from where the first women's rights conventions were held to which states have elected women as treasurers. Each table provides a somewhat different perspective, all intended to put the political process in order. Chapter 6, on women in the U.S. House, has the most. In chronological order, its twelve tables aim to create a sense of how the election of women happened—and what is happening now.

Women in American Politics is not merely a book of lists, however. Tables are accompanied by analyses of the complex and sometimes contradictory trends behind the facts of women's political milestones. The narrative describes how women achieved what they did in the differing categories of elective and appointive office. It puts elections in the context of their times and explains the ways in which differing political issues—as well as economic and social patterns—affected whether or not women won at the polls. Much of the information in this reference will surprise researchers and readers.

Along the way, sidebars offer stories illuminating the drama (and sometimes comedy) of political life—everything from a U.S. representative from Kentucky whose husband ran against her to Ambassador Florence "Daisy" Hurst Harriman's flight from fascists in Norway. Chapter 13 explicates how women entered the judiciary, and readers will learn that the first woman admitted to the bar in the Washington Territory was motivated to become a lawyer after being tried for murdering her husband. Among the sidebars are interviews with some contemporary women in politics, such as Florida's chief financial officer Alex Sink and Michigan governor Jennifer M. Granholm.

In addition to sidebars, each chapter has a section of biographies on women who may be famous (Hillary Rodham Clinton, for example, in the chapter on presidential candidates) or obscure. Among those who are obscure—but should not be—are Wyoming's Estelle Reel, the first woman appointed to a position high enough to require Senate confirmation; New Mexico's Soledad Chávez Chacón, the first female state secretary of state; and Utah's Martha Hughes Cannon, a polygamist physician and the nation's first female state senator. In Chapter 14, on state judiciaries, readers will discover that Florence Allen organized her fellow feminists to be elected to the Ohio Supreme Court in 1922. The chapter on mayors has a biography of Bertha Landes, elected in Seattle in 1926, and the chapter on cabinet officials highlights Frances Perkins, who, as labor secretary in the 1930s, implemented Social Security.

Familiar names include those from the past, such as Susan B. Anthony and Elizabeth Cady Stanton, to the modern, including Republicans Elizabeth Dole and Condoleezza Rice and Democrats Geraldine A. Ferraro and Nancy Pelosi.

NOTES ON POLITICAL TERMINOLOGY

Political terminology is a map for understanding the framework in which women have approached issues. Conservative means to conserve, to keep as is, to oppose change. In a political context, conservative implies an attachment to traditional behaviors and systems, which means, by definition, that conservatives can be expected to resist broad social and political movements such as feminism. Leading conservatives who opposed the right to vote are a feature of in Chapter 1. Like Phyllis Schlafly in the 1970s, anti-suffragists were well known in 1920 but because the change that they fought proved popular, these conservatives became obscure. A second example of this pattern is Iris Faircloth Blitch, a U.S. representative from Georgia who opposed racial integration in the 1950s and 1960s. Her reputation declined, and she is largely forgotten. Those who championed change, such as U.S. representative Shirley Anita Chisholm, are remembered as more heroic.

Those who worked for racial integration in the mid-twentieth century and for the abolition of slavery a century earlier were classified as liberal, which by dictionary definition means forwarding-thinking and open to new ideas. Its definition in terms of political science also stresses belief in gradual reform and planned, democratic change, as opposed to impulsiveness, violence, censorship, and armed force. Liberalism is not restricted to one party. Many of the initial Republican women in Congress were more liberal, especially on race, than their Democratic counterparts. Great variation can exist even within a party. Montana Republican Jeannette Rankin, the first woman in Congress, worked for the vote full time and was such a thorough-going pacifist that she opposed both World War I and World War II. The second woman in the U.S. House, Oklahoma's Mary Alice Robertson, also was a Republican but so inherently conservative that she had opposed her own right to vote.

The least ambiguous political term was adopted by Progressives, or Populists, who were vital to changing political discourse from the 1880s to the 1920s. As befits champions of progress toward improved democracy, the Progressive Party supported the vote and included women in leadership. The clearest examples of Progressive success were the two constitutional amendments ratified in 1913, predating women's full enfranchisement. The Sixteenth Amendment gave Congress the authority to collect income taxes, overturning U.S. Supreme Court action declaring such taxes unconstitutional. The Seventeenth Amendment provided for the direct election of U.S. senators, who up until that point had been elected by state legislatures.

Possibly a victim of its own success, the Progressive Party died out soon after the 1920 amendment that enfranchised all women, but many minor parties—with participation from women—have influenced politics both before and after it. Women from major political parties were a minority among the first female legislators, in Colorado during the 1890s. The nine included no Democrats but represented the Populist, Silver Republican, Fusion, and other parties. From the American (Know-Nothing) Party of the 1840s to the left-leaning Green Party and the right-leaning Tea Party of the 2000s, some women inevitably join some men in marching to the different drummers of minor parties.

Some of these women are mentioned at the end of the book, where the state-by-state guide emphasizes the pioneer women's movement, mainly because the myriad details of that older story are the least accessible today. While the state section expends more words on the nineteenth and early twentieth centuries, modern women are more likely to be covered in the first eighteen chapters. Each chapter also has a fairly lengthy bibliography about the topic—women in the federal judiciary, for instance, or female activists in the political parties—while the individual states have much shorter bibliographies directly related to that state.

The name and subject indexes should prove a useful guide for finding specific information. For example, the narrative about Vermont in the state section refers to Consuelo Northrop Bailey. The indexes take users to Chapter 5 on state senators, where readers will discover that she was the nation's first female senate president, as well as Speaker of the Vermont House. That might lead to curiosity about whether Bailey's speakership also was a national first. Chapter 4, on state representatives, will answer the question: Vermont was preceded by North Dakota.

The indexes are the bridge connecting pieces of an individual woman's history. For example, March Fong Eu appears in the California profile in the state section, and the indexes lead users to her biography in Chapter 3, on the first women elected to statewide executive offices. The Pennsylvania narrative mentions Kathleen "Kathy" Dahlkemper, and the indexes lead to Chapter 6, where readers learn that her husband was the first man to be president of the Congressional Spouses Club.

SPECIAL CHALLENGES IN RESEARCHING WOMEN'S HISTORY

That leads to marriage and marital honorifics. Sometimes they are used because the only name that can be found for a woman is that of her husband. This is particularly true for the tables in Chapter 1 of prominent suffragists and anti-suffragists. Even when a woman's full name is known, marital honorifics can be helpful to researchers, which is why they especially are used with the generally unknown women listed among the states as the first presidents of the League of Women Voters. A researcher looking for more on Connecticut's Miss Mabel Washburn, for example, may appreciate being aware that her name might have changed a few years later.

Name change is one of the most serious problems in doing women's history. All too often, meritorious women have been forgotten simply because historians found it too difficult to track them in the newspapers and other documents of their lives, when their names may have differed. Women who married and changed names after their moment of fame are particularly difficult to trace.

Some cases still are confused. For example, more research needs to be done before it can be said with assurance that Nettie C. Tator, who applied to the California bar in 1872, was the same person as Annette W. Cronise, who was admitted to the Ohio bar in 1873. She probably left her brief marriage, practiced with her sister, Florence Cronise, and became Nettie Cronise Lutes after a second marriage. The book provides many such starting points for young historians and political scientists.

Even more intriguing questions occur about possible conflict between kinswomen. Was Delaware's Emily P. Bissell, who was perhaps the nation's strongest anti-suffragist, from the same family as Hannah S. Bissell, a supporter in Ohio? Was Mrs. Garrett A. Hobart, a New Jersey anti-suffragist, kin to Baltimore's Mary Garrett or New York's Mary Garrett Hays, who were leading supporters? And was Elizabeth Boynton Hobart, a pioneer feminist in Illinois and Indiana, related to New Jersey's anti-feminist Hobart?

Some other relations, especially mother and daughter teams, are known. The first woman elected to a legislature in the South was Mississippi's Nellie Nugent Somerville in 1922. Her daughter, Lucy Somerville Howorth, won a seat during the next decade. Mamie Shields Pyle was South Dakota's prominent suffragist, and her daughter, Gladys Pyle, was the only woman elected to significant offices in that state. Ohio representative Frances Payne Bolton served at the same time as her son, Oliver Payne Bolton. He was not nearly as good a politician, however, and her tenure was much longer.

Modern examples also exist, sometimes with the same name and sometimes different. Missouri's Jean Carnahan and daughter Robin Carnahan both won major elections, but is it much harder to tell that Nevada treasurer Patty Cafferata is the daughter of Rep. Barbara Farrell Vucanovich. They managed a notable political feat in 1982, when both won their positions in the same election cycle. But even in the Internet age, such questions recur. Perhaps an Oregon historian can explain what, if any, is the connection between three women named Roberts who held high office there in the 1980s and 1990s.

The state sketches also list pioneer feminist publications. The known ones range from none in many states to four in Indiana. I trust that when researchers visit their state archives, they will appreciate knowing, for example, that Rhode Islander Anna W. Spencer began publishing *Pioneer and Woman's Advocate* in 1852, and Arkansans could subscribe to *Woman's Chronicle* in 1888.

A final area of women's history that is hugely important, but is not often explored, is the effect of pregnancy, especially unintended pregnancy, on careers. Was, for example, future emissary Mary McLeod Bethune pregnant when she married and added that surname? It seems probable, as her husband dropped out of her life almost immediately. Rep. Ruth Bryan Owen may have been pregnant instead of merely rebellious when, at barely eighteen, she left college and married a much older man. Women's history is more complicated than "men's history," and researchers have only begun to look seriously for its lessons.

ACKNOWLEDGMENTS AND NOTES ON SOURCES

The primary source of historical information up to 1922 is the *History of Woman Suffrage*. The first three of these six tomes—one of which exceeds a thousand pages—were written by Susan B. Anthony, Elizabeth Cady Stanton, and Matilda Joslyn Gage. Although the least known, Gage arguably was the best writer and theorist among the three women. She definitely was the most knowledgeable about women's global history. Those volumes were published in the 1880s, and Gage split with Anthony and Stanton in 1890, forming her own Woman's National Liberal Union. A few years later, the National American Woman Suffrage Association formally condemned Stanton, its former president, for her *Woman's Bible* (1895). Thus Anthony saw to publication of the fourth volume in 1902 on her own, with assistance from her secretary and publicist Ida Husted Harper. Harper wrote the remaining volumes, published in 1922. Those last two volumes are the source for much of the information in Chapters 1 through 3, especially for political women prior to the Nineteenth Amendment, as well as for many of the women in the section on states.

Several individuals helped dig out the mostly unknown women featured in Chapters 2 and 3, especially Phillip J. Roberts of the University of Wyoming —who replied to my inquiry from Dubai—as well as Dan Chavez of the University of New Mexico and Sarah Walker of the North Dakota State Archives. Because North Dakota elected the first woman to statewide office, in 1892, and other western states followed with women as state superintendents of schools, the National Council of State School Officials also was a source. Throughout the book, but especially in Chapter 3, a great deal of thanks is due to the Center for Women and Politics at Rutgers University, which has been maintaining excellent records of women elected to statewide offices and to Congress for many years. It is a fundamental source for anyone interested in the topic, and the same may be said of the Carrie Chapman Catt Center for Women and Politics at Iowa State University, which also has answered my inquiries.

Chapters 4 and 5, on state legislators, owe a tremendous debt to Elizabeth M. Cox's extremely detailed *Women State and Territorial Legislators, 1895–1995: A State-by-State Analysis, with Rosters of 6,000 Women,* which was published by McFarland and Co. in 1995. A second source is *Women Wielding Power,* a "cyber-exhibit" by the National Women's History Museum (NWHM) in Washington, DC. Although I was the curator for this 2007 work, NWHM's program director, Nikki Emser, did its graphics, much of the research, and all of the supervision of interns who worked on the project. Robin Read, longtime executive director of the National Federation of Women Legislators, also was helpful for these chapters. Special thanks is due, too, to Lois Ricciardi for her research on one of the biographies, that of Florida's Mary Lou Baker.

More than any other source, Chapters 6 and 7 depend on *Women in Congress, 1917–1990,* which was issued by the Office of the House Historian in 1991. The House committee officially in charge of its publication was chaired by Rep. Corinne Claiborne "Lindy" Boggs of Louisiana. The House subsequently updated that work, publishing more than a thousand pages in *Women in Congress, 1917–2006,* with that committee headed by Rep. Marcia Carolyn

"Marcy" Kaptur of Ohio. Second to congressional sources is *Almanac of American Politics,* which began publishing its biannual volumes on members of Congress in 1972, as well as the biographies of women members of Congress that were written by Mary Ellen Snodgrass in the four-volume encyclopedia *A History of Women in the United States: A State-by-State Reference,* of which I was general editor.

Bruce Calvin and Ann S. Kelly of the National League of Cities provided information for Chapter 9 on mayors, as did Frances S. Pollard and Joan Crigger of the National Conference of Mayors. Special thanks for Chapter 10 again are due to Nikki Emser of the National Women's History Museum, who supervised interns in creating "First But Not Last: Women Who Ran for President," which was launched early in 2008. I was a consultant on this project, and Kristen Blake created lesson plans.

The American Bar Association was helpful with the chapters on the judiciary, and the last chapters on organizations, parties, and political action committees are based largely on information provided directly by the groups profiled. In the section on states, those who answered obscure questions include Mary Libby Payne of Mississippi, and South Carolina historians Marjorie Spruill, Keller H. Barron, and Sheila Henry. My friend from graduate school days, retired judge Bea Ann Smith of Austin, provided answers and colorful context on Texas.

Hilary Poole and Valerie Tomaselli of MTM Publishing have been my faithful business associates for more than a decade, and I greatly value both their editorial skills and their steadfast encouragement. It goes without saying, but perhaps should be said, that thanks always are due to my wonderfully supportive husband, Roy Weatherford, and our daughter, Margaret Prater, who is a law librarian with the Department of Justice. They not only are personally important, but often are helpful with difficult points of research and computer competence.

This is a book for dipping into, for moving around in, for discovery of one little tidbit that leads to another interesting scenario, and so on—until you gain a broader picture of American politics and its evolving place for women.

Doris Weatherford
Seffner, Florida
December 2011

PRESIDENTIAL AND VICE PRESIDENTIAL CANDIDATES

As of 2011, fifty-six presidential elections have taken place, one every four years. Some presidents served multiple terms, others died in office prior to finishing a term, one president resigned, and another ascended to office without being elected. In total, forty-four men have been president of the United States, and forty-seven men have been vice president.

Most American women got the vote with the Nineteenth Amendment in 1920, more than nine decades ago. In contrast, most of the world's women had to wait until after World War II, with many not winning the vote until the second half of the twentieth century. Yet the world's first elected female head of state was in Ceylon (now Sri Lanka) in 1960. Other countries steadily followed, and more than three dozen have passed that milestone prior to the United States. Five nations—Argentina, India, Ireland, the Philippine Islands, and Sri Lanka—have twice chosen a woman to lead them, while Americans have yet to set the precedent.

NINETEENTH-CENTURY PIONEERS

When VICTORIA WOODHULL audaciously ran for president in 1872, the only political jurisdictions in the world where women could vote were the Wyoming Territory, which had granted the in right late 1869, and the Utah Territory, which followed a few weeks later, early in 1870.[1]

President Ulysses S. Grant, the general who arguably won the Civil War for the Union, was up for reelection in 1872. The war had been over for a mere seven years, and the Fifteenth Amendment, which was intended to assure

the vote to former slaves, had been added to the Constitution on March 10, 1870. Less than a month after that, on April 2, Victoria Woodhull sent a notice to the *New York Herald* announcing her candidacy for president.

She was too intelligent ever to believe that she had any chance of winning, but Woodhull was a master of the field that, in the future, would become known as public relations. She chose the campaign as a method of gaining publicity for her argument that the Constitution, and its newly adopted amendment, used gender-neutral language and should include women as voters.

Most people, women included, scoffed at Woodhull, but the was one era of radical change. A decade earlier, in 1862, when the War between the States was raging, it was far from certain that human bondage based on skin color would be abolished just three years later. To Woodhull, arguing for the legal equality of men and women was no more far-fetched than arguing for racial freedom. She reinforced her logic by choosing African American leader Frederick Douglass as her running mate. He neither accepted the nomination nor in any way associated himself with her. Douglass had political friendships with Lucretia Mott, Susan B. Anthony, Elizabeth Cady Stanton, and other pioneer feminists, but by the presidential election year of 1872, these progressives would see Woodhull as a dangerously radical newcomer.

Anthony initially had been charmed by Woodhull, who blazed through the women's movement of the 1870s like a fast-burning comet. Woodhull had no public profile until January 1870, when she and her sister, Tennessee Claflin, opened a successful brokerage firm in New York City, using money they obtained from multimillionaire Cornelius Vanderbilt. They also sporadically published a newspaper, *Woodhull & Claflin's Weekly*, in which they promoted avant-garde views. Woodhull called other women to

---

[1] See Chapter 1: Battle for the Vote.

Table 10.1 Notable Female Presidential Candidates, by Year

Year	Name	Residence	Party
1872	Victoria Woodhull	New York	Equal Rights
1884	Belva Lockwood	Washington, DC	National Equal Rights
1964	Margaret Chase Smith	Maine	Republican
1972	Shirley Anita Chisholm	New York	Democratic
1972	Patsy Takemoto Mink	Hawaii	Democratic
1976	Ellen McCormack	New York	Democratic; Right to Life
1984	Sonia Johnson	Utah	Citizens; Peace and Freedom
1988	Lenora Branch Fulani	New York	New Alliance
1988	Patricia Scott Schroeder	Colorado	Democratic
2000	Elizabeth Dole	North Carolina; Washington, DC	Republican
2004	Carol Moseley-Braun	Illinois	Democratic
2008	Hillary Rodham Clinton	Illinois; Arkansas; New York	Democratic

Source: Compiled by author.

Table 10.2 Notable Female Vice Presidential Candidates, by Year

Year	Name	Residence	Party
1924	Lena Jones	Tennessee	Democratic
1952	India Edwards	District of Columbia	Democratic
1972	Frances Farenthold	Texas	Democratic
1972	Theodora "Tonie" Nathan	Oregon	Libertarian
1984	Geraldine A. Ferraro	New York	Democratic
1996	Winona LaDuke	Minnesota	Green Party
2008	Sarah Palin	Alaska	Republican

Source: Compiled by author.

political action by establishing an Equal Rights Party, with herself as the nominee for president.

Although she had no formal education, Woodhull was not entirely a gadfly. She understood the political process and was capable of writing with all the formal logic of a lawyer. She also merits credit for instigating the first feminist testimony in Congress. According to Josephine Griffing, who moved from Ohio to Washington, DC, to help implement the Freedman's Bureau for ex-slaves, it was Woodhull, not more established feminists, who took the lead in forcing Congress to listen to women's plea for the vote. Summarizing the year 1870, Griffing wrote:

Mrs. Victoria C. Woodhull of New York City memorialized Congress for the exercise of the elective franchise, which memorial was read in the House of Representatives by Hon. George W. Julian, early friend of the cause, referred to the Judiciary Committee and ordered to be printed.

This action on the part of Mrs. Woodhull was taken without consultation with, or even knowledge of the [feminist leaders]. . . . With some difficulty she obtained permission for a hearing before the Judiciary Committee. (Stanton, Anthony, and Gage 1882, 484)

Table 10.3 Elected Female Chief Executives, by Nation and Year

Year	Nation	Name
1960	Ceylon (Sri Lanka)	Sirimavo Bandaranaike
1966	India	Indira Gandhi
1969	Israel	Golda Meir
1974	Argentina	Isabel "Evita" Peron
1979	United Kingdom	Margaret Thatcher
1980	Iceland	Vigdis Finnebogadottir
1982	Malta	Agatha Barbara
1986	Philippines	Corazon Aquino
1986	Norway	Gro Brundtland
1988	Pakistan	Benazir Bhutto
1990	Barbados	Nita Ruth Barrow
1990	Ireland	Mary Robinson
1990	Nicaragua	Violetta Chamorro
1992	Poland	Hanna Suchocka
1993	Canada	Kim Campbell
1993	Turkey	Tansu Ciller
1994	Sri Lanka	Chandrika Kumaratunga
1997	Guyana	Janet Jagan
1997	Ireland	Mary McAleese
1997	New Zealand	Jenny Shipley
1999	Latvia	Vaira Vike-Feiberga
1999	Indonesia	Megawati Sukarnoputri
1999	Panama	Mireya Moscoso
2000	Finland	Tarja Halonen
2001	Philippines	Gloria Macagapal Arroyo
2005	Germany	Angela Merkel
2006	Chile	Michelle Bachelet
2006	Liberia	Ellen Johnson-Sirleaf
2007	India	Pratibha Patil
2007	Argentina	Cristina Fernandez de Kirchner
2009	Lithuania	Dalia Grybauskaite
2010	Australia	Julia Gillard
2010	Brazil	Dilma Rouseff
2010	Costa Rica	Laura Chincilla
2011	Denmark	Helle Thorning-Schmidt

Source: Compiled by author, primarily based on "Timeline: Women in World History" in Doris Weatherford, *Women's Almanac 2002* (Westport, CT: Oryx Press, 2002), 307–340.

Note: Countries are listed alphabetically within each year.

Victoria Woodhull reading her argument in favor of women being allowed to vote to the Senate Judiciary Committee on January 11, 1871. She would go on to declare her candidacy for president in 1872.

Seeing that Woodhull would make the first appearance on Capitol Hill to advocate for the vote, not themselves, Griffing, Susan B. Anthony, and a half-dozen other feminist leaders joined her before the House Judiciary Committee on January 11, 1871. Washingtonians crowded into the hearing room for a glimpse at the notorious Mrs. Woodhull and were surprised to see a beautifully dressed, soft-spoken lady whose words made good sense. Some suffragists welcomed her into their fold, and Griffing reported that "thousands of tracts" with Woodhull's speech had been printed and "are being sent to the whole country" (Stanton, Anthony, and Gage 1882, 486).

But, by May 1872, when Anthony and Stanton led the annual convention of the National Woman Suffrage Association (NWSA), any friendship had dissolved. Perhaps feeling threatened by the way that the infamous newcomer seemed poised to take over the movement in which she had labored for three decades, Anthony gaveled down Woodhull's speech. With the platform in an uproar, Anthony adjourned the session and ordered the janitor to extinguish the lights.

Worse was to come, as presidential candidate Woodhull grabbed attention by plunging the women's movement into sensationalist scandal. It revolved around the

Rev. Henry Ward Beecher, an extremely popular preacher who was a leader in the American Woman Suffrage Association (AWSA), along with his sister, famed author Harriet Beecher Stowe. Their American association was emerging as a rival to the National association, Anthony and Stanton's group. The American was Boston-based, and with leaders such as the Beecher family, Julia Ward Howe, and Louisa May Alcott, it incorporated much more religiosity.

Woodhull, who was not at all religious, despised hypocrisy, and she saw Reverend Beecher as a hypocrite. She knew that Beecher had had an affair with Lib Tilton, a married member of his congregation. Susan B. Anthony was close to Tilton, often stayed at the Tilton home when she was in New York City, and knew about the romance. The relationship was over by the time Woodhull revealed it in *Woodhull & Claflin's Weekly*, but Theodore Tilton nonetheless sued Beecher for alienation of his wife's affection. The case dragged on over four years, until Beecher finally was acquitted (by an all-male jury) in 1876.

The immediate response to the newspaper story was dramatic. Copies of the paper sold for as much as $40, and postal authorities arrested Woodhull and Claflin on

Some people in the Victorian Age were so offended by Victoria Woodhull's beliefs that she was called "Mrs. Satan," the title of a 1967 biography on her. Although she rocked the world of her time, her congressional testimony now sounds so legalistically reasoned that it probably would bore a modern audience. This speech to the House Judiciary Amendment was in 1871, just months before her quixotic presidential campaign in 1872. Woodhull argued that if the gender-neutral language of the Fifteenth Amendment to the U.S. Constitution did not apply to either black or white women, then a Sixteenth Amendment should be added to spell out that women of any race were, in fact, citizens and therefore entitled to vote. Her "memorial" to the House committee covers a half-dozen pages of fine print, but this excerpt is part of the logical case that Woodhull built.

The sovereign will of the people is expressed in our written Constitution, which is the supreme law of the land. The Constitution makes no distinction of sex. The Constitution defines a woman born or naturalized in the United States, and subject to the jurisdiction thereof, to be a citizen. It recognizes the right of citizens to vote. It declares that the right of citizens of the United States to vote shall not be denied or abridged by the United States or any State on account of "race, color, or previous condition of servitude."

Women, white and black, belong to races.... The right to vote can not be denied on account of color. All people included in the term color have the right to vote unless otherwise prohibited....

All people of both sexes have the right to vote.... Women, white and black, have from time immemorial groaned under what is properly termed in the Constitution "previous condition of servitude." Women are the equals of men before the law, and are equal in their rights as citizens....

The citizen who is taxed should also have a voice in the subject matter of taxation. "No taxation without representation" is a right which was fundamentally established at the very birth of our country.... Women constitute a majority of the people of this country—they hold vast portions of the nation's wealth and pay a proportionate share of the taxes. (Stanton, Anthony, and Gage 1881, 443)

Woodhull came a little closer to touching on the sexual and, especially, the emotional when she alluded to male dependence on females. Although psychology was not yet an academic field and Sigmund Freud had yet to appear, Woodhull already had grasped some of his basic principles. As he would later, she asserted that many men's problems were rooted in their subconscious rejection of having once been completely reliant on mothers. As boys grew into men, Woodhull suggested, they often transferred that emotional dependence to wives and other female confidants, seeking comfort unavailable in the competitive world of men, especially political men. Changing that status by granting political equality to women therefore was threatening. Woodhull reasoned:

Women bear, rear, and educate men; they train and mould their characters; they inspire the noblest impulses in men ... ; they are the secret consolers, the best advisers, the most devoted aides in the most trying periods of men's lives, and yet men shrink from trusting them in the common questions of ordinary politics. Men trust women ... in all other places, but when they propose to carry a slip of paper with a name upon it to the polls, they fear them. (Stanton, Anthony, and Gage 1881, 447–448)

Woodhull's 1872 "presidential campaign" in fact was more nearly what modernists call "consciousness raising." She knew that she was not considered a serious contender for the nation's top job, but she also understood that the first step in any cause is speaking about it—and accepting the ridicule that always is hurled at the first to promote change.

the federal charge of using the mail to distribute obscenity. The presidential candidate spent election day of 1872 in jail. There is no record of her winning any votes.

Belva Lockwood had been present when Victoria Woodhull addressed the Judiciary Committee in 1871, but the two women were not closely affiliated.[2] Nevertheless, Lockwood emulated Woodhull by running for president in 1884 and chose a very similar name for her small party. Her new National Equal Rights Party shared no connection with the even smaller Equal Rights Party that Victoria Woodhull had begun in 1872. Adherents to Lockwood's party lived primarily in the nation's capital, where Lockwood lived, and in San Francisco, where she occasionally visited. Lockwood was a more plausible candidate than Woodhull. She not only had a spotless personal reputation, but she also had been an elected school superintendent in rural New York and was among the nation's first women to earn a law degree.

Lockwood's quest for full citizenship was complicated by the fact that she moved to Washington, DC, where citizens lack full representation in Congress. She worked to enhance the civil rights of Washingtonians and, in 1871, participated in caucuses that chose a congressional delegate. She also was part of an 1871 demonstration

---

[2] For Lockwood's biography, see Chapter 13: Pioneers in the Judiciary.

in which some seventy Washington women marched to city hall and unsuccessfully attempted to register to vote.

Her battle first to study and then to practice law took the entire decade of the 1870s. When the U.S. Supreme Court backed a lower court decision that a woman could not practice law in the District of Columbia, she turned to political action. Lockwood persistently lobbied both the U.S. House and the U.S. Senate, and in 1879, Congress passed a bill requiring federal courts to recognize female attorneys. Doing all of this a half-century before most women got the vote required incredible endurance, self-confidence, and faith in democratic ideals.

Lockwood also established a network of political allies outside of her milieu. As early as 1870, she drafted a bill for gender equity in federal civil service—far ahead of anyone else. She went to New York to lobby for female employment rights, and when the nation celebrated its first centennial in 1876, she was part of the Philadelphia event that drew attention to the inclusion of women. In 1880, she attended the Republican National Convention in Chicago, again lobbying its male delegates on behalf of women. She worked to hire female guards in women's prisons and represented female journalists in their quest for news access.

Lockwood had enough of a national network that, when the National Equal Rights Party nominated her for president in 1884, its membership was largely in California, not on the East Coast. Her running mate was San Franciscan Marietta L. B. Stowe, who also had struggled to become an attorney. Although California women would not win the vote until 1911, they explained their strategy as "getting one elector" in the state's electoral college delegation, "so that person will become the entering wedge" (Stanton, Anthony, and Gage 1886, 757). The party platform not only addressed feminist issues, but also took positions on current foreign and domestic questions. Its most innovative idea, which never came close to adoption, was the federalization of family law, so that women and children would not lose rights when they moved across state lines.

Back East, Susan B. Anthony and other feminists reacted to Lockwood's campaign as they had to Woodhull's: Despite her qualifications, the easterners were embarrassed by her ambition and lack of realism. They feared that her quixotic crusade made them look ridiculous by association and distracted from the seriousness of their efforts to win the vote for less egocentric women. They also suspected that Lockwood's campaign was what would today be called a publicity stunt, intended to benefit her increasingly lucrative law practice.

Lockwood's 1884 presidential campaign yielded 4,149 votes in six states out of the ten million total votes cast. Claiming she had been defrauded of many more, Lockwood ran again in 1888. That went even less well, but far from seeing it as ignominious defeat, Lockwood moved on to international issues, especially the promotion of peace through law, and she continued to insist on her right to participate in both the judicial and political systems.

She won $5 million for displaced Cherokees in 1906, arguing before the U.S. Supreme Court at age seventy-six. The year before her 1917 death, she campaigned for Woodrow Wilson, much to the chagrin of Alice Paul and others in the National Woman's Party, who viewed Wilson as a foe.[3]

To those who criticized her audacity in mounting presidential campaigns, Belva Lockwood responded:

Why not nominate women for important places? Is not Victoria Empress of India? Is not history full of precedents of women rulers? We shall never have equal rights until we take them, nor respect until we command it. (Stanton, Anthony, and Gage 1886, 809)

THE FIRST CANDIDATES OF THE TWENTIETH CENTURY

Both Victoria Woodhull and Belva Lockwood were fully aware of the fact that they could not vote for themselves, nor did they truly expect men to elect them. After women in all states got the vote in 1920, a few on the fringes of politics emulated Woodhull and Lockwood by declaring themselves candidates. During the remainder of the century, at least thirty-five women would run for the presidency as nominees of small parties, including the Socialist Party, the Greenback Party, the Workers' League Party, and even such oddities as the Looking Back Party and the Surprise Party.

In the early twentieth century, the most credible of these candidates was Marie C. Brehm, who was a sixty-five-year-old lecturer for the Women's Christian Temperance Union in 1924, when she won the vice presidential nomination of the Prohibition Party at its national convention. That, however, was after the Eighteenth Amendment banned the alcohol sales throughout the nation, and success left Prohibitionists without a significant platform.

At the 1924 Democratic National Convention, Lena Jones Wade Springs of Tennessee was honored by having her name placed in nomination for vice president. She

---

[3] See Chapter 1: Battle for the Vote.

Table 10.4 Major Party Presidential Tickets That Nominated or Considered Nominating Women, since 1952

Year	Republican Ticket	Republican Women Considered	Democratic Ticket	Democratic Women Considered
1952	Dwight D. Eisenhower and Richard M. Nixon	Margaret Chase Smith	Adlai E. Stevenson and John J. Sparkman	India Edwards for vice president
1972	Richard M. Nixon and Spiro T. Agnew		George S. McGovern and R. Sargent Shriver	Shirley Chisholm for president; Frances Farenthold for vice president
1976	Gerald R. Ford and Bob Dole		Jimmy Carter and Walter F. Mondale	Ellen McCormack for president
1984	Ronald Reagan and George H.W. Bush		Walter F. Mondale and Geraldine A. Ferraro	Geraldine A. Ferraro nominated for vice president
2008	John McCain and Sarah Palin	Sarah Palin nominated for vice president	Barack Obama and Joseph R. Biden Jr.	

Source: Compiled by author.

THE LITERATI, HUMORISTS, AND WOMEN

Like countless women before and after her, Margaret Chase Smith expected that reporters covering her political activities would first describe her dress, hat, and jewelry. Journalistic obsession with female appearance never ceased, but by the 1960s, most newsmagazines were learning to move beyond that to political coverage that was not blindly biased against a woman because she was a woman.

A curious exception was with literary magazines that ventured into politics—and especially their humorists. This had been the case in World War II also, when magazines found women's new roles to be great subject matter for cartoons. As the war intensified, most newsmagazines moved on to serious treatment that was generally favorable. The magazines that most thoroughly objected to new roles for women were aimed at well-read audiences of the classically educated. Modern people forget that until the GI Bill made college possible for the middle class, most of the educational elite was not only male, but also conservative and protective of its privilege. Members of this cohort were most apt to ridicule objections to the status quo using the cruel guise of humor.

Cleveland Amory was a star with that sort of reader. Although later known for his work in animal rights, in the 1960s he was still very much a member of the literati. He began his career with the *Harvard Crimson*, and his column in the *Saturday Review of Literature*, which ran for twenty years, was considered mandatory reading for the avant-garde. But the era was one in which near-misogyny passed for humor, and when Margaret Chase Smith announced her presidential quest, he began his opposition to that by ridiculing the entire notion of a female president. He wrote:

In this country still, thank heaven, some people are born strong and some are born girls. Some people are born intelligent and some are born girls. Some are born of good character, and some are born girls. (Sherman 2000, 187)

Painful though this must have been to read, Margaret Chase Smith clipped Amory's column and saved it in a scrapbook. She did the same with other hateful words penned by respected men who projected an image of open-mindedness while blindly assigning all women to the category of "other." Often educated in sex-segregated boarding schools, their experience taught them to view women as so innately different from men, so much less than equal human beings, that they openly publicized their anti-female views in a way that they never would have done with ethic minorities, the handicapped, or others who have no choice about their status in life. Without examining their prejudices, such men simply concluded that no woman—presumably including their wives, daughters, and sisters—ever could be capable of top office.

Jim Bishop, a best-selling author of books such as *The Day Christ Died* (1957), wrote a piece that Senator Smith also kept, with a title that demonstrated his automatic prejudice against her: "A Woman President? NO!" She saved the assertion of *Los Angeles Times* writer Richard Wilson: "the fundamental emotionalism of women does not suit them for the White House" (Sherman 2000, 269).

In an era when such views were considered acceptable and even amusing, Smith's presidential quest was a profound contribution to female progress. Her campaign pioneered the way for other women, and when—less than twenty years later—Shirley Chisholm ran for president, no respected journalist or humorist dared to so easily dismiss her. That might have been partly because she was African American, but as white women followed down the path to the presidency in the future, they would encounter less and less evidence of misogyny. By the millennium, almost no one would see Amory's column as funny.

chaired the party's important Credentials Committee that year, but she did not intend to be a genuine nominee. The same was true for Izetta Jewell Brown, who was nominated for vice president by her West Virginia delegation. After 1924, however, even honorary gestures such as these declined.

Almost three decades later, Democrats again placed a woman, India Edwards, in nomination for vice president at their 1952 convention. Once more, it was intended as an honor, not a serious move, although this time the woman was more qualified. Edwards had been a reporter for the *Chicago Tribune,* a notoriously anti-Democratic newspaper, until her son was killed in World War II. She then moved to Washington, D.C., became a strong supporter of the Democratic Roosevelt administration, and when Franklin D. Roosevelt died at the war's end, became close to the new president, Harry S. Truman. She used her access to the White House to encourage his appointment of women such as Helen Eugenie Moore Anderson as ambassador to Denmark and Georgia Neese Clark as treasurer of the United States.[4]

Truman made Edwards head of the Women's Division of the Democratic Party, and he thought so much of her that, in 1951, he offered its chairmanship to her. By then, though, she had had enough of dealing with the men who still dominated party politics, and she turned him down. Placing her name in nomination at the 1952 convention thus was an honor to a woman whose career was winding down along with Truman's. Such symbolic gestures, however, played only a small part of conventions then, as they were truly business meetings, not the televised spectacles of today. Unlike in contemporary times, relatively few states held presidential primaries. In most states, political parties chose delegates to national conventions at caucuses, and national party conventions were decision-making bodies. Delegates truly chose their party's nominees for president and vice president at the convention, sometimes casting dozens of ballots over many days to reach agreement.[5]

Interest in both state-level presidential primaries and television news was growing in 1952, and that year's convention would be the last in which delegates had much individual authority. Democrats nominated Illinois governor Adlai E. Stevenson for president and Sen. John J. Sparkman of Alabama for vice president. Republicans chose Dwight D. Eisenhower to head their ticket, with Richard M. Nixon as his running mate. The 1952 Republican National Convention was the first that was scripted for cameras, leaving little room for Maine senator Margaret Chase Smith and the attempt of Republican women to nominate her for vice president.[6]

Smith was a hero to the National Federation of Business and Professional Women's Clubs (BPW), the era's most feminist organization. BPW members organized Republican delegates from several states who wanted to set the precedent of nominating a woman. Rep. Clare Booth Luce of Connecticut wrote a nomination speech, seated herself with Maine's delegation, and arranged to be recognized by the chairman.[7] However, nominee-in-waiting Dwight Eisenhower sent word that "under no circumstances should Margaret Smith's name be placed in nomination for Vice President" (Schmidt 1996, 227). He wanted no challenges to his choice of California senator Richard Nixon and feared that even a symbolic effort could open the gate for Nixon's opponents. When the chairman called on Luce, she made a hurried speech that left her, Smith, and BPW members feeling embarrassed.

Twelve years later, when Smith announced for the presidency, she made sure that the circumstances were under her own personal control. Thus, the first presidential candidacy of a woman that the mainstream media took seriously was that of Margaret Chase Smith in 1964.

The first woman to serve in both the U.S. House and in the U.S. Senate, Smith was very popular with her constituents and with women generally. She had something of a national network through BPW, as well as with female veterans of World War II, because she had sponsored the legislation that admitted women into the non-nursing units of the U.S. Navy, Marine Corps, and Coast Guard. In 1964, when she announced her intention to seek the top job, Senator Smith was a childless widow who had been in Congress for twenty-three years.

Lyndon B. Johnson of Texas was the incumbent, having risen from the vice presidency when John F. Kennedy was assassinated in November 1963. Prior to his death, Presidential Kennedy had acknowledged the political skill of the female senator from Maine. When the president was questioned—in what turned out to be his last press conference—about his upcoming reelection and rumors that Smith might seek the Republican nomination, he replied that he "would not look forward to campaigning against Margaret Chase Smith. . . . She is very formidable as a political candidate" (Sherman 2000, 181). Smith had, in fact, entertained the idea of running against Kennedy but instead she went ahead against the new incumbent, Johnson.

---

[4] See Chapter 12: Ambassadors and Chapter 11: Cabinet and Subcabinet.

[5] See also Chapter 16: Political Parties and Conventions.

[6] For Smith's biography, see Chapter 7: United States Senators.

[7] For Luce's biography, see Chapter 12: Ambassadors.

She announced her candidacy at a luncheon meeting of the Women's National Press Club on January 27, 1964. At the end of a long speech on the state of the nation and the pros and cons of running for its top post, she committed herself to the presidential primaries in New Hampshire and Illinois. She met the gender issue head on, acknowledging that many people believed the White House was no place for a woman. But, she said, that in addition to believing that her moderate record was one that the Republican Party needed, she wanted to "pioneer the way for a woman," as "women before me pioneered the way for me" (Vallin 1998, 109).

Smith added that times were changing rapidly. Making the analogy to racial bias, she proclaimed, "Who can deny that the rights of Negroes are greater in 1964 than they were in 1954? Who can deny that there has been much progress?" (Schmidt 1996, 293). She reminded her audience that she had won repeated elections without party backing or expensive campaigns and said she was eager to see if that could be replicated at the national level. She also insisted that she was not seeking the vice presidency, although many reporters—including female ones—quickly leapt to that conclusion.

The importance of personal contact in the New Hampshire presidential primary is a given of modern political science, but that was not the case in 1964, and Smith merits credit for helping to establish the tradition. More accustomed to cold than many candidates, she opened her campaign near the Canadian border on a morning that was well below zero. Smith also promoted a new style of one-on-one connection without advertising. She deliberately established no campaign office and did not hire any professional political help. The strategy failed, however. Greatly outspent by the male candidates, she came in second-to-last even in this New England state so close to her home, where she had expected to do well.

Voters went for another neighbor, Henry Cabot Lodge of Massachusetts. New Hampshire voters chose him over both less privileged men and a woman who had worked her way up from nothing. The vote tallies were Henry Cabot Lodge, 33,521; Barry Goldwater, 21,775; Nelson A. Rockefeller, 19,496; Richard M. Nixon, 15,782; Margaret Chase Smith, 2,812; and Harold E. Stassen, 1,285.

The results cannot be interpreted as anything other than a humiliating defeat for Smith, but her name already was on the Illinois ballot, and she kept her commitment to run there. She had supporters there, with one group led by women who spontaneously backed her and another dominated by men who wanted her as vice president,

intending to balance the ticket in the moderate direction if extremist Goldwater ended up as the nominee.

Neither group of supporters got any financial help from Smith, as she decided to return all contributions with thanks. This probably was a strategically sound decision: Her fund-raising capabilities were not sufficiently developed to make a real dent in the costs of running in a big state such as Illinois, and by returning the money, she could serve as a model for a different style of politics. She also did not spend much time campaigning. Smith was proud of never missing a Senate vote, and with the historic 1964 Civil Rights Act under debate, she spent only two weekends in Illinois. Voters seemed pleased with this low-key approach, however, and she carried a quarter of a million votes in the April balloting—approximately 30 percent of the total and appreciably better than she had done in New Hampshire.

Women in Oregon and California, many of them members of BPW, encouraged her to run in their primaries, but she chose not to accept the expense of campaigning in these distant states even though her name was on their ballots. After she came in fifth in the Massachusetts primary, which was won by its native son Henry Cabot Lodge, Smith knew that her poor showings in her own region prevented any chance of ultimate success. She probably had realized that from the beginning, when countless New Hampshire voters enthusiastically greeted her but told reporters that they would not vote for her or any other woman.

The California women nonetheless organized events to honor Smith when she arrived in San Francisco for the Republican National Convention in July 1964. Vermont senator George D. Aiken nominated her, and among those who seconded the nomination was Rep. Frances Payne Bolton of Ohio.[8] Hundreds of people participated in a floor demonstration on her behalf, but Smith won the votes of just twenty-seven convention delegates from seven states. That, however, was better than three of the male contestants, including, ironically, Henry Cabot Lodge. Barry Goldwater carried the convention by a lopsided majority but went on to lose to Johnson by the widest margin of any presidential race to that point.

Keenly aware that she was making history for women, Smith expressed no regrets about her failed quest. She had more Washington experience than all of her opponents added together, she often said, and when a reporter asked why she had decided to run, Sen. Margaret Chase Smith reasonably replied, "There was nowhere to go but the presidency" (Schmidt 1996, 300).

---

[8] For Bolton's biography, see Chapter 6: United States Representatives.

The 1964 Republican National Convention was boisterous by Republican standards, but Democratic convention that year and the two following it, in 1968 and 1972, were riotous.[9] As Republicans grew more conservative with the nominations of Goldwater and Nixon, in 1968 and 1972, respectively, Democrats grew more liberal and especially more diverse than any party ever had been—but not without internal pain.

The key to the transformation of the two parties was race. Beginning with Abraham Lincoln, most voting blacks lived in the North and were Republicans. Party registration in the North began to change as the Franklin D. Roosevelt administration, and especially first lady Eleanor Roosevelt, reached out to African Americans during the Great Depression and World War II. Democratic President Harry Truman added to that record by desegregating the military, as did John Kennedy and Lyndon Johnson with the civil rights legislation that ensured voting rights, integrated public accommodations, and more. Integration and voter registration drives—led by black women such as Arkansas's Daisy Bates, Alabama's Rosa Parks, and Mississippi's Fannie Lou Hamer—forced the issue of African American political participation in the South.

Courts ruled against "white primaries" that effectively had barred blacks from meaningful ballot access, and the Democratic Party sided with the protestors against the exclusionary whites in state party affiliates. In 1964, when Republicans nominated their most conservative candidate, Barry Goldwater, the Credentials Committee of the Democratic Party upheld Fannie Lou Hamer's protest against the all-white Mississippi delegation. A black plantation worker and civil rights activist, Hamer had been beaten and jailed for leading voter registration drives. This made her an icon among Mississippi blacks and with whites who supported their cause. At the 1964 Democratic convention, she led a demand that Mississippi's delegation be integrated to represent the true population of the state. After a disruptive fight, the convention seated the African Americans, and party realignment began. In the 1968 election, Republican Richard Nixon added to the transformation with his "Southern strategy," which used race as a wedge issue to entice white Southern Democrats to change parties.

The 1964 Democratic convention was tumultuous, but the next one, in Chicago in 1968, was downright violent, as police physically attacked demonstrators outside the convention hall. In 1972, the Democratic convention in Miami was less violent than in 1968 but nonetheless chaotic. South Dakota senator George S. McGovern, a strong war critic, was nominated and would go on to lose to incumbent Nixon by an even greater margin than Goldwater lost to incumbent Johnson in 1964. With the nation deeply divided over the war and other issues, including women's rights, three women launched campaigns for the top of the ticket in 1972: Theodora Nathalia Nathan, called "Tonie," was the vice presidential nominee of the Libertarian Party and Patsy Takemoto Mink and Shirley Anita Chisholm ran in Democratic presidential primaries.[10]

Libertarians held their first presidential nominating convention that year, aiming to create a new third party. Their philosophy appeals to people who are economic conservatives and social liberals, and with increasing inflation because of the Vietnam War, their minimalist approach to government spending became increasingly attractive. Many more in the era's counterculture society liked the Libertarian platform on social issues. Libertarians want to lessen government intrusion into personal lives, including matters related to sexuality and reproduction as well as drug use and other victimless crimes. The U.S. political system presents many barriers to new parties, however, and the Libertarian ticket won fewer than four thousand votes in the presidential election.

Yet, when the electoral college met in December 1972, Tonie Nathan had the distinction of being the first woman to win an electoral college vote—in this case, for vice president. She was the running mate of John Hospers, a philosopher at the University of Southern California. The single vote was cast by Roger McBride, a Virginia member of the electoral college. He was a Republican, but with the assured victory of the Republican ticket of Richard M. Nixon and Spiro T. Agnew, McBride chose to cast his electoral vote for the Libertarian ticket. Tonie Nathan, an Oregon talk-show host, continued to run for various offices during the next two decades, but she never won more than 14 percent of the vote in any race.

Patsy Mink and Shirley Chisholm were U.S. representatives firmly affiliated with the Democratic Party, and both reflected its new diversity. Chisholm was an African American from New York City, and Mink's maiden name—which she rarely used—was Takemoto. Her parents had been born in Japan, which was the American enemy as young Patsy grew up in Hawaii's Maui during World War II. Beyond being female, therefore, both women faced additional barriers in their presidential

---

[9] See Chapter 16: Political Parties and Conventions.

[10] For Mink's biography, see Chapter 5: State Senators, for Chisholm's biography, Chapter 6: United States Representatives.

quests. Mink's candidacy aimed especially at protesting the Vietnam War. As an Asian American, she understood its negative nature, and her predictions of American defeat soon turned out to be true. Chisholm's candidacy aimed to legitimize new roles for African Americans.

Just as liberal Republicans had asked Margaret Chase Smith to run in their states' presidential primaries in 1964, a group of liberal Democrats asked Patsy Mink to run in 1972. Students at Oregon colleges were particularly active against the war, and they knew of Mink's leadership in Congress on the issue. U.S. representative Julia Butler Hansen, a Democrat from Washington, also played a low-key role in encouraging Mink.[II] As it turned out, however, a conservative Democrat, John Goemens, filed to run against her for Congress, and Mink soon had to set aside any presidential ambitions to concentrate on Hawaii and her House reelection. Like Smith in the 1964 New Hampshire presidential primary, Mink came in second-to-last in Oregon, winning just 2 percent of the vote in the May balloting.

Three years later, on October 8, 1975, she told the Honolulu *Star Bulletin* that she had no regrets about this or any other aspect of her independent ideology. "It is easy enough," she said, "to vote right and consistently be with the majority. But it is more often more important to be ahead of the majority, and this means being willing to cut the first furrow in the ground and stand alone for a while if necessary."

Mink competed in just one state, but Shirley Chisholm's candidacy was intended to be truly national. She even internationalized her race somewhat, frequently pointing out that Sri Lanka, India, and Israel had elected women to their top posts and arguing that American women should be equally assertive. Although she was just in her second congressional term, Chisholm's 1968 election as the first black woman in the U.S. House gave her wide name recognition, and she jumped into the 1972 presidential race intending a real contest, not merely a symbolic gesture.

She announced her candidacy on January 25, 1972, using the slogan of "Unbought and Unbossed," the title of her 1970 biography. Although most of her supporters were newcomers to politics, countless grassroots feminists tried to find ways to help on the "Chisholm Trail to 1600 Pennsylvania Avenue." In that era, "Ms." was a new term of address, intended to be the equivalent of "Mr." in not revealing anything about marital status, and buttons appeared that said "Ms. Chis. for Pres." Her campaign recruited enough volunteer petition gatherers to put her name on the ballot in several states, with her first contest in Florida on March 14.

Florida remained very much a Southern state in 1972, with major school districts that were only beginning racial integration despite the fact that it had been almost twenty years since the Supreme Court ruled on the issue in 1954. There were enough emerging feminists to ensure that Chisholm attracted crowds, but she won just 4 percent of the vote. She also campaigned in the Southern state of North Carolina, as well as her own New York and nearby New Jersey and Massachusetts. She flew to California for its June primary and visited Illinois, Minnesota, and Michigan in between, but she did not have enough time or money to campaign in Wisconsin, where she also was on the ballot. Additional voters in states where her name was not on the ballot made the effort to write in her name, so Chisholm ended up with measurable support in more than a dozen states. More of that came from white women than from black men, as a number of male African American leaders—including the Rev. Jesse Jackson, powerful California Assembly leader Willie Brown, and DC House delegate Walter E. Fauntroy—instead endorsed white men, especially eventual nominee George McGovern.

When the Democratic Party met for its national convention in July, McGovern's emergence as the nominee was not a foregone conclusion. Chisholm had 28 delegates pledged to her, and as the sole black candidate, she pinned her hopes of increasing her numbers on the convention's black caucus. She won some converts, especially after Hubert H. Humphrey dropped out and about 90 of his delegates switched to Chisholm. When the roll of states was called, Chisholm had 151 votes when McGovern reached the majority needed to win. Delegates then moved to make the nomination unanimous, so Chisholm never knew how many more delegates from additional states might have supported her. In any case, her 151 votes were historic: No woman before, or for a long time after, had won as many in a major party convention.

In addition to that milestone, the 1972 Democratic convention featured the nomination of Texan Frances Farenthold for vice president. Often called "Sissy," Farenthold was a Vassar College graduate, attorney, and member of the Texas House. She also was a founder of the National Women's Political Caucus (NWPC), and NWPC leaders, especially celebrated feminist Gloria Steinem, were extremely active at the convention. Part of what made the convention so chaotic was that George McGovern did not orchestrate the choice of his running mate, instead allowing the delegates to make their own choice. Thus, after the presidential nomination played out

[II] See Chapter 6: United States Representatives.

late at night, television audiences on the next night were treated to a genuine race for vice president.

Women who were disappointed in the way that Shirley Chisholm had been shunted aside rallied around Farenthold, and she won 404 votes for vice president—more than most male candidates, including future president Jimmy Carter. Her tally was enough to make Farenthold second in the balloting, which was won by Missouri senator Thomas F. Eagleton. Less than three weeks later, after it was revealed that Eagleton had been under psychiatric care, McGovern dropped him from the ticket—but did not replace him with the woman who had come in second at the convention balloting.

Instead, McGovern's choice was former Peace Corps head R. Sargent Shriver. Shriver's wife was Eunice Kennedy Shriver, whose brothers, John F. Kennedy and Robert F. Kennedy, had been assassinated in 1963 and 1968, respectively. Another brother, Massachusetts senator Edward M. Kennedy, refused McGovern's invitation for the vice presidency and instead advocated for his brother-in-law as the running mate. In the November general election, the McGovern-Shriver ticket carried only Massachusetts and the District of Columbia. Even McGovern's own South Dakota deserted him. As Democrats lost in a landslide to incumbents Richard Nixon and Spiro Agnew, some Democratic delegates regretted not voting for Sissy Farenthold for vice president, as she might have carried the big state of Texas.

No woman with sound elective credentials ran for president in 1976, the year that Democrat Jimmy Carter took the White House from unelected Republican president Gerald Ford, who had become an unelected vice president when Agnew resigned and then succeeded Nixon after he resigned. One feature of the Democratic primary contest was the candidacy of Ellen McCormack, who ran on a right-to-life platform. A New York grandmother, McCormack differed from previous Democratic candidates in that she did not pretend to be qualified for the presidency. Instead, she was akin to Victoria Woodhull in using the electoral system to publicize her views—in McCormack's case, on abortion.

She was a pioneer in this area, undertaking her quest less than three years after *Roe v. Wade* legalized early-term abortions. In addition to her antiabortion stance, McCormack opposed war and the death penalty. And, although she had no pretensions to political experience, she was more astute about getting on state ballots and winning commitments from delegates than some who had political experience.

McCormack qualified for Democratic primary ballots in eighteen states, more than any woman to that point. She received Secret Service protection and was the first woman to qualify for matching campaign funds from the federal government. This enabled her to run targeted television ads, and McCormack won a total of 238,027 primary votes — more than some well-known Democratic men. The final result, though, was just twenty-two committed delegates at the convention that nominated Jimmy Carter, fewer than Margaret Chase Smith in 1964 or Shirley Chisholm in 1972.

McCormack subsequently dropped her Democratic affiliation and formed the Respect for Life Party, which later became known as the Right to Life Party, and largely dropped any opposition to war and execution. She ran unsuccessfully for lieutenant governor of New York in 1978 and again campaigned for the presidency in 1980. As a minor-party candidate, she was less successful at getting on ballots than she had been as a Democrat. She ran in just three states: her own New York, as well as New Jersey and Kentucky. She and her running mate, Carroll Driscoll, won just 32,327 votes in 1980, a year in which no credible female candidate in either major party campaigned for the presidency.

HOLDING PATTERN: THE 1980S

At a highly divided 1980 convention in New York City, Democrats renominated President Jimmy Carter, who was weakened by a primary challenge from Sen. Edward Kennedy. This internal Democratic dissent eased the way for Republican victory, led by California governor Ronald Reagan, in the general election. Although he was the nation's first divorced president and although he did not then have good relationships with the children from either of his marriages, Reagan's campaign focused on family values. He defeated Carter, a longtime Sunday school teacher with a solid family life.

This was the first campaign in which the term "family values" became a code used against Democrats, and it was the first time that a gender gap between men and women appeared, with men being more likely to vote for family values and Republicans.[12] The Republican transformation can be seen clearly in the first ladies. Betty Ford supported the Equal Rights Amendment (ERA) and other feminist causes, but Nancy Reagan did not. In addition, Republicans campaigned to reverse *Roe v. Wade*, but they proposed no constitutional amendment to do so in this or future convention platforms.

More than a century earlier, feminists had learned with *Minor v. Happersett* (1875)—the case in which the U.S. Supreme Court ruled that the Fifteenth Amendment,

---

[12] See also Chapter 16: Political Parties and Conventions.

which assured the vote to "all citizens" but denied it to those born female—that the only way to overrule a Supreme Court decision is (1) to hope that a future Court reverses it or (2) to amend the Constitution, which requires approval by two-thirds of both houses of Congress and three-quarters of the state legislatures.[13] The fact that Republicans never have proposed a specific amendment to reverse *Roe v. Wade* indicates to some that they are unwilling to take on this challenge. Public opinion on this personal issue appears too unsettled to even draft language for such an amendment, but the party nonetheless used the topic as a wedge issue for decades to come.

In 1984, Republicans renominated incumbent Reagan and his vice president, George H. W. Bush, but the Democratic convention, held in San Francisco, was historic for women. GERALDINE A. FERRARO became the first woman nominated for vice president by a major party. Feminists throughout the nation threw spontaneous celebrations when the presumptive Democratic presidential nominee Walter F. Mondale, who had been vice president under Jimmy Carter and a U.S. senator from Minnesota, announced his choice of Ferraro, a U.S. representative from New York. She later wrote:

What a high that night was. As I looked out over the convention floor, I saw the faces of America: farmers, factory workers, young professionals, the elderly, business executives, blacks, whites, Hispanics . . . and so many women. No one wanted to leave. Even my normally more sobersided peers and colleagues were caught up in the euphoria.

Did I think we could win the election? Sure did. The Democratic party had already bucked the odds by selecting a woman as the vice presidential candidate. We never seemed more together.

There wasn't a cloud on my horizon as we left the Moscone Center to celebrate with Joan and Fritz Mondale. What I didn't know then was the personal agony that lay ahead, an agony that at times would seem almost unbearable. More than once in the next four months as the euphoria faded and the highs were equaled by the lows I would remember my mother's words to me when I was young. . . . "Don't forget your name," she would tell me. *"Ferro* means iron. You can bend it, but you can't break it. Go on." (Ferraro 1985, 23)

It was her mother's reaction that most worried Ferraro as the campaign wore on. Perhaps the most harmful attacks came courtesy of Rupert Murdoch's News Corporation, publisher of the *New York Post*, which assailed the business history of Ferraro's husband, John Zaccaro, and went on to other scurrilous charges, tarring even her father, who had died when Ferraro was eight. Encouraged

by ethnic-based innuendo, many voters saw her Italian background as a negative, while the Roman Catholic leadership criticized her pro-choice stance much more than they did with male Catholic candidates.

Comparatively fewer personal attacks were made on Mondale, as Ferraro, an outsider to the established image of presidents, became the media lightning rod. Mondale and Ferraro lost to Reagan and Bush by approximately fifty-four million to thirty-eight million votes. Although the Mondale-Ferraro ticket lost with women, too, especially older women, the election results demonstrated a growing gender gap: A whopping 64 percent of men voted Republican.

The attention to Ferraro's vice presidential candidacy late in 1984 meant that Sonia Johnson's presidential quest earlier that year was largely overlooked. An English professor, the mother of four, and a fifth-generation Mormon, Johnson was troubled by her church's strong opposition to the Equal Rights Amendment. People of the Mormon faith, or The Church of Jesus Christ of Latter-day Saints (LDS Church), had been politically active against the ERA since at least 1973, when they bussed hundreds of women to a Florida conference on the status of women, where the LDS women voted en masse against their own constitutional equality. The ERA made Johnson something of a celebrity. Her 1981 book, *Housewife to Heretic*, detailed her 1979 trial for heresy and her ex-communication from the church because of her disagreement with Mormon elders on the equality of women. "I'm a feminist to the core," she wrote, "and will be until I die, fiercely, passionately, reverently, and totally committed to justice to my sisters on this earth" (Johnson 1981, 112).

Two minor parties, the Peace and Freedom Party and the Citizens Party, nominated Sonia Johnson for president. She won approximately sixty thousand votes, mostly in California and Pennsylvania. Some ninety-five hundred were in Louisiana, and eighty-seven Texans took the trouble to write in her name. She raised enough money under the Citizens Party banner to make history, as on July 25, 1984, Johnson became the first minor-party candidate of either gender to qualify for federal matching funds. By then, Democrats had nominated Walter Mondale and Geraldine Ferraro, and their campaign obtained $40 million in matching funds from the Federal Election Commission (FEC). FEC records show that just a month later, on August 23, commissioners ruled that Johnson was not a viable candidate for the general election, canceling further eligibility for matching funds.

In the end, her 1984 candidacy was much like that of Belva Lockwood a hundred years earlier. In 1884, the National Equal Rights Party was too small and its leaders,

---

[13] See Chapter 1: The Battle for the Vote.

Lockwood and Marietta L. B. Stow, too egocentric to be viable. As with Lockwood, many women not only believed that Johnson's crusade was unrealistic, but also excessively personal. She focused on her own life issues at least as much as those of voters, and most feminists instead supported Walter Mondale, especially after he named Geraldine Ferraro as his running mate.

Like Ferraro and Johnson in 1984, the 1988 contest saw two female candidates, one a major party stalwart and the other from a minor party. PATRICIA SCOTT SCHROEDER was a firm Democrat, and Lenora Branch Fulani was the standard-bearer for the New Alliance Party (NAP), which she founded. Fulani, a psychologist, was akin to Democrat Shirley Chisholm in being a black woman from New York. Fulani differed from Chisholm, though, in believing that neither Democrats nor Republicans were capable of addressing the issues that most concerned millions of Americans. Arguing that corruption permeated both political parties, she wanted a "new alliance" of the alienated.

She made her first bid for office in 1982, when the NAP nominated her for lieutenant governor of New York. In 1985, she ran as its nominee for mayor of New York City, and the following year, she attempted the governorship. Undeterred, Fulani entered the presidential arena in 1988, saying in her stump speech that hers was a "militant crusade for fair elections and democracy . . . with the goal of changing the electoral process."

For most African Americans, the focus of the 1988 presidential primaries was on Jesse Jackson, who made a significant bid for the Democratic nomination. Fulani and her party nonetheless had enough political skill that she was the first African American and the first woman to be on the general election ballot in all fifty states. She carried some 225,000 votes, or 0.2 percent. Although this percentage was tiny, it stood as the highest number for any female presidential candidate in a general election. Fulani would run again in 1992, less successfully than she had in 1988.

Much more media attention for the 1988 contest went to Representative Schroeder, Democrat of Denver. She had been elected to the U.S. House on an antiwar platform in 1972 and was a veteran of the Nixon impeachment and other crises of that troubled era. More than anyone else, Schroeder came to symbolize women's issues in Congress, as she took up the leadership on the ERA, maternity leave, fair credit, child care, and more. Appointed to the House Armed Services Committee in her first term, Schroeder was a leading critic of defense spending and the chief proponent of fairness for women in the military.

Her sixteen years in Congress made her as well qualified as any of the male candidates running for president in the 1988 election. The Republican nominee would be George H. W. Bush of Texas, vice president under Ronald Reagan, whose two terms were ending. The Democratic field was open after the 1984 loss of Vice President Walter Mondale and Rep. Geraldine Ferraro.

As Democrats began their exploratory campaigns in 1987, Schroeder supported the candidacy of her Colorado colleague, Sen. Gary Hart. She and her husband, Jim Schroeder, were friends and neighbors with Gary and Lee Hart. Although Pat Schroder heard the persistent rumors of Gary Hart's womanizing, she discounted them. She was sufficiently supportive of him that she hurriedly rearranged her schedule to go to California when he asked her to substitute for him at newspaper interviews. Upon arriving on the West Coast, she turned on the television and saw film of Hart cavorting with a woman on a yacht in Bimini. "This," she exclaimed later, "was the pressing business that prevented him from making the trip" (Schroder 1998, 203).

In June 1987, a month after Gary Hart dropped out of the race, someone leaked to the *New York Times* that Schroeder was considering running. She was on a plane traveling between Washington and Colorado, and the press ambushed her when she arrived in Denver. She later recalled that, at the airport, "the world was there. I never had to call a press conference" (Schroeder 1998, 205). Being backed into her announcement in this way, however, proved something of a disadvantage, as Schroeder did not have a chance to analyze her campaign's chances fully, especially the fund-raising aspect that remained so difficult for women. The National Organization for Women pledged some $400,000 to get her on the ballot in several states, but money would remain Schroeder's greatest problem.

She campaigned nationally throughout the summer, traveling from Oregon to Florida and attracting good crowds of empathetic feminists—but not enough support from party regulars. Many were of the type that she described as "the Democratic state chairman in a southern state." Without naming him, Schroeder wrote of his comments at a party dinner in the South. He introduced her "glowingly," even offering the high praise that she "knew more about national defense than all of the other candidates combined." Then he burst her balloon by adding, "Of course I can't vote for her because I have a problem with a man for First Lady" (Schroeder 1998, 211).

Other contenders for the Democratic nomination were Gov. Michael S. Dukakis of Massachusetts, former governor Bruce Babbitt of Arizona. Sen. Paul Simon of Illinois, Sen. Joseph R. Biden Jr. of Delaware, Sen. Al Gore of Tennessee, Rep. Richard A. Gephardt of Missouri, and civil rights leader Jesse Jackson of Illinois. A *Time* magazine poll showed Schroder running third among these well-qualified men, but her biggest problem was her congressional colleague, Gephardt. Democratic House Speaker Jim Wright of Texas strongly supported Gephardt, and few congressional colleagues had the courage to resist Wright's influence.

Sen. Gary Hart, for whom Schroeder had done so much, repaid her by endorsing New York governor Mario M. Cuomo, who was not even a candidate. Cuomo's Italian background did not prevent others from trying to draft him, as gender proved more of an obstacle than ethnicity: In debates about Democratic chances, the comparison was between Geraldine Ferraro and Pat Schroeder, not Ferraro and Cuomo. Even feminist Democrats argued that it was too soon after Ferraro's loss to consider another woman at the top of the ticket.

Among the few dissenters from this "reasoning" were Nancy Pelosi and Barbara Kennelly, who helped with fund-raisers in their home states of California and Connecticut, respectively. Instead, said Schroeder, "most of my colleagues reacted like Congressman Les Aspin, who kept asking if I had lost my mind" (Schroeder 1998, 207). Despite qualifications equal to other candidates, even her political colleagues could not envision her as president. By the time Congress resumed work in September, Schroder decided that she could do more good by returning to the House leadership and retaining her power there than she could by continuing a seemingly doomed presidential quest.

Hers was the last presidential campaign by a significant female candidate in the twentieth century, but another woman ran twice for vice president. President Clinton was up for reelection in 1996, when the Green Party nominated consumer activist Ralph Nader for president and Winona LaDuke for vice president. Born in 1959 in Los Angeles, LaDuke was a descendent of Minnesota's Ojibway (Chippewa) tribe. Her father, a Native American, was a film actor, and her Jewish mother was an artist. After graduation from Harvard University, LaDuke moved to Minnesota, where much of the land near the Canadian border remains Indian reservations.

According to a Green Party press release dated June 25, 1996, when the party met in Denver for its convention, LaDuke was "probably the only vice presidential candidate in history to be nursing a newborn baby." She especially spoke to issues of poverty and environmentalism, and she accused the Clinton administration of being too supportive of corporate interests. This was the first time that the Green Party competed in the presidential race, and its ticket was on the general ballot in twenty-one states. Nader and LaDuke won 4 percent of the vote in Oregon, which was the ticket's highest number. They would try again in 2000—again without success—but

with much more serious national effect, due to the closely fought race between Vice President Al Gore and Texas governor George W. Bush.

AT THE MILLENNIUM

Twelve years passed between Patricia Schroeder's bid for the 1988 Democratic nomination and that of Elizabeth Dole for the Republican nomination in 2000.[14] Dole was the first Republican woman to make the attempt since Margaret Chase Smith sought the nomination in 1964, thirty-six years earlier.

Dole came to the decision to run because many people encouraged her to do so in 1996. In that election, her husband, Kansas senator Bob Dole, challenged President Bill Clinton. Dole was the second divorced man nominated by Republicans, something that was little noted as the party continued its focus on family values. His running mate was Jack F. Kemp, who had been secretary of housing and urban development under George H. W. Bush as well as a member of the U.S. House. Many people pointed out that Elizabeth Dole was a better campaigner than either of the Republican nominees.

A native North Carolinian, she was the first woman to serve in two cabinet positions under two different presidents. Elizabeth Dole was head of the American Red Cross in 1996, when she took a leave of absence to campaign for her husband. She did so again when she campaigned for herself in 1999 for the 2000 contest. She never had run for any office when she set out for the top one, but Dole had broad name recognition from her appointive positions and from her husband's campaigns.

She conducted a national quest for seven months of 1999, and early polls showed her running second, with only Texas governor George W. Bush outpacing her. Dole was particularly innovative with televised town hall meetings, when she often moved from the stage to interact with the audience. Attendees loved this personal touch, but it nonetheless made it easy for reporters to emphasize Dole's graceful style over substance on the issues.

Her husband also proved less supportive than she had been of him. When he told the *New York Times* that he wanted to donate to Arizona senator John McCain, one of her competitors, because McCain had been helpful to him, many people saw that as evidence that Bob Dole had no faith in his wife's campaign. Lack of donors ultimately forced Elizabeth Dole to drop out. In October, when Bush had raised $57 million and she had less than $5 million in

---

[14] For Dole's biography, see Chapter 11: Cabinet and Subcabinet.

her war chest, she abandoned her quest. She left the race prior to the 2000 presidential primaries, so there is no objective measure of how much support she might have had, but whatever she had appeared to be slipping. In an autumn straw poll of Iowa Republicans, she came in third, behind Bush and Delaware multimillionaire Steve Forbes.

Many experts predicted that Bush, the son of the former president, would chose Elizabeth Dole as his running mate when he won the 2000 Republican nomination, but instead he opted for former Wyoming representative Dick Cheney. In many ways, the Cheneys and Doles were similar Republican power couples, as Lynne Cheney, too, had held high appointive positions, including a controversial tenure as head of the National Endowment for the Humanities. Democrats nominated Vice President Al Gore and Connecticut senator Joseph I. Lieberman. Neither of their wives ever held public office. The Green Party again chose Ralph Nader and Winona LaDuke, who together proved a spoiler to the Democratic ticket.

Hillary Clinton at Baruch College in New York on June 3, 2008, on final primary night.

Nader and LaDuke won 2,882,955 votes in 2000, or 2.7 percent of the general election tally. This was enough to make a real difference in the very close race between the major parties. (Democrats won the popular vote, but the Constitution provides that the electoral college, with representatives from each state equal in size to its congressional delegation, chooses the president. After the US Supreme Court halted the recount of disputed ballots in Florida, Bush had more electoral votes than Gore.) In 2004, Winona LaDuke did not join Nader in continuing to carry the Green Party banner. Instead, she endorsed the Democratic nominee, Massachusetts senator John Kerry.

Kerry had emerged as the 2004 winner after besting several other candidates, including former Illinois senator Carol Moseley-Braun.[15] After earning a law degree from the prestigious University of Chicago, she was a federal prosecutor and then won election to the Illinois House in 1978. Although she had risen in the leadership there, her 1992 race for the U.S. Senate surprised pundits. With financial help from feminists all over the country, she

defeated an incumbent, winning a comfortable 53 percent of the vote in the big state. The first black woman in the Senate, she was just its second elected African American, following only Massachusetts's Edward W. Brooke, who won three decades earlier.

Moseley-Braun lost her 1998 reelection bid, and after service as an ambassador during the Clinton administration, she explored the possibility of a 2004 presidential quest. She announced her candidacy at Washington, DC's historic black institution, Howard University. But she made the announcement on September 11, 2003, the second anniversary of the terrorist attacks on the United States. The choice of date in itself caused some to question her political sagacity.

Moseley-Braun pointed out that her elective qualifications were better than some of the other candidates. They included black activist Al Sharpton, who never held office; North Carolina senator John Edwards, who was still in his first term; and Howard Dean, who was the former governor of Vermont, a state with fewer residents than her Cook County, Illinois. Moseley-Braun had won elections at the local, state, and federal level and, as the representative of the United States in New Zealand, even had some modest international credentials.

Moseley-Braun debated with the eight male candidates and was interviewed by national media but, like other female candidates, had trouble raising money. She garnered only $72,000 during the last quarter of 2003. She also publicized her effort to get on the Virginia ballot by petition, and when the campaign failed to collect enough

---

[15] For Moseley-Braun's biography, see Chapter 7: United States Senators.

signatures by the deadline, that proved an embarrassment. Four days prior to the Iowa caucuses, on January 15, 2004, Moseley-Braun used her appearance on *The Daily Show with Jon Stewart* to drop out and endorse Howard Dean. The Federal Election Commission kept an open file on Moseley-Braun's presidential campaign, largely because of $262,000 in unpaid debts.

As George W. Bush's two terms were coming to an end after the 2008 election, the presidential field was open in both parties. Virtually no Republicans urged the nomination of Vice President Richard Cheney, and no viable woman entered the Republican primaries. Arizona senator John McCain would be the nominee, and his choice of Alaska governor SARAH PALIN as his running mate made history for Republicans. She was the party's first vice presidential nominee and the nation's first since Democrat Geraldine A. Ferraro in 1984, almost a quarter-century earlier.

Democrats also set a historic milestone, as their primaries became a close race between the nation's first potential female president, HILLARY RODHAM CLINTON, and its first potential African American president, Barack Obama. Bumper stickers said "Make History—Vote Democratic," as either choice would be unprecedented. Other candidates threw their hats into the ring, including former vice presidential nominee and former senator John Edwards, former vice presidential nominee and sitting senator Joseph Lieberman, and retired U.S. Army general Wesley Clark, but the race narrowed down to the two individuals who were not white men.

Hillary Clinton had been the most politically active first lady since Eleanor Roosevelt, and in 2000, she exceeded Roosevelt's record by winning election as the first female senator from New York. She had many feminist fans throughout the world but was often a lightning rod for controversy during her husband's two terms as president. Thus, some senators were surprised that Clinton was a hard-working, thoughtful colleague who had her own identity and set of achievements, separate from those of her husband, former president Bill Clinton.

She launched her campaign for the presidency on January 20, 2007, the anniversary of her husband's 1992 inauguration. "I'm in," she said, "and I'm in to win!" She campaigned vigorously for the next eighteen months, winning twenty-one primaries and more than eighteen million votes, more than any other candidate in the history of presidential primaries. She raised $212 million, significantly more than any previous woman. But, from the beginning, the bar for Hillary Clinton was set high, and because she was portrayed as the frontrunner at the start, she had nowhere to go but down. Analysis by

political scientists Regina G. Lawrence and Melody Rose summarized the media coverage:

Following the late October 2007 debate . . , critic Stanley Fish observed that "everyone was writing her political obituary ten seconds after the last word was spoken. . . . They were all standing over the body and taking bets on whether or not it could be revived."

Thus before the first caucus was held . . . , the media and pundits relentlessly described the tightening of the pre-election opinion polls in terms of Clinton losing her place . . . , although she still held a commanding lead in most national polls. . . .

When Clinton and Obama each won some victories on Super Tuesday, the media's game-framed narrative continued. . . . According to media critic Howard Kurtz . . . , the narrative that she was losing the nomination left Clinton "drowning in a sea of negative coverage."

Though Clinton won the Texas and Ohio primary contests, the loser theme continued. . . . The pundits, led by [Tim] Russert, thus declared her bid over a full month before Clinton actually suspended her campaign—and before all the primary voters had cast their ballots. (Lawrence and Rose 2010, 185–186)

Clinton arguably made a mistake by focusing the majority of her time and campaign funds on the states that held primaries and not on those that held caucuses or conventions. Iowa held its caucus on January 3, 2008, and when Clinton did not carry the voting there, it damaged the frontrunner image that the media had created. She won the traditionally first primary, in New Hampshire on January 8, but by only 3 points, which was not enough to quell the media critiques.

Both major parties traditionally have treated the Iowa caucuses and the New Hampshire primary with special respect, and these states are nearly all white, Northern states had been allowed the first shot at winnowing out presidential candidates. Democrats sought to address this lack of diversity by permitting Nevada and South Carolina to also vote in January. Clinton won the popular vote in the Nevada caucuses on January 19, but internal party rules were such that Obama garnered more Nevada delegates to the Democratic National Convention in the summer, where the real nomination occurs. On January 26, Obama carried South Carolina.

More important than these four small states, though, were the large states of Florida and Michigan. Democratic National Committee chairman Howard Dean protected the primacy of Iowa and New Hampshire, as well as Nevada and South Carolina, by announcing that the voting results of states holding a primary prior to February 5, or Super Tuesday, would be considered unofficial and that delegates to the nominating convention from that state would not be seated. Michigan and Florida defied that ruling; especially in Florida, Democrats had no choice but to hold their primary on the "illegal" day, as the new date was set by law in a legislature that was dominated by Republicans. Clinton delegates in those two states would wait months to know whether or not they would be able to vote for her at the convention.

The race continued through the spring, and Clinton eventually won 18,046,007 popular votes, compared with 17,869,542 for Obama. As with the electoral college, however, popular votes do not necessary matter in the even more obscure world of presidential primaries. Like Gore in the popular versus electoral college vote of 2000, Clinton won the votes of more people in 2008, but Obama outpaced her in the delegate count. Finally, on May 31, the Democratic Rules Committee dealt with the issue of the "too early" primaries in Florida and Michigan. Committee members largely backed their chairman, awarding Obama a larger share of delegates than he had won to punish Clinton for allowing her name to remain on the ballot in those states. In effect, said authors Chuck Todd and Sheldon Gawsier, the committee's decision meant that Clinton's victories in these large, ethnically diverse states were "hollow" (Todd and Gawsier 2009, 14).

On June 7, 2008, a week after the Rules Committee meeting, Hillary Clinton halted her historic march toward the presidency, as it became clear that her Senate colleague, Illinois's Barack Obama, had enough pledged delegates to secure the nomination at the Democratic National Convention. Held in Denver August 25–28, the convention honored her unprecedented quest, as well as her plea for unity. Many Democrats urged what they called a "dream ticket" of Obama for president and Clinton for vice president, but Obama chose Delaware senator Joseph R. Biden Jr. as his running mate. In November, Obama was elected as the nation's first African American president, defeating the Republican ticket of John McCain and Sarah Palin. Upon assuming office in 2009, Obama appointed Clinton as secretary of state, further increasing her international visibility. Her 2008 race as potentially America's first female president also raised the status of women and was a strong factor in McCain's choice of a woman as his running mate on the Republican ticket.

Although Sarah Palin's experience was limited to less than a full term as governor of one of the nation's least populous states, she provided a contrast to Biden, seen by many as an insider white male. Some Republican men seem to have been attracted to Palin's good looks, while many women found inspiration in her story of going from the mother of five young children to the governorship to potentially the White House. As the economy collapsed in the last months of the Bush administration, however, McCain's weakness on economic issues was exposed, and although Palin brought an undeniable energy to the Republican ticket, they lost.

Important for the long-term cause of female equality, even after they lost, no pundits said that sharing the slate with a woman was in itself a factor in McCain's defeat. Palin was not blamed for the defeat in the way that Geraldine Ferraro had been in 1984. That faulting of Ferraro especially was excessive compared with Palin because Ferraro and Mondale ran against an incumbent and, thus, were even less likely to have been successful. The fact that Palin was not blamed to the same extent may indicate that Republicans are less likely than Democrats to criticize their losers, but it almost certainly shows that the public grew more comfortable with the idea of a woman in the top spot between 1984 and 2008.

But Sarah Palin lost, as had Hillary Clinton earlier in the year and other women for more than a century prior to 2008. Clinton famously said that the eighteen million votes she won were "18 million cracks in the glass ceiling" that allows women to see, but not yet reach, the highest heights. When she and other women daringly took on challenges, the result was that those challenges appear less daunting, especially for youthful women who have not experienced the level of prejudice against women that has been routine throughout America's history. If the glass ceiling of the White House has eighteen million cracks, then it seems inevitable that someday a woman will shatter that final barrier.

PROFILES OF NOTABLE PRESIDENTIAL AND VICE PRESIDENTIAL CANDIDATES

Several notable women made their mark in presidential politics. **Hillary Rodham Clinton** *became the first woman to run for president in all fifty state primaries or caucuses.* **Geraldine A. Ferraro** *was the first female nominee for vice president.* **Sarah Palin** *was the first Republican female nominee for vice president.* **Patricia Scott Schroeder** *was well qualified for her 1988 race;* **Victoria Woodhull** *was the first woman to run for president. (Among the other women who ran for president or vice president, Patsy Takemoto Mink is profiled in Chapter 5; Shirley Chisholm, in Chapter 6; Carol Moseley-Braun and Margaret Chase Smith, in Chapter 7; Elizabeth Dole, in Chapter 11; and Belva Lockwood, in Chapter 13.)*

HILLARY RODHAM CLINTON (1947–)

In 2008, Hillary Diane Rodham Clinton came closer to winning the presidency than any other woman.

Born in the Chicago suburb of Park Ridge, Illinois, to Hugh and Dorothy Rodham, she grew up with two younger brothers in a middle-class Methodist family. Like most of her suburban neighbors, she was a Republican. Interested in politics as a teenager, she volunteered in the failed presidential bids of Richard M. Nixon in 1960 and Barry Goldwater in 1964. She excelled at school and was accepted at Massachusetts's prestigious Wellesley College, a pioneering institution for women where she became a Democrat.

After her 1969 graduation, she went on to elite Yale Law School, and was chosen for the editorial board of *Yale Law Review and Social Action*. She also volunteered on cases affecting women and children, as well as migratory workers. Through this, she met Marian Wright Edelman, founder of the Children's Defense Fund, as well as Anne Wexler, who would be a Democratic power during the Carter administration. Wexler offered Rodham her first paid political job.

The Yale law degree that she earned in 1973 still was unusual for a woman in that era. Discrimination against female attorneys was routine, but there was more acceptance in the public arena than in the private. Rodham moved to Washington, DC, and worked as a staff attorney with the House Judiciary Committee when it considered the impeachment of Richard Nixon.

She had met Bill Clinton at Yale in 1971, and he repeatedly had proposed marriage. In August 1974, after Nixon's resignation meant that she would have to seek a new job, Rodham said that she "followed her heart" to his home in Fayetteville, Arkansas, where they married on October 11, 1975. She kept her maiden name, and both she and her husband taught law at the University of Arkansas. When he was elected attorney general in 1976, they moved to Little Rock, and she joined the Rose Law Firm, an old Arkansas establishment, and soon became its first female partner. She also continued her work with the Children's Defense Fund, as well as other pro bono causes, including the nationally based Legal Services Corporation, which serves clients too poor to hire lawyers.

Her husband was elected governor in 1978, and their daughter, Chelsea, was born in February 1980. In the Republican sweep at the polls in November of that year, Bill Clinton lost the governorship to Republican Frank D. White. Hillary supported the family while Bill found his political footing again. They returned to the governor's mansion after Bill Clinton was reelected in 1982, and he never lost another election.

In 1992, President George W. Bush ran for a second term, and Bill Clinton decided to challenge the incumbent. Arkansans had been fine with a first lady who used her maiden name, but when the couple started campaigning nationally, more media referred to her as "Hillary Rodham Clinton," and in time, the "Rodham" was dropped. They often campaigned together in the early stages, and especially at the bellwether Florida Democratic convention straw poll in autumn 1991, people flocked to her as much as to him. No other candidate's wife was comparable, and such occasions led Bill Clinton to say on television that, in electing him, the nation would "get two for the price of one."

When he defeated the incumbent president, Bill Clinton did what he had done with some Arkansas initiatives and put his wife in charge of a task force to propose major changes in health care policy. The task force bogged down in details, however, and Clinton was unable to garner the public support that Congress needed for such historic action.

Hillary Clinton understood that health care and many other issues are closely linked to the status of women, and in 1995, she was the first first lady to attend one of the international meetings that the United Nations holds on women's issues every five years. It was held in Beijing in 1995, and although conservatives loudly objected to her attendance, millions of women throughout the world admired her leadership.

Bill Clinton's alleged infidelity arose as an issue during the 1992 presidential campaign. More serious and proven accusations, with more serious consequences, were made while he was in the White House, exposing the couple to years of embarrassing disclosures and white-hot media attention. Through it all, Hillary Clinton remained at the center of the storm, criticized by some on the left for staying in the marriage and by some on the right for alleged business improprieties.

Her years as first lady were winding down when New York senator Daniel Patrick Moynihan announced his retirement and recruited Hillary Clinton to succeed him. New York had set a precedent in 1964, when it elected Robert F. Kennedy as its U.S. senator even though he had not lived there, and Moynihan believed that both the state and the United States would benefit from a similar election of Hillary Clinton. As Kennedy had earlier, Clinton established residence in New York in anticipation of running for the Senate. She conducted a yearlong listening tour, traveling through the small towns and big cities of the large state, and New Yorkers elected her in 2000. She carried 55 percent of the vote, compared with 43 percent for the Republican nominee. Over the next six years, she surprised many of her detractors with her thoughtful and humble service to the state of New York. In 2006, she won reelection with a strong 67 percent.

Those numbers in a state that is very diverse boded well for her presidential campaign in 2008, and Hillary Clinton came very close to being the first female president. She withdrew in favor of Barack Obama in June, campaigned for him in the summer and fall, and soon after his January inauguration, he appointed her secretary of state. Secretary Clinton has garnered respect even in right-wing quarters that once were fiercely critical.

GERALDINE A. FERRARO (1935–2011)

The first female nominee of a major party for vice president, Geraldine Anne Ferraro was born in Newburgh, New York, to Italian-speaking parents. Her immigrant father died when she was eight, leaving her mother, Antonetta Corrieri Ferraro, to support the family by working in the garment industry.

She attended Catholic schools for girls and worked part time prior to graduating from New York City's Hunter College in 1956 with a degree in English. Ferraro then taught public elementary school while putting herself through law school at Fordham University, earning her law degree in 1960—more than a decade before significant numbers of women entered law schools. She was one of just two women in her class. She also married businessman John Zaccaro in 1960 and, again, uncommon for that era, retained her maiden name.

She bore three children while also working as an attorney in her husband's real estate business. They prospered, and she was able to devote more time to Democratic politics and her personal career. Her peers elected her president of the Queens County Women's Bar Association in 1970, and in 1974, she entered the public arena with a job as an assistant district attorney. New York had few female prosecutors at the time, and as her cousin headed the district attorney's office, Ferraro was accused of being the beneficiary of nepotism. She proved herself, however, as a tough prosecutor specializing in sex crimes that previously had been ignored. Moreover, despite the rumors of unfair treatment in her hiring, she discovered that she was being paid less than male prosecutors. Her superiors were unembarrassed to say that lower pay was acceptable because she was married.

That turned her attention to making change in a broader way, and in 1978, she ran for a vacant congressional seat representing a blue-collar district in Queens. With support from feminists and young people, as well as an emphasis on her tough experience as a prosecutor, she won the Democratic nomination with 53 percent of the

vote. Crime was the major issue in the general election, too, and she defeated the Republican nominee by 10 points.

Quickly promoted by House Speaker Thomas P. "Tip" O'Neill, she rose in the party hierarchy and served on the powerful House Budget Committee. A firm feminist, she sponsored the 1981 Economic Equity Act and other legislation to correct injustices toward women in salaries, pensions, and other areas of finance. Remembering her widowed mother's struggle to support a family, she especially emphasized the needs of older women. She also worked for environmental issues that the Reagan administration tried to sidetrack and, after visiting Central America, spoke out against the secret war the Reagan administration promoted there.

She was the first woman to chair the Democratic Platform Committee, which sets party policy, for the 1984 national convention. In both parties, the Committee meets for months prior to the convention to settle on issues to be proposed for adoption by delegates. Her role as committee chair gave Ferraro an opportunity to demonstrate her comprehension of national needs, and that was a factor when former vice president Walter F. Mondale, the presidential nominee, chose her as his running mate. The choice initially was popular, and Mondale soared in the polls immediately afterward. But, as the campaign went on in the fall, media scrutiny of Ferraro and especially of John Zaccaro proved damaging. The media had no precedent for how to handle the husband of a major candidate, and much innuendo about Zaccaro's businesses reflected negatively on her. Beyond gender, Ferraro's ethnicity and her pro-choice Catholicism became campaign issues.

After the Mondale-Ferraro ticket lost, she wrote her memoir *Ferraro: My Story* (1985). Ferraro attempted to return to politics in 1992, seeking the Democratic nomination to run against New York's Republican senator Alfonse M. D'Amato. Republicans feared her candidacy the most of any Democratic challenger because she would cut into D'Amato's Italian base, but after a bruising primary battle that included Rep. Elizabeth Holtzman and male candidates, she lost the nomination by less than 1 point.

President Bill Clinton appointed Ferraro to several posts with the United Nations (UN), including ambassador to the UN Commission on Human Rights. She also taught at prestigious universities and was a frequent political commentator on television, especially the CBS talk show *Crossfire*, which she cohosted in 1996 and 1997.

Given the narrow margin by which she had lost the 1992 Democratic Senate nomination, it was reasonable for Ferraro to try again in 1998. This time she lost by a wider margin. New York Democrats nominated Charles E. Schumer instead, and he decisively defeated D'Amato in the fall. Finally, in 2000, the state's Democrats would nominate a woman to run for the U.S. Senate, Hillary Rodham Clinton, who went on to victory on election day. Ferraro would support Clinton when she ran for president in 2008.

Countless feminists who could not vote for Geraldine Ferraro in New York found inspiration in her story, especially in the courageous battle against cancer that she waged for more than a decade. Ferraro finally lost that battle in March 2011, at age seventy-five.

SARAH PALIN (1964–)

Born in 1964 in Sand Point, Idaho, Sarah Louise Heath competed in sports and beauty contests as a teenager. She attended four colleges in Hawaii, Alaska, and Idaho and graduated from the University of Idaho in 1987. After marrying Todd Palin the next year, she bore five children while working with him in his commercial fishing business and as a sports reporter.

Elected to the city council of the small town of Wasilla, Alaska, in 1992, she became mayor in 1996. From there, she made the remarkable leap to statewide office. Palin lost the Republican nomination for lieutenant governor in 2002 but won the 2006 gubernatorial nomination, in the process defeating incumbent governor and former U.S. senator Frank H. Murkowski. She defeated another former governor in the general election, stunning Alaska's political establishment. At forty-two, she was the youngest governor in the youthful state's history.

Palin made a huge splash as John McCain's running mate during the 2008 presidential race, and her near–rock star status among the Republican base breathed life into the campaign which nonetheless was defeated by the Democratic ticket. She did not resign as governor of Alaska for the campaign, but her return to that office proved disappointing for supporters. On the July 4 weekend of 2009, she stunned observers with an announcement that she would resign the governorship at the end of the month.

She explained that her family had taken a vote and asked her to resign the governorship. Her husband, five children (the youngest of whom has Down's syndrome), and a grandchild born to her unwed daughter continued to live in Wasilla, some six hundred miles from the capital at Juneau, where she was supposed to work full time. Conservative commentators applauded the resignation, hoping aloud that this would allow Palin more time to develop a national network. Palin, however, did not enter the 2012 presidential race and instead became an author, speaker, and television commentator.

PATRICIA SCOTT SCHROEDER (1940–)

Considered the most important congressional sponsor of feminist legislation in American history, Patricia Nell Scott Schroeder had enough expertise in other public policy areas that she was a well-qualified candidate for president in 1988.

Born in Portland, Oregon, in 1940, her parents were adventurous Nebraskans who roamed the West and Midwest just before and during World War II, primarily buying and rehabilitating wrecked airplanes. They settled in Des Moines, Iowa, where she graduated from high school, and she continued working for the family business while attending the University of Minnesota. She earned enough in this part-time work not only to pay her tuition, but also to buy an expensive new car. She graduated Phi Beta Kappa in 1961.

She had intended to major in aeronautical engineering, but counselors believed that area to be too unconventional for a woman, so she studied history and the Chinese language. With no firm career goals as graduation neared, she applied to Harvard Law School and was one of fifteen women accepted for admission, in a class of five hundred, over the objections of the dean. Not surprisingly, given such animosity toward female students, Patricia Scott was unhappy at Harvard until Jim Schroeder, also a Midwesterner, introduced himself. They married and, after their mutual graduations, decided to establish themselves in Denver in 1964.

While Jim built a private law practice, Pat worked for the National Labor Relations Board. During this time, she nearly died twice as a result of pregnancy-related problems. The first time, doctors had ignored her complaints until she delivered twins, one stillborn and the other dying soon afterward. The second time, she nearly bled to death. Both experiences profoundly shaped her view that every woman has the right to control her own medical decisions. Ultimately, the Schroeders became the happy parents of Scott, a boy named for her family, and Jamie, a girl named for Jim. They were ages six and two when their mother was elected to Congress in 1972.

Denver was more leftist than many cities in the troubled era of the Vietnam War and the civil rights movement, and the Schroeders were part of a progressive coalition of young professionals seeking an alternative to the incumbent U.S. representative. Pat Schroeder emerged as a plausible candidate to draw attention to the issues, but no one truly expected that she would win the Democratic nomination, let alone the general election. Operating on a shoestring budget and with the help of hundreds of volunteers, the campaign drew enough discontented voters to the polls so that at age thirty-two—and to her own surprise—Pat Schroeder was elected to the U.S. House.

An even greater surprise came when this anti-war advocate was named to the House Armed Services Committee. Although California's Florence Kahn was the first woman appointed to the committee in 1929, it since had become an all-male bastion to the point that Washingtonians believed no woman ever had served on it. A certain truth was that none had won the powerful slot in her first term. Much later, Schroeder discovered that this surprising appointment was due to the long-suffering wife of Wilbur D. Mills, a powerful Democratic representative from Arkansas. He had been pulled over by police late at night in the company of an Argentine stripper named Fanne Foxe, who fled the car, jumped into Washington, DC's Tidal Basin, and had to be rescued. After that career-endangering experience, Mills apparently acceded to his wife's demand that House leadership put the unconventional woman from Colorado—whom she never had met—on the Armed Services Committee. The appointment was made over the objections of the committee head, F. Edward Hebert of Louisiana, who initially forced Schroeder and Ronald V. Dellums of California, the first African American on the committee, to share one overstuffed chair at the committee room's table.

Despite the obstacles, Schroeder stayed on Armed Services to much success. She not only was a persistent watchdog on wasted Pentagon money, but also improved life for ordinary soldiers, especially women. It was not coincidental that the U.S. Army and the U.S. Navy finally had its first female generals and admirals in the 1970s, while she was gaining power on this powerful committee. She would lead the quest for the admission of women to the ancient military academies and force the Pentagon to accept women as pilots and in other roles previously denied to them.

She also championed pioneer legislation in gender equity for civilians, including Social Security, child care, and maternity leave. She repeatedly dogged the National Institutes of Health because it excluded women from its general health studies and refused to conduct inquiries into female diseases. Until her involvement, for example, even breast cancer studies had been limited to male breasts. Her 1988 presidential campaign interrupted this congressional work only briefly, and Denver residents consistently reelected Patricia Schroeder to the House until she chose not to run in 1996.

Schroeder became president of the Association of American Publishers in 1997. Her memoir, *24 Years of Housework . . . and the Place Is Still a Mess: My Life in Politics,* was published in 1998. She and her husband frequently travel together supporting Democratic candidates, especially women.

VICTORIA WOODHULL (1838–1927)

Often accompanied by her sister Tennessee and her daughter, Zula Maude, Victoria Woodhull romped through the Victorian Age like a character released from a bawdy novel. Her astonishing life—and the widespread publicity that it received— was a giant exception to general rules about female behavior and set precedents in business and politics.

Born in Licking County, Ohio, when that still was a frontier, she grew up in a traveling medicine show run by her one-eyed father, Buck Claflin. It featured his ten children, with one of Victoria's brothers posing as a cancer doctor, while she and Tennessee practiced "psychic medicine." The sisters soon grew adept at séances, palm readings, and other spiritualistic techniques, which Victoria always claimed were guided by a higher power.

At fifteen, she began a relationship with "Doctor" Canning Woodhull. She bore two children, but this did not mean settling down. The young family traveled as far as California before Dr. Woodhull disappeared in an alcoholic haze. Victoria gave up her mentally challenged son for adoption and, with Tennessee and Zula Maude, worked at various disreputable enterprises throughout the Midwest. The women were charged with prostitution, blackmail, and other criminal offenses in several places, but their usual strategy was to promise to move on, and they served no lengthy jail time. The most serious of their legal problems was when they fled Illinois after Tennessee was charged with manslaughter when a patient on whom she practiced psychic medicine died. She was accused of causing the death by neglecting genuine medical care.

Victoria secured a divorce from Woodhull in St. Louis in 1866, but if she married her lover, "Colonel" James Blood, no documentary evidence has been found. She apparently considered her name recognition to be valuable, as she continued to be known as "Mrs. Woodhull." Blood also advocated open marriage and what the era called "free love." He completely supported his unconventional partner and followed her to New York City when she and Tennessee moved there in 1868.

They might have remained petty miscreants for the rest of their lives but for railroad magnate Cornelius

Vanderbilt. His wife had recently died, and the sisters had no problem charming the lonely old man and fulfilling his hopes of contacting his late wife in the great beyond. From there, however, they departed from their usual snake-oil deceit. With backing from Vanderbilt, the women became serious investors, first in real estate and then in the stock market.

By January 1870, they were successful enough to open their own brokerage firm at 44 Broad Street, with well-decorated offices in the midst of the financial district. In addition to their brokerage, they began producing a newspaper, *Woodhull & Claflin's Weekly*, in 1870. Published until 1877, it never achieved a true weekly schedule. The paper promoted many advanced ideas: among its editorial policies was a healthy diet, reform of the era's restrictive dress for women, and even an international language. It ran Karl Marx's *Communist Manifesto* and promoted feminism and the Equal Rights Party.

Woodhull announced her presidential ambitions in the spring of 1872, but by election day, she and Tennessee were in jail. They were arrested for using the postal service to spread obscenity because they published in their newspaper the true story of Rev. Henry Ward Beecher's infidelity. The indictment eventually was dropped. In 1877, four years after their release from prison, the sisters and Zula left for London, amid rumors that the trip was paid for by the chief Vanderbilt heir, who wanted them out of the country when the estate was contested. The sisters issued a farewell copy of their newspaper and reinvented themselves abroad.

Tennessee, who sometimes spelled her name "Tennie C.," transformed herself via marriage into Lady Cook, and Victoria married an affluent Englishman, John Biddulph Martin. With Zula, she developed *Humanitarian* magazine and demonstrated that she could run a longtime business and educational enterprise by keeping it in regular publication from 1892 to 1910.

With occasional visits to her native land, Victoria Woodhull lived on through World War I and most of the Roaring Twenties, when her ideas sounded much less outrageous than they had a half-century earlier. By then, both American and British women could vote, and although it still would be a long time coming, the notion of a female president was less improbable than it had been when she pioneered the idea in 1872.

REFERENCES AND FURTHER READING

Chisholm, Shirley. 1973. *The Good Fight*. New York: Harper and Row.

Clift, Eleanor, and Tom Brazaitis. 2003. *Madam President: Women Blazing the Leadership Trail*. New York: Routledge.

Clinton, Hillary Rodham. 2003. *Living History*. New York: Simon and Schuster.

Falk, Erika. 2008. *Women for President: Media Bias in Eight Campaigns*. Urbana: University of Illinois Press.

Ferraro, Geraldine A., with Linda Bird Francke. 1985. *Ferraro: My Story*. New York: Bantam Books.

Frisken, Amanda. 2004. *Victoria Woodhull's Sexual Revolution: Political Theater and the Popular Press in Nineteenth-Century America*. Philadelphia: University of Pennsylvania Press.

Goldsmith, Barbara. 1998. *Other Powers: The Age of Suffrage, Spiritualism, and the Scandalous Victoria Woodhull*. New York: A.A. Knopf.

Han, Lori Cox, and Caroline Heldman, eds. 2007. *Rethinking Madam President: Are We Ready for a Woman in the White House?* Boulder, CO: Lynne Rienner Publishers.

Johnson, Johanna. 1967. *Mrs. Satan: The Incredible Saga of Victoria C. Woodhull*. New York: Putnam.

Johnson, Sonia. 1981. *Housewife to Heretic*. New York: Doubleday.

Lawrence, Regina G., and Melody Rose. 2010. *Hillary Clinton's Race for the White House: Gender Politics and the Media on the Campaign Trail*. Boulder, CO: Lynne Rienner Publishers.

Morrison, Susan, ed. 2008. *Thirty Ways of Looking at Hillary: Reflections by Women Writers*. New York: HarperCollins.

Norgren, Jill. 2007. *Belva Lockwood: The Woman Who Would Be President*. New York: New York University Press.

Schmidt, Patricia L. 1996. *Margaret Chase Smith: Beyond Convention*. Orono, ME: University of Maine Press.

Schroeder, Patricia. 1998. *24 Years of House Work . . . and the Place Is Still a Mess: My Life in Politics*. New York: G.K. Hall.

Sherman, Jannan. 2000. *No Place for a Woman: A Life of Margaret Chase Smith*. New Brunswick, NJ: Rutgers University Press.

Stanton, Elizabeth Cady, Susan B. Anthony, and Matilda Joslyn Gage. 1881. *History of Woman Suffrage*. Volume 1. New York: Fowler and Wells. Reprint, New York: Arno Press, 1969.

Stanton, Elizabeth Cady, Susan B. Anthony, and Matilda Joslyn Gage. 1882. *History of Woman Suffrage*. Volume 2. New York: Fowler and Wells. Reprint, New York: Arno Press, 1969.

Stanton, Elizabeth Cady, Susan B. Anthony, and Matilda Joslyn Gage. 1886. *History of Woman Suffrage*. Volume 3.

Rochester, New York: Charles Mann Printing Company. Reprint, New York: Arno Press 1969.

Todd, Chuck, and Sheldon Gawiser. 2009. *How Barack Obama Won*. New York: Vintage Books.

Vallin, Marlene Boyd. 1998. *Margaret Chase Smith: Model Public Servant*. Westport, CT: Greenwood Press.

Watson, Robert P., and Ann Gordon, eds. 2003. *Anticipating Madam President*. Boulder, CO: Lynne Rienner Publishers.

Wertheimer, Molly Meijer, and Nichola D. Gutgold. 2004. *Elizabeth Hanford Dole: Speaking from the Heart*. Westport, CT: Praeger.

CABINET AND SUBCABINET

The U.S. Constitution does not provide for a presidential cabinet, but George Washington set the precedent by creating the first one in 1789 when he chose five men as his advisors. Collectively dubbed "the cabinet," they were Thomas Jefferson, who headed the Department of State; Henry Knox, head of the Department of War (now the Department of Defense); Alexander Hamilton, chief of the Department of the Treasury; Attorney General Edmund Randolph, who headed what became known as the Department of Justice; and Postmaster General Samuel Osgood. (The Post Office would cease to be part of the cabinet in 1971.).

The cabinet grew very slowly, with no positions added from 1789 until 1849, when Congress created the Department of the Interior. The meaning of that name has now changed, but, at the time, "interior" referred to the unsettled West. The first secretary of the interior was appointed the year after the United States won its war with Mexico, which meant the acquisition of California and additional land in the southwest. Vast areas around the Mississippi River basin had been added in 1803, with the Louisiana Purchase from France; Florida was purchased from Spain in 1819; and, when the boundary of "the Oregon Country" was peacefully settled with Canada, the outlines of what would be the contiguous United States were becoming clear. The Interior Department was created to manage this land and—after War Department officials forced Indians to sign treaties with the U.S. government—to govern its natives.

National change can be seen in the forty years that passed between the 1849 creation of the Interior Department and the 1889 establishment of the Department of Agriculture (USDA). It was the first agency that could be dubbed "special interest," and, ironically, it was created when farming was no longer the prime American

occupation. The remainder of the new executive departments followed this occupational or economic model. As of 2011, there were fifteen departments. Other agencies began to be created fairly frequently starting at the end of the nineteenth century.

This chapter covers both female cabinet members and some of the lesser or subcabinet positions. All of these women held positions sufficiently important to require Senate confirmation.

PIONEERING AT LOWER LEVELS

The first appointment of a woman to a federal position that was high enough to require Senate confirmation occurred in 1898, when Republican president William McKinley named Estelle Reel of Wyoming as head of the nation's schools for Native American children. McKinley was assassinated in 1901, and his vice president, Theodore Roosevelt, succeeded him in office. During Roosevelt's tenure, in 1903, Congress enacted legislation to establish an eighth cabinet-level department, the Department of Commerce and Labor. A federal Children's Bureau was created within the department in 1912, and President William Howard Taft, a Republican elected in 1908, appointed Julia Lathrop as its first head.[1]

Part of the Illinois coalition of activists headed by Jane Addams, Lathrop was the second woman to hold a federal position high enough to require Senate confirmation. Unlike Estelle Reel, however, Lathrop was not

---

[1]For more on Lathrop and Reel, see Chapter 2: Female Officeholders Prior to the Nineteenth Amendment.

Table 11.1 Women in the Cabinet, by Year

Tenure	Name	Department	Appointed By	Party	Notes
1933–1945	Frances Perkins	Labor	Franklin D. Roosevelt	Democrat	Department was twenty years old
1953–1955	Oveta Culp Hobby	Health, Education, and Welfare (HEW)	Dwight D. Eisenhower	Republican	Inaugurated department
1975–1977	Carla Anderson Hills	Housing and Urban Development (HUD)	Gerald R. Ford	Republican	HUD was ten years old
1977–1979	Juanita M. Kreps	Commerce	Jimmy Carter	Democrat	Appointment of woman to highest-ranking department to date
1977–1979	Patricia Roberts Harris	Housing and Urban Development	Jimmy Carter	Democrat	African American; in the cabinet with Juanita M. Kreps, for the first time two women served simultaneously
1979–1980	Patricia Roberts Harris	Health, Education, and Welfare	Jimmy Carter	Democrat	Second female secretary of HEW
1980–1981	Patricia Roberts Harris	Health and Human Services (HHS)	Jimmy Carter	Democrat	Inaugurated department
1979–1981	Shirley M. Hufstedler	Education	Jimmy Carter	Democrat	Inaugurated department
1983–1985	Margaret M. Heckler	Health and Human Services	Ronald Reagan	Republican	Second female secretary of HHS
1983–1987	Elizabeth Dole	Transportation	Ronald Reagan	Republican	Department was twelve years old
1987–1989	Ann Dore McLaughlin	Labor	Ronald Reagan	Republican	Second female secretary of labor
1989–1990	Elizabeth Dole	Labor	George H.W. Bush	Republican	Third female secretary of labor
1991–1993	Lynn Martin	Labor	George H.W. Bush	Republican	Fourth female secretary of labor
1992–1993	Barbara Franklin	Commerce	George H.W. Bush	Republican	Second female secretary of commerce
1997–2001	Madeleine K. Albright	State	Bill Clinton	Democrat	First female secretary of state; position created in 1789
1993–2001	Janet Reno	Attorney general (Justice)	Bill Clinton	Democrat	First female attorney general; position created in 1789
1993–2001	Donna E. Shalala	Health and Human Services	Bill Clinton	Democrat	Third female secretary of HHS
1993–1997	Hazel R. O'Leary	Energy	Bill Clinton	Democrat	Only female Clinton appointee who did not serve eight years
1997–2001	Alexis M. Herman	Labor	Bill Clinton	Democrat	African American; fifth female secretary of labor
2001–2006	Gale A. Norton	Interior	George W. Bush	Republican	First female secretary of interior; department created in 1849
2001–2005	Ann M. Veneman	Agriculture	George W. Bush	Republican	First female secretary of agriculture; department created in 1889
2001–2009	Elaine L. Chao	Labor	George W. Bush	Republican	Asian American; fifth female secretary of labor
2005–2009	Condoleezza Rice	State	George W. Bush	Republican	African American; second female secretary of state
2005–2009	Margaret Spellings	Education	George W. Bush	Republican	Second female secretary of education
2006–2009	Mary E. Peters	Transportation	George W. Bush	Republican	Second female secretary of transportation
2009–	Hillary Rodham Clinton	State	Barack Obama	Democrat	Third female secretary of state
2009–	Hilda L. Solis	Labor	Barack Obama	Democrat	Hispanic; sixth female secretary of labor
2009–	Kathleen Sebelius	Health and Human Services	Barack Obama	Democrat	Fourth female secretary of HHS
2009–	Janet Napolitano	Homeland Security	Barack Obama	Democrat	First female secretary of homeland security

Source: Compiled by author.

Note: Within years, cabinet secretaries listed in order of rank.

Table 11.2   Notable Presidential Appointments below Cabinet Level, by Year

Year Appointed	Name	Title, Agency	Appointed By	Notes
1898	Estelle Reel	National superintendent of Indian schools, Interior Department	William McKinley	First female appointee to require Senate confirmation
1912	Julia Lathrop	Director, Children's Bureau, Labor Department	William Howard Taft	Second female appointee to require Senate confirmation
1919	Mary Anderson	Director, Women's Bureau, Labor Department	Woodrow Wilson	Headed agency for twenty years
1920	Helen Hamilton Gardener	Member, Civil Service Commission	Woodrow Wilson	Highest female appointee to date
1933	Nellie Tayloe Ross	Director, U.S. Mint	Franklin D. Roosevelt	Former governor of Wyoming
1935	Mary McLeod Bethune	Director, Division of Negro Affairs, National Youth Administration, Works Progress Administration	Franklin D. Roosevelt	First African American; Depression-era agency
1949	Georgia Neese Clark	U.S. treasurer, Treasury Department	Harry S. Truman	First woman to have her name on U.S. currency
1950	Anna Rosenberg	Assistant secretary of defense, Defense Department	Harry S. Truman	Requested by Defense Secretary George C. Marshall
1962	Katie Louchheim	Deputy assistant secretary of state, State Department	John F. Kennedy	Highest State Department position to date
1964	Virginia Mae Brown	Chair, Interstate Commerce Commission	Lyndon B. Johnson	First woman to head an independent federal agency
1964	Mary Gardener Jones	Member, Federal Trade Commission	Lyndon B. Johnson	Consumer protection agency, begun in 1914
1969	Nancy Hanks	Chair, National Endowment for the Arts	Richard M. Nixon	Agency was four years old
1972	Dixy Lee Ray	Member, Atomic Energy Commission	Richard M. Nixon	Scientist; later governor of Washington
1973	Barbara Franklin	Vice chair, Consumer Product Safety Commission	Richard M. Nixon	Agency was new
1975	Betty Southard Murphy	Member, National Labor Relations Board	Gerald R. Ford	First woman on board, which rules on labor disputes
1978	Anne Wexler	Special assistant to the president for public outreach, White House Office of Public Liaison and Intergovernmental Affairs	Jimmy Carter	Powerful political position within the White Office
1978	Nancy H. Teeters	Member, Board of Governors, Federal Reserve System	Jimmy Carter	First woman on board that regulates interest rates
1981	Anne Burford Gorsuch	Administrator, Environmental Protection Agency	Ronald Reagan	First female administrator; forced to resign
1985	Jackie Strange	Deputy postmaster general, U.S. Postal Service	Ronald Reagan	Highest female appointee since the post office began in colonial days
1986	Lynne Cheney	Chair, National Endowment for the Humanities (NEH)	Ronald Reagan	First woman and second NEH chair
1988	Elaine L. Chao	Chair, Federal Maritime Commission	Ronald Reagan	Chinese American; agency regulates ocean-bound shipping
1990	Antonia Novello	Surgeon general, Public Health Service Commissioned Corps	George H.W. Bush	Hispanic; position established during the Civil War
1991	Bernadine P. Healy	Director, National Institutes of Health	George H.W. Bush	Promoted research on women's health issues
1993	Carol M. Browner	Administrator, Environmental Protection Agency	Bill Clinton	Served entire eight years of the Clinton administration
1993	Doris Meissner	Commissioner, Immigration and Naturalization Service	Bill Clinton	First female commissioner; agency established in 1903
1993	Margaret Richardson	Commissioner, Internal Revenue Service	Bill Clinton	Tax-collecting agency with roots in the Civil War
1993	Laura D'Andrea Tyson	Chair, Council of Economic Advisers	Bill Clinton	First female chair

Table 11.2   (Continued)

Year Appointed	Name	Title, Agency	Appointed By	Notes
1993	Sheila Widnall	Secretary of the Air Force, Defense Department	Bill Clinton	Highest female appointee at the Pentagon
1994	Mary L. Shapiro	Chair, Commodities Futures Trading Board	Bill Clinton	Agency regulates trading in agricultural products
1997	Aida Alvarez	Administrator, Small Business Administration	Bill Clinton	Hispanic; first female administrator since agency created in 1953
1997	Charlene Barshefsky	U.S. trade representative, Executive Office of the President	Bill Clinton	First female trade representative; develops U.S. trade policy and conducts trade negotiations
2001	Condoleezza Rice	National security adviser, Executive Office of the President	George W. Bush	Advises president on national security matters; serves on the National Security Council
2001	Christine Todd Whitman	Administrator, Environmental Protection Agency	George W. Bush	Former governor of New Jersey
2006	Sheila Bair	Head, Federal Deposit Insurance Corporation	George W. Bush	Agency began 1933 to insure bank deposits
2009	Mary L. Shapiro	Chair, Securities and Exchange Commission	Barack Obama	Agency began in 1934 to regulate stock trading
2010	Elizabeth Warren	Assistant to the president and special adviser to the secretary of the Treasury	Barack Obama	Set up Consumer Financial Protection Bureau, but was not appointed to it when it was authorized in 2011

Source: Compiled by author, with assistance from 50-50 by 2020, an organization devoted to equal representation for women in government.

appointed head of an ongoing agency but instead began a wholly new bureau—something that other women also would do. This ability of women, who organized executive programs from idea to implementation, merits more acknowledgment from historians.

As America matured into an industrialized nation, the interests of commerce and labor often were diametrically opposed. In 1913, the Department of Commerce and Labor was divided into the Department of Commerce and the Department of Labor, with the Children's Bureau becoming part of Labor. Newly inaugurated president Woodrow Wilson, a Democrat, reappointed Lathrop as head of the Children's Bureau, and she continued in that position until 1921, when Grace Abbott, another progressive Chicagoan for immigrants and working people, succeeded her.

The primary goal of the Children's Bureau was a national ban on child labor. Congress tried twice, in 1916 and 1919, to discourage employment of children, but the U.S. Supreme Court subsequently ruled both acts unconstitutional. A constitutional amendment giving Congress the authority to outlaw child labor was submitted to the states in 1924 but was not ratified. The problem finally was resolved during the Great Depression, when the Court did not strike down a ban on child labor that was part of the 1937 Fair Labor Standards Act.

Beyond child labor, the Children's Bureau also concerned itself with health issues and was briefly successful with the Sheppard-Towner Maternity and Infancy Protection Act, which provided free health care for pregnant women and young children. The Republican Congress denied funding for the program in 1929, when mothers most needed it as the economy collapsed.

The Department of Labor also housed the Women's Bureau. With a labor shortage during World War I, President Wilson created a task force to recruit women for more jobs outside the home, and Congress authorized its existence under the Labor Department, where it was bureaucratically akin to the Children's Bureau. The first chief of the nascent bureau was Mary Van Kleeck, who had been named to several commissions by both Democrats and Republicans. She served more as a policymaker than an administrator, however, and resigned the post in 1919 in favor of her assistant, Mary Anderson. In 1920, Congress formalized the Women's Bureau of the Department of Labor, and Anderson headed it for the first quarter-century of its existence.

When Democrats lost the 1920 election, Republican women rallied to support Anderson and the Women's Bureau, and the three successive Republican presidents during the Roaring Twenties kept her in the office. A Swedish immigrant who began life in America as a factory

Table 11.3 First Women Cabinet-level Positions, by Year of the Department's Creation

Year Department Created	Title	President in Office at Creation	First Woman	Year She Took Office	Appointing President	Party
1789	Attorney general	George Washington	Janet Reno	1993	Bill Clinton	Democrat
1789	Secretary of war (later secretary of defense)	George Washington	None			
1789	Secretary of state	George Washington	Madeleine K. Albright	1997	Bill Clinton	Democrat
1789	Secretary of the Treasury	George Washington	None			
1789	Postmaster general	George Washington	None			
1849	Secretary of the interior	Zachary Taylor	Gale A. Norton	2001	George W. Bush	Republican
1889	Secretary of agriculture	Grover Cleveland	Ann M. Veneman	2001	George W. Bush	Republican
1913	Secretary of commerce	Woodrow Wilson	Juanita M. Kreps	1977	Jimmy Carter	Democrat
1913	Secretary of labor	Woodrow Wilson	Frances Perkins	1933	Franklin D. Roosevelt	Democrat
1953	Secretary of health, education, and welfare	Dwight D. Eisenhower	Oveta Culp Hobby	1953	Dwight D. Eisenhower	Republican
1965	Secretary of housing and urban development	Lyndon B. Johnson	Carla Anderson Hills	1975	Gerald R. Ford	Republican
1967	Secretary of transportation	Lyndon B. Johnson	Elizabeth Dole	1983	Ronald Reagan	Republican
1977	Secretary of energy	Jimmy Carter	Hazel R. O'Leary	1993	Bill Clinton	Democrat
1979	Secretary of health and human services	Jimmy Carter	Patricia Roberts Harris	1979	Jimmy Carter	Democrat
1979	Secretary of education	Jimmy Carter	Shirley M. Hufstedtler	1979	Jimmy Carter	Democrat
1989	Secretary of veterans affairs	George H.W. Bush	None			
2003	Secretary of homeland security	George W. Bush	Janet Napolitano	2009	Barack Obama	Democrat

Source: Compiled by author.

Note: The postmaster general ceased being in the cabinet in 1971, when the U.S. Postal Service was established as an independent agency.

worker, she understood labor issues and was very popular with her constituency. Democrat Franklin D. Roosevelt reappointed her when he entered the White House, and in 1933, he put Anderson in charge of a delegation to the International Labour Organization in Geneva. She served throughout the Great Depression and most of World War II, resigning in 1944 at age seventy-two.

In addition to Van Kleeck at the Women's Bureau, President Wilson promoted other women. He named several to special commissions that dealt with war-related issues. Among them was Anna Howard Shaw, the former president of the National American Woman Suffrage Association. The highest of such appointments was Florence "Daisy" Hurst Harriman, who, under Franklin Roosevelt, would be the nation's second female ambassador.[2]

In 1920, just months prior to the Nineteenth Amendment's final ratification, Wilson appointed the first woman—Helen Hamilton Gardener—to the Civil Service Commission, an extant body that, significantly, dealt with issues not necessarily connected to women or children. Founded in 1883, the commission's purpose, as mandated by Congress, was to make federal employment less political and more professional. Over time, the office

developed and administered civil service examinations that formed the basis for fair hiring. Gardener lived in Washington, DC, next door to House Speaker Champ Clark. They became good friends, and her influence with him was incalculable in congressional passage of the Nineteenth Amendment, which granted all women the vote. Carrie Chapman Catt and other mainstream leaders for the vote were aware of Gardener's quiet but astute political abilities, and Wilson's appointment of her went smoothly. She served a five-year term, ending in 1925.

Calvin Coolidge, a Republican, was president by then, having succeeded Warren Harding after his sudden death in 1923. Neither Harding nor Coolidge appointed women to significant new positions. The third Republican president of the Roaring Twenties, Herbert Hoover, did not appoint any women, either. The first appointment of a woman to be in the cabinet would have to wait until the election of Democrat Franklin Roosevelt.

THE FIRST TWO: 1933 AND 1953

Women had voted for thirteen years and the Labor Department was twenty years old when Franklin Roosevelt named FRANCES PERKINS as its head. She was

---

[2] See Chapter 12: Ambassadors.

not only the first female member of the cabinet, but also the most important labor secretary and one of the most important cabinet members of all time. Under her administration of the department, the nation implemented its first federal legislation on minimum wages and maximum hours, unemployment compensation, Social Security, and other historic changes related to labor issues.

More than anyone else, Molly Dewson, the head of the Women's Division of the Democratic Party, pushed Roosevelt to make the unprecedented cabinet appointment. Dewson repeatedly lobbied the president-elect and quietly organized a letter-writing campaign throughout the nation for Perkins. Then, Dewson had to persuade Perkins to accept the position: Perkins was a naturally quiet and modest person who valued her privacy and that of her family. Perkins later said that her primary motivation for accepting the position was feminist.

I have always felt that it was not I alone who was appointed to the Cabinet, but that it was all the women of America; and I have been happy that so many women have shared with me the sense of gratification that this time has come. . . . The overwhelming argument and thought which made me do it in spite of personal difficulties was the realization that the door might not be opened to a woman again for a long, long time, and that I had a kind of duty to other women to walk in and sit down on the chair that was offered. (Ware 1987, 179)

Although Roosevelt and other cabinet members understood that Perkins's qualifications were as legitimate as those of any man, her appointment was not without controversy. Many leaders in the American Federation of Labor (AFL) and the Congress of Industrial Organizations (CIO) grumbled about the Labor Department being headed by a woman. The president stuck to his resolution, though, and Perkins repaid him with loyalty. She was one of just two cabinet members who served throughout Roosevelt's tenure. The other was Harold Ickes, secretary of the interior, and the cabinet's only Jewish member.

The nation's economic condition was so severe that the administration set to work on inauguration day, and Frances Perkins took the oath of office only a few hours after the president did, on March 4, 1933. In May, she played a key role in passage of the Federal Emergency Relief Act. June brought the beginning of the U.S. Employment Service, as well as the creation of the National Labor Relations Board that settled grievances. Thus, in her first three months, Frances Perkins accomplished more than most government officials during their entire careers. In 1934, she led the United States into the International Labour Organization, which was part of the Geneva-based League of Nations, and in 1935, Social Security was implemented. In 1937, the Fair Labor Standards Act ensured the right of collective bargaining, set federal maximum hours and minimum wages, and banned child labor.

Mainstream journalists tended to ignore news about racial minorities, but among the many scattered agencies that the Roosevelt administration used to deal with the Great Depression was the National Youth Administration (NYA). It aimed to give employment skills to young people, especially African Americans and Native Americans. Unlike the Civilian Conservation Corps, which was restricted to young white men, the NYA was integrated by both race and gender. In 1935, to help run the organization, President Roosevelt appointed the nation's first African American of either gender to a top federal position, Mary McLeod Bethune. As the 1905 founder of what became Florida's Bethune-Cookman College, she was an excellent choice for introducing innovative ideas. Bethune traveled thirty-five thousand miles in just one year, speaking for equal opportunity for minority youth—including Native Americans, Mexican Americans, and African Americans. Although she was the only woman in the "black cabinet," a handful of mostly male African Americans that informally advised the president, she was its acknowledged leader. The group held its weekly meetings at her Washington home.

Bethune would serve until World War II brought an end to the NYA. Labor secretary Perkins also faced a different set of economic problems after war broke out in Europe in 1939. Instead of dealing with unemployment, millions of additional workers had to be recruited for factories that were being retooled from producing civilian goods to military materiel. During the next few years, the nation saw the largest entrance of women and racial minorities into the labor force of any time in its history, and again, Perkins spearheaded the effort. She faced critics—including some women—who thought that while it was fine for her to hold this cabinet position in peacetime, she should surrender it to a man in wartime.

She resigned on July 1, 1945, a few months after Roosevelt died and when the war in Europe was over. Vice President Harry S. Truman succeeded Roosevelt as president, and he did not appoint any women to his cabinet. He did, however, appoint Kansas banker Georgia Neese Clark as the first female U.S. treasurer—but this is a largely ceremonial position, not to be confused with the powerful post of secretary of the Treasury. Every president since Truman has followed his precedent by appointing women to the lesser post, but none yet has headed the Treasury Department.

Truman also made one other significant appointment, but that precedent largely has been forgotten. Anna Rosenberg was a highly paid labor-relations consultant in New York City when President Roosevelt recruited her to

In 1946, after Frances Perkins resigned as secretary of labor, President Harry S. Truman appointed her to the Civil Service Commission. Its job is to hear cases involving disputes between federal employees and their managers, with commissioners acting as judges to rule on whether or not a federal employee can be fired. According to biographer George Martin, Perkins's most upsetting case, which seems almost bizarre now, was not so unusual in an era when moral turpitude was grounds for dismissal from government employment. Saying that the case "concerned a Washington policeman and a woman working for the government," Martin used delicate language in his description.

The policeman asked the woman to perform on him what has sometimes been considered an unnatural sex act. Later the man felt remorse and confessed the act to his priest. . . . The priest advised the man to report the woman to her superiors, which the man did after receiving a promise that his name would not be used. Charges were made against the woman and her case came before the commission.

Perkins . . . thought that the man's moral character was so "degraded" that, as a policeman, with the right to enter people's homes, he was "a threat to the community." But she was still more upset that commissioners should accept evidence from a source who refused to be identified. Again and again she urged her fellow commissioners to report the man . . . so that he, too, might be dismissed. But they refused: he had been promised immunity. She interviewed the man, pointing out that for a mutual, private act, which he had made public, the woman would lose both job and reputation while he would retain both. To her astonishment, he could see no injustice in what was happening. (Martin 1976, 478)

Even though the activity was private and unconnected to her federal employment, the anonymous woman lost her job, while her sexual partner retained his—and Perkins was powerless to do anything about this inequity.

accept one of the dollar-a-year jobs that he offered his advisers. Roosevelt liked to send incognito representatives to check on his administrators, and Rosenberg traveled thousands of miles during the war to assess soldier morale. She slept on the ground, ate GI (government issue) rations, and according to Eleanor Roosevelt, "knew more Army privates than anyone else" (Roosevelt 1954, 169).

General George C. Marshall, who was the U.S. Army's chief of staff during World War II, got to know Rosenberg via her reports. In 1950, when he became secretary of defense [after the 1947 name change from Department of War to Department of Defense (DOD)], Marshall asked President Truman to appoint Rosenberg to the high rank of assistant secretary of defense. She did a good but low-profile job as its expert in personnel. No woman since has reached this level at the Pentagon.

At the cabinet level, eight years passed between Perkins's 1945 resignation and the 1953 appointment of OVETA CULP HOBBY. She was the second woman in the cabinet and the first to inaugurate a new department. Starting a major project from scratch was not new for Hobby, as she had built the Women's Army Corps (WAC) from its implementing legislation in 1942 to 100,000 volunteer female soldiers in 1945, when World War II was won. No other military corps met so much success so quickly, but although Hobby's responsibilities meant that she should have been a general, Congress limited the corps' head to the rank of colonel. Dwight D.

Eisenhower noticed the exceptional abilities of Army women early in his command of the North African and European Theaters of Operations, and a few months after his 1953 inauguration as president, he chose Hobby to head the new Department of Health, Education, and Welfare (HEW).

The idea for such an executive agency had been around for a long time. Among those who proposed such a post was Florida representative Ruth Bryan Owen, who introduced legislation to create a Department of Home and Child soon after she entered Congress in 1929.[3] More than two decades passed between Owen's proposal and HEW's beginning, and then many saw the new department as more a matter of streamlining extant agencies than as a commitment to new policy.

The name Department of Health, Education, and Welfare spelled out its disparate responsibilities. Health issues, for example, had been addressed by Congress as early as 1798, when, during the John Adams administration, it passed an Act for the Relief of Sick and Disabled Seamen. The Office of the Surgeon General grew out of the Civil War, and the U.S. Public Health Service began in response to epidemics in the late nineteenth century, but it was not officially authorized until 1912. Other agencies with similar aims grew similarly haphazardly.

---

[3] See Chapter 6: United States Representatives.

Although most politicians rhetorically argued that educational issues were the province of the states, federal aid to education had begun with the Northwest Ordinance of 1787, when the federal government set aside revenue from land sales in the new territories for the benefit of schools. By the time of HEW's establishment, a number offices dealt with education concerns, especially schools for Native Americans and for the disabled.

Finally, the Constitution's preamble says that one of the federal government's chief responsibilities is "to provide for the general welfare," but even more than education, the federal government left welfare programs to the states and to private charities. The Great Depression, however, necessitated more federal activism for the needy, and even World War II, with its rationing and allotments to soldiers' dependants, validated the idea that the federal government had obligations to assist those without income. These disparate matters of health, education, and welfare were combined under the purview of HEW.

Oveta Culp Hobby began the task of sorting them out in April 1953. As in the WAC, she took an organization from conceptual beginning to established operation, in this case with a budget of $5.4 billion and a staff of thirty-five thousand, appreciably fewer than she commanded in the war. She had the president's support, not only because of their mutual war service, but also because Eisenhower believed in the principles of the new department. Indeed, he may have been the only president who could have made it work. A Democrat such as Roosevelt, Truman, or Kennedy might have been accused of excessive liberalism in birthing HEW, but Eisenhower was a Republican whose life in the military accustomed him to a federal government that provided for the health, education, and welfare of himself and his family. Eisenhower thus was able to disregard objections from politicians, especially white Southern men, who saw HEW as an intrusion into states' rights.

Eisenhower, however, turned out to lack the political skills to support Hobby in the way that Roosevelt had supported Perkins. Many of those who opposed HEW were open racists, and beyond their objections to welfare in general, they also objected to Hobby's appointment of a black woman as her top assistant. Jane M. Spaulding, an officer in the National Association of Colored Women, had a background similar to Hobby's and was an excellent administrator, but her appointment was another negative for conservatives.

The problem that overwhelmed Hobby's tenure, though, should have been a good thing. Serious epidemics of polio had swept the postwar nation, and with support from the new March of Dimes Foundation, Dr. Jonas Salk developed the first vaccine to prevent the disease.

Formally called infantile paralysis, it especially attacked children. Many victims died, and others could live only by being confined in an iron lung that forced breathing. Polio was contagious and terrifying to many parents, who eagerly awaited the Salk vaccine.

Distribution of the vaccine became a paradigm for Eisenhower's—and the nation's—confused thinking on health care. As a military man accustomed to free health care, he assured the public that the vaccine would be free, but as a Republican who believed in free enterprise, he also responded positively to pharmaceutical companies and physicians who intended to charge for vaccinations. Hobby was left to figure out this economic contradiction. She also had to reassure the public that the vaccine was safe, after a bad batch of vaccine from one California laboratory caused deaths. Hobby shut down the lab immediately, assembled an inspection team within two days, and instituted a tedious batch-by-batch review of all vaccine, but she nonetheless received more than her share of the blame.

Questions of safety thus forced federal control of the vaccine's distribution, and the inoculation program was well on its way when Hobby resigned on July 13, 1955. Her stated reason for leaving was that her husband was critically ill, but he did not die until a decade later, and many believed that the polio fiasco was the real cause. Although no evidence exists that Eisenhower asked for her resignation, he failed to support her in a clear and consistent way, and he did not refuse to accept the resignation.

A point that historians generally have overlooked in Hobby's relative failure at HEW is a decline in female power after the war, especially in Congress.[4] When Hobby headed the WAC, the new corps had strong defenders in Massachusetts representative Edith Nourse Rogers and other female members of Congress who deflected criticism. HEW, however, was not strongly identified with any woman in Congress, and that absence meant that all attacks were aimed at Hobby. Frances Perkins, too, had benefited from support from women such as Rep. Mary T. Norton, who chaired the House Labor Committee during Perkins's tenure. Because women's networks had declined by the 1950s, Hobby had no female defenders. Neither the American Nurses Association nor any other organization of women spoke out on her behalf.

THE MODERN ERA BEGINS, 1955–1980

President Eisenhower did not appoint another woman to the cabinet after Hobby's 1955 resignation, and his eight

---

[4] See, especially, Chapter 6: United States Representatives.

years in office ended in January 1961. His vice president, Richard M. Nixon, narrowly lost to Democrat John F. Kennedy in the 1960 election. President Kennedy did not immediately appoint a woman to cabinet rank, either. He did, however, begin the nation's first Presidential Commission on the Status of Women in late 1961, naming former first lady Eleanor Roosevelt as its chair and urging governors to set up similar state commissions.[5] Future presidents maintained the commission until 1981, when Republican Ronald Reagan did not make appointments to the federal body, and it died.

The commission was created in response to lobbying by consumer activist Esther Peterson, and Kennedy also chose Peterson to head the Women's Bureau of the Department of Labor. He set a precedent, too, with the first appointment of a woman, Dr. Janet Travell, as White House physician. Finally, he named Democratic activist Katie Louchheim as a deputy assistant secretary at the State Department over objections from its diplomats, who saw even this lowly appointment as unsuitable for a woman.[6]

After Kennedy's 1963 assassination, Democrat Lyndon B. Johnson of Texas became president. Congress created two new cabinet-level departments, Housing and Urban Development (HUD) in 1965 and Transportation (DOT) in 1967. Both were at least somewhat analogous to the Departments of Agriculture and Commerce, in that they were established largely in response to lobbying by the affected industries. Although complaints about excessive government were as frequent then as now, the reality is that most people in private enterprise want government agencies that specialize in their field. These bodies not only conduct research and promote their interests at taxpayer expense, but also because such agencies have the force of law in controlling unfair competition. A seat at cabinet meetings is an additional plus.

No women were appointed to these or other cabinet positions by either Johnson or his Republican successor, Richard Nixon. However, both men did make some unprecedented appointments at the subcabinet level. In 1964, Johnson appointed Virginia Mae Brown to the Interstate Commerce Commission, an agency that regulated trade. The president had not even contacted Brown when he announced the appointment in a speech to the Women's National Press Club. She accepted nevertheless and, in routine rotation, rose to chair the commission in 1969, making her the first woman to head an independent administrative commission of the federal government. She used her position to impose reformist rules such as

forbidding employees from accepting gifts from private contractors. Her term expired after Nixon's 1968 election, and he did not reappoint her.

He did appoint scientist Dixy Lee Ray to the Atomic Energy Commission. She later would become governor of Washington.[7] Barbara Franklin also would go on to higher office. Her career began when Nixon appointed her as vice chair of to the new Consumer Product Safety Commission in 1973. Nixon also appointed Virginia Knauer as the first U.S. consumer advocate. A 1937 graduate of the University of Pennsylvania and the first woman elected to the Philadelphia City Council, Knauer was a widow in 1966, when she moved to Washington, DC, to lobby for the handicapped. She was appointed to the new consumer position in 1969. Both she and Franklin retained their posts after Nixon's resignation and later advised other presidents on consumer issues.

Nixon resigned in disgrace in 1974 and was succeeded by Gerald R. Ford. When Ford appointed the cabinet's third woman, CARLA ANDERSON HILLS, twenty years had passed since Hobby's 1955 resignation. In 1975, Hills became secretary of the Department of Housing and Urban Development. She moved there from her position as chief of the Civil Division of the Department of Justice, and her experience was almost entirely limited to law, not urban planning or construction. Senate confirmation, therefore, was not entirely smooth, but the nation was in such turmoil from the Nixon scandals that senators allowed the new, unelected president to have his choice.

From its beginning, HUD was known for its cost overruns and fiscal mismanagement, and Hills's reputation for integrity helped improve that image. Several mayors criticized her as too unwilling to promote investment in urban redevelopment, but the era was one of great inflation, and Hills wanted to hold the line on spending. In any case, she did not have much time to make major changes, as her tenure ended after Ford lost the 1976 election.

Even though Democrat Jimmy Carter, the former governor of Georgia who defeated Ford, would serve only one term, he became the first president to appoint more than one woman who would join the cabinet—promoting an unprecedented three during his four years in office. PATRICIA ROBERTS HARRIS succeeded Carla Hills at HUD, Juanita M. Kreps was the first woman to head the long extant Department of Commerce, and Shirley M. Hufstedler would be the inaugural chief of the new Department of Education. In addition to the precedent of naming three women as secretaries, Carter merits credit

---

[5] See Chapter 17: Interest Groups.

[6] For more, see Chapter 12: Ambassadors.

[7] See Chapter 8: Governors and Lieutenant Governors.

for appointing the first female racial minority in the cabinet, as Harris was African American.

Juanita Kreps's appointment came first, with Carter announcing his choice soon after the election. Kreps was an economist teaching at North Carolina's prestigious Duke University, and she had been the first woman on the governing board of the New York Stock Exchange. Formally named Blair Juanita Morris, she had grown up poor in coal mining Kentucky, the daughter of a divorced mother. She attended Kentucky's Berea College, an institution founded in the nineteenth century on the premise that students would work on the college farm to pay their tuition. She graduated with honors in 1942, the first full year of American involvement in World War II. Because most young men were in the military, universities opened doors to women that they never had done before, and she was able to earn a master's degree in 1944 and a doctorate in 1948 at Duke, both in economics. Meanwhile, she married Clifton Kreps, who also had a doctorate in economics, and bore three children.

Dr. Juanita Kreps rose in academia from a first teaching job in Ohio to Hofstra University and Queens College in New York before returning to Duke, where she became the university's first female vice president. She also served on the boards of such major corporations as J. C. Penney, Nabisco, and Chrysler, where male colleagues admired her clear thinking and aggressive approach to new business opportunities, especially abroad.

Some in Congress were trying to dismantle the Commerce Department in this era because it had become a collection of disparate agencies that lacked coordination. Its divisions included everything from the Bureau of the Census to the National Weather Service, but Kreps was determined to stop in-fighting between bureaucrats and to improve the department's coordination in the interest of a more holistic economy. She succeeded to the point that, by the end of her tenure, talk of eliminating the department had stopped.

Kreps may have stayed with the Carter administration for its full tenure, but her husband was mentally ill. She resigned in 1979 after he attempted suicide. Returning to North Carolina, she served on the boards of additional corporations and earned some twenty honorary degrees prior to dying just short of her ninetieth birthday.

Carter's other 1977 appointee already was known to the public and the press. Patricia Roberts Harris had served as ambassador to Luxembourg under Democrat Lyndon Johnson.[8] Unlike Kreps, Harris grew up in a more financially secure family, which helped compensate somewhat for the era's routine discrimination against her and other

people of color. Because Carla Hills had set the precedent of a woman at HUD, little controversy arose when Harris succeeded her in the top spot. Harris was so talented that she turned out to be Carter's utility-player, filling in as needed. During his four-year tenure, she held three cabinet positions: secretary of HUD, secretary of HEW, and secretary of the Department of Health and Human Services (HHS). HEW was split in 1980 into HHS and the Department of Education.

At HUD, Harris worked to end the Nixon era approach known as slum clearance and instead emphasized redevelopment of urban historic areas that had deteriorated. At her confirmation hearing, she reminded senators that, for most of her life, she would not have been able to buy a house in many neighborhoods because of her skin color, and she worked to end housing discrimination. She also developed the concept of urban homesteading, an overdue reminder of the advantages that the federal government had given a century earlier to rural dwellers, when the 1862 Homestead Act offered free land.

Harris left HUD to take over the Department Health, Education, and Welfare in 1979. The following year, HEW was divided into the Department of Education and the Department of Health and Human Services. Harris thus oversaw the dismantling of her department, and when HHS became a separate entity, she was its first secretary.

Shirley Hufstedler was the third woman to launch a new executive department, joining Harris and Oveta Culp Hobby, who had done so back in the 1950s. Partly because the legislation establishing the Department of Education only narrowly passed, Carter chose a lawyer, not an educator, as secretary. Members of the National Education Association and other teachers organizations initially were skeptical that a nonteacher could understand their profession, but Hufstedler soon won them over. She successfully supervised some seventeen thousand employees and administered a $14 billion budget until she had to resign early in 1981, after President Carter lost his reelection to Republican Ronald Reagan.

Hufstedler got the Department of Education off to a fine start, and although Reagan and other Republicans periodically threatened to abolish it, Congress never has seriously considered doing so. The Education Department is especially valued for its research into problems such as dyslexia and other learning disabilities that previously were unknown. Despite women's prominence in the field of education, though, no other woman would head the department for a quarter-century, from the end of Hefstedler's tenure early in 1981 to 2005.

Carter also made some significant appointments of women at the subcabinet level. Learning from his

---

[8] See Chapter 12: Ambassadors.

experience with Juanita Kreps, he appointed another female economist, Nancy H. Teeters, as a governor of the Federal Reserve Board, which regulates banking and, importantly, changes rates of interest on loans. A 1952 graduate of Ohio's Oberlin College, she was typical of women who grew up in an era when few female students, no matter how talented, were encouraged to pursue advanced degrees. She became an economist only after her in-laws financed her graduate studies.

Finally, in addition to Patricia Harris as the first African American woman in the cabinet, Carter appointed Mary Frances Berry, a black woman, to two prominent positions beneath that level. In 1977, his first year in office, he named her assistant secretary for education at HEW. At that time she was chancellor of the University of Colorado and the first black woman to lead a research university. In 1980, his last full year in office, Carter added Berry to the Civil Rights Commission. These appointments required some political courage because Berry was uncompromising in her passion for minorities and women. Although she earned a doctorate in history at the University of Michigan and was well regarded in academia, conservatives saw her as a radical and loudly voiced their objections. When Republican Ronald Reagan became president, he tried to remove Berry from the commission. She went to court and won the right to serve out her full term and later chaired the panel.

REAGAN AND BUSH ADMINISTRATIONS, 1981–1993

Republican Ronald Reagan, who defeated Jimmy Carter in 1980, would appoint three women during eight years in office, in contrast to Carter, who appointed them to five positions in four years.

No women were part of Reagan's initial cabinet, but he made a subcabinet level appointment that soon became controversial. The Environmental Protection Agency (EPA) had been created in 1970, during the Nixon administration, when the public was outraged by the fact that petroleum pollution on Ohio's Cuyahoga River was so bad that, at the point where it enters Lake Erie, the water caught fire. In May 1981, President Reagan appointed Anne Burford, an attorney and Colorado legislator, as EPA's first female chief. Neither Reagan nor Burford shared the goals of most environmentalists, and she soon ran into trouble with Congress.

On December 16, 1982, the full House voted 205 to 105 to cite Burford for contempt—something that never before had been done at that level of office. She was following White House orders when she refused to release records on the EPA's management of its $1.6 billion Superfund for hazardous waste cleanup. The House sought to check on the use of the funding. In February, the Reagan administration diverted attention from the EPA chief—whose name changed to Anne Burford Gorsuch with marriage that month—by firing Rita Lavelle, the head of EPA's Solid Waste Division. Lavelle was dismissed after news stories revealed that she harassed EPA employees for doing their jobs, while accepting gifts from the industries that she was charged with regulating. The negative headlines on EPA did not end, however, and Gorsuch, too, was forced to resign in March 1983.

In the same year, President Reagan named Margaret M. Heckler to head HHS. She was the department's third secretary and its second woman, following Patricia Roberts Harris, who headed HHS at its beginning. The only woman in her Boston College Law School class, she won the coveted position of editor of *Annual Survey of Massachusetts Law* and graduated in 1956. Because women were unwelcome at major law firms, she formed a partnership with other women in the affluent Boston suburb of Wellesley. She also married stockbroker John Heckler and bore three children before being elected to Congress in 1966, representing the area southwest of Boston.

In the U.S. House, Heckler supported the Equal Rights Amendment and particularly worked for child care and equal access to credit. She lost a close 1982 race to Democrat Barney Frank. Frank's sister, Ann Lewis, was a Democratic Party powerhouse and helped him defeat Heckler, a Republican.[9]

Heckler was widely respected by her peers in Congress, and the three senators who voted against her confirmation as head of HHS did so because they thought her insufficiently opposed to abortion. Her HHS tenure avoided restrictions in that area, though, while giving the first attention to acquired immune deficiency syndrome (AIDS). Heckler successfully advocated for the National Organ Transplant Act and supported funding for Alzheimer's disease research. Under her administration, HHS also developed guidelines for SSI, or Supplemental Security Insurance for the disabled.

However, Heckler apparently had trouble getting along with Reagan's staff, and she soon found herself shut off from access to the president before being removed from HHS entirely in 1984. Some of Heckler's difficulties may have been based in the fact that she was more liberal than those in the White House. A second factor probably was that Heckler's husband filed for divorce in 1984. Reagan was up for reelection that year, and even though he was the nation's first divorced president, different standards

---

[9] For more on Lewis, see Chapter 16: Political Parties and Conventions.

for women meant that the headlines about her divorce proved embarrassing. This, plus the administration's desire for a conservative man at HHS, meant that she was reassigned—with a pay cut—and became ambassador to Ireland in December 1985.[10]

Reagan appointed ELIZABETH DOLE as secretary of transportation in 1983. She was the first—and, as of 2011, the only—woman to head that traditionally male department. Her husband was Kansas senator Bob Dole. He also chaired the Senate Finance Committee, but senators had no problem with potential conflicts of interest when they confirmed her. Elizabeth Dole would go on to become the first woman to serve in two different cabinet positions under two different presidents.

DOT at that time had 100,000 employees and a $27 billion budget, constituting a much larger bureaucracy than HHS and Education, which covered areas that are traditionally associated with women. Dole's predecessor had recently implemented a heavy-use tax on trucks, and during her first week in office, Dole dealt with a strike of independent truckers. She went on to defy the usual Republican agenda by imposing more safety regulations, especially mandating brake lights on rear windows and air bags in new cars. She also dogged the Federal Aviation Administration (FAA) on safety issues and irritated airline executives with demands for more on-time flights.

Her department imposed the first random drug tests of its employees, and the initial testing showed that the agency had a drug and alcohol addiction rate of over 5 percent. Dole also aimed to increase the number of women in nonclerical jobs in the mostly male agency. DOT's workforce was 81 percent male when she arrived, and almost all of the 19 percent who were female were in clerical positions. She managed to increase the number of women in managerial jobs, but only by a few percentage points.

That, plus her drug-testing policy, made enemies within DOT, but more important were business enemies, especially in the airline and automobile industries. She resigned on September 30, 1987, well before the end of Reagan's second term. Most pundits, including feminists, believed that her chief reason for resigning was that she was being pressured by her husband's aides to campaign full time for his failed attempt to win the 1988 Republican presidential nomination.

At the same time that Dole was promoting women, another early Reagan appointee resigned because she believed the administration was insufficiently respectful of women. Barbara Honegger had campaigned for Reagan

and Bush in 1980 and was appointed to a political position in the Civil Rights Division of the Justice Department. She resigned in 1983, denouncing the department's antidiscrimination work as nothing but a sham. Several news sources reported that the White House press office responded to inquiries by calling Honegger a "low level Munchkin" and implying that her only role in the administration was to dress as a bunny for the annual White House Easter egg roll.

Critics of the Reagan administration were more concerned about one of his appointments the following year. Linda Chavez became head of the Civil Rights Commission and implemented an agenda that in many ways ran in direct opposition to the aims of its congressional enabling act. Under her chairmanship, the commission began backing off of its support of affirmative action, bilingual education, and other programs to ensure equity for minorities and women. At the time, some governmental entities were studying the concept of comparable worth, which examined public jobs for required credentials and responsibility levels, and then implemented salary scales to ensure, for example, that nurses were paid as much as garbage collectors. Chavez denounced the idea as too radical. Chavez left her post to pursue a 1986 Senate race in Maryland, which she lost to Democrat Barbara Mikulski.[11]

Also in 1986, Reagan made another controversial appointment when he chose Lynne Cheney to head the National Endowment for the Humanities (NEH). The wife of Wyoming representative and future vice president Dick Cheney, she had earned a doctorate in British literature from the University of Wisconsin, but many scholars who were associated with NEH viewed her as too willing to limit freedom of expression. She spoke out frequently against the depiction of sex and violence in art forms from film to music. Cheney also distressed NEH clientele by adhering to the administration's antigay views. She eventually would be supportive of her daughter, then a teenager and later an open lesbian. She was the first female head of NEH, and as of 2011, none has followed.

The third woman appointed to the cabinet by Reagan was Ann Dore McLaughlin, who became secretary of labor at the end of 1987. Like Lynne Cheney, McLaughlin was connected to a political husband. John McLaughlin had been a speechwriter for the Nixon administration and went on to be a conservative talk-show figure, hosting *The McLaughlin Group*, among other shows. Ann McLaughlin had been appointed to executive positions in the Treasury and Interior departments.

---

[10] See also Chapter 6: United States Representatives and Chapter 12: Ambassadors.

[11] See Chapter 7: United States Senators.

Unlike most female cabinet appointees, Elizabeth Dole's resignation was at least as controversial as her nomination had been. She resigned as head of the Department of Transportation (DOT) in 1987 to assist in her husband's bid for the presidency. Many feminists complained publicly about her giving up a chance to transform DOT, with most portraying her resignation as abandonment of a rare career opportunity for traditional wifely duty.

Authors Molly Meijer Wertheimer and Nichola D. Gutgold quoted feminist icon and syndicated columnist Ellen Goodman: "Elizabeth Dole is taking off ahead of schedule. . . . The woman is leaving to become—heaven help her—a frequent flier in the presidential campaign of her husband." Others, including some men, echoed the thought.

Journalist Stephen C. Fehr reported that many women were debating the pros and cons of Dole's resignation. . . . Some said that in a two-career marriage, it is the woman who must give up her job. Irene Natividad [of the National Women's Political Caucus] was quoted as saying that Dole's decision was really "sexism rearing its ugly head," while other women pointed out that it was fine for a woman to have a career and contribute to the family income, but it was too difficult when her career was too demanding. Ruth Mandel, director of the Center of American Women in Politics at Rutgers, put the point well when she said that Dole and her decision to resign reminded her of the Roman god Janus, whose face looked both backward and forward. (Wertheimer and Gutgold, 2004, 90-91)

Their points were valid, but another argument also can be made. Bob Dole may have been the primary reason that Elizabeth Dole's career flourished after her initial experience in the Nixon administration. Although she was qualified for the top job at DOT and the other federal positions she held, similarly qualified women did not win such high-level posts—and, without her influential husband, she, too, might have been passed over for cabinet positions. His Washington, DC, tenure predated hers; he was both a strong senator and a strong Republican, rising to majority leader and minority leader; and the two presidents who appointed his wife to their cabinets doubtless included his position in the Senate as a factor in their decisions.

Journalists also largely ignored the fact that the DOT budget during her tenure was strongly affected by his chairmanship of the Senate Finance Committee. This axiomatic conflict of interest was not scrutinized, and the precedent that the Doles set was overlooked a few years later, when another power couple arrived in Washington. Although Hillary Rodham Clinton, too, was well qualified and although she was not paid for her services, she was widely criticized for overseeing a task force to devise a health care reform proposal. Both Doles were well paid with federal tax dollars, but they never endured such criticism. Proper roles of political wives continued to be debated, and, like Janus, people look both backward and forward simultaneously, stumbling on their conflicting attitudes toward strong women married to strong men.

By 1987, when Elizabeth Dole resigned from DOT, feminists were sufficiently powerful that the Reagan administration understood the public relations damage that could result from an all-male cabinet. Dole resigned on September 30, and McLaughlin became head of the Department of Labor on December 14. She would serve slightly more than a year, until January 1981. The second female head of that department, she was seen as a caretaker and seemed to accept that role. McLaughlin undertook no major policy efforts, making her tenure a great contrast to the first female labor secretary, Frances Perkins.

Although he also was a Republican, newly elected president George H. W. Bush did not reappoint McLaughlin to Labor. Instead, he chose Elizabeth Dole, whose husband had dropped out of the 1988 presidential race that Bush won. The Senate vote to confirm her was 99–0, and she was the third female secretary of labor. She served only from January 1989 to November 1990, a much briefer tenure than she had as head of the Department of Transportation.

As was the case at DOT, Dole did not entirely please conservatives when she headed the Labor Department. During her tenure, the department produced the study that popularized the phrase "glass ceiling," denoting the invisible but routine barriers to female careers. "We aim," she wrote, "to give a 'wake-up call' to businesses, to alert them to the fact that the next 'fair-haired boy' of their organization just might be a woman" (Grossman 2000, 751). Such feminist emphasis was new to organized labor as well as to business, and neither bloc was enthusiastic about Dole. Lacking support from the White House as well, she resigned to become president of the American Red Cross.

Her successor at the Department of Labor was another woman: Lynn Martin, formally named Judith Lynn Morley Martin. She had represented a northern Illinois district in the U.S. House since 1981, rising quickly in the Republican leadership and serving on powerful congressional committees.[12] In 1990, she accepted the Republican Party's invitation to challenge Illinois senator Paul Simon. Despite being a moderate who supported the Equal Rights Amendment and abortion rights, she lost badly to the popular Democratic man, with Martin winning a mere 35 percent of the vote. Just as they had done when Margaret Heckler lost to Barney Frank in Massachusetts, Republican leaders in Washington restored Lynn Martin's career by making her labor secretary.

Martin carried on Elizabeth Dole's glass ceiling work and set an example by promoting women in her department. She also addressed the workplace problems of sexual harassment and drug use, and she implemented educational programs to train workers for new jobs in a computerized world. She served until after President Bush lost the 1992 election. Her Democratic successor, Robert B. Reich, arguably was the most activist labor secretary since Frances Perkins, and he worked with Martin on Educating to Compete, a national response to an increasingly globalized workforce.

Probably because her tenure was brief, George H. W. Bush's third female cabinet appointee has been largely overlooked, but Barbara Franklin, named in 1992, was well qualified to head the Department of Commerce. She was the second woman in this position, following Juanita Kreps. Born Barbara Hackman, she earned a master's degree in business administration at Harvard University in 1962, where she was one of a dozen women in a class of more than six hundred men. Like Kreps, she served on the boards of major businesses while also teaching—in Franklin's case, at the Wharton School of the University of Pennsylvania, a top institution in that field. She recruited women for appointments in the Nixon administration, and in 1973, the year before he resigned, Nixon named her to the Consumer Product Safety Commission, which was another case of a woman leading a newly created agency.

Although she was a Republican and he a Democrat, Carter allowed Franklin to stay on when he became president, and for six years, she implemented new safety regulations. She especially concentrated on products intended for use by children and on cancer-causing food additives. President Ronald Reagan, who defeated Carter in 1976, appointed Franklin to the President's Advisory Commission on Trade Negotiations in 1982, and she continued that service under George H. W. Bush. He also offered her appointments to both the Small Business Administration and the Federal Reserve System, but Franklin rejected them to continue her private career. She accepted,

however, when he offered her the cabinet-level position of secretary of the Department of Commerce. She was sworn in on February 27, 1992, but just eight months later, Bush lost his reelection. During her short time at Commerce, Franklin concentrated on trade with China, and after leaving office, she continued to specialize in foreign trade as a business consultant.

The Office of the Surgeon General, which has existed since the Civil War, is just below cabinet level, and Antonia Novello, a Puerto Rican, became the first female surgeon general in 1990, also under President George H. W. Bush. A well-credentialed pediatrician, she gave a new focus to health, even calling violence a national epidemic. Dr. Novello pointed out that many emergency room patients sought treatment as a result of violent acts, and she argued that violence in the home, workplace, and streets should be addressed with the same educational campaign that was lowering tobacco use.

The following year, Bernadine P. Healy became the first woman to head the National Institutes of Health (NIH). Presumably because she was Catholic, Dr. Healy did not face the litmus test questions on abortion that often were the center of such confirmation hearings, but she nonetheless was controversial at NIH. Its primary mission is research, and, in her brief tenure prior to Bush's 1992 loss, she began to insist that more women's diseases be included in medical trials.

UNPRECEDENTED NUMBERS: CLINTON ADMINISTRATION, 1992–2000

Democrat Bill Clinton defeated incumbent president George H. W. Bush in 1992 partly by promising to create an administration that "looks more like America." When Clinton took office in 1993, more than five hundred men but just fourteen women had served in presidential cabinets. All but one of those women had been white, and Clinton vowed to make appointments that reflected the nation's diversity. He did so, appointing an unprecedented five women, including racial minorities—and appreciably more at the subcabinet level.

No woman had been attorney general since George Washington created the post in 1789, more than two centuries earlier. Clinton's first nomination as attorney general was corporate attorney Zoë Baird, but she withdrew from the confirmation process after it was revealed that she had not paid Social Security taxes on an undocumented immigrant who worked as a nanny for her children. In an opinion piece published on January 25, 1993, *New York Times* columnist Anthony Lewis concluded that

---

[12] See Chapter 6: United States Representatives.

much of the hostility against nominee Baird was gender-based. The lack of attention to male roles, indeed, was reinforced by his title: "What If It Were Mr. Baird?"

For his second choice, Clinton turned from a business lawyer to the judiciary and named federal judge Kimba M. Wood, but she withdrew, too. While Wood had hired an undocumented worker, she broke no laws. She had not only paid the required taxes but also employed the immigrant before it was illegal to do so. She decided to spare herself the turmoil of the confirmation process, however, and instead retained her lifetime appointment on the bench.[13] Wood's baby-sitter had not been an issue when a Republican president, Ronald Reagan, appointed her as a federal judge.

The attorney general heads the Department of Justice, and while the debate on the top job was ongoing, Clinton attempted to name his choice for a lower-level DOJ position, the head of the department's Civil Rights Division. Lani Guinier, who was of Jewish and Jamaican heritage and the first black woman tenured at Harvard Law School, endured a storm of hostility. Conservatives opposed the appointment because of Guinier's written works on affirmative action and especially her proposals for alternative forms of voting that would strengthen minorities—including ideological minorities, such as those on the far right. One such method, cumulative voting, was used for city council races in Cambridge, Massachusetts, where Harvard is located. It allows a voter to split votes among candidates, depending on the passion one feels about them. For example, if five council seats are on the ballot, a voter may cast all five of his or her votes for one candidate or divide them between different candidates. The idea was too complex to even be open to debate among traditional politicians and they portrayed it as evidence of Guinier's radicalism. Although Guinier was willing to fight for confirmation, Clinton decided that the administration did not need another distraction from its major goals and abandoned the appointment. That drew criticism from leftists and some African Americans.

The president did stick with his resolution to appoint the nation's first female attorney general and on March 12, 1993, the Senate finally approved JANET RENO. A long-time elected state attorney for Florida's Miami–Dade County, Reno proved successful in reducing crime via methods that did not add to Florida's overcrowded prisons. The Teen Court that she implemented, where other teenagers served as jurors, turned around many young lives before it was too late. It and her Drug Court became models elsewhere. Reno had a spotless reputation for integrity, but she soon became a target for other reasons.

Because of her physical appearance and unmarried status, many accused her of lesbianism.

Reno's tenure as attorney general was tumultuous. She faced her first crisis immediately upon taking office, when Federal Bureau of Investigation (FBI) agents attempted to arrest members of a religious cult, the Branch Davidians, near Waco, Texas. After a six-week siege, a fire broke out in the cult's compound resulting in eighty-six deaths, including both Branch Davidians and FBI agents. The fact that the action was planned before Reno took office was lost in the controversy, and she was blamed.

Conservatives also criticized her when she refused to appoint a special proscecutor to investigate what they called "Whitewater," a decade-old Arkansas land investment on which the Clintons lost money. Meanwhile, the left criticized Reno when the Clintons' partner in the venture, Susan McDougal, was imprisoned for refusing to testify against her old friends. Reno stayed loyal to her commitment and finished out her eight years as head of the Department of Justice. She was the first attorney general to do so since William Wirt in the early nineteenth century.

Donna E. Shalala was the third female head of the Department of Health and Human Services, following Democrat Patricia Harris under Carter and Republican Margaret Heckler under Reagan. Shalala, whose parents were immigrants from Lebanon, is considered the first Arab American in the cabinet. She had served in the Carter administration as an assistant secretary of housing and urban development. When Clinton appointed her to head HHS, Dr. Shalala, who held a Ph.D. in political science, was chancellor of the University of Wisconsin, where she was the nation's second female head of a major public research university.

At HHS, she worked to increase funding for AIDS research and to ensure the vaccination of all children. Like Reno, Shalala served the entire eight years of the Clinton administration, longer than any previous HHS head. She then became president of the University of Miami, and in 2008, his last full year in office, George W. Bush presented her with the Presidential Medal of Freedom.

Hazel R. O'Leary, an African American born in Virginia, was the first woman to head the Department of Energy. The post was added to the cabinet in 1977, under President Jimmy Carter. The new department was a merger of the Atomic Energy Commission and other subcabinet level agencies related to the national need for new sources of fuel.

Hazel O'Leary was the least successful of Clinton's female appointees. An attorney by training, she had worked in the Carter administration as head of Energy's consumer issues. Her credentials led to an easy Senate confirmation, but she failed to accomplish much before

[13] See Chapter 15: Federal Courts.

being subtly forced to resign because of excessive spending, much of it on apparently unnecessary travel. She apologized to Congress in 1996 for outspending her budget and resigned at the beginning of Clinton's second term in 1997. O'Leary's most important contribution at the Energy Department probably was the release of previously secret information on nuclear tests.

The president put another African American woman in his cabinet at the beginning of his second term: Alexis M. Herman, the fourth female head of the Department of Labor. Complicating her confirmation was that the AFL-CIO supported male candidates as secretary of labor and Republicans charged that she had raised funds illegally for Clinton's presidential campaign. The Senate confirmed her by 85–13 on April 30, 1997, but continued allegations led Attorney General Janet Reno to appoint a retired judge to investigate. Although he cleared Herman of the charges, the controversy prevented her from accomplishing much during her relatively brief tenure. Her most noted action was the settlement of a strike by the Teamsters union against United Parcel Service. She went on to serve on the boards of several international corporations.

Warren M. Christopher was Clinton's first secretary of state and resigned at the beginning of Clinton's second term. The appointment of MADELEINE K. ALBRIGHT to succeed Christopher as head of the State Department was historic. Because the secretary of state outranks the attorney general in cabinet protocol, Albright's appointment was the highest of all time. Her tenure at the State Department and, earlier, as U.S. ambassador to the United Nations, was especially notable because, with the help of North Atlantic Treaty Organization (NATO) allies, the United States led a major military mission to bring peace and restore human rights in Bosnia—with no American soldier killed by hostile fire.[14]

Until the success of that operation, many pundits accused Albright of misjudging the situation. Other critics assumed that she could not handle problems in the Middle East fairly because she was Jewish—something that she, the daughter of a Czech diplomat, did not know until researchers discovered it during her confirmation. The Middle East has seemingly intractable difficulties, though, and her Republican successors did not criticize Albright's diplomacy. Historians increasingly view Albright as a highly successful secretary of state.

In addition to these five women in the cabinet, Clinton made more subcabinet-level appointments than previous presidents. His most successful subcabinet appointee probably was Carol M. Browner, the head of the Environmental Protection Agency. Clinton elevated her to cabinet

rank, and she served his entire eight years. Browner is considered by many environmentalists to have been the most effective EPA chief ever.

Female economists also played major roles during the strong economic growth of the Clinton administration. Laura D'Andrea Tyson headed his Council of Economic Advisers (CEA) until 1995, when he appointed her to the National Economic Council. She was succeeded at CEA by Janet Yellen, who served from 1997 to 1999. No woman would chair CEA again until 2009, when President Barack Obama appointed Christina Duckworth Romer. In between, six men chaired the council as the economy collapsed in the first decade of the new millennium. Alice M. Rivlin, perhaps the era's most respected female economist, was director of the Office of Management and Budget (OMB) during the Clinton administration, from 1994 to 1996. She went on to serve as a member and as vice chair of the Federal Reserve System.

Charlene Barshefsky garnered favorable press in the role of U.S. trade representative (1997–2001), while Aida Alvarez, a native of Puerto Rico, was the first Hispanic woman to head the Small Business Administration (1997–2001). Clinton included both women in cabinet meetings, as well as Janice Lachance, who was director of the Office of Personnel Management from 1997 to early 2001.

Margaret Richardson headed the tax-collecting Internal Revenue Service from 1993 to 1997. Doris Meissner was chief of the Immigration and Naturalization Service for the entirety of Clinton's tenure, from 1993 to 2001, an era in which immigration, especially from Mexico, was increasingly controversial. The actor Jane Alexander chaired the National Endowment for the Arts from 1993 to 1997, and Clinton's 1993 choice for director of the Women's Bureau of the Department of Labor was Karen Nussbaum, founder of the clerical workers' union Nine-to-Five. Also in 1993, Dee Dee Myers became the first female White House press secretary—a role that is highly visible on television. Joycelyn Elders, an African American from Arkansas, became surgeon general in 1993. After a controversial fifteen months in office, conservatives forced her firing after Dr. Elders made some frank comments on teenage sexuality.

Mary L. Shapiro also generated headlines as chair of the Commodity Futures Trading Commission (CFTC). This agency regulates agribusiness and brokers as they buy and sell crops and livestock in futures that have not yet been physically delivered. Both farms and trading floors were strongly dominated by men, and Shapiro's 1994 appointment came as a shock to them. Several news sources reported that after she turned down a request from the Chicago Board of Trade for exemptions to some regulations, its president said that he would not be "intimidated by some blonde, 5-foot-2 girl." Shapiro responded

---

[14] See Chapter 12: Ambassadors.

Madeleine K. Albright was U.S. representative to the United Nations when Washington, DC, gossip turned to the subject of a vacancy in the top job at the State Department. As usual, a number of powerful men wanted the position and were campaigning for the appointment with White House staff. Albright also had supporters, including President Bill Clinton's political director, Ann Lewis. Still, choosing a woman for this highest cabinet post would be unconventional, and Clinton agonized over the decision. According to Albright biographer Thomas Blood:

The debate raged on in the Old Executive Office Building throughout the weekend. . . . During the next few days several events unfolded to Albright's advantage. First, out of nowhere, Senate Foreign Relations Committee Chairman Jesse Helms [Republican of North Carolina] weighed in, giving his strong support to Ambassador Albright. . . .

The second major development came when several key players in the women's movement began pressuring the White House. . . . Friends like [former vice presidential nominee Geraldine A.] Ferraro counseled her to move aggressively. . . . On the other hand, Health and Human Services Secretary Donna Shalala and other allies were adamant that Albright not be seen as self-promoting. . . . Throughout the selection process, the President recalled Senator

[Barbara] Mikulski's assessment of Albright: "A lot of diplomats may grasp the complexities of [war in] Bosnia, but only Albright could explain why we were there in a way that the local grocer could understand." . . .

Reaching Albright at her Georgetown house at 7:46 AM, the President wasted no time, telling her that . . . some members of the diplomatic corps had strong reservations concerning her ability to deal with . . . Muslim leaders. While his tone was serious, he tried to lighten the subject by joking about her making a "no *cojones*" speech. . . .

Characteristically, Albright didn't miss a beat. "You know what they say, Mr. President," she said. "They can't cut 'em off if you don't have them." Her retort broke both of them up. . . . The President, amazed once again at her unflappable manner, asked her, "So you really think you can handle the likes of Assad?" "Are you kidding, Mr. President? Compared to Jesse Helms, that guy is a puppy dog." With that, the deal was done. (Blood 1997, 19–34)

Albright's tenure was almost universally acknowledged to be a success, especially her settlement of the war in Bosnia without the loss of a single American soldier under hostile fire. Presidents George W. Bush and Barack Obama followed Clinton's precedent by also naming women as secretary of state.

that she was 5'5" and, at thirty-nine, not a girl. He apologized, and she continued to do her regulatory job.

Among the lower-level controversial appointments was that of Roberta Achtenberg as assistant secretary of housing and urban development. The daughter of immigrants from the Union of Soviet Socialist Republics and Quebec, Canada, Achtenberg had been elected to the San Francisco Board of Supervisors in 1990. Her Senate confirmation in 1993 was the first of an openly gay person at this level of government.

Finally, Clinton's most historically significant—yet little heralded—appointment may have been that of Sheila Marie Evans Widnall as secretary of the Air Force. The first woman to head a branch of the military, she was a rocket scientist. Widnall researched and taught aeronautics at the prestigious Massachusetts Institute of Technology (MIT). She took office on August 6, 1993, after a Senate confirmation that was quiet compared with those of earlier Clinton appointees. Her priorities were training and personnel improvements within the Air Force, as well as modernization of technology. Widnall headed the Air Force through Clinton's 1996 reelection, resigning on October 31, 1997, to return to MIT.

THE NEW MILLENNIUM

George W. Bush, who became president in 2001, appointed three women who would serve in his first-term cabinet and added three more in his second term. Two of his appointees were the first women to head their departments.

The Department of the Interior was more than 150 years old in 2001, when Bush appointed Gale A. Norton as its first female chief. A Colorado attorney, she had been active in the Libertarian Party in the 1970s and was a strong proponent of its philosophy of limited government regulation and expansive private enterprise. Her mentor was James G. Watt, the highly controversial head of the Interior Department in the Reagan administration who famously objected to a Beach Boys concert on the National Mall in Washington, DC, proclaiming their music too radical.

Norton became a federal employee in Reagan era, working in both the Agriculture Department and the Interior Department. She returned to Colorado in 1988 and was elected state attorney general in 1990. After her tenure in that post, she lobbied in Washington for businesses, especially mining and petroleum interests that wanted access to public land. Although environmentalists objected to her nomination as interior secretary, she had enough contacts as a lobbyist that Senate confirmation went smoothly.

From then on, however, Norton's time in office was plagued by controversy over development in wilderness areas, cutting old-growth forests, and mining on public land. She and the department also were accused of corruption. In 2002, American Indians sued the department for mismanagement of their tribal funds, and Norton was charged with contempt of court for failing to respond. When she resigned early in 2006, Norton said she wanted to spend more time in the mountains that she loved, but even western newspapers that generally support Republicans greeted her departure gleefully. The Missoula, Montana, *Independent*, for example, headlined its story "End of an Error: Saying Good Riddance to Gale Norton."

Secretary of Agriculture Ann M. Veneman, the first woman to hold that position, had a résumé similar to Norton's but was more successful. In addition to a law degree, Veneman earned a graduate degree in public policy at the University of California at Berkeley and then was a California state employee until 1980, when she joined a private firm. In 1986, during the Reagan administration, she moved to Washington and worked in the Foreign Agricultural Service of the Department of Agriculture. She negotiated trade deals and tariffs on imported food. California governor Pete Wilson, a Republican, appointed her as the state's first female agriculture chief.

George W. Bush appointed Veneman to head the Department of Agriculture; her Senate confirmation posed no problems; and she was sworn in on January 20, 2001, the same that day he was as president. By then, the department greatly reflected the power of agribusiness. With more than 110,000 employees, it was larger than other departments that more directly relate to governance. According to the USDA, its $113 billion budget in fiscal year 2002 was higher than all but five of the nation's private corporations. Much of its money traditionally has gone to farmers as crop support subsidiaries, that is, payments for limiting the amount they plant so that food prices stay high.

Veneman was a broader thinker and more innovative than most in the industry, something that was reflected in her goal-setting book *Food and Agriculture: Taking Stock for a New Century* (2001). It discussed such nontraditional issues as attention to obesity, feeding the world's malnourished, and improved nutrition for schoolchildren. She resigned in 2005 and then became head of the United

Nations Children's Fund (UNICEF), a career that ended with a similar lack of publicity in 2010.

Elaine L. Chao, the first Chinese American in the cabinet, was the only female appointee to serve through the Bush administration's eight years. The fifth woman to head the Department of Labor, she was akin to earlier labor secretaries Republicans Ann Dore McLaughlin and Elizabeth Dole, in that Chao's husband doubtless was a factor in her appointment. In 1993, she had married Republican senator Mitch McConnell of Kentucky, who would go on to the top Republican post in the Senate.

Elaine Chao was born on the island of Taiwan and grew up on Long Island, New York, where her father was in the shipping business. She earned a graduate degree at Harvard Business School in 1979 and, after Republicans won the White House and the Senate majority in the 1980 election, moved to Washington to work for the Department of Transportation. In 1988, she served a one-year term as head of the Federal Maritime Commission, and the next year, President H. W. Bush appointed her as deputy secretary of the DOT. After he lost to Bill Clinton in 1992, Chao first headed the United Way and then worked for the Heritage Foundation, a Washington-based conservative think tank, until George W. Bush appointed her as secretary of labor in 2001. This was the first time that a woman succeeded another woman of the opposite party in a cabinet office, as Chao followed Democrat Alexis M. Herman.

Chao was perhaps the least progressive of the female labor chiefs. As with earlier Republican appointments, unions were not pleased with her business orientation, and she did not work to benefit nonunion women as Elizabeth Dole and Lynn Martin had. Chao was not accused of corruption in the way that Gale Norton was, but she was criticized for her seeming indifference to the workers that were the department's clientele. The Government Accountability Office (GAO), which is independent of political influence, announced in 2007 that Chao's department was ignoring some seventy thousand cases of workers who had been underpaid by their employers. In another report, the GAO concluded that her department gave Congress misleading information on the alleged benefits of workforce outsourcing. Even the department's own inspector general reported in 2008 that employees of the Occupational Safety and Health Administration, who enforce the Occupational Safety and Health Act, systematically ignored dangerous workplace conditions, especially in coal mines.

The Labor Department thus had been headed by five women, more than any other executive department, despite having a traditionally male constituency. The Department of Education, meanwhile, covers an area closely associated with women, but until 2005, it had only one woman in the top position—the first, Shirley Hufstedler, appointed by Democrat Jimmy Carter in 1979. Because he lost the next year's election, her tenure was brief, and no woman followed until 2005. Although women dominate the field of education, all of the education secretaries for a quarter-century had been men.

At the beginning of his second term, George W. Bush appointed Margaret Spellings to head the Education Department. She replaced an African American man, Rod Paige. Spellings had helped create the Bush education policy of No Child Left Behind and soon encountered opposition from teachers, especially because of Republican advocacy of merit pay.

A century earlier, the salaries of individual teachers often varied according to the whim of school board members and administrators, leaving much room for sexual harassment and racial discrimination. By the late twentieth century, teachers in every state had unionized and created pay scales that did not allow such behavior. Advocates of merit pay began arguing that teaching quality would be improved if such standard salaries were displaced with monetary incentives for better student performance, as measured by new standardized tests. Strong arguments have been posed on both sides of the issue, and Spellings's task was to deliver the White House's point of view. Often that view was the opposite of positions taken by delegates to the annual conventions of the American Federation of Teachers and the National Education Association, which represent millions of classroom teachers.

A Texan, Spellings was close to George W. Bush, and she worked in the White House during his first term. Her credentials were slim, as she held only a bachelor's degree from the University of Houston. It was in political science, and she never had taught. Spellings also was charged with allowing banks to profit excessively from college student loans that were guaranteed by the Department of Education. After Democrats won the 2008 elections, she left politics and started an educational consulting business in Washington.

Also during Bush's second term, Mary E. Peters headed the Department of Transportation. An Arizonian with a background in management, Republican governor Jane Dee Hull had appointed Peters as chief of the state transportation department. She moved to Washington in 2001 to head the Federal Highway Administration, a DOT division, and was promoted to the top job in autumn 2006. Her confirmation was quiet, and Peters never attracted much press, despite promoting an agenda of privatizing public roads and creating more toll highways. Unions did protest against opening U.S. borders to commercial trucks, especially from Mexico, without inspections. When Republicans lost the 2008 presidential

election, Peters returned to Arizona and considered running for governor, but she backed off in favor of fellow female Republican Jan Brewer.[15]

Bush, like Clinton, elevated both the administrator of the Environmental Protection Agency and the U.S. trade representative to cabinet rank. In his first term, he appointed New Jersey governor Christine Todd Whitman to head the EPA. Disappointed with the White House's failure to support the agency's mission, she resigned less than two years into her tenure.[16] In 2006, he appointed Susan C. Schwab to the trade position. Well educated, she held a doctorate in public administration from George Washington University, had worked and studied in Asia, and had private corporate experience. During her relatively brief tenure prior to the 2008 election, she strongly defended the North American Free Trade Agreement (NAFTA) with Canada and Mexico, and she developed additional trade with Latin America. Schwab attracted little media attention until just days before her tenure ended, when she tripled some tariffs on European products. Some Europeans, especially the French, saw this as retaliation for their lack of support for the war in Iraq.

Also at the subcabinet level, Bush appointed Sheila Colleen Bair to head the Federal Deposit Insurance Corporation (FDIC), which was created during the Great Depression to ensure that depositors did not lose their savings when banks collapsed. Appointed in 2006, she had both academic and corporate experience as an economist and continued to be well regarded under the Obama administration.

By far the most prominent female appointment of the Bush-Cheney administration was Secretary of State CONDOLEEZZA RICE. The second woman to hold this top position, she did not directly succeed Clinton appointee Madeleine Albright but instead followed the State Department's first African American chief, retired general Colin L. Powell. He resigned at the beginning of Bush's second term, and Rice was the first secretary of state to be both African American and female. She was extremely well credentialed, having risen from segregationist Alabama—where one of her friends was killed in the 1963 Birmingham bombing of a black church by whites—to high posts in both academia and government.

In his first term, George W. Bush had appointed Rice as national security adviser, the most powerful of several

---

[15] For more on Hull and Brewer, see Chapter 8: Governors and Lieutenant Governors.

[16] For more on Whitman, see Chapter 8: Governors and Lieutenant Governors.

Running for office and losing can be a good exercise in humility—and that can be an asset later, when greater modesty encourages one to ask questions and foresee what may be going wrong.

In 1990, Sheila Colleen Bair, a Republican, ran for Congress from Kansas and lost. Young and self-confident at the time, she said, "I couldn't believe it." She was working for Kansas senator Bob Dole, and she said, "he told me the reason I lost was because I was a woman, and I was unmarried. And that made me all the more determined to take on new challenges." By 2006, she was chairman of the Federal Deposit Insurance Corporation (FDIC), which insures bank accounts.

In a speech at the John F. Kennedy Presidential Library and Museum in Massachusetts, where she accepted a 2009 Profile in Courage Award, Bair spoke about when the economy crashed under the Bush-Cheney administration.

I wanted to make sure our policies helped the average homeowner on Main Street, not just the large financial institutions on Wall Street. We could see the train wreck coming and working families needed protection, too.

Robert Frost liked to say that a banker is someone who gives you an umbrella when the sun is shining and takes it away when it starts to rain. Well, we set out to prove that adage wrong at Indy-Mac bank. During the time we were conservator, we restructured loans for over 13,000 families to keep them in their homes. . . .

We weren't trying to do something great or even courageous. We were just trying to do something that seemed like basic common sense. But seeing what was happening, we couldn't stand on the sidelines and be insignificant, doing nothing. . . .

True leaders are willing to lock arms with the foot soldiers. And true heroes are willing to do what's right regardless of credit. (Bair 2009, n.p.)

In its press release on her award, the library said: "Sheila Bair has been called 'a lone voice in the wilderness' for her early warnings about the sub-prime lending crisis and for her dogged criticism of both Wall Street's and the government's management of the subsequent financial meltdown." Bair left the FDIC post at the end of her six-year term in 2011.

federal positions that deal with spying and the intelligence it produces. Although she held this office when the nation suffered its worse security breach ever with the attacks of September 11, 2001, Rice initially avoided much of the scrutiny for what went wrong. In the spring of 2004, however, the national commission investigating the attacks asked her to testify. She refused at first but subsequently did so under pressure. By then it was clear that she either was uniformed or prevaricating when she justified the invasion of Iraq by saying that it had weapons of mass destruction. Because Rice had encouraged the war in Iraq and its expansion to Afghanistan, some senators objected to her as head of the State Department—where the intended mission is peace. Her confirmation vote was 85–13, with California senator Barbara Boxer especially arguing for greater accountability.

Her tenure at the State Department was affected by her previous tenure as national security adviser, and especially after news stories revealed the use of secret torture, many questioned Rice's role in its authorization. Having a black woman as the United States' chief representative abroad, however, was an undeniable positive with the majority of the world's population, and she traveled widely to reinforce that. Rice never lacked for substance and was better informed on international details than most of her predecessors. She returned to that scholarly role at Stanford University after Democrats won the 2008 presidential election. Hillary Rodham Clinton succeeded her at State, setting a milestone as the cabinet's highest-ranking position passed from one woman to another.

Hillary Clinton became secretary of state when Barack Obama, her former rival for the Democratic nomination, named her soon after his 2008 election.[17] As a senator from New York, she had earned the respect of her Senate colleagues, and her confirmation was smooth. The third female head of the State Department, she has garnered praise from previous critics.

Obama appointed four women, including Clinton, to his initial cabinet. The Department of Labor had its sixth female head in Hilda L. Solis. The daughter of immigrants from Mexico and Nicaragua, she was representing the East Los Angeles area in the U.S. House when Obama chose her to be the first Hispanic woman in the cabinet.[18] Previous to that, she was the first Hispanic

---

[17] For Clinton's biography, see Chapter 10: Presidential and Vice Presidential Candidates.

[18] See Chapter 6: United States Representatives.

woman in the California Senate. Solis had not grown up privileged. She was the first in her family to go to college, something that gave her a keen awareness of working-class life.

As labor secretary, Solis invigorated the department's mission, increasing enforcement of overtime pay and other wages legally due to workers. She supported extension of unemployment benefits during the Great Recession, and she rescinded a number of policies from Elaine Chao's administration that favored corporate interests over those of employees. Especially after the worst mining disaster in decades, when twenty-nine miners were killed in West Virginia in 2010, Solis beefed up enforcement of the Occupational Safety and Health Act. She also took the lead internationally, hosting the first meeting between labor officials in major nations on how globalization was affecting workers.

Hilda Solis was the sixth female head of the Labor Department, while Kathleen Sebelius, the second female governor of Kansas, became the fourth woman to head the Department of Health and Human Services.[19] No woman had held the top post at HHS since Donna Shalala in the Clinton administration. During Sebelius's first two years in office, HHS joined with the Department of Agriculture to require more nutritional information on food labels. She also had the unenviable task of heading the executive department most relevant to health care reform legislation, which passed in 2010. Implementation of the complex law falls under HHS, and according to a November 12, 2010, report by Bloomberg News, Sebelius aimed to carry on despite a new Republican majority elected in the House, many of whom campaigned against what they disparagingly dubbed "Obamacare."

Like Sebelius, Janet Napolitano had been a governor. Arizonans elected her to both that position and, earlier, state attorney general.[20] The agency that she headed in the Obama administration, the Department of Homeland Security, was created after the September 11 attacks, and she was its first female head. An early supporter of Barack Obama, he named her soon after his election, and despite the masculine culture in the field of security, her January confirmation was much easier than that of Solis or Sebelius.

As of 2011, the Department of Homeland Security has merited credit for preventing deaths in several planned terrorist attacks. Its mission requires Napolitano to walk a fine line between those concerned about invasions of privacy and those who would require even more invasive tracking of people, especially airline passengers and those who cross borders. On August 25, 2010, the *Washington Post* called Janet Napolitano "a tough pragmatic with bipartisan credibility."

Like Clinton and George W. Bush, Obama gave the EPA administrator cabinet rank. Lisa P. Jackson was the first person of African heritage to hold the post. A chemical engineer with a graduate degree from prestigious Princeton University, Jackson married and had two children before developing a career in environmentalism, working in Washington, New York City, and New Jersey.

Confirmed by a voice vote in the Senate, she announced that her top priority was greenhouse gases, which lead to warmer temperatures that melt polar ice caps and thus cause sea levels to rise. Most of the scientific community agreed with Jackson that carbon emissions must be limited, lest the world risk permanent flooding of its coasts. Despite that consensus, a major meeting in Copenhagen, Denmark, in December 2009 did not reach agreement on how to implement lifestyle changes to avoid the foreseen crisis. Congress also failed to act on proposed legislation to limit emission of these gases within the United States. Jackson's more successful priorities included joining with both the Department of Transportation and the Department of Housing and Urban Development to improve air and water quality, as well as clean up toxic waste.

Like Clinton, Obama appointed a woman, Christina Duckworth Romer, to chair the Council of Economic Advisers and included her in cabinet meetings. With a doctorate in economics from MIT, Romer taught at Princeton University and the University of California at Berkeley, specializing in the causes of the Great Depression. That was certainly relevant as the economy collapsed at the end of the Bush administration, but her 2009 appointment nonetheless was controversial. Romer resigned from the CEA in September 2010, when Obama asked her to serve on his President's Economic Recovery Advisory Board.

That was at the same time he chose Elizabeth Warren to head a proposed position within the Securities and Exchange Commission (SEC) to protect consumers from fraud in financial transactions. Wall Street strongly opposed Warren, a Harvard University economist, and because both the agency's creation and her confirmation would be difficult, Obama gave her a title that did not require confirmation. When Congress authorized the Consumer Financial Protection Bureau in 2011, the president appointed a less controversial man, Richard Cordray, as its head. Warren announced her candidacy for the U.S. Senate in 2012, running against Republican Scott Brown.

[19] For more on Sebelius, see Chapter 8: Governors and Lieutenant Governors.

[20] See Chapter 8: Governors and Lieutenant Governors and Chapter 3: Statewide Elective Officeholders.

Time, in an article in its May 24, 2010, issue, called Warren "a new sheriff in town" for the policing of financiers, and the magazine added Mary Shapiro and Sheila Bair to its list of "new sheriffs." Shapiro had gotten the attention of financiers during the Clinton administration, when she regulated commodities futures, and Obama appointed her to head the Securities and Exchange Commission, which was created to regulate the stock market after Wall Street fell in 1929. The third of the "new sheriffs" named by *Time* was Sheila Bair, a Republican who had been appointed to head the Federal Deposit Insurance Corporation in 2006. The financial mess that became apparent in 2008 was similar to that of the 1930s, but, unlike during the Great Depression when Frances Perkins was quite alone, many more women were empowered to clean up the Great Recession.

PRECEDENTS YET TO BE SET

One of George Washington's five cabinet members was the secretary of war, a position that was renamed secretary of defense after World War II. Begun in 1789, the Department of War long handled the needs of both active soldiers and veterans. In 1989, during the administration of George H. W. Bush, Congress authorized a separate Department of Veterans Affairs. Two hundred years apart in age, these two departments share a commonality in that neither has been led by a woman.

Throughout the history of the Veterans Administration (VA), which had existed at a sub-cabinet level since 1930, never has a woman held its top job—even though millions of women have served in the military. Women who rose close to the top at the VA included Dorothy Starbacks, who set a record for longevity as director of benefits from 1977, at the beginning of the Carter administration, to 1985, in the Reagan administration. During the Clinton administration, in the 1990s, Mary Lou Keener was the VA's top legal counsel. She became a lawyer after service as a Navy nurse during the Vietnam War.

The nation's dedication to its military is clear in the fact that, when the Department of Veterans Affairs was created, the VA was the federal government's largest independent agency and its budget was second only to that of the largest executive department, the Department of Defense (DOD). It also never has had a woman nominated for its top post. The closest that women have been to the pinnacle at the Pentagon was in 1950, when Harry S. Truman appointed Anna Rosenberg as an assistant secretary, and in 1993, when Bill Clinton named Sheila Widnall as secretary of the Air Force. Even though three women have served as secretary of state, and even though

Table 11.4 Female U.S. Treasurers, by Year of Appointment

Year	Name	Appointing President
1949	Georgia Neese Clark	Harry S. Truman
1953	Ivy Baker Priest	Dwight D. Eisenhower
1961	Elizabeth Rudel Smith	John F. Kennedy
1963	Kathryn O'Hay Granahan	John F. Kennedy; Lyndon B. Johnson
1969	Dorothy Andrews Elston Kabis	Richard M. Nixon
1971	Romana Acosta Banuelos	Richard M. Nixon
1974	Francine Irving Neff	Richard M. Nixon; Gerald R. Ford
1977	Azie Taylor Morton	Jimmy Carter
1981	Angela Marie Buchanan	Ronald Reagan
1983	Katherine D. Ortega	Ronald Reagan; George H.W. Bush
1989	Catalina Vasquez Villalpando	George H.W. Bush
1994	Mary Ellen Withrow	Bill Clinton
2001	Rosario Marin	George W. Bush
2005	Anna Escobedo Cabral	George W. Bush
2009	Rosa Gumataotao Rios	Barack Obama

Source: Compiled by author, using data from the Department of the Treasury.

the military now has many female generals and admirals, none has received serious consideration as secretary of defense.

The other cabinet position that dates back to George Washington and has never been held by a woman is the secretary of the Treasury. This milestone may well be the next to be passed, as many modern female economists have the experience and credentials to hold this top post.

Treasury secretary is different from the U.S. treasurer. The U.S. treasurer's name appears on paper money, but the position, which is within the Department of the Treasury, is advisory and largely ceremonial. It has become stereotypically female since Democrat Harry Truman appointed the first woman, Kansas banker Georgia Neese Clark, in 1949. His successor, Dwight D. Eisenhower, appointed Republican activist Ivy Baker Priest in 1953. Future presidents followed with female appointees, usually chosen because of their political activism and not because of their fiscal knowledge.

The first Hispanic woman to be U.S. treasurer was Romana Acosta Banuelos, chosen by Republican Richard M. Nixon in 1971. Five more Hispanic women have followed her. Democrat Jimmy Carter named the first African American treasurer, Azie Taylor Morton, in 1977. She served through the Carter administration and, as of 2011, remains the only African American of either gender to serve as U.S. treasurer. Legislation passed in 1981 put the U.S. Mint under the umbrella of the U.S. treasurer.

Franklin Delanor Roosevelt appointed Nellie Tayloe Ross (right) as head of the U.S. Mint in 1933. She held the job for 20 years. She is pictured here with Marion Glass Banister, the Assistant U.S. Treasurer, in March 1938. Mrs. Banister was the sister of Sen. Carter Glass of Virginia.

Former Wyoming governor Nellie Tayloe Ross headed the Mint under Democrat Franklin D. Roosevelt, serving through the Great Depression and World War II.[21]

In addition to the secretary of the Treasury and the secretary of war, George Washington included the postmaster general in his cabinet. The post was downgraded from the cabinet in 1971, during the Nixon administration, when the U.S. Postal Service was established as an independent agency. No woman has ever headed the nation's postal service. As with the U.S. treasurer, the position of postmaster general historically was deemed a reward for presidential campaign supporters, but some holders have been major assets in the cabinet. This was especially true of James A. Farley, a close policy adviser to Franklin Roosevelt who also introduced the first free delivery of mail to rural residents.

Women certainly have demonstrated their ability, successfully running post offices in many small towns and some major cities. After the Civil War, for example, President Ulysses S. Grant in 1869 rewarded Elizabeth Van Lew for the risks she took as a Union spy by appointing her postmistress in Richmond, Virginia, the capital of the defeated Confederacy. Women's history in this field dates back to colonial days, when Mary Katherine Goddard was postmistress of Baltimore (1775–1789).

Women's records of service to presidents, in fact, dates back to the nation's earliest years. Yet, while nearly six hundred men have been appointed as cabinet officers, just

[21] See Chapter 8: Governors and Lieutenant Governors.

twenty-six women have held those positions. As of 2011, three of George Washington's original five-member cabinet positions—those dealing with war, revenue, and the post office—never had been held by a woman.

PROFILES OF CABINET AND SUBCABINET MEMBERS

*The women profiled here are notable for their service in the cabinet. **Frances Perkins** was the first female cabinet member, **Oveta Culp Hobby** was the second, and **Carla Anderson Hills** was the third. **Elizabeth Dole** was the first woman to hold two cabinet positions under two different presidents. **Patricia Roberts Harris** was the first black woman on the cabinet. **Madeleine K. Albright** was the first female secretary of state, and **Condoleezza Rice** was the first African American woman in that role. **Janet Reno** was named the first female attorney general, more than two hundred years after George Washington appointed his cabinet.*

MADELEINE K. ALBRIGHT (1937–)

The first female secretary of state, the cabinet post that deals with other nations, Madeleine K. Albright has lived an international life from the beginning.

Born Marie Jana Korbelova in Prague, she was nicknamed "Madlenka." Her mother was Mandula Spiegel, and her father, Josef Korbel, was a diplomat. They were Jewish, which was why the family fled Czechoslovakia when she was just a baby. Albright, however, would not find out about her Jewish heritage until her nomination as secretary of state. Baptized as Roman Catholics, the family spent the war years in England. Madlenka grew up in the exile community there, thinking that she was a Catholic Czech, then often called Bohemian. She was eight in 1945, when the Allies won the war. The family moved back to continental Europe, and Josef Korbel became Czechoslovakia's ambassador to Yugoslavia.

At boarding school in Switzerland, she was exposed to more languages, something that helped with her ability as an adult to speak a half-dozen fluently. She also adopted the French version of her nickname, Madeleine. Soon, the family had to flee again, as Communists took over Czechoslovakia and her father was forced to resign in 1948. While he escaped via Kashmir, her mother and siblings went to London; months later, they were reunited in New York. Josef Korbel became a professor at the University of Denver, and Madeleine spent her teenage years in Colorado. She became a U.S. citizen in 1957, while a scholarship student at Massachusetts's elite Wellesley

College. Active in College Democrats of America, she graduated with a degree in political science in 1959.

Like most young women of that era, she married soon after graduation. She changed her religion as well as her name, converting from Catholic to Episcopalian. Her husband, Joseph Medill Patterson Albright, was related to families that owned the *Chicago Tribune* and other newspapers. Even privileged young men were subject to the military draft in 1959, and the newlyweds spent their first months at Fort Leonard Wood, Missouri. Madeleine Albright found employment at a newspaper in Rolla, Missouri, and she worked for *Encyclopedia Britannica* after they moved to Chicago in 1960. The following year, they moved to New York and he was on the staff at *Newsday*. During this time, she gave birth to twin daughters and she had a third daughter in 1967. Living subsequently in both Washington, DC, and New York, she pursued graduate studies at Johns Hopkins University and Columbia University. The latter school awarded her a doctorate in political science in 1975.

The next year, Jimmy Carter was elected president. His national security adviser was Zbigniew Brzezinski, one of Albright's former professors. He recruited her to the White House as his congressional liaison in 1978, and after Carter lost the 1980 election, she found a home with the Woodrow Wilson International Center for Scholars. She specialized in Poland, which then was moving from a Soviet satellite to an independent democracy. Partly because of her youthful experience in fleeing Europe when Soviets took over Czechoslovakia, Albright was known as a strong anticommunist, as well as an active Democrat.

After twenty-three years of marriage, Joseph Albright fell in love with another woman, and the couple divorced in 1982. That same year, Madeleine Albright joined the faculty of Georgetown University, which long had been known as the most likely point of entry for people who wish to enter the diplomat corps. She continued her Democratic Party roles, including advising Geraldine A. Ferraro, the 1984 nominee for vice president, on international issues. This background and more gave Albright the credentials to be appointed as the U.S. ambassador to the United Nations (UN) by President Bill Clinton.

She served at the UN until the beginning of Clinton's second term, when he chose her as the nation's first woman to head the State Department. As a Clinton appointee for eight years, her major success was the settlement of war in the Balkans, ending ethnic cleansing and persecution of Muslims there. Her major failure— something that both she and Clinton have repeatedly stated that they regret—was not trying to stop similar ethnic atrocities in Africa, especially genocide between tribes in Rwanda.

When Republican George W. Bush entered the White House in 2001, some speculated that Albright would return to her birthplace and assist the development of the new Czech Republic. Although its president encouraged her, she did not accept. Instead, she began a consulting business that included former Environmental Protection Agency administrator Carol M. Browner, who brought her expertise in global warming and pollution that knows no borders. Retaining her professorship at Georgetown, Albright also served in many other capacities, including a director of the Council on Foreign Relations, a member of the board of the New York Stock Exchange, and chair of the Council of Women World Leaders.

She supported her good friend Hillary Rodham Clinton for the 2008 Democratic nomination and has informally advised President Barack Obama on international issues. From the beginning of her career, Albright wrote many books on foreign affairs and added more after leaving the State Department: *Madam Secretary* (2003), *The Mighty and the Almighty: Reflections on America, God, and World Affairs* (2006), and *Memo to the President-Elect: How We Can Restore America's Reputation and Leadership* (2008).

ELIZABETH DOLE (1936–)

The only woman to serve in the cabinets of two presidents, Elizabeth Dole was the first female head of the Department of Transportation and the third at the Department of Labor.

Born in Salisbury, North Carolina, Elizabeth Hanford, sometimes called "Liddy," was an outstanding student. She graduated from Duke University, arguably the best school in the South, in 1958, and went on to study at England's Oxford University. Upon returning to the United States, she taught high school in Massachusetts for a year and then earned a master's degree in education from Harvard University. Teaching was not to be her career, however, and she went on to Harvard Law School, graduating in 1965—when few women were accepted to law schools, especially one that prestigious.

A Democrat then, Hanford campaigned for John F. Kennedy and Lyndon B. Johnson in 1960. After graduating from law school, she joined the Johnson administration. Her mentor in Washington, DC, was Virginia Knauer, who headed the White House Office of Consumer Affairs when Republican Richard M. Nixon succeeded Johnson in 1969. Although still a registered Democrat, Hanford stayed at the White House, where she specialized in consumer affairs until 1973, when Nixon appointed her to the Federal Trade Commission

(FTC), an agency that dates to the early twentieth-century consumer movement.

Elizabeth Hanford met Robert Dole, Republican senator from Kansas, in 1972. He divorced later that year, and she changed parties when they married in 1975. Nixon had resigned by then, and Gerald R. Ford had assumed the presidency. When Bob Dole, as he usually was called, ran for vice president with President Ford in 1976, Elizabeth Hanford Dole—as she then was known—took leave from the FTC to campaign for the Republican ticket. Both parties supported the Equal Rights Amendment at that time. Republicans Elizabeth Dole and first lady Betty Ford joined Democrats Rosalynn Carter, soon to be first lady, and Joan Mondale, wife of vice presidential nominee Walter Mondale, in giving positive attention to women's issues. Dole especially focused on equal access to credit and mortgages.

When the Republican ticket lost to Carter and Mondale, Dole went back to serving her seven-year term on the FTC. She resigned early to campaign again when her husband unsuccessfully sought the 1980 Republican presidential nomination. Ronald Reagan, after his general election victory, chose Elizabeth Dole as head of the White House Office of Public Liaison and Intergovernmental Affairs. This was the first time that a woman succeeded a woman in that position, as Anne Wexler held it during the Carter administration.[22]

Dole served there from 1981 to 1983, when Reagan appointed her as the first woman to head the Department of Transportation (DOT). She resigned from DOT in 1987, when she once again helped her husband in his presidential quest. He lost the Republican nomination to George H. W. Bush. After winning the general election in 1988, Bush chose Elizabeth Dole to head the Department of Labor. Her most lasting contribution there was the "glass ceiling study", which demonstrated systematic discrimination against women in the white-collar workforce.

She resigned as labor secretary late in 1990 to head the American Red Cross. Dole was its first female president since founder Clara Barton retired in 1904, and some considered Dole's tenure controversial. Anonymous people at the Department of Defense complained that she gave orders on what the Red Cross would and would not do for soldiers in a way that would have been unacceptable without her status as the wife of a powerful senator. She took a leave of absence from the Red Cross to campaign for her husband in 1996, when Bob Dole, as the Republican nominee, made his last unsuccessful bid for the White House, losing to incumbent Bill Clinton.

Many people had told the Doles that she was a better campaigner than he, and in 1999, she resigned from the Red Cross to run for president. Elizabeth Dole never had run for anything in her own right, as all of her experience was in appointive, not elective, office. Meanwhile Republicans had become less receptive to a woman who advocated for women's rights than they had been decades earlier. She withdrew from the race, and although some predicted that the winner, George W. Bush, would choose her for vice president, he instead opted for former secretary of defense Dick Cheney. Dole then began planning a campaign for senator from North Carolina, which she won in 2002. Elizabeth and Bob Dole coauthored *The Doles: Unlimited Partners* during his 1996 campaign, and her *Hearts Touched by Fire: My 500 Most Inspirational Quotations* was published in 2004. After losing her 2008 Senate reelection to Democrat Kay Hagan, Elizabeth Dole retired.

PATRICIA ROBERTS HARRIS (1924–1985)

The first woman to hold more than one cabinet position, Patricia Roberts Harris also was the nation's first African American woman in the cabinet and the first African American woman to be an ambassador.

She was born in Matton, Illinois, into a middle-class family. Her father was a railroad employee in an era when unionization made that one of the most remunerative occupations open to black men. Her family sent her to Howard University in Washington, DC, the nation's most prestigious institution for African Americans, and the city would become her home for the rest of her life. She helped integrate its public facilities with what probably was the civil rights movement's first sit-in, at a lunch counter in 1943. She graduated summa cum laude in 1945.

After graduate work at the University of Chicago and at Washington's American University, Patricia Roberts married attorney William Beasley Harris in 1955 and worked for several progressive causes. With his encouragement, she earned her law degree from George Washington University in 1960, graduating first in her class at the predominantly white school, where future first lady Jacqueline Kennedy had been a student in the 1950s.

Harris worked briefly for the Department of Justice when Robert F. Kennedy was attorney general. His brother, President John F. Kennedy, appointed her as cochair of the Women's National Commission for Civil Rights. She rose rapidly in Democratic politics and seconded the nomination of Lyndon B. Johnson for his first term as president in his own right at the 1964 Democratic National Convention. At this same convention, another black woman, Mississippi's Fannie Lou Hamer, led a successful protest that ended discrimination against African

American delegates. Harris's speech was unifying, and in 1965, President Johnson rewarded her with appointment as ambassador to Luxembourg.

She served in that post until after Republican Richard M. Nixon won the 1968 presidential election and then returned to Washington, becoming dean of the Howard University School of Law in 1969. Harris won her first major corporate appointment in 1971, when IBM added her to its board, again a pioneering achievement for African American women. She left Howard University for the private practice of law in 1972, which enabled increased Democratic activism, and she chaired the Credentials Committee of the 1976 Democratic National Convention that nominated Jimmy Carter. He appointed her as head of the Department of Housing and Urban Development immediately upon taking office, making her not only the first African American woman in the cabinet but also the first African American woman in the line of presidential succession.

Her Senate confirmation was relatively easy, with the only objections being that she might have been too successful to understand the problems of blacks in ghettos. Harris assured senators that she had encountered discrimination and had overcome her share of problems. Confirmation was even easier in 1979, when Carter asked her to resign from HUD and take over the transformation of the Department of Health, Education, and Welfare into two cabinet-level departments. The Senate did not require a third confirmation when she became secretary of the Department of Health and Human Services, which officially began on May 4, 1980. President Carter lost that November's election to Republican Ronald Reagan, which meant that Harris's cabinet service ended early in 1981.

Just fifty-six then, Harris taught at the George Washington University Law School. She ran unsuccessfully for mayor of the District of Columbia in 1982, when, again, her problem was that too many people saw her as too successful and therefore unable to identify with them. Gender also was a factor, and Washington, as of 2011, would have only one female mayor. She was Sharon Pratt Dixon, elected in 1990, who had learned politics by managing Harris's 1982 campaign.

Patricia Roberts Harris died of breast cancer at age sixty. She has received posthumous honors, including being featured on a stamp issued by the U.S. Postal Service in 2000.

CARLA ANDERSON HILLS (1934–)

The third woman to serve in the cabinet, Carla A. Hills had excellent educational qualifications. After studying at England's Oxford University, she graduated from Stanford University in her native California and then earned her law degree from Yale University in 1958—a time when few women were admitted to such prestigious law schools. Although she graduated in the top twenty of her class, her experience was akin to other women in that no major law firm offered her a job. She had been born to an affluent family in Beverly Hills and did not need to earn a living, but she was passionate about practicing law.

When Carla Anderson married lawyer Roderick Hills in 1958, she would use both her maiden and married names, but without a hyphen, and she often was called by the surname Hills. Bearing four children did not slow her down, although she later said that she was careful to arrange her schedule so that she did not miss events important to her son and three daughters. During the first twelve years after graduation and marriage, she worked as a federal prosecutor in Los Angeles, became a partner in a private law firm, taught as an adjunct at the University of California at Los Angeles, and served as president of the National Women Lawyers Association.

Hills specialized in antitrust law, and the family moved to Washington, DC, when she became head of the Civil Division of the Department of Justice (DOJ). The department originally recruited her husband, but her abilities were quickly recognized, and she became a star there. In 1975, President Gerald R. Ford chose Hills as secretary of the Department of Housing and Urban Development (HUD), thus making her the third woman to be a member of the cabinet. Although her qualifications for HUD were somewhat questionable, Hills's impeccable reputation for following the law turned out to be what HUD and the nation needed.

After Ford lost the 1976 election to Jimmy Carter, she returned to private practice during the Carter and Reagan administrations. She was considered too moderate a Republican for the Reagan White House, but in 1989, President George H. W. Bush, her fellow Yale alumnus, appointed Hills as the U.S. trade representative, the nation's chief trade negotiator. She was the top person responsible for the North American Free Trade Agreement (NAFTA). Although the agreement was supported by President Bill Clinton, such appointments are typically partisan, and Hills again returned to private life after Bush lost to Clinton in 1992.

Returning to Los Angeles, Carla Anderson Hills served on a number of national and international boards and, with Democrat Robert E. Rubin, cochaired the Council on Foreign Relations. The author of several books on law, she continued to write and lecture in retirement. Yale University granted her an honorary degree in 2008.

OVETA CULP HOBBY (1905–1995)

In addition to being the second woman in the cabinet, Oveta Culp Hobby was an outstanding lawyer and publisher, and she commanded the first female unit of the American military that was not for nurses.

Born in Kellen, Texas, Oveta Culp was encouraged by her father, an attorney. She graduated from the University of Texas while still in her teens, and by age twenty, she was serving not only as an assistant city attorney in Houston, but also as parliamentarian for the state legislature in Austin. She held the latter post from 1926 to 1931, while also writing a textbook on parliamentary procedure. At age twenty-one, she codified the state's laws on banking, systematically compiling all laws the legislature had passed that pertained to banks.

She married William P. Hobby in 1931, when she was twenty-six. A former governor of Texas and the publisher of the *Houston Post*, he was much older, but he consistently supported her independent career. While bearing two children—one of whom, William P. Hobby Jr., would become lieutenant governor of Texas—she educated herself in journalism. Beginning as a research assistant, she rose up the ranks to executive vice president of the *Houston Post* by 1938. Much later, in 1960, her colleagues nationally would honor her as Publisher of the Year.

Six months before the attack on Pearl Harbor, Hobby took one of the dollar-a-year jobs that President Franklin D. Roosevelt offered his top policy advisers and became head of the Women's Interests Division of the U.S. Army's Public Relations Bureau. From there, a logical step was for her to head the Army's new unit for women who were not nurses, which came to be known as the Women's Army Corps (WAC). The idea was controversial, and many were especially skeptical that the corps could be launched by a civilian woman who was just thirty-seven years old. Hobby proved her abilities, recruiting nine women of similar age and background and delegating responsibilities among them. Eventually she won over both the press corps and military men.

Because, as WAC director, every decision she made—from soldiers' bra color to their deployment to the Pacific—was policy setting, it would have been easy to be overwhelmed by minutia. Hobby in fact routinely worked fourteen-hour days and often slept just a few hours a night. By 1944, she had to be hospitalized for exhaustion. She kept that quiet, however, and thus was criticized when she resigned in July 1945, after the war in Europe was over but before it ended in Asia. Because Hobby had taken care to groom her successor, the WAC continued to perform smoothly.

Returning to Houston, she expanded the family business from print news to television. She also served on the board of the new Corporation for Public Broadcasting, as well as on the boards of other businesses, including General Foods. She returned to Washington in 1953 at the request of President Dwight D. Eisenhower, who appointed her as head of the new Department of Health, Education, and Welfare (HEW). She was the second woman in the cabinet, and the first chief of HEW.

Hobby was fifty when she resigned from the position in 1955, and she never again accepted a governmental appointment. She concentrated on her businesses and, after her husband's 1964 death, assumed the title of publisher of the *Houston Post*. In 1983, she sold the paper for approximately $100 million. Hobby supported a number of cultural and educational causes, and she earned more than a dozen honorary degrees. Oveta Culp Hobby died at age ninety.

FRANCES PERKINS (1882–1965)

The first woman in the cabinet, Frances Perkins remains one of the most significant executive department secretaries of all time. Revolutionary changes took place during her tenure as secretary of labor, including such fundamentals of the economy as the establishment of Social Security.

A Boston native, she grew up in a Republican family and graduated from Massachusetts's Mount Holyoke College—arguably the nation's oldest college for women—in 1902. Perkins moved to Illinois and taught high school science in suburban Chicago, while also volunteering with immigrant settlement houses, including Jane Addams's famed Hull House. Her interests switched from science to the problems of the working poor, and she returned east to earn a master's degree in sociology and economics from New York City's prestigious Columbia University in 1910. Except for when she lived in the nation's capital, New York City would be her home.

While employed by the National Consumers League, she volunteered with the movement for women's right to vote, and it was in that work, she said, that she learned leadership and oratory skills. After personally witnessing the horrific Triangle Shirtwaist Factory fire in New York's garment district, Perkins sought and won a salaried position investigating this and other hazardous employment.

Frances Perkins retained her maiden name when she married economist Paul Wilson in 1913. She bore two daughters, losing one in infancy. She stayed loyal to her marriage, even as the relationship became increasingly a burden. Despite his background in finance, Wilson lost their savings gambling on the gold market. After that, he never was steadily employed. He displayed the behavior of a manic-depressive and would spend much of his later life in sanitariums.

Fortunately, Perkins increasingly was able to afford his expensive treatment, as New York governor Al Smith appointed her to the State Industrial Commission in 1919. She was the highest-salaried woman on the state payroll. The governor supported Perkins as she intervened on behalf of labor in strikes and supervised settlements. While workers in most of the nation lost power during the Roaring Twenties, Perkins led progressive legislation in New York, including a reduction in the standard work-week from fifty-six to forty-eight hours. When as the national economy collapsed in 1929, she went to Europe to study unemployment compensation systems, as the U.S. government had nothing similar.

Perkins's work was her life from 1933, when President Franklin D. Roosevelt appointed her as labor secretary, until she resigned on June 30, 1945, a few months after his death. She had written numerous articles for magazines, including women's magazines, throughout her career, and her book, *The Roosevelt I Knew,* was published in 1946. It turned out to be a bestseller and provided her with the financial security that she long had sought. In September 1946, President Harry S. Truman appointed her to the Civil Service Commission, which deals with federal employees. She served there until after Democrats lost the 1952 election. She was seventy-two years old by then, and her husband died the same year—but she returned to her original profession of teaching. Perkins was age eighty-five and on the faculty of a Cornell University labor studies program when she died in 1965.

Modest as well as hard-working, she did not receive the awards that she was due. Neither colleges nor women's organizations nor labor unions made her the recipient of the honorary degrees and other awards that should have been granted to the innovator of unemployment insurance, Social Security, and other fundamentals of the modern economy. However, a new Labor Department headquarters, on Washington's Pennsylvania Avenue, was named the Frances Perkins Building.

JANET RENO (1938–)

The nation's first female attorney general, Janet Reno served the entire eight years of the Clinton administration.

She was born in Miami, Florida, and grew up close to the Everglades in a house that her mother built. Her mother, Jane Wood Reno, wrote for the *Miami News,* and her father, a Danish immigrant, was a reporter for the *Miami Herald.* That newspaper was owned by the family of Marjorie Stoneman Douglas, an early twentieth-century environmentalist and Florida icon who lived to 107. She also influenced young Janet Reno.

Reno traveled from tropical heat to frigid upstate New York, where she graduated from Cornell University in 1960 with a degree in chemistry, an unconventional field for women at the time. The same was true when she switched fields and won acceptance at Harvard Law School, in an era when very few women did so. She earned her law degree in 1963, two years ahead of another woman who would serve in a future cabinet, Elizabeth Dole.

Returning to Florida, Reno worked in small Miami firms until 1971, when she became staff director of the House Judiciary Committee in Tallahassee. This was an exciting time in state government, as the Florida League of Women Voters reformed the judicial system and the legislature adopted model acts on open government and financial disclosure. Reno assisted with those efforts and, in the Florida Senate, was lead counsel for the committee that revised the criminal code.

Crime would be the focus of her reforms when she moved back to Miami and worked as a prosecutor. She sought especially to implement important changes in juvenile justice. After two years with one of Florida's largest private firms, she became prosecutor for Dade County, which is centered in Miami and is Florida's most populous county. Governor Reubin Askew appointed Reno as state attorney when the incumbent resigned in 1978. It was an innovative appointment, as few women in the nation and none in the state had held this position. Indeed, Florida would elect a female attorney general before most counties elected a female prosecutor. Reno won reelection five times, from 1978 to 1993, and she reduced crime among Miami's heterogeneous population during turbulent times.

With the strong recommendation of U.S. senator and former Florida governor Bob Graham, President Bill Clinton chose Janet Reno to head the Department of Justice after his first choices ran into confirmation difficulties. Easily confirmed, she was sworn into office on March 12, 1993. Because of the earlier failed nominations, the media focused on the attorney general more than usual, and Reno got more than her share of negative attention.

Reno stuck it out through a sometimes controversial tenure, serving during the two terms of the Clinton administration despite hints from some White House staffers that they would not be disappointed to see her leave. Especially after the Republican Congress tried to remove the president from office, some Democrats thought that Reno could have done a better job of protecting his civil rights. Her naturally dispassionate judicial temperament also served her badly as a statewide candidate. After returning to Florida in 2001, she lost the 2002 Democratic nomination for governor. Although afflicted with Parkinson's disease, she maintained her activism for justice and feminism as a private citizen and, in retirement, continued to live in the house that her mother built.

CONDOLEEZZA RICE (1954–)

The second woman to head the State Department and the first African American woman to do so, Condoleezza Rice was born to middle-class black parents in Birmingham, Alabama. She was just eight years old when racists bombed a black church there, killing her playmate Denise McNair during Sunday school.

Despite this challenging background, "Condo," as her father called her, excelled. Both of her parents were talented educators, and she was their only child. They introduced her to foreign languages, ice-skating, and, especially, music. Her goal was to be a classical pianist, and she would maintain her abilities to perform with outstanding musicians while in political office.

The family moved to Denver in 1967, where her father became an administrator at the University of Denver. She enrolled there at age fifteen. She majored in political science, and one of her most influential professors was Josef Korbel. Decades later, his daughter, Madeleine K. Albright, would precede Rice as the first female secretary of state. Just nineteen when she graduated in 1974, Rice was voted the outstanding senior woman.

She earned a master's degree at Indiana's University of Notre Dame and then worked at the State Department during the Carter administration. Although Carter was a Democrat, Rice became a Republican. She was influenced by her father, who had experienced severe discrimination from conservative Democrats in Alabama, as well as by Colorado's moderate brand of Republicanism. Returning to the University of Denver, she earned a doctorate in political science, with a specialty in the Soviet Union, in 1981.

Dr. Rice immediately joined the faculty of California's respected Stanford University, which would be her academic home for the rest of her career. She connected with Brent Scowcroft, who had been national security adviser under President Gerald R. Ford, when Scowcroft visited Stanford in 1985. After George H. W. Bush took office in 1989, Scowcroft returned to that position and invited Rice to join his staff. Stanford allowed only two years of leave,

and she thus went back to California in 1991, before Bush lost the 1992 election to Democrat Bill Clinton.

While at Stanford, she joined the Hoover Institution on War, Revolution, and Peace, a conservative think tank. Mentored there by former secretary of state George P. Shultz, the Hoover Institution enabled Rice to network with powerful Republicans, including some in private enterprise. Chevron, a petroleum company, named an oil tanker for her, and she joined its board as well as those of other major corporations, while also rising in academia.

Rice served on the search committee for Stanford's new president, and after Gerhard Casper took the job in 1992, he appointed her provost—the second-highest position at universities—in 1993. Ironically, because of her frequent absences from the classroom, she had not yet earned tenure, but both tenure and a promotion to full professor came with the provost position. This was very much the reverse of the usual university promotion path, and some professors expressed resentment at what they saw as exceptionalism for a political favorite. They also objected to her decision as provost to eliminate affirmative action as a factor in future tenure decisions. She did earn praise for eliminating Stanford's budgetary deficit. Rice was the first woman, the first African American, and the youngest person to be the private university's provost.

Her association with the Hoover Institution enabled her to become acquainted with the Bush family, and Laura Bush, wife of George W. Bush, began including Rice on social occasions. After the elder Bush's 1992 loss, the family groomed Jeb Bush for the presidency until he lost his 1994 attempt to unseat Democratic Florida governor Lawton Chiles. The focus then switched to George W. Bush, who was governor of Texas when Democrat Clinton's two terms were coming to an end. During this time, Rice was treated much as a family member and, on numerous visits to Texas, coached George W. Bush about international issues.

Rice resigned from Stanford in 2001 when Bush named her national security adviser. She faced some opposition in the Senate when Bush appointed her secretary of state at the beginning of his second term. Several news sources noted that the thirteen votes against her was the most negative tally against a nominee for secretary of state since 1825.

Her term at the State Department included a number of ideological controversies, especially over the war in Iraq, but no charges of corruption or self-interest. After Democrat Barack Obama won the 2008 election, Rice returned to the Hoover Institution and Stanford. She moved from the university's political science department to its business school, where she concentrated on international business. She had published academic works on

Russia and Eastern Europe earlier, and in 2010, Rice issued reflections on her childhood with *Extraordinary, Ordinary People: A Memoir of a Family*.

REFERENCES AND FURTHER READING

Anderson, Paul. 1994. *Janet Reno: Doing the Right Thing.* New York: John Wiley and Sons.

Bair, Sheila. 2009. "Acceptance Speech." John F. Kennedy Presidential Library and Museum, Profiles in Courage Award. May 19. www.jfklibrary.org/Events-and-Awards/Profile-in-Courage-Award/Award-Recipients/Sheila-Bair-2009.

Blackman, Ann. 1998. *Seasons of Her Life: A Biography of Madeleine Korbel Albright.* New York: Scribner.

Blood, Thomas. 1997. *Madam Secretary: A Biography of Madeleine Albright.* New York: St. Martin's.

Borrelli, Mary Anne. 2002. *The President's Cabinet: Gender, Power, and Representation.* Boulder, CO: Lynne Rienner Publishers.

Burford, Anne M. 1986. *Are You Tough Enough? An Insider's View of Washington Power Politics.* New York: McGraw-Hill.

Colman, Penny. 1993. *A Woman Unafraid: The Achievements of Frances Perkins.* New York: Atheneum.

Dobbs, Michael. 1999. *Madeleine Albright: A Twentieth-Century Odyssey.* New York: Henry Holt.

Dole, Robert, and Elizabeth Dole, with Richard Norton Smith. 1988. *The Doles: Unlimited Partners.* New York: Simon and Schuster.

Grossman, Mark. 2000. *Encyclopedia of the United States Cabinet.* Volumes 1–3. Santa Barbara, CA: ABC-Clio.

Kessler, Glenn. 2007. *The Confidante: Condoleezza Rice and the Creation of the Bush Legacy.* New York: St. Martin's.

Lippman, Thomas W. 2000. *Madeleine Albright and the New American Diplomacy.* Boulder, CO: Westview Press.

Lucas, Eileen. 1998. *Elizabeth Dole: A Leader in Washington.* Minneapolis: Millbrook Press.

Mabry, Marcus. 2007. *Twice as Good: Condoleezza Rice and Her Path to Power.* New York: Modern Times.

Mackenzie, G. Calvin, ed. 2001. *Innocent Until Nominated: The Breakdown of the Presidential Appointments Process.* Washington, DC: Brookings Institution Press.

Martin, George. 1976. *Madam Secretary: Frances Perkins.* Boston: Houghton Mifflin.

Melich, Tanya. 1996. *The Republican War against Women.* New York: Bantam Books.

Perkins, Frances. 1946. *The Roosevelt I Knew.* New York: Viking.

Reich, Robert B. 1997. *Locked in the Cabinet.* New York: Knopf.

Roosevelt, Eleanor. 1954. *Ladies of Courage.* New York: G. P. Putnam's Sons.

Ware, Susan. 1987. *Partner and I: Molly Dewson, Feminism, and New Deal Politics.* New Haven, CT: Yale University Press.

Wertheimer, Molly Meijer, and Nichola D. Gutgold. 2004. *Elizabeth Hanford Dole: Speaking from the Heart.* Westport, CT: Praeger.

12

AMBASSADORS

In the nation's earliest days, such luminaries as Benjamin Franklin, Thomas Jefferson, and John Adams were authorized to speak for the infant republic in the monarchial courts of Europe, especially Paris. Without their diplomatic success, which brought France as an ally into the war against Britain, the architects of U.S. independence could have been hanged as traitors instead of honored as heroes.

The first secretary of state, Thomas Jefferson, took the lead in developing the State Department to deal with all peaceful international interactions, including issuing of passports, protecting the rights of Americans away from home, and negotiating treaties, especially commercial ones that increase trade, as well as to pursue the department's most important goal—avoiding war through diplomacy.

As the United States grew and presidential campaigns became increasingly costly, ambassadorships,—particularly to European countries,—became patronage rewards for major donors. At the same time, finding qualified people willing to serve as ambassadors to poor nations in Africa, Asia, and Latin America became more difficult. Thus has evolved a distinction between ambassadors who are political appointees and those who are career diplomats. In impoverished and war-torn nations, U.S. representatives often are not political appointees but professional employees of the State Department.

Every diplomatic office, of course, is staffed with nonpolitical appointees, some of whom are employed there for decades. Professional State Department employees sometimes spend most of their lives abroad, while politically appointed ambassadors come and go with changes in the occupant of the White House. Staffs can include Americans and English-speaking natives, often women who can speak more than one language. This staff carries on the day-to-day work of granting visas, assisting visiting

Americans, and so on. Meanwhile, politically appointed ambassadors and professional diplomats deal with commercial deal-making and policy questions.

One of the chief duties of foreign service officers (FSOs) is to report on political and military conditions in their assigned nation. The State Department has a long history of transmitting secret cables, in which FSOs provide detailed information about issues and personalities that might cause problems for the United States.

Even more than in other executive departments, the highest-ranked officials of the State Department traditionally have been white men, often educated in the Ivy League and personally wealthy enough to subsidize entertaining at their embassies. But, over the course of the twentieth century, women slowly entered their domain. Many women worked for years at ranks below ambassador, handling the cases of American citizens aboard year in and year out. Sometimes they lived in dangerous conditions that required them to remain within walled compounds to prevent takeovers by anti-American natives.

This chapter emphasizes those who became ambassadors as a result of political appointments over those who have risen to be ambassadors because of longtime employment in the State Department. Job titles traditionally have been ranked based on the prestige of the nation assigned, and these vary from ambassador to the lesser statuses of minister, consul, emissary, and chargé d'affaires. For simplification, the term "ambassador" is used here for any woman who headed an American mission in another nation, whether that was an embassy, legation, or consulate.

FSOs are sworn into office the same way that other high-ranking personnel in the federal government are. They take an oath of loyalty to the United States upon graduation from State Department training, and if they reach high rank, they formally present their credentials to

Table 12.1 Precedent-Setting Political Appointments of Female Ambassadors, by Year

Year	Country or Body	Name	Appointing President	Party
1933	Denmark	Ruth Bryan Owen	Franklin D. Roosevelt	Democrat
1937	Norway	Florence "Daisy" Hurst Harriman	Franklin D. Roosevelt	Democrat
1949	Luxembourg	Perle Mesta	Harry S. Truman	Democrat
1949	Liberia	Mary McLeod Bethune	Harry S. Truman	Democrat
1953	Italy	Claire Booth Luce	Dwight D. Eisenhower	Republican
1962	Bulgaria	(Helen) Eugenie Moore Anderson	John F. Kennedy	Democrat
1974	Ghana	Shirley Temple Black	Gerald R. Ford	Republican
1976	United Kingdom	Anne Legendre Armstrong	Gerald R. Ford	Republican
1981	Switzerland	Faith Whittlesley	Ronald Reagan	Republican
1981	United Nations	Jeane J. Kirkpatrick	Ronald Reagan	Republican
1983	Austria	Helene A. von Damm	Ronald Reagan	Republican
1983	UN Agency for Food and Agriculture (Rome)	Millicent Hammond Fenwick	Ronald Reagan	Republican
1985	Ireland	Margaret M. Heckler	Ronald Reagan	Republican
1989	Czechoslovakia	Shirley Temple Black	George H.W. Bush	Republican
1993	France	Patricia Churchill Harriman	Bill Clinton	Democrat
1993	Jamaica	Shirley Anita Chisholm	Bill Clinton	Democrat
1994	Micronesia	March Fong Eu	Bill Clinton	Democrat
1994	Portugal	Elizabeth Frawley Bagley	Bill Clinton	Democrat
1997	Vatican City	Corinne Claiborne "Lindy" Boggs	Bill Clinton	Democrat
1999	New Zealand	Carol Moseley-Braun	Bill Clinton	Democrat
2006	African Union	Cindy Courville	George W. Bush	Republican
2008	European Union	Kristen Silverberg	George W. Bush	Republican
2009	Ambassador-at-large for global women's issues, State Department	Melanne Verveer	Barack Obama	Democrat
2010	El Salvador	Mari Carmen Aponte	Barack Obama	Democrat
2011	Ambassador-at-large for international religious freedom, State Department	Suzan Johnson Cook	Barack Obama	Democrat

Source: Compiled by author.

Note: The table contains only political appointees, not career diplomats. Only the first female ambassador to a nation or international body is listed.

the foreign nation where they serve and take a separate oath for that assignment.

Like members of the federal judiciary and executive department secretaries, presidential nominees for ambassadorships must be confirmed by the Senate. More than other such posts, however, senators are inclined to allow presidents to choose ambassadors without much interference. The opinion that matters most is that of the secretary of state, to whom ambassadors report, as well as that of the receiving nation.

INFORMAL PIONEERS, 1840S TO 1920S

Jane McManus Storm Cazneau, whose pseudonym as a newspaper correspondent was Cora Montgomery, probably would have been an ambassador had she been male. She was Jane Maria Eliza McManus and twenty-five years old in 1832, when her family in Troy, New York, fell into bankruptcy. Her father sent her to visit Aaron Burr, a friend, former U.S. vice president, and a longtime advocate of national expansion. She talked with Burr about opportunities for her family outside of the borders of the United States. Acting on Burr's recommendation, she went to Texas, then part of Mexico. There she learned Spanish and, during the next two decades, became sufficiently respected as a news writer on the Southwest that she frequently traveled between there and New York.

When war loomed with Mexico in 1847, she traveled to Mexico City with President James K. Polk's emissary, Moses Yale Beach, who had been specially appointed by Polk to deal with the coming war. She served as Beach's translator, and some historians believe that she even was responsible for his appointment. She knew the president better than Beach did and visited the White House just prior to his appointment. Her surname had changed to Storm by then, but marriage did not slow her international career. After the United States expanded with the acquisition of formerly Mexican land between Texas and

California, Storm continued to support the new national policy of Manifest Destiny by focusing on potential American expansion into Cuba, Haiti, and other parts of the Caribbean. The borders of the United States still were being defined in the 1850s, and acquisition of Caribbean islands was an especially popular idea in the American South. Slavery had proven financially unrewarding in the North and West, but it was profitable in the island tropics.

Marrying for a final time in 1849, Jane Cazneau moved with her new husband to New Mexico. After five years there, William Cazneau, who had served in the founding legislative body of the Republic of Texas, obtained a State Department appointment to Santo Domingo. However, the *New York Post* asserted that it was she who was the "real commissioner" (May 1979, 399).

Jane Cazneau soon was in the thick of Caribbean politics, writing to three U.S. presidents during the 1850s about business opportunities in the islands. Unlike abolitionists, she urged the State Department to put an end to the only black-run government in the Western Hemisphere, Haiti. Despite this racism, the Cazneaus did not join the Confederacy and instead stayed loyal to the Union when the Civil War began. In fact, the couple had to flee to Jamaica in 1863. Emboldened by the war, Spanish officials in Santo Domingo looted their estate, which functioned as the American embassy. They returned to Santo Domingo at the war's end, and after William's 1877 death, Jane continued her activism for increased trade with Caribbean nations. She was sailing back to the islands from New York when she died in a shipwreck at age seventy-one.

Marilla Ricker's life was less adventurous, but she had enough interest in Latin America that she made a more formal attempt to enter the diplomatic corps. Ricker had been a young, wealthy New Hampshire widow in the 1870s, when she filed one of several court cases averring that women were eligible to vote under the Fifteenth Amendment.[1] A pioneering attorney, too, she moved to Washington, DC, and established a law practice. Ricker sought a diplomatic assignment in the late 1890s. As her feminist friends in New Hampshire reported in the 1900 volume of the *History of Woman Suffrage,* she "was a candidate for U.S. Minister to Colombia. New Hampshire was one of six States which petitioned for her appointment. Ex-Senator [Henry William] Blair exerted himself in her behalf, but it is hardly necessary to say that she was not appointed" (Anthony and Harper 1902, 816).

Female employment within the federal government had begun with the needs of Civil War. Although men still held the majority of even clerical jobs in the early twentieth century, one exception existed at the State Department. According to department historian Elmer Plischke, Marion Letcher rose to be "Chief of the Office of the Foreign Trade Advisor" in 1917 (Plischke 1999, 309). She worked her way to the top under Secretary of State William Jennings Bryan, whose daughter, RUTH BRYAN OWEN, later would become the department's first female emissary.

THE FIRST AMBASSADORS

The Nineteenth Amendment, ratified in 1920, granted equal voting rights, but other forms of equality would be debated for decades. None of the three Republican presidents in the 1920s—Warren G. Harding, Calvin Coolidge, and Herbert Hoover—appointed a woman to a major diplomatic position, although some rose within the State Department. In 1922, Lucille Atcherson became "the first woman Foreign Service officer" (Calkin 1978, 338) but was not allowed to go overseas. Her State Department boss, Wilbur J. Carr, recommended that Congress amend federal law on State Department employment to add "women, Negroes, and naturalized citizens as classes who could not be certified as eligible to take the exams" for duty abroad (Vickers 2009, 124). Atcherson eventually won her bureaucratic battle to be a foreign service officer, and she joined the American legation in Switzerland in 1925. Other women followed at this limited level, including Ruth B. Shipley, who became chief of the Passport Division in 1928.

The precedent of appointing a woman to a top foreign post was not set until Democrat Franklin D. Roosevelt named Ruth Bryan Owen as minister to Denmark soon after his 1933 inauguration. Owen was the first female U.S. representative from the South.[2] She lost reelection to her Florida seat to another Democrat in 1932, however, and Roosevelt responded by setting this diplomatic precedent for women. Owen was very well qualified. She spoke German, which is related to Danish, and had been living in Germany when she met her English husband. They also lived in Jamaica and Egypt and had circled the globe before he died in Miami.

Owen's appointment was not without controversy. Some objected because of the usual gender conservatism, but others thought the choice was politically poor. Florida's *Everglades News* thought that Owen had not done enough work for Roosevelt to merit the appointment,

---

[1] See Chapter 1: Battle for the Vote.

[2] See Chapter 6: United States Representatives.

while one Mrs. Allison from Nebraska wrote a letter to the president also objecting to his appointment, but on the opposite grounds. In her view, Owen was so valuable to the Democratic Party that her presence could not be spared.

May I be pardoned in the liberty I am taking in telling you so many of our people are very much disappointed that you are sending Mrs. Ruth Bryan Owen to a foreign county. We just can't feel it is giving her a square deal, (as) she has been such a material help to the country at large. . . . She did more toward swinging this traditional republican (sic) state of Nebraska over to the Democratic Party last fall than any or all other speakers the party had in the field. . . . Now if you can't find a niche somewhere in this new administration for this woman of all women and keep her at home, I am afraid great numbers of women on these western prairies are not going to forget about it in . . . November of 1936. (Vickers 2009, 126)

Owen was thrilled with the appointment, as were some eight hundred people—including famed aviator Amelia Earhart and first lady Eleanor Roosevelt—who celebrated at a bon voyage dinner in New York. Three of Owen's four young adult children accompanied her to Copenhagen, and the *Berlinske Tidende* clearly saw her appointment as a new and favorable thing. The *Extrablader* put its editorial in both a past and future context, and it even concluded that the traditionally feminine attributes of tact and compromise could result in a more peaceful world.

This is the first time that (the) United States has sent out a lady as Minister to a foreign country, and Denmark is the happy country upon which the honor is bestowed. . . . There can be no doubt but that the experiment will be crowned with success. . . . Who knows whether it will not some day be considered an advantage that the most important diplomatic posts be occupied by ladies? (Vickers 2009, 132)

Denmark had granted women the vote earlier than in the United States (in 1908 for local elections and 1915 in all elections), and Owen loved the small but progressive nation. She heaped praise on the country back in America, using her annual leave to speak all across the nation, but especially to Danish heritage groups. She also was the first American diplomat to visit Greenland, which was a Danish colony, and later wrote a book about it. She learned Danish and especially worked to improve trade. Like other Europeans, Danes had been offended by high tariffs that Congress imposed in the early days of the Great Depression, which had been a factor in causing the economic collapse to become worldwide.

Table 12.2   Female Ambassadors, Both Political Appointees and Career Diplomats, 1933 to 1993

Tenure	Nation	Name	Status	Administration	Notes
1933–1936	Denmark	Ruth Bryan Owen	Political appointee	Franklin D. Roosevelt	First female ambassador
1937–1940	Norway	Florence "Daisy" Hurst Harriman	Political appointee	Franklin D. Roosevelt	Escaped from Nazis
1949–1953	Luxembourg	Perle Mesta	Political appointee	Harry S. Truman	
1949–1953	Denmark	(Helen) Eugenie Moore Anderson	Political appointee	Harry S. Truman	
1953–1956	Italy	Clare Boothe Luce	Political appointee	Dwight D. Eisenhower	First former woman U.S. representative
1953–1957	Switzerland	Frances E. Willis	Career diplomat	Dwight D. Eisenhower	First female career diplomat
1957–1961	Norway	Frances E. Willis	Career diplomat	Dwight D. Eisenhower	
1960–1961	Congo	Clare H. Timberlake	Career diplomat	Dwight D. Eisenhower	First in Africa
1961–1964	Ceylon (Sri Lanka)	Frances E. Willis	Career diplomat	John F. Kennedy	First in Asia
1962–1964	Bulgaria	(Helen) Eugenie Moore Anderson	Political appointee	John F. Kennedy	First to a communist nation
1964–1968	Denmark	Katherine White	Career diplomat	Lyndon B. Johnson	
1964–1969	Norway	Margaret Joy Tibbetts	Career diplomat	Lyndon B. Johnson	
1965–1967	Luxembourg	Patricia Roberts Harris	Political appointee	Lyndon B. Johnson	First African American
1966–1973	Nepal	Carol C. Laise	Career diplomat	Lyndon B. Johnson	
1969–1974	Barbados	Eileen R. Donovan	Career diplomat	Richard M. Nixon	First in Caribbean
1972–1976	Zambia	Jean Mary Wilkowski	Career diplomat	Richard M. Nixon	
1973–1976	Luxembourg	Ruth Lewis Farkas	Political appointee	Richard M. Nixon	
1974–1976	Ghana	Shirley Temple Black	Political appointee	Gerald R. Ford	
1974–1976	Togo	Nancy V. Rawls	Career diplomat	Gerald R. Ford	

(Continued)

Table 12.2 (Continued)

Tenure	Nation	Name	Status	Administration	Notes
1975–1979	New Guinea and Solomon Islands	Mary Seymour Olmsted	Career diplomat	Gerald R. Ford	
1976–1977	Cape Verde Islands	Melissa Foelsch Wells	Career diplomat	Gerald R. Ford	
1976–1977	Luxembourg	Rosemary L. Ginn	Political appointee	Gerald R. Ford	
1976–1979	Mali	Patricia M. Byrne	Career diplomat	Gerald R. Ford	
1976–1977	Nepal	Marquita Moseley Maytag	Political appointee	Gerald R. Ford	
1976–1977	United Kingdom	Anne Legendre Armstrong	Political appointee	Gerald R. Ford	United Kingdom considered the most prestigious appointment
1977–1980	Cameroon and Guinea	Mabel Murphy Smythe	Career diplomat	Jimmy Carter	
1977–1980	Finland	Rozanne Ridgway	Career diplomat	Jimmy Carter	
1977–1980	Honduras	Mari-Luci Jaramillo	Career diplomat	Jimmy Carter	First Hispanic American
1977–1981	Belgium	Ann Cox Chambers	Career diplomat	Jimmy Carter	
1978–1981	Netherlands	Geri M. Joseph	Career diplomat	Jimmy Carter	
1978–1981	Togo	Marilyn P. Johnson	Career diplomat	Jimmy Carter	
1979–1983	Burma	Patricia M. Byrne	Career diplomat	Jimmy Carter	
1979–1980	Suriname	Nancy Ostrander	Career diplomat	Jimmy Carter	
1979–1981	Caribbean	Sally A. Shelton	Career diplomat	Jimmy Carter	Included eight island nations, from Barbados to St. Vincent
1979–1981	Mali	Anne Forrester	Career diplomat	Jimmy Carter	
1979–1981	Malta	Joan M. Clark	Career diplomat	Jimmy Carter	
1979–1981	New Zealand	Anne Clark Martindell	Career diplomat	Jimmy Carter	
1979–1983	Ivory Coast	Nancy V. Rawls	Career diplomat	Jimmy Carter	
1980–1981	Malaysia	Barbara M. Watson	Career diplomat	Jimmy Carter	
1980–1983	Burundi	Frances Cook	Career diplomat	Jimmy Carter	
1980–1983	Sierra Leone	Theresa Healy	Career diplomat	Jimmy Carter	
1981–1984	Bangladesh	Jane Abell Coon	Career diplomat	Ronald Reagan	
1981–1984	New Guinea and Solomon Islands	M. Virginia Shafer	Career diplomat	Ronald Reagan	
1981–1985	United Nations	Jeane J. Kirkpatrick	Political appointee	Ronald Reagan	
1981–83; 1985–89	Switzerland	Faith Whittlesey	Political appointee	Ronald Reagan	
1983–1985	Austria	Helene A. von Damm	Political appointee	Ronald Reagan	
1983–1985	East Germany	Rozanne Ridgway	Career diplomat	Ronald Reagan	
1983–1986	Laos	Theresa Till	Career diplomat	Ronald Reagan	
1985–1990	Luxembourg	Jean S. Gerard	Career diplomat	Ronald Reagan	
1986–1989	Laos	Harriet W. Isom	Career diplomat	Ronald Reagan	
1986–1989	Madagascar	Patricia G. Lynch	Career diplomat	Ronald Reagan	
1987–1991	Mozambique	Melissa Foelsch Wells	Career diplomat	Ronald Reagan	
1988–1990	Swaziland	Mary C. Ryan	Career diplomat	Ronald Reagan	
1989–1992	Cameroon	Frances Cook	Career diplomat	George H.W. Bush	
1989–1992	Czechoslovakia	Shirley Temple Black	Political appointee	George H.W. Bush	
1989–1991	Iraq	April C. Glaspie	Career diplomat	George H.W. Bush	
1989–1993	Malta	Sally J. Novetzke	Political appointee	George H.W. Bush	
1989–1992	Mauritius	Penne Percy Korth	Political appointee	George H.W. Bush	
1989–1993	Nepal	Julia Chang Bloch	Career diplomat	George H.W. Bush	First Asian American
1990–1993	Micronesia	Aurelia Brazeal	Career diplomat	George H.W. Bush	
1991–1994	Algeria	Mary Ann Casey	Career diplomat	George H.W. Bush	
1991–1993	Zaire	Melissa Foelsch Wells	Career diplomat	George H.W. Bush	

Source: Compiled by author, with some data from Ann Miller Morin, *Her Excellency: An Oral History of American Women Ambassadors* (New York: Twayne Publishers, 1995); Elmer Plische, *U.S. Department of State: A Reference History* (Westport, CT: Greenwood Press, 1999); Homer L. Calkin, *Women in American Foreign Affairs* (Washington, DC: U.S. Government Printing Office, 1977); and Homer L. Calkin, *Women in the Department of State* (Washington, DC: U.S. Government Printing Office, 1978).

Note: The table highlights notable pioneers in foreign service during the first sixty years after the precedent was set and covers up to 1993, when Bill Clinton took office as president of the United States.

"IN NO SENSE CAN A WOMAN APPOINTEE GO AS FAR AS A MAN . . ."

When Ruth Bryan Owen left her position as the nation's first female diplomat amid controversy over her recent marriage, the *New York Times* editorialized on September 1, 1936:

Mrs. Owen had no prejudice to overcome in a country [Denmark] where sex equality is taken for granted, and where her task was only to increase, as she did with conspicuous success, the real friendship and admiration of the Danes for the United States. But while it is quite customary for men in the American diplomatic service to marry foreigners and while the wives of foreign envoys to this country are often Americans, a foreign husband for an American official abroad brings up questions for which there is no answer in protocol. In the present case these questions are complicated by the fact that the husband is himself an official of the King's household.

Apparently Mrs. Owen has been content to break one precedent without raising the next point that must be met if diplomacy as a career is ever to be really open to women. It is also apparent that unless Washington follows the example of some of the other Governments in forbidding all diplomatic representatives to marry foreigners, in no sense can a woman appointee go as far as a man in the field of international relations.

It was true: A woman never could go as far as a man if marriage was a barrier for her, but not for him. Both in the diplomatic field and in other professions, the nation needed to take a long look at the old legal truism that a marriage contract knitted two into one—and that one was the man.

In a January 21, 1934, *New York Times* article, Owen strongly suggested that America could learn from Denmark in dealing with the Great Depression. At a time when many Americans, especially racial minorities, had little or no education, she pointed out that "illiteracy was practically non-existent" in Denmark, adding that "social insurance of every type gives the people a sense of dignity and security." She concluded that "the extraordinary agricultural efficiency of the Danes is due to their ability and willingness to cooperate."

She also fell in love with a Dane, nobleman Borge Rohde. Even though they married in the United States, no one in the State Department pointed out that the union would have legal consequences for her career. Under Danish law, she became a Danish citizen with marriage and thus, according to State Department officials, could not keep her position as minister from the United States. Attorneys who complained about the marriage after the fact probably were aware of this consequence, but they failed to warn her. As complaints about the marriage mounted, Owen became concerned with the political damage she might do to the president. After exchanges with the White House via telegraph, she decided to remove herself from the gender-based controversy. She resigned about a month after her wedding, on August 29, 1936, and spent the autumn campaigning for Roosevelt's reelection.

After winning by a wider margin than even his 1932 triumph, Roosevelt appointed the second female foreign diplomat, FLORENCE "DAISY" HURST HARRIMAN, who became ambassador to Norway in 1937.

Meanwhile, in Washington, women began to rise at the State Department. Blanche R. Holla became chief of its Office of Coordination and Review in the same year as Harriman's appointment. Secretary of State Cordell Hull, who had objected to Ruth Bryan Owen's marriage, also set a precedent by sending Margaret Hanna to Geneva as a credentialed foreign service officer. Ella A. Logsden rose to be chief of the State Department's Office of Fiscal and Budget Affairs in 1940. The era's major achiever, however, was Daisy Harriman.

A longtime liberal Democrat, Harriman grew up wealthy and married into a very prominent New York family. She nonetheless supported the largely immigrant garment workers who went on strike in 1910. When she joined their picket line, she was assaulted by police and arrested. In court, the judge quickly dismissed the charges and assured Mrs. J. Borden Harriman, as the newspapers called her, that the police never would have arrested her if they had known who she was. Despite her socialite status, Harriman worked in several posts to promote public good.

President Woodrow Wilson appointed her to the Federal Industrial Relations Commission in 1913, which was before women in eastern states could vote.[3] The only woman on the commission, she served a four-year term and traveled the country investigating causes of worker discontent. When the United States entered World War I in 1917, she chaired the federal committee

---

[3] See Chapter 11: Cabinet and Subcabinet.

During World War II, Germany never invaded Sweden, the nation to its north across the Baltic Sea, partly because the Nazis saw the advantages of having a neutral nation that was closely related in language and partly because Sweden remained willing to make its resources, especially coal, available to German buyers. Adolph Hitler's troops did, however, invade the country that connects to Sweden by land—Norway, which is strategically across the North Sea from the fascists' major enemy, Britain.

When the attack came at dawn on April 9, 1940, snow was still on the ground. Some roads through Norway's mountains remained impassable, and more soon could not be traversed because of the Nazis. Florence "Daisy" Hurst Harriman, U.S. ambassador to Norway, told the story of the evacuation she led from the Norwegian capital, Oslo, to the Swedish border. The trek, about one hundred miles on a direct route and in a car capable of going as fast as today's cars, took five terrifying days.

At half past eleven that night, Oslo sounded the air raid alarm, but as the street lights were not turned off for some time, we, at the Legation did not take it very seriously. Members of the staff telephoned in to ask if I thought they ought to come round and take shelter in our new bomb-proof room in the basement. It had been finished only three days before and we had joked about it. . . .

At 3:00 A.M. the telephone made me jump out of bed. Sir Cecil Dormer asked if I would take over the British Legation, as German warships were coming up the fjord. . . . We got off a cable to the Department of State. . . . We suddenly became aware that the voice of the Oslo telegraph operator, who was saying that perhaps our message would not get through to Washington, was . . . more German than Norwegian. . . .

German bombers whirred overhead. . . . My own instructions [were] to follow the [Norwegian] Government. . . . By 9:45 we were all in our cars . . . and joined the procession that was steadily streaming out of town. . . . Behind us the Nazis had occupied Oslo. . . .

We suddenly realized we were in a trap. Every available road . . . was barricaded. . . . The Germans flying at low attitude were almost in my hair. The deafening roar was terrifying. But so intent were they on laying waste any town in which the King might be, that it was not until several days later that their shrapnel began to rake the roads. . . .

For all the sun, it was freezing cold, and the way was long until we reached the border. The young man at the [Swedish] Customs was not one to be lightly taken in. A woman the American Minister to Norway? No, Madam, he would telephone to Headquarters before he let us pass. . . . [Finally], my unlikely story was verified, and I was welcomed across the border. (Harriman 1941, 250–269)

The shock of Hitler's troops attacking peaceful Norwegians was a motivating factor for many Scandinavian Americans to volunteer for duty in World War II. Daisy Harriman's testimony of her experience especially rallied women to the cause.

Women in Industry, and after Republicans won the White House and the majority in both houses of Congress in the 1920 election, she concentrated on building Democratic Women's Clubs for newly enfranchised women. All of this and more made her a logical choice to be the nation's second woman to head a diplomatic mission abroad.

Harriman's experience as minister to Norway was less controversial within the United States than that of Owen to Denmark. But, abroad, it would prove anything but routine. While Norwegians proved somewhat reluctant to accept a female minister, Harriman quickly won them over. Although in her late sixties by then, she swam their fjords and skied their mountains. After Germany attacked Poland in September 1939 and thus began World War II, she negotiated the release of an American ship, *The City of Flint*, from Germans who captured it on the Baltic Sea. She served from 1937 to 1940, when Nazis invaded Norway—and Harriman then demonstrated her true mettle. Enduring the surprise bombing of Oslo, she slowed her own evacuation to help others escape. After reaching neutral Sweden, she spent her seventieth birthday working to see that all Americans were out of Nazi-occupied Norway. Despite the tumult and physical danger of serving in this place and time, Daisy Harriman proved that a female diplomat could do everything that would be expected of a man—and do it well and without complaint.

FROM THE 1940S TO THE 1960S

A decade after her resignation as the nation's first female diplomat, President Roosevelt sent Ruth Bryan Owen Rohde to the State Department to work on the creation of the United Nations (UN). While attending a founding conference in 1945, she would have seen MARY McLEOD BETHUNE, a fellow Floridian who was the world's only woman of color at the assembly, which was held in San Francisco that summer.

Four years later, in 1949, Democratic President Harry S. Truman set a significant but largely unheralded precedent by naming Bethune as a special envoy to Liberia. Bethune represented the United States at the inauguration of Liberian president William Tubman, whose family, former American slaves, had taken the name of American abolitionist Harriet Tubman. Bethune returned to Liberia in 1952, when she was the first woman of any nation to receive its highest medal, Commander of the Order of the Star of Africa. She also was honored by Haiti, another nation founded by former American slaves. Truman's appointment as a special envoy, however, did not make Bethune head of the American mission to Liberia, as this was an era when white men continued to head diplomatic legations, even in the world's black-majority countries.

The third appointment of a woman as head of a mission abroad was in keeping with the State Department's criteria for male ambassadors: those who were personally wealthy and especially those who had contributed substantially to presidential campaigns. She was Perle Mesta, long known as Washington's "hostess with the mostest." Born as Pearl Skirvin to an affluent Michigan family, she wed George Mesta, a Pittsburgh industrialist, in 1917. He was a government consultant on machinery for World War I, and the Mestas frequently traveled in Europe on business.

She learned enough about his business that, when he died in 1925, she not only took over the metal company, but also expanded into real estate, ranching, and petroleum. Although she lived in Washington, Mesta became active in Oklahoma politics because of her oil interests there, and when Oklahoma Republican Alfred M. Landon ran for president against Franklin Roosevelt in 1936, she campaigned for Landon. She switched over to the Democratic Party in 1940, however, and President Harry S. Truman appointed her as minister to Luxembourg in 1949.

Although a tiny nation, Luxembourg had established itself as a major steel producer, and Mesta had contacts there from her years as a Pittsburgh businesswoman. She set a precedent by being the first female diplomat to present her credentials to a female head of state, as Grand Duchess Charlotte reigned in Luxembourg. Mesta had the same formal title that Owen and Harriman had in Denmark and Norway, respectively: envoy extraordinary and minister plenipotentiary.

Despite her business qualifications to serve in Luxembourg, the press portrayed Mesta's appointment as merely a reward for her role as a Democratic hostess in Washington. These comments had the ring of truth: Her parties,

Mary McLeod Bethune listening to Eleanor Roosevelt speak out against lynching on January 13, 1939. A decade later, Bethune would become the first African American to represent the United States abroad, in the African nation of Liberia.

in fact, were helpful to President Truman and Democrats because Bess Truman disliked entertaining. In contrast to the first lady, Mesta reveled in the public eye. Perle Mesta served five successful years in Luxembourg, until the Republican Eisenhower administration replaced her in 1953.

Truman also appointed Minnesota Democrat Helen Eugenie Moore Anderson, who always was called "Eugenie," as the second woman to represent the United States in Denmark. She served from 1949 to 1953 and, like Ruth Bryan Owen before her, learned Danish. Denmark was impoverished after World War II, and Anderson made a point of not traveling in an embassy car, instead riding a bicycle like most Danes. Her husband accompanied her to Copenhagen, and Anderson set another precedent for women in 1951, when she was the first to have her signature on a commercial treaty.

President Dwight D. Eisenhower made three significant ambassadorial appointments of women during his

The status of the world's women was not yet sufficiently high for many to be official representatives of their nations at the founding meetings of the United Nations (UN), but some American women were more deeply involved in its creation than most realize.

Women had proposed the idea of world government as a way to end war at least as early as 1848, when Scottish reformer Frances Wright wrote a prescient book on the subject. Frenchwoman Jeanne de Hericourt did the same in 1869. Women such as Jane Addams and Emily Greene Balch led major efforts for peace during and after World War I. They and others sustained the Women's International League for Peace and Freedom during the isolationism of the 1920s and 1930s. World War II demonstrated that the United States could not live apart from the rest of the globe, and even during the war, Americans and their allies began referring to themselves as the "United Nations."

President Franklin D. Roosevelt saw to it that at least some American women were included in its formal founding. In addition to Ruth Bryan Owen, he appointed Virginia Gildersleeve, the president of New York City's elite women's college, Barnard. She was the only woman in the U.S. delegation in the first planning meeting, which took place in February 1945, before the war was over. Anne O'Hare McCormick, the first woman on the editorial board of the *New York Times*, served even earlier. She was part of a secret committee that advised Roosevelt on postwar policy, and he appointed her as a delegate to initial international meetings.

After Roosevelt's April death, President Harry S. Truman appointed Mary McLeod Bethune, a Floridian, as the world's only woman of color with official status at the founding meeting of the UN in San Francisco that summer. Dr. Edna Fluegel of Georgetown University also served as a special assistant to the U.S. delegation to the United Nations, and another little known woman, Vera Whitehouse, worked on specifics such as atomic energy control, the development of an effective international court, and the creation of the United Nations Educational, Scientific, and Cultural Organization (UNESCO). Alice Paul, founder of the National Woman's Party during the struggle for the vote, played a particularly important role in seeing that the UN's founding documents avoided masculine nouns and pronouns.

Finally, President Truman insisted that former first lady Eleanor Roosevelt accept a leading role. Despite her comments to the press after her husband's death that she was a nobody, New Year's Eve of 1945 found her packing for London and the first full meeting of the unprecedented organization. The male diplomats and members of Congress in attendance were skeptical about her presence, but unlike most of them, she was fluent in French and knowledgeable about many international issues and personalities. Indeed, more than any other single person, it was Eleanor Roosevelt who is the author of the Universal Declaration of Human Rights.

---

eight years in office. The least prestigious was that of Mary Pillsbury Lord, a liberal Republican from the Minnesota grain-milling family, who was appointed to the UN Commission on Human Rights. She had campaigned for Eisenhower and was a longtime advocate for the world's children. Eleanor Roosevelt, a Democrat, said that Lord was so effective a lobbyist that, when she was appointed to the UN, Lord "knew personally almost every senator or member of the House who had ever had anything to do with the United Nations" (Roosevelt 1954, 242).

Frances E. Willis set a precedent as the first female foreign service officer to hold full ambassadorial rank when President Eisenhower appointed her ambassador to Switzerland in 1953. Willis had been in Belgium when Nazis overran it in 1940. She escaped to Britain, where she joined many other representatives of European governments-in-exile. When the war ended, she continued to rise in the FSO ranks. She served in Finland and then became the second female minister to Norway. This made her the first nonpolitical female minister from the United States (Daisy Harriman, who also escaped from Nazis, had been a political appointee). Willis ultimately would end her career in Ceylon (now Sri Lanka) in 1961, when that nation had a female head of state.

Other women also rose at the State Department, and historian Elmer Plischke, who was an insider with the diplomatic corps, said that "by 1953, there were forty-three women Foreign Service Officers" (Plischke 1999, 512). These were career professionals, usually multi-lingual, who were certified to go abroad and represent the United States, but did not head the embassy to which they were assigned. They began to create a pathway for other women to gain experience, leading to a greater pool of female diplomats eligible for nonpolitical appointments at top levels in the 1970s and beyond.

The Eisenhower administration's most significant appointment was both more prestigious and more controversial than the other two. The president named CLARE

BOOTHE LUCE as ambassador to Italy. A political appointee, she was the second woman to hold that rank and the first assigned to a country considered a major nation. A Republican and former U.S. representative from Connecticut, Luce also was a playwright and a celebrity from the 1930s through the 1950s. She was married to Henry Luce, perhaps the era's most powerful magazine publisher. Henry accompanied Clare on her assignment and ran his worldwide publications from Italy. When they arrived, women especially greeted the new ambassador enthusiastically.

Thousands of Neapolitans, most of them women, shouted and applauded the first woman envoy to Rome as she landed on the Italian ship *Andrea Doria*. Completely ignored in the bedlam were her husband . . . and the mayor, (who) looked crestfallen. Mrs. Luce read a prepared statement in Italian. (Shadegg 1970, 237)

The women's reaction to Luce was not typical of the governing class, however, as the press criticized even the fact that she took the *Andrea Doria*, which docked in Naples, instead of arriving at the capital of Rome. Most men reacted like the crestfallen mayor, and according to Luce's sympathetic biographer, Stephen Shadegg, "the Italian press was filled with expressions of displeasure and embarrassment. Unidentified government figures stated that the appointment of a woman . . . was an indication that Eisenhower regarded Italy as a third-rate power" (Shadegg 1970, 233).

More than a little justification existed for this view. Eisenhower had led World War II troops from North Africa through Italy to depose its fascist leader, Benito Mussolini, and Italy lost considerable global prestige as a result of its alliance with Nazi Germany. Moreover, just as most Italians promoted Mussolini's rise, they almost voted to return to authoritarian government after the Allies liberated them. Other nations in southeastern Europe were adopting totalitarianism, and Americans reasonably feared that Italy would do the same.

Luce would make a difficult political situation worse by making it clear which presidential candidate she favored in the upcoming Italian election. Voters did not heed her advice on whom they should elect, and the unsurprising result was that Luce never came close to success as a diplomat. Poor health was her ostensible reason for resigning, but late in her tenure, she committed another diplomatic faux pas by going to see Italy's new president without making an appointment. In fact, "when Ambassador Luce left Italy, the newspaper *Europae* published a list of her diplomatic blunders" (Shadegg 1970, 269).

Nevertheless, President Eisenhower continued to solicit financial support from the Luces, receiving $60,000 for his 1956 reelection campaign. In February 1959, Eisenhower appointed Clare Boothe Luce as ambassador to Brazil. This time, the Senate confirmation was not routine. Wayne Morse, a Democrat from Oregon who soon would lead opposition to the Vietnam War, was troubled by the Luces' increasingly right-wing views, especially derogatory comments on Latin America in Luce publications. J. William Fulbright, a senator from Arkansas who was a top expert on foreign affairs, also objected to the appointment. Joseph S. Clark of Pennsylvania was most damning.

There is nothing in her record to indicate to me that Mrs. Luce is qualified to be a diplomat. The role for which I believe she is very well qualified is that of a political hatchet man. She does very well at making inflammatory, demagogic political speeches. She and her husband contribute heavily to the Republican coffers, and for this she is being rewarded with an Ambassadorship. (Shadegg 1970, 282)

The Senate nonetheless confirmed her on April 28 by a vote of 79 to 11—but the Luces had decided during the contentious debate that, as soon as she won the fight, she would withdraw. On May 1, 1959, the White House announced that Clare Boothe Luce would not be going to Brazil, as the president had reluctantly accepted her resignation.

FROM KENNEDY TO CARTER, 1960–1977

In the years after the end of World War II, many countries in Asia and Africa threw off the European colonialism that had dominated them prior to the war. One such was the Congo, which earlier had been the Belgian Congo. Clare H. Timberlake, a career diplomat with the State Department, became ambassador to the new nation in 1960. In 1961, Frances E. Willis, who already had been ambassador to Switzerland and Norway, became ambassador to the Indian Ocean nation called Ceylon by British imperialists; now it is Sri Lanka.

John F. Kennedy won the White House for Democrats in 1960, and he appointed Katie Loucheim as deputy assistant secretary of state, the highest rank yet for a woman. His most important appointee was Eugenie Anderson, who had been ambassador to Denmark under President Truman. Her 1962 appointment to Bulgaria, though, was much more significant than the Danish appointment, as it made Anderson the first female ambassador to a communist nation. It was even more unusual in that Anderson was not a career diplomat, but instead an activist in the League of Women Voters. Wealthy through her marriage to a cereal heir, she had run for Congress in 1944, against an incumbent who was an isolationist in this most difficult year of the war. Although she lost the election, her internationalism did not wane, and when Democrats regained the White House with the 1960 election, she made herself available for the unrewarding post of Bulgaria.

One of the poorest of the poor countries in southeastern Europe, Bulgaria's history is ridden with violence. It still had a king at the beginning of World War II, and he sided with Hitler. Therefore, the Union of Soviet Socialist Republics (USSR)—which was an ally of the United States—successfully invaded. Soviets continued their occupation after the war ended, and Bulgarian politicians were puppets who often executed their opponents. The government closed foreign schools, banned foreign news, and persecuted Christians. In February 1950, Bulgaria insisted that the American minister be recalled because he was suspected of spying. After the United States severed diplomatic relations, Bulgarian employees of the legation were imprisoned and tortured.

The embassy did not reopen until 1959, and President Kennedy demonstrated great respect for Eugenie Anderson by appointing her to this turbulent position just three years later, in 1962. She served in Sophia for the next two years, even though the Bulgarian government sent thugs to throw rocks at the embassy. She also defied local police who tried to stop her from distributing American information. She returned to the United States in 1964, after Kennedy's assassination, and President Lyndon B. Johnson then appointed Anderson to positions with the United Nations, including the Trusteeship Council, in the late 1960s.

Johnson also made a historic choice when he sent Patricia Roberts Harris to Luxembourg. The precedent of a female diplomat had been set in this nation by Perle Mesta, but Harris was the first female African American to head a legation anywhere in the world. She performed this duty from 1965 through 1967, when she returned to United States and campaigned for Democrats in 1968. When Democrat Jimmy Carter won the White House in 1976, she would serve in three cabinet positions during his administration.[4]

Harris was a political appointee, but three other career women rose to significant posts during the Johnson years. In 1964, Katherine White became the third female ambassador to Denmark, and Margaret Joy Tibbetts became the third to Norway. In 1966, Carol C. Laise became ambassador to a more unconventional place, Nepal. Although not violent like Bulgaria, Nepal certainly was not noted for luxury. A small nation between India and China, this mountainous area historically has been both geographically and culturally disconnected from the rest of the world.

Laise had been a career diplomat since the 1940s, and her rise to a top position in the State Department showed the beginnings of a new enlightenment and a specific intent by the Johnson administration to appoint women. Laise not only was the first ambassador to an Asian nation, but she also set another precedent in 1967, when she married Ellsworth Bunker, a widower who was ambassador to Vietnam. He had headed the embassy in Italy just prior to Clare Boothe Luce. When the Bunkers returned home in 1973 at the end of the Vietnam War, Carol Laise Bunker became the first female assistant secretary of state, the highest rank yet for a woman.

Lyndon Johnson did not seek reelection in 1968, and Republican Richard M. Nixon won the presidential election of that turbulent year.[5] Two career women rose to top posts in the early years of his administration. Eileen R. Donovan was named ambassador to Barbados in 1969, making her the first woman with that title in the Western Hemisphere. According to her *New York Times* obituary, published on December 15, 1996, she never married, and her career, which began in 1948, took her to the Philippines, Italy, and Japan before she went to the Caribbean.

In 1972, Jean Mary Wilkowski, also a career diplomat, became ambassador to Zambia. A Wisconsin native, Wilkowski benefited indirectly from World War II, when the shortage of male employees allowed her to be the first female acting ambassador in Latin America, where she served in Trinidad. Wartime promotions such as that often were temporary, however, and it took most of Wilkowski's thirty-five-year career to rise to a genuine post as an ambassador.

Nixon made only one political appointment of a female ambassador, and it became controversial. According to historian Ann Miller Morin, Ruth Lewis Farkas was qualified to be the third female representative to Luxembourg. She had been active in the United Nations since a 1961 appointment by President Kennedy, and Lyndon Johnson, another Democrat, had considered her as ambassador to Costa Rica. But her husband, in Farkas's own words, "thought a great deal of Richard Nixon," and when the couple contributed $300,000 to his 1972 reelection campaign, many accused them of "buying" the Luxembourg appointment (Morin 1995, 76 and 78). Farkas detailed the role that money had played, referring to calls between her husband and Nixon campaign aides, while justifying it as only a small percentage of their net worth. She presented this explanation when she had to fly back to Washington from Luxembourg to testify before an

---

[4] See Chapter 11: Cabinet and Subcabinet.

[5] See Chapter Ten: Presidential and Vice Presidential Candidates.

Carol C. Laise got her start in the foreign service because of World War II, when many women found occupational opportunities that had been closed to them previously. She detailed the beginning of her career in an interview with author Ann Miller Morin.

Women were in demand because there was no danger of their being drafted. . . . I spent three years in Washington. . . . [A call] came to help out in London. . . . That was 1946. . . . When I got to London, there was considerable shock that I turned out to be a woman. . . .

I felt that Asia was important to the future of the United States. . . . I also found . . . that where the traditions were shaped by British administration, it was easier to relate and function as a woman. And equally, I felt that in India there was a goal of hospitality. . . . In the embassy in Delhi, my colleagues were extremely helpful and kind. . . . I was there for four years . . . [and] got to know Mrs. [Indira] Gandhi. (Morin 1995, 59)

Laise also met Vice President Lyndon B. Johnson when he visited India in 1961, and she soon was promoted to deputy director of South Asian affairs. It was, she said, "a traumatic time," with the assassination of President John F. Kennedy in 1963 and that of Indian leader Jawaharlal Nehru in 1964. After Johnson succeeded Kennedy, Lasie said: "I began to get indications from the White House that they thought that since the President was interested in appointing more women ambassadors, I ought to be considered for one such post." The White House decided on Nepal, and Laise arrived there late in 1966, when she had plans to marry.

On Christmas Day, I informed His Majesty that I would be getting married to Ellsworth Bunker on the third of January. He seemed thunderstruck at the idea. . . . [But] Nepalese seemed to take it as a proper acknowledgment of their importance that, in effect, there were two American ambassadors resident at Kathmandu. (Morin 1995, 61–70)

Because Ellsworth Bunker was highly prominent during the Vietnam War and because women were strongly attuned to news about that unpopular war, the marriage drew more attention than otherwise would have been the case. For many young women, it was their first awareness of female diplomats, and Carol Laise Bunker thus inspired some of those who followed her career path later in the century.

investigating committee. When Gerald R. Ford succeeded Nixon as president in August 1974, Farkas followed State Department protocol and submitted her resignation. The new administration was busy with many other things, however, and did not take action until February 1976. Ambassador Farkas was in New York at the time, taking a grandson to lunch, and learned that she had been replaced when she read about it in the newspaper.

During the administration of Republican Gerald Ford, three career women were promoted to head legations abroad. They were Nancy V. Rawls in the African nation of Togo, Mary Seymour Olmsted in the South Pacific's Solomon Islands and New Guinea, and Melissa Foelsch Wells in the Cape Verde Islands, which are off the coast of North Africa.

Ford made four political appointments during his brief tenure. Three of the four political women he appointed were named in 1976, the year in which he ran for election in his own right—and lost. Thus, they had less than a year in office. Party activist Rosemary L. Ginn was a Missourian who became the nation's fourth female ambassador to Luxembourg in 1976. California fund-raiser Marquita Moseley Maytag went to Nepal that year, following the precedent set by career diplomat Carol C. Laise (later Carol Laise Bunker) in 1966. Two others were better-known Republicans. Anne Legendre Armstrong won the most coveted assignment of all, ambassador to Great Britain, and Shirley Temple Black, ambassador to Ghana, was Ford's first appointment, in 1974, and the first noncareer woman to head an embassy in Africa.

Shirley Temple was perhaps the most popular child actor of the twentieth century. Her movies inspired both a hairstyle and a nonalcoholic drink that was named for her. As Shirley Temple Black, she discovered that stardom has its limits, as she was not popular enough with Californians to win nomination for a U.S. House seat in 1968. More conservative than her Republican rival, she lost to a then unknown trial lawyer and Vietnam War opponent, Paul N. "Pete" McCloskey Jr. Black continued to be active in the Republican Party, though, and Richard Nixon appointed her to a position with the UN in 1969. Gerald Ford promoted her as ambassador to Ghana.

Ghana was an unconventional choice for a celebrity such as Black, but it traditionally has been more prosperous than most African nations. Until 1957, it was called "the Gold Coast" both because the mineral was mined there and because, during earlier centuries, it was a very profitable exporter of slaves. By the 1970s, the capital of

Accra had wide, landscaped boulevards with modern cars and air-conditioned buildings. Black served until mid-1976, when she returned to the State Department and became its first female protocol chief. As such, she was in charge of arrangements for the inauguration of Jimmy Carter on January 20, 1977, and her resignation was effective the next day.

Anne Legendre Armstrong, who rarely used her maiden name, cochaired the Republican National Committee from 1971 to 1973, during the period when Richard Nixon was reelected. A Texan, she was a 1949 graduate of Vassar College, and like most Republican women prior to the Reagan era, she supported the Equal Rights Amendment. Her tenure as ambassador to Britain was brief, however, as Republican Gerald Ford appointed her just months before he lost the 1976 election. As diplomatic protocol requires, Armstrong resigned when the Carter administration began. No woman since has held this prestigious appointment with America's most faithful ally.

WOMEN RISING, 1977–1992

President Jimmy Carter consciously avoided making traditional political diplomatic appointments, and, during his four-year tenure, more career women at the State Department rose in diplomatic status than ever before. The most significant was Lucy W. Benson, the first undersecretary in the department's history and the highest position then held by a woman. Moreover, she worked in a nontraditional area, undersecretary for arms control and international security.

More than a dozen American women were promoted to head missions abroad during the Carter years, including posts far from the traditional ones in Europe, where women led the diplomatic corps in Belgium, Finland, and the Netherlands, as well as the Mediterranean island of Malta. To the south, career women took over in the African nations of Cameroon and Guinea, as well the Ivory Coast, Mali, and Togo. In Southeast Asia, they represented the United States in Bangladesh, Burma, and New Zealand. In the Caribbean, Sally A. Shelton was responsible for eight islands, and Nancy Ostrander represented the United States in Suriname.

Mari-Luci Jaramillo, assigned to Honduras in 1977, was America's first female Hispanic ambassador. Jaramillo was a university professor in New Mexico when—to her surprise—Warren M. Christopher, who would head the State Department in President Bill Clinton's first term, sought her out.

Rozanne Ridgway, often called "Roz," was more typical of the State Department career diplomats who were appointed to ambassadorial rank in the Carter years. She had served under Margaret Tibbetts in Norway, was an expert in oceans and fisheries, and turned down an ambassadorship to Trinidad and Tobago before accepting the position in Finland, the final Scandinavian nation to have a female ambassador from the United States. Her tenure as ambassador to Finland ended in 1980, and three years later Ridgway took on the tough assignment of ambassador to East Germany, which lasted until 1985.

The closest that President Carter came to a female political appointee probably was Barbara Newell—and even that was not partisan. An economist educated at Vassar College and the University of Wisconsin, Newell had been president of Wellesley College and would become chancellor of Florida's university system. In between, she served in Paris as the U.S. representative to the United Nations Education, Scientific, and Cultural Organization (UNESCO). Appointed in 1979, she had to resign early in 1981, after Carter lost his 1980 reelection to Republican Ronald Reagan.

During Reagan's first year in office, Joan M. Clark rose to be the first female director general of the foreign service, a nonpolitical position that she held until 1983. A much more political appointee was Faith Whittlesley, who twice served as ambassador to Switzerland. A former Pennsylvania legislator, she was a strong Reagan supporter and White House adviser. She specialized in seeking congressional funds for parochial schools and worked with Reagan supporters who opposed abortion.

Ambassador Whittlesley served in Switzerland from 1981 to 1983 and then again from 1985 to 1988. She generally was considered successful, especially for her attempts to open that nation's traditionally secret international banking system. Whittlesley nonetheless was controversial because of charges that she offered favors in exchange for contributions to her entertainment fund. An Associated Press article syndicated on December 12, 1986, began publicizing these accusations. Several journalists followed up, including famed William F. Buckley, and the consensus of insider opinion was that the negative leaks on Whittlesley came from disgruntled Republican men in the White House. The Subcommittee on International Operations of the House Foreign Affairs Committee investigated the charges, but its results were not published in 1988, the last full year of Reagan's tenure in office. Meanwhile, Attorney General Edwin Meese III—who also was controversial—found no cause for action, and Whittlesley remained in Switzerland.

Helene A. von Damm also was a longtime Reagan supporter, and he named her ambassador to Austria, a first for women. She was herself Austrian, having come to Michigan in 1959 as a soldier's wife. After divorcing and moving to California, she worked as Reagan's private secretary as early as 1966 and went with him to the White House in 1981. Von Damm left the White House for the Austrian capital of Vienna in 1983 and, soon after divorcing her third husband, married the owner of that city's historic Hotel Sacher. She resigned her ambassadorship in June 1985—apparently without mentioning her plan to the president, whom she had seen just weeks earlier—and married for a fourth time.

Reagan's most significant appointment was a great contrast to von Damm's escapades, as JEANE J. KIRK-PATRICK was a foreign policy expert who took her duties as the first female U.S. ambassador to the United Nations very seriously. She was an academic with a long list of publications on international issues and was affiliated with Georgetown University, an institution with strong links to the State Department. Reagan read one of Kirkpatrick's articles prior to his election, and even though she was a registered Democrat, he sought her out and eventually appointed her to this top position. Many earlier women held appointments with the UN in supportive roles—including even some members of Congress, who did double duty as UN delegates during its early days—but none had held the title of ambassador.

Kirkpatrick's academic credentials made her well qualified, but some worried that she lacked real-world experience. Others, especially on the left, could not accept the thesis that attracted Reagan's attention. She drew a distinction between "authoritarian" governments and "totalitarian" ones, finding the latter unacceptable and the former satisfactory. In the eyes of her critics, the label "totalitarian" consistently was attached to leftist governments, even those that had some evidence of free elections, while "authoritarian" governments led by right-wingers were worthy of U.S. protection, despite a lack of free elections. In Kirkpatrick's view, enthusiastically adopted by Reagan, economic socialism was more dangerous to U.S. interests than political oppression.

This doctrine saw its clearest execution in Central America. where the Reagan administration in 1981 secretly provide money and weapons through the Central Intelligence Agency (CIA) to counterrevolutionary forces, known as contras, who subverted elected governments there. Secret U.S. military units and the CIA, for example, targeted Daniel Ortega, whom most observers believed had won election in Nicaragua, as well as future Nobel Peace Prize winner Oscar Arias in Costa Rica, a nation without an army. Despite Costa Rica's resolute antimilitarism, according to political scientist Walter LaFeber, "Jeane Kirkpatrick urged that the Pentagon and CIA be allowed to train a force that could become part of the spreading conflagration" (LaFeber 1993, 341). Had this been widely known at the time, most of Kirkpatrick's UN

colleagues would have seen it as a betrayal of the UN mandate for peace.

Kirkpatrick's biggest success was that she encouraged satellites of the Soviet Union in Eastern Europe to begin to establish independence that had been lost to them since World War II. Poland led the way, and other Slavic nations followed in a largely peaceful transition to democracies. This was seen by many to have justified Kirkpatrick's anticommunist stance, while the violence in Central America remained unknown to most Americans—and when it was revealed, most focus was on an obscure colonel, Oliver L. North, whose work in the White House basement was seen as not necessarily authorized at higher levels.

Kirkpatrick may have been unaware of North's operation, as she was excluded from White House decision-making. Even in her first year at the UN, she threatened to resign because she felt that Reagan's staff ignored her. According to the June 14, 1982, issue of Time, Kirkpatrick told the president that she felt undermined by Secretary of State Alexander M. Haig Jr., who had served as Nixon's White House chief of staff. In any case, she ended her UN tenure in 1985, soon after Reagan's second inauguration. She won accolades from most. Even those who disagreed with her philosophy respected her knowledge, honesty, and toughness in negotiation.

Reagan made two final appointments in the tradition of naming election losers to ambassadorships. After Republican Millicent Hammond Fenwick gave up her affluent New Jersey House seat to run for the Senate in 1982 and lost to a Democratic man, Reagan appointed her to the UN Agency for Food and Agriculture, headquartered in Rome. She held the rank of ambassador. In 1985, he named former Republican representative Margaret M. Heckler as ambassador to Ireland. She had lost her Massachusetts seat in 1982 to Democrat Barney Frank. Reagan appointed Heckler to head the Department of Health and Human Services, but when headlines appeared about her messy divorce, he sent her to Ireland. She was the first female U.S. ambassador there, and being of Irish heritage (her maiden name was O'Shaughnessy) and having many Irish connections in Massachusetts, her tenure was happy.[6] In addition, billionaire Leonore Annenberg, called "Lee," was briefly chief of protocol for the State Department during Reagan's first year in office.

Vice President George H. W. Bush succeeded Reagan in the White House, and his most visible political appointment was that of Shirley Temple Black, the

---

[6] See also Chapter 6: United States Representatives and Chapter 11: Cabinet and Subcabinet.

former movie star who had been ambassador to Ghana under Gerald Ford. He appointed her ambassador to Czechoslovakia, a more suitable embassy for her than Ghana, and Black enjoyed an uncontroversial tenure there. She served from August 1989 to July 1992, resigning shortly before Bush lost his reelection.

Bush also appointed the first Asian American woman as an ambassador, Julia Chang Bloch. Born in China, she came to the United States as a child and earned a master's degree in Asian studies at Harvard University. She then worked for several Washington agencies, including as a Senate staffer specializing in world hunger and food distribution. She was the third female ambassador to Nepal, following Carol Laise Bunker and Marquita Maytag, and served throughout Bush's four years in office.

Another career woman was entrusted with a significant mission during those years, but: April C. Glaspie remains little known. She was ambassador to Iraq when the United States went to war with that nation in 1990 in defense of the tiny kingdom of Kuwait, where women could not vote. Iraq at the time was headed by Saddam Hussein, who would be overthrown and subsequently executed during a second U.S. war with Iraq under the second President Bush.

Glaspie had been a State Department employee since 1966. Educated at California's historic institution for women, Mills College, she became an expert on the Middle East and served in Egypt and Syria as well as Kuwait prior to being named ambassador to Iraq in 1989, the first year of George H.W. Bush's administration. Despite the prominence of her position as the first female ambassador to an Arab nation, she made few headlines. Diplomatic histories also generally exclude her, including the massive tome of more than six hundred pages written by the State Department's Elmer Plischke that was published in 1999, a decade after Glaspie's historic appointment.

One exception is Jeane Kirkpatrick, who mentioned Glaspie in her 2007 book, *Making War to Keep Peace*. Kirkpatrick spoke of Ambassador Glaspie's efforts to prevent Saddam's invasion of Kuwait by issuing "official assurances that the United States desired 'to improve relations with Iraq'" (Kirkpatrick 2007, 12). Glaspie, however, had been in Iraq almost two years before she had her sole— and major—private meeting with Saddam.

The September 23, 1990, international edition of the *New York Times* contained a transcript of the meeting. While issuing calls for peace and gently inquiring as to why Iraqi troops were assembling on the Kuwait border, she also said: "We have considerable sympathy for your quest for higher oil prices, the immediate cause of your confrontation with Kuwait." Some, including Hussein himself, took this as permission for the invasion. Glaspie

subsequently contended, in testimony before the Senate Foreign Relations Committee, that the transcript was "disinformation."

After Glaspie's service in Iraq ended, she was assigned to the UN until her 2002 retirement. As history played out, if April Glaspie's intentions were to seek peace, she had little effect. Militarism displaced diplomacy, and her personal career never recovered.

THE MILLENNIUM AND BEYOND, 1993–2010

George H.W. Bush lost the 1992 election to Democrat Bill Clinton, who appointed more women to more offices than any previous president. This also was true at the State Department, where Clinton named an uncommon number of women with political experience to top diplomatic posts.

New Yorker Shirley Anita Chisholm, the first African American female member of Congress was named ambassador to Jamaica in 1993.[7] Her first husband, Conrad Chisholm, had been born there, and her parents had emigrated from the Caribbean. Chisholm's health was poor, though, and she served only briefly before suffering a stroke and resigning. Another black woman, Carol Moseley-Braun, became ambassador to largely white New Zealand after she lost her 1998 Senate reelection.[8] Moseley-Braun served until after Democrat Al Gore lost the 2000 presidential election.

Former Vermont governor Madeline M. Kunin was ambassador to Switzerland.[9] The first female Jewish governor, she was the first ambassador to seriously undertake returning property to Jewish victims of World War II. As a result of Kunin's attention to the issue, Swiss banks reviewed their records from a half-century earlier, and upward of thirty thousand American Jews were able to claim deposits that their families had made when they fled from the Nazis. Kunin's mother's bank account even turned up on a list of "unclaimed assets."

Clinton appointed Jean Kennedy Smith, the sister of the late president, as ambassador to Ireland. She had a link to that nation through her family heritage, and in the 1930s, her father had been ambassador to the United Kingdom. The president also had Irish roots and prioritized bringing peace to Ireland. Both he and his ambassador

---

[7] See Chapter 6: United States Representatives.

[8] See Chapter 7: United States Senators.

[9] See Chapter 8: Governors and Lieutenant Governors.

Table 12.3 Female Ambassadors by Country, 1993 to 2010

Nation	Name	Tenure	Nation	Name	Tenure
Albania	Marisa R. Lino	1996–1999		Aldona Wos*	2004–2006
	Marcie B. Reis	2004–2007	Ethiopia	Aurelia Brazeal	2002–2005
Algeria	Mary Ann Casey	1991–1994		Vicki Huddleston	2010–
	Janet Sanderson	2002–2003	Finland	Bonnie McElveen-Hunter*	2001–2003
Angola	Cynthia Efird	2004–2007		Marilyn Ware*	2005–2209
Argentina	Vilma Socorro Martinez*	2009–	France	Pamela Churchill Harriman*	1993–1997
Armenia	Marie Yovanovitch	2008–	Gabon	Elizabeth Raspolic	1995–1998
Austria	Swanee Hunt*	1993–1997		Eunice Reddick	2007–2010
	Kathryn Walt Hall*	1997–2001	Ghana	Kathryn Dee Robinson	1998–2001
	Susan R. McCaw*	2006–2007		Nancy Jo Powell	2001–2002
Australia	Genta Hawkins Holmes	1997–2000		Mary Carlin Yates	2002–2005
Azerbaijan	Anne Derse	2006–2009		Pamela Bridgewater	2005–2008
Bahamas	Nicole Avant	2009–	Guatemala	Marilyn McAfee	1993–1996
Bangladesh	Mary Ann Peters	2000–2003		Prudence Bushnell	1999–2002
	Patricia A. Butenis	2006–2007	Guinea	Joyce E. Leader	1999–2000
	Judith Ann Chambers	2010–		Peggy Blackford	1995–1998
Barbados	Jeanette W. Hyde*	2000–2003		Marcia Bernicat	2009–
	Mary Kramer*	2003–2006	Haiti	Janet Sanderson	2006–2009
	Mary Ourisman*	2006–2009		Geraldine H. Mu	2009–
Belarus	Karen B. Stewart	2006–2008	Hungary	Nancy Goodman Brinker*	2001–2003
Belgium	Brenda Schoonover	2010–		April H. Foley*	2006–2009
Belize	Carolyn Curiel	1997–2001		Eleni Tsakopoulous-Kounalakis	2009–
Benin	Ruth A. Davis	1992–1995			
	Pamela E. Bridgewater	2000–2002	Iceland	Barbara J. Griffiths	1999–2002
	Gayleatha B. Brown	2006–2009		Carol van Voorst	2006–2009
Bolivia	Donna Hrinak	1998–2000	Ireland	Jean Kennedy Smith*	1993–1998
Botswana	Katherine Hubay Canavan	2006–2008	Jamaica	Shirley Anita Chisholm*	1993
Brazil	Donna Hrinak	2002–2004		Sue McCourt Cobb*	2001–2005
Bulgaria	Nancy McEldowney	2008–2009		Brenda LaGrange Johnson*	2005–2009
Burkina Faso	Sharon P. Wilkinson	1996–1999	Kazakhstan	A. Elizabeth Jones	1995–1998
	Jeanine Jackson	2006–2009	Kenya	Aurelia Brazeal	1993–1996
	Cynthia Akuetteh	2010–		Prudence Bushnell	1996–1999
Burundi	Theresa Ann Tull	1993–1996	Korea (South)	Kathleen Stephens	2008–
	Sylvia Gaye Stanfield	1999–2002	Kosovo	Tina Kaidanow	2008–2009
	Patricia Moller	2006–2009	Kuwait	Deborah Jones	2007–
	Pamela Slutz	2010–	Kyrgyz Republic	Eileen Malloy	1994–1997
Cambodia	Carol Rodley	2008–		Anne M. Sigmund	1997–2000
Cameroon	Janet Garvey	2007–2010		Marie Yovanovitch	2005–2008
Cape Verde Islands	Marianne Myles	2008–		Tatiana Gfoeller	2008–
Central African Republic	Mosina Jordan	1995–1997	Laos	Wendy Chamberlin	1996–1999
				Patricia Haslach	2004–2007
	Mattie R. Sharpless	2001–2002		Karen B. Stewart	2010–
Colombia	Anne W. Patterson	2000–2003	Latvia	Catherine Todd Bailey*	2004–2007
	Robin R. Sanders	2002–2006		Judith Gail Garber	2009–
Cote d'Ivoire	Arlene Render	2001–2002	Lebanon	Michele Sison	2008–2010
Costa Rica	Anne Slaughter Andrew	2009–		Maura Connelly	2010–
Czech Republic	Mary Thompson-Jones	2009–2010	Lesotho	Katherine H. Peterson	1998–2001
Denmark	Laurie Fulton	2009–		June Carter Perry	2004–2007
Djibouti	Marguerita Dianne Ragsdale	2003–2006	Liberia	Linda Thomas-Greenfield	2008–
Dominican Republic	Donna Hrinak	1994–1997	Lithuania	Anne E. Derse	2009–
Ecuador	Gwen C. Clare	1999–2001	Luxembourg	Ann L. Wagner*	2005–2009
	Kristie Kenney	2002–2005		Cynthia Stroum	2009–
	Linda Jewell	2005–2008	Madagascar	Vicki Huddleston	1995–1996
	Heather Hodges	2008–		Shirley Elizabeth Barnes	1998–2001
Egypt	Margaret Scobey	2008–		Wanda Nesbitt	2001–2004
El Salvador	Anne W. Patterson	1997–2000	Malawi	Amelia Ellen Shippy	1998–2000
	Rose M. Likins	2000–2003	Malaysia	Marie T. Huhtala	2001–2004
	Mari Carmen Aponte*	2010–	Maldives	Patricia A. Butenis	2009–
Estonia	Melissa Foelsch Wells	1998–2001	Mali	Vicki Huddleston	2002–2005

(Continued)

Table 12.3 (Continued)

Nation	Name	Tenure	Nation	Name	Tenure
	Gillian A. Milovanovic	2009–	Paraguay	Maura Harty	1997–1999
Malta	Kathryn Haycock Proffitt*	1997–2001		Liliana Ayalde	2008–
	Molly H. Bordonaro	2005–2009	Philippines	Kristie Kenney	2006–2009
Marshall Islands	Joan M. Plaisted	1995–2000	Portugal	Elizabeth Frawley Bagley*	1994–2001
	Greta N. Morris	2003–2005	Qatar	Elizabeth D. McKune	1998–2001
	Martha Campbell	2010–		Maureen Quinn	2001–2004
Mauritania	Dorothy Myers Sampas	1994–1997	Rwanda	Margaret K. McMillion	2001–2004
Mauritius	Mary Jo Wills	2009–	Senegal	Harriet L. Elam-Thomas	1999–2002
Micronesia	Aurelia Brazeal	1990–1993		Marcia Bernicat	2007–
	March Fong Eu*	1994–1996	Serbia	Mary Bruce Warlick	2009–
	Cheryl A. Martin	1996–1999	Sierra Leone	June Carter Perry	2007–2010
	Diane Watson*	1999–2002	Singapore	Patricia L. Herbold	2005–2009
	Suzanne K. Hale	2004–2007	Slovenia	Nancy Halliday Ely-Raphel	1998–2001
	Miriam Hughes	2007–2009	South Africa	Jendayi E. Frazier	2004–2005
Moldova	Mary Pendleton	1992–1995	Sri Lanka	Terrisita Currie Schaffer	1992–1995
	Pamela Hyde Smith	2001–2003		Patricia A. Butenis	2009–
	Heather M. Hodges	2003–2006	Suriname	Marsha E. Barnes	2003–2006
Mongolia	Pamela Slutz	2003–2006		Lisa Bobbie Schreiber Hughes	2006–2009
Morocco	Margaret Tutwiler*	2001–2003			
Mozambique	Sharon P. Wilkinson	2000–2003	Switzerland	Madeline M. Kunin*	1993–2001
	Helen Meagher La Lime	2003–2006		Pamela P. Willeford*	2003–2006
Namibia	Joyce Barr	2004–2007	Syria	Margaret Scobey	2003–2006
	Gail Mathieu	2007–	Tajikistan	Tracey Ann Johnson	2006–2009
Nepal	Sandra Vogelgesang	1994–1997	Thailand	Kristie A. Kenney	2009–
	Nancy Jo Powell	2007–2009	Timor	Judith Fergin	2010–
Netherlands	Cynthia Schneider*	1998–2001	Togo	Brenda Schoonover	1997–2000
	Fay Hartog-Levin	2009–	Trinidad & Tobago	Patricia McMahon Hawkins	2008–
New Guinea	Arma Jane Karaer	1997–2000		Beatrice Wilkinson Welters	2010–
	Susan S. Jacobs	2000–2003	Tunisia	Mary Ann Casey	1994–1997
	Leslie V. Rowe	2006–		Robin Lynn Raphel	1997–2000
New Zealand	Carol Moseley-Braun*	1998–2001	Turkmenistan	Laura E. Kennedy	2001–2003
Nicaragua	Barbara C. Moore	2002–2005		Tracey Ann Johnson	2003–2007
Niger	Barbro Owens-Kirkpatrick	1999–2002	Uganda	Nancy Jo Powell	1997–1999
	Gail Mathieu	2002–2005	United Arab Emirates	Marcella Wahba	2001–2004
	Bernadette Allen	2006–		Michele Sison	2004–2008
Nigeria	Robin R. Sanders	2007–2010	Vatican City	Corinne Claiborne "Lindy" Boggs*	1997–2001
Norway	Robin Chandler Duke*	2000–2001		Mary Ann Gledon*	2008–2009
Oman	Frances D. Cook	1996–1999	Venezuela	Donna Hrinak	2000–2002
Pakistan	Wendy Jean Chamberlin	2001–2002	Yemen	Barbara Bodine	1997–2001
	Nancy Jo Powell	2002–2004		Marjorie Ransom	2001
	Anne W. Patterson	2007–	Zambia	Arlene Render	1996–1999
Panama	Linda Ellen Watt	2002–2005		Carmen M. Martinez	2005–2008
	Barbara Stephenson	2006–2010			
	Phyllis M. Powers	2010–			

Source: Complied by author, using data from the American Foreign Service Association, the Council of American Ambassadors, and the U.S. State Department.

Note: Table contains both political and career appointees. An asterisk (*) indicates a political appointee.

encouraged diplomatic agreements that began to end centuries of anti-English violence. Smith had some critics, however, as controversy arose over her recommendation that Gerry Adams, leader of the Irish political party Sinn Féin, receive a visa to visit the United States. Her view eventually won out, and Adams did a national tour. In terms of women's history, Jean Kennedy Smith set a nice precedent: when Mary Robinson was elected as Ireland's first female president in 1997, Smith was able to present her credentials as ambassador to another woman—a first for the two nations.

Pamela Churchill Harriman, a Democratic activist who married into the same railroad-owning Harriman family as diplomatic pioneer Daisy Harriman, received the plum assignment of first female ambassador to France. She was well suited for the position. Born into English nobility as Pamela Digby, she married Randolph Churchill, the son of Sir Winston Churchill. She had lived in France both before and after World War II and was well accustomed to Paris and its high society. After marrying Averill Harriman, one of the most distinguished American diplomats of the twentieth century, she became a U.S. citizen in 1971 and, by 1993, when Clinton appointed her, was so well known as a Washington hostess that no senators objected.

Except for her celebrity status, which made a huge splash, her tenure was unremarkable. The most significant achievement during her tenure was the ratification of the Dayton Accords, so named because the treaty, which ended the war in Bosnia, had begun with negotiations in Dayton, Ohio. As has been the case for centuries, this major international agreement was signed in Paris, in 1995. Two years later, Harriman died suddenly from a stroke. The ambassador's funeral at Washington's National Cathedral was packed by the political elite.

Former Democratic vice presidential nominee Geraldine A. Ferraro was ambassador to the UN Commission on Human Rights from 1993 to 1996.[10] Madeleine K. Albright became the second woman, following Jeane Kirkpatrick, to represent the United States as the chief ambassador to the United Nations.[11] In 1994, Clinton appointed Elizabeth Frawley Bagley, an attorney specializing in international law and trade, as ambassador to Portugal. The Portuguese were very pleased with Bagley, and they awarded her several honors.

In his second term, Clinton promoted Madeleine Albright as the nation's first female secretary of state, in charge of the entire diplomat corps. Clinton also set another precedent in his second term, when he named the first woman as ambassador to the Vatican. She was Corinne Claiborne "Lindy" Boggs, a feminist Catholic who had represented Louisiana in the House for many years.[12] Although Boggs was eighty-one when Clinton made this historic appointment, she served at the Holy See in Rome from 1997 to 2001. Also in 1997, Clinton named Genta Hawkins Holmes, a California professor of diplomatic history, as the first female ambassador to Australia—a longtime ally of the United States.

State Department historian Plischke in 1999 summarized the twentieth century for women in diplomacy. "Over the years," he wrote, "women were appointed to represent the United States in at least seventy-five countries, including eighteen in Europe, sixteen in the Western Hemisphere, many in Africa, and a few in Asia, the Mideast, and the Indian and Pacific Oceans" (Plischke 1999, 515). Several nations welcomed more than one female

emissary from the United States, with Norway, Denmark, and especially Luxembourg having the most. In addition to assignments with the UN, career women represented the United States in the Organization of American States, which deals with issues in the Western Hemisphere. The pioneers there were Harriet C. Babbitt and Gale W. McGhee—names that indicate progress for women, but probably not for Hispanics.

George W. Bush became president in 2001. His national security adviser, Condoleezza Rice, exercised a great deal of influence on foreign policy.[13] Another well known appointee during Bush's first term was Nancy Goodman Brinker. The founder of the Susan Komen Foundation for Breast Cancer Research, she served as ambassador to Hungary from 2001 to 2003. Ruth A. Davis, a careerist with the State Department, became director general of the foreign service in 2001.

In the midterm elections of 2002, Maryland representative Constance A. Morella, a liberal Republican, lost her Washington suburb seat to a Democratic man.[14] Bush subsequently appointed her as permanent representative to the Organisation for Economic Co-operation and Development (OECD), which is based in Paris. The OECD is the bureaucratic descendant of the Marshall Plan, named for former secretary of state George C. Marshall, which rebuilt Europe after World War II.

Condoleezza Rice became secretary of state during Bush's second term, and the number of women appointed to new types of ambassadorships rose under her leadership. Cindy Courville, an African American originally from Louisiana, was ambassador to the African Union from 2006 to 2009. Although a political appointee, Dr. Courville had vast experience in the federal government. Kristen Silverberg was the first female ambassador to the European Union, but her appointment came late in the Bush administration, and she served only from July 2008 to January 2009. The Bush administration also followed the precedent of the Clinton administration by appointing a woman, Mary Ann Glendon, as ambassador to the Holy See. Glendon's tenure lasted only from 2008 to President Obama's inauguration in early 2009.

Perhaps the most unusual appointments of career woman during the George W. Bush administration were in Pakistan, where three women served. Wendy Chamberlin and Nancy Jo Powell, both longtime State Department professionals, were ambassadors there early in the decade, and Anne W. Patterson took on the tough assignment in 2007. She would stay on after the assassination of

---

[10] See Chapter 10: Presidential and Vice Presidential Candidates.

[11] See Chapter 11: Cabinet and Subcabinet.

[12] See Chapter 6: United States Representatives.

[13] See Chapter 11: Cabinet and Subcabinet.

[14] See Chapter 6: United States Representatives.

former Pakistan prime minister Benazir Bhutto late that year, as well as after Democrat Barack Obama won the White House in 2008.

Just prior to the Pakistan appointment, Patterson had been acting U.S. ambassador to the UN. She was well prepared for the post in Pakistan by her service in two Latin American nations, El Salvador and Colombia. Both frequently were the scene of violent opposition to U.S. foreign policy. She allegedly was targeted for assassination when she escorted Minnesota senator Paul D. Wellstone, a liberal Democrat, in Colombia—a major exporter of illegal drugs. Patterson's Pakistan tenure ended in October 2010, and Cameron Munter succeeded her. But, during the tenure of both women, "special ambassadors"—all male—were the ones who garnered media attention in these troubled regions.

Just before Congress recessed for election year campaigning in the summer of 2008, Republican senator Sam Brownback lifted his objection to the confirmation of Kathleen Stephens as the nation's first female ambassador to South Korea. A career diplomat, Stephens had served in the southern part of the Korean peninsula as a Peace Corps volunteer more than three decades earlier. Her return as ambassador was fulfilling both for herself and for Koreans.

The 2008 election of Barack Obama, whose father was Kenyan, was of tremendous significance to international relations, as people all around the globe were gratified to see America elect a black leader. Obama appointed his rival for the Democratic nomination, Hillary Rodham Clinton, to head the State Department.[15] The transition from Secretary of State Condoleezza Rice to Secretary of State Hillary Clinton also was a first.

This marked a huge change in the State Department's history, a change that began in the 1990s with advocacy by women in Congress. Aiming to make the department more diverse and inclusive, they insisted that the relevant panel, the House Post Office and Civil Service Subcommittee on the Civil Service, hold hearings on the subject. The report, *Under-representation of Women and Minorities in the Foreign Service,* was published in 1990—during the George H.W. Bush administration—and gave the State Department a mandate to create a diplomat corps that looked more like the world to which it was assigned. Two decades later, those foreign service officers had risen in the ranks to reach the status of ambassadors.

At the political, as opposed to civil service, level, President Obama appointed Susan Rice as ambassador to the UN, succeeding the contentious John R. Bolton. He also

named Melanne Verveer to a newly created State Department position, ambassador-at-large for global women's issues. Verveer had studied Russian and other languages at Georgetown University and served as first lady Hillary Rodham Clinton's chief of staff. Obama also set a precedent by appointing Vilma Socorro Martinez as the first female ambassador to Argentina.

These and other Obama appointees were not particularly controversial, but the Senate nonetheless was extremely slow to approve his nominations, to the State Department and other executive departments and agencies, as well as to the judiciary. The Senate allows any member to put an anonymous hold on legislation and nominations, and some Republicans used this tactic to delay Obama's choices throughout 2009 and 2010. Stymied by the Senate, Obama finally used the congressional recess of August 2010, when Congress recessed for the mid-term elections, to bypass confirmation for some appointees. The most noteworthy of these was Mari Carmen Aponte, a former president of the Hispanic National Bar Association, as ambassador to El Salvador. Two right-wing senators, Republicans Jim DeMint of South Carolina and Jim Risch of Idaho, had put a hold on Aponte's appointment, but Robert Menendez, Democrat of New Jersey, strongly defended her.

Obama nominated Suzan Johnson Cook, a Bronx pastor who offered comfort to the victims of the September 11 attack in Manhattan, as ambassador-at-large for international religious freedom. The first woman and the first African American to serve as chaplain for the New York Police Department, she had served as a domestic policy adviser to President Bill Clinton. Her confirmation also was held up in the Senate, but finally went through in spring 2011. Dr. Cook was the first woman appointed to this comparatively new post, which was established by the International Religious Freedom Act of 1998.

Other embassy slots continued to need attention. The conservative *Washington Times* reported on July 10, 2010, that about 11 percent of U.S. ambassadorships were vacant because of the Senate's slowness to confirm Obama's appointees. Little reason existed—other than politics—for this reluctance. Of those that were filled, Obama's choices were largely career State Department employees, with just 26 percent termed political. This was less than George W. Bush's record. According to the American Foreign Service Association, 30 percent of his ambassadors were political.

In all aspects of government, debate has been long running on the virtues of professionals versus politicians. Many believe that most government officials should have credentials of education and experience to best fulfill their jobs, while others believe that no experience is equivalent to that of directly representing the populace by winning

---

[15] See Chapter 10: Presidential and Vice Presidential Candidates.

elections and implementing the voters' will. Like other bodies that implement national policy, the State Department, too, continues this debate.

The tradition of making political appointments gives presidents an opportunity to influence foreign relations by naming ambassadors whose views reflect the results of recent elections. An African American president and a female secretary of state, however, were unprecedented, and some senators tried to claim the moral high ground by refusing to acknowledge the long history of political appointments—and their participation in it. But whether for good or ill, professionals, not politicians, are increasingly in charge of the American image abroad, and the percentage of ambassadors who were careerists rose to almost three-fourths in the early years of the Obama administration.

On the whole, the gradual evolution from political appointees to professional diplomats not only has increased opportunity for women, but also is slowly improving relations abroad from the days of imperialism. Earlier ambassadors were much more likely to be businessmen who had a self-interest in, for example, going to South Africa for its diamonds or to Colombia for its coffee and, thus, improving their personal commercial situation at taxpayer expense. Few had the interest of the people of the host nation at heart, compared with today's professionals, who are carefully groomed by the State Department to understand national histories, languages, and cultures.

THE PAST MEETS THE FUTURE: PRECEDENTS YET TO BE SET

The status of women in foreign relations has improved since Ruth Bryan Owen became the first female diplomat in 1933, but more milestones have to be passed before American women can say that they are equally represented abroad. The United States has diplomatic relations with almost two hundred nations but less than one-quarter of the available ambassadorial slots are held by women.

No woman, for example, ever has served as ambassador to the major Asian nations of Japan and China. No woman has represented the United States in Moscow, not when it was the capital of the USSR or the modern nation of Russia. Although India is a major power and had a woman, Indira Gandhi, as a founding president, no woman has spoken for the United States there.[16] Even

America's peaceful neighbor to its north, Canada, which also has preceded the United States in having a female head of state, never has had a woman as ambassador from the United States. The same also is true of its southern neighbor, Mexico.

While women have won appointments to new nations such as Benin, Burundi, and Cameroon, none has had the top post in Greece, an ancient nation, or its eastern neighbor, Turkey. To the west, Italy has had one female ambassador—appointed in 1953, more than a half-century ago. More than a quarter-century also has passed since the brief tenure of a woman in Great Britain, which, unlike the United States, has had female heads of state, both before and after its emergence as a democracy. Spain's powerful Queen Isabella played a founding role in America, with the first European explorers funded by her. Her daughter, Juana, also was a coequal monarch, but no woman ever has spoken for the United States in Madrid.

Women also rarely are utilized in trouble spots such as Indonesia and the Middle East, even though social scientists agree that women are more likely than men to have well-developed negotiating skills. Israel is another nation that had a prominent female founder, Golda Meir, and a strong alliance with the United States, but no American woman has held the ambassadorship. None has been appointed to war-torn Afghanistan, with which the United States has had diplomatic relations since 1935. Although Roz Ridgway did some of the tough negotiations that merged East Germany and West Germany in the 1980s, neither she nor any other woman has been ambassador to a unified Germany, either before or after World War II. Many milestones have yet to be passed.

PROFILES OF AMBASSADORS

The women profiled here were political appointees, not diplomats with careers in the State Department. **Ruth Bryan Owen** *and* **Florence "Daisy" Hurst Harriman** *were the first and second female ministers abroad, respectively.* **Clare Boothe Luce** *was the first female ambassador to a major nation—Italy.* **Mary McLeod Bethune** *was the first African American to represent the United States as an envoy.* **Jeane J. Kirkpatrick** *was the first woman appointed U.S. permanent representative to the United Nations.*

MARY MCLEOD BETHUNE (1875–1955)

The first African American woman to represent America abroad, Mary Jane McLeod was born to freed slaves a decade after the Civil War ended. As a young person, she

---

[16] For a list of nations with elected female chief executives, see Chapter 10: Presidential and Vice Presidential Candidates.

aspired to be a missionary to Africa but found no mission society willing to sponsor her. The closest she came was when she was in her seventies, when she twice was a special envoy to Liberia.

The youngest of seventeen children and raised in Sumter County, South Carolina, Mary worked in cotton fields after finishing the basic curriculum in a one-room school funded by Presbyterians. Through its teacher, she obtained patronage from a young Colorado teacher and Quaker, Mary Chrissman, who provided both financial and emotional support in a correspondence that lasted fifty years, although the two did not meet until 1930.

With her tuition secured, twelve-year-old Mary McLeod took a train—which she never before had seen—to Scotia Seminary in North Carolina. There she benefited from an integrated faculty, which was uncommon at the time. When she graduated in 1894, she went to the Chicago school that later became the famed Moody Bible Institute. That institution was unable to find a church willing to accept a black American as a missionary to Africa. Returning to the South, she taught in Georgia and South Carolina before marrying Albertus Bethune in May 1898. Their only child, Albert McLeod Bethune, was born the following February. They moved to the timber town of Patlaka, Florida, where Albertus found work. The marriage quickly dissolved. Although they never formally divorced, he was a factor in her life only briefly.

In 1904, she and her young son moved to Daytona Beach, which she would call home for the rest of her life. That year, with five initial students and almost no cash, she began the Daytona Beach Literary and Industrial School for Girls. The girls helped her clean trash from the former dump in which the boarding school was located. Sometimes Bethune and her students were so poor that they did not know how their next meal could be obtained. Her strong Christian views and disciplined curriculum attracted support, though, especially from black mothers who needed to board their daughters when they accompanied their wealthy white employers to summer homes in the North. In winter, when these families came back to Florida, Bethune trained her girls to sing for donations. She eventually gained financial support from such winter residents as John D. Rockefeller Jr., and by 1941, her school consisted of fourteen buildings on thirty-two acres of land. Its curriculum also evolved from its vocational roots and, after merging with a male school, became Bethune-Cookman College.

By then, Florida woman had the vote, and Bethune organized black residents to register and vote, despite threats from racists in the 1920s. When, in the 1930s, the Roosevelt administration signaled its willingness to promote black causes, Bethune helped lead the historic realignment of African Americans from Republican, the party of Lincoln, to Democratic, the party of Franklin D. Roosevelt and Eleanor Roosevelt. Bethune had become a friend of the first lady by then, and the president appointed her to head the Office of Negro Affairs of the National Youth Administration (NYA), a New Deal education and employment agency. The highest government appointment yet for an African American woman, she moved to Washington, DC, and led meetings of Roosevelt's "black cabinet" in her home. These were informal gatherings of black leaders, primarily men, who had contacts with white government officials, including Roosevelt, which they used to advocate for greater minority opportunity.

The NYA disbanded when the United States entered World War II, and Bethune served on the advisory committee that created the Women's Army Corps (WAC). She played a strong but quiet role in the corps' acceptance of black recruits and also helped see that they were trained in a variety of occupational specialties, not merely assigned to kitchens and laundries. She toured Europe in 1944, inspecting the work of blacks WACs and arguing for integrated housing, something that President Harry S. Truman began in 1948.

At the war's end, Bethune was the only woman of color in the world to have an official status at the founding conference of the United Nations. She was vice president of the National Association for the Advancement of Colored People, which was just one of many organizations in which she was active. The founding president of the National Council of Negro Women, she also served terms as president of the National Association of Colored Women, the National Association of Teachers in Colored Schools, and the Association for the Study of Negro Life and History. She was an officer in integrated organizations, too, including Planned Parenthood. In addition, Bethune was a businesswoman, having cofounded Central Life Insurance with African American men in 1923, a time when white-owned companies did not sell life insurance to blacks. By 1952, all thirteen male cofounders had died, and Bethune became the only female president of an insurance company in America.

Bethune's national reputation was established already by 1931, when she was tenth on a list of America's fifty most influential women. Rollins College, a private institution for women in Orlando, awarded her an honorary doctorate in 1949, and she received dozens of other honorary degrees and awards before her death at eighty. Mary McLeod Bethune is buried on the grounds of Bethune-Cookman College. The U.S. Postal Service issued a stamp in her honor in 1985.

FLORENCE "DAISY" HURST HARRIMAN
(1870–1967)

The nation's second female representative abroad was called "Daisy" from childhood and never used her formal name, Florence. Daisy Jaffray Hurst was born into an elite New York family, and she devoted her life to Democratic activism.

Her mother died when she was three, and Daisy grew up in a mansion on New York's Fifth Avenue, educated largely by governesses. She wed banker J. Borden Harriman at nineteen and endured several miscarriages before bearing her only child, a daughter named Ethel. By the turn of the century, Harriman had begun a life that would make her far more than a socialite.

In 1904, she was a founder of the Colony Club, the first private club for wealthy women in New York that was comparable to the clubs long available to men. Networking with such women, she was able to attract financial supporters for women's right to vote, and in 1917, New York would be the first eastern state to enfranchise its women.[17] Meanwhile, though, Harriman achieved much more, and in unconventional areas.

Most notably, she accepted a 1906 appointment as manager of the New York State Reformatory for Women at Bedford, and she stuck with that inglorious position for twelve years. During great strikes in the garment industry, she was one of the society women who boycotted non-union clothing manufacturers and donated to the Women's Trade Union League. She also worked for the Democratic Party, and when Woodrow Wilson became president in 1913, he appointed her to the Federal Industrial Relations Commission (FIRC), a major precedent in presidential appointments.

Her husband died the next year, and it was commission work that motivated her move from New York to Washington, DC, where she lived on Foxhall Road in Georgetown for the rest of her life. After her four-year term on FIRC ended, Wilson appointed her to chair the World War I committee Women in Industry. She also helped found the Red Cross Motor Corps and encouraged women to drive its ambulances. Harriman went to France in 1918 to implement the program with some five hundred vehicles, the first wartime ambulances not powered by horses or mules.

Although widowhood and the Great Depression made her less wealthy, Harriman nonetheless was a very popular Washington hostess. Invitations to her Sunday night salons were prized by both liberals and conservatives. She made the only real mistake of her political career in 1932,

---

[17] See Chapter 1: Battle for the Vote.

when she initially failed to support Franklin D. Roosevelt as the Democratic nominee. He was too astute to hold this against her, however, and she ardently campaigned for him thereafter. In 1937, he rewarded her with appointment as minister to Norway.

After escaping from the invasion of Norway by Germany in April 1940, Harriman worked in neutral Sweden to see that all Americans were out of occupied Norway. She returned to the United States, which still was neutral, in September, along with Crown Princess Martha of Norway. In her seventies by then, Daisy Harriman lived out her retirement in Washington but continued to be a Democratic activist. President John F. Kennedy presented her with a Citation of Merit for Distinguished Service in 1963. She died four years later at ninety-seven. Her daughter had predeceased her in 1953.

JEANE J. KIRKPATRICK (1928–2006)

The first female U.S. ambassador to the United Nations, Jean Duane Jordan Kirkpatrick had nothing in her Midwestern background or even her early adulthood that would have predicted international fame.

Born to a blue-collar family living amongst Oklahoma's oilfields, she used her middle name, Duane, and graduated from high school in Mount Vernon, Illinois. Admission to New York's Barnard College, the historic women's affiliate of Columbia University, began to change her life. She graduated from Barnard in 1948, three years after the end of World War II. After earning a master's degree at Columbia, she went to work at the State Department in Washington, DC. It was a particularly unfortunate time, as the department was under attack from Sen. Joseph R. McCarthy and other ultra-conservatives. After a year of study in France, she married Evron Kirkpatrick, called "Kirk," in 1955 and had three children, all boys.

The Kirkpatricks lived in Washington, and her husband was a political scientist who had been in the wartime Office of Strategic Services, the forerunner of the Central Intelligence Agency (CIA). His espionage experience probably influenced her foreign policy views, which ultimately would be shaped by CIA spies almost as much as by State Department diplomats. Kirk also encouraged Jeane to do graduate work, and she earned her doctorate in 1968, twenty years after her Barnard graduation.

She thus was forty when she joined the faculty of Georgetown University. By then, Dr. Kirkpatrick's first book had been published. She was editor of a group of essays, *The Strategy of Deception: A Study of World-wide Communist Tactics* (1963), and in 1971, she turned her doctoral dissertation into a book on Argentina during its dictatorship under Juan Peron. She also consulted with the State Department and other organizations, while teaching and continuing her extensive list of publications. For *Political Woman* (1974), her only venture into sociology and feminism, she contacted forty-six state legislators who responded anonymously to more than a hundred questions, including many inquiring into how women blended personal and political life. She returned to more traditional political science with *The New Presidential Elite: Men and Women in National Politics* in 1976 and wrote frequent articles for opinion journals aimed at the politically influential.

One of Ronald Reagan staffers brought to his attention a Kirkpatrick article in *Commentary,* and Reagan chose her to be the first female ambassador to the United Nations (UN) largely because of that piece. As a Georgetown professor, she had the respect of many Washingtonians, and she was easily confirmed by the Senate. Kirkpatrick continued to publish while at the UN. Many of her views during this time can be seen in the titles of her publications, such as when she attacked the Carter administration's foreign policy in *Double Standards in Human Rights* (1981).

She spoke at the Republican National Convention that renominated Reagan in 1984 and somewhat belatedly changed her voter registration from Democratic to Republican in 1985. Her resignation from the UN post after Reagan's 1984 reelection was not unexpected by Washington insiders who had seen some Republican men align against her. Later, when Reagan considered naming her as his national security adviser, Secretary of State George P. Shultz was so opposed to her that he threatened to resign if Reagan made the appointment.

After leaving the UN, Kirkpatrick briefly considered a presidential race in 1988. She quietly explored the possibility of competing against the eventual Republican nominee, Vice President George H.W. Bush, but her party loyalty was far from clear and she found few supporters. She thus continued to teach and write. Perhaps the most telling of her books in this era was *The Withering Away of the Totalitarian State—and Other Surprises* (1992). Popular as a speaker with audiences arranged by conservative organizations, she enjoyed appreciable income.

Her personal life generally was happy, although a son rejected his mother's politics by becoming a Buddhist lama (a chief or high priest). The Kirkpatricks were married for forty years when Kirk died in 1995. Jeane lived on another decade, during which time she also served as a secret envoy to Saudi Arabia for George W. Bush. This was not revealed until after her death, which came at age eighty in the Washington suburb of Bethesda, Maryland.

CLARE BOOTHE LUCE (1903–1987)

Clare Boothe Luce held the most significant ambassadorship of any woman of her time, as she represented the United States in Italy.

Born in New York City, she was educated at finishing schools on Long Island and in Tarrytown, New York. She studied dance and was talented enough to do some acting as a child. She later became social secretary to multimillionaire and feminist Alva Vanderbilt Belmont. Boothe married millionaire George Brokaw in 1923, bore a daughter the following year, and divorced her alcoholic husband in 1929.

Returning to her maiden name, she worked in top editorial positions for Conde Nast publications, including *Vogue* and *Vanity Fair*. These sophisticated magazines and her first book, *Stuffed Shirts* (1931), were indicative of her well-developed sense of fashion, as well as her literary savior faire. In 1935, she married publishing tycoon Henry Luce. Among his hugely popular magazines were *Time* and *Life*. From then on, it would be difficult for the public to judge if Clare Boothe Luce's celebrity status was based on her ability or on the fact that many reporters were employed—or hoped to be employed—by her husband.

Her play *The Women* (1936) depicted upper-class women, most of whom were vacuous, jealous, and lived vicariously through their husbands. Critics liked it more than audiences at the time, but since its revival in the 1970s, *The Women* has run both on stage and in screen adaptations. Other plays followed, including the comedic hit *Kiss the Boys Goodbye* (1938) and a self-described melodrama, *Margin for Error* (1940). Both then and later, Clare Boothe Luce was both the author and the subject of countless articles in newspapers and magazines.

She wrote an important nonfiction book, *Europe in the Spring* (1941), which explicated the rise of fascism. With U.S. entrance into World War II, Luce successfully ran for the U.S. House in 1942.[18] Her district was an affluent suburban Connecticut area that previously was represented by her stepfather. Her congressional colleagues quickly promoted Luce, as she won a seat on the important Military Affairs Committee and gave the keynote speech at the Republican National Convention in 1944. Reelected that year, she chose not to run in 1946, largely because she had not gotten over the great trauma of her life. Her daughter, Ann Clare Brokaw, was a student at Stanford University when she was killed in a car accident in 1943. Luce stayed out of politics until 1952 but continued to write. Among her works were *The Twilight of God* (1949) and *Saints for Now* (1952).

---

[18] See Chapter 6: United States Representatives.

Dwight D. Eisenhower won the White House for Republicans in 1952, and he appointed Luce as ambassador to Italy in 1953. It was the first appointment of a woman with ambassadorial rank to a major nation. She served three years, returning to the United States in 1956. Eisenhower then named her ambassador to Brazil in 1959, but Luce resigned just a month after winning a bitter senatorial fight for confirmation.

The Luces moved from New York City to Arizona and later to Hawaii. Her increasingly rabid anticommunism lacked the wit that she formerly displayed, and she objected to a range of progressive changes during the 1950s and 1960s. She returned to the mainland to second the nomination of conservative Republican Barry Goldwater in 1964. He lost in a landslide. Her husband died in 1967, and she returned to writing, including a play, *Slam the Door Softly* (1971), and a nonfiction book, *The Eisenhower Administration* (1973).

Luce supported Ronald Reagan's winning 1980 campaign and returned to Washington, DC, where he appointed her to his Foreign Intelligence Advisory Committee. Like her, he was a member of the stage and screen community, and he honored her with the Presidential Medal of Freedom in 1983. The recipient of many awards and honorary degrees, Clare Boothe Luce died in Washington at age eighty-four.

RUTH BRYAN OWEN (1885–1954)

Ruth Bryan Owen led a complex life, with three marriages and name changes. She also had three distinctive government careers: Between the 1920s and the 1950s, she was the first woman elected to Congress from the South, the first female diplomat, and an architect of the United Nations.

Born in Illinois to politician William Jennings Bryan and pioneering attorney Mary Baird Bryan, she had role models in both parents. The family, which included a younger brother, soon moved to Nebraska, and from an early age, Ruth participated in politics as her father rose to eventually become the only three-time Democratic nominee for president. Fewer people noticed her extraordinary mother. Mary Baird Bryan attended college, studied law, and passed the Nebraska bar exam in 1888, when Ruth was three. Mary Baird Bryan was the first young mother in the world to be credentialed as an attorney.

By age eleven, Ruth was handling some of her father's political correspondence. She entered the University of Nebraska in 1901, when she was just sixteen, but left two years later to marry William Homer Levitt, an artist much older than she. She might have been pregnant at the time. In any case, she would bear two children, Ruth and John Baird, in quick succession. She and Levitt divorced after a five-year marriage, some of which she and the children spent with her parents.

She was in Germany studying voice when she met Reginald Owen, an English military officer. They wed, and she accompanied him to Jamaica before bearing her third child, Reginald, in England in 1913. When World War I began the next year, she took a course in nursing and went to the British colony of Egypt, where she worked for three years in a Cairo hospital. In 1918, near the end of the war, her husband became critically ill with kidney disease that he had ignored during months of combat at the Dardanelles, the Aegean Sea strait long claimed by both Greece and Turkey.

Doctors told him that he would not recover. Ruth Bryan Owen, pregnant with her fourth child, who would be named Helen Rudd, led her family around the globe traveling east through Asia to the Miami suburb of Coconut Grove. Her parents had retired there after her father resigned as secretary of state in 1915 because he opposed American involvement in the war.

Despite their abilities, the Bryans had not accumulated wealth in their decades of politics, and Ruth Bryan Owen became the chief breadwinner for not only her four children, but also a disabled husband, an aging father, and a mother who eventually would be crippled by arthritis. Owen discovered that she had inherited her family's oratorical skills, and she joined the national lecture circuit. She also taught speech at the new University of Miami and soon became involved in Florida politics.

In 1926, just six years after Florida women won the vote, she ran for a seat in the U.S. House. The district was huge, stretching hundreds of miles along the east coast of Florida from the Georgia border to Key West. Her mother plotted strategy, and Ruth traveled with other women—driving her own car, with "The Spirit of Florida" emblazoned on it, at a time when driving still was new for women. But Florida was not feminist. It had not ratified the Nineteenth Amendment enfranchising women, and, in fact, some Floridians were so opposed that they filed suit to have the amendment declared invalid. Beyond that, her father died the previous year, and so men in the Democratic Party (the only party that mattered in the South then) felt free to oppose her. Despite these obstacles, Owen lost by a mere eight hundred votes.

Her husband died in 1927, and she prevailed in the 1928 election, defeating the incumbent, William Sears. He, however, could not accept his loss and argued to the House that, because Owen had been married to an Englishman, she was not a U.S. citizen, although she—and generations of her family—had been born in the United

States. This situation never applied to men, of course, and Congress corrected the injustice with the 1922 Cable Act, but Sears argued that the seven-year waiting period for citizenship had not quite passed when Owen was elected. The House Elections Committee accepted his complaint, and Owen had to state her case to the lawyer-filled membership of the entire House. Amidst national publicity and with women as voters, the representatives had the sense to seat her. Sears continued to complain, and the House ultimately barred him from the floor, a privilege extended to former members.

Owen won a precedent-setting seat on the House Foreign Affairs Committee, worked to preserve the Florida Everglades, and proposed a cabinet-level Department of the Home and Child.[19] She lost her reelection bid in 1932, when anti-incumbent sentiment and the issue of Prohibition—for which her father had been highly visible—were factors working against her. President Franklin D. Roosevelt appointed her minister to Denmark the next year, and she served until 1936, when her third marriage again resulted in problems of citizenship that forced her to resign.

Owen had written *The Elements of Public Speaking* (1931) while in Congress, and in 1935, while an ambassador, she issued *Leaves from a Greenland Diary*. She continued in this genre with three books in the late 1930s on Scandinavia and its folklore, and she would add another in 1949 on the Caribbean, where she had lived early in her second marriage. In between, she wrote the book that most reflected her political views: *Look Forward, Warrior* (1942) was a plea for global harmony that came out in the first full year of American involvement in World War II.

She and her husband, Borge Rohde, lived in the United States, and at this time in her life she was usually called Ruth Bryan Rohde. As World War II wound down, President Roosevelt appointed her to the State Department, from which her nemesis, Secretary of State Cordell Hull, had resigned. Roosevelt saw her as an excellent choice to work on drafting the charter for the new United Nations (UN), and after the president's death in April 1945, President Harry S. Truman appointed her as an alternate delegate to the UN General Assembly. She served the UN creditably and, beginning in 1948, chaired a committee for international speakers.

Owen died of a heart attack at age sixty-eight in Copenhagen, Denmark, where she had gone to receive the Order of Merit from the Danish king for her contributions to global understanding.

---

[19] See Chapter 6: United States Representatives and Chapter 11: Cabinet and Subcabinet.

REFERENCES AND FURTHER READING

Anthony, Susan B., and Ida Husted Harper, ed. 1902. *History of Woman Suffrage*. Volume 4. Indianapolis: Hollenbeck Press. Reprint, New York: Arno Press, 1969.

Calkin, Homer L. 1977. *Women in American Foreign Affairs*. Washington, DC: U.S. Government Printing Office.

Calkin, Homer L. 1978. *Women in the Department of State*. Washington, DC: U.S. Government Printing Office.

Craig, Gordon A. 2008. *Tact and Intelligence: Essays on Diplomatic History and International Relations*. Palo Alto, CA: Society for the Promotion of Science and Scholarship

Crapol, Edward P., ed. 1992. *Women and American Foreign Policy: Lobbyists, Critics, and Insiders*. 2nd ed. Wilmington, DE: SR Books.

Finger, Seymour M. 2002. *Inside the World of Diplomacy: The U.S. Foreign Service in a Changing World*. Westport, CT: Praeger.

Gerson, Allan. 1991. *The Kirkpatrick Mission: Diplomacy without Apology; America at the United Nations, 1981–1985*. New York: Free Press/Macmillan.

Harriman, Florence Jaffray. 1923. *From Pinafores to Politics*. New York: Henry Holt and Company.

Harriman, Florence Jaffray. 1941. *Mission to the North*. Philadelphia: J.B. Lippincott.

Haskins, James. 1988. *Shirley Temple Black: Actress to Ambassador*. New York: Viking.

Hudson, Linda S. 2001. *Mistress of Manifest Destiny: A Biography of Jane McManus Storm Cazneau, 1807–1878*. Austin: Texas State Historical Association.

Ivins, Molly. 1993. *Nothin' But Good Times Ahead*. New York: Random House.

LaFeber, Walter. 1993. *Inevitable Revolutions: The United States in Central America*. New York: W.W. Norton.

Kirkpatrick, Jeane J. 2007. *Making War to Keep Peace*. New York: HarperCollins.

May, Robert E. 1979. "Lobbyists for Commercial Empire: Jane Cazneau, William Cazneau, and U.S. Caribbean Policy, 1846–1878." *Pacific Historical Review* 48, no. 3 (August).

McCluskey, Audrey, and Elaine M. Smith, eds. 1999. *Mary McLeod Bethune: Building a Better World*. Bloomington: Indiana University Press.

Morin, Ann Miller. 1995. *Her Excellency: An Oral History of American Women Ambassadors*. New York: Twayne Publishers.

Morris, Sylvia Jukes. 1997. *Rage for Fame: The Ascent of Clare Boothe Luce*. New York: Random House.

Plischke, Elmer. 1999. *U.S. Department of State: A Reference History.* Westport, CT: Greenwood Press.

Roosevelt, Eleanor. 1954. *Ladies of Courage.* New York: G. P. Putnam's Sons.

Shadegg, Stephen. 1970. *Clare Boothe Luce: A Biography.* New York: Simon and Schuster.

U.S. State Department. 1990. *Under-representation of Women and Minorities in the Foreign Service–State Department: Hearings before the Subcommittee on the Civil Service.* Washington, DC: U.S. Government Printing Office.

Vickers, Sarah (Sally) Pauline. 2009. *The Life of Ruth Bryan Owen: Florida's First Congresswoman and America's First Woman Diplomat.* Tallahassee: Sentry Press.

Wilkowski, Jean M. 2008. *Abroad for Her Country: Tales of a Pioneer Woman Ambassador in the U.S. Foreign Service.* Notre Dame, IN: University of Notre Dame Press.

13

PIONEERS IN THE JUDICIARY

Lawmaking is integral to the practice of politics, and women long were excluded from the field of law. Therefore, before women could assume their rightful place in the political sphere, they had to carve out an equal space under the law.

In early twentieth-century America, a married woman did not own her own clothes in some states. Even if she wove the cloth and sewed the garments herself, legal possession was held by her husband. The marital contract made a man and a woman one—and that one was the man. At marriage, a woman became feme covert, a female covered by the male, without legal existence of her own.

The battle for equality in the legal field is complicated by the fact that states control who is allowed to practice law, which means that every state had to address the issue of admitting women to its legal bar. The legal profession clearly professed the belief that women were less than full human beings and that states' rights were more important than the rights of half of the population. By the twenty-first century, nearly half of all law school graduates were women, but most were the first generation of female lawyers in their families.

IN COURT, BUT NOT LAWYERS, 1647–1869

Margaret Brent often is called the nation's first female attorney, but she was much more than that. In effect, she was briefly the ruler of Maryland, when it was a proprietary colony, wholly owned by England's Lord Baltimore. His younger brother, Leonard Calvert, represented Baltimore in America, and when Calvert died in 1647, he made Brent the executor of his will and, thus, in charge of the colony. The honor, however, also brought problems, as Calvert had not paid his debts to the soldiers who had helped him put down a rebellion. When the soldiers threatened revolt, it was Brent who averted a civil war. Many sources quote the letter that the legislature sent to Lord Baltimore, which summarizes that, without her, "all would have gone to ruin" (Smith 1901, 117).

Because she appeared in court and exercised powers of attorney, some modern feminists cite Brent as the nation's first female lawyer. However, her legal activity was not in the role of a lawyer for hire. In no way did she attempt to practice law. Instead, she set an important precedent as a woman who was highly capable of governing.

Although the average colonial woman could not practice law per se, women did use courts even for trivial matters. They sued each other as well as men, with complaints ranging from roaming pigs to profanity use. Even indentured servants, who lived in a near-slave status, brought charges against employers. A female servant might argue in court, for instance, that she was not provided with adequate clothing or food, and judges often supported such plaintiffs.

An African American woman, Lucy Terry Prince, also assumed that she had a right to represent her family in a lawsuit. They were free people of color in Vermont, and in 1797, she successfully argued a boundary dispute with a neighbor before a circuit-riding representative of the U.S. Supreme Court. She won, and Justice Samuel Chase is said to have commented that she did as good a job as any Vermont lawyer.

After the colonies became states, however, women's freedom to go to court increasingly was constrained by state laws that "protected" them from suing and being sued. Laws restricting the property rights of married women and widows were the initial focus of the women's rights movement.

Table 13.1 First Women Admitted to the Bar, by State or Territory

Year	State or Territory	Name	Notes
1869	Iowa	Arabella "Belle" Mansfield	Unmarried; did not practice
1870	Illinois	Ada (or Adah) H. Kepsey	Married; practiced with husband
1870	Missouri	Helena "Lemma" Barkaloo	Unmarried; died young
1871	Michigan	Sarah Kilgore	Married; practiced with husband
1871	Arkansas	Phoebe Couzins	Unmarried; admitted in several states
1872	District of Columbia	Charlotte E. Ray	Unmarried; African American
1872	Kansas	Phoebe Couzins	Unmarried; admitted in several states
1872	Maine	Clara Hapgood Nash	Married; practiced with husband
1872	Utah Territory	Phoebe Couzins	Unmarried; admitted in several states
1872	Utah Territory	(Cora) Georgianna Snow	Unmarried; father was attorney general
1873	Ohio	Annette W. "Nettie" Cronise (later Lutes)	Practiced with sister, who was Ohio's second female attorney
1875	Indiana	Elizabeth Jane Eaglesfield	Unmarried; long practice
1875	Wisconsin	Elsie B. Botensek	Little known
1875	Wisconsin	Lavinia Jane Goodell	Unmarried; died young
1878	Minnesota	Martha Angle Dorsett	Married; practiced with husband
1878	North Carolina	Tabitha A. Holton	Practiced with father and brothers
1879	California	Laura de Force Gordon	Unmarried; national feminist leader
1879	California	Clara Shortridge Foltz	Married; independent practitioner
1879	Virginia	Belva Lockwood	Practiced in Washington, DC
1882	Connecticut	Mary Hall	Practiced in Hartford; suffragist
1882	Nebraska	Ada M. Bittenbender	Married; leader in agriculture and temperance
1884	Pennsylvania	Carrie S. Burnham (later Kilgore)	Long struggle to be admitted; tested the right to vote
1885	Washington Territory	Mary A. Leonard	Became a lawyer after being tried for murdering husband
1886	New York	Kate Stoneman	Unmarried; suffragist; practiced in Albany
1886	Oregon	Mary A. Leonard	Became a lawyer after being tried for murdering husband
1888	Hawaii Territory	Almeda Eliza Hitchcock	Unmarried; parents were missionaries to Hawaii
1890	Montana	Ella Knowles (later Haskell)	Unmarried; Populist Party nominee for attorney general in 1892
1890	New Hampshire	Marilla Ricker	Widow; pioneer in voting tests; practiced in Washington, DC
1882	Massachusetts	Lelia J. Robinson	Unmarried; complied state laws affecting women
1893	Nevada	Laura May Tilden	Unmarried; first of four women admitted to the Nevada bar in the 1890s
1893	South Dakota	Nellie A. Douglass	Little known
1894	New Jersey	Mary Philbrook	Led lobbying; organized Women's Lawyers Club, Philadelphia, 1899
1895	Idaho	Helen Louise Young	Admitted five years after statehood and one year before Idaho enfranchised women
1895	Kentucky	Sophonisba Breckenridge	World's first female Ph.D. in political science, 1901
1896	Colorado	Mary Lathrop	Long career; admitted to U.S. Supreme Court in 1917
1896	West Virginia	Agnes J. Morrison	Practiced in Wheeling with husband
1898	Florida	Louise Rebecca Pinnell	Corporate attorney for railroad company
1898	Louisiana	Betty Runnels	Little known; Tulane University graduate
1898	Oklahoma	Laura Lykins	Little known
1899	Wyoming	Grace Raymond Hebard	Feminist; Wyoming pioneer; a civil engineer and historian
1902	Maryland	Etta Maddox	Active suffragist
1902	Vermont	Jessie D. Bigwood	Studied at Boston University; practiced in Burlington
1905	North Dakota	Helen Hamilton	More than a decade after North Dakota elected a woman to statewide office in 1892
1907	Tennessee	Marion Scudder Griffin	Rejected by Tennessee Supreme Court in 1901
1908	Alabama	Maud McLure Kelly	Father was a judge; practiced in Birmingham; attorney with the Interior Department
1910	Texas	Hortense Ward	Active suffragist
1912	Arizona	Sarah Sorin	Same year as statehood
1914	Mississippi	Lucy H. Greaves	Little known; from Gulfport
1917	New Mexico	Catherine Mabry	After statehood (1912), but before enfranchisement (1920)
1918	Georgia	Stella Akin	Unmarried; young; founder of Savannah League of Women Voters
1918	South Carolina	Claudia J. Sullivan	Little known
1920	Rhode Island	Ada L. Sawyer	Unmarried; young; practiced in Providence
1921	Alaska Territory	Aline Chenot Baskerville Bradley Beegler	Widow; several careers
1923	Delaware	Sybil Ward; Evangelyn Barsky	Three years after Nineteenth Amendment granted enfranchisement to all women

Source: Compiled by the author, with some information from Carolyn Sleeth of Stanford University's Legal History Biography Project and Barbara Allen Babcock, who holds the Judge John Crown distinguished professorship at Stanford University School of Law.

THE DECADE THAT MADE THE DIFFERENCE, 1869–1879

The Civil War provided an opportunity for women to demonstrate executive abilities that never before had been attributed to them. One who did so was MYRA COLBY BRADWELL. Soon after the war, she began publishing the *Chicago Legal News*, which grew rapidly into a nationally circulated weekly aimed at lawyers. She took the bar examination in 1869 and passed, but the Illinois Supreme Court refused to admit her to the bar on the grounds of gender.

Bradwell v. Illinois went to the U.S. Supreme Court, whose justices agreed with those in Illinois. In 1873, the highest court ruled that states were free to exclude women from the legal profession. The Court would use the same reasoning again in *Minor v. Happersett* (1875), declaring that states were free to define their voters. These hugely important cases meant that women had no existence under federal law. Instead, they had to undertake innumerable battles in each state.[1]

Generally speaking, the older the state, the more likely its judiciary was exclusionary. Iowa was still a frontier in 1869 when it became the first state to admit a woman to the practice of law—Arabella Mansfield, called "Belle." A judge who had been following Myra Bradwell's case in neighboring Illinois encouraged Mansfield to take the bar examination, which she easily passed. He determined that the masculine pronouns in Iowa law on bar admission were no more meaningful than masculine language in other state laws that nonetheless applied to women, and the legislature soon followed up by eliminating the restrictive pronouns. One factor that made the precedent go smoothly may have been that Mansfield, who was just twenty-three when she passed the bar, made it clear that she had no intention of practicing. She took the exam to prove the feminist point and returned to her career as a literature professor.

The power wielded by individual judges was illustrated again in the case of Ada (or Adah) H. Kepsey, who—to the awareness of almost no one—became the first female lawyer in Illinois. Like Bradwell, Kepsey was married to an attorney. She worked in his practice before graduating from Chicago's Union Law School in 1870. A local judge simply failed to consider precedents before he admitted her to the bar that year, and she quietly practiced law in Effingham, a small town near Champagne, unnoticed by those working on Bradwell's long-running case.

The most significant reformer of Illinois law was Alta M. Hulett, a young unmarried woman who had worked in

a law office and, as was customary with young men at the time, read law under an experienced attorney. She joined Bradwell in lobbying for change, and the legislature removed masculine pronouns in the section pertaining to

---

[1] See Chapter 1: Battle for the Vote.

Table 13.2   Admission of Women to the Bar, by State

State	Entrance into Union	First Female Bar Admission	Years Between
Alabama	1819	1908	89
Alaska	1959	1921	Prior to statehood
Arizona	1912	1912	0
Arkansas	1836	1871	35
California	1850	1879	29
Colorado	1876	1896	20
Connecticut	1788	1882	94
Delaware	1787	1923	136
Florida	1845	1898	53
Georgia	1788	1918	130
Hawaii	1959	1888	Prior to statehood
Idaho	1890	1895	5
Illinois	1818	1870	52
Indiana	1816	1875	59
Iowa	1846	1869	23
Kansas	1861	1872	11
Kentucky	1792	1895	103
Louisiana	1812	1898	86
Maine	1820	1872	52
Maryland	1788	1902	114
Massachusetts	1788	1882	94
Michigan	1837	1871	34
Minnesota	1858	1878	20
Mississippi	1817	1914	97
Missouri	1821	1870	49
Montana	1889	1890	1
Nebraska	1867	1882	15
Nevada	1864	1893	29
New Hampshire	1788	1890	102
New Jersey	1787	1894	107
New Mexico	1912	1917	5
New York	1788	1886	98
North Carolina	1789	1878	89
North Dakota	1889	1905	16
Ohio	1803	1873	70
Oklahoma	1907	1898	Prior to statehood
Oregon	1859	1886	27
Pennsylvania	1787	1884	97
Rhode Island	1790	1920	130
South Carolina	1788	1918	130
South Dakota	1889	1893	4
Tennessee	1796	1907	111
Texas	1845	1910	65
Utah	1896	1872	Prior to statehood
Vermont	1791	1902	111
Virginia	1788	1879	91
Washington	1889	1885	Prior to statehood
West Virginia	1863	1896	33
Wisconsin	1848	1875	27
Wyoming	1890	1899	9

Source: Compiled by author.

Because a few women insisted on the right to practice law, female defendants eventually had at least some chance of obtaining a female lawyer. Getting a true jury of her peers—much less a female judge—would take much longer. However, even without the vote, persistent women, many of them attorneys, managed to reform laws that discriminated against them.

Nowhere was the legal subordination of women more clear than in the adjudication of insanity. Myra Colby Bradwell, the editor of *Chicago Legal News*, wrote on November 21, 1868:

Married women and [legal] infants, who, in the judgment of the medical superintendent [of the Illinois State Hospital for the Insane] are evidently insane or distracted, may be entered or detained in the hospital on the request of the husband of the woman or the guardian of the infant, without the evidence of insanity required in other cases. (Friedman 1993, 203)

Over the years, Bradwell extensively cited the case of Elizabeth Parsons Packard, who was incarcerated in the asylum at Jacksonville, Illinois, for three years and was legally defenseless against her husband's will to keep her there. Packard wrote in 1875:

It was a great surprise to find so many in the Seventh Wards, who like myself, had never shown any insanity while there, and these were almost uniformly married women, who were put there either by strategy or by force. None of these unfortunate sane prisoners had had any trial or chance for self-defense. . . . Another fact I noticed was that [the superintendent] invariably kept these wives until they begged to be sent home. This led me to suspect that there

was a secret understanding between the husband and the doctor; that the *subjection* of the wife was the cure. . . . Time and time again have I seen these defenseless women sent home only to be sent back for the sole purpose of making them the unresisting slaves of their cruel husbands. (Friedman 1993, 205)

Packard's friends eventually obtained a writ to release her, and a trial showed her to be sane. Her husband immediately packed up most of their possessions and, with their children, moved to Massachusetts. Myra Bradwell concluded her editorial by reminding her readers of how such law developed.

This section [of the state legal code] was passed upon the supposition that a married woman had not the same right to liberty that her husband had. . . . . Let the husband think the wife insane, or wish to get rid of her, all he had to do was to seize and bind her, take her to the insane asylum in this condition, which would make a sane woman . . . appear to be insane. . . . Scores of married women were "incarcerated." (Friedman 1993, 206)

Susan B. Anthony, too, intervened during the 1850s in a case of a woman who fled with her daughter to New York, escaping their abusive husband and father—who also was a Massachusetts state senator. Anthony hid the mother and child with a Quaker woman and resisted her political allies, including abolitionist William Lloyd Garrison, when they tried to convince her that she should return the refugees in accordance with the law. Such men saw no contradiction between urging their followers to resist the federal Fugitive Slave Act of 1850 while, at the same time, insisting that state laws on women be obeyed. The entrance of women into the legal profession helped change that.

the judiciary in 1873, the same year that the U.S. Supreme Court ruled that state law, not the U.S. Constitution, was preeminent in the case of women. For Hulett, however, victory was achieved. She was just nineteen when she was admitted to the bar on June 4, 1873, and began practicing in Chicago. Her milestone could not be fully developed, though, because she died six years later.

While Illinois was grappling with Bradwell's case, men associated with Washington University in St. Louis, Missouri, sought female students capable of setting the precedent for a coeducational law school. In 1869, they accepted Phoebe Couzins, whose father was a federal marshal in St. Louis. Helena "Lemma" Barkaloo joined Couzins. Having heard about this opportunity in the Midwest, Barkaloo moved from Brooklyn, New York. She had studied law on her own and applied unsuccessfully to Columbia University. Because she was well prepared, she graduated with a

law degree from Washington University in 1870. Unfortunately, Lemma Barkaloo died of typhoid fever just months after her bar admission—beginning a myth that women were not physically capable of practicing law.

Couzins, who graduated the following year, went on to be admitted to the bars of nearby Arkansas and Kansas, as well as that of the Utah Territory, where women won the vote in 1870. Couzins nevertheless often was portrayed as the first female law school graduate because of Barkaloo's early death. Lemma Barkaloo, however, should be remembered not only as the first female law school graduate, but also the first female lawyer to try a case in court.

These pioneer bar admissions were in the heartland, in five states with connecting borders. The first exception to the geographical rule was Washington, DC: Although not a state, it was the first eastern jurisdiction to accept a female lawyer, and she was an African American.

When Phoebe Couzins earned her law degree in 1870, thousands of women greeted her graduation with joy. But Couzins proved to be a prima donna. By the end of her life, she had alienated most of those who once were her champions.

The young Couzins was much admired by feminists. One, whose initials were F. E. B., wrote of the 1874 annual meeting of the National Woman Suffrage Association in Washington, DC:

The fascinating St. Louis lawyer, Miss Phoebe Couzins, whose logic is as sound as her wit is sparkling, was introduced, and delivered an address on "Woman as Lawyer," a subject which, in most hands, would have put the audience to sleep, but in hers, kept them wide awake with laughter and applause at her brilliant sallies. (Stanton, Anthony, and Gage 1882, 542)

Couzins seemed to prefer the attention of speaking about law to the drudgery of practicing it. Although she holds legitimate claim to being the first female federal marshal because she replaced her father in that position for two months in 1887, she did not develop a career in law enforcement, either. Instead she attempted to support herself on the lecture circuit, with limited success. With almost no income by the turn of the century, she desperately needed the paid job of secretary to the Board of Lady Managers for the 1893 World's Fair in Chicago. She nonetheless clashed with the board's chairman, Bertha Palmer, to the point that the board fired her.

In 1897, Couzins turned against her fellow suffragists, accepting employment with the United Brewers' Association to lecture and lobby against women's right to vote. Brewers were worried that female voters would ban alcohol, and the association kept Couzins on its payroll for more than a decade. She spoke against the principles she once professed.

Phoebe Couzins died impoverished in St. Louis, Missouri, and was spared a grave in a potter's field only because of a childhood friend who remembered happier days. Someone thoughtfully put on her chest the federal marshal's badge that she had worn for two months in her prime.

Charlotte E. Ray graduated from the law school of Howard University, a new institution for blacks that began after the Civil War. Born free in 1850, she was the daughter of educated abolitionists living in New York City and taught in a prep school associated with Howard University. She graduated in 1872, less than five years after the university began, and was admitted to the bar in the District of Columbia on April 23, 1872.

Ray's ascent was meteoric compared with that of Myra Bradwell and other white women. Unfortunately, that may have been because the legal profession did not take a black woman seriously enough to bother to oppose her. Ray was young and unconnected, and by 1879, she had abandoned the profession, returning to New York and teaching.

Later in 1872, Maine became the first eastern state to admit a woman to the bar. Clara Hapgood Nash of Columbia Falls, a seaboard town near the Canadian border, was motivated to become an attorney because of cases of injustice against women. "Scarcely a day passes," she wrote, "but something occurs in our office to rouse up my indignation afresh by reminding me of the utter insignificance with which the law, in its every department, regards women" (Stanton, Anthony, and Gage 1886, 358).

The final precedents of 1872 were in the Utah Territory, which admitted two women to its bar. One was Phoebe Couzins, who never practiced there, and the other was Cora Georgianna Snow, called "Georgia" and "Georgie." She was a true daughter of Utah, a member of a founding family. She read law with her father, Zerubbabel Snow, who had been elected attorney general of the territory in 1869. Both she and Phoebe Couzins were admitted to the bar on Saturday, September 21, 1872, in a courthouse ceremony attended by Utah's governor.

Major Charles H. Hampstead, who formally sponsored Snow's admission, said that she had not previously applied for the bar because, despite her "brilliant intellect," she was "timid." The Salt Lake City Daily Tribune noted: "Miss Snow doubtless will render invaluable service to her sex in the future as counsel where delicacy is a fundamental element of consultation" (Staker and Staker 1993, 10 and 11). Almost no other opinion makers raised that point, as the advantage of having a female attorney in sexual abuse cases rarely was mentioned. Modesty was a much more important value in the case of women.

Despite five striking precedents in 1872, the next year brought just one: Ohio admitted Annette W. Cronise (later Lutes) to its bar in April 1873. Called "Nettie," her identity has been intertwined with that of Nettie C. Tator, who applied unsuccessfully for admission to the California bar in 1872. The two probably were one. She appears to have been Nettie Tator when she went to California, but

Belva Lockwood was admitted to the Court in 1879 and argued her best, and last case, in 1906. She was 76 years old.

Missouri's Lemma Barkaloo and Illinois's Alta Hulett also died young (and also were unmarried), some conservatives argued that women could not endure the practice of law. This ignored the fact that none of the married women, including some who bore children, died because of mental strain, but the argument nonetheless was effective with some. The extent to which debate focused on women's bodies can be seen in the dissent written by Wisconsin Supreme Court justice C. J. Ryan. Unable to argue legalistically after the legislative reform, he used biology in his 1875 decision.

The law of nature destines and qualifies the female sex for the bearing and nurturing of the children of our race and for the custody of the homes of the world and their maintenance in love and honor. . . .

[Women should be shielded] from all the nastiness of the world which finds it way into courts of justice; all the unclean issues, all the collateral questions, of sodomy, incest, rape, seduction, fornication, adultery, pregnancy, bastardy, legitimacy, prostitution, lascivious cohabitation, abortion, infanticide, obscene publication, libel and slander of sex, impotence, divorce—and all the nameless indecencies. (Sleeth 1997, n.p.)

Ryan seemed to ignore the fact that women were affected by his list of "indecencies" at least as much as men and were more likely to be victims.

His argument did not slow progress. Indiana's Elizabeth Jane Eaglesfield was admitted to the bar in 1875 and, perhaps because she was a graduate of the prestigious University of Michigan Law School, did not face obstacles. Called "Bessie," Eaglesfield practiced in Terre Haute and in Indianapolis, as well as, briefly, in Brazil. She appears to have retained her maiden name after marrying James M. Ashley Jr. and ended her career back in Michigan, where she also became the first woman licensed as a ship captain on the Great Lakes. According to Terre Haute historian Mike McCormick, Bessie Eaglesfield became Indiana's first female attorney at age twenty-two "without fanfare" (McCormick 2005, 53). This was despite language in the state's legal code requiring attorneys to be voters. Again, a state judiciary demonstrated inconsistency, as Indiana women did not win the vote until 1920, with ratification of the Nineteenth Amendment.

The final Midwestern state to admit a woman to its bar in the decade that changed everything was Minnesota. She was Martha Angle Dorsett, a graduate of Iowa College of Law, who was admitted to the Iowa bar in June 1876. Her husband also was an attorney, and when they moved to Minneapolis, his application quickly was approved. She, however, was turned down by a judge who said: "The work of wives and mothers forbids that they

then she soon returned east. She also encouraged her sister, Florence Cronise, who, in September 1873, became Ohio's second female attorney. They worked together in Tiffin, Ohio, until 1880, when Nettie married attorney Nelson Lutes and practiced with him as Lutes & Lutes. After his death in 1900, their daughter, Evelyn Lutes, joined her. Nettie Lutes practiced law for more than four decades.

Wisconsin, still another Midwestern state, admitted Lavinia Jane Goodell and, perhaps, Elsie B. Botensek in the same era. Botensek remains in need of historical research, but Goodell's case attracted much attention. An unmarried woman, Goodell was admitted to the First Judicial Circuit Court on June 17, 1874, and began practicing in Janesville. The next year, she handled a case that merited appeal to the Wisconsin Supreme Court, which refused to hear her. The state's highest court did not reject Goodell because of marital status but, instead, went further, declaring any female lawyer to be unacceptable. That motivated some newspaper editors to support her, and the legislature in 1877 passed a law that no one could be refused the right to argue before the state's courts because of gender. Kate Kane and Angie J. King followed in 1879, and Cora Hurtz Oshkosh joined them in 1882.

Lavinia Goodell practiced in Janesville for the next three years, until her premature death in 1880. Because

The great underpinning of judicial conservatism is that, if no precedent exists, a proponent's case must be dismissed. That was the reasoning used when the U.S. Supreme Court ruled on Belva Lockwood's admission to practice before it: Because no woman had, none could.

In an 1877 speech to the convention of the National Woman Suffrage Association in Washington, DC, Lockwood pointed out the absurdity of this line of reasoning, which absolutely blocks progress of any sort. "It is the glory of each generation," she said, "to make its own precedents."

Elizabeth Cady Stanton was not a person who offered praise lightly. As a logical thinker and a fine orator herself, she recognized that Lockwood possessed the innate abilities of leadership—abilities that would have made Lockwood presidential material had she been male. She praised Lockwood's speaking style and could not resist commenting on her appearance.

As Mrs. Lockwood—tall, well-proportioned, with dark hair and eyes, in velvet dress and train, with becoming indignation at such injustice—marched up and down the platform and rounded out her glowing periods, she might have fairly represented the Italian Portia at the bar of Venice. No more effective speech was ever made on our platform.

In January 1878, the U.S. Senate Committee on Elections invited Connecticut's Isabella Hooker—sister to Harriet Beecher Stowe and Rev. Henry Ward Beecher—to address the members. Perhaps they feared that Lockwood or other Washingtonians would try to join in, because the senators on the committee stipulated that "none but congressmen will be admitted to the hearing room." While Hooker spoke on the vote, Lockwood sent a written statement to all senators. She pointed to female leadership in the highest offices, with examples of excellent reigns by female monarchs. On the lower end of the scale, and in response to the argument that "admission to the bar constitutes an office," she noted that "every woman postmaster, pension agent, and notary public throughout the land is a bonded officer of the government."

She finally was able to reverse the Supreme Court's ruling by successfully lobbying Congress for legislation that effectively ordered the Court to permit women to practice law before it. When the bill passed both houses, the *New York Nation* wrote on February 8, 1879:

The bill was carried through by the energetic advocacy of Senators [Joseph E.] McDonald, [Aaron A.] Sargent, and [George F.] Hoar, whose oratorical efforts were reinforced by the presence of Mrs. Lockwood. After the struggle was over, all the senators who advocated the bill were made the receipts of bouquets. . . . This is a pleasing omen of that purification of legal business which it is hoped will flow from the introduction of women to the courts. It was not flowers that used to be distributed at Washington and Albany in the old corrupt times.

Hope for an end to corruption proved premature, but it is incontestable that female participation in government and reform walked hand in hand through the next century. Although progress has been slow, the League of Women Voters and other such women's groups have successfully demanded many changes in governmental procedure that have extended democracy.

Much of the credit is due to Belva Lockwood, who insisted that precedents must be set and that women have the right to practice law and even run for president. Most presidents began their careers as lawyers, and many consider that background to be a prerequisite for the presidency. Whether or not a law degree is essential to becoming president, Belva Lockwood made a huge contribution to the advancement of women.

shall bestow that time and labor so essential in attaining the eminence to which the true lawyer should ever aspire" (Sleeth 1997, n.p.). Again, legislators proved more equitable than judges, and in its 1877 session, the Minnesota Legislature amended the state's legal code to include women. The vote was 63–30 in the House and 26–6 in the Senate. Dorsett practiced with her husband and went on to work for women's rights

In the Far West—after a struggle—California admitted two women in 1879. Both Laura de Force Gordon and Clara Shortridge Foltz were active feminists. Gordon had begun the California suffrage movement in 1868. In Stockton, she headed what was believed to be the only daily newspaper in the world edited and published by a woman. She was unmarried, unlike Foltz, whose contemporaries referred to her as "Mrs. Clara S. Foltz, a brilliant young woman who had begun the study of law in San Jose" (Stanton, Anthony, and Gage 1886, 757).

Both Gordon and Foltz were aware of Nettie C. Tator's unsuccessful application to the California bar in 1872. In 1877 they sued for admission to the new Hastings College of Law of the University of California. The courts would rule in their favor in 1879, but meanwhile Foltz drafted a legislative bill that would permit women to practice law. State senators passed it by a wide margin in 1878, and the California Assembly followed in a close vote after several heated debates. Gordon later reinforced this weak legislative mandate. During an 1879 revision of the state constitution, she led a successful effort to add language that said "no person shall, on account of sex, be disqualified from entering upon . . . any lawful business, vocation or profession."

The 1878 admission of Tabitha A. Holton to the North Carolina bar was both exceptional and quiet. Her mother died when she was young, and her father, an attorney, reared her in the legal profession along with his three sons. They practiced in Dobson, a small town in western North Carolina near the Tennessee border. North Carolina thus was the first state of the former Confederacy to have a female lawyer—something that most other Southern states would not do for decades.

Finally, the bar admission of BELVA LOCKWOOD, who eventually became the most famous of the era's female lawyers, absorbed the entire decade. Charlotte Ray, an unmarried African American, had been accepted to the bar of the District of Columbia in 1872, but Lockwood, a white woman who was both married and widowed during the decade, endured a long struggle to practice in the District. First she had to fight for the degree that she earned from a Washington law school. Then, after technical admission to the DC bar, she had another long fight to appear in federal courts, which was essential to practicing in a place with no state government. Lockwood had to lobby Congress for legislation to authorize her ultimately very successful career.

THE 1880S AND ONWARD

Nebraska admitted Ada M. Bittenbender to the bar in 1882, but the 1888 admission of Mary Baird Bryan was more notable. The wife of Democrat William Jennings Bryan, she studied law at the University of Nebraska when her daughter—later known as Ruth Bryan Owen, the first woman from the South in the U.S. House —was three years old.[2]

Nebraska's neighbor, Kansas, had set the precedent in 1872 with Phoebe Couzins, and in 1889, Attorney General L. B. Kellogg appointed his wife, who had been in private practice with him, as an assistant attorney general. In the same year, the legislature authorized Ella Cameron to serve out the term of her deceased father as a probate judge.

A 2008 book about New York State's pioneer female lawyer Kate Stoneman deemed her "unprecedented" (Salkin 2008, 16), but many precedents had been set in other states before her, and her admission to the bar was comparatively easy. The process in Albany took less than a year for Stoneman, from taking the bar exam in the summer of 1885 to legislative reform, led by Stoneman, in the spring of 1886.

Massachusetts took more than a decade to admit Lelia J. Robinson. Unmarried, she graduated from the Boston University School of Law. The Massachusetts Supreme Court ruled against her in 1881, and the legislature did not amend the law to allow for her admission to the bar until 1892. Meanwhile, Robinson worked for the vote and compiled a report on the legal status of Massachusetts women.

New York and Massachusetts were among the original thirteen states, while the Hawaii Territory would not become a state until 1959. It nonetheless admitted Almeda Eliza Hitchcock in 1888, and the firm that she founded remains in business in the twenty-first century. Montana became a state in 1889 and had its first female lawyer the same year. Ella Knowles, moreover, was the first woman to run for state attorney general. She was the Populist Party nominee in 1892.[3] Later married and divorced, she also is known as Ella Haskell. In the same year that Knowles was admitted to the Montana bar, MARILLA RICKER was the first woman admitted in New Hampshire. She had a long activist history and lived in Washington, DC. Ricker developed "an extensive practice" in the nation's capital, as well as in New Hampshire (Stanton, Anthony, and Gage 1886, 106).

Oregon entered the Union in 1859, earlier than most western states. Its first female attorney, Mary A. Leonard, was exceptional. Born in France to Swiss parents, she apparently emigrated alone. She was living in Portland by 1870 and married Daniel Leonard in 1875. In 1878, after attempting unsuccessfully to divorce him, she was tried—and found not guilty—of his murder. Leonard moved to Seattle, where she read law. Although it would be another three years before the Washington Territory became a state, she was admitted to its bar in 1885. Oregon initially refused admission when she returned to Portland, but after the legislature amended the legal code, she became the first female lawyer in her home state.

Kentucky, which would be a conservative state in the late twentieth century, admitted a woman to the bar in 1895. Sophonisba Breckinridge was from a politically powerful Kentucky family. She lived most of her life in Chicago but did not practice law in either place. Instead, she was a pioneer for women in the field of political science. Along with Jane Addams and other politically active women, she was a founder of social science departments at the new and coeducational University of Chicago.

---

[2] See Chapter 6: United States Representatives and Chapter 12: Ambassadors.

[3] See Chapter 3: Statewide Elective Officeholders.

Dr. Breckinridge was particularly influential in reforming juvenile justice systems and in introducing ideas implemented with President Franklin D. Roosevelt's New Deal.

As the nineteenth century ended, perhaps the most important milestone was that Michigan men elected a woman as a prosecuting attorney in 1899. Although it would not grant women the vote until 1918, Michigan had been the fourth state to admit women to its bar, in 1871, and several practiced at the turn of the century. Merrie Hoover Abbott practiced with her husband in Ogemaw County, and voters there elected her as prosecutor in 1898. Sworn in on January 1, 1899, she successfully served until October, when the Michigan Supreme Court ruled that a woman could not hold the job. The law required prosecutors to be "electors," and because Abbott could not vote, male voters could not vote for her.[4]

As the century ended, Southern states continued to be more conservative than others, but in 1898, Florida admitted Louise Rebecca Pinnell of Jacksonville. She was an attorney for a powerful railroad and not notably feminist. Florida would wait until the 1940s for a truly activist female attorney, Mary Lou Baker of St. Petersburg. The second woman in the state legislature, she also retained her maiden name at marriage and was pregnant as a legislator.[5] Even after World War II, Baker was unable to get a law passed allowing women to serve on juries. It passed after she lost her 1946 reelection, but, even then, jury service was voluntary for women. They were exempted unless they took the initiative to volunteer. As late as 1961, eighteen states "protected" women from jury duty with such automatic exemptions and three states did not allow female jurors at all. Florida was one of the eighteen, and in *Hoyt v. Florida*, the U.S. Supreme Court upheld such exclusionary juries.

Female attorneys could be seriously handicapped by being forced to argue to all-male juries. Especially in cases involving sex, such juries made it much more difficult to convince female victims and witnesses to come forward. Not until 1975 did the Supreme Court reverse itself, ruling in *Taylor v. Louisiana* that exempting women violated the right of a defendant to a jury of her peers. It was not until 1994, moreover, that the highest court decided that trial attorneys could not use their peremptory challenges to exclude jurors on the basis of gender. Ironically, in this Alabama case, it was a man who objected to his dismissal from a jury that was considering a paternity case.

The question of jury duty would drag on through most of the twentieth century, just as the issue of inclusion of women in other aspects of the justice system did. At the Department of Justice, for example, the first female attorney general, Janet Reno, was not appointed until 1993, but the first barrier had been broken in 1915.[6] That year, young Annette Adams, head of the California Democratic Women's Club, was sworn in as the nation's first federal assistant attorney general over the objections of her boss in San Francisco, even though California women had won the vote in 1911. In 1920, Adams transferred to the Department of Justice in Washington, but she lost her position after Democrats lost that year's election. Republicans replaced her with another California woman, Mabel Willebrandt, who became quite well known as a federal attorney.

Very little has been written about Violette Neatly Anderson, a Chicago lawyer who became the first African American woman to argue before the U.S. Supreme Court, in 1926, almost fifty years after the first black man was accorded this privilege in 1880. About the same length of time had passed since a white woman, Belva Lockwood, was admitted to practice before the highest court in 1879. The double burden of race and gender meant that black women ran about a half-century behind white women for most achievements in the legal profession.

Even at the end of the twentieth century, the legal profession's slowness to adopt principles of equality could be seen in the pondering pace of electing women to positions within the American Bar Association (ABA). The association, which began in 1878, did not admit women at all until 1919—decades after women were accepted in the judicial systems of many states.

The first female ABA president, Roberta Cooper Ramo of New Mexico, overcame obstacles of poverty and racism, as well as gender. She was the only graduate of her 1967 class at the University of Chicago who could not get a job, as many firms refused even to interview a woman. Upon her election as head of the 375,000-member ABA in 1995, she said that her most satisfying case involved freeing civil rights workers led by the Rev. Dr. Martin Luther King Jr. from jail. She was so poor at the time that she had to borrow cab fare from her clients. Once the barrier was broken, several women followed her as ABA presidents in the new millennium. Martha Barnett of Florida, president in 2000, offered strong feminist leadership. A Tallahassee attorney, she was a driving force behind Florida's belated compensation for victims of a 1923 massacre in an African American town, Rosewood.

Karen Mathis of Denver became president in 2006, and she raised the ABA's profile internationally with rule-of-law initiatives in developing democracies. After her term,

---

[4] See Chapter 2: Officeholders Prior to the Nineteenth Amendment for examples in other states of women elected by male voters and not removed from office.

[5] See Chapter 4: State Representatives.

[6] See Chapter 11: Cabinet and Subcabinet.

Mathis used her legal skills in the Czech Republic and then became head of Big Brothers-Big Sisters of America. Carolyn Lamm, who was inaugurated in 2009, practices in Washington, DC, and like Mathis, also emphasized globalism. The 2011-2012 president-elect is Lauren Bellows. She is a Chicagoan—something that *Chicago Legal News* pioneer Myra Bradwell doubtless would find satisfiying.

POLITICAL ACTION VERSUS COURT ACTION

Two general political axioms can be learned from this history. One, legislators were more responsive to the needs of female lawyers (and of the general effect of justice for women) than judges. Legislatures are elected bodies, whereas judges may be elected or appointed according to the law of a particular state. The greater liberalism of legislators shows that democracy works, even in a time before half of the nation's citizens could vote.

Despite modern complaints about activist judges, the judiciary showed itself to be much less willing to implement reforms regarding female lawyers than legislatures were. This may be as it should be, but it also shows that the right to assemble and petition and speak—provisions of the U.S. Constitution that women always assumed applied to them equally with men—would be effective if the petitioners are persistent.

Two, the rights of American women, much more than those of American men, have been limited by where a woman lives. This continues to be so, especially with reproductive law. The power of geography clearly is demonstrated in the varieties of results in the long struggle to become lawyers. Many courts repeatedly said that states' rights were more important than human rights.

Five jurisdictions accepted women as lawyers prior to statehood, while they were territories. All were in the Far West. The slowest states to make the change were those of the original colonies in the East. They were not necessarily the Southern states usually stereotyped as conservative. South Carolina and Georgia share a 130-year gap between statehood and their first female bar admission with the northern state of Rhode Island. Massachusetts has a 114-year gap. Except for insular Tennessee and Kentucky, all of the states that took more than a century to approve female lawyers are on the East Coast. The slowest state was Delaware, which calls itself The First State because it was the first to ratify the Constitution. After 136 years, it was the last state to admit a woman to its bar of justice.

The history of the legal profession's long discrimination against women is infrequently discussed in law schools. Too few courses provide students with information on women's major civil rights cases, not even those as important as *Minor v. Happersett* or *Bradwell v. Illinois.* Without this knowledge, the question of states' rights versus women's rights goes unnoticed, even as it continues to be fundamental in debates on current laws. Cases on reproductive issues could especially benefit from greater awareness of this history.

PROFILES OF JUDICIARY PIONEERS

The three women profiled here hold pioneering status as attorneys and as political activists on behalf of women's rights. **Myra Colby Bradwell** *filed the first court case on women's right to practice law.* **Belva Lockwood,** *who endured a long struggle to practice law, was the first woman to argue before the U.S. Supreme Court. Attorney* **Marilla Ricker** *was a pioneer in testing women's right to vote under the Fifteenth Amendment, which enfranchised black men.*

MYRA COLBY BRADWELL (1831–1894)

The case that Myra Bradwell brought to the U.S. Supreme Court in 1873 set a precedent that affected women negatively for decades. In *Bradwell v. Illinois,* the Court ruled that states could exclude women from the legal profession on the grounds of gender.

Myra Colby was born in Vermont to liberal, abolitionist parents. The Colbys moved to Illinois in 1843, and Myra taught school in Cook County until her 1852 marriage to James Bradwell. After studying law for years, he passed the Illinois bar in 1855 and joined Myra's brother in a successful firm, Bradwell & Colby. Myra bore four children, and James was elected as a county judge in 1861.

The Civil War began that year, and Myra Bradwell worked with the U.S. Sanitary Commission, a forerunner of the American Red Cross. She also was the founding president of the Chicago Soldiers' Aid Society, led construction of a home for disabled veterans, and served on the board of the state industrial school for girls.

In 1868, when she was thirty-seven, Bradwell began publishing the *Chicago Legal News,* which soon had a national audience. She took the bar exam in 1869 and, when the Illinois Supreme Court refused to admit her, spent the next four years appealing the decision to the U.S. Supreme Court. Meanwhile, she was rising as a major figure in Illinois legal circles.

When suffragists organized in Chicago in 1869, Bradwell obtained support from all of the city's judges.

She drafted bills protecting the property rights of married women and widows and, with help from American Woman Suffrage Association leader Mary Livermore and others, lobbied the legislature in Springfield until they became law. Bradwell also wrote bills that granted equal guardianship to mothers, made women eligible for election to school boards, and authorized their service as notaries public.

Over the years, she crusaded for improved court procedures, higher standards for lawyers, and specialization by legal field. *Chicago Legal News* pointed out the need for reform in corporate law, especially regarding monopolistic railroads, and her paper advocated the first zoning regulations. Because of her own discrimination case, the legislature passed a law making women eligible for any occupation in 1872. The Illinois bar also made Bradwell an honorary member that year, and she would serve four times as its vice president.

By the time that the highest court's decision came down in *Bradwell v. Illinois*, the state had admitted two women as lawyers. Bradwell did not reapply. In 1890, twenty-one years after her original application, the Illinois Supreme Court acted on its own initiative and admitted her to the bar. In 1892, the U.S. Supreme Court admitted her.

That, however, would be just two years prior to her death from cancer at age sixty-three. Meanwhile, *Chicago Legal News* flourished, and the Bradwells became wealthy enough to build a Michigan Avenue mansion and travel to Europe. Daughter Bessie Bradwell graduated at the top of her 1882 class at the law school later affiliated with Northwestern University and, as Bessie Helmer, continued her mother's newspaper until 1925.

BELVA LOCKWOOD (1830–1917)

The second woman to announce her candidacy for the presidency, under the banner of the National Equal Rights Party, Belva Ann Bennett McNall Lockwood was as credentialed as some male candidates, but she had no chance of winning her 1884 campaign—or the one she waged in 1888.

A native of Niagara County, New York, she was akin to other bright young women of the time in that she began teaching school at age fifteen. At eighteen, she married Uriah McNall and bore a daughter. He was killed in a sawmill accident, and she was left, at age twenty-three in 1853, a widow with a child to support. Instead of accepting the usual fate of such women—quick remarriage—she was determined to go to college.

Belva McNall was fortunate to live in western New York, which was a hotbed of unconventional behavior in the 1850s, and she managed to graduate with honors from Genesee College, later Syracuse University, in 1857. She was elected as preceptress (or principal) of Union School in Lockport, New York. Popular with her students and faculty, the town kept her in this post despite her development of an innovative curriculum that included physical exercise, nature walks, and public speaking, even for girls. She also met Susan B. Anthony, who lived and had taught in the same area.

In 1866, when her daughter was seventeen, they moved to Washington, DC. That was the year after the Civil War ended, and McNall sought a less parochial life than rural New York offered. The capital had been transformed by the war, and her decision to move there would prove key to her future achievement. She opened one of its first private coeducational schools and also drew attention from Ezekiel Lockwood, a dentist appreciably older than she. Their 1868 marriage provided the financial security she long had sought. She endured a pregnancy in her late thirties, only to see the child die in infancy. Soon afterward, she began applying to law schools.

Georgetown University, then a Catholic (Jesuit) institution for men, not surprisingly rejected her on the grounds of gender. However, that also was the reason given by Columbian College (now George Washington University) and the new Howard University, established by Congress for blacks. They claimed having a woman in class would be distracting for male students, even though Lockwood by then was over forty and had long classroom experience in coeducational schools. Finally, she was accepted by National University Law School, in Washington, a new institution looking for students. When she finished her coursework in 1873, however, the school refused to grant a degree to a woman. Lockwood appealed to President Ulysses S. Grant, who was an honorary official of the school. Grant admired the work he had seen women do during the Civil War, and he successfully intervened on her behalf.

Even after she passed the bar examination, she faced more obstacles, as federal courts refused to allow a woman to practice before them. When Lockwood's husband died in 1877, her goal became even more important, as, once again, she was a widow who needed to earn a living. She honed her political skills by successfully lobbying for a bill to reverse the judiciary, and by the 1880s—when she was in her fifties—Lockwood was able to begin her life in the law.

She eventually built a substantial practice, and her presidential aspirations in the 1884 and 1888 elections may even have helped it. Evidence exists that she provided sound legal advice for women who never had heard of a female attorney before Lockwood's campaigns. She wrote articles for national magazines on her experience as a lawyer and as a presidential candidate. Lockwood took unusual cases, including lobbying, and she accepted African Americans and immigrants as clients. She capped her career in 1906 with a major case before the U.S. Supreme Court on behalf of Cherokees in western North Carolina and eastern Tennessee, winning a $5 million settlement for them. Syracuse University honored her in 1909.

Belva Lockwood, who overcame so many barriers, died three years short of ratification of the Nineteenth Amendment, which granted the vote to all American women. She was buried in Washington's Congressional Cemetery. George Washington University took over National University Law School, where she had earned her degree, and women there now celebrate an annual Belva Lockwood Week.

MARILLA RICKER (1846–1920)

A pioneer attorney in both Washington, DC, and her native New Hampshire, Marilla Ricker also was one of the first women to vote.

Born near Dover, Marilla Young was educated at private Colby Academy in New London, New Hampshire. She taught school until her 1863 marriage to John Ricker, described as an intelligent farmer who was twice her age. He died five years later, leaving her a wealthy twenty-eight-year-old widow.

The Fifteenth Amendment, which was intended to grant the vote to black men but made no mention of gender, was ratified on March 30, 1870, and Marilla Ricker tested its gender-neutral language in that spring's municipal elections in Dover. Probably because she owned a significant amount of property, she registered to vote without problem, but when she attempted to cast her ballot, she was refused. She began plans to sue the election officials, but "being strongly opposed by her republican friends, she silently submitted to the injustice." The next year, with the Fifteenth Amendment clearly accepted, "she saw that her name was on the registry list and her vote was received without opposition" (Stanton, Anthony, and Gage 1882, 506–507).

Ricker traveled in Europe from 1872 to 1876, learning several languages. After that, she spent her winters in Washington, DC, an exciting place in the 1870s, when the nation struggled to redefine itself after the Civil War. Wealthy enough that she did not have to earn a living, Ricker began assisting people in jail with their legal cases—a century before courts would rule that indigent defendants had the right to an attorney.

She went on doing her charitable work in jails, albeit handicapped by an inability to notarize documents or bring her cases to court. She read law and was admitted to the DC bar in 1882, having earned the highest score on the bar examination. In the same year, President Chester A. Arthur appointed her as a notary public. The District's judges in 1884 appointed her to the quasi-judicial post of examiner in Chancery Court, making her the first woman to hold that position. Ricker also advocated prison reform. At a time when jails and prisons employed few or no female guards, female prisoners were especially subject to sexual abuse.

She also traveled to lobby for the vote, including an 1888 trip to California. An officer in both New Hampshire and national suffrage organizations, she was friends with fellow Washington lawyer Belva Lockwood and supported Lockwood's National Equal Rights Party in the 1880s.

Ricker thus was more familiar with state laws and especially the criminal justice system than most applicants when she applied to the New Hampshire bar in 1890. She was fifty years old and influential enough that the state's officials admitted her without a struggle. She continued to practice in Washington, too, and was admitted to practice before the U.S. Supreme Court in 1891. She subsequently turned increasingly from criminal law to banking and labor law on behalf of the poor.

Marilla Ricker continued to engage in consciousness-raising political efforts, including an attempt to be an ambassador and an attempt to run for governor of New Hampshire in 1910. Her filing fee was rejected because without the right to vote, the state's attorney general said, she had no right to run. Even in the states where women had the vote, none was elected governor until 1924.[7]

She also made annual protests against New Hampshire's lack of full enfranchisement when she paid her property taxes. For fifty years, from 1870 to 1920, Ricker filed an objection at tax time. She barely lived to see the day when that no longer would be necessary. The Nineteenth Amendment was added to the U.S. Constitution on August 26, 1920, and Marilla Ricker died the following November 12.

REFERENCES AND FURTHER READING

American Bar Association. 1997. *Elusive Equality: The Experiences of Women in Legal Education.* Chicago: American Bar Association.
American Bar Association. 1998. *Facts about Women and the Law.* Chicago: American Bar Association.

American Bar Association. 1989. *Women and the ABA: A History of Women's Involvement with the American Bar Association, 1965–1989.* Chicago: American Bar Association.

Babcock, Barbara Allen. 2011. *Woman Lawyer: The Trials of Clara Foltz.* Palo Alto, CA: Stanford University Press.

Buckley, Anna J. 1990. *Mistress Margaret Brent.* Annapolis: Maryland State Archives.

Chester, Ronald. 1985. *Unequal Access: Women Lawyers in a Changing America.* South Hadley, MA: Bergin and Garvey Publishers.

Drachman, Virginia. 1998. *Sisters in Law: Women Lawyers in Modern America.* Cambridge, MA: Harvard University Press.

Drobac, Jennifer. 1998. *In Search of Nettie C: The Mystery of Two Nineteenth Century Lawyers.* Stanford, CA: Stanford University Press.

Dusky, Lorraine. 1996. *Still Unequal: The Shameful Truth about Women and Justice in America.* New York: Crown.

Epstein, Cynthia Fuchs. 1993. *Women in Law.* Urbana: University of Illinois Press.

Fox, Mary Virginia. 1975. *Lady for the Defense: A Biography of Belva Lockwood.* New York: Harcourt Brace Jovanovich.

Friedman, Jane M. 1993. *America's First Woman Lawyer: The Biography of Myra Bradwell.* New York: Prometheus Books.

Gaza, Hedda. 1996. *Barred from the Bar: Women in the Legal Profession.* New York: F. Watts.

Golemba, Beverly E. 1992. *Lesser-Known Women: A Biographical Dictionary.* Boulder, CO: Lynne Rienner Publishers.

Loquesto, Wendy, ed. 2000. *Celebrating Florida's First 150 Women Lawyers.* Tallahassee: Florida Bar Association.

McCormick, Mike. 2005. *Terre Haute: Queen City of the Wabash.* Mount Pleasant, SC: Arcadia Publishing.

Morello, Karen Berge. 1986. *The Invisible Bar: The Woman Lawyers in America: 1638 to the Present.* New York: Random House.

Mossman, Mary Jane. 2006. *The First Women Lawyers: A Comparative Study of Gender, Law, and the Legal Professions.* Oxford, UK: Hart Publishing.

Newman, Cynthia. 1984. *Maud McLure Kelly: Alabama's First Woman Lawyer.* Birmingham, AL: Birmingham Printing and Publishing.

Norgrin, Jill. 2007. *Belva Lockwood: The Woman Who Would Be President.* Foreword by Ruth Bader Ginsburg. New York: New York University Press.

Salkin, Patricia E. 2008. *Pioneering Women Lawyers: From Kate Stoneman to the Present.* Chicago: American Bar Association.

Sleeth, Carolyn. 1997. *First Women Lawyers in the United States.* Stanford University, Stanford, CA.

Smith, Helen Ainsley. 1901. *The Thirteen Colonies. Part 2: New Jersey, Delaware, Maryland, Pennsylvania, Connecticut, Rhode Island, North Carolina, South Carolina, Georgia.* New York: G. P. Putnam.

Smith, J. Clay, Jr., ed. 1998. *Rebels in Law: Voices in History of Black Women Lawyers.* Ann Arbor: University of Michigan Press.

Staker, Steven L., and Colleen Young Staker. 1993. "Utah's First Women Lawyers: Georgianna Snow and Phoebe Wilson Couzins." *Utah Bar Journal* (December).

Stanton, Elizabeth Cady, Susan B. Anthony, and Matilda Joslyn Gage. 1881. *History of Woman Suffrage.* Volume 1. New York: Fowler and Wells. Reprint, New York: Arno Press, 1969.

Stanton, Elizabeth Cady, Susan B. Anthony, and Matilda Joslyn Gage. 1882. *History of Woman Suffrage.* Volume 2. New York: Fowler and Wells. Reprint, New York: Arno Press, 1969.

Stanton, Elizabeth Cady, Susan B. Anthony, and Matilda Joslyn Gage. 1886. *History of Woman Suffrage.* Volume 3. Rochester, New York: Charles Mann Printing Company. Reprint, New York: Arno Press 1969.

14

STATE COURTS

From informal colonial roots—when women freely went to court and argued before judges who were their neighbors—the American judicial system grew into a much less accessible system after ratification of the U.S. Constitution. States varied in the types of legal systems they implemented, and the complex workings of the judicial branch can make it somewhat indecipherable.

Some states have municipal courts, while others have only county courts. Justices of the peace, who often were the only judges in the Wild West, largely have disappeared. The same is true of urban night courts, in which a judge quickly disposed of after-hour arrests. Some modern systems have informal courts in which citizens can argue for themselves before a judge; others have mediation systems, in which opposing sides in a civil suit can meet and allow a court-appointed arbitrator to impose a settlement.

The nature of an alleged crime determines the court in which a case is first heard. Misdemeanors go to municipal or county courts, and felonies, which are more serious crimes, can go immediately to circuit courts. Civil suits, wherein citizens sue each other, usually are assigned by the jurisdiction's chief judge according to the complicity of the case and its monetary value.

The manner of how judges arrive on the bench also varies from state to state. In most, lower-level judges are elected, usually by county. Circuit courts are the next level, and those judges also may be elected or, in some states, appointed by the governor. Circuit court judges, or whatever this intermediate level is termed, are expected to have better credentials and more experience than those at the lower level.

Appellate courts are for those who have lost a case but want to continue their argument. For example, in Florida, a case might go from county court to circuit court and then to one of several regional appellate courts before the case might ultimately end up at the state supreme court in Tallahassee. Appellate courts are not trial courts, in that the case is not reheard by a judge or jury. Instead, lawyers write briefs and make oral arguments that the appellate or the supreme court justices consider.

The highest court in a state usually is called the Supreme Court, but other names, such as Superior Judicial Court, sometimes are used. The judges (usually called justices) often were elected in the past, but, as the twentieth century progressed, many states changed their laws to make the highest levels of their judicial systems appointed, not elected. This follows the federal model, in which the president is the appointing authority, and the U.S. Senate confirms his nominations, which are for life. State senators likewise usually confirm gubernatorial appointments.

A significant number of states still elect their highest judges, and a few even hold partisan elections with primaries and runoffs. Arkansas and Oregon are among the few states that bucked the overall trend of moving toward appointments. Both states once appointed supreme court justices but returned to electing them. Arkansas, which was one of the first states to admit a woman to its bar, also is a relative pioneer with women on its highest court under both the elected and appointed systems.[1] Arkansas's Elsijane Trimble Roy was the nation's second woman appointed to a state supreme court, in 1975; Annabelle Tuck, the first under the new elected system, in 1997. In Oregon, Betty Roberts was the first female appointee, in 1982; Virginia Linder, the first elected, in 2006. Linder defeated Jack Roberts, a former Republican gubernatorial nominee.

---

[1] See Chapter 13: Pioneers in the Judiciary.

Table 14.1 First Women on State Supreme Courts, by State

State	Year	Name
Alabama	1974	Janie Shores
Alaska	1996	Dana Fabe
Arizona	1960	Lorna Lockwood
Arkansas	1975	Elsijane Trimble Roy
California	1977	Rose Elizabeth Bird
Colorado	1979	Jean Dubofsky
Connecticut	1978	Ellen Ash Peters
Delaware	2000	Peggy L. Ableman
Florida	1985	Rosemary Barkett
Georgia	1992	Leah Ward Sears
Hawaii	1993	Paula A. Nakayama
Idaho	1992	Linda Copple Trout
Illinois	1992	Mary Ann G. McMorrow
Indiana	1995	Myra C. Selby
Iowa	1986	Linda Neuman
Kansas	1977	Kay McFarland
Kentucky	1993	Janet Stumbo
Louisiana	1992	Catherine "Kitty" Kimball
Maine	1983	Caroline Duby Glassman
Maryland	1979	Rita Charmatz Davidson
Massachusetts	1977	Ruth Abrams
Michigan	1972	Mary Stallings Coleman
Minnesota	1977	Rosalie Ervin Wahl
Mississippi	1982	Lenore L. Prather
Missouri	1987	Ann K. Covington
Montana	1989	Diane G. Barz
Nebraska	1998	Lindsey Miller-Lerman
Nevada	1995	Miriam Shering
New Hampshire	2000	Linda Stewart Dalianis
New Jersey	1982	Marie Garibaldi
New Mexico	1984	Mary Coon Walters
New York	1993	Judith S. Kaye
North Carolina	1962	Susie Marshall Sharp
North Dakota	1984	Beryl J. Levine
Ohio	1922	Florence Allen
Oklahoma	1982	Alma Bell Wilson
Oregon	1982	Betty Roberts
Pennsylvania	1996	Sandra Schultz Newman
Rhode Island	1979	Florence Kerins Murray
South Carolina	1988	Jean Hoefer Toal
South Dakota	2002	Judith Meierhenry
Tennessee	1995	Holly M. Kirby
Texas	1992	Rose Spector
Utah	1982	Christine Durham
Vermont	1990	Denise R. Johnson
Virginia	1997	Cynthia Dinah Fannon Kinser
Washington	1981	Carolyn Reaber Dimmick
West Virginia	1988	Margaret L. Workman
Wisconsin	1976	Shirley S. Abrahamson
Wyoming	2000	Marilyn S. Kite

Source: Compiled by author.

Appointed judges in some states also have term limits, usually between six and ten years, and these are staggered so that a new governor is likely to be in office when a justice's term expires. Judges in Hawaii and Maryland, for example, have ten-year terms and must be reappointed by whomever is governor a decade later. New York's terms are for fourteen years. Judith S. Kaye, for instance, was the first woman on that state's highest court when Gov. Mario M. Cuomo appointed her in 1993. Gov. Eliot Spitzer reappointed her in 2007.

Other states, including California, do not require reappointment but, instead, use merit retention. In this system, after a judge has sat on the bench for a specified period—again, usually six to ten years—his or her name goes on the ballot and voters are asked: "Should Justice ABC be retained?" In most cases, voters retain judges by huge margins. However, women have been more likely to be targeted for such recall elections than men.

Because the organizational structures of lower courts vary, the clearest way to measure the status of women in state judiciaries is by focusing on the first women who served on a state's highest court. The first was elected in 1922, and the last woman to achieve this milestone in the fifty states was appointed in 2002—an eighty-year span. How much systems have changed can be measured by the fact that the first five women on state supreme courts were elected, while the last five were appointed.

PIONEERS, 1870–1970

Esther Morris is considered the first female judicial officer. The governor of the Wyoming Territory appointed her as justice of the peace in 1870.[2] Other women were slow to follow the precedent, and even after women were admitted to state bars in the 1870s and 1880s, they rarely became judges. According to historian Karen Berger Morello, at the turn of the century,

Only a few more women were appointed to the bench. These included Helen Jaeger, who served as a police judge in Tacoma, Washington; Catherine Waugh McCulloch, twice appointed justice of the peace of Evanston, Illinois; Othilia Beals, justice of the peace in Seattle; Frances Hopkins, temporary probate judge of Jefferson County, Missouri; Lydia Beckley Pague, a county court judge in Eagle, Colorado; and Reah Whitehead, a justice of the peace in Seattle. . . .

[Whitehead participated] in the first case . . . in which a felony was prosecuted and defended by women lawyers. In *State of Washington v. Raymond* in 1913, Reah Whitehead and defense lawyer Leola May Blinn tried a case to a hung jury of ten women and two men. (Morello 1986, 224)

Because Washington, DC, lacks a state government, the president appoints its judiciary, and Democrat Woodrow Wilson named Kathryn Sellers to the municipal court in 1918, before the Nineteenth Amendment ensured women's

---

[2] See Chapter 2: Female Officeholders Prior to the Nineteenth Amendment.

Table 14.2 First Women on State Supreme Courts, by Year

Year	State	Name	Notes
1922	Ohio	Florence Allen	Elected, with networking by suffragists
1960	Arizona	Lorna Lockwood	Elected; first female chief justice in 1965
1962	North Carolina	Susie Marshall Sharp	Appointed by Terry Sanford (D); subsequently elected as chief justice
1972	Michigan	Mary Stallings Coleman	Elected; chief justice in 1979
1974	Alabama	Janie Shores	Elected; considered for the U.S. Supreme Court by President Bill Clinton
1975	Arkansas	Elsijane Trimble Roy	Appointed by David Pryor (D)
1976	Wisconsin	Shirley S. Abrahamson	Appointed by Patrick J. Lucey (D); subsequently elected
1977	California	Rose Bird	Appointed by Jerry Brown (D); lost 1986 recall
1977	Minnesota	Rosalie Ervin Wahl	Appointed by Rudy Perpich (D)
1977	Kansas	Kay McFarland	Appointed by Robert Bennett (R)
1977	Massachusetts	Ruth Abrams	Appointed by Michael S. Dukakis (D)
1978	Connecticut	Ellen Ash Peters	Appointed by Ella Tambussi Grasso (D); first appointment of a woman by a woman
1979	Colorado	Jean Dubofsky	Appointed by Richard D. Lamm (D)
1979	Maryland	Rita Charmatz Davidson	Appointed by Acting Governor Blair Lee (D)
1979	Rhode Island	Florence Kerins Murray	Appointed by J. Joseph Garrahy (D)
1981	Washington	Carolyn Reaber Dimmick	Appointed by Dixy Lee Ray (D); went on to federal court
1982	Mississippi	Lenore L. Prather	Appointed by William Winter (D)
1982	New Jersey	Marie Garibaldi	Appointed by Thomas H. Kean (R) [thanks]
1982	Oklahoma	Alma Bell Wilson	Appointed by George Nigh (D)
1982	Oregon	Betty Roberts	Appointed by Victor G. Atiyeh (R)
1982	Utah	Christine Durham	Appointed by Scott M. Matheson (D)
1983	Maine	Caroline Duby Glassman	Appointed by Joseph E. Brennan (D)
1984	New Mexico	Mary Coon Walters	Appointed by Toney Anaya (D)
1985	North Dakota	Beryl J. Levine	Appointed by George Sinner (D); subsequently elected
1985	Florida	Rosemary Barkett	Appointed by Bob Graham (D); went on to federal court
1986	Iowa	Linda Neuman	Appointed by Terry E. Branstad (R)
1987	Missouri	Ann K. Covington	Appointed by John Ashcroft (R)
1988	West Virginia	Margaret L. Workman	Elected; chief justice in 1993
1988	South Carolina	Jean Hoefer Toal	Elected; twice chief justice
1989	Montana	Diane G. Barz	Appointed by Stan Stephens (R)
1990	Vermont	Denise R. Johnson	Appointed by Madeline M. Kunin (D)
1992	Idaho	Linda Copple Trout	Appointed by Cecil D. Andrus (D)
1992	Georgia	Leah Ward Sears	Appointed by Zell Miller (D); African American
1992	Illinois	Mary Ann G. McMorrow	Elected
1992	Louisiana	Catherine "Kitty" Kimball	Elected
1992	Nevada	Miriam Shering	Elected
1992	Texas	Rose Spector	Elected; lost in 1998
1993	Hawaii	Paula A. Nakayama	Appointed by John Waihee III (D); reappointed by Linda Lingle (R)
1993	New York	Judith S. Kaye	Appointed by Mario M. Cuomo (D); reappointed by Eliot Spitzer (D)
1993	Kentucky	Janet Stumbo	Elected
1995	Indiana	Myra C. Selby	Appointed by Evan Bayh (D); chief justice 1997
1995	Tennessee	Holly M. Kirby	Appointed by Don Sundquist (R); elected 1996
1996	Alaska	Dana Fabe	Appointed by Tony Knowles (D); barely survived a 2010 recall by anti-choice groups
1996	Pennsylvania	Sandra Schultz Newman	Elected
1997	Virginia	Cynthia Dinah Fannon Kinser	Appointed by George Allen (R)
1998	Nebraska	Lindsey Miller-Lerman	Appointed by Ben Nelson (D)
2000	Delaware	Peggy L. Ableman	Appointed by Thomas R. Carper (D)
2000	New Hampshire	Linda Stewart Dalianis	Appointed by Jeanne Shaheen (D)
2000	Wyoming	Marilyn S. Kite	Appointed by Jim Geringer (R)
2002	South Dakota	Judith Meierhenry	Appointed by John Hoeven (R)

Source: Compiled by author.

Note: All appointments were made by governors. (D) means Democrat and (R) means Republican.

Florence Allen's mother had been an Ohio suffragist. The future judge is shown holding a flag at suffrage headquarters in Cleveland in 1912. Florence Allen was both the first woman on a state supreme court and the first in the federal court system (see Chapter 15).

right to vote. Republican president Warren Harding emulated Wilson by appointing Mary O'Toole to this court in 1921. An attorney, O'Toole was president of the local Equal Suffrage Association during the crucial years between 1915 and 1920.

Most female judicial pioneers in the early twentieth century were appointed to courts related to children, so-called orphans' courts. These courts almost invariably were in big cities. Among them was Memphis, Tennessee, where Camille Kelley was appointed in 1921. Public social service systems to keep kids out of court had yet to be developed, and in a 1931 interview, Kelley said that she already had handled some twenty-five thousand cases of delinquent and neglected children. Chicago judge Mary Bartelme also received publicity for her legal efforts on behalf of teens. Friends during the 1930s called Bartelme "Suitcase Mary," as she tried to provide each young woman released from her custody with a suitcase of new clothing (Morello 1986, 226).

The low-level, stereotypically feminine nature of these appointments appears to show that officials were slower to recognize female ability than voters. The best example of this thesis is FLORENCE ALLEN, who was elected to the Ohio Supreme Court in 1922, at the first opportunity for such a victory to occur. Allen's mother had been a suffragist, and she organized Ohio women to elect her daughter to the state's highest bench. Allen had won her first election as a local judge in Cayahoga County (Cleveland)

in 1920, two months after ratification of the Nineteenth Amendment. After just two years at the local level, she filed for the Ohio Supreme Court with petitions, getting her name on the fall ballot after the party primaries were over. She freely credited women with her amazing success. "The women were my organization," Judge Allen said later.

They simply got in touch with the women in every county who had been active in the suffrage movement. They handled my publicity, wrote letters to the newspapers, arranged my meetings, and distributed my very meager campaign literature. We had little money . . . and won by a 350,000 vote majority. (Roosevelt 1954, 197–198)

Reelected to another six-year term in 1928, she was the first woman in the world to sit on a court of last resort. Allen would set other precedents in the federal judiciary, but none of the era's women successfully emulated her.[3] The same was true of an unusual precedent set in 1925, when Miriam "Ma" Ferguson was governor of Texas and a case was heard by an all-female panel of judges. Its beginnings were in 1924, when Ferguson was running for office and Democrat Pat Neff was governor. *Johnson v. Darr* had been appealed to the Texas Supreme Court in Austin from a lower court in El Paso, and one of the parties was Woodmen of the World, an organization that sold insurance.

Because the Texas Supreme Court had only three members, all of whom had a personal investment in the outcome, they recused themselves. The governor then appointed three women who were ineligible for membership in the all-male Woodmen. They were Ruth Brazill of Galveston, who had been an anti-suffragist; Hortense Ward of Houston, who was the first female lawyer in Texas; and Nellie Gray Robertson, county attorney for Hood County and the chief justice of the special court. All three met the requirements of the state's legal code, which specified that judges be at least thirty years old, have practiced in Texas for seven years, and be able to swear that they never had participated in a duel. Their first session was in January, and no objection was made when the women upheld the El Paso decision in May. But news of this all-female court spread nationally via syndi-

_____

[3] See Chapter 15: Federal Courts.

As was the case with many early female attorneys, Susie Marshall Sharp's father was a lawyer. She had had his unconditional support her whole life, and so the hostility of young men in law school came as a shock. Because she had attended a single-sex college, she did not have male classmates until the University of North Carolina School of Law. "The boys that didn't ignore me," she told historian Karen Berger Morello, "treated me rudely."

"They would leave little anonymous notes on my chair containing citations to certain North Carolina cases. For example, one day I received a note about a case and I went hurrying to the library to read it. It turned out to be a decision upholding the right of a husband to use reasonable force to beat his wife. . . . The notes continued for a little while longer, but when they realized I meant business and had no designs on them, I stopped being a good joke." The last note left on her chair indicated the beginnings of a changing attitude: "If you are going to stay, get some rubber for those high heels." (Morello 1986, 241)

Democratic governor Terry Sanford, who appointed Sharp to the highest court in 1962, was perhaps the most liberal Southern governor of his time. Some of his constituents, including newspaper editors, had yet to grasp the changes that were beginning to take hold with the Kennedy administration, and one wrote a particularly irrational editorial about Sanford's appointment of Sharp. He railed, "What if she were forced with trying a case of rape? Wouldn't that be too much for her delicate sensibilities?"

Judge Sharp responded with a letter to the newspaper. She pointed out that "there could have been no rape had not a woman been present" and added "I consider it eminently fitting that one be in on the 'pay-off'" (Morello 1986, –242).

cation from the *Dallas Morning News,* which said on January 2, 1925: "It was a healthy New Year gift of recognition to the woman barrister of today. This is the first instance a woman has been appointed to sit on the supreme bench; it is the first time a higher court is to be composed entirely of women."

Although the Roaring Twenties greatly expanded women's social freedoms, women regressed politically. All too many young women saw feminism as passé, as their mother's outdated cause. The Great Depression of the 1930s limited female opportunity in all fields. Although World War II opened economic doors, only exceptionally skilled political women surged forward in the war and postwar years.[4] Some, however, got training that ensured a future career. This was true, for example, for Florence Kerins Murray, who was the youngest lieutenant colonel in the Women's Army Corps and went on to be the first woman on the Rhode Island Supreme Court.

But not until 1960 did a second woman again sit on the highest court of a state—and she become the first female chief justice. LORNA LOCKWOOD of Arizona, was like Ohio's Florence Allen in that she was elected, not appointed. Prior to her election, she served on the Maricopa County Superior Court, where her most heralded case involved the rape of a four-year-old girl. Lockwood "was certain of the defendant's guilt, [but] the jury didn't agree, and Lockwood was furious at their acquittal" (Morello 1986, 240). She also was Arizona's first woman to sentence a man to death, and voters easily elected her to the Arizona Supreme Court in 1960. President Lyndon B. Johnson considered her for the U.S. Supreme Court twice, but the positions went instead to Abe Fortas, the son of Russian Jews, and Thurgood Marshall, the Court's first African American.

The third woman on a highest state court came just two years after Lockwood's election. She was SUSIE MARSHALL SHARP of North Carolina, and she initially was appointed by Democratic governor Terry Sanford, later a presidential candidate. The 1962 appointment was for a vacancy, and Sharp had to run in the next election. Voters supported her, as they did again in 1975, when she became chief justice. North Carolina directly elects its chief justice, and she was the nation's first woman elected to the position. As with its first female bar admission in 1878, North Carolina led the Old South with Sharp's precedents and was decades ahead of other states that often consider themselves more liberal.

THE REVOLUTIONARY 1970S

Michigan, too, had been a pioneer with female admission to the bar. Sarah Kilgore was the first in 1871. A century later, it still was a pioneer with women on its highest court, with the seating of Mary Stallings Coleman in

---

[4] For state and legislative posts, see, especially, Chapter 4: State Representatives, Chapter 5: State Senators, Chapter 6: United States Representatives, and Chapter 7: United States Senators.

1972. The fourth woman on a state supreme court, Coleman led the way for ten other women who also passed this milestone during the revived feminism of the revolutionary 1970s.

The next, the fifth woman on a state supreme court, was Janie Shores of Alabama, who won election as a Democrat in 1974. She served until retirement in 1999, and President Bill Clinton considered her for the vacancy that Ruth Bader Ginsburg ultimately filled. According to a story in the *Birmingham News* on March 29, 1995, Clinton had come across Shores on his own, and the chief reason that she was not appointed was that Washington insiders did not know her.

Thus, of the first five women on state supreme courts, two were in former Confederate states, two were in the Midwest, one was in the Far West, and none was from the old centers of legal learning in the Northeast. The pattern continued until 1977, when Ruth Abrams of Massachusetts became New England's first female justice. At the decade's end, the precedent had been set in fourteen states. The Midwest led the way with five, in Kansas, Michigan, Minnesota, Ohio, and Wisconsin. Each of the other three regions had three: the West, with Arizona, California, and Colorado; the South, with Alabama, Arkansas, and North Carolina; and in the Northeast, they were Massachusetts, Maryland, and Rhode Island.

The best known of these female justices doubtless was California's Rose Elizabeth Bird. Appointed by Democratic governor Jerry Brown as chief justice in 1977, she survived recall attempts until conservatives ousted her from the court a decade later. In a highly political campaign, her opponents distributed bumper stickers that read "Bye-Bye Birdie." They called her soft on crime, despite a record very similar to those of male justices, and tagged her as "communist." In 1986, California voters rejected three sitting justices: Rose Bird, Cruz Reynoso, and Joseph Grodin. Stanley Mosk, whose opinions usually agreed with the others, was not targeted. As of 2011, Rose Bird remains the only female chief justice to lose a merit retention election, but she lost decisively. The vote was 67 percent to 33 percent against her. Her relative youth may have been a negative factor, too, as she was just sixty-three when she died in 1999.

The revolutionary 1970s included the first female supreme court justice to be appointed by a female governor. She was Ellen Ash Peters, who was named to Connecticut's highest court by Governor Ella Tambussi Grasso in 1978; she became chief justice of the court in 1984. Peters had been a law professor at Yale University, and in remarks she made at her 1999 retirement, Peters recalled that she almost did not take the governor's call because she thought that Grasso wanted to name her to still another policy committee.

The second woman appointed by a woman almost was part of the decade that changed everything: Washington governor Dixy Lee Ray named Carolyn Reaber Dimmick to the Washington Supreme Court in January 1981, just days before Ray had to leave the office because she lost the 1980 election. The Washington Heritage Center reported that Dimmick was "pretty and youthful." She went on to the federal bench in 1985 and still was serving at age seventy-nine when the center quoted her: "I never met a legal job I didn't love."

Twelve women became state supreme court justices in the 1970s. As the trend toward appointing instead of electing justices grew, just two were elected in the 1970s. The phenomenon of female justices still was rare, and voters who changed their state constitutions to appoint, instead of elect, their highest judges generally were thinking of judges as male. So many unqualified men, in fact, had been elected simply by spending the most money that the reform was considered good government.

Had so many states not switched to appointments, however, more women likely would have been elected sooner. Voters almost invariably supported women in judicial campaigns when they appeared on the ballot. The real problem was that so few women had the credentials to run in the 1970s. To be on a supreme court then meant that a woman probably would have had to go to law school in the 1950s or earlier, and there were not yet enough qualified women, or at least not enough who were willing to put themselves on the ballot.

The major parties were notably different in setting the highest state judicial precedent. Five Democratic governors appointed women to this position before any Republican did. Robert Bennett, the Republican governor of traditionally Republican Kansas, appointed Kay McFarland in 1977. He was singular. The eight other men and one woman who set this precedent during the 1970s were Democrats.

CONTINUED GROWTH: THE 1980S

Sixteen states put a woman on their highest court in the 1980s, and like the 1970s, the majority were appointed, not elected. Political acceptance of female justices can be seen in that partisanship evaporated in the eighties. Appointing a woman was no longer seen as risk-taking, and an almost equal numbers of Democratic and Republican governors did so. Of the decade's sixteen women, eight were chosen by Democrats, six by Republicans, and two were elected.

The two women who won elections in the 1980s both were Southerners. West Virginia voters chose Margaret L. Workman, and South Carolinians voted for Jean Hoefer Toal. Both have gone on to serve as chief justice, which is not the case in most states. As of 2011, Toal had twice been chosen by her peers for their top post.

Beryl J. Levine was unusual in that she joined the North Dakota Supreme Court in 1985, before any women were on the bench of the state's circuit courts. Born in Canada, she moved to the United States in 1955. She was appointed to a vacancy in 1985 and won election in 1986. In the March 24, 1986, issue of *People* magazine, Levine said that when she applied to law school at the University of North Dakota she was thirty-five years old. A dean told her: "You've got five kids. You're married to a doctor. You won't come to class." Yet Levine drove the eighty-five miles from her Fargo home to the campus in Grand Forks every day, and she graduated first in her class. While on the court, she established a commission on gender fairness in state law.

Rosemary Barkett led the same effort in Florida, and she served on the Florida Commission on the Status of Women even after she held the highest judicial position.[5] Barkett also was similar to Levine in that both were immigrants. Barkett was born in Mexico to Syrian parents, and when her family moved to Miami during World War II, she spoke no English. She entered a convent at seventeen and became a Catholic nun, but she left the order after eight years to enter the law school of University of Florida, in 1970. She was the first woman named as the school's outstanding senior. After a decade of private practice, she was appointed as a circuit judge in 1979. In 1985, she became the first woman on the Florida Supreme Court. Like other women perceived as liberal, she was targeted by conservatives for removal, but Barkett worked hard to retain her seat. Feminists joined her in campaigning, and she survived the challenge. In 1993, President Bill Clinton appointed Rosemary Barkett to the federal court in Atlanta, Georgia.

APPROACHING THE MILLENNIUM AND BEYOND

In the last decade of the twentieth century, fifteen more states added women to their highest courts, leaving just four to set the precedent in the twenty-first century.

_____

[5] For more on these commissions, see Chapter 17: Interest Groups.

Democrat Bill Clinton was in the White House during most of the 1990s, and the era returned to the pattern of Democratic governors appointing more women to courts. Eight Democratic governors set the precedent of appointing the first woman on their state supreme courts, as opposed to two Republicans. The decade also saw the return of women winning their seats through elections. Five women—in Illinois, Kentucky, Louisiana, Nevada and Pennsylvania—became the first female justice in their state via election.

Illinois is especially notable because its voters share many political characteristics with Ohio, but Illinois trailed Ohio in this precedent by seventy years: Ohio voters chose Florence Allen in 1922, but it was 1992 when Mary Ann G. McMorrow won in Illinois. Pennsylvania's Sandra Schultz Newman was the most controversial of these elected justices. Unlike most, she was open about her Republican partisanship and barely won reelection. The most successful may have been Louisiana's Catherine "Kitty" Kimball, who went on to be chief justice in the next decade.

Georgia was the first state to have a female African American justice. Zell Miller, a populist Democrat, named Leah Ward Sears in 1992. The first Asian American woman at this level was Paula A. Nakayama in Hawaii. That state is unusual in requiring that judges be reappointed at the expiration of ten-year terms, and Nakayama is unique among women in being appointed first by a Democratic governor and then by a Republican governor. John Waihee III chose Nakayama in 1993, and Linda Lingle would reappoint her in 2003.

Madeleine M. Kunin had named Denise R. Johnson to the Vermont court in 1990, becoming the third female governor to name a woman to this highest post. The fourth such case was in New Hampshire, where governor Jeanne Shaheen appointed Linda Stewart Dalianis in 2000. When Dalianis went on to be chief justice in 2010, Jeanne Shaheen had moved from governor to U.S. senator. All of the female governors who appointed the first female justices in their states were Democrats.

Besides Shaheen's New Hampshire, two other states had the first women on their highest court in 2000. The others were Delaware and Wyoming, and the very last state, where the milestone was set in 2002, was South Dakota. Some irony exists in each of these latecomers. Delaware calls itself The First State because it was first to ratify the U.S. Constitution. However, it lagged historically on women's rights, even though it has had a female governor. The Wyoming Territory was the first to grant women the vote in 1869, but it was slow to elect them in the twentieth century. South Dakota did not elevate a

Table 14.3 Women on State Supreme Courts, by State, 2010

State	Court Size	Number of Women	Women in Leadership Positions
Alabama	9	3	Chief Justice Sue Bell Cobb
Alaska	5	1	
Arizona	5	1	
Arkansas	7	1	
California	7	4*	
Colorado	7	3	
Connecticut	8	3	
Delaware	5	1	
Florida	7	2	
Georgia	7	1	Chief Justice Carol W. Hunstein
Hawaii	4	1	
Idaho	5	0	
Illinois	7	3	
Indiana	5	0	
Iowa	4	0	
Kansas	7	2	
Kentucky	7	2	Deputy Chief Justice Mary C. Noble
Louisiana	7	3	Chief Justice Catherine "Kitty" Kimball
Maine	7	2	Chief Justice Leigh Ingalls Saufley
Maryland	7	2	
Massachusetts	7	2	
Michigan	7	3	
Minnesota	7	2	Chief Justice Lorie Skjerven Gildea
Mississippi	9	1	
Missouri	7	3	
Montana	7	2	
Nevada	7	2	
Nebraska	7	1	
New Hampshire	5	2	Chief Justice Linda Stewart Dalianis
New Jersey	7	3	
New Mexico	5	1	
New York	7	3	
North Carolina	7	3	Chief Justice Sarah Parker
North Dakota	5	2	
Ohio	7	4*	Chief Justice Maureen O'Connor
Oklahoma	7	1	
Oregon	7	2	
Pennsylvania	7	2	
Rhode Island	5	1	
South Carolina	5	1	
South Dakota	5	1	
Tennessee	5	3*	Chief Justice Janice Holder
Texas	9	2	
Utah	5	2	Chief Justice Christine Durham
Vermont	5	2	
Virginia	7	1	
Washington	9	4	Chief Justice Barbara Madsen
West Virginia	5	2	Chief Justice Margaret L. Workman
Wisconsin	7	4*	Chief Justice Shirley S. Abrahamson
Wyoming	5	1	Chief Justice Marilyn Kite

Source: Compiled by author.

Note: An asterisk (*) indicates a female majority.

woman to its highest court until 2000, while its sister state, North Dakota, had been the first to elect a woman to statewide office back in 1892.

As 2011 began, New Hampshire's Dalianis was one of fifteen women who were the chief justice of their state. These included both appointed and elected women, and they covered the alphabetical range of states from Alabama to Wyoming. Dalianus was the only one in the Northeast. The South had by far the most, with female chief justices in seven states: Alabama, Georgia, Kentucky, Louisiana, North Carolina, Tennessee, and West Virginia. The Midwest had three (Minnesota, Ohio, and Wisconsin) and the Far West had four (California, Utah, Washington, and Wyoming).

Four of the fifteen states with female chief justices also had a majority of women on the court. In California, the 1986 election in which Rose Bird was removed from office proved the acme of conservatism, and in 2011, Tani Goree Cantil-Sakaye presided over its seven-member court. A Filipino American, she led four women and three men, one of whom was Hispanic and another Asian. Wisconsin shared the same record of four women on a seven-member court and also had a female chief justice, Shirley S. Abrahamson. Tennessee also held this status, but with a smaller court. Three of its five members were women, and the chief justice was Janice Holder.

Finally, Ohio, too, had a female majority of four women on a seven-member court in 2011, also with a female chief justice. Despite the League of Women Voters' longtime effort for judicial nonpartisanship, Ohio's contests continued to be between party nominees. Three of the four women were Republicans; the sole Democrat also was African American. The 2011 court marked the third time that women outnumbered men, a fitting legacy for Ohio's Florence Allen, elected in 1922 as the first woman on a state supreme court.

While four states—California, Ohio, Tennessee, and Wisconsin—had a majority of women on their highest court in 2011, three others had none. Idaho, Indiana, and Iowa had women on their courts at some point in the past but, as the second decade of the millennium began, included none. No discernable pattern emerges by geography or political history for either trend. The courts with female majorities range from western California to eastern Ohio, and from liberal to conservative. The three without any women are in the West or Midwest and generally are conservative—but Iowa, which lacked any woman in 2011, had been the very first state to admit a woman to its bar back in 1869. As with other offices, the most compelling reason that women do or do not rise to the highest places appears to depend on individual initiative and the creation of viable feminist networks. In any case, women still have ground to cover before they are truly judged by their peers.

⟨⟨⟨ PROFILES OF STATE SUPREME COURT JUDGES

The women profiled here set milestones on state supreme courts. **Florence Allen** *was the first to be elected to any court of last resort.* **Lorna Lockwood** *was the first to be appointed chief justice.* **Susie Marshall Sharp** *was the first to be elected chief justice.*

FLORENCE ALLEN (1884–1996)

The first woman in the world elected to a court of last resort, Florence Ellinwood Allen had the benefit of being raised by a mother who believed not only in her daughter but also in women's rights. Corrine Tuckerman Allen was the first woman on the enrollment records of Massachusetts's Smith College. When that single-sex institution began classes in 1875, higher education for women was considered radical.

Florence Allen was born in Salt Lake City, Utah, when the West still was a frontier. She was descended from New England pioneers, including Ethan Allen, famous for capturing Fort Ticonderoga with the Green Mountain Boys in the American Revolution. Her grandparents had been pioneers in Ohio, and she was sent there for education. She had no thought at the time of becoming a judge and studied music at Ohio's Case Western Reserve, in its affiliated college for women.

After graduation in 1904, she went to Berlin, Germany, for intensive training in piano, but her hopes of being a concert pianist ended with an injury to her hand. Allen returned to Ohio and wrote music criticism for *The Plain Dealer* (Cleveland) for three years, while also earning a master's degree in political science. It was fashionable in that era for upper-class young women to spend some time working in settlement houses, which had been founded to aid the flood of immigrants arriving from Europe. Allen went to New York City and worked at the Henry Street Settlement that had been started by famed Lillian Wald in 1893.

This experience brought her attention to the range of legal problems endured by many immigrants and the urban poor, especially women. Rejected by several law schools because of gender, Allen finally won admission to New York University. After graduating, she again returned to Ohio, where she was admitted to the bar in 1914. Then thirty years old, she used her position as a lawyer to work on behalf of female enfranchisement, and that activity paid off personally. In 1919, before Ohio women had the vote, she was appointed as an assistant prosecutor for Cuyahoga County, which is centered in Cleveland. The next year, in the first election in which all American women could vote, she won election to a local judgeship.

Showing remarkable confidence in both herself and the voters, Allen ran for the Ohio Supreme Court in the next election, in 1922. With her campaign run by the network of women who had worked for the vote, she won by a wide margin. Reelected in 1928 with an even bigger majority, Judge Allen set another precedent in 1934, when President Franklin D. Roosevelt appointed her to the U.S. Court of Appeals, which is just beneath the U.S. Supreme Court. She stayed there, serving as chief justice from 1958 until her retirement the following year. Justice Florence Allen died at eighty-two in Waite Hill, Ohio.

LORNA LOCKWOOD (1903–1977)

Arizona's Lorna Elizabeth Lockwood was the first female chief justice of a United States court.

No known kin of famed attorney Belva Lockwood, she was born near the border of Mexico, in the small town of Douglas.[6] Her parents moved to Tombstone when she was four, and she graduated from high school there. She said that she knew from girlhood that she wanted to be a lawyer like her father, who was elected to the Arizona Supreme Court in 1924. She graduated from law school at the University of Arizona in 1925, but she had difficulty finding a job. Most of her work was as a legal secretary, not as an attorney, until she began an affiliation with Arizona's first female lawyer, Sarah Sorin.

A Democrat, Lockwood was more political than many pioneer female attorneys, and won election to the Arizona House in 1938. She represented Phoenix until after the 1946 election, rising to chair the House Judiciary Committee, one of the most powerful of committees in state legislatures. In addition to the part-time legislative service, she was an attorney for the World War II Office of Price Administration. That agency set retail prices to prevent wartime inflation, and the experience was excellent for learning to make judicious decisions. Price control was particularly needed in Phoenix, which grew exponentially during the war because troops headed for desert climates trained near there. It is the center of Maricopa County, and Lockwood won appointment as a judge to the Maricopa County Superior Court in 1951.

---

[6] For more on Belva Lockwood, see Chapter 13: Pioneers in the Judiciary.

She was more active in civic causes than many judges, including holding office in the National Federation of Business and Professional Women's Clubs. That and other organizations provided a network for her to win election to the Arizona Supreme Court in 1960. She also served on the Governor's Commission on the Status of Women, was president of the state association of judges, and in rotating duty, was three times the court's chief justice.

Lockwood was considered for the U.S. Supreme Court in the early 1960s, during the Kennedy/Johnson years. When the first woman finally joined the Court in 1981, she was fellow Arizonan Sandra Day O'Connor. Lockwood, however, did not live to see that day. She died of complications of pneumonia in 1977.

SUSIE MARSHALL SHARP (1907–1996)

The first woman elected to the position of chief justice of a state supreme court, Susie Marshall Sharp was a lifelong North Carolinian.

She was born in Rocky Mount to a family that had settled there centuries earlier, and her father was an attorney and active Democrat. She attended North Carolina College for Women in Greensboro and entered law school in 1926 at the University of North Carolina. Sharp was the only female student, and her male classmates initially harassed her but stopped when they saw how serious she was about the legal profession. She graduated with high honors and began practicing with her father as Sharp & Sharp.

After two decades of practice, including being the city attorney for the town of Reidsville, Gov. William Kerr Scott in 1949 appointed Sharp as a special judge for the Superior Court of North Carolina. This position required significant travel to courthouses throughout the state. She performed her duties well and future governors reappointed her. In 1962, Gov. Terry Sanford appointed her to a vacancy on the state's highest court. She subsequently was elected to the vacancy and then to a full term. North Carolina voters chose her as chief justice in 1974, and she served until mandatory retirement, in 1979.

Time named Susie Sharp as one of the twelve most influential women in the nation in 1975, and North Carolina senator Sam J. Ervin Jr.—who was known as a constitutional scholar—recommended her to Richard M. Nixon for the U.S. Supreme Court. However, the president's four Court appointments between 1969 and 1971 all went to white men.

North Carolina law required justices to retire at age seventy-two. Sharp then devoted time to speaking out on issues that she could not raise on the bench. One was an amendment to the state constitution requiring that candidates for judicial positions be lawyers. Her 1974 opponent had no legal training; he was a salesman for a fire equipment company. Sharp also had gained attention earlier in her career for insisting that restroom facilities be modified for female judges. She died just short of her ninetieth birthday in Raleigh and was buried in Rockingham County's Greenview Cemetery.

REFERENCES AND FURTHER READING

Allen, Florence Ellinwood. 1965. *To Do Justly*. Cleveland: Case Western Reserve University Press.

Baum, Lawrence. 2008. *American Courts: Process and Policy*. Boston: Houghton Mifflin.

Council of State Governments. 2009. *The Book of the States*. Volume 41. Lexington, KY: Council of State Governments.

Gaza, Hedda. 1996. *Barred from the Bar: Women in the Legal Profession*. New York: F. Watts.

Hayes, Anna. 2008. *Without Precedent: The Life of Susie Marshall Sharp*. Chapel Hill: University of North Carolina Press.

Morello, Karen Berger. 1986. *The Invisible Bar: The Woman Lawyers in America: 1638 to the Present*. New York: Random House.

Quantz, David M. 1986. *Lorna Lockwood: A Dynamic Woman in Changing Times*. Tucson: University of Arizona Press.

Roberts, Betty. 2008. *With Grit and by Grace: Breaking Trails in Politics and Law*. Corvallis: Oregon State University Press.

Roosevelt, Eleanor. 1954. *Ladies of Courage*. New York: G. P. Putnam's Sons.

Salkin, Patricia E. 2008. *Pioneering Women Lawyers: From Kate Stoneman to the Present*. Chicago: American Bar Association.

Stolz, Prebe. 1981. *Judging Judges: The Investigation of Rose Bird and the California Supreme Court*. New York: Free Press.

Stumpf, Harry P., and John H. Culver. 1992. *The Politics of State Courts*. New York: Longman.

15

FEDERAL COURTS

The U.S. Constitution, ratified in 1789, gave both the president and Congress a good deal of authority in the creation of the third branch of government, the judiciary. Each state also developed its own judicial system for enforcing state laws, while the Constitution provided for a U.S. Supreme Court and such lower courts as Congress wished to create. It also spelled out the jurisdiction of federal courts, which primarily is to enforce federal law and to deal with international and interstate cases.

The Constitution further mandated that nominations for federal judgeships were to be made by the president, with confirmation by the Senate. The appointments were for life, which gave judges the independence that is vital to making decisions without regard to short-term politics. The Constitution says that federal judges serve for life "during good behavior," and, because of that, no mandatory retirement age is set. Many judges never retire but, instead, take senior status, which means that they remain eligible to be recalled to the bench if a particular need arises.

Members of the U.S. Supreme Court are based in Washington, DC, but, when the nation began, they also rode circuit, with individual justices hearing cases in districts outside of the capital city. As the population grew, Congress increased the number of courts. The biggest change in the system was in 1891, when nine courts of appeal were established between the district and Supreme Court levels; two more since have been added. (Because these additional courts led to changes in geographical jurisdictions, courts mentioned below generally are not referred to by numbers, but instead by the city in which the court is based.)

Since 1869, the U.S. Supreme Court has had nine members. Immediately beneath it are regional courts of appeals, often called district or federal circuit courts. They have 179 members in eleven regional jurisdictions. Presidents also appoint 677 federal judges who serve on the lowest federal level, district courts. A president can appoint hundreds of federal judges, all of whom can serve for life. In modern times, Gerald R. Ford had the fewest appointments, with 62; Ronald Reagan, the most, with 376.

Finally, some federal judges specialize in particularly narrow areas of law, such as patents and bankruptcy. Admiralty courts, for example, historically dealt with issues on the high seas, and customs courts—customs as in taxes on imports—became courts of international trade in 1980. The very first woman to serve on a federal court was on a customs court, in the inland city of Cleveland, Ohio, which receives foreign imports from shipping routes along the Great Lakes. President Herbert Hoover appointed Genevieve R. Cline, an activist in the General Federation of Women's Clubs, in 1928. She succeeded the judge for whom she had worked as a merchandise appraiser. Cline was middle-aged when she earned her law degree, in 1921, and one of her first cases as a judge set a precedent on whether or not a married woman could declare a domicile separate from that of her husband. A feminist, Cline ruled in favor of the woman.

In 1968, Congress created the position of federal magistrate, which is filled through appointment by district judges to act as judges in cases that are less than felonies. A number of women are federal magistrates, but this chapter concentrates on pioneer women who were federal judges, especially at the appellate level, as well as the four women who have served on the U.S. Supreme Court, the final arbiter of the law of the land.

Table 15.1 Female Federal Judges, 1928–1980

Year	Name	Type of Court	Base	Appointing President	Notes
1928	Genevieve R. Cline	Customs	Cleveland, Ohio	Calvin Coolidge (R)	First on a customs court
1934	Florence Allen	Appellate	Cleveland, Ohio	Franklin D. Roosevelt (D)	First elected to a state supreme court—Ohio, 1922
1950	Burnita Shelton Matthews	District	Washington, DC	Harry S. Truman (D)	First on a federal district court
1955	Mary Donlan Alger	Customs	New York, New York	Dwight D. Eisenhower (R)	Former U.S. House candidate
1961	Sarah Tilghman Hughes	District	Dallas, Texas	John F. Kennedy (D)	Administered the oath of office to Lyndon B. Johnson after Kennedy's assassination
1966	Constance Baker Motley	District	New York, New York	Lyndon B. Johnson (D)	First African American woman
1968	Shirley M. Hufstedler	Appellate	San Francisco, California	Lyndon B. Johnson (D)	First on the West Coast
1968	June Lazenby Green	District	Washington, DC	Lyndon B. Johnson (D)	Succeeded Burnita Shelton Matthews
1970	Cornelia Groefsema Kennedy	District	Detroit, Michigan	Richard M. Nixon (R)	First in the Midwest; elevated by Jimmy Carter (D) in 1979
1976	Mary Anne Riley	District	Phoenix, Arizona	Gerald R. Ford (R)	World War II veteran
1977	Phyllis A. Kravitch	District	Eastern Georgia	Jimmy Carter (D)	Elevated to appellate court in Atlanta by Carter in 1979
1977	Elsijane Trimble Roy	District	Western Arkansas	Jimmy Carter (D)	First woman on the Arkansas Supreme Court
1978	Patricia Jean E. P. Boyle	District	Eastern Michigan	Jimmy Carter (D)	Resigned in 1983 to serve on Michigan Supreme Court
1978	Ellen Bree Burns	District	Connecticut	Jimmy Carter (D)	Graduated Yale Law School in 1947; became chief justice in 1988
1978	Mary Johnson Lowe	District	Southern New York	Jimmy Carter (D)	LL.M. (master of law) from Columbia University in 1955
1978	Mariana Pfaelzer	District	Central California	Jimmy Carter (D)	Known for protecting undocumented immigrants
1978	Norma Levy Shapiro	District	Eastern Pennsylvania	Jimmy Carter (D)	Law degree from University of Pennsylvania, 1951
1979	Ruth Bader Ginsburg	District	Washington, DC	Jimmy Carter (D)	Became the second woman on the U.S. Supreme Court
1979	Barbara Brandriff Crabb	District	Western Wisconsin	Jimmy Carter (D)	Chief judge 1980–1996
1979	Orinda Dale Evans	District	Northern Georgia	Jimmy Carter (D)	Chief judge 1999–2006
1979	Joyce Hens Green	District	Washington, DC	Jimmy Carter (D)	Later served on U.S. Foreign Intelligence Surveillance Court
1979	Shirley Brannock Jones	District	Maryland	Jimmy Carter (D)	Earned law degree in 1946; served on Baltimore orphans court
1979	Diana E. Murphy	District	Minnesota	Jimmy Carter (D)	Elevated to appellate court in St. Louis, Missouri, by Bill Clinton (D)
1979	Sylvia H. Rambo	District	Middle Pennsylvania	Jimmy Carter (D)	Chief judge 1992–1998
1979	Mary Lou Robinson	District	Northern Texas	Jimmy Carter (D)	Previously chief judge of a Texas court of civil appeals
1979	Barbara Jacobs Rothstein	District	Western Washington	Jimmy Carter (D)	Later head of the Federal Judicial Center in Washington DC
1979	Anna Diggs Taylor	District	Eastern Michigan	Jimmy Carter (D)	African American; law degree from Yale University, 1957; noted for rulings on wiretaps
1979	Anne Elise Thompson	District	New Jersey	Jimmy Carter (D)	African American; previously held judgeships in Trenton, New Jersey
1979	Zita Leeson Weinshienk	District	Colorado	Jimmy Carter (D)	Previously held judgeships in Denver, Colorado
1979	Veronica DiCarlo Wicker	District	Eastern Louisiana	Jimmy Carter (D)	Served until her 1994 death
1979	Rya Weickert Zobel	District	Massachusetts	Jimmy Carter (D)	Native of Germany; law degree from Harvard University, 1956

Table 15.1 (Continued)

Year	Name	Type of Court	Base	Appointing President	Notes
1979	Betty Binns Fletcher	Appellate	San Francisco, California	Jimmy Carter (D)	Her son was named to the same court by Bill Clinton (D)
1979	Dorothy Wright Nelson	Appellate	San Francisco, California	Jimmy Carter (D)	Popularized mediation
1979	Mary M. Schroeder	Appellate	San Francisco, California	Jimmy Carter (D)	First female federal chief justice at appellate level
1979	Amalya Lyle Kearse	Appellate	New York City	Jimmy Carter (D)	First African American woman on an appellate court
1979	Carolyn Dineen King	Appellate	Houston, Texas	Jimmy Carter (D)	As of 2011, had written more than four thousand opinions
1979	Stephanie Kulp Seymour	Appellate	Denver, Colorado	Jimmy Carter (D)	Became chief justice in 1994
1979	Delores Korman Sloviter	Appellate	Philadelphia, Pennsylvania	Jimmy Carter (D)	Became chief justice in 1991
1979	Patricia McGowan Wald	Appellate	Washington, DC	Jimmy Carter (D)	Additional career in international law
1980	Ann Aldrich	District	Northern Ohio	Jimmy Carter (D)	Long career as an attorney in many places and legal areas
1980	Susan H. Black	District	Northern Florida	Jimmy Carter (D)	Elevated to U.S. Court of Appeals for the Eleventh Circuit in 1992
1980	Helen J. Frye	District	Oregon	Jimmy Carter (D)	Previously served on Oregon courts
1980	Susan O'Meara Getzendamer	District	Northern Illinois	Jimmy Carter (D)	Law degree from Loyola University, 1966; resigned in 1987 for private practice
1980	Norma Holloway Johnson	District	Washington, DC	Jimmy Carter (D)	High-profile cases; chief justice 1997–2001
1980	Judith Nelsen Keep	District	Southern California	Jimmy Carter (D)	Chief justice 1991–1998
1980	Marilyn Hall Patel	District	Southern California	Jimmy Carter (D)	Much publicized; ruled on behalf of female firefighters

Source: Compiled by author, with some data from the Federal Judicial Center.

Note: (D) means Democrat and (R) means Republican.

THE PIONEERS, 1934–1976

Democrat Franklin D. Roosevelt set precedents in many areas, including the appointment of the first woman in the cabinet, the first female ambassador, and the first female federal judge. Florence Allen of Ohio in 1922 had been the first woman on a state supreme court.[1] Voters elected the Ohio Supreme Court, and Allen used networks of suffragists to win this prestigious post just two years after Ohio women won the vote. Roosevelt elevated her to the federal bench in 1934, his second year in office. Judge Allen was the nation's first woman on a state supreme court and the first on a federal appellate court. With the exception of Cline on the comparatively obscure Cleveland customs court, Allen was the first on a federal bench. She served on the U.S. District Court of Appeals

[1] For Allen's biography, see Chapter 14: State Courts. For other Roosevelt appointees, see Chapter 11: Cabinet and Subcabinet and Chapter 12: Ambassadors.

for the Sixth Circuit, based in Cleveland, until her retirement in 1959.

Allen was singular as the only woman among Roosevelt's 193 judicial appointees. His successor, Harry S. Truman, also a Democrat, set a second precedent when he chose BURNITA SHELTON MATTHEWS for the U.S. District Court for the District of Columbia. President Truman appointed her in October 1949, and the Senate confirmed her in April 1950. Matthews's appointment was at a lower level than Allen's 1934 appointment. It was not an appellate court, as was Allen's position, but a federal trial court.

Like Roosevelt, Truman named only one woman; Matthews was alone among the 122 federal judges he appointed. President Dwight D. Eisenhower also appointed only one—and that was to a specialized court, the Customs Court of New York City. She was Mary Donlan Alger, a native of western New York and a 1920 graduate of Cornell University Law School. Eisenhower was a Republican, and his appointee also was an activist

Bernita Shelton Matthews was appointed to the U.S. District Court for the District of Columbia in October 1949. She was confirmed by the Senate in April 1950. She was the first woman to gain a life-tenured trial court judgeship in the nation and the only woman named by President Truman.

Republican. She had lost a 1940 congressional race to Democrat Caroline O'Day.[2] Alger's judicial career was limited to this one court, where she served from 1955 to 1966. Her position was unusually significant, though, because of the great amount of federal tax revenue that enters through the huge port of New York City.

Women's path in the federal judiciary thus regressed, as the two female appointees under Truman and Eisenhower in the 1950s were of lower status than the first, under Roosevelt two decades earlier. Democrat John F. Kennedy narrowly won the 1960 election, and, during his approximately one thousand days in office, he named 124 men and one woman to federal judgeships.

The woman was Sarah Tilghman Hughes, who was appointed to the federal court for the Northern District of Texas in 1961. Hughes had attended George Washington University Law School at night and worked as a police officer during the day. She moved to Texas with her husband, George Hughes, in 1922 and practiced in Dallas. A Democrat, she served in the Texas House in the 1930s. In 1935, she became Texas's first female state judge, and she thus had long experience when Kennedy appointed her. Judge Hughes drew national attention two years later, when she administered the oath of office to Vice President Lyndon B. Johnson after Kennedy's assassination in Dallas. As of 2011, she remains the only woman to have sworn in a president.

In 1966, President Johnson, a Democrat from Texas, appointed the first African American woman to a federal court, CONSTANCE BAKER MOTLEY. She served on one of the nation's most intellectually challenging courts, the Southern District of New York, which tries complex financial cases based in Manhattan. Motley became well respected in judicial circles, and feminists in the 1970s often cited her as a potential U.S. Supreme Court justice. Being both black and female, however, proved too much of a barrier, even though Lyndon Johnson set several records for diversity. He made 168 appointments, including that of Thurgood Marshall, the first African American on the Supreme Court.

Johnson also was the first president to name more than one woman to federal judgeships. In addition to Motley in 1966, Johnson appointed two women in 1968, one on each coast. Shirley M. Hufstedler joined the Ninth Circuit Court of Appeals, which covers the Northwest from Montana to Alaska. Headquartered in San Francisco, it also includes Hawaii. Hufstedler left her lifetime post in 1979 to become the first head of the Department of Education under President Jimmy Carter.[3] When he lost the next year's election to Republican Ronald Reagan, she lost her career. Speculation was widespread at the time that Hufstedler would be the first woman on the Supreme Court, but no vacancies opened up during Carter's four years in office.

President Johnson named June Lazenby Green to the district court for Washington, DC. She filled the vacancy created by the retirement of Burnita Matthews, who had been appointed by President Truman. A graduate of the law school of American University in Washington, Judge Green served from 1968 to 1984, when she took senior status, which she still held when she died in 2001.

Republican Richard M. Nixon won the 1968 election and had a powerful impact on the courts—appointing 231 judges, more than any other president thus far—during less than two terms in office. Before resigning in disgrace in 1974, he had the rare opportunity to appoint four members of the Supreme Court. All were white men. At lower levels, he made only one appointment of a woman, Cornelia

---

[2] See Chapter 6: United States Representatives.

[3] See Chapter 11: Cabinet and Subcabinet.

Table 15.2 Number of Female Federal Judges, by Appointing President, in Chronological Order

Appointing President	Total	Women	Percentage
Franklin D. Roosevelt (D)	193	1	< 1
Harry S. Truman (D)	132	1	< 1
Dwight D. Eisenhower (R)	179	1	< 1
John F. Kennedy (D)	105	1	< 1
Lyndon B. Johnson (D)	168	3	1.8
Richard M. Nixon (R)	231	1	< 1
Gerald R. Ford (R)	62	1	1.6
Jimmy Carter (D)	259	36	13.9
Ronald Reagan (R)	376	27	7.2
George H.W. Bush (R)	192	34	17.7
Bill Clinton (D)	373	105	28.2
George W. Bush (R)	325	69	21.2
Barack Obama (D)	132	52	39.4
Total	2,727	332	12.2

Source: Compiled by author.

Note: President Barack Obama's appointments refer to the first two years of his presidency. (D) means Democrat and (R) means Republican.

Groefsema Kennedy, who was named a judge for the Eastern District of Michigan. Nixon appointed her to the federal district court in 1970, and Jimmy Carter, a Democrat, would elevate Kennedy to the U.S. Court of Appeals for the Sixth Circuit in 1979.

Vice President Gerald R. Ford became president upon Nixon's resignation, and his tenure of less than two years allowed only sixty-two appointments to the federal judiciary. Just one was a woman, Mary Anne Richey of Arizona, who had been a pilot in the Women's Air Service Pilots (WASP) during World War II. She entered public employment as an attorney for Pima County and moved up the ranks to be a federal attorney there. She became a state appellate judge in 1964. Ford nominated her for the U.S. District Court for the District of Arizona on June 2, 1976. Senators, focused on creating a positive impression for female voters in that fall's close election, confirmed her on June 16. Judge Richey served until her death in 1983.

Thus, in the forty-two years between Franklin Roosevelt's 1934 precedent and this 1976 appointment by Gerald Ford, only nine women were appointed to the federal bench, among thousands of appointments of men. Six women were appointed by Democratic presidents; three, by Republicans. Even more significant is the fact that, with the exception of Shirley Hufstedler, whose service was brief, these women held less prestigious positions than the first, Florence Allen. Her outstanding career was based in the networks of women who won the vote in 1920, and more than a half-century later, it would take another revival of feminism to shake up the nation's systems of justice.

THE UNHERALDED CARTER REVOLUTION, 1976–1980

Feminism revived in the late 1960s and early 1970s with the formation of the National Organization for Women (NOW) and other organizations. But few noticed the quiet revolution that feminists and Democratic President Jimmy Carter brought to the nation's judicial system.

Although he had no opportunity to affect the all-male composition of the U.S. Supreme Court, Carter made a huge difference in the number of women appointed to lower courts. Indeed, he made so many appointments that the focus here is on the higher positions of appellate courts. Of Carter's 259 judicial appointees, 36 were women—four times the nine women chosen by the seven prior presidents. He did have somewhat more opportunity than other presidents because Congress added two new circuits during his tenure. However, most of his appointments of women were traditional ones in which a woman succeeded a man in a vacant seat. Because judges are appointed for life, Jimmy Carter's legacy lived on long after he returned to Georgia.

His first significant appointments were in 1977, his first year in office, when he chose two Southern women. Phyllis A. Kravitch, a 1943 graduate of the prestigious University of Pennsylvania Law School, joined the district court in eastern Georgia. Carter had been governor of Georgia, and this was the first appointment of a woman in a president's home state. In 1979, he elevated her to the U.S. Court of Appeals in Atlanta. He also named Elsijane Trimble Roy to the Western District of Arkansas. She had been the first woman on the Arkansas Supreme Court.[4]

Carter gave opportunities to a number of other women who later became major figures in the justice system. Among them was Ruth Bader Ginsburg, who Carter appointed to the U.S. Court of Appeals for the District of Columbia Circuit. Under President Bill Clinton, she would become the second woman on the U.S. Supreme Court. Often nonpartisan in his approach, Carter, a Democrat, promoted Cornelia Kennedy from the federal district court in Detroit, to which she had been appointed by Republican Gerald Ford. Carter elevated her to Sixth Circuit Court of Appeals, which considers cases from parts of Michigan, Ohio, Kentucky, and Tennessee.

Patricia McGowen Wald served on the U.S. District Court of Appeals for the District of Columbia for twenty years, from Carter's 1979 appointment until her 1999 retirement. She was its chief justice from 1986 to 1991. Born in 1928, Wald had been a pioneer woman at Yale Law School, from which she graduated in 1951. She took a

---

[4] See Chapter 14: State Courts.

break to rear five children, campaigned for Carter, and worked in the White House until her appointment. She did not slow down after retirement. President Clinton appointed Wald to the International Criminal Tribunal for the Former Yugoslavia, and she also has served on quasi-judicial bodies investigating issues regarding Iraq and Guantánamo.

In 1979, Carter appointed three women to the Ninth District Court of Appeals. Although based in San Francisco, it covers a huge geographical area and has become known as the nation's most liberal court. Betty Binns Fletcher earned her law degree at the University of Washington in 1956. She wrote major opinions for the court, particularly on behalf of women, gays, and American Indians. Dorothy Wright Nelson, based in Los Angeles, had been a law professor at the University of California at Los Angeles, and she served until taking senior status in 1995. Finally, Mary M. Schroeder had been one of six women in her 1965 law school class at the University of Chicago. Judge Schroeder went on to be the first female chief justice in the federal system and presided over several major cases, including compensation for Japanese Americans who were interned during World War II.

Stephanie Kulp Seymour also became chief justice of a federal appellate court, presiding over the court based in Denver. Born in 1940 in Battle Creek, Michigan, she had the best college credentials of any female federal judge to that point. She was a 1962 graduate of Massachusetts's elite Smith College and of Harvard Law School in 1965. The law school only recently had begun admitting women, and she was one of 23 female students in a class of 550. She practiced in Boston, Massachusetts, Tulsa, Oklahoma, and Houston, Texas, until Carter appointed her to the newly configured Tenth Circuit, which handled cases from Colorado, Kansas, New Mexico, Oklahoma, Utah, and Wyoming. The first woman on that court, she also served as chief justice from 1994 to 2000.

Dolores Korman Sloviter, who was of Jewish heritage, served on the U.S. Court of Appeals for the Third Circuit, headquartered in Philadelphia. Born in that city in 1932, she earned her law degree at Pennsylvania State University in 1956. She married, practiced privately, and taught at Temple University until Carter appointed her in 1979. She served as chief justice from 1991 to 1998 and, as of 2011, remained on the court.

Carter emulated fellow Southerner Lyndon Johnson in naming an African American to the federal bench, Amalya Lyle Kearse. She served on the Second Circuit Court of Appeals based in Manhattan, which also heard cases from nearby states. She was a New Jersey native whose mother was a physician. She attended Wellesley College in Massachusetts and went on to the elite student editorship of the law review journal at the University of Michigan Law School. Returning east after her 1962 graduation, she rose to be a partner at a prestigious Wall Street firm. President Carter appointed her in 1979, and she served on the appellate court until taking senior status in 2002.

Three dozen women were appointed to the federal courts in the four exceptional years between 1977 and 1980. Because feminists pushed for their appointments, and because President Carter responded, these women permanently changed the face of federal justice.

THE SUPREME COURT AND MORE, 1980–1992

Just as Democrat Jimmy Carter bested Republican Gerald R. Ford at the polls in 1976, Carter was defeated in 1980 by Republican Ronald Reagan. During the 1980s, the Republican Party dropped its support for the Equal Rights Amendment and asserted a conservative ideology that, among other things, rejected affirmation action.

In office for two full terms, Reagan made more judicial appointments than any other president, giving him a long-lasting impact on the courts. His 376 appointments would be more numerous than future presidents who also served eight years. By far his most significant appointment was that of the first woman to the highest court, SANDRA DAY O'CONNOR. When he appointed her, 101 men had served during the Court's 191-year history. The nation was so eager to see its first female representative on the Supreme Court that virtually no opposition arose to O'Connor, and the Senate confirmed her 99–0. She went on to justify women's high hopes, gaining a reputation as an excellent, unbiased justice while also speaking openly about the gender bias she had suffered.

Although she had held elective office as a Republican in Arizona, Justice O'Connor did not vote in a predictably partisan way, and she ultimately became the swing vote among the court's nine members, offering the balance-tipping

Table 15.3   Female Supreme Court Justices

Tenure	Name	Appointing President	Confirmation Vote
1981–2005	Sandra Day O'Connor	Ronald Reagan (R)	99–0
1993–	Ruth Bader Ginsburg	Bill Clinton (D)	96–3
2009–	Sonia Sotomayor	Barack Obama (D)	68–31
2010–	Elena Kagan	Barack Obama (D)	63–37

Source: Compiled by author.

Note: (D) means Democrat and (R) means Republican.

By dedicating her 2003 book, *The Majesty of the Law: Reflections of a Supreme Court Justice*, to her law clerks, U.S. Supreme Court justice Sandra Day O'Connor demonstrated the importance of mentoring the next generation. She had plowed her own professional path largely alone, but she was grateful for the one female role model that she had: Justice Lorna Lockwood of the Arizona Supreme Court (see Chapter 14). In the chapter "Women in Judging," O'Connor addressed the question of whether female judges are fundamentally different from male judges in the way they work.

My intuition and my experience persuade me that having women on the bench . . . is extremely important. . . . I am often asked whether women judges speak with a different voice. . . . Undaunted by the troubling history of their view, many writers have suggested that women practice law differently than men. . . . The so-called new feminism is interesting but troubling, precisely because it so nearly echoes the old Victorian myth of the "true woman"—the myth that worked so well to keep women out of the professionals for so long. . . .

Theoretical discussions are ongoing today—particularly in academic circles—about differences in the voices women and men

hear, or in their moral perceptions. . . . Generalizations . . . cannot guide me reliably in making decisions about particular individuals. . . . I was a law teacher until I became a judge. In class or in grading papers over seventeen years, and now in reading briefs and listening to arguments in court for fourteen years, I have detected no reliable indicator of distinctly male or surely female thinking. . . .

Judge Pat Wald of the Court of Appeals for the District of Columbia, said recently, "We may be almost at the gates of real equality—when we can judge and be judged by the same standards. . . ." Justice Jeanne Coyne, formerly of the Minnesota Supreme Court, . . . says that "a wise old man and a wise old woman reach the same conclusion." Are women from Venus and men from Mars? Or, as [journalist] Ellen Goodman says, "aren't we all living here together on earth?" (O'Connor 2003, 186–193)

Both inside and outside of judicial circles—and even within the same person—debate continues on whether women think and behave differently from men. What is no longer debatable, however, is that all humans, regardless of gender, are entitled to equal justice.

opinion among justices who were evenly divided. Thus, especially during the administrations of Democrat Bill Clinton and Republican George W. Bush, Justice O'Connor effectively made final decisions for the nation's citizens.

With the public desire for a woman on the court fulfilled, Reagan did not appoint a second one. Instead, he chose Antonin Scalia and Anthony M. Kennedy, while also naming William H. Rehnquist as chief justice. All three were white males, and they adhered to the conservative philosophy that challenged reproductive rights women had won with decisions on birth control in the 1960s and on abortion in the 1970s. After O'Connor's appointment, these rights, which affect women much more than men, became central to court confirmation battles.

Of the hundreds of appointments made during his eight years, Reagan chose just twenty-seven women for courts lower than the Supreme Court. This compares with thirty-six by Carter, who had half as much time as president. Of the twenty-seven, Reagan made twenty-one appointments of women at the district level, the lowest, and three female corporate attorneys won appointments to specialty courts in bankruptcy, patents, and international trade.

Just three women—compared with Carter's eight—joined appellate courts based on geography, in California, Pennsylvania, and Texas. The most notable may have been

Edith Hollan Jones. At age thirty-six, she was promoted from her position as general counsel for the Republican Party to the circuit court based in Houston. She later wrote an opinion in *McCorvey v. Hill* (2004), a follow-up case to famed *Roe v. Wade* (1973), that very much reflected her party's position.

Although unknown at the time, Reagan's most notable appointment at the district level probably would be Kimba M. Wood. Harvard educated, she went on to preside over several highly publicized cases in Manhattan. Although easily accepted by the Senate when Republican Reagan nominated her, Wood ran into trouble when Democrat Bill Clinton attempted to appoint her as attorney general.[5]

Like Jimmy Carter, George H. W. Bush, who was vice president under Reagan, would serve just one term. Despite two vacancies during his four years, he did not take the opportunity to appoint a second woman to the nine-member Supreme Court. However, during his four years in office, he appointed thirty-four women at lower levels, more than Ronald Reagan had done with twice as much time.

Bush not only was more moderate than his predecessor, but he also had the benefit of many more qualified

[5] See Chapter 11: Cabinet and Subcabinet.

women, as female law school enrollment soared in the late 1960s and the 1970s. By the time that he took office in 1989, these women had the credentials for judicial appointments. More than men, they were likely to go into public employment and especially were apt to seek service on criminal cases. Encouraged by feminism and other progressive movements, many of these women wanted to be judges in areas of laws that dealt with people more than property. At the federal level, these were criminal issues such as interstate custody, kidnapping, and prostitution. While old offenses, they represented a newly expanded area of law, especially federal law.

Thus the Bush administration, from 1989 to 1993, had the advantage of many more women in the appointment pipeline. Of his total forty-two choices at the appellate level, seven were women. Pamela Ann Rymer, his first female appointee, had been rejected by the Senate for elevation to the Ninth District Court in California in 1987, under Reagan, but was accepted under Bush in 1989. The others appointed at the appellate level were Alice Batchelder (Cincinnati), Susan H. Black (Atlanta), Karen Henderson (Washington, DC), Jane Richards Roth (Philadelphia), Ilana Diamond Rovner (Chicago), and Karen J. Williams (Richmond). Rovner is especially notable because she was born in Latvia and her mother fled from Nazis. Except for Black, who was appointed as a federal judge for the Northern District of Florida by Jimmy Carter, these women either had been initially appointed by Reagan or came directly from state courts or private practice.

At the district level, George H.W. Bush made 142 total appointments, 27 of whom were women. The most notable would be SONIA SOTOMAYOR, later named to the U.S. Supreme Court by President Barack Obama. Another woman whose appointment demonstrates the relative nonpartisanship of this administration was Susan Webber Wright, named as a district judge in Arkansas. In 1998, she dismissed the sexual harassment case that Paula Jones brought against President Bill Clinton. Despite his brief tenure, George H. W. Bush managed to have significant impact on the courts. His total of 192 judicial appointments during four years was just one fewer than Franklin Roosevelt had in more than twelve years.

CLINTON ADMINISTRATION AND BEYOND, 1993 TO 2011

Bill Clinton won the presidency in 1992, putting Democrats in the White House for the first time since Carter's defeat. Twelve years had passed since Sandra Day O'Connor joined the Supreme Court in 1981. During that time, Republican administrations had added five more men—a majority of the court. At the first opportunity, in August 1993, Clinton appointed RUTH BADER GINSBURG, the second woman on the highest court and its first Jewish woman. Her Senate confirmation vote was 96–3.

Clinton named significantly more women to executive offices than any previous president, and the same was true for judicial appointments.[6] In specialty courts, he chose two women for the U.S. Court of International Trade and one for the U.S. Tax Court, but his major contribution was the promotion of eighteen women to traditional appellate courts—more than twice as many as any predecessor. Six of Clinton's first ten appellate appointments were women, a record that no other president came close to matching.

At the district level, too, his very first appointments went to women, one of whom was Martha Vazquez, named as a federal judge in New Mexico. In total, women accounted for 82 of his 305 appointees at the district level. Not only did he begin to fulfill the promise of a government that "looked more like its people," but he also knew more of his judicial appointees personally, largely because of Hillary Rodham Clinton's long activism in national legal associations. Of Clinton's sixty-six appellate court appointees, sixteen endured the nervous tension of a roll call vote in the Senate, and of those sixteen, four were women.

Rosemary Barkett, a former nun whose parents were Syrian, had been the target of a recall from the Florida Supreme Court.[7] Her confirmation to the court in Atlanta was the closest among Clinton's female appointees, with a vote of 61–37. Sonia Sotomayor, who had Hispanic roots, drew only slightly less opposition. Her confirmation vote for the Manhattan-based court was 67–29. Marsha Siegel Berzon, who had a Jewish heritage, was approved 64–34 for the U.S. Court of Appeals for the Ninth Circuit, based in San Francisco. The least opposition among these roll calls was in the case of the only woman without an ethnic background viewed as different. Mary Margaret McKeown, called "Margaret," joined Marsha Berzon on the West Coast's U.S. appeals court. McKeown was confirmed by 80–11. It was not so much her personal résumé that forced her nomination into a roll call; some senators said that they wanted to send a message to the increasingly liberal San Francisco court.

Clinton was succeeded in 2001 by George W. Bush, son of the former president. The younger Bush had two

---

[6] See, especially, Chapter 11: Cabinet and Subcabinet and Chapter 12: Ambassadors.

[7] See Chapter 14: State Courts.

When interviewed in the summer of 2011, Rosemary Barkett had just returned from North Africa. As chair of one of the American Bar Association's (ABA) Rule of Law Initiatives, she led American attorneys who acted as advisers for developing judiciaries in Morocco, Tunisia, and Egypt. The Arab Spring had just occurred in Egypt, making it a particularly propitious time to encourage democratic, secular court systems.

Barkett traveled a long personal route to get to the point where she could lead an ABA entourage. Born in Mexico, she grew up in Miami, part of a Catholic family that encouraged her to enter a convent as a teenager. Moving from that cloistered life to the overwhelmingly male atmosphere of the University of Florida—where Gator football reigned supreme—was another major transition.

The Florida Supreme Court was all-male when she joined it in 1985. Asked how these men treated her, she responded: "They were extremely welcoming. I'm still amazed at that." Because all justices worked in the same Tallahassee building and saw each other daily, "it became really rather intimate, like a little family." Because, ethical restrictions limit the socializing that judges can do, they often entertained in each other's homes. With the men's wives and children joining in, it became "very comfortable, like an extended family. In retrospect," she added, "they were just very sweet."

The federal court to which she was elevated in 1993 differed. Its judges see each other only when the court formally convenes in Atlanta, Georgia. Members live and work throughout Alabama, Georgia, and Florida, leaving little opportunity to socialize or meet each other's families. Barkett spends most of her time in Miami, where she is an admitted workaholic who enjoys delving into new cases. Asked about the difference between state and federal courts, she replied that, although "the process is pretty much the same," federal law differs in fundamental ways from state law. She cited federal environmental law and intellectual property rights as interesting new challenges.

Discrimination against women, she said, is much more subtle now than it was when she began practicing law four decades ago. Nonetheless, she has noticed that both men and women remain much more likely to address female justices by their first names than they do with male justices.

When questioned about the paucity of women as ABA presidents, she explained that those most likely to rise to that position are the managing partners of large law firms. Being elected as a managing partner by peers who specialize in argumentation and competition, she concluded, still seems to require "a lot of testosterone." The situation, however, is improving (See Chapter 13).

For Barkett, the deepest satisfaction lies in the opportunity to develop new case law, "to think though the complexities that people face—and everything is complex. There often is validity to many sides of an issue, and my greatest reward is that I find this fascinating."

---

opportunities to appoint women to the Supreme Court. Instead, he chose Samuel A. Alito Jr. and John G. Roberts Jr. He elevated Roberts to chief justice upon William H. Rehnquist's death. Bush briefly nominated his personal attorney, Harriet Miers of Texas, to the Court, but she withdrew after encountering criticism of her slim qualifications. Sandra Day O'Connor retired soon after Bush's 2004 reelection, leaving Ruth Bader Ginsburg as the only woman among eight men.

In total, George W. Bush made 325 judicial appointments. Of these, 62 were at the appellate level, with 16 of the 62 being women. Although he nominated just one woman to a specialty court, that appointment set a precedent. Mary J. Schoelen was the first woman on the Court of Appeals for Veterans Claims. At the district level, 52 of his 261 appointees were women. Like his father, Bush was more apt to nominate women who were in private practice. None of his appellate choices was promoted from previous federal experience as a Clinton appointee.

Unlike his father, but like Bill Clinton, George W. Bush encountered opposition to his choices in the Senate. Five of his sixteen female appellate appointees faced roll call votes, a much higher percentage than any previous president. The first was in 2003, when Deborah L. Cook won her seat on the Akron-based court with a 66–25 tally. Whether or not it was related, Judge Cook also is noted for being the only woman to play on an otherwise all-male golf course in Ohio.

Other senators objected to Diane Schwerm Sykes, a Wisconsin judge who was appointed to the federal court based in Chicago. Her ex-husband was a controversial conservative radio host, her biggest negative in the confirmation process. She was confirmed in 2004 by a vote of 70–27. In May and June of 2005, Priscilla Owen and Janice Rogers Brown made the news. Owen's confirmation to the court based in New Orleans was held up by Democrats because of her association with petroleum companies and her anti-choice views. Brown, although African American, also was considered too conservative by some. Owen was approved on a 55–43 tally; Brown, 56–43.

Increased partisanship especially showed in the case of the era's last female appellate appointee, Helene White. A Michigan jurist, she waited more than a decade for the chance to serve on the appellate court based in Cincinnati. The Clinton administration nominated her in 1997, but Michigan Republican senator Spencer Abraham objected, and in his personal vendetta against Clinton, Abraham also blocked the 1999 nomination of Katherine McCree Lewis. Both women thus were pawns in another game, but Lewis died before the game was over.

George W. Bush renewed Clinton's 1997 nomination of the well-qualified Helene White, but it took until 2008, Bush's last year in office, for her to win the judgeship. Facing another election cycle, senators allowed White's confirmation to a new vacancy on the Cincinnati court by a 63–32 margin. Her nemesis was no longer in the Senate to oppose her, as Republican Abramson had lost his reelection to Democrat Deborah Ann Stabenow. The case demonstrates the power of an individual senator, especially one from a nominee's home state, to control judicial appointments.

Democrat Barack Obama defeated Republican John McCain in 2008, and among the precedents set by the nation's first African American president was the nomination of two women to the Supreme Court during his first two years in office. The two previous presidents who had appointed women to the highest level, Reagan and Clinton, appointed only one among several opportunities. Obama merited much credit from feminists for using both of his early chances to begin to balance the court by gender. George W. Bush had appointed no woman to the highest court during his eight years, and only Ruth Bader Ginsburg, a Clinton appointee, remained when Obama took office. He nominated Sonia Sotomayor in 2009 and, less than a year later, chose Elena Kagan.

Neither confirmation went smoothly, certainly nothing like the unanimous vote that Sandra Day O'Connor won in a less partisan 1981. Although she was an open Republican who had been in elective politics, no Democrats had opposed O'Connor, as Republicans did with Sotomayor and Kagan, who had been in the nonpartisan judicial system all of their lives. The point was particularly clear with Sotomayor, who was sufficiently nonpolitical that she initially was appointed to the federal bench by noted conservative Ronald Reagan. That fact was nearly forgotten as she went from one senatorial office to another, doing the necessary lobbying to earn the final tally of 68–31.

Elena Kagan came to the Supreme Court from the post of solicitor general, to which Obama had appointed her the previous year. The solicitor general leads the office that represents the United States before the Supreme Court, and Kagan was the first woman to hold the position. She attracted even more negative votes than Sotomayor, winning confirmation by a mere 63–37.

In addition to two women on the Supreme Court, Obama set a precedent by elevating the first woman to be chief justice of a specialty court. He appointed Emily C. Hewitt as chief of the U.S. Court of Federal Claims. This court, in Washington DC, differs from all others in that the United States is the defendant, not the prosecutor, and citizens may use it to sue for redress of monetary claims. In the centuries since its creation, no female voice ever had been heard on its bench. At the appellate level, Obama had appointed six women to the bench; as of early 2011, four were awaiting confirmation. Twenty-four of his district-level female appointees had been confirmed, while fifteen waited for Senate action.

Of those who were confirmed, none was opposed as seriously as were the women he named to the Supreme Court. Some senators may have sought publicity by speaking out on the highly visible appointees, while ignoring the less publicized nominations. With just one exception, none of the six confirmed appellate judges attracted any negative votes. The exception was Jane Branstetter Stranch, Obama's choice for the court based in Cincinnati. A Tennessean, her practice before federal courts had been on behalf of clients who lost their pensions due to reckless fiduciary managers, and twenty-one senators voted against her.

Of the thirty-nine women Obama named to district court benches, twenty-four were confirmed and fifteen were awaiting confirmation in early 2011. Only one drew serious senatorial debate. Benita Y. Pearson had served as a federal magistrate for the Northern District of Ohio and was confirmed as a judge on that court by a 56–39 tally. She was its first female African American judge, and although the majority of her bar association colleagues deemed her well qualified, just one Republican voted for her—Sen. George V. Voinovich of her home state.

Thus, as he headed into the second half of his first term, Barack Obama had nominated a total of forty-nine women to traditional courts, as well as two to the Supreme Court and one to a specialty court. That total of fifty-two women is a higher proportion than any previous president. As of early 2011, Obama had nominated 132 judges at all levels, meaning that almost four of every ten were women.

In the long view of the century, the United States had gone from no female judges at all in 1911 to near equality in 2011, at least in terms of new appointments at the lower levels. In 1911, a female defendant in a federal trial always faced an all-male jury, and she had no chance whatever of seeing the robed figure behind the bench as akin to herself. Her appellate brief would be considered only by men, and no one on the Supreme Court shared her life experience. In 2011, American women could foresee a future in which all courts, especially federal courts, truly would be composed of their peers.

PROFILES OF FEDERAL COURT JUDGES

*These women were all pioneers in the federal judiciary. **Burnita Shelton Matthews** was the first female federal trial judge. **Constance Baker Motley** was the first African American woman to be a federal trail judge. **Sandra Day O'Connor, Ruth Bader Ginsburg, Sonia Sotomayor,** and **Elena Kagan** the first women on the U.S. Supreme Court.*

RUTH BADER GINSBURG (1933–)

The second woman on the U.S. Supreme Court, Ruth Bader Ginsburg was born in Brooklyn, New York, to Jewish parents. Her mother succumbed to cancer when Ruth was a teen, and her only sibling, an older sister, also died young. She attended New York's Cornell University, where she majored in government, and graduated in 1954. She then was admitted to Harvard Law School, where she was one of nine women in a class of more than five hundred.

After marrying Martin Ginsburg, she moved to New York City and bore the first of two children before finishing her legal education at Columbia University, tying for valedictorian, in 1959. Ginsberg was the first woman to serve on the law review journals of two prestigious universities, Harvard and Columbia. In the 1960s, she learned Swedish to work on a study of Swedish judicial procedure.

While teaching at Rutgers University, she founded the women's rights section of the American Civil Liberties Union. Jimmy Carter appointed her to the appellate court in Washington, DC, in 1980, and she served there until President Bill Clinton appointed her to the Supreme Court in 1993, his first year in office. She was the second woman on the nine-member court and served with Sandra Day O'Connor until 2005, when O'Connor retired. She then was the court's only woman until 2009. Ginsberg's husband died in 2010, but she continues to serve on the nation's highest bench.

ELENA KAGAN (1960–)

The fourth woman on the U.S. Supreme Court and its youngest member, Elena Kagan was born in New York City to Jewish parents. She earned a distinguished education at three universities — Oxford, Princeton, and Harvard — and then clerked at both the appellate level in Washington, DC, and at the Supreme Court.

Kagan began teaching law at the University of Chicago in 1991 and, in 1995, became a policy adviser in the Clinton administration. In 1999, President Bill Clinton nominated her to the appellate court in Washington, DC, but Senate Judiciary Committee chair Orrin G. Hatch, Republican of Utah, refused to schedule a hearing, and the nomination expired at the end of Clinton's administration.

Students had insisted that the University of Chicago grant tenure to Kagan in 1995, but when the university refused to rehire her, she obtained a visiting professorship at Harvard Law School. Her colleagues there were more appreciative of her abilities, and in 2003, she became its first female dean.

Within days of his inauguration, President Barack Obama announced that he was appointing Kagan as solicitor general, the office that intervenes on behalf of the United States in virtually every case in which the federal government is a party. No woman had held this position before, and some of the men who did were controversial, especially Kenneth W. Starr at the end of the George H.W. Bush administration and Theodore Olson under George W. Bush. Senators particularly grilled Kagan about her views on gay rights, but they approved Obama's nomination of her for solicitor general by 61–31 on March 19, 2009.

The next year, Obama nominated Sonia Sotomayor to the Supreme Court, making her its third female member. No president ever had named two women at this highest level, but on April 9, 2010, Obama announced that he intended to elevate Elena Kagan from solicitor general to the Court. Her Senate confirmation vote was 63–37, with the tally largely on party lines—but two female Republican senators, Olympia J. Snowe and Susan Collins of Maine, supported Kagan. As of 2011, she still must recuse herself from some cases because they were filed under her name when she was solicitor general.

BURNITA SHELTON MATTHEWS (1894–1988)

Appointed by President Harry S. Truman to the federal district court in Washington, DC, Burnita Shelton Matthews was the first woman to preside over federal trials. Her 1949 appointment came later than that of Florence Allen in Ohio, whom Roosevelt appointed in 1934, but

Allen was at the appellate level, while Matthews served at the district level, where cases are tried.

A Mississippi native, she grew up with a knowledge of the judicial system because her father was the clerk of court for Copiah County. After her mother died when she was sixteen, she became the female head of a household with four brothers. Her father sent her to Cincinnati to train as a pianist—a suitable vocation for women, in his view—but, unlike Florence Allen, who did the same, Burnita Shelton was not seriously interested in music.

She had always wanted to be a lawyer, and she found her path when she married Percy Matthews and moved to Washington, DC, in 1917. She supported herself by working as a clerk for the Veterans Administration (VA). While her husband served in World War I, she took night classes at the National University Law School, which later became the George Washington University Law School. It was the same institution that initially refused to grant Belva Lockwood her degree in the 1870s.[8]

Women had made some progress in the fifty years since then, but after Matthews passed the bar examination and applied for admission to the bar association in the District of Columbia, her 1920 dues check was returned uncashed. Even though a number of women had practiced law in Washington at the time, Matthews had to fight for acceptance. The VA that had employed her as a clerk refused to hire her as an attorney, and so Matthews founded her own law firm with two other women.

Active with the era's National Woman's Party and a drafter of the 1923 Equal Rights Amendment, Matthews worked to include women on juries.[9] In this era of transition after the Nineteenth Amendment was ratified in 1920, she wrote a number of model legislative bills on women's legal rights that were adopted by state legislatures. She attended a 1926 meeting of the International Woman Suffrage Alliance in Paris and was president of the National Association of Women Lawyers in 1934. After Truman's precedent-setting appointment in 1949, Matthews served on the DC court for nearly twenty years. A number of high-profile cases passed through her courtroom, including a trial involving Teamsters leader Jimmy Hoffa in 1956.

The first woman on the federal bench, Ohio's Florence Allen, never married but devoted her whole life to the law. Burnita Matthews married but never had children. She was quoted as saying that a woman could not have both a legal career and children.

Judge Matthews took senior status in 1968, just prior to the death of her husband. In this semiretired position, she heard some significant cases, including one in 1971 in which she ruled that Social Security benefits to the disabled could not be terminated without a hearing. She died just short of her ninety-fourth birthday.

CONSTANCE BAKER MOTLEY (1921–2005)

The first black woman on the federal judiciary, Constance Baker Motley set a number of precedents.

Her parents had emigrated from the Caribbean island of Nevis, and she was one of the twelve children they raised in New Haven, Connecticut. While her mother reared the family, her father worked as a cook at Yale University. It would be years before Yale admitted any women, though, let alone a black woman. A New Haven man who was impressed with her academic ability paid her way to Fisk University, a historic black college in Nashville, Tennessee. She decided, though, that she preferred the racially integrated education of the Northeast and returned to earn degrees at New York University (1943) and Columbia University Law School (1946). Most of that period was during World War II, when many colleges opened doors to women because their classrooms were empty. Millions of college-age men were serving in the military.

A 1946 marriage changed her name, and she bore a son, Joel Motley III. She had volunteered for the National Association for the Advancement of Colored People (NAACP) as a student and began practicing law under the best of mentors: Thurgood Marshall, who, in 1967, would become the first African American on the U.S. Supreme Court. She was the first female attorney on the NAACP's legal staff in New York during the postwar era when the civil rights movement began, a time when it took real courage to file and argue a lawsuit based on race.

The NAACP took up the Topeka, Kansas, case of Linda Brown, a black girl who lived in an integrated neighborhood but was forced to attend a segregated school further from her home. Motley drafted the arguments for *Brown v. Board of Education* (1954), which, along with *Roe v. Wade* (1973), may be among the most important court cases in the twentieth century. The Court struck down state laws that mandated racial segregation in schools, and Motley went on to win other major civil rights victories. Among them was one involving Charlayne Hunter (later Gault), the first African American admitted to the University of Georgia, in 1961.

The Hunter case did not generate nearly as much publicity as did the 1962 case of James Meredith, who integrated the University of Mississippi. Motley successfully argued his case before the U.S. Supreme Court and soon became nationally known as an effective lawyer before the

---

8. See Chapter Thirteen: Introduction to the Judiciary.
9. See Chapter Seventeen: Special Interests.

highest court. She was not the first black woman admitted to argue before the Supreme Court—that had been Chicago's Violette Neatly Anderson in 1926—but the event still was so uncommon in 1962 that many media sources named Motley as the first. She won other similar cases, integrating both universities and public accommodations such as restaurants throughout the South.

Motley's political rise was even more meteoric than her legal career had been. A Democrat, she was the first black woman elected to the New York State Senate, and at the time, in 1964, she was the only female senator of any color in Albany. She resigned to accept the presidency of the Borough of Manhattan, to which she was unanimously elected in 1965. The next year, President Lyndon B. Johnson, who guided the historic 1964 Civil Rights Act through Congress, appointed Constance Baker Motley as the first black woman on the federal bench.

She served as a judge on the district court in Manhattan for the next twenty years, from her 1966 appointment to her retirement from full-time work in 1986. From 1982, she was its chief justice, again a milestone for black women. Throughout that period, many predicted that she would be the first African American woman on the U.S. Supreme Court, but that never happened. As of 2011, there still has been no black woman on the highest court. Constance Baker Motley died in New York at age eighty-four.

SANDRA DAY O'CONNOR (1930–)

The first woman on the U.S. Supreme Court, Sandra Day O'Connor inspired millions of young women.

Sandra Day grew up in isolated Arizona and later titled her biography *The Lazy B* (2002) for the family ranch. Because no high school was nearby, her family sent her to live with her grandmother in El Paso, Texas, where she graduated at age sixteen. She entered California's Stanford University and completed both college and law school in five years. A youthful but outstanding student, she was in the top 10 percent of her law school class and served on the law review journal. In 1952, she married John Jay O'Connor, who was still a law student. After working briefly, she accompanied him during his U.S. Army service to Germany. The couple had three sons.

In 1965, O'Connor returned to the full-time practice of law and became active in Republican politics. This resulted in an appointment to a vacancy in the Arizona Senate, where she succeeded another woman, in 1969. Appointed by Republican governor John Richard Williams, she was elected in her own right in 1970 and rose to be majority leader in just five years. She was not the

nation's first woman to hold this position, but she certainly was a pioneer among female leaders in state senates.[10]

O'Connor left the legislative branch of state government for the judicial branch after she won election in 1974 as a judge in Phoenix. Democratic governor Bruce Babbitt appointed her to the Arizona State Court of Appeals in 1979. A mere two years later, Republican president Ronald Reagan named her to the U.S. Supreme Court. Arguably other women had stronger credentials for this vacancy, but O'Connor's moderate record made her an acceptable choice to both ends of the political spectrum. A few on the far right briefly objected to her as insufficiently conservative, but the Senate confirmed her 99–0.

At age fifty-one, she was young by the standards of Supreme Court justices, but she was old enough to remember when she, a top graduate of a prestigious law school, was offered jobs only as a legal secretary. That kind of life experience, unshared by the Court's men, doubtless was a factor in moving O'Connor from the conservative intentions of some involved with her appointment to her later status as the court's swing vote.

She announced her retirement on July 1, 2005, and President George W. Bush appointed Samuel A. Alito Jr. to fill the vacancy, despite publicized opinions from first lady Laura Bush and others that O'Connor's seat be taken by another woman. In retirement, she served on the board of the Philadelphia museum dedicated to the history of the U.S. Constitution, as well as other groups. Her husband died in 2009, after suffering for two decades with Alzheimer's disease. She also worked for that cause.

SONIA SOTOMAYOR (1954–)

The third woman on the U.S. Supreme Court, Sonia Maria Sotomayor was its first Hispanic member.

She was born in New York City to Puerto Rican parents. Her father died when she was nine, and her mother had to support the family. She overcame these hardships to graduate with highest honors from Princeton University in 1976. She went on to Yale Law School, where she earned her degree in 1979 and was editor of the prestigious *Yale Law Review*. After five years as an assistant district attorney in New York City, she went into private practice but continued her advocacy on behalf of Hispanics. She was a board member on the Puerto Rican Legal Defense Fund.

President George H.W. Bush, a fellow Yale graduate, appointed Sotomayor to the court for the U.S. District Court for the Southern District of New York in 1991. Confirmed by the Senate, she served there until 1997,

---

[10.] See Chapter Six: State Senates.

when President Bill Clinton elevated her to the region's appellate court. Senate approval was slower this time but eventually came in 1998. Meanwhile, she also taught law at Columbia University and at New York University.

President Barack Obama named Sotomayor to the U.S. Supreme Court in May 2009, and she conducted personal interviews with many senators prior to her confirmation. The August 6 vote was 68–31, largely along party lines. Hispanics particularly rejoiced, and the Bronx housing development in which she grew up was renamed for her. As of 2011, Sotomayor can look forward to a long future on the highest court in the land.

REFERENCES AND FURTHER READING

Biskupic, Joan. 2005. *Sandra Day O'Connor: How the First Woman on the Supreme Court Became Its Most Influential Justice.* New York: ECCO.

Comiskey, Michael. 2004. *Seeking Justices: The Judging of Supreme Court Nominees.* Lawrence: University of Kansas Press.

Leahy, James E. 1999. *Supreme Court Justices Who Voted with the Government: Nine Who Favored the State over Individual Rights.* Jefferson, NC: McFarland and Co.

O'Connor, Sandra. 2003. *The Majesty of the Law: Reflections of a Supreme Court Justice.* New York: Random House.

Parry-Giles, Trevor. 2006. *The Character of Justice: Rhetoric, Law, and Politics in the Supreme Court Nomination Process.* East Lansing: Michigan State University Press.

Perry, Barbara Ann. 1991. *A Representative Supreme Court? The Impact of Race, Religion, and Gender on Appointments.* New York: Greenwood Press.

Songer, Donald R. 2000. *Continuity and Change on the United States Courts of Appeals.* Ann Arbor: University of Michigan Press.

16

POLITICAL PARTIES AND CONVENTIONS

The nation's founders wanted to avoid the creation of political parties, but already by the end of George Washington's presidency in 1797, rival factions had begun to emerge. The Federalist Party, which was centered on the political ideas of Alexander Hamilton and John Adams, supported a strong centralized government. Believing that concept too similar to the British monarchical structure they had rebelled against, Thomas Jefferson, James Madison, and others founded the Democratic-Republican Party (later the Democratic Party).[1]

Locally, parties often were based more on personalities than on ideology. For example, it was warring party bosses who in 1807 caused New Jersey women to lose the voting rights they briefly held.[2] At the national level, Federalists withered to the point that Democrat James Madison drew only one negative electoral vote in his 1820 reelection. Former Federalists evolved into Whigs, the American (Know-Nothing) Party, the Constitutional Union Party and others. Today's Republican Party began in the 1850s, but leaders of all parties long opposed women's right to vote.

Male politicians generally were correct in believing that women voters would lessen their power. Unlike many men, few women were willing to sell their vote for a shot of whisky, an exchange that was common in the nineteenth century, especially in immigrant sections of big cities and in frontier saloons. Parties created tickets of their candidates, and men, many of whom were illiterate, routinely voted according to ticket color or symbols, not by marking individual names on an unbiased ballot.

---

[1] Throughout this chapter, useful reference may be made to Chapter 10: Presidential and Vice Presidential Candidates, as well as Chapter 17: Interest Groups and Chapter 18: Political Action Committees.

[2] See Chapter 1: Battle for the Vote.

All across the country and well into the twentieth century, thousands of men in small towns aspired to be the local version of New York's William "Boss" Tweed, a Democrat, or Ohio's George "Boss" Cox, a Republican, two party leaders who were so powerful that they were near-dictators of their states. Party bosses achieved this power largely by controlling elections with patronage, especially government jobs. Bosses were a factor in presidential races, too, and the national party conventions that chose nominees thus were of great importance to such men. State parties selected their delegates to these conventions, and until the Nineteenth Amendment ensured women of the vote, virtually all delegates were male. For most of American history, national party conventions—which meet every four years—not only selected the presidential nominees, but also set policy, including many issues affecting women.

PIONEERS: FROM THE CIVIL WAR TO THE TWENTIETH CENTURY

The first American woman to play a highly visible part in party politics was JESSIE BENTON FREMONT, daughter of powerful Missouri senator Thomas Hart Benton and wife of John Charles Fremont, the first presidential nominee of the new Republican Party, in 1856. The young party created lapel buttons featuring her face and saying "Jessie and Our Fremont." Fremont would lose the election to Democrat James Buchanan of Pennsylvania. As president, Buchanan did so little to stop the looming Civil War that he was not even re-nominated in 1860.

That election marked a crucial turning point. It featured four candidates. The Democratic Party split into Northern and Southern factions, each with its own nominee, and the Constitutional Union Party also had a credible candidate,

Table 16.1 National Conventions of Major Political Parties, 1868–2008

Year	Party	Nominee	Location	Noteworthy Events
1868	Democratic	Horatio Seymour (NY)	New York, NY	Susan B. Anthony attended, the first of many for her
	Republican	Ulysses S. Grant (IL)	Chicago, IL	Susan B. Anthony attended
1872	Democratic	Horace Greeley (NY)	Baltimore, MD	Isabella Beecher Hooker and Laura de Force Gordon joined Anthony
	Republican	Ulysses S. Grant (IL)	Philadelphia, PA	Anthony, Hooker, and Gordon attended
1876	Democratic	Samuel Tilden (NY)	St. Louis, MO	Phoebe Couzins and Virginia Minor spoke to committee
	Republican	Rutherford B. Hayes (OH)	Cincinnati, OH	Couzins, Minor, Sara Andrews Spencer, and Elizabeth Boynton Harbert spoke to committee
1880	Democratic	Winfield Hancock (PA)	Cincinnati, OH	Suffragists presented platform plank to committee
	Republican	James A. Garfield (OH)	Chicago, IL	Suffragists presented platform plank to committee
1884	Democratic	Grover Cleveland (NY)	Chicago, IL	Cleveland won, despite issue of his youthful illegitimate fatherhood
	Republican	James G. Blaine (ME)	Chicago, IL	Employed anti-suffragist ghostwriter Mary Abigail Dodge
1888	Democratic	Grover Cleveland (NY)	St. Louis, MO	Cleveland's marriage to a much younger woman became an issue
	Republican	Benjamin Harrison (IN)	Chicago, IL	Convention adopted a plank regarding the vote but did not apply it to women
1892	Democratic	Grover Cleveland (NY)	Chicago, IL	Campaign featured first lady Frances Folsom Cleveland on posters
	Republican	Benjamin Harrison (IN)	Minneapolis, MN	First female delegate, Wyoming's Theresa A. Jenkins
1896	Democratic	William Jennings Bryan (NE)	Chicago, IL	Female delegates from Utah, including Dr. Martha Hughes Cannon, a state senator
	Republican	William McKinley (OH)	St. Louis, MO	Lillie Devereux Blake and J. Ellen Foster spoke to committee
1900	Democratic	William Jennings Bryan (NE)	Kansas City, MO	Elizabeth M. Cohen of Utah seconded Bryan's nomination
	Republican	William McKinley (OH)	Philadelphia, PA	Colorado and Idaho sent female delegates
1904	Democratic	Alton B. Parker (NY)	St. Louis, MO	Women spoke to committee with no result
	Republican	Theodore Roosevelt (NY)	Chicago, IL	Women spoke to committee with no result
1908	Democratic	William Jennings Bryan (NE)	Denver, CO	Anna Howard Shaw led effort for party endorsement of suffrage
	Republican	William Howard Taft (OH)	Chicago, IL	First female electoral college member, Utah's Margaret Zane Cherdon
1912	Democratic	Woodrow Wilson (NJ)	Baltimore, MD	"Daisy" Harriman and other women worked for Wilson
	Republican	William Howard Taft (OH)	Chicago, IL	Had the least support among feminists
	Progressive	Theodore Roosevelt (NY)	Chicago, IL	Chicago's Jane Addams seconded the nomination
1916	Democratic	Woodrow Wilson (NJ)	St. Louis, MO	Large demonstration remembered as "the golden lane"; convention endorsed the vote for women
	Republican	Charles Evans Hughes (NY)	Chicago, IL	Huge parade, but the plank adopted was equivocal
1920	Democratic	James M. Cox (OH)	San Francisco, CA	Izetta Jewell Brown of West Virginia seconded nomination; adoption of "equal division"
	Republican	Warren G. Harding (OH)	Chicago, IL	Suffrage plank; seven women appointed to the Republican National Committee
1924	Democratic	John W. Davis (WV)	New York, NY	Lena Jones Wade Springs of South Carolina chaired Credentials Committee; her name and that of West Virginia's Izetta Jewell Brown were placed in nomination for vice president
	Republican	Calvin Coolidge (MA)	Cleveland, OH	African American Hallie Q. Brown spoke

Table 16.1 (Continued)

Year	Party	Nominee	Location	Noteworthy Events
1928	Democratic	Al Smith (NY)	Houston, TX	First Catholic nominee; Eleanor Roosevelt network developed
	Republican	Herbert Hoover (CA)	Kansas City, MO	No notable feminist achievements
1932	Democratic	Franklin D. Roosevelt (NY)	Chicago, IL	Strongly supported by Democratic Women's Clubs, led by Molly Dewson
	Republican	Herbert Hoover (CA)	Chicago, IL	Ruth Hanna McCormick and Alice Roosevelt Longworth led women for Hoover
1936	Democratic	Franklin D. Roosevelt (NY)	Philadelphia, PA	Landslide victory empowered many women, especially Dewson
	Republican	Alfred M. Landon (KS)	Cleveland, OH	Disastrous loss brings Marion Martin of Maine to try to organize Republican women
1940	Democratic	Franklin D. Roosevelt (NY)	Chicago, IL	Eleanor Roosevelt mediated dispute over vice presidency
	Republican	Wendell Wilkie (NY)	Philadelphia, PA	Platform was isolationist, which encouraged "mother's clubs" opposed to Roosevelt
1944	Democratic	Franklin D. Roosevelt (NY)	Chicago, IL	Endorsed the Equal Rights Amendment; Dorothy Vredenburgh Bush became longtime secretary
	Republican	Thomas E. Dewey (NY)	Chicago, IL	Endorsed the Equal Rights Amendment
1948	Democratic	Harry S. Truman (MO)	Philadelphia, PA	India Edwards delivers keynote speech
	Republican	Thomas E. Dewey (NY)	Philadelphia, PA	Push to the right led by anticommunist Betty Farrington
1952	Democratic	Adlai E. Stevenson (IL)	Chicago, IL	India Edwards delivers another keynote, becoming the first woman to make two; Edwards also was nominated for vice president
	Republican	Dwight D. Eisenhower (NY)	Chicago, IL	Eisenhower won votes from women because he supported military women in World War II
1956	Democratic	Adlai E. Stevenson (IL)	Chicago, IL	Women regressed from the days of Roosevelt and Truman
	Republican	Dwight D. Eisenhower (PA)	San Francisco, CA	No notable feminist achievements
1960	Democratic	John F. Kennedy (MA)	Los Angeles, CA	Patsy Takemoto Mink of Hawaii spoke for minorities; platform featured strong civil rights plank
	Republican	Richard M. Nixon (CA)	Chicago, IL	Platform included an antidiscrimination plank
1964	Democratic	Lyndon B. Johnson (TX)	Atlantic City, NJ	Fannie Lou Hamer of Mississippi led credentials fight for blacks
	Republican	Barry Goldwater (AZ)	San Francisco, CA	Margaret Chase Smith of Maine ran for president
1968	Democratic	Hubert H. Humphrey (MN)	Chicago, IL	Violent convention; Shirley Chisholm of New York led women and blacks
	Republican	Richard M. Nixon (CA)	Miami, FL	Some violence; rule reform for minority outreach
1972	Democratic	George S. McGovern (SD)	Miami, FL	Jean Miles Westwood of Utah chaired the Democratic National Committee
	Republican	Richard M. Nixon (CA)	Miami, FL	Anne Legendre Armstrong of Texas made keynote address
1976	Democratic	Jimmy Carter (GA)	New York, NY	Corinne Claiborne "Lindy" Boggs of Louisiana was the first woman to preside at a convention
	Republican	Gerald R. Ford (MI)	Kansas City, MO	Mary Louise Smith of Iowa chaired the Republican National Committee
1980	Democratic	Jimmy Carter (GA)	New York, NY	Feminists split between Carter and Kennedy factions
	Republican	Ronald Reagan (CA)	Detroit, MI	Party drops the Equal Rights Amendment from platform; had been included since 1944

(Continued)

Table 16.1 (Continued)

Year	Party	Nominee	Location	Noteworthy Events
1984	Democratic	Walter F. Mondale (MN)	San Francisco, CA	Martha Layne Collins presided; Geraldine A. Ferraro chosen for vice president
	Republican	Ronald Reagan (CA)	Dallas, TX	Keynote speech by U.S. Treasurer Katherine Ortega
1988	Democratic	Michael S. Dukakis (MA)	Atlanta, GA	Popular keynote by Ann W. Richards of Texas; Susan Estrich managed campaign
	Republican	George H.W. Bush (TX)	New Orleans, LA	Pro-choice women made unsuccessful attempt to change platform
1992	Democratic	Bill Clinton (AR)	New York, NY	Ann W. Richards presided; Barbara Jordan, an African American, gave keynote speech
	Republican	George H.W. Bush (TX)	Houston, TX	Marilyn Quayle, wife of Vice President Dan Quayle, spoke
1996	Democratic	Bill Clinton (AR)	Chicago, IL	Hillary Rodham Clinton spoke, the first first lady to do so
	Republican	Bob Dole (KS)	San Diego, CA	Keynote address by Susan Molinari of New York
2000	Democratic	Al Gore (TN)	Los Angeles, CA	Campaign manager was Donna Brazile, an African American
	Republican	George W. Bush (TX)	Philadelphia, PA	Speakers included Elaine L. Chao, Elizabeth Dole, and Condoleezza Rice
2004	Democratic	John Kerry (MA)	Boston, MA	Fewer women featured than in the past
	Republican	George W. Bush (TX)	New York, NY	First lady Laura Bush spoke
2008	Democratic	Barack Obama (IL)	Denver, CO	House Speaker Nancy Pelosi of California presided
	Republican	John McCain (AZ)	St. Paul, MN	Sarah Palin chosen for vice president

Source: Compiled by author.

but Abraham Lincoln gave the Republican Party its first victory. He did not win a majority of the popular vote, but when the electoral college met in December, it gave him 180 of its 303 votes. Within days, Southern states began seceding from the Union, forming the Confederate States of America.

Republicans promised an end to the expansion of slavery in territories but did not promise to end slavery in the states where it existed. Abolitionists, including many prominent women, worked to force Lincoln to adopt a stance of full emancipation. Under the umbrella of their Loyal League, Susan B. Anthony and Elizabeth Cady Stanton collected almost 400,000 petitions that both proclaimed loyalty to the Union and urged Lincoln to abolish slavery everywhere. These politically astute women also charged a penny per petition, which not only gave them their first significant funding, but also created an invaluable file of contacts.

Lincoln won reelection in 1864, although the Democratic nominee, former Union general George McClellan, won an appreciable number of the all-Northern, all-male voters. Lincoln was assassinated the next year, and Vice President Andrew Johnson took office. After his own Republican Party impeached him, he was not a candidate in 1868. War hero Ulysses S. Grant won the 1868 presidential election, and most feminists worked for him and the Republican ticket. As Massachusetts author Harriet Hanson Robinson wrote of the election, "Republican women did as much effective work during the campaign as if each one had been 'a man and a voter.' They did everything but vote. All this agitation was a benefit to the Republican party, but not to woman suffrage" (Stanton, Anthony, and Gage 1886, 279).

Grant was reelected in 1872, and most feminists continued to think of themselves as Republicans – even though the Democratic nominee was New York journalist Horace Greeley, a longtime supporter of women's rights and other progressive causes. By then, though, he had quarreled with Elizabeth Cady Stanton and other "radical" suffragists over the Fifteenth Amendment, which granted black men the vote but was interpreted to deny it to women of any race.[3] Although Anthony had attended the 1872 Democratic National Convention in Baltimore in hopes of reaching out to that party, Republicans ensured Anthony's loyalty by hiring her as a speaker, and she campaigned against her former friend Greeley.

---

[3] See Chapter 1: Battle for the Vote.

The Republican Party was threatened with a schism that year, with "Liberal Republicans" holding a convention in Cincinnati while "Republicans" convened in Philadelphia. According to Anthony, pressure to avoid this internal split forced "the first mention of woman in the platform of either of the great political parties." A plank read:

The Republican party, mindful of its obligation to the loyal women of America, expresses its gratification that wider avenues of employment have been open to women, and it further declares that her demands for additional rights should be treated with respectful consideration. (Stanton, Anthony, and Gage 1882, 317)

According to Anthony, "Philadelphia has spoken and woman is no longer ignored" (Stanton, Anthony, and Gage 1882, 317).

Liberal Republicans pointed out that this vague statement promised nothing. Some even joined Democrats in supporting Greeley, who had a much longer history of supporting minorities. Anthony, however, stayed with the main Republican group and Grant. Even though she "recognized" the "meagerness" of the plank, she saw it as "promising" (Stanton, Anthony, and Gage 1882, 317). Indeed, it would be the best that national party conventions offered to feminists for a long time.

Feminists not only made a great demonstration at the July the Fourth centennial in Philadelphia, but also at the 1876 national political conventions. Matilda Joslyn Gage drafted separate resolutions that were presented to each party, tailoring the points to be most effective to the men of each.[4] Republicans nominated Rutherford B. Hayes of Ohio. In the fall 1876 election, he lost the popular vote to Democratic Samuel Tilden of New York by 4,300,590 to 4,036,298. Stunned by their first loss since 1860, congressional Republicans created a special commission that nullified some of the ballots, especially in the former Confederacy, and the electoral college awarded the presidency to Hayes by 185–184. Feminists hoped that Republican first lady Lucy Hayes would endorse their platform, but she never did.

Despite their inability to vote, women played a sufficiently important part in politics that both major parties established convention committees on women's rights in 1880. No results of these committee hearings made it into party platforms, but speaking to such committees constituted another milestone. Representatives of the National Woman Suffrage Association (NWSA) sent delegates to the conventions of four parties in 1880.

Susan B. Anthony led seventy-six NWSA members to the Republican convention in Chicago, Illinois. They were welcomed at the city's great hotel, the Palmer House, operated by multimillionaire feminist Bertha Honore Palmer. Attorney Belva Lockwood drafted a resolution to put a plank in the Republican platform: "Resolved, That we pledge ourselves to secure to women the exercise of their right to vote."[5] A delegate from Arkansas offered it to the convention. Anthony reported that "not only were the Arkansas delegation of Republicans favorable to the recognition of women . . . but Southern delegates were largely united in their demand" (Stanton, Anthony, and Gage 1886, 177–178). Republicans in the South in that era were liberals, however, and they were easily outmaneuvered by the conservatives who increasingly dominated the party in other states.

Many of the feminists who attended the Chicago Republican convention also attended the Democratic one in Cincinnati, where Anthony said they were "better treated" (Stanton, Anthony, and Gage 1886, 181). Democrats gave them reserved seats, free headquarters space, and a committee hearing with no time limit. But, she reported, "although the platform committee sat until 2 A.M., no result was reached . . . [because], it was said, of the objection of the extreme Southern element which feared the political recognition of negro [sic] women."[6] Anthony nonetheless sat on the Democratic dais, while a clerk read a lengthy resolution written by Matilda Joslyn Gage.

Some women also attended the 1880 convention of the Greenback Party, which promoted putting more money into circulation by taking the dollar off the gold standard. Others went to the convention of the Prohibition Party, where they had been specifically invited and received the most serious political attention. Even that party, however, did not add a feminist plank to its platform. Anthony paid a personal visit to the Ohio home of Republican nominee James A. Garfield to lobby him, but that also was to no avail.

Garfield was assassinated by Charles Guiteau, a mentally ill former supporter who was not given a patronage job that he thought he deserved, and Vice President Chester A. Arthur became president in 1881. Arthur did not win his party's nomination in 1884; instead Republicans chose James G. Blaine. He became the first Republican to lose the White House in the twenty-four years since Abraham Lincoln won it in 1860. The margin was very narrow, as Democratic nominee Grover Cleveland won 4,874,986 votes to Blaine's 4,851,981. The electoral

---

[4] See Chapter 1: Battle for the Vote.

[5] See Chapter 13: Pioneers in the Judiciary.
[6] See Chapter 1: Battle for the Vote.

At the 1880 Republican National Convention in Chicago, pioneer attorney Belva Lockwood of Washington, DC, presented this "memorial," requesting that the attendees reconsider their position on woman suffrage.

To the Republican Party in Convention assembled, Chicago, June 2, 1880:

Seventy-six delegates from local, State, and National suffrage associations, representing every section of the United States, are here to-day to ask you to place the following plank in your platform:

Resolved, That we pledge ourselves to secure to women the exercise of their right to vote.

We ask you to pledge yourselves to protect the rights of one-half of the American people, and thus carry your own principles to their logical results. The thirteenth amendment of 1865, abolishing slavery, the fourteenth of 1867, defining citizenship, and the fifteenth of 1870, securing United States citizens in their right to vote . . . stand as enduring monuments. . . . But the great duty remains of securing to woman her right to have her opinions on all questions counted at the ballot box.

You cannot live on the noble words and deed of those who inaugurated the Republican party. . . . You must have a new, vital issue to rouse once more the enthusiasm of the people. Our question of human rights answers this demand. The two great political parties are alike . . . upon general questions. . . .

The essential point in which you differ from the Democratic party is national supremacy [as opposed to states' rights], and it is on this very issue we make our demand. . . . [We] ask that our rights as United States citizens be secured by an amendment to the national constitution. . . . Your pledge to enfranchise ten millions of women will rouse an enthusiasm which must count in the coming closely contested election. But above expediency is right, and to do justice is ever the highest political wisdom." (Stanton, Anthony, and Gage 1886, 177–178)

Many things have changed since Lockwood's time, especially the reversal of the parties on states' rights. That was a Democratic priority in the nineteenth century, but it became a Republican rallying crying in the mid- and late twentieth century. Lockwood's basic point, however, remains as ever: The best advice for politicians—even when controversies are hot and the majority may not agree—is to do what is equitable and just.

---

college tally, however, was 219 to 182. Newspaper columnist Mary Abigail Dodge was a longtime ghostwriter for Blaine. Dodge was not a suffragist, and neither major-party candidate had much appeal for feminists.

The Prohibition Party first endorsed the vote for women at its 1884 convention. Many women considered this a victory, but it was a negative, not a positive, with the two major parties. Both were strongly influenced by the liquor lobby, and in endorsing enfranchisement, Prohibitionists seemed to prove what the major parties feared—that female voters would outlaw alcohol.

The presidential tables turned in 1888, as Republican Benjamin Harrison ousted Democrat Cleveland from the White House. Susan B. Anthony's aide, Ida Husted Harper, said "women were wholly disregarded" at the Republican conventions in 1880 and 1884. Their hopes briefly rose in 1888, when delegates adopted a plank that stated: "We recognize the . . . right of every lawful citizen to cast one free ballot in all public elections." Suspecting that this was aimed at black men rather than women, "the leaders of the woman suffrage movement at once telegraphed to Chicago . . . , asking if this statement was intended to include 'lawful women citizens.'" The convention chairman wired back, "I do not think the platform is so construed." (Anthony and Harper 1902, 436).

Male voters reversed themselves in 1892, and Cleveland returned to the White House after defeating Harrison. The most notable thing from a feminist perspective about the 1892 Republican convention was the first presence of a voting female delegate. She was Theresa A. Jenkins of Wyoming, a largely Republican state. Women in the Wyoming Territory had won the vote in 1869, but although women were elected at the state level, none was a convention delegate until after statehood. Wyoming was admitted as a state in 1890, and Jenkins was a delegate in 1892, the first opportunity. That convention was held in Minneapolis, and Susan B. Anthony led a successful effort for a plank that endorsed the vote for "every citizen, be he rich or poor, native or foreign, black or white" (Anthony and Harper 1902, 436). Republicans chose to take the "he" seriously, and as the plank did not mention women, it was another hollow victory.

The Rev. Dr. Anna Howard Shaw accompanied Anthony to Omaha in 1892, where the Progressive Party had its first convention. Feminists had high hopes for this ideologically compatible new party, but "to their amazement they were refused permission even to appear before on the Committee on Resolutions, a courtesy which by this time was usually extended at all political conventions" (Anthony and Harper 1902, 437). The rejection may have been a personal jab against Easterners Anthony and Shaw.

Other women, especially from the inland states where Progressives were best organized, were delegates and sat on committees at conventions in both 1892 and 1896. The Progressive Party convention achieved a milestone in 1892 by adopting a plank supporting "equal rights . . . for all men and women" (Anthony and Harper 1902, 438). Mary Ellen Lease of Kansas, famous for her advice to farmers to "raise less corn and more hell," was one of the party's most popular speakers.

The 1896 Democratic convention was historic, as the party took a decided turn to the left, adopting many Progressive Party goals and nominating populist William Jennings Bryan of Nebraska. Many women supported Bryan, including wealthy Bertha Honore Palmer, who sat on the dais when Bryan made his famous "Cross of Gold" speech, deriding bankers and capitalists while supporting farmers and the working class. Utah women were the first delegates to a Democratic convention. They had won the vote and lost it, but with statehood in 1896, women were voting delegates to that year's convention. Among them was Dr. Martha Hughes Cannon, who voted differently from her husband.[7]

At the 1896 Republican convention, Lillie Devereux Blake and J. Ellen Foster spoke to the Resolutions Committee on behalf of women's right to vote. A New Yorker, Blake had been active in the suffrage movement for decades, while Foster had roots in the conservative wing of the Women's Christian Temperance Union (WCTU). When Foster split with progressive WCTU president Frances Willard, Republican politico James Clarkson hired her as a speaker in 1888.[8] He authorized Foster's creation of the National Woman's Republican Association, which was not truly a grass-roots organization, but a vehicle for Republican men to reach out to women. Funded by John D. Rockefeller Jr., Foster even went to Ireland to deliver her antialcohol message. She spoke to more issues than temperance and women's rights and ran her pro-business operation with "a secretary, a publicity director, and 300 field workers. Republican leaders apparently covered all expenses, including travel funds and elegant headquarters in New York" (Edwards 1997, 84).

The major parties conducted very different races in 1896. Bryan campaigned vigorously across the nation, while Republican nominee William McKinley stayed at his Ohio home, conducting a front-porch style campaign—and won. The Republican strategist was Mark Hanna, and his daughter, Ruth Hanna McCormick, would be elected to Congress from Illinois in 1928, in the

same year that William Jennings Bryan's daughter, Ruth Bryan Owen, was elected from Florida.[9] Of the two young women named Ruth, Bryan played the stronger role in the 1896 campaign. Democrats nominated her father again in 1900 but, again, McKinley defeated him.

Just months later, the postwar generation suffered its third presidential assassination, when an anarchist shot McKinley. Theodore Roosevelt thus became president in 1901. A Roosevelt presidency never was desired by Mark Hanna and other Republican insiders. When they engineered Roosevelt's vice presidential nomination, it was because they wanted to end his activist governorship of New York, not because they hoped he would lead the party, much less the country. Nevertheless, Roosevelt became the most modern of presidents to that point, although his political ideology still did not include endorsing women's right to vote.

THE CRUCIAL DECADES, 1900–1920

The century started with a milestone at the 1900 Democratic convention, when delegate Elizabeth M. Cohen of Utah had the honor of seconding the nomination of William Jennings Bryan. A married woman, Cohen is another player in women's history whose biography is in need of more research. Works on Jewish women mention her, and Jane Addams also referred to Cohen in 1912, when Addams became the second woman to second a presidential nomination.

Despite his defiance of party insiders, Theodore Roosevelt proved so popular with voters that the 1904 Republican convention had no choice but to nominate him. Democrats chose Alton B. Parker of New York. He would lose the election by more than two million votes. Third-party candidates also garnered significant votes that year, especially Socialist Eugene V. Debs, even though he was in prison on election day. Women's right to political participation was an inherent part of Socialist philosophy, and its platform said so from the party's American beginning in 1901.

Most feminists supported Roosevelt in 1904, not so much because he was a Republican, but because he was a progressive. Although he never endorsed women's right to vote, he did invite Susan B. Anthony to the White House. At the 1904 convention nominating Roosevelt, five women spoke to the relevant committee, but ultimately their words had no impact on the party platform. They were Harriet Taylor Upton and Elizabeth Hauser of Ohio,

---

[7] See Chapter 5: State Senators.

[8] For more on the WCTU and Willard's biography, see Chapter 17: Interest Groups.

[9] See Chapter 6: United States Representatives.

Chicago attorney Catherine Waugh McCulloch, and two ordained clergy women, the Reverends Celia Parker Wooley of Massachusetts and Olympia Brown of Michigan. At the Democratic convention, delegates heard from Kate Gordon of New Orleans, Priscilla Hackstaff of New York, and Louise Worth of St. Louis, with the same polite but ineffectual result.

Suffragists organized better in 1908, and women at the Republican convention were led by Jane Addams. Samuel Gompers, president of the American Federation of Labor, spoke on behalf of a plank endorsing female enfranchisement but "was ignored" (Harper 1922, 5:703). At the Democratic convention, suffragists were sufficiently visible that thousands of people, mostly male delegates, received a lengthy written appeal on arrival. It was signed by the Rev. Dr. Anna Howard Shaw and other prominent women, but again feminists were unsuccessful. In the fall, Republican candidate William Howard Taft defeated William Jennings Bryan. This was the last time that Democrats chose the great orator as their nominee.

The 1912 election changed everything. Dissatisfied with his successor, Theodore Roosevelt bolted to the Progressive Party. Republicans renominated Taft, and Democrats chose New Jersey governor Woodrow Wilson. Women worked in all three campaigns, but they were least active for Republican Taft. At the GOP convention, Wisconsin senator Robert M. La Follette, whose wife, Belle La Folette, worked hard for the vote, presented a suffrage plank. It was voted down, and two days later, the La Follettes and other liberal Republicans joined Theodore Roosevelt in the Progressive Party.

Progressives held their official convention in August, and Jane Addams seconded Roosevelt's nomination. In addition to endorsing the vote, the party included women on committees. Roosevelt initially proposed a national referendum to determine whether or not women wanted to vote, but Sen. Albert Beveridge of Indiana prevailed, arguing "votes are theirs as a matter of natural right" (Harper 1922, 5:706).

Because of this split between liberal and conservative Republicans, Wilson became the first Democrat to win the White House in twenty years. The Democratic platform did not endorse the vote, and suffragists Anna Howard Shaw and Dora Lewis had such difficulty getting a hearing that Lewis later became a leader in the anti-Wilson National Woman's Party.[10] At the same time, though, many women supported the intellectual and reformist Wilson, formerly president of Princeton University. "Daisy" Harriman worked especially hard for his nomination, and

he would reward her with a significant federal appointment. She went on to be the nation's second female ambassador.[11]

No one agonized over the 1912 election more than Alice Roosevelt Longworth. The daughter of Teddy Roosevelt, she married Cincinnati representative Nicholas Longworth at the White House in 1906. He not only was less progressive than his father-in-law, but also was very close to Ohio's powerful Taft family, with President William Howard Taft as a registered voter in Longworth's district. Father and son-in-law viewed the split in the Republican Party pragmatically, and together, they asked Alice to sit out the campaign. She wanted to campaign for Progressives, but her in-laws strongly opposed her father and his new party, so she suffered miserable months in the Longworths' Cincinnati home for her husband's sake. Like her father, her husband lost to the Democratic nominee. Although his career recovered, their marriage was damaged. Not surprisingly, she never was accepted in the town she called "Cincin-nasty" (Cordery 2007, 224).

Ohio women did not win the vote, but women elsewhere formed a substantial voting bloc by the 1916 election. They had full rights in eleven states, all in the West, as well as the right to vote for president in several others. Illinois granted women presidential suffrage in 1913, and other states soon emulated that half-loaf approach, probably because allowing women to vote in presidential elections only was an easy way for state politicians to placate women without threatening their own positions. By the time Wilson ran for reelection in 1916, enough women could vote in the presidential race that both parties had to pay attention.

Carrie Chapman Catt organized a massive demonstration in Chicago, where Republicans met. Despite cold, rain, and wind, some twenty-five thousand women marched through Grant Park to the convention. Feminist Ida Husted Harper wrote:

Just as Mrs. A. J. George of Brookline, Massachusetts was asserting, "there is no widespread demand for woman suffrage," hundreds of drenched and dripping women began to pour into the hall. . . . Thousands of converts were made among those who witnessed the courage and devotion of the women in facing this storm. Representatives of the National American Woman Suffrage Association had a half hour [at the committee hearing], the National Association Opposed to Woman Suffrage the next half hour, and the Congressional Union a final half hour. . . .

The strongest possible influence was brought to bear by the party leaders. . . . Nevertheless it carried by 26 to 21. Within a half hour defeat again threatened when seven absent members

[10] See Chapter 1: Battle for the Vote and Chapter 17: Interest Groups.

[11] For Harriman's biography, see Chapter 12: Ambassadors.

The terms "liberal" and "conservative" have been used as labels for several decades, but it seldom is pointed out that views can vary even within the same person. One can hold conservative views about politics or economics, while behaving as a social liberal—or vice versa. Cousins Eleanor Roosevelt and Alice Roosevelt Longworth are the perfect illustration. Alice was conservative in her political and economic views, but so liberal that she was nearly libertine in her behavior. Eleanor was the opposite, a liberal in economics and politics, but conservative in her lifestyle.

Although part of aristocratic New York society, they had similarly sad childhoods. Alice's mother died on the day she was born, and her mourning father, future president Theodore Roosevelt, absented himself from her early childhood. Eleanor's mother also died when she was very young, and with an alcoholic father, she was reared by a disapproving maternal grandmother. She did have the advantage of being sent to Europe for finishing school, where she found role models in her teachers.

Alice grew into a rebellious teenager, so much so that her father famously said he could either govern the country or govern Alice, but he could not do both. She invited friends to smoke cigarettes on the White House roof, drank champagne at all-night parties, and drove her new car at dangerous speeds in the exclusive summer resort town of Newport, Rhode Island. She played poker with men and, most notoriously, bet at a racetrack where photographers snapped her. Nor did her behavior become more cautious as she aged. When, after two decades of marriage to Republican representative Nicholas Longworth, she bore her first child, almost no one believed that he was the father.

Thus, despite their similar backgrounds, the cousins—who never were very close—evolved into very different political beings. Alice enjoyed politics, but for her it was a game, a highly personal one that was not based in a strong or consistent philosophy. Known for her biting wit and behind-the-scenes power, she would be a dominant Washington, DC, presence for decades. Invitations to her home were more sought after than invitations to the White House.

Eleanor avoided politics as a young wife, and she never saw it as a game. She honed her skills after Franklin was crippled by polio in the 1920s, and she traveled as his "eyes and ears." Friendships with reformers such as Frances Perkins and Molly Dewson led her deeper into activism on behalf of the downtrodden, while Alice frequently belittled reformers. Eleanor's economic and political views were generously liberal, but her social philosophy was conservative. She believed, for example, that men should be paid well enough that women could avoid paid employment and make children their priority. She did not smoke and dressed traditionally, but she also socialized with other cultures and classes—people who never would be invited to Alice's salons.

Thus, two girls reared in the same tradition evolved differently, but both were strong influences in defining their parties. Eleanor did far more to organize Democratic women, yet Alice arguably had more influence with the men of her party. She attended conventions, and some say that the phrase denoting insider politics—"smoke-filled room"—originated at her hotel suite when Republican leaders settled on Ohio's Warren G. Harding as the 1920 presidential nominee.

Alice did not admire Harding, but the compromise was consistent with her philosophy, in which the primary goal was winning the party game. Eleanor in contrast, was quite nonpartisan and said many good things in her numerous publications about Republican women who shared her views. Alice thus provided a role model for the social liberation of the Roaring Twenties, while Eleanor was a model for expansion of political and economic democracy during the Great Depression and World War II.

of the committee came and asked for reconsideration. After repeated parlays . . . , the final vote was 35 to 11. . . . But it read, "The Republican party . . . favors the extension of the suffrage to women but recognizes the right of each State to settle this question for itself." (Harper 1922, 5:710–711)

Again, this was a hollow victory for Republican women, in the sense that Democratic President Wilson and most of his cabinet had endorsed the vote for women in 1915. Democratic women took nothing for granted, however, and they made a huge demonstration at the 1916 convention in St. Louis. Called "the golden lane," six thousand women dressed in yellow and white formed a lane between the convention hall and the major hotel. In addition, "on the steps of the Art Museum . . . were women in black typifying the non-suffrage States; those in gray representing the partial suffrage States; those in red, white, and blue representing the States where political equality prevailed" (Harper 1922, 6:349). The chief manager of this brilliant stroke of publicity was Emily Newell Blair, a Missouri journalist and Democratic Party activist.

Despite the show, some men still objected, and debate on the issue lasted all night. When the Resolutions Committee adjourned at 7:15 A.M., the plank was a full endorsement of female enfranchisement. When it went to the floor, "yells and catcalls were met with the cheers of the women who filled the gallery and waved their banners and yellow parasols" (Harper 1922, 5:713). When a minority report, signed by only four of the fifty-member committee, was rejected 888 to 181, Democratic women knew their victory was complete.

Led by Alice Paul, the Congressional Union Party, later called the National Woman's Party, nonetheless continued to demonstrate against Wilson—to the point that some feminists thought that it was a secret arm of the Republican Party.[12] Among those who voiced this suspicion was Democrat Mary Baird Bryan, wife of William Jennings Bryan, who worked hard for the vote after the adoption of the 1916 Democratic platform.

In 1917, New York became the first Eastern state to enfranchise women, and in 1918, the Midwestern states of Michigan, Oklahoma, and South Dakota followed. With presidential rights in still more states, both parties were forced to focus on women at their 1920 conventions. By June 1919, both houses of Congress had passed the Nineteenth Amendment to the U.S. Constitution, and by the following June, when party conventions met in 1920, only one more state remained to meet the required three-fourths for ratification.

Republicans gathered in Chicago (for the fifth consecutive time), and Mary Garrett Hay, a field organizer for the National American Woman Suffrage Association, led the charge. Feminists demanded an unequivocal endorsement of suffrage in the platform as well as an equal number of male and female officials within the party. They did not get nearly that, but seven seats on the National Republican Executive Committee were reserved for women.

Democrats met in San Francisco later in June. They not only reaffirmed their 1916 plank but also adopted a resolution urging specific Democratic governors to call legislative sessions to provide the last essential state for ratification of the Nineteenth Amendment. Tennessee's governor responded, and on August 26, the amendment was added to the Constitution. Democratic women achieved a further victory with what was called "equal division." The 1920 convention changed party rules to require "full sex equality" in delegates to national conventions, as well as on the national committee that governed between conventions. The new rules said that the Democratic National Committee (DNC) "hereafter shall include one man and one woman from each State" (Harper 1922, 5:719). Beyond that, West Virginia's Izetta Jewel Brown became the third woman to second a presidential nomination when she spoke to the convention in support of nominee James M. Cox.[13]

Millions of women who never worked for the vote—and some who worked against it—voted in November 1920. Among those who presented herself as supportive but who, in fact, never had helped suffragists was Ohio's Florence Harding. Her husband, Warren G. Harding, was the 1920 Republican nominee. Democratic nominee Cox also was from Ohio. Socialists again chose Eugene Debs, who won almost a million votes. Harding soundly carried the election, as the post–World War I public—including some tired suffragists—wanted a break from Wilson's reforms and internationalism. Voters effectively put an end to the Progressive Era, opting instead for Harding's campaign theme, "return to normalcy."

BUILDING POWER, 1921 TO 1964

By 1922, both parties added a female vice chairman to their governing national committees, and both created local clubs for women. Missouri writer Emily Newell Blair used the skills she learned in the General Federation of Women's Clubs to organize thousands of Democratic Women's Clubs across the nation. The DNC hired Marion Glass Banister of West Virginia and Texas suffragist Minnie Fisher Cunningham to assist Blair. Their paid counterparts who developed the Republican Women's Clubs also were former suffragists, Mary Garrett Hay and Harriet Taylor Upton. Upton was from Ohio, as was President Harding, who referred to her as a good choice to replace the more liberal Hay because Upton was "safe and sane" (Freeman 2000, 97).

Harding died suddenly in 1923, and the new president, prim New Englander Calvin Coolidge, was the natural choice for Republicans in 1924. They also adopted equal division at this convention, and a committeewoman joined a committeeman from each state on the Republican National Committee (RNC). Upton nonetheless left the RNC to run (unsuccessfully) for Congress because, she said, she was only "allowed to do . . . about one tenth of what I ought to do" (Freeman 2000, 97).

Most of the era's African Americans considered themselves Republicans, as the party still was known as "the party of Lincoln." The 1924 convention heard from Hallie Q. Brown, who at age seventy-four was president of the National Association of Colored Women. Nannie Helen Burroughs, an innovative educator and writer in Washington, DC, was the first president of the National League of Republican Colored Women. The organization flourished only in the Roaring Twenties, however. It would not survive the Great Depression of the next decade.

The Democratic convention of 1924 was the longest in American history. It took 103 ballots to decide on a

---

[12] For Paul's biography, see Chapter 1: Battle for the Vote.

[13] For more on Brown, see Chapter 7: United States Senators.

"Daisy" Harriman was not the least tired by the long 1920 Democratic National Convention. Instead, the tight contest for the nomination offered an unusual opportunity to exercise her zeal for politics. Although born into New York's elite, she empathized with the poor and was an active, ever-optimistic reformer. She kept a daily journal at the San Francisco gathering attended by thousands of Democrats.

Thursday, July 1st. Yesterday was a perfect day, as Conventions go. The nominating speeches were excellent and the demonstrations amounted to pandemonium! Al Smith is the greatest governor New York has ever seen, and he was a fish peddler in his youth! . . .

When [William] McAdoo was put in nomination I really believe there was more spontaneous enthusiasm for him than for anyone. The [San Francisco] papers are poisonous about him, and I suppose most of the [New York] ones are too, but that only proves the Republicans are afraid of him. I am working hard for him. . . .

12:30. Mrs. Brown of West Virginia seconds Davis' nomination. She is very good looking, and has a charming voice. . . . The most finished and perfect speech I have ever heard a woman make.

1:00. One poor woman from the Philippines is putting Burton Harrison in nomination. Thank goodness her voice is such that one can't hear her.

Evening session . . . 8:05. Word has just come up that the Resolutions Committee won't be ready to report until 9 PM, and then the session will last until 5 AM. I wish I had taken a nap this afternoon. . . .

9:15. Mrs. Castleman, silver-haired National Committeewoman from Kentucky, 78 years old, is singing "My Old Kentucky Home." Dear thing, she is for McAdoo. Oh! I wouldn't have missed this convention for anything! It is wonderful.

11:45. Suffrage plank brings on a great demonstration. All states join in procession except Maryland and South Carolina.

12:05. All the planks of the League of Women Voters included in the platform.

Saturday. Nobody knows anything, and everybody lies every minute! Mrs. Bass calls me on to the platform . . . because McAdoo has lost ground to [James M.] Cox. . . .

Midnight. Adjournment until Monday. . . .

July 5th. Well, it's over. Now we must be good sports. . . .

(Harriman 1923, 326–338)

Daisy Harriman's conclusion that "we must be good sports" was integral to her personality and was a factor in her success as the nation's second female ambassador. She understood that, even more than winning, losing can build character for people and for parties. It often leads to better public service later.

---

presidential nominee, and after that much dissention, John W. Davis had almost no chance of winning the general election, especially against an incumbent. His candidacy was a compromise between Al Smith, the first Catholic to rise to that level of politics, and William McAdoo, son-in-law of the late President Wilson. Eleanor Wilson McAdoo had been a strong supporter of women's right to vote, and most feminists supported her husband.

This Democratic convention also was notable because it saw the first votes for a woman as vice president. Male delegates long had been honored with nominations as favorite sons, by which state delegations nominate their beloved members for president or vice president. Speeches are made and applause garnered, but no one intends the nomination as anything more than a gesture of respect. Two women were favorite daughters at the 1924 Democratic convention, as their names were placed in nomination for vice president. The West Virginia delegation named Izetta Jewell Brown, who was a U.S. Senate candidate and had seconded the 1920 presidential nomination

of John W. Davis. South Carolina's delegation nominated Lena Jones Wade Springs. Born in Tennessee and educated in Virginia, she was an English professor and feminist who began representing South Carolina on the DNC in 1922. More significant than the vice presidential gesture, Springs chaired the convention's Credentials Committee. That post is vital to conventions, as the committee handles questions on whether a delegate has been duly elected.

The nominations for Brown and Springs were courtesies, but the Prohibition Party truly did nominate Marie C. Brehm for vice president in 1924. She was then a sixty-five-year-old lecturer for the Women's Christian Temperance Union, to which she had devoted her whole life. The Eighteenth Amendment that banned alcohol was in effect during the 1920s, and because the party's platform lacked other meaningful goals, it did not attract the votes that it had in the past.

Incumbent Republican Coolidge won by a strong margin in 1924, but the taciturn president chose not to run in 1928. Republicans nominated Herbert Hoover, who had made a name for himself by handling food distribution to millions of Europeans who were in danger of starvation during World War I. His wife, Lou Henry Hoover, was unconventional in that she earned a degree in geology and met her husband while both studied at the London School of Mines. They worked together all over the world, including China, where she defied native belief that the presence of a woman in a mine would cause a cave-in. She did not emphasize this feminism in the campaign, however. Instead, the Hoover name would be inextricably linked to the Great Depression, which began when Wall Street fell just months after he took office.

The 1928 Democratic convention was in Houston, Texas, the first time that a city in the former Confederacy hosted a convention. It also was notable because delegates nominated New York governor Al Smith, and his Catholicism became the paramount issue in the general election. Many voters in the usually Democratic Solid South deserted the party because of the nominee's religion and because the platform advocated repeal of Prohibition. Smith was an old friend of Eleanor Roosevelt and other prominent feminists, and they worked hard for him, to no avail.

This campaign would prove excellent training, though, especially for MOLLY DEWSON, who organized Democratic Women's Clubs and oversaw workshops that trained some 100,000 party women in campaign techniques. She pushed equal division, insisting that chairmanships and vice chairmanships be shared by women and men, and prevailed in 1932, when Franklin D. Roosevelt ousted President Hoover by a huge majority.

Roosevelt won by an even larger majority in 1936, as he trounced Republican nominee Alfred M. Landon—called "Alf" and the father of future Kansas senator Nancy Landon Kassebaum—with 523 electoral votes to 8.[14] Again, Dewson's organizing of Democratic women proved key, as did Roosevelt's recognition of women by appointing the first to high positions. A black minister gave the invocation at the 1936 Democratic convention, an indication of how many African Americans had switched to the Democratic Party during the Roosevelt administration. They were motivated by New Deal programs and especially because Eleanor Roosevelt reached out to them as no other political leader ever had done.

Conventions of both parties throughout this era debated a federal approach to prosecuting Ku Klux Klan members and others who lynched African Americans with impunity, but such legislation did not pass until modern laws were enacted against hate crimes. Jessie Daniel Ames, a white woman from Texas, was a largely unheralded activist against lynching. Among black

women, the strongest probably was journalist Ida Wells-Barnett. Because of threats against her life, she was forced to leave Memphis, Tennessee, for Chicago.

World War II had broken out by 1940, when Roosevelt ran for an unprecedented third term. Some Democrats objected, and controversy also arose over the vice presidency. Because presidents do not traditionally attend conventions until after all issues are settled, Eleanor Roosevelt preceded Franklin to Chicago and mollified the warring factions. Vice President John Nance Garner of Texas refused to stay on the ticket, famously saying that the "vice presidency is not worth a bucket of warm spit," and Eleanor convinced Southern delegates to accept Henry Wallace of Iowa, whom many considered too leftist.

Republicans also met in Chicago, and their 1940 nominee was a surprise. Wendell Wilkie was a former Democrat and internationalist, something that turned out to have little appeal for mostly isolationist Republicans. He was derided within his own party as "One World Wilkie," and the result was that even though many people were concerned about breaking the two-term precedent, they supported Roosevelt. He won with 449 electoral votes to Wilkie's 82. Yet so many Republican women were motivated by isolationism in 1940 that groups such as the Mothers of Sons sprang up, especially in the Midwest. Although they were more against Roosevelt than for peace, most also refused to support Wilkie.

The same wartime reasoning brought Roosevelt's reelection in 1944, although Harry S. Truman of Missouri replaced Henry Wallace in the vice presidential slot. The Republican nominee was Thomas E. Dewey, who, like Roosevelt and Al Smith, had been governor of New York. The League of Women Voters made a strong effort to get ballots to the millions of soldiers overseas, and most came back marked for the incumbent. Dewey managed to get only 99 electoral votes against Roosevelt's 432.

Both parties endorsed the Equal Rights Amendment (ERA) in 1944. Democratic women had been ambivalent about the ERA because it would nullify state protective labor laws for women that they had worked hard to pass, but the entrance of millions of women into the wartime labor force eased this concern. The largest political factor for Democrats, though, was the knowledge that the ERA's sponsors in the National Woman's Party were largely Republicans. When they convinced mainstream Republicans to endorse the ERA, Democrats had to follow.

The 1944 Democratic convention featured another milestone, as Dorothy Vredenburgh Bush called the roll of the states when votes were taken. A 1938 graduate of the Mississippi College for Women, she would serve as secretary of the DNC for the next forty years. She handled the vote counts for twelve conventions, some of them raucous. Party

---

[14] See Chapter 7: United States Senators.

chairmen came and went, but Bush never had a reelection opponent. She combined a Mississippi accent with great fairness and efficiency at the lectern and retired to acclaim in 1988. In her December 23, 1991, *New York Times* obituary, Bush was quoted as having said: "I was born a Democrat like most people were born into a religion."

Although her tenure was shorter, Katherine Howard was akin to Bush as secretary of the Republican National Committee. Soon after Howard was elected to the RNC, she found her name on party literature in Massachusetts as a member of the Finance Committee, although she never had been invited to any of its meetings. She objected and soon found herself in charge of a Special Gifts Committee that raised $54,000 for the 1948 campaign. As a result, she became the first female secretary of the RNC. Marion Martin was the chief professional in charge of organizing Republican women in this era of Democratic dominance, but many RNC women "simply did not like Martin" (Rymph 2006, 95), and she was fired in 1946. President Truman, however, admired Martin so much that he considered appointing her to the Federal Communications Commission. Democratic women, appalled at the idea that he would give this unprecedented opportunity to a woman of the opposite party, talked him out of it.

The 1948 election centered on Harry Truman, who became president soon after his inauguration as vice president, when Roosevelt died early in 1945. Almost every pundit predicted that Republican Dewey, who had challenged Roosevelt in 1944, would prevail in 1948. Voters differed, however, and chose Democrat Truman. The electoral count was 303–189, with another 39 electoral votes going to third parties.

Part of the reason for Truman's success was INDIA EDWARDS and Perle Mesta, who followed Molly Dewson as the most prominent Democratic women. Truman rewarded Mesta with appointment as the third female ambassador.[15] Edwards became the strongest voice in the White House on behalf of women. Largely because she was one of the few professional politicians who believed that Truman could win in 1948, she became the first female party official with full access to the White House. Truman referred to his wife, Bess Truman, as "the Boss," and he insisted that DNC men similarly view Edwards as their boss. Several times he backed her when conflicts arose with men unaccustomed to a woman in charge.

Republicans began drifting right ideologically at their 1948 convention, as anticommunism became the party's chief theme. Betty Farrington, who was elected president of the Republican Women's Federation in 1948, held this view. For her, "Christianity and anticommunism were inseparable" (Rymph 2006, 112).

At the next election, 1952, more moderate Republican women helped their party retake the White House for the first time in twenty years. The convention nominated World War II hero Dwight D. Eisenhower, who only recently had declared a party affiliation, and he benefited from campaign work led by Ivy Baker Priest and Bertha Atkins. A Utah Mormon, Priest had a long career in Republican politics. She ran unsuccessfully for Congress in 1934 and 1950, but she would win election as California's treasurer in 1966. In 1952, she played a strong enough role for Eisenhower that he followed Truman's precedent and appointed her as the first Republican woman in the largely ceremonial position of U.S. treasurer.[16]

Eisenhower was the much better known candidate because of the war, and many women supported him, in no small part because he had supported women in the military. Democrats chose Illinois senator Adlai E. Stevenson, who promised to carry on Roosevelt and Truman's New Deal policies, but most voters wanted a change of direction. The same two men faced each other again in 1956, with the same result. Democrats, though, added a platform plank encouraging equal employment opportunities for minorities in 1952 and one for school integration in 1956.

Eisenhower's vice president, Richard M. Nixon of California, was the Republican nominee in 1960, and Democrats chose Sen. John F. Kennedy of Massachusetts. It was a very close election; one vote per precinct nationally would have changed the result. Kennedy won, proving that Catholicism was not the barrier for him that it had been for Al Smith in 1928. It would be the last campaign for Eleanor Roosevelt, who worked for Kennedy, as she had for Stevenson in the previous decade. Katie Louchheim also was a DNC power in this era, and Kennedy went over the heads of career men in the State Department to give her the highest position yet granted to a woman there.

Kennedy would be assassinated in 1963, and the question at the 1964 Democratic convention was not who would be the nominee – that was assumed to be new president Lyndon B. Johnson—but, instead, who would be a delegate.

FROM THERE TO HERE: CHANGING PARTIES, 1964–2011

Democratic conventions had come close to splitting up over the issue of race for decades, and without Eleanor Roosevelt to intervene, that happened in 1964. As the

---

[15] See Chapter 12: Ambassadors.

[16] See Chapter 3: Statewide Elective Officeholders and Chapter 11: Cabinet and Subcabinet.

years went on, more and more white Southern Democrats left for the Republican Party; most blacks did the opposite. To a somewhat lesser extent, the same would be true for feminists.

Fannie Lou Hamer, a black woman from rural Mississippi, was the face of this change at the 1964 Democratic convention. Although she was poor and poorly educated, Hamer was a fierce activist who had endured beatings while trying to vote. She appealed to the Credentials Committee to refuse to accept Mississippi's all-white convention delegation. For days, the convention was disrupted by hearings on whether or not to decertify white Mississippians and replace them with black delegates. The committee's ambiguous decision satisfied neither faction. All but three of the white delegates walked out, and when the blacks attempted to take their empty seats, guards forcibly removed them. The stage was set for a riotous convention in 1968.

The 1964 Republican convention was much quieter, and comparably less media attention focused on Margaret Chase Smith of Maine, who was the first woman to receive convention votes for president.[17] She had dropped out of the competition by then, but some delegates cast ballots for the feminist senator in the first round of voting at the convention that nominated Arizona conservative Barry Goldwater. In the fall, he lost to Texas Democrat Lyndon Johnson in a landslide.

Responsibility for the disastrous nomination and campaign loss divided Republicans, including women. Political scientist Catherine E. Rymph wrote that the word "'rancor' quite aptly describes the struggle for control of the National Federation of Republican women" (Rymph 2006, 177). As first vice president of the federation, PHYLLIS SCHLAFLY expected to become its president in 1966, but moderate Republican women kept the very conservative Schlafly from being promoted. Incumbent president Dottie Elson, with help from RNC professional Elly Peterson, organized to defeat what they called the "nut fringe" of Republican women (Rymph 2006, 179).

By the 1960s, more and more states were conducting presidential primaries in the spring, and summer conventions thus became increasingly less important as decision makers. With that development and the advent of television, conventions became less about debates between potential nominees and more about showcasing an already known nominee. Instead of truly discussing issues and choosing candidates, convention delegates became orchestration for prime-time television.

Television also brought traumatic events into every living room in 1968, as Democrats Martin Luther King

Jr. and Robert F. Kennedy were assassinated in the spring. In the summer, violence erupted outside both conventions. Anger about overdue civil rights for blacks melded with protests against the Vietnam War and thousands of mostly young people flooded the streets of the host cities, trying to influence the policymakers inside the conventions. In Miami, Florida, riots greeted Republicans, who nominated Richard Nixon, their unsuccessful nominee in 1960. In response to the protestors, the party instituted some rule reform intended at greater inclusion, as its delegates were overwhelmingly white and male. Women constituted just 30 percent of the delegates that year, and African Americans accounted for 3 percent. Only one in every one hundred delegates was under thirty years of age.

Young people went to Chicago and the Democratic convention, where the violence was much worse. Many protestors were jailed, and women were prominent among both the demonstrators and the delegates. Vice President Hubert H. Humphrey was chosen as the Democratic presidential nominee. When Humphrey continued to back Johnson's war policy, many Democrats refused to vote in the election or they cast their ballots for alternative candidates. Nixon won by a substantial margin in 1968 and would do so again in 1972.

Democrats in 1972 nominated South Dakota senator George S. McGovern at a convention so disorganized that he began his acceptance speech after midnight, missing the prime-time electronic audience. The chief reason that the convention was chaotic was that the party reformed its structure, giving much more weight to newcomers, especially feminists and other progressives. Texan Frances Farenthold received some votes for vice president that year, and in 1971, Jean Westwood of Utah had become the first female chair of the DNC.[18] Her chairmanship lasted less than a year, however, as Democrats were trounced in 1972. Richard Nixon was renominated at a Republican convention featuring Texan Anne Armstrong as the keynote speaker.

Public sentiment in 1972 proved more anti-McGovern than pro-Nixon. As reporters dug into crimes such as the Republican burglary of Democratic headquarters at Washington's Watergate complex, Nixon was forced to resign in 1974. Nixon's vice president, Spiro T. Agnew, already had resigned because of corruption charges and had been succeeded by House minority leader Gerald R. Ford, also a Republican. Thus, when Nixon left, Ford became president. Republicans spent much of 1974 attempting to reform their negative image. That year, Mary Louise Smith, a moderate from Iowa, was chosen to head the RNC. She served through Ford's tenure, from

---

[17] See Chapter Presidential and Vice Presidential Candidates, as well as Chapter 7: United States Senators.

[18] For more on Farenthold, see Chapter Ten: Candidates for President and Vice President.

1974 to 1977 and, as of 2011, remained the only woman to head the party.

First lady Betty Ford of Michigan was a moderate and supported the ERA, as did Rosalynn Carter, wife of the 1976 Democratic nominee Jimmy Carter of Georgia. That Democratic convention set a precedent as the first presided over by a woman, Corinne Claiborne "Lindy" Boggs of Louisiana, and Rep. Barbara Jordan, an African American from Houston, used her powerful oratorical skills in the keynote speech.[19] In a very close election with feminists on both sides, Carter prevailed. Anne Wexler and Midge Constanza, both strong feminists, did an outstanding job in the Carter White House of emulating the outreach done earlier by Molly Dewson and India Edwards. Wexler's *New York Times* obituary, which appeared on August 8, 2009, said that insiders termed her "the most competent woman in Democratic politics in this country."

Southern Jimmy Carter never had been very popular in the Northeast, and Massachusetts senator Edward M. Kennedy, brother of the late president, ran against him for the 1980 Democratic nomination. Carter had the majority of delegates, but Kennedy did not surrender until the convention—and that division cost Democrats in the fall. California Republican Ronald Reagan ousted Carter from the White House, setting the stage for greater Republican conservatism. The 1980 Republican convention dropped its longtime ERA plank from the platform, and its candidates increasingly spoke out against *Roe v. Wade*, the 1973 Supreme Court decision that limited the power of states to criminalize early stage abortions. The Democratic platform, in contrast, again endorsed the ERA and then went further by promising to withhold financial support from any anti-ERA candidates.

Ratification time for the Equal Rights Amendment had expired by 1984, when Republicans renominated Reagan. Democrats chose Sen. Walter F. Mondale of Minnesota, who made history by choosing a feminist woman, New York representative Geraldine A. Ferraro, for his vice presidential running mate.[20] Kentucky governor Martha Layne Collins presided over the convention, and Joan Mondale was much more feminist than first lady Nancy

Jimmy Carter and Barbara Jordan at the Democratic National Convention podium in 1976. Rosalyn Carter and Joan Mondale are barely visible to the left.

Reagan, but voters opted to retain the incumbent. In the 1986 midterm election, pollster Celinda Lake proclaimed a "gender gap," as more women began voting Democratic, while more men cast ballots for Republicans.

Louisiana RNC member Virginia Martinez was largely responsible for bringing Republicans to the New Orleans Superdome in 1988. Pro-choice Republican women tried to soften their party's position on abortion, but they failed to convince other Republicans, both women and men. Democrats that year chose Massachusetts governor Michael S. Dukakis, the first Greek Orthodox nominee. He set a precedent by naming a woman as his campaign manager. She was young lawyer and future media commentator Susan Estrich. In the fall, Dukakis lost badly to George H. W. Bush, who withstood criticism by his fellow Texan, Democratic governor Ann W. Richards.[21] In the third keynote speech by a woman at a Democratic convention, she famously said that the affluent Bush had been born "with a silver foot in his mouth."

To the surprise of most pundits, Bush lost his 1992 reelection bid to Arkansas governor Bill Clinton. Democrats nominated Clinton at a convention in which women were highly visible. Ann Richards presided; Hillary Rodham Clinton, a strong feminist, presented a generational contrast to first lady Barbara Bush; and Ann Lewis proved an excellent campaign strategist.[22] In contrast, political scientist Catherine Rymph wrote:

[19] For more on Boggs and Jordan, see Chapter 6: United States Representatives.

[20] For Ferraro's biography, see Chapter 10: Presidential and Vice Presidential Candidates.

[21] For Richards's biography, see Chapter 8: Governors and Lieutenant Governors.

[22] See Chapter 10: Presidential and Vice Presidential Candidates, as well as Chapter 7: United States Senators.

Vice Presidential candidate Sarah Palin signing photos at a campaign rally in Carson, California, in 2008.

During the 1990s, moderate, feminist Republicans watched in dismay as their party shifted ever more to the right and ever further away from the concerns of Republican feminists. . . [Former RNC chair] Mary Louise Smith spoke out until her death in 1997 against her party's positions on women's issues and civil rights, its general drift away from its moderate wing. . . . [She] was shunned by key party leaders. (Rymph 2006, 237)

Clinton did not shun feminists, and Chicago peace activist Debra DeLee chaired the DNC in 1994–1995. He was reelected in 1996, despite the efforts of Elizabeth Dole on behalf of her husband, Republican nominee Robert Dole of Kansas.[23] Rep. Susan Molinari of New York delivered the keynote speech at the Republican convention, and Hillary Clinton became the first first lady to formally address a party convention. One prime-time session was devoted to the nation's children and families, with five female Democratic senators joining Clinton as speakers.

Donna Brazile became the first African American woman to manage a presidential campaign in 2000, when she was hired by Vice President Al Gore, the Democratic nominee. The election was historic in the way that 1876 contest had been, as Americans were reminded that the president is chosen by the electoral college, not by individual voters. Gore won the popular vote, with 50,999,897 to 50,456,002 for Republican George W. Bush of Texas. The son of the former president, he also was the brother of Florida governor Jeb Bush. When the U.S. Supreme Court ordered Florida to stop recounting disputed ballots

and awarded all of its electoral votes to Bush, he narrowly won the electoral college tally.

The 2004 Democratic nominee, Massachusetts senator John Kerry, did not include as many women in visible positions as at past conventions. He lost to incumbent Bush, as women in both parties arguably regressed during the first years of the new millennium. Democrats returned to female visibility in 2008 with the strong primary campaign of Hillary Clinton, and House Speaker Nancy Pelosi presided over the convention that nominated the first African American president, Barack Obama.

Republicans also made history in 2008, as they followed the precedent established by Democrats in 1984 and nominated a woman for vice president. Alaska governor Sarah Palin joined Vietnam War hero and Arizona senator John McCain as the Republican nominees.[24] Like 1984 with Geraldine Ferraro, a female presence on the ticket was not a determining factor, and McCain and Palin lost to Obama and his vice presidential running mate, Joseph R. Biden Jr.

Both parties scheduled the 2012 conventions for unconventional cities in the South. Republicans chose Tampa, Florida, and Democrats opted for North Carolina's historic Charlotte. In the spring of 2011, President Obama selected Debbie Wasserman Schultz, a young representative from Florida, to head the Democratic Party.[25] As with his appointments of women to the cabinet and the judiciary, this marked a historically significant change.

Among Republicans, Ann Wagner, who had been cochair of the RNC during the administration of George W. Bush, ran for chair in 2011 but withdrew after six rounds of balloting. Sharon Day, who opposed party leadership in Florida, replaced Wagner as RNC cochair. In the rules of both parties, that secondary position goes to a woman when a man is in the top spot. That has been the case for Republican women except for the brief tenure of Mary Louise Smith in the late 1970s.

The League of Women Voters and other nonpartisan organizations faithfully follow the intention of the nation's founders to avoid political parties. That remains a grand ideal, but the nation's past shows that parties can be very powerful, and feminists ignore them at their peril.

---

[23] See Chapter 10: Presidential and Vice Presidential Candidates, as well as Chapter 7: United States Senators.

[24] See Chapter 8: Governors and Lieutenant Governors and Chapter 10: Presidential and Vice Presidential Candidates.

[25] See Chapter 6: United States Representatives.

*The two Republican women profiled here represent a long span of time, with **Jessie Benton Fremont** setting precedents in the nineteenth century and **Phyllis Schlafly** making her mark in the twentieth century and continuing her cause into the twenty-first century. The biographies of the two Democrats, **Molly Dewson** and **India Edwards**, both active in the mid-twentieth century, are presented here because they were the first female party officials to have true personal access to the president.*

MOLLY DEWSON (1874–1962)

Formally named Mary Williams Dewson, Molly Dewson was the most visible female party activist in the decades immediately after women got the vote in 1920.

Her Boston family was wealthy enough to send her to private Miss Ireland's School and then to all-female Wellesley College, where the 1897 class prophecy said she would be president of the United States—more than twenty years before that was even a possibility. She did become senior class president and was already demonstrating innate political skills.

Like many young affluent women in the Progressive Era, Dewson worked full time on behalf of the needy. In her case, first was the Women's Educational and Industrial Union, a privately supported institution in Boston, and then the publicly supported Massachusetts Industrial School for Girls. She developed innovative methods to measure success in criminology and social work, and this ability to analyze statistics led to her next position as secretary of the Massachusetts Minimum Wage Commission. In 1912, Dewson led passage of the first minimum-wage law in the nation.

Despite job offers, she took a chance on a wholly different kind of endeavor. With the woman who would become her life partner, Mary G. Porter, she ran a dairy farm near Worcester for five years. When the nation entered World War I in 1917, Dewson—at age forty-three—traveled overseas to work for the Red Cross, leading operations to assist refugees in the Mediterranean zone.

After returning to the United States in 1919, she joined the National Consumers League and worked with future Supreme Court justice Felix Frankfurter on issues for both consumers and workers. When the Court struck down their attempt to create a federal minimum-wage law in *Adkins v. Children's Hospital* (1923), she was so dispirited with the national scene that she concentrated on reforms in New York, where progressive Democrat Al Smith was governor.

She became close friends with New Yorkers Eleanor Roosevelt and Frances Perkins, who would be the first woman to serve in the cabinet, as secretary of labor. In 1928, Dewson campaigned for Franklin D. Roosevelt for governor, and four years after that, she went to Washington, DC, with the Roosevelts. Employed by the Democratic Party, she was the first female operative of either party to be given genuine support by a president. Roosevelt's was the first Democratic administration since all women were empowered to vote, and Dewson integrated the Democratic Women's Clubs, which had been founded in 1922, into a vital part of party structure. Strongly committed to the "equal division" concept that required affirmative action on behalf of female party volunteers, she also lobbied for presidential appointment of women to federal offices.

Dewson left party employment in 1937 to sit on the new board that implemented Social Security, something she had supported since her early days as a social worker. She served there through World War II, when a bad heart caused her to retire to Maine with Mary Porter. Even in retirement, though, Molly Dewson was available to Democrats in election years. She died at the age of eighty-eight in 1962, after John F. Kennedy returned the White House to the Democrats.

INDIA EDWARDS (1895–1990)

A valued part of campaigns for Democratic presidents from Franklin D. Roosevelt in the 1940s to Lyndon B. Johnson in the 1960s, India Edwards began her career as a journalist for the *Chicago Tribune*, a highly Republican newspaper.

Born in Chicago as India Walker, she grew up in Nashville and was educated in St. Louis. She married in 1917, but her husband, John Sharp, soon was killed in World War I. Her second husband was financier Jack Moffett. They had a son and a daughter. Jack lost the family money, along with his self-esteem, when Wall Street crashed. India supported the four of them, plus both of their mothers, on her earnings as a music critic and society reporter for the *Tribune*. He drank and dated other women, and after seventeen years of marriage, she divorced him in 1937.

Five years later she married Herbert Edwards, a filmmaker who would win the first Academy Award for a feature-length documentary. He had made advertisements for 1936 Republican nominee Alfred M. Landon, but despite that and the *Tribune*'s anti-Democratic stance, she always viewed herself as a Democrat, and Herbert soon became very supportive of her career as a professional Democrat.

They wed in 1942, the first full year of World War II. Her son, John Moffett, enlisted in the U.S. Army Air

Forces, and he was killed in a plane accident in 1944. Because her husband had accepted a job with the Office of War Information, Edwards left the *Tribune* and moved to Washington, DC. Vowing to make meaningful both her son's death and that of her first husband, she dedicated herself to the internationalism that brought the United Nations. Ironically, she was inspired to work for Democrats after hearing a speech by Rep. Clare Booth Luce, a Republican.[25]

Edwards rose quickly and soon was named head of the Women's Division of the National Democratic Committee (DNC). With full access to the White House, she specialized in recommending qualified women to President Harry S. Truman. Among his most significant female appointees were Eugenie Anderson as ambassador to Denmark and Georgia Neese Clark as the first female U.S. treasurer.[26] Edwards's obituary, syndicated by the *San Francisco Chronicle* on January 17, 1990, quoted her: "Sometimes I'd feel like a ghoul.... I'd read the obituaries and as soon as a [political] man had died, I'd rush over to the White House and suggest a woman to replace him."

She turned down Truman's offer of the party chairmanship, believing that the battles she would have to fight against sexism would distract from the party's success. Her obituary quoted her as telling a reporter, "if I had wanted to advance myself, I suppose I could have [accepted the chairmanship], but what I really wanted was a lot of jobs for a lot of women—and I got them."

Truman also offered Edwards the unusual opportunity to be the keynote speaker at two national conventions. She spoke in 1948 and again in 1952. The topic of the second speech, she said, came to her in the middle of the night, when she remembered

Emperor Haile Selassie of Ethiopia standing alone before the League of Nations in 1936 to warn that the unchecked aggression against his homeland [had] world wide consequences.... I suddenly knew that I must talk about the importance of the Korean War. I had to speak as a woman—a wife who wore a Gold Star in World War I and a mother who wore a Gold Star in World War II. (Edwards 1977, 152)

She dedicated her 1977 book, *Pulling No Punches: Memoirs of a Woman in Politics*, to Harry Truman, as well as to her "liberated mother," India Thomas Walker Gillespie, and her daughter, India Moffett Williams. One of her five granddaughters also was named India.

Edwards later said that her only political regret was briefly leaving the Democratic Party in 1976, when she supported John B. Anderson, a U.S. representative from her home state of Illinois. He left the Republican Party to run an unsuccessful presidential campaign as an independent.

She attended her last Democratic convention in 1984, when she was eighty-nine, and saw the nomination of Geraldine A. Ferraro as vice president. Retired to California, India Edwards died in Sebastopol at ninety-four.

JESSIE BENTON FREMONT (1824–1902)

Because she was the daughter of a powerful senator and her husband was the first Republican presidential nominee, Jessie Ann Benton Fremont was at the heart of politics in the mid-nineteenth century. If she had been a man, she probably would have risen high. But, even without electoral opportunity, she was influential.

She was born four years after the Missouri Compromise allowed slavery in that state, and her father, Thomas Hart Benton, was a longtime Missouri senator. She grew up with homes in St. Louis and Washington, DC, but because the vast majority of women did not go to college then, she taught herself history and politics by reading in the Library of Congress. Tutors taught her French and Spanish, but she rebelled against the domestic arts at Miss English's School in the Georgetown section of Washington.

True to her spirited self, Jessie Benton eloped at seventeen with John Charles Fremont, a talented but poor U.S. Army officer. He was beginning to build a reputation as an explorer of still unmapped western territories, and after Senator Benton reconciled himself to the upstart groom, he promoted Fremont's military career. Jessie's sense of drama was evident in their first year of marriage, when she helped write her husband's 1842 report on his explorations. She added such flair to the report that the government document became a bestseller. She did the same again in 1846, and the Fremont name soon became inextricably linked to the opening West.

The role that she played promoting her husband's career went far beyond the era's traditional boundaries of "wifely behavior." While still just nineteen years old, she had the temerity to hide orders from the War Department that could have slowed his career. She claimed that the orders had not been delivered until after he left for the post that she wanted him to have. During war with Mexico in the late 1840s, she furthered his ends with information that she got from translating confidential letters from Mexico for the secretary of state. She was fearless about lobbying presidents on behalf of her husband. Not surprisingly, many people, including some feminists, criticized her for excessive ambition.

Meanwhile she bore five children, three of whom survived infancy, and made her first, difficult trek to the West in 1849. The family began calling California their home that year, when the discovery of gold began transforming that area from its long Mexican heritage. Again, her Spanish was helpful, and the Fremonts bought land that soon made them wealthy. They played a major role in bringing California into the nation as a free state in 1850, as well as in building the new Republican Party, which was committed to ending the expansion of slavery.

When John Charles Fremont was the first Republican nominee for president in 1856, Jessie Benton Fremont was just thirty-two years old. She probably was the first woman to gain a substantial number of votes for her husband, as her smiling face appeared on campaign illustrations. After his electoral loss, they sojourned in Europe but returned to the United States when the Civil War began.

John was appointed to command the Union armies of the West but was demoted when, true to the abolitionist principles that they both held, he emancipated slaves owned by Missourians who supported the Confederacy. This was in 1861, two years before President Abraham Lincoln issued the Emancipation Proclamation. Jessie traveled to Washington to argue her husband's case, but Lincoln's War Department was more interested in neutrality for the border state of Missouri than in freeing slaves.

She was too protective of her husband's career to openly affiliate herself with the women's rights movement, but she quietly supported it. While John continued with the war, Jessie stayed in the East and worked with the abolitionist Loyal League that Elizabeth Cady Stanton and Susan B. Anthony organized. Fremont also wrote *The Story of the Guard* (1863), about the war's first years, and when she could afford it later, she sent checks to Anthony.

Like many families after the Civil War, the Fremonts suffered financial reverses. Theirs came to a head during the 1873 national depression. To help restore the family fortune, Jessie returned to writing. For the rest of the century, she published a multitude of articles for popular magazines that made her one of the best-known women in the country.

John was appointed as governor of the Arizona Territory in 1878, and the Fremonts moved there. Their daughter, Elizabeth Benton Fremont, wrote of Arizona in *Recollections* (1912). From the 1840s through the 1890s, Jessie Benton Fremont's writing encouraged many Americans to move west. She consistently presented an optimistic, progressive view of politics but never deserted her original Republican Party, even though the Progressive Party came to better represent her views. Jessie Benton Fremont died in Los Angeles at age seventy-eight, soon after Theodore Roosevelt—who shared much of her western-oriented, expansive philosophy— became president. Less than a decade after her death, California women would win the vote.

PHYLLIS SCHLAFLY (1924–)

More than any other woman, Phyllis Schlafly was responsible for pushing the Republican Party to the right during the late twentieth century. She was especially successful in her crusade against the Equal Rights Amendment (ERA).

Phyllis McAlpin Stewart was born in Alton, Illinois, across the Mississippi River from St. Louis. Her parents were educated, but her attorney father found it impossible to support the family during the Great Depression. Her mother worked as a teacher and librarian to pay for Phyllis's education in Catholic schools. World War II brought increased prosperity to the family, and Phyllis graduated with honors from Washington University in St. Louis in 1944. She went east to earn a master's degree in political science from Radcliffe College, the female affiliate of Harvard University, in 1945. At that point she promoted some Democratic goals, including the formation of the United Nations. She became more conservative after going to work for the American Enterprise Institute, which was founded in 1943 to lobby against Democratic initiatives.

In 1949, at age twenty-five, Phyllis Stewart married John Schlafly Jr., an attorney and a member of a St. Louis family affluent enough that servants allowed her much free time. In 1952, just three years after her wedding, she made the first of three unsuccessful bids for Congress. While rearing six children, she remained active in Republican politics and ran for Congress again in 1960 and in 1970. In 1964, she strongly supported Arizona senator Barry Goldwater for the presidency, and her self-published book on him, *A Choice, Not an Echo* (1964), played a key role in his nomination.

Goldwater badly lost the election, and after a bitter fight, Schlafly lost the presidency of the National Federation of Republican Women. She briefly joined the ultra-right John Birch Society, and then, in 1972, she established her own group, the Eagle Forum.[27] Its influence was strongest in the 1970s, as especially older Republican women reacted negatively to social change. With Schlafly as the only president in its history, the Eagle Forum opposed the Equal Rights Amendment, sex education, and reproductive choice. It also took stands on nonfeminist issues and especially supported a strong military. The Eagle Forum proved very influential within the Republican Party during the 1980s.

Schlafly wrote almost two dozen books on a variety of subjects. The most notable was *The Power of the Positive Woman* (1977). She earned her law degree from Washington University in 1978. In both writing and speeches, she consistently asserted the primacy of homemaking as women's proper full-time role. Critics pointed out that she hired nannies while flying across the country telling other women to stay home.

She maintained a home in Washington, DC, and faithfully supported Republican nominees until 2008. She refused to endorse anyone that year, despite the presence of a conservative woman, Alaska governor Sarah Palin, on the Republican ticket. Schlafly also made the news earlier in 2008, when Washington University trustees voted to give her an honorary degree. She received the degree but, faced with protestors who decried her as anti-intellectual, the university gave her no speaking opportunity. Aged eighty-seven in 2011, Phyllis Schlafly continues to influence people through her Eagle Forum.

REFERENCES AND FURTHER READING

Anthony, Susan B., and Ida Husted Harper, eds. 1902. *History of Woman Suffrage.* Volume 4. Indianapolis: Hollenbeck Press. Reprint, New York: Arno Press, 1969.

Byrne, Gary C. 1976. *The Great American Convention: A Political History of Presidential Campaigns.* Palo Alto, CA: Pacific Books.

Cordery, Stacy. 2007. *Alice: Alice Roosevelt Longworth, from White House Princess to Washington Power Broker.* New York: Viking.

Edwards, India. 1977. *Pulling No Punches: Memoirs of a Woman in Politics.* New York: G. P. Putnam's Sons.

Edwards, Rebecca. 1997. *Angels in the Machinery: Gender in American Party Politics from the Civil War to the Progressive Era.* New York: Oxford University Press.

Fitzgerald, Sara. 2011. *Elly Peterson: Mother of Moderates.* Ann Arbor: University of Michigan Press.

Freeman, Jo. 2000. *A Room at a Time: How Women Entered Party Politics.* Lanham, MD: Rowman and Littlefield.

Harper, Ida Husted, ed. *History of Woman Suffrage.* 1922. Volumes 5–6. New York: J. J. Little and Ives.

Harriman, Florence (Daisy). 1923. *From Pinafores to Politics.* New York: Henry Holt and Co.

Jeansome, Glen. 1996. *Women of the Far Right: The Mothers Movement and World War II.* Chicago: University of Chicago Press.

Knight, Louise. 2010. *Jane Addams: Spirit in Action.* New York: W. W. Norton.

Laas, Virginia Jeans. 1999. *Bridging Two Eras: The Autobiography of Emily Newell Blair, 1877–1951.* Columbia: University of Missouri Press.

Louchheim, Katie. 1983. *The Making of the New Deal: The Insiders Speak.* Cambridge, MA: Harvard University Press.

Melich, Tanya. 1996. *The Republican War against Women: An Insider's Report from behind the Lines.* New York: Bantam Books.

National Party Conventions, 1831–1992. 1995. Washington, DC: CQ Press.

Panagopoulos, Costas, ed. 2007. *Rewiring Politics: Presidential Nominating Conventions in the Media Age.* Baton Rogue: Louisiana State University Press.

Roosevelt, Eleanor. 1954. *Ladies of Courage.* New York: G. P. Putnam's Sons.

Rymph, Catherine E. 2006. *Republican Women: Feminism and Conservatism from Suffrage to the Rise of the New Right.* Chapel Hill: University of North Carolina Press.

Sanbonmatsu, Kira. 2003. *Democrats, Republicans, and the Politics of Woman's Place.* Ann Arbor: University of Michigan Press.

Stanton, Elizabeth Cady, Susan B. Anthony, and Matilda Joslyn Gage. 1886. *History of Woman Suffrage.* Volume 3. Rochester, NY: Charles Mann Printing Company. Reprint, New York: Arno Press 1969.

Smith, Larry David. 1991. *Cordial Concurrence: Orchestrating National Party Conventions in a Telegenic Age.* New York: Praeger.

Ware, Susan. 1987. *Partner and I: Molly Dewson, Feminism, and New Deal Politics.* New Haven, CT: Yale University Press.

Wolbrecht, Christina. 2000. *The Politics of Women's Rights: Parties, Positions, and Change.* Princeton, NJ: Princeton University Press.

17

INTEREST GROUPS

When the United States was founded, no organizations of women existed, and that remained the case for many decades. Although George Washington could and did belong to many groups—including the fraternal lodge the Freemasons—Martha Washington could not have joined anything. Even the Eastern Star, the Masonic affiliate for wives, was not founded until 1875, more than a century after she might have been a member.

The first organizations of cause-oriented women were missionary societies affiliated with churches, which began with liberal Protestant denominations in the first half of the nineteenth century. Another century would pass before more conservative faiths created such groups. A few women organized female moral reform societies in the early nineteenth century, especially in Ohio, where liberal education flourished, albeit primarily for men. These societies focused on the elimination of prostitution and other vices, even publishing the names of men who visited brothels in local newspapers during the 1830s. As Victorian attitudes grew, acknowledging such sexual reality became improper for ladies, and by the 1850s, the groups had faded.

Reform-minded women—often led by Quakers, who implemented real self-governance in their meeting houses—began antislavery societies during the 1830s. From those roots, women's rights societies evolved. The first women's rights meeting was in 1848, in Seneca Falls, New York.[1] This was radical, however, and national organizations of middle-class women pursuing acceptable goals did not begin until their work in the Civil War taught women the importance of female association. Many learned their first organization skills through raising funds for the U.S. Sanitary Commission and other war-related activities.

---

[1] See Chapter 1: Battle for the Vote.

Historians believe Anna Ella Carroll may have been the first American woman to earn a living by working for political interests. A member of an old Maryland family fallen on hard times, she lived in Washington, DC, and supported herself as a lobbyist before the Civil War. The War Department, too, paid Carroll significant fees for pro-Union writing and advocacy. Her legalistic treatise on why states had no constitutional right to secede was distributed to every member of Congress.

A few other women followed Carroll as paid lobbyists after the war, but they came up through the ranks of their particular cause and their motivation was not money. The most important were Emmeline B. Wells and Angela Newman, who opposed each other's causes. Wells lobbied for the right of Utah women to both vote and to stay in their polygamous marriages. Newman, a Nebraskan hired by Methodist women, walked congressional halls countering Well's arguments on polygamy. Newman may be credited with obtaining the first federal appropriation directly for women. In 1885, she won $40,000 for a Salt Lake City shelter for women leaving polygamous marriages. For years thereafter, Congress funded its annual operating expenses.

GROWING INTEREST GROUPS

During the latter half of the nineteenth century, millions of women learned the skills that men had used for centuries: how to form an organization, define its goals into resolutions and platforms and by-laws, collect dues, elect officers, and do all the communication work that is necessary to speak with a common voice.

Aside from the antislavery societies, the first organizations with a directly political purpose were the National

Members in front of General Federation of Woman Clubs sometime between 1918 and 1928. Almost a century later, the GFWC maintains excellent archives on women's history at its headquarters in Washington, DC.

Founders of the League of Women Voters pose with their recommendations for the Democratic Party platform. Although the date of the photograph is unknown, the issues on the sign make it likely that it was at the 1920 convention in San Francisco (See Chapter 16).

What historians call "the club movement" coalesced into the General Federation of Women's Clubs (GFWC) in 1890. Most such clubs originated from the fact that women long had been barred from colleges, and during the late nineteenth century, they organized study clubs to educate themselves in subjects they had missed in their youth. This led to interest in contemporary issues, and many study clubs evolved into civic organizations that improved local cultural opportunities, especially schools and libraries. Although too often denigrated as mere clubwomen, GFWC members took political stands on issues and lobbied especially for environmentalism, public sanitation, and literacy.

Other organizations, especially the League of Women Voters, as well as the National Federation of Business and Professional Women's Clubs (BPW), began as a direct result of winning the vote in 1920. The same was true for female auxiliaries of the major political parties.[2] A half-century later, these organizations continued while a new brand of feminism arose. The late 1960s and 1970s saw the formation of the National Organization for Women (NOW), the National Women's Political Caucus (NWPC), and other left-leaning organizations. Conservative women countered with new groups in the 1980s. Because Congress adopted new laws on organizational political spending in this era, BPW, NOW, and other older organizations created legal arms known as political action committees, or PACs. Newer groups of conservative women were more likely to organize as PACs from the beginning (see Chapter 18: Political Action Committees).

Woman Suffrage Association and its sometimes rival, the American Woman Suffrage Association. Women who did not necessarily support that then-radical goal also formed organizations in the 1870s to work on other issues that can be considered political.

The Association for the Advancement of Women was dedicated to educational equality, and it evolved into today's American Association of University Women.

The following offers brief histories of the most influential of hundreds of political organizations that have promoted women's causes. Listed in alphabetical order, they were chosen for inclusion on the basis of several criteria, the first of which is whether or not they are aimed directly at advancing the status of women. Some

---

[2] See Chapter 16: Political Parties and Conventions.

Table 17.1 The Establishment of Major Women's Interest Groups, by Year of Founding

Year Founded	Name	Prominent Early Leaders
1848	Women's rights societies	Lucretia Mott; Elizabeth Cady Stanton
1869	National Woman Suffrage Association (NWSA)	Susan B. Anthony; Elizabeth Cady Stanton
1869	American Woman Suffrage Association (AWSA)	Lucy Stone; Julia Ward Howe
1873	Association for the Advancement of Women (later the American Association of University Women)	Jane Cunningham Croly; Maria Mitchell
1874	Women's Christian Temperance Union	Annie Wittenmyer; Frances Willard
1890	National American Woman Suffrage Association	Merger of NWSA and AWSA
1890	General Federation of Women's Clubs	Jane Cunningham Croly; Julia Ward Howe
1896	National Association of Colored Women	Mary Church Terrell
1899	National Association of Women Lawyers	Rosalie Loew; Burnita Shelton Matthews
1903	Women's Trade Union League	Leonora O'Reilly; Mary Kenny O'Sullivan; Rose Schneiderman
1915	Women's International League for Peace and Freedom	Jane Addams; Emily Greene Balch
1919	National Federation of Business and Professional Women's Clubs	Lena Madesen Phillips; Margaret Hickey
1919	League of Women Voters	Carrie Chapman Catt; Maud Wood Park
1921	Planned Parenthood	Margaret Sanger; Mary Ware Dennett
1935	National Council of Negro Women	Mary McLeod Bethune; Dorothy I. Height
1963	President's Commission on the Status of Women	Eleanor Roosevelt; Esther Peterson
1966	National Organization for Women	Betty Friedan; Wilma Scott-Heide
1971	National Women's Political Caucus	Gloria Steinem; Bella Abzug
1974	MANA: A Latina National Organization	Alma Morales Riojas

Source: Compiled by author.

Note: For more information on the National American Woman Suffrage Association and its two earlier constituent groups, both founded in 1869, see Chapter 1: Battle for the Vote. Neither the Women's Trade Union League, founded in 1903, nor the National American Woman Suffrage Association, and its two constituent groups, is extant.

groups—such as the American Federation of Teachers and the American Nurses Association—are large organizations composed primarily of women and frequently support feminist aims, but they are excluded because their chief purpose is to promote their profession.

An overwhelming criterion for inclusion is whether or not the women's organization is national and is politically active, especially in lobbying Congress and state legislatures. Worthy charities composed of women that are not primarily political in aim, such as the Junior League, are excluded. That also is the case for organizations with a religious affiliation, such as the National Conference of Catholic Women.

Taking stands on issues and actively lobbying also means the exclusion of academic think tanks on women. Some, especially the Center for American Women and Politics at Rutgers University, do an excellent job of maintaining records on elected women. It and other such bodies, such as Iowa's Carrie Chapman Catt Center and the Washington, DC-based White House Project, conduct workshops and seminars that enable women to run for office effectively, but lobbying on issues is a prime criterion for inclusion here.

New groups that operate largely in cyberspace also are excluded. Groups such as Women's Media Center and Women's E-News often ask readers to advocate on issues, but they cannot yet be considered historical organizations of women. Even the Ms. Foundation, which dates to an earlier era, is excluded because of its ties to the famous feminist magazine. Influential though that publication and others are, the concentration here is on organizations, not feminist presses.

Organizational nonpartisanship is another factor. The below groups began prior to the creation of modern political action committees, which endorse candidates and contribute financially to campaigns. Although some included organizations may have later developed PACs, that was not their original aim. Modern groups that began with the direct purpose of influencing elections through endorsements and contributions— such as EMILY's List, Concerned Women for America, and the Eagle Forum— are in Chapter 18.

With the exception of the suffrage associations and the historically important Women's Trade Union League, these organizations are extant. No attempt has been made to include the many groups that support a specific historical purpose, such as the preservation of Susan B. Anthony's home or roadway signs that relate to women's history.[3]

---

[3] For hundreds of such groups, see Doris Weatherford, ed., A History of Women in the United States: *A State-by-State Reference*, Vols. 1–4 (Danbury, CT: Grolier Academic Reference, 2004).

American Association of University Women

IIII 16th Street NW
Washington, DC 20036
800-326-AAUW
www.aauw.org

The modern American Association of University Women (AAUW) began as the Association for the Advancement of Women (AAW). AAW grew out of Sorosis, a sorority formed by professional women in New York City in 1868, after female journalists were banned from a function for English author Charles Dickens. A national group from its beginning, AAW aimed to promote the entrance of women into scholarship and the professions.

The leader of Sorosis, JANE CUNNINGHAM CROLY, convened AAW in 1873 in New York City, at a meeting that was attended by four hundred women. Boston's Mary Livermore of the American Woman Suffrage Association was its first president. Famous author Julia Ward Howe of Massachusetts and future Women's Christian Temperance Union president FRANCES WILLARD of Illinois were founding vice presidents. AAW also paid a good deal of attention to science, and self-taught astronomer Maria Mitchell, who discovered a comet in 1847, also was a founder. Although some colleges were available to women by the 1870s, when AAW began, almost none of its early members had had a chance to go to college in their youth in the 1840s. Many had succeeded without the benefit of a formal education, but they profoundly understood what a handicap it was to be banned from classroom and laboratories. Because many of the era's physicians averred that female bodies could not stand the strain of higher education, they wanted to demonstrate the opposite.

As young women took advantage of the new colleges that opened after the Civil War, enough women were college graduates to form the American Association of University Women in 1881. Female students still were a distinct minority, as even in the 1890s and early 1900s few families of upper-class women encouraged higher education. Sociologist Emily Greene Balch, for example, would win the Nobel Peace Prize in 1946, but, when she was young, she had to leave Boston and study at Pennsylvania's Bryn Mawr College because her father was embarrassed to have his friends know that he had a daughter in college.

Thus, when AAUW began in 1881, the majority of American women did not personally know a single female college graduate. AAUW offered companionship for these higher education pioneers, providing an important venue for women to network with others akin to themselves. The older AAW faded and died in the 1890s. Its purpose had been to advocate for higher education, and as that was achieved, the AAUW, which required members to be college graduates, replaced it.

The need for AAUW's pursuit of educational equity remained real, as even in the 1960s and 1970s some colleges barred female students from departments such as horticulture. Because of these and other inequities, AAUW lobbied for the Equal Rights Amendment. It also has been deeply involved with the implementation of Title VII of the 1964 Civil Rights Act, which ostensibly abolished such discrimination, and it has supported affirmative action in scholarships, sports, and other educational equity. AAUW regularly lobbies to implement its motto: Breaking Barriers for Women and Girls.

Business and Professional Women

1718 M Street NW
Washington, DC 20036
202-293-1100
www.bpwfoundation.org

Founded in 1919, just before women got the vote, the National Federation of Business and Professional Women's Clubs, usually called "BPW," was a response to the new job openings that World War I offered to women.

During the war, which ended in 1918, women had entered the world of commerce in increasing numbers and, they understandably felt a need to network with each other. The League of Women Voters also began in 1919, but BPW differed from it in focusing on economic self-sufficiency for women. It soon became the era's most effective female lobbying force.

Pioneer BPW clubs were most popular in the Midwest, and the first president of the organization was Lena Madesen Phillips of Kentucky. Margaret Hickey of St. Louis soon became BPW's best-known leader. During the Great Depression, she led BPW in not only lobbying for women's fair share of New Deal programs, but also for more women at the managerial level of government. BPW devised a talent bank of women qualified for federal appointments, and its leaders used their connections with Department of Labor officials Frances Perkins and Mary Anderson, as well as first lady Eleanor Roosevelt, to promote the careers of female professionals.[4]

Although BPW did not officially endorse candidates, its members have a long history of working in political campaigns. In 1952, Republican women in BPW pushed

---

[4] See Chapter 11: Cabinet and Subcabinet.

hardest for the presidential candidacy of Maine senator Margaret Chase Smith.[5] BPW first endorsed the Equal Rights Amendment in 1937, and it was the major force behind the Equal Pay Act—first introduced in 1945 but not passed until 1963. At the signing ceremony, President John F. Kennedy recognized the primacy of BPW's sponsorship by giving the first pen used for signing the bill to the organization, whose president then was Virginia Allen. He had also acknowledged BPW's long-time advocacy of commissions on the status of women in 1961 when he created the nation's first such body at the federal level.

BPW worked for comparable worth in the 1970s, when feminists tried to persuade local and state governments to reevaluate job categories by gender so that, for instance, professional social workers and librarians—most of them women—would not be paid less than maintenance men and bus drivers, usually men with no hard-won credentials. BPW also joined other organizations in campaigning for the Equal Rights Amendment. It continues to work against sexual harassment and for pay equity, health care reform, and other issues that affect women and their families.

Commissions on the Status of Women

National Association of Commissions on Women
300 San Mateo Blvd.
Albuquerque, NM 87108
505-222-6613
www.nacw.org

Although hundreds of similarly titled organizations exist, not all are necessarily affiliated with the National Association of Commissions on Women. All commissions on the status of women, however, have their roots in the founding of the United Nations (UN) at the end of World War II. In the decades since, commissions have spread internationally and to local and state governments within the United States.

Eleanor Roosevelt, who was appointed by President Harry S. Truman as a UN delegate, led the charge for women at the UN's first meeting in London early in 1946. She was the chief drafter of the Universal Declaration of Human Rights, and with encouragement from American feminist Alice Paul, Roosevelt insisted that the declaration's language—unlike the Declaration of Independence—be written without masculine words.[6] UN founders also created a global Commission on the Status of Women, which

has continued without interruption since 1946. Especially notable gatherings of this commission have been held in Mexico City (1975), Narobi, Kenya (1985), and Beijing, China (1995).

Fifteen nations, ranging alphabetically from Australia to Venezuela, developed such commissions in 1947, but the political climate for similar women's commissions within the United States was not hospitable until Democrat John F. Kennedy won the 1960 election. In his first year in office, he created the President's Commission on the Status of Women, with Roosevelt as chair.

The twenty-six-member commission had sixteen women and ten men. Most of the women were organizational presidents, and most of the men were governmental officials. Their first goal was enactment of the Equal Pay Act, which had lingered in Congress since 1945. It passed in 1963, prior to Kennedy's assassination that year. The commission issued its first major report in 1965, a study of women in the United States that was led by famed anthropologist Margaret Mead. It found that—more than four decades since the Nineteenth Amendment was ratified—women still suffered much legal discrimination, including unequal access to credit and insurance, disqualification from jury service, and restricted educational and employment opportunity.

Because most legal discrimination was based in state laws, President Kennedy asked governors to establish state commissions on the status of women. Most did, including conservative states in the South. Southern governors of the era remained Democrats, and Kennedy was a Democrat. His successor, Texan Lyndon B. Johnson, also was a Southern Democrat, and he, too, urged governors to follow up with state commissions on the status of women.

In some states, the commissions were highly successful in analyzing women's needs and in changing law accordingly. Iowa, for example, published a lengthy report verifying the unequal status of its women, while in Florida, commission women in the 1960s delved into such neglected problems as the near-slave status of female farm workers. Many states performed studies on the status of their homemakers. Attorney Sarah Weddington, of *Roe v. Wade* fame, wrote the Texas report.

County and city governments also created commissions in the 1970s. They brought attention to topics that previously were seen as too shameful for public discussion, giving public voice to new terms such as "domestic violence" and "sexual harassment." Countless commissions played a strong role in the creation of shelters for battered women and "displaced homemakers"—another new term for a previously neglected issue, those of divorced or widowed women who had no employment skills. On both the state and local level, commissioners worked to redefine rape

---

[5] See Chapter 10: Presidential and Vice Presidential Candidates.

[6] See Chapter 1: Battle for the Vote.

American feminists did not limit their organization building to U.S. borders. The International Congress of Women began in Paris, France, in 1878, with two hundred women representing twelve European nations, from England to Rumania. Encouraged by Paris resident Theodore Stanton, son of Elizabeth Cady Stanton, the American attendees included Julia Ward Howe, Mary Livermore, and Lucy Stone. The group, which was called both the "congress" and the "council" of women, met in 1883 in Liverpool, England, and in Washington, DC, in 1888.

The international body's most active leader was May Wright Sewall of Indiana. Sewall presided over a massive meeting in Chicago in 1893, when the World's Fair was held. During one week of May, a convocation attracted 150,000 women from twenty-seven countries who heard 330 scheduled speakers. Countless feminist networks grew from that gathering.

The global women's movement convened in London in 1899 and three years later in Washington. The issue of female enfranchisement came to a head in 1904 in Berlin, Germany. The German government offered generous sponsorship, but Katherine Anthony, Susan's niece, wrote that she believed its aim was to keep women from pursuing any political agendas by overscheduling them with entertainment events. Politically oriented women responded with the International Woman Suffrage Alliance, devoted to winning the vote.

When the alliance met in Copenhagen, Denmark, in 1906, new members came from Australia and Canada. The 1908 gathering in Amsterdam, Netherlands, led by Dutch physician Aletta Jacobs, had representatives from twenty nations. Australia, Finland, and Norway were honored because they had granted voting rights. At the 1911 convention in Stockholm, Sweden, the Rev. Dr. Anna Howard Shaw preached in an ancient church with a women's choir and a female organist

and composer. The 1913 convention was the acme, as the Austro-Hungarian Empire welcomed women to Budapest, Hungary, with the government paying much of the alliance's expenses. The organizer was Rosika Schwimmer, a Budapest resident who attracted 240 delegates from twenty-two nations. The Chinese Woman Suffrage Society joined, giving the alliance representation on five continents.

But World War I erupted the next year, and the alliance did not gather until after its end. British and American women won the vote soon after the war, and without their impetus, the organization never would be the same. Nonetheless, those still struggling for basic rights met in Geneva, Switzerland, in 1920 under the aegis of the new League of Nations.

Delegates from nearly every European nation attended, as well as ten from India and one from Japan. Some American women attended, including Ida Husted Harper, who had been Susan B. Anthony's press aide. Harper wrote of the many goals adopted, which included the following.

Equal status of women with men on legislative and administrative bodies; full personal and civil rights for married women. . . . Equal pay for equal work. . . . The right to work of women, married or unmarried, shall be recognized and no special regulations shall be imposed contrary to the wishes of the women themselves. . . . Resolutions were adopted against traffic in women. (Harper 1922, 6:871)

Almost a century later, the United Nations holds similar conferences, but they are neither frequent nor well funded. Many of needs, however, remain the same. The sale of women and girls continues to plague society, even in the United States, and a disproportionate number of women still are uneducated and underemployed. Some nations do not allow women to vote or drive cars; many do not allow them to file for divorce.

and to insist that law enforcement officers take it seriously. They also pushed for more women in law enforcement and in other public safety professions.

Some commissions succeeded in extending school board responsibilities to preschool, building government-sponsored child care centers. They also worked with private enterprise to create child care within parental workplaces. Commissions took the lead on reforming common practices such as disallowing a woman's income in mortgage applications; they repealed laws that compelled women to change their names at marriage; and they championed the needs of women ranging from those in prison to those in universities.

The year 1977, when President Jimmy Carter supported a national feminist gathering in Houston, Texas, proved the zenith of such commissions, and the conservative trend signaled by the 1980 election of Republican Ronald Reagan brought an end to many. Both state and local governments defunded the commissions' meager budgets, and some governors allowed them to die by simply failing to making appointments. At the federal level, the president's commission that had existed through the administrations of Democrats Kennedy, Johnson, and Carter, as well as under Republicans Nixon and Ford, died under Reagan.

In some states during the 1980s and 1990s, women were successful with legislation that made commissions permanent, no longer subject to the whim of a governor. With the White House failing to support them, disparate local and state commissions also began the private National Association of Commissions on Women. President Bill Clinton revived the concept with the White House Office on Women's Initiatives, but his successor, George W. Bush, closed that office in 2001.

The political pendulum swung again with the 2008 election, and on March 9, 2009, during Women's History Month, Democrat Barack Obama signed an executive order creating the White House Council on Women and Girls. Two years later, that body issued *Women in America: Indicators of Economic and Social Well-Being* (2011), the first comprehensive report on the status of American women in the half-century since Margaret Mead's 1965 report.

General Federation of Women's Clubs

1734 N Street NW
Washington, DC
202-347-3168
www.gfwc.org

Founded in 1890 by Jane Cunningham Croly, the General Federation of Women's Clubs (GFWC) united local women's clubs that had grown from the 1870s onward. Representatives of sixty-three clubs attended the founding meeting in New York City. Many were study clubs, in which women who had not had the opportunity to attend college joined together in self-education projects. Other clubs aimed more at civic improvement than self-improvement, and some of those became active in local government.

On the national level, GFWC's first success was passage of federal Pure Food and Drug Act. The 1906 law provides the basic framework for the Food and Drug Administration. Prior to its enactment, for example, milk often was diluted with water and chalk. It was not refrigerated, causing illness and even death of thousands of children every summer. Lobbyists for GFWC worked less successfully for a national ban on child labor and for an eight-hour workday, especially for female workers.

By 1915, so many women were willing to get involved with these issues that the federation had more than two million members in many thousands of local clubs. Virtually every community with a population of a thousand or more had a GFWC affiliate, usually named for the town. In Florida, for example, in addition to the Tampa Woman's Club, there was the nearby Ruskin Woman's Club and the Brandon Woman's Club. Many built clubhouses, some of which still are extant. Members pushed city and county governments to build parks and playgrounds. They lobbied school boards for hot lunches. Even without the vote, they worked for installation of water and sewer systems.

Environmentalism, a new movement at the turn of the century, also was a GFWC priority. Members were especially successful in convincing other women to stop wearing hats adorned with feathers. The fashion caused the near-extinction of many species of exotic birds that were shot to provide feathers. GFWC clubs also bought and preserved wilderness land, and they often financed local projects, especially libraries. Using grants from multimillionaire Andrew Carnegie, they founded about 75 percent of the nation's libraries and lobbied governments for operating funds thereafter.

Their awareness of the disappearing natural environment led GFWC to recognize the plight of Native Americans, and they worked for improved conditions on reservations. The early federation also had some clubs of black women and a few integrated clubs. Like the clubs of white women, these worked for civic improvements in their communities, demonstrating how to use government for the greater good.

During World War II, members sold enough government bonds to purchase more than four hundred airplanes. In 1944, the war's last full year, the federation endorsed the Equal Rights Amendment, and in 1945, it sent representatives to the founding meetings of the United Nations.

As modern women have less time for volunteerism, and as the organization's goals became more conservative than other groups such as the League of Women Voters, membership had fallen from millions to about 350,000 at the end of the twentieth century. GFWC never has endorsed candidates and remains nonpartisan, but many individual members are politically influential in their communities. In the 1990s, the national federation played a role in the passage of two laws, the Violence against Women Act and the Family and Medical Leave Act. GFWC also has adopted positions supporting gun control. Its Washington, DC, headquarters features a Women's History and Resource Center.

League of Women Voters

1730 M Street, NW
Washington, DC 20036
202-429-1965
www.lwv.org

The League of Women Voters (LWV) has its first roots in the National Council of Women Voters, which formed in 1911 in states—all in the West—where women could vote. That group never achieved significant national status, however. Consequently, the modern LWV dates itself to 1919, the year that both houses of Congress passed the Nineteenth Amendment.

National American Woman Suffrage Association (NAWSA) president Carrie Chapman Catt proposed the idea for an organization to encourage women to participate in civic life at the 1917 convention, and plans were finalized at the 1919 convention.[7] Catt soon became the honorary president, and the league's first genuine president was MAUD WOOD PARK. Like Catt, she was an exceptionally skilled lobbyist and played a major role in the league's first congressional successes.

In 1921, LWV joined with the General Federation of Women's Clubs and other groups to lobby successfully for the Sheppard-Towner Maternity and Infancy Protection Act, which provided federal funding for the care of pregnant women and their babies. The following year, also with lobbying support from LWV, Congress passed the Cable Act, which modified federal law that forced a woman to surrender her citizenship if she married a foreign man.

The Roaring Twenties were socially liberal but politically conservative, and those two bills turned out to be the only successful ones of an original thirty-eight-item league agenda. Future presidents were not as adept as Park, and because NAWSA had been a single-issue organization focusing solely on the vote, many women did not see the multi-issue league as necessary in the way that NAWSA had been. Membership dropped sharply. Only one in every ten of NAWSA's two million members chose to join LWV. As the years went by, the organization increasingly lost touch with its feminist roots and fell into the habit of studying political activity, not leading it. In the 1920s and 1930s, for example, LWV issued reports on the numbers of women elected to office that showed a decline, not growth. Yet the league neither endorsed candidates nor encouraged its members to run for office, and the few who did so often found themselves ostracized as "too political."

Disagreement about the Equal Rights Amendment also split the organization, and LWV increasingly was dominated by women who avoided controversy. Instead, they immersed members into studies of issues, usually unrelated to women's needs. The league focused on technical improvements in governance reform and on voter outreach. But, even in that area, it did not take on registration of black voters. During World War II, instead of lobbying for equal pay for factory workers or child care for the millions of mothers who entered the labor force, the league's major activity was sending absentee ballots to (mostly male) soldiers abroad. At conventions between 1942 and 1944, members confirmed their opposition to the Equal Rights Amendment.

Feminism revived in the 1960s with the National Organization for Women and other groups, and the league then returned to more of its early century purpose. It encouraged men to join, and it worked with other organizations to support the Equal Rights Amendment and for repeal of state laws discriminating against women. Its major emphasis, though, continued to be elections, as league members regularly ensured honesty by volunteering at the polls. At the national level, it worked for the use of voter machines instead of paper ballots, as well as for publicly financed campaigns to lessen the power of big donors. Most significant, no other organization has played such an important role in televised political debates. Leaguers from national to local levels have specialized in moderating them, thus providing voters a direct look at candidates.

As the new millennium began, the LWV had more than twelve hundred chapters throughout the nation. It maintains its nonpartisan nature and does not endorse candidates, but its members have led countless campaigns on state and local issues. In many places, league members have brought down corrupt public officials with their careful research and attendance at public meetings. A reputation for absolute honesty has earned these women the respect of law enforcement officials, editorial writers, and others who have curtailed the careers of political bosses.

Equally important, the organization has served as a training ground for thousands of women in office. It does lengthy, unbiased studies on issues prior to adopting positions on them at annual conventions. In 2011, the national LWV prioritized fighting repeal of the health care reform law enacted during the Obama administration and damaging amendments to the older Clean Air Act.

Mana: A Latina National Organization

1725 K Street NW
Washington, DC 20006
202-833-0060
www.hermana.org

Founded in 1974, MANA reflected the era's expansion of civil rights to both women and racial minorities. Originally the Mexican-American Women's National Association, it soon expanded to include Spanish-speaking women of other nationalities.

---

[7] See Chapter 1: Battle for the Vote.

Now the largest pan-Hispanic women's organization, it works to empower women through both leadership development and issue advocacy. Its membership has roots in Central and South American nations, as well as the Caribbean, and MANA chapters have been established throughout the United States.

It does not endorse candidates, but MANA actively lobbies Congress and state legislatures. It gained attention, for example, in 2009, when members protested against depicting the Mexican border as a terrorist threat. Immigration reform is among its highest priorities, but MANA also has feminist priorities and especially applauded the confirmation of Sonia Sotomayor to the U.S. Supreme Court. Among its legislative goals in 2011 was protecting educational access for Spanish speakers from budget cuts.

National Association of Colored Women's Clubs

1601 R Street NW
Washington, DC 20009
202-667-4080
www.nacwc.org

Formally begun in Washington, DC, on July 21, 1896, the National Association of Colored Women's Clubs (NACWC) grew out of a Boston meeting held the previous year.

Bostonian Josephine St. Pierre Ruffin—who also was active in the mostly white General Federation of Women's Clubs (GFWC)—pulled together leaders of the Colored Women's League (founded 1893) and the National Federation of Afro-American Women (founded 1895) that agreed to merge. Margaret Murray Washington, wife of famed Booker T. Washington, was the temporary chairman, and MARY CHURCH TERRELL was the first president. Delegates from twenty-five states, representing about five thousand women, were at the founding meeting, which occurred just six years after GFWC united similar clubs for white women.

Although few realized it, NACWC's goals predated those that white feminists would adopt decades later, when white women began to enter the workforce in large numbers. Most black women always had worked, and NACWC's goals centered around employment issues. Because "so many families are supported entirely by our women," Terrell said, the NACWC would focus on "equality of pay" and "care for the children of absentee mothers" (Terrell 1940, 169). Child care for black mothers, though, was often a profoundly different issue than it was for white women. Black women who worked for upper-class families often were expected to travel with them for months at a time. Even middle-class white families moved to summer homes in mountains or at the seashore and expected their servants to go along, which would leave the children of maids and cooks without care. Providing child care thus became a priority for NACWC much earlier than for white women.

Membership rose to fifteen thousand in less than a decade. Some of its twelve departments were devoted to self-improvement in art and literature, but Terrell also anticipated the consciousness raising and women's shelters that white feminists created in the 1970s. She imaginatively but largely unsuccessfully proposed counseling centers for black women. Other goals were more political, with a strong emphasis on ending lynching and the convict labor system that reduced black prisoners in the Deep South to near-slave status. Members also worked to end public transportation policies that forced blacks—no matter how wealthy or educated—into segregated accommodations.

Although NACWC forged links with white organizations, it was not a major player in the movement for the vote. Terrell personally was active for the cause, but she recognized that having the organization take up the issue of the vote was too risky for most of her members—not only because of opposition from employers, but also from husbands, most of whom were social conservatives. Furthermore, many suffrage leaders saw black women as a political liability. Nonetheless, under the leadership of its fourth president, Elizabeth Carter Brooks, NACWC endorsed female enfranchisement at its 1912 convention. At that same convention, delegates began a scholarship fund with an initial endowment of $50,000.

The issues that most motivated NACWC were local and practical. Members worked for child care and health care, as well as for vocational education for black women, especially in nursing. Because they had little influence with local governments, they raised their own money to support such facilities. Members built the first nursery school for black children in the South, in Atlanta, and by the middle of the twentieth century, virtually every branch owned property. In Kansas, a state without a major black population, NACWC in 1954 owned a clubhouse and a home for unwed mothers in Topeka, as well as the Phyllis Wheatley Home in Wichita.

NACWC also worked to keep black history alive, building a monument to Harriet Tubman in Albany, New York, and naming buildings in Los Angeles, California, for abolitionist Sojourner Truth and businesswoman Madame C. J. Walker. The organization celebrated its one-hundredth anniversary in Detroit, Michigan, in 2006 and has chapters in thirty-two states.

National Association of Women Lawyers

321 North Clark Street
Chicago, IL 60654
312-988-6186
www.nawl.org

The National Association of Women Lawyers (NAWL) began in 1899, thirty years after Iowa became the first state to admit a woman to the practice of law. Most states had their first female attorneys by then, but because such women remained highly unusual, NAWL was an early feminist organization.[8]

Unlike organizations for teachers, librarians, and especially nurses, women in the legal field had to fight for decades to obtain permission from courts to do their jobs. Beyond that, these pioneers made a huge contribution to other feminist organizations, as their legal skills were key to success in the many lawsuits that had to be filed (or defended) in the quest for the vote and other civil rights.

NAWL began as the Women Lawyers Club, with eighteen members in New York City and Rosalie Loew as president. From this club in 1899, it expanded to become an association in 1911, when it also began to publish *Women Lawyer Journal*. The organization's current name, adopted in 1923, reflected an expansion to the entire nation. Its members were active in the suffrage movement, and after that 1920 victory, they emphasized reform of state laws affecting women, especially on juries. A 1939 report showed that only twelve states had laws on jury duty that were equal for men and women. All others either automatically exempted women unless they made an active effort to volunteer or they completely barred women as jurors. More than two decades would pass before laws were changed in every state.

NAWL also worked to end the many legal barriers that married women faced, especially in business, and it supported a constitutional amendment to ban child labor. It endorsed the Equal Rights Amendment in 1935 and, in 1939, announced that thirty-seven women had been appointed to significant positions within the prestigious American Bar Association (ABA), which had admitted its first two female members in 1918. NAWL became an ABA affiliate in 1943, in the midst of World War II. During the war, many NAWL members did pro bono work for soldiers and their families. NAWL members also were appointed to positions on the status of women in the early United Nations, and at the war's end, they organized events to network with female lawyers internationally.

NAWL revived its support for the Equal Rights Amendment in the 1960s, worked for the 1963 Equal Pay Act, and played a major role in the era's reform of state divorce laws. In some states, it remained almost impossible to obtain a divorce.

As women began to enter law schools in large numbers in the 1970s and 1980s, NAWL's membership grew exponentially. It elected its first African American president, Mahala Ashley Dickerson, in 1983, and watched with pride as New Mexico's Roberta Cooper Ramo became the first female ABA president in 1995. Florida's Martha Barnett was the second in 2000, and Kathy Castor, president of Florida's NAWL branch, was elected to Congress in 2006. These women serve as examples of the excellent networking that NAWL provides, even as it continues to work on issues that affect women—in a profession that long resisted them.

National Council of Negro Women

633 Pennsylvania Avenue NW
Washington, DC 20005
202-737-0120
www.ncnw.org

Founded on December 5, 1935, at a meeting called by Florida's Mary McLeod Bethune, the National Council of Negro Women (NCNW) merged a number of organizations.[9] NCNW differed from the extant National Association of Colored Women Clubs (NACWC), which focused on local charities and long had Republican leaders. The new organization leaned Democratic and its goals were more clearly political. NCNW especially emphasized equal employment opportunity.

During World War II, NCNW played a particularly strong role for blacks in the Women's Army Corps (WAC). Although black women, like black men, lived in segregated barracks, the WAC offered nearly equal employment opportunity and did not limit black women to kitchen and laundry duty. Bethune served on the advisory committee that formed the WAC, and she was influential in bringing its second training facility to Daytona Beach, Florida, where there was a substantial black population.

After the war, NCNW worked for a permanent Fair Employment Practices Commission, as well as federal

---

[8] See Chapter 13: Pioneers in the Judiciary.

[9] For Bethune's biography, see Chapter 12: Ambassadors.

legislation that would take the crime of lynching out of negligent state courts in the South. When Bethune retired from its presidency in 1949, the organization had some eight thousand members and would grow stronger with the civil rights movement of the next decades, as desegregation of schools and public accommodations became the key issues.

For forty years, from 1970 to her 2010 death at age ninety-eight, Dorothy I. Height was NCNW president. In addition to focusing on racial prejudice, especially in employment, she assisted organizations aimed at gender bias. Height was among the women who witnessed President John F. Kennedy's 1963 signing of the Equal Pay Act, and President Bill Clinton awarded her the Medal of Freedom in 1994.

By then, NCWC's Washington office had more than fifty staff members serving some 250 local groups. It conducted programs in Africa and published two house organs, *Black Women's Voice* and *Sisters Magazine*. Members also preserved Mary McLeod Bethune's Washington, DC, home at 1713 Vermont Avenue and, in 1995, bought a historic headquarters on prestigious Pennsylvania Avenue—in a neighborhood that once featured a slave market.

National Council of Women's Organizations

714 G Street NW
Washington, DC 20003
202-293-4505
www.ncwo.org

An umbrella body for some two hundred organizations of women, the National Council of Women's Organizations was an outgrowth of the 1983 defeat of the Equal Rights Amendment and especially was energized by the United Nations' feminist gathering in Beijing, China, in 1995.

The council unites women's organizations for a progressive agenda focused on economic and educational equity, child care, reproductive rights, fairness in Social Security, and other evolving issues. The coalition is diverse, representing religious groups and homemakers, as well as lesbians and women of color. Its head since 2005 has been Susan Scanlan, who drafted legislation that admitted women to the historic military academies early in her Capitol Hill career. She also helped found the Congressional Women's Caucus.

The council unifies political action on issues, but, according to its website, membership in the coalition is not open to "for-profit organizations or those whose purpose is to elect candidates from a single party."

National Organization for Women

1100 H Street NW
Washington, DC 20005
202-628-8669
www.now.org

From its 1966 beginning, the National Organization for Women (NOW) has emphasized the "for" in its name and always has included male feminists. It soon became the preeminent group revitalizing the feminist movement that had faded in the 1920s. Especially in the 1970s and 1980s, NOW made a larger contribution to female equality than any other organization.

The cultural catalyst for NOW was Betty Friedan's best-selling book *The Feminine Mystique* (1963), and Friedan served as NOW's first president. Its founding on October 29, 1966, took place at meeting chaired by University of Wisconsin political scientist Kathryn Clarenbach, an associate of women's history giant Gerda Lerner. Most of the three hundred attendees at the Washington, DC, gathering were, like Clarenbach, affiliated with commissions on the status of women. Because these were governmental bodies, they often were barred from actions that commissioners wanted to take—endorsing legislative bills or filing lawsuits, for example—and women wanted a private body that they could control without interference from politicians.

NOW provided that organizational vehicle, and it grew rapidly. When Friedan stepped down in 1970, after only a little more than three years, 750 delegates from 118 chapters attended that year's convention. Delegates also promoted a one-day national strike by women on August 26, 1970, which was the fiftieth anniversary of the ratification of the Nineteenth Amendment granting all women the vote. Women's history was so little known that almost no one was aware of the anniversary, and the event got a great deal of press attention. Not all of it was positive, as conservatives objected to the one-day strike, but the overall effect for NOW was excellent, and membership soared.

One early success was pressuring newspapers to end employment ads that routinely segregated jobs by gender. Classified ad sections read "Help Wanted—Men" and "Help Wanted—Women," instead of today's "sales," "professional," and so on. A great deal of attention went to education, and NOW can claim major credit for ending school practices that routinely routed girls into home economics and secretarial classes, while boys studied agriculture or business. NOW pressured publishers to eliminate similar stereotypes in textbooks, and chapters spent years lobbying school boards to provide equity for girls in athletics. In some cities, the first women hired as anchors on television and the first female firefighters and police officers were because NOW chapters filed lawsuits.

Reform of state divorce laws probably was its easiest early success, but after the U.S. Supreme Court's 1973 decision on abortion rights, the organization has continually defended reproductive freedom. NOW also lobbied successfully for contraceptive availability, especially in Connecticut and Massachusetts, the last two states to restrict access to birth control pills. In some places, NOW members built women's centers and shelters for victims of domestic violence, and everywhere, they reformed laws on rape and insisted that it be treated like other crimes. At the time, for example, a victim had to pay for an expensive medical kit that gathered the material evidence to prosecute the alleged rapist.

NOW was not an entirely political organization, as many members felt a stronger attraction to consciousness raising, that is, group discussions of how gender bias permeates all aspects of life. Some boycotted products whose advertising denigrated women, and others emphasized dress reform—the press, for example, fixated on so-called bra burnings. Without breaking from NOW, many women whose interests were more political than social formed the National Women's Political Caucus in 1971.

NOW's presidency rotates frequently. Aileen Hernandez briefly succeeded Friedan, Wilma Scott-Heide became the third president in 1971, and Karen DeCrow followed. Eleanor Smeal was the first salaried president in 1977, as membership grew to approximately a half-million, with a thousand chapters all across the nation. Pennsylvanian Molly Yard took over from Smeal in 1987. The daughter of missionaries to China, Yard had seen the most horrific results of gender bias, including female infanticide. When Yard suffered a stroke in 1991, attorney Patricia Ireland became president. She had the longest tenure, between 1991 and 2001, and Ireland's book *What Women Want* (1996) provided an excellent encapsulation of the era's feminist issues.

NOW has sponsored many parades and demonstrations to draw attention to current issues. Its 2004 March for Women's Lives attracted well over a million people to the National Mall in Washington, DC, for the cause of protecting women's reproductive health from government interference. NOW's current agenda focuses on promoting economic and political equality, ethnic diversity, and equal rights for lesbians, as well as ending sex discrimination and violence against women.

National Women's Political Caucus

P.O. Box 50476
Washington, DC 20091
202-785-1100
www.nwpc.org

Founded in 1971, the National Women's Political Caucus (NWPC) was largely an outgrowth of the National Organization for Women (NOW). No animosity existed between NOW and NWPC leadership, and many feminists joined both organizations. The aim of the caucus was more specialized, as it provided a new feminist vehicle in mainstream politics.

Its primary leaders were celebrated journalist Gloria Steinem, as well as New York representatives Bella Abzug and Shirley Chisholm. Although they were Democrats, the caucus was bipartisan, and some of its subsequent presidents were Republicans. NWPC was particularly active at Democratic conventions in 1976 and 1980, and it merits much of the credit for the 1984 nomination of Geraldine A. Ferraro as the Democratic candidate for vice president.

State and local chapters endorsed candidates of both parties from the organization's beginning, but national rules limited them to women. Endorsing only women proved a negative in NWPC's aim of ratifying the Equal Rights Amendment (ERA), as the inability to offer political support to male ERA sponsors caused some chapters to break from the national organization.

After the ERA ran out of time for ratification in 1983, the caucus concentrated more on electing women to state and local offices. Among its first successes was Kathy Whitmire, a member who was elected as mayor of Houston, Texas, in 1981.[10] NWPC members regularly conducted workshops on how to run a successful campaign.

The caucus has supported Senate ratification of the United Nations (UN) treaty to eliminate discrimination against women since the UN drafted that pact in 1980. It was more successful in supporting the 1994 Violence against Women Act, which passed during the administration of Democratic president Bill Clinton, as well as the 2009 Paycheck Fairness Act under Democratic president Barack Obama. As the caucus celebrated its fortieth anniversary in 2011, its goals included protection of reproductive rights and health care reform.

Planned Parenthood

1-800-230-PLAN
www.plannedparenthood.org[11]

Planned Parenthood has a long history of both political controversy and personal courage.

In 1916, Margaret Sanger, a credentialed nurse, midwife, and the married mother of three, began the nation's first

---

[10] See Chapter 9: Mayors

[11] Because of attacks on its clients and employees, Planned Parenthood does not publicize the address of its national headquarters. See Chapter 9: Mayors

birth control clinic with her sister, Ethel Byrne, in poor neighborhood of Brooklyn, New York. Women's demand for knowledge and control of their bodies was clear in that almost five hundred clients showed up on opening day. They were eager to learn about the diaphragms that Sanger had smuggled into the United States from Holland. But Sanger and Byrne soon were arrested and jailed. Speaking about birth control was equated to obscenity, and the cause would be tied up in court litigation for many years.

The organization also owes a great historical debt to Mary Ware Dennett, who joined Sanger in forming the National Birth Control League in 1915. A descendant of an old Massachusetts family, Dennett also was the mother of three. Her ancestors included Lucretia Coffin Mott and Martha Coffin Wright, leaders of the first women's rights meeting in Seneca Falls, New York, in 1848. Dennett had held the nascent birth control movement together while Sanger researched the issue in Europe—after fleeing from arrest in 1913, when the Post Office Department deemed her article on syphilis to be obscene.

Under Dennett's leadership the organization took the name Voluntary Parenthood League, but she and Sanger split in 1925. Court decisions had made Sanger more pragmatic, while Dennett remained more feminist. Dennett continued to argue for free speech, while Sanger accepted judicial rulings that only physicians could dispense information on how to prevent pregnancy.

Sanger and her second husband, wealthy industrialist John Slee, moved to Arizona in 1937, but she never fully retired. After two decades as the Voluntary Parenthood League, the organization changed its name to Planned Parenthood in 1942, the first full year of U.S. entry in World War II. Public health officials in that war were more realistic about preventing venereal disease than they had been in World War I, and many soldiers overseas took advantage of free condoms that the military distributed.

International Planned Parenthood began in 1952, and Sanger traveled widely raising funds for research on the birth control pill. It went on the market in 1960. When Sanger died in 1966, millions of women were taking "the pill" everyday. Just a few decades earlier, it had been illegal even to discuss pregnancy prevention.

After Sanger, Mary Steichen Calderone emerged as Planned Parenthood's most prominent leader. A Quaker and also the mother of three, Dr. Calderone had excellent credentials in medicine and public health. She pioneered sex education in schools and saw the expansion of Planned Parenthood's services, as contraception began to be accepted as routine in the 1960s and 1970s. The U.S. Supreme Court's 1973 decision on early abortions in *Roe v. Wade* marked another milestone for female health and privacy, but there soon was a backlash.

Planned Parenthood unsuccessfully fought the 1976 Hyde Amendment, named for Republican representative

---

STATUS OF WOMEN: AGE OF CONSENT

Lawmaking bodies composed entirely of men seldom addressed issues related to women, especially if those issues involved sexuality. Every state, though, had to have laws under which rape could be prosecuted. Discussion of rape and other sex crimes frequently was used as an argument against women's involvement in "dirty" politics and as a justification for excluding women from the judiciary, particularly as jurors.

Towards the end of the nineteenth century, some women defied decorum and forced legislators to deal with the need for legal reform. These lobbyists usually volunteered at the request of the Women's Christian Temperance Union (WCTU). Although the WCTU focused on alcohol abuse, it also had a long list of other concerns, including child abuse. The WCTU had chapters in every state by the turn of the century, and these women ran a national—albeit quiet—campaign to lobby state legislatures into raising the age of consent, also termed the age of protection.

This is the minimum age at which a person is considered legally competent to consent to sex. Until the WCTU's

campaign, that age was set shamefully low. In Delaware, for example, until 1895, a "woman" could give her consent to sex at age seven.

In Georgia, in 1899, a bill to raise the age from ten to twelve was defeated. In several states that raised the age, lawmakers nonetheless added clauses spelling out to future (male) jurors that they could not convict a man merely on the testimony of the victim. Even in New York, the legal age of consent remained ten in 1900, as legislators failed to respond to lobbying.

The WCTU conducted a well-organized national campaign (see Table 17.2). Except for California, every state reporter provided age of consent information when Susan B. Anthony and Ida Husted Harper requested it for their end-of-the-century compilation on the status of women. Many state reporters included information on later legislation that raised the age higher. Although Oregon had led the way in 1864, before WCTU began, most states did not address the issue until women brought it to their attention, if then.

Table 17.2 Age of Consent Reform, 1864–1900

State	Year of First Reform	Change in Age
Alabama	1897	10 to 14
Arizona	1887	10 to 14
Arkansas	1893	12 to 16
California	Not recorded	
Colorado	1891	10 to 16
Connecticut	1887	10 to 14
Dakota Territory	1887	10 to 14
Delaware	1895	7 to 18
District of Columbia	1889	12 to 16
Florida	1900	10 to 16
Georgia	1899	House bill to raise from 10 to 12 was defeated, 71–77
Idaho	1893	10 to 14
Illinois	1887	10 to 14
Indiana	1900	Remained at 14
Iowa	1886	10 to 13
Kansas	1900	18 (no record available on how long age of consent had been 18)
Kentucky	1900	Remained at 12
Louisiana	1896	none to 16
Maine	1887	10 to 13
Maryland	1899	14 to 16
Massachusetts	1886	10 to 13
Michigan	1887	10 to 14
Minnesota	1891	10 to 16
Mississippi	1900	Remained at 10
Missouri	1889	12 to 14
Montana	1887	10 to 15
Nebraska	1885	10 to 12
Nevada	1889	12 to 14
New Hampshire	1887	10 to 13; as of 1900, girls could marry at 12
New Jersey	1887	10 to 16
New Mexico	1887	10 to 14
New York	1900	Remained at 10
North Carolina	1900	Remained at 10
Ohio	1887	10 to 12
Oklahoma	1890	None to 14
Oregon	1864	10 to 14
Pennsylvania	1887	10 to 16
Rhode Island	1889	10 to 14
South Carolina	1895	10 to 14
Tennessee	1893	10 to 16
Texas	1891	10 to 12
Utah	1888	10 to 13
Vermont	1886	10 to 14
Virginia	1896	12 to 14
Washington	1893	12 to 16
West Virginia	1900	Remained at 12
Wisconsin	1887	10 to 14
Wyoming	1882	10 to 14

Source: Compiled by author, from information in Susan B. Anthony and Ida Husted Harper, eds., *History of Woman Suffrage*, Vol. 4 (Indianapolis, IN: Hollenbeck Press, 1902; reprint, New York: Arno Press, 1969).

Note: No data are available for Alaska or Hawaii as they were not yet states. For North Dakota and South Dakota, see Dakota Territory. States continued to make adjustments to their ages of consent in the twentieth century.

Henry J. Hyde of Illinois. It prohibited the use of Medicaid funds to terminate pregnancies. Faye Wattleton became the organization's president in 1978, and she led it through many lawsuits and legislative battles during the conservative 1980s. The gag rule imposed by the Reagan administration prohibited overseas physicians who received federal funds from even discussing the topic with their patients.

The theoretical "war on abortion" became literal in some instances, and Planned Parenthood facilities were bombed in several cities. Dr. David Gunn was killed outside a clinic in Pensacola, Florida, in 1993. Dr. John Bayard Britton was assassinated there the next year. Two female Planned Parenthood employees, neither of them abortion providers, were shot later in 1994. Gloria Feldt courageously took on the presidency in 1996, and she saw the organization through a decade with hundreds of assaults on Planned Parenthood employees and clients, including forty bombings.

At the beginning of the new millennium, Planned Parenthood had approximately 750 clinics throughout the country. Almost a century after the crusade began, Planned Parenthood continues to work on behalf of women's health, even as eliminating federal funding from the organization became a central battle in the budget debates of 2011.

Woman's Christian Temperance Union

1730 Chicago Avenue
Evanston, IL 60201
800-755-1321
www.wctu.org

The Woman's Christian Temperance Union (WCTU) began almost spontaneously in the winter of 1873–1874, when a Woman's Crusade against alcohol swept through Ohio.

Americans today seldom realize how much their ancestors drank, but records show that great quantities of alcohol were consumed. Early colleges supplied their male students with daily beer, and soldiers and sailors received regular rum rations. Loving mothers pacified their babies with alcohol-based elixirs that were viewed as medicinal. The nation's first civil unrest, the Whiskey Rebellion during the presidency of George Washington, was caused by a new tax on liquor. At the same time, the status of women was so low that they had no protection from alcoholic men. Drunken husbands not only could beat their wives and children with impunity, but they also were free to spend the family income without any legal restraint. Divorce was almost impossible, and thus, as the women's rights movement gained strength, a political movement to prohibit alcohol grew.

The WCTU was women's strongest organization in that movement. Beginning with women who prayed and sang hymns in front of Ohio saloons, it formalized in Cleveland in the summer of 1874. The Midwest would remain its stronghold, and the WCTU's first president was Annie Wittenmyer of Iowa. She had worked during the Civil War for the U.S. Sanitary Commission and developed great organizational skills. In the five years of her presidency, the WCTU built a network of more than a thousand local units with some twenty-six thousand members. She also created a publication, *Our Union*, which was edited by Frances Willard, who, in 1879, was elected president over the more politically conservative Wittenmyer.

Willard and the WCTU soon were synonymous, and she was one of the century's most popular women. Her election signaled a victory for WCTU members who supported causes beyond temperance, and under Willard's "do everything" platform, the organization expanded to other feminist issues, including prostitution. Nonfeminist goals also were adopted. As Willard networked with advocates for such causes as labor, peace, and prison reform, the organization had thirty-nine different issue-oriented departments.

The most politically successful may have been Social Purity, which managed to raise the age of consent in almost every state. The age of consent, sometimes called the age of protection, is the age at which a man can argue in court that he is not guilty of rape because a "woman" consented to sex. Before the WCTU worked to reform these state laws, it was as low as seven. (See Table 17.2)

By 1891, when the World Women's Christian Temperance Union (World WCTU) began with a meeting in Boston, the organization garnered seven million signatures on a polyglot petition to governments throughout the world, urging them to control narcotics, including tobacco, as well as alcohol. WCTU also reached out to black women and had an organizational department devoted to building chapters of African Americans, especially in the South. It had less outreach to immigrant women, many of whom came from European cultures in which daily use of beer and wine was routine. Most of those women were Catholic, and the use of "Christian" in its name was not truly meaningful, as Jewish women were more likely to join the WCTU than Catholic women.

As the number of immigrants increased and the nation became more cosmopolitan in the early twentieth century, the WCTU—centered as it was in small towns in the Midwest—became increasingly parochial. Even before Willard's 1898 death, signs appeared that members were beginning to reject her progressivism. The tactics of temperance extremist Carry Nation, who infamously attacked saloons with a hatchet in Kansas during the early twentieth century, also brought the organization into political disrepute. The WCTU never had another prominent president after Willard, and it increasingly emphasized Protestant religiosity and the single issue of Prohibition. By about 1910, its political strategy was less independent than it had been earlier, and it became much more subordinate to male-dominated Prohibition groups.

The Eighteenth Amendment, which provided for a federal ban on alcohol, was added to the U.S. Constitution in January 1919. At that time, WCTU had some 800,000 members, but success kills a single-issue organization, and its membership rapidly declined. Repeal of the Eighteenth Amendment in 1933 (with the Twenty-first Amendment) did not revive it. Most Americans, women as well as men, concluded that the Noble Experiment had demonstrated its failure during the Roaring Twenties. In the decades afterward, WCTU members still made themselves available to lecture to schoolchildren on temperance, including addictions to tobacco and caffeine, as well as illegal drugs and alcohol. Its Protestant orientation limited that audience, too, especially after court decisions ruled against sectarian prayer in public schools.

When substance abuse again became an issue in the 1970s, WCTU's membership was too small to be an asset in antidrug coalitions. Operating out of Willard's historic home in Evanston, Illinois, it continued to publish *Signal Press,* but the WCTU no longer could be considered a viable political organization. It nonetheless merits respect for the attitudinal change that it led in an era when drunkenness was excused, even in politically prominent men, while women suffered in legal silence.

Women's International League for Peace and Freedom

777 UN Plaza
New York, NY 10017
212-682-1265
www.wilpfinternational.org

Founded in January 1915 by Jane Addams, the Women's International League for Peace and Freedom (WILPF) began as the Woman's Peace Party.

With Carrie Chapman Catt, prominent physician Alice Hamilton, and others, Addams led an attempt to end the war that had broken out in Europe in August 1914. Even though most of these women lived in states where they could not vote, they went abroad as diplomats for peace. Forty-two American women crossed the submarine-infested Atlantic Ocean for an international conference at the Hague, and some of them went on to meet with representatives of governments as far away as Russia. They returned home to work on maintaining U.S. neutrality, and Emily Greene Balch spent an hour debriefing President Woodrow Wilson on her meetings with top officials, including the king of Norway.

Nevertheless, in 1917, Congress declared war on Germany and the Austro-Hungarian Empire. Some representatives voted against it, including Rep. Jeannette Rankin of Montana.[12] When, in 1918, the United States proved to be on the winning side of World War I, the women's attempt for peace was seen as treasonous, and Wellesley College fired Professor Balch, a pioneer sociologist who also had a degree in economics from the University of Berlin. At age fifty-two, she lost her pension as well as her job.

The Woman's Peace Party transformed itself into WILPF in 1921, with Addams as president. It was truly international, with headquarters in traditionally neutral Switzerland. The membership included many of America's leading women. Among them were Sophonisba Breckinridge, an economist with the University of Chicago, Florence Kelley, whose legal work won important employment cases for women, and Mary Church Terrell, founder of the National Association of Colored Women's Clubs.

Addams won the Nobel Peace Prize in 1931 and retained the WILPF presidency until her 1935 death. Balch then led the organization, and she became the second American woman to win the Nobel Peace Prize in 1946. That was the year after World War II, a horrific conflict that WILPF worked hard to prevent. Balch joined other WILPF leaders in Geneva, where they spent the years of fascist domination assisting refuges who fled from other parts of Europe.

In the postwar period, Republicans such as Joseph R. McCarthy and Richard M. Nixon persuaded many Americans that working for peace was nearly synonymous with working for communism, and WILPF members found themselves targeted by the House Un-American Activities Committee. WILPF was politically powerless to prevent the Korean War's fifty thousand deaths.

Younger women revived the organization in the 1960s and 1970s to oppose the Vietnam War. WILPF focused on assisting those who refused to be drafted. It organized many demonstrations to oppose that war, and its lobbying played a part in ending the draft.

WILPF affiliated with the United Nations (UN) as a nongovernmental organization (NGO) when that opportunity arose, and at the beginning of the new millennium,

most of its leadership comes from nations other than the United States. Its U.S. office is in the UN Plaza in New York, and it has chapters throughout the nation, especially in places with major universities. Philadelphia members, with their long pacifist Quaker tradition, are particularly active. They have worked for the UN's commitment to prosecute rape as a war crime, and WILPF continues to lobby for U.S. ratification of the 1980 UN treaty to eliminate all forms of discrimination against women.

Women's Trade Union League

The Women's Trade Union League (WTUL) began in 1903 at a convention of the American Federation of Labor (AFL) in historic Faneuil Hall in Boston, Massachusetts. Female delegates there revolted against the dismissal of their issues by the male-dominated AFL, and they formed their own organization.

The WTUL was led by Leonora O'Reilly of the United Garment Workers and Mary Kenny O'Sullivan, who began her labor activism with the Woman's Bookbinders Union in Chicago, Illinois. It was unprecedented in that, unlike male-run unions, the WTUL sought support from women who were not working class. Lillian Wald, a settlement house founder and public nursing advocate, provided the WTUL with a network of wealthy supporters in New York, while Jane Addams did the same in Chicago. Another wealthy woman, Margaret Drier Robins, gave O'Reilly a lifetime annuity so that she could quit her ten-hour factory days and organize full time. Robins and her sister, Mary Elizabeth Drier, devoted their lives to progressive causes, and in 1905, Robins became WTUL president.

This unity of the upper class and working class showed its value in 1909, when women in the garment industry went on strike. Led by Robins in Chicago and Drier in New York, some twenty thousand women left their sewing machines and walked off of their badly paid jobs. Clothing manufacturers refused to settle with the International Ladies Garment Workers Union, and the strike went on for most of two years. Mayors in both cities encouraged the police to arrest picketers, and many of the mostly young and immigrant women were physically assaulted and jailed. Affluent WTUL supporters not only provided bail money, but they also stopped buying clothing. Women from such influential New York families as the Belmonts, Harrimans, and Morgans finally forced the manufacturers to negotiate with the union.

By 1911, the WTUL had branches in eleven cities, from Boston to Denver, Colorado. The league was a factor in the 1912 strike against textile mills in Lawrence, Massachusetts,

---

[12] For Rankin's biography, see Chapter Six 6: United States Representatives.

where out-of-control police killed Annie LoPizzo, the mother of eight. The WTUL supported women in strikes that ranged from Milwaukee breweries to Connecticut corset makers.

The WTUL was especially important in the aftermath of the tragic Triangle Shirtwaist Factory fire in New York City. The factory had been one of the few dressmakers that did not recognize a union after the 1909 strike, and it kept its doors locked lest a labor organizer slip in. When fire broke out, 146 workers, most of them young immigrant women, either burned to death behind the locked doors or were killed when they jumped from the eighth-floor windows. The WTUL followed through with a four-year study of similar factories elsewhere, and because of their lobbying, New York passed model laws to grant worker rights and outlaw unsafe conditions.

World War I largely put an end to the political reforms of the Progressive Era, and the Women's Trade Union League never again was so effective. Rose Schneiderman, a Jewish garment worker born in Russia, became president in 1926, and she would lead the WTUL for the remainder of its existence.

Wall Street crashed soon after Schneiderman became president, and the Great Depression of the 1930s wrought serious harm to all female employment, affecting working-class women most seriously. Few could afford to pay dues, and although Schneiderman was a friend of Franklin D. Roosevelt and Eleanor Roosevelt, the WTUL continued to decline. During World War II, management needed middle-class workers enough that it made the changes WTUL had promoted. With less need for the organization, it disbanded soon after the war's end.

Young Women's Christian Association

2025 M Street NW
Washington, DC 20036
202-467-0802
www.ywca.org

The Young Women's Christian Association (YWCA) is America's oldest and largest national organization for women. For more than a century, it has lobbied to advance opportunity for young women in education, employment, and more.

Both it and its male counterpart, the Young Men's Christian Association (YMCA), originated with evangelical Protestants in London. Britain's male organization began in 1844; its female counterpart, in 1851. In America, the catalyst for women was the Civil War. That emergency required many women to travel for the first time without male escort, and safe havens for such women arose in several cities because of the war. Soon after the war's end, the YWCA formalized in Boston, in 1866.

As the nation urbanized in the late nineteenth century, the YWCA's chief mission was to provide dormitories where young women could stay upon their arrival in a city. The assumption was that such women could not earn enough to stay in hotels, and, in any case, reputable hotels were wary of renting rooms to a lone woman, assuming that she was a prostitute. YWCA housing offered a place to live under close supervision, allowing rural families to send their daughters to seek urban employment under morally safe conditions.

The late nineteenth and early twentieth centuries saw great fear of what was termed "white slavery," the kidnapping of young women who were forced into prostitution. This was less likely to happen than many believed, but women in several organizations, including the YWCA, took up the cause of prevention. They lobbied for laws, especially the 1910 Mann Act, which made it a federal crime to transport a woman between states for immoral purposes.

YWCA representatives met trains that brought rural women to cities and, with the blessing of federal officials, stationed themselves at immigration centers to prevent exploitation of newly arrived women. Sometimes caseworkers went too far in their good intentions. For example, in their efforts to be sure that no young woman left Ellis Island without "male protection," occasionally a woman who could not speak English was wed against her will.

The YWCA also reached out to minorities. It built chapters at black colleges in the Deep South, and the first YWCA dormitory for black women was in Dayton, Ohio, in 1893. Similar facilities were built in Baltimore, Maryland, Washington, DC, Philadelphia, Pennsylvania, and New York City. In addition to running employment bureaus, the organization itself provided job opportunities for professional women. Its first paid black employee was Addie Hunton in 1907. One of her most notable successors was Crystal Bird Fauset, the first black women elected to a state legislature.[13] In 1890, as the former Indian Territory became the Oklahoma Territory, it opened a facility there for Native American women.

The YWCA held its first interracial conference in Louisville in 1915, and in the era between World War I and World War II, the YWCA showed more political courage on racism than many organizations. The resolution adopted at its 1934 convention against lynching was more progressive than most other women's groups. It also adopted pro-union positions that ultimately led the economy out of the Great Depression.

---

[13] See Chapter 4: State Representatives.

During World War II, YWCA members expanded the overseas mission they had undertaken during the first war; in both, the organization specialized in assisting refugees. On the World War II home front, the YWCA greatly expanded its efforts against racism. Because of its long work with young immigrant women, YWCA awareness of bias based on ethnicity was so profound (and exceptional) that its chapter in Portland, Oregon, went to court on behalf of Japanese Americans who were interned during the war. YWCA representatives also provided important legal and social work services in those internment camps.

Fascists suppressed the World's Young Women's Christian Association (World's YWCA) in Asia and Europe, but members nonetheless did heroic work with non-Christian refugees. This not only saved lives, but also further expanded intellectual horizons. The YWCA supported the United Nations and played a part in the civil rights movement of the 1960s. By 2011, the World's YWCA had some twenty-five million members in 106 nations; in the United States, about 2.6 million members in approximately three hundred affiliates. Its primary mission had changed from moral protection and safe travel to positive action for careers, ethnic inclusion, and ending violence. Despite the retention of "Christian" in its formal name, the YWCA long has been open to women of all faiths or none.

WOMEN'S ORGANIZATIONS: PAST AND FUTURE

As the twenty-first century began, some organizations—for example, the Women's Trade Union League and WCTU—had died or virtually died. Others evolved far from their nineteenth-century roots. Some, like the YWCA, became more progressive, while others were akin to GFWC in becoming more conservative. But no group had the large political network that had once been active for the vote, when two million people paid dues to the National American Woman Suffrage Association just prior to the 1920 ratification of the Nineteenth Amendment.

That issue attracted a truly large political bloc. Moreover, the NAWSA was one of several organizations for the cause, and the nation's population base was much smaller than today. Proportionally, women were much more politically active then than later. Success often kills a single-issue organization, but even with broader agendas later in the twentieth century, the same would be true of the National Organization for Women and the National Women's Political Caucus. As they achieved their goals, their membership declined.

Two groups that formed late in the twentieth century, however, merit attention, as both attempt to lead into the future by remembering the past. The California-based National Women's History Project (NWHP) was sufficiently political that it succeeded in getting presidential and congressional attention to proclaim March as Women's History Month. Since the late 1970s and 1980s, the NWHP has influenced the views of millions by providing educational materials and conferences on America's significant women. Its most prominent leaders were Molly Murphy McGregor and the late Mary Ruthsdotter.

The National Women's History Museum (NWHM) is based in the nation's capital. It began in 1997, when a group led by Karen Stasser and Susan Jollie succeeded in moving a statue of Lucretia Mott, Elizabeth Cady Stanton, and Susan B. Anthony from obscurity in the Capitol basement to prominence in its rotunda. As of 2011, NWHM's president is Joan Bradley Wages, and its goal is to build a museum on American women on or near the National Mall in Washington, DC.

Things have changed tremendously from the time when Martha Washington had no organization to join. Today's women have a plethora of opportunities to unite their views with those of others and, by taking political action, to create the world they want.

PROFILES OF FOUNDERS OF WOMEN'S INTEREST GROUPS

*These women were founders of the largest organizations for women. All were pioneers in the field of issue advocacy and were successful at turning opinion into political action. **Jane Cunningham Croly** founded the General Federation of Women's Clubs. **Maud Wood Park** was the first president of the League of Women Voters. **Mary Church Terrell** was the founder of the National Council of Colored Women. **Frances Willard** was the second president of the Women's Christian Temperance Union, but by far its most influential leader.*

JANE CUNNINGHAM CROLY (1829–1901)

The founder of the General Federation of Women's Clubs, newspaper columnist Jane Cunningham Croly was known to her many readers as "Jennie June."

The Cunninghams emigrated from England to rural New York when Jane was twelve. After her father's death in 1854, she moved to New York City and freelanced with several newspapers, and her columns soon were published in other cities. In her job at the *New York World*, she was one of the first women to work in a newspaper office, as opposed to being a correspondent who wrote at home and sent in her copy. Moreover, she defied convention by continuing to work after her 1856 marriage and also after becoming a mother, which was extremely unusual. Four of her children lived to adulthood. Her husband was David Croley, and while he was managing editor of the *World* in the 1860s, she edited its women's section.

Croly had published two books and was part of New York's literary society when, in 1868, she was involved in an incident that became a catalyst for feminist organizing. Because she was a woman, she was excluded from a press function for English author Charles Dickens. In response, with others of the city's female writers, she founded Sorosis. The nation's first organization of professional women, it later merged into the Association for the Advancement of Women.

Croly organized both the New York Woman's Press Club and the General Federation of Women's Clubs, which brought together disparate local civic organizations. Energetic and enthusiastic, she also edited several women's magazines, traveled to organize hundreds of women's clubs, and wrote the massive *History of the Women's Club Movement in America* (1898). Most of this was achieved in the 1890s, when Croly was in her sixties.

Much more liberal than many of the women who came to dominate the movement, Croly's writing advocated fair treatment of blacks, liberation from confining fashions, and especially educational and employment opportunity. By the time she died just days after her seventieth birthday, her work had influenced the opinions of millions.

MAUD WOOD PARK (1875–1955)

The first president of the League of Women Voters, Maud Wood Park was the most skilled congressional lobbyist in the movement for female enfranchisement.

An affluent Bostonian, Maud Wood joined the movement for women's right to vote while a student at Radcliffe College, Harvard University's female affiliate. She graduated in 1898, a year after secretly marrying Charles Edward Park. Announcing the marriage would have meant expulsion from school. They lived near the Denison House, Boston's most important settlement house for immigrants, and she continued her political activism.

She was the youngest delegate at the 1900 convention of the National American Woman Suffrage Association (NAWSA) and, in 1901, succeeded Alice Stone Blackwell, the daughter of Lucy Stone, as president of the Massachusetts Woman Suffrage Association. Charles Park died in 1904. The young widow continued with her work, even helping to organize Boston's first parent-teacher association,

although she was childless. In 1906, the year that Susan B. Anthony died, Park began the college-based Equal Suffrage League. For several years, she traveled around the country organizing women on college campuses. This would prove vital to reviving an aging suffrage movement.

Park remarried in 1908, but it was an extremely modern arrangement. She neither took Robert Hunter's name nor lived with him. They shared summers in her Maine home, but few of her political associates knew that she was married. Instead of honeymooning, she joined her friend Mabel Willard in 1909 on a global trip to investigate the status of women. Funded by Boston philanthropist Pauline Shaw, they especially visited Asian countries. When she returned in 1911, Park earned appreciable fees for lectures about the deplorable conditions of women abroad.

Meanwhile Alice Paul and other younger women were rebelling against NAWSA president Rev. Dr. Anna Howard Shaw. Carrie Chapman Catt, who succeeded Shaw in 1915, valued Park's political sophistication. Park moved to Washington, DC, lived at NAWSA headquarters, and spent almost every day on Capitol Hill until the Nineteenth Amendment was ratified in 1920.[14]

The League of Women Voters began the previous year with Catt as honorary president, and Park was its first genuine president. Her lobbying played a major role in two congressional successes: the 1921 Sheppard-Towner Maternity and Infancy Protection Act, which provided free maternal health care until its 1929 defunding; and the 1922 Cable Act, which equalized men and women in citizenship. Prior to it, an American woman lost her citizenship if she married a foreigner, but a man did not.

The new organization also adopted a long list of other legislative aims, but Park met less success as the Roaring Twenties became socially liberal but politically conservative. One of the era's most debated issues was a constitutional amendment to ban child labor, but it ran out of time for ratification in 1924. In that same year, Congress passed the Immigration Act, virtually closing America's doors to newcomers. Depressed and ill with a bacterial infection, Park resigned the league presidency.

She continued to lecture at colleges and supported the era's effort for international governance through the League of Nations. Living in Maine, she returned to drama—her major at Radcliffe—and wrote a play on Lucy Stone that was published in 1936. She also coauthored a related book, *Victory: How Women Won It* (1940). Her book *Front Door Lobbying* (published posthumously in 1960) remains instructive for coalescing the aims of a

---

[14] See also Chapter 1: Battle for the Vote.

large organization into law. Maud Wood Park died in Melrose, Massachusetts, at age eighty-four.

MARY CHURCH TERRELL (1863–1954)

The founding president of the National Association of Colored Women (NACW), Mary Church Terrell lived a long life of activism in Washington, DC. Terrell's motto was: "Keep on going, keep on insisting, keep on fighting injustice" (Terrell 1940, 269).

She could have passed for white, as her father, Robert Church, was the son of his master, and her mother, Louisa Ayres Church, had white grandfathers. Both were freed by the 1863 Emancipation Proclamation, shortly before their daughter, called "Molly," was born. They lived in Memphis, Tennessee.

A talented hairdresser, Louisa Church earned enough that she soon bought a house and carriage. She and her husband sent Molly from Memphis to Ohio at age seven because of better educational opportunities available there. They divorced, and Louisa moved to New York, where she was successful in the cosmetic industry. Molly remained close to her father, spending summers with him, and he made a fortune buying and then reselling property when Memphis residents fled from a mosquito-caused epidemic in 1879.

In 1884, when Church finished at Ohio's Oberlin College—the world's first to admit blacks and women—she was one of no more than two dozen black female college graduates in the world. Her father insisted that she come home to Memphis, but she found society life vacuous and defiantly returned to Ohio. She taught at Wilberforce University, a black institution, and in 1888, when she earned a master's degree from Oberlin, Mary Church probably was the world's best-educated black woman.

Oberlin offered her the position of registrar, but she turned it down to live in Washington, DC, where she taught at what was called "the Colored High School." In 1891, at age twenty-eight, she married Robert Terrell, a Harvard University graduate whose color was even lighter than hers. He earned a law degree, while she lost three babies before Phyllis—named for black poet Phillis Wheatley—survived infancy. In 1905, she would adopt her niece and namesake, Mary Church. The family was wealthy enough to vacation in Europe, where Terrell kept diaries in the language of the country she was visiting.

Her sense of justice, though, motivated political action. The first cause she took up was in 1892, when African Americans she had known in Memphis were attacked by white rioters. The victims included journalist Ida Wells-Barnett, and like her, many black residents left the city permanently. Young Mary Church Terrell joined aging Frederick Douglass at the White House to appeal to President Benjamin Harrison for federal intervention, to no avail.

She then led a merger of extant organizations for black women, combining them to found the National Association of Colored Women's Clubs in 1896. She served three two-year terms as president before accepting the honorary presidency. Terrell also spoke to several conventions of the nearly all-white National American Woman Suffrage Association. Her greatest oratorical triumph was in 1905, when she spoke to the International Council of Women in Berlin, Germany. She repeated the speech in English, French, and German.

During service on the school board for the District of Columbia from 1895 to 1911, her priority was enforcement of the U.S. Supreme Court's "separate, but equal" decision in *Plessy v. Ferguson* (1896). She tried, without much success, to equalize schools for blacks and whites in terms of teacher pay, textbooks, and other aspects. She also met with Secretary of War (and future president) William Howard Taft about mistreatment of black soldiers, and she was a founding member of the National Association for the Advancement of Colored People (NAACP).

As part of women's efforts in World War I, Terrell took a position in the War Department but resigned when she saw that no one wanted her to do anything. After the war, she joined the Women's International League over Peace and Freedom (WILPF), choosing it over the more moderate League of Women Voters. She attended WILPF's first postwar meeting in Zurich, Switzerland, again speaking in other languages.

While the Nineteenth Amendment enfranchised other American women, District of Columbia residents remained without the vote. Because she could not register there, the likelihood is that Terrell registered at her Maryland summer home as a Republican. She was a member of the Republican National Committee during the 1920s. She campaigned for Illinois's Ruth Hanna McCormick and kept her Republican registration until 1952, after most blacks left that party for the Democrat's New Deal.[15] Mary McLeod Bethune led that shift, and conflicting party affiliation was a factor in Bethune's 1935 formation of the National Council of Negro Women, which was more openly supportive of Democrats than the NACW.[16]

After Terrell's husband died in 1925, she concentrated on her autobiography. Famed author H. G. Wells concentrated on the preface for *A Colored Woman in a White World* (1940). She returned to greater activism in the 1940s but

---

[15] See Chapter 6: United States Representatives.

[16] See Chapter 12: Ambassadors.

had to sue the American Association of University Women (AAUW) to restore her lapsed membership. After she won, most AAUW members ostracized her. That doubtless was a reason that she spent less time with women's organizations and instead led the civil rights movement in the nation's capital.

Well before others, Terrell conducted boycotts of businesses that barred black customers. She picketed and may have created the "sit-in" when she persuaded a few other blacks to sit with her at Washington's Thompson's Restaurant. When they were not served, she sued on the basis of a Reconstruction law that never had been repealed. At nearly ninety, Terrell was a party to a 1953 case that desegregated Washington's eateries. Even more creatively, she surreptitiously bought large numbers of theater tickets and distributed them to African Americans. They arrived just before curtain time, forcing managers to integrate the audience or play to an empty house.

Death came while she was planning to go to Georgia to protest the execution of a black woman who killed her white male assailant. Mary Church Terrell died just weeks before the Supreme Court ruled in *Brown v. Topeka Board of Education* that segregated schools were inherently unequal.

FRANCES WILLARD (1839–1898)

The legacy of Frances Elizabeth Caroline Willard, one of the most influential women of the nineteenth century, is inseparable from the Woman's Christian Temperance Union (WCTU).

Willard was not the political conservative that the terms "Christian" and "Temperance" may suggest. Her upbringing encouraged fresh ideas. While her father babysat, her mother took courses at Ohio's Oberlin College after Frances was born, which was extremely rare for a new mother to do in the early 1840s. Oberlin was a very liberal institution, and Mary Thompson Willard probably was the world's first woman to combine motherhood and college.

Her parents were pioneer settlers in Wisconsin in 1845, where Frances enjoyed outdoor life with her brothers, even calling herself "Frank." Their father became a state legislator and succeeded in getting a school for the area when she was fifteen. At seventeen, she attended Milwaukee Female College and went on to Illinois, where she graduated from Northwestern Female College in 1859.

Willard spent the Civil War years teaching in Illinois and Pennsylvania and then headed an academy for girls near Seneca Falls, New York, where she was exposed to the area's feminism. A wealthy friend paid for Willard to accompany her on a two-year European trip in the late 1860s. They went as far as Turkey, and articles on this trip were Willard's first publications.

Upon her return, she was named president of the Evanston College for Ladies, a new school founded in 1871 with links to Northwestern University, which soon absorbed it. Willard then became dean of women at this growing university, making her a pioneer female administrator at a major coeducational institution. Willard was nationally recognized in 1873, when she was invited to be a cofounder of the Association for the Advancement of Women. It was not this organization, however, but the WCTU that would become her life's work. Supported by a network of Chicago women, she organized Illinois women into the WCTU in June 1874 and, just weeks later, was elected corresponding secretary at its first convention in Cleveland, Ohio.

She earned a living on the lecture circuit, where she was very popular with Midwestern audiences. In 1879, she began lobbying for Illinois women's right to vote in referenda on liquor sales. Using the strategy of gathering petitions at her speeches, she collected some 180,000 signatures. The effort was so impressive that she was elected WCTU president that same year.

Then age forty, she would head the WCTU for the rest of her life. Willard not only demonstrated uncommon organizational skills, but also was one of the century's best-liked women. She had an unusual capacity to take up radical causes and yet retain a conservative image. Her sense of humor and oratorical ability made her a natural politician who was not seen as a political ideologue. She organized WCTU chapters in every state in the nation by 1883, less than a decade after the organization began.

In an era when being a WCTU member was itself controversial, Willard supported women's right to vote. Calling herself "a conservative woman devoted to the idea of the ballot" (Willard 1889, 169), she presented 200,000 petitions to Congress for that right in 1887. She went beyond mere issue advocacy to participate in the election of candidates who furthered her cause, cloaking this radicalism in the more comforting language of "home protection."

Willard also managed to befriend Susan B. Anthony while officially belonging to Lucy Stone's rival suffrage organization. Unlike Anthony, who sometimes alienated her natural allies, Willard was a genius at welcoming others to political networks.

She further demonstrated this ability with organizations primarily composed of men. She was a cofounder of the Prohibition Party, which captured a substantial portion of male votes in every election from 1884 to its achievement of the Eighteenth Amendment early in 1920.

Nor did she limit herself to male organizations that supported temperance. Willard worked with the agrarian Grange, the Knights of Labor, and other farmer, union, and populist organizations that emerged during the early Progressive Era. By the late 1890s, she was beginning to see alcoholism less as a sin and more as an understandable result of hopelessness, much of which was grounded in inequality. She envisioned an essentially socialist economy, with no great division of rich and poor.

Willard wrote several books, but none was as popular as her autobiography, *Glimpses of Fifty Years* (1889). It sold well enough to make her financially secure for the last decade of her life. She succumbed to chronic anemia at age fifty-eight in a New York City hotel. Her body was returned to Chicago, where more than twenty thousand people paid their respects. In 1905, Illinois honored Frances Willard with one of the two statues that every state is allowed to display in the Capitol.

REFERENCES AND FURTHER READING

Addams, Jane, Emily G. Balch, and Alice Hamilton. 1915. *Women at the Hague: The International Congress of Women and Its Results.* New York: Macmillan.

Anthony, Katherine. 1954. *Susan B. Anthony: Her Personal History and Her Era.* New York: Doubleday.

Blair, Karen J. 1989. *The History of Women's Voluntary Associations, 1810–1960.* Boston: G. K. Hall.

Croly, Jane Cunningham. 1898. *The History of the Women's Club Movement in America.* New York: H. G. Allen.

Davis, Evelyn Jean. 1984. *The Socialization of Women into Politics: A Case Study of the League of Women Voters.* Ann Arbor, MI: University of Michigan Press.

Harper, Ida Husted, ed. 1922. *History of Woman Suffrage.* Volumes 5–6. New York: J. J. Little and Ives.

Hoyt, Kenneth B. 1978. *The National Federation of Business and Professional Women and Career Education.* Washington, DC: U.S. Government Printing Office.

Laughlin, Kathleen A., and Jacqueline L. Castledine. 2011. *Breaking the Wave: Women, Their Organizations, and Feminism, 1945–1985.* New York: Routledge.

Levine, Susan. 1995. *Degrees of Equality: The American Association of University Women and the Challenge of Twentieth-Century Feminism.* Philadelphia: Temple University Press.

Martin, Theodora Penny. 1987. *The Sound of Their Own Voices: Women's Study Clubs, 1860–1910.* Boston: Beacon Press.

Minkoff, Debra. 1995. *Organizing for Equality: The Evolution of Women's and Racial-Ethnic Organizations in American, 1955–1985.* New Brunswick, NJ: Rutgers University Press.

Rice, Anna. 1947. *A History of the World's Young Women's Christian Association.* New York: New Woman Press.

Schneiderman, Rose. 1967. *All for One.* New York: Paul S. Eriksson.

Seymour-Jones, Carole. 1994. *Journey of Faith: History of the World YWCA, 1945–1995.* London: Allison and Bushby.

Stuhler, Barbara. 2000. *For the Public Record: A Documentary History of the League of Women Voters.* Westport, CT: Greenwood Press.

Terrell, Mary Church. 1940. *A Colored Woman in a White World.* Washington, DC: Randell. Reprint, New York: Arno Press, 1980.

Wells, Marguerite Milton. 1940. *A Portrait of the League of Women Voters.* Washington, DC: National League of Women Voters.

Willard, Frances. 1889. *Glimpses of Fifty Years: The Autobiography of an American Woman.* Chicago: Woman's Christian Temperance Publishing Association.

Young, Louise M. 1989. *In the Public Interest: The League of Women Voters, 1920–1970.* New York: Greenwood Press.

18

POLITICAL ACTION COMMITTEES

Individuals and businesses have used money to influence elected officials ever since elections began. For most of American history, this practice was completely unregulated. Even at the beginning of the twentieth century, politicians still took the connection between money and votes so much for granted that some did not hesitate to put into writing the fees they charged for sponsoring a particular bill.

In the Progressive Era beginning in the late nineteenth century, when women also began to vote in some states, the link between campaign-funding and vote-promising increasingly came to be seen as a form of bribery, and politicians became somewhat more careful about revealing who was funding their campaigns. Still, bribery was difficult to prove, especially on the federal level, which is distant from most constituents, and very few states required any reporting of campaign income or expenses. Women in the movement for the vote witnessed countless cases of elections being bought, especially by the liquor and tobacco industries. Even railroads spent money trying to defeat referenda that enfranchised women. They did not want reformers to upset the status quo of a comfortable political game between affluent players.

Campaign accountability, therefore, was one of the goals of the League of Women Voters. During the 1920s and 1930s, thousands of newly enfranchised women worked for state and local reforms that would require candidates to report who was funding their campaigns. The league and its organizational ancestor, the National American Woman Suffrage Association, had no concerns about revealing who funded their own issue-oriented electoral efforts. They received millions of small donations from those who wanted honest government.

The league did not endorse candidates or donate to them, but as the economy recovered from the Great Depression, other organizations with millions of members began to pool their resources to affect elections. By doing so, working-class people could begin to match the longtime political power of the wealthy. The first unified action of the sort that became known as a political action committee began with the 1944 election, when the Congress of Industrial Organizations (CIO) created the first. In fact, it coined the term "PAC."

The leadership of the CIO, a federation of 5.5 million unskilled industrial workers, feared that the nation would plummet back into poverty when war production ended. Victory was in sight by 1944, and so the CIO organized its members to register, vote, and elect a Congress that would adopt a New Frontier of economic values, including expanded education, affordable housing, and medical care. The PAC did not donate directly to candidates but instead spent money to influence voters in key congressional districts. Its message was progressive, as CIO leaders predicted that, without such a unified effort: "We can expect groups to be incited against groups, whites against Negroes, farmers against factory workers, women workers against men workers, and all of them against organized labor" (Gaer 1994, 81). The campaign succeeded in defeating more than a dozen members of Congress, all of them male.

The CIO merged with the American Federation of Labor (AFL), which was composed of craftsmen such as carpenters and bricklayers, in 1955. Thereafter known as the AFL-CIO, the affiliation of various unions had millions of members, and even with an expenditure of just a few dollars per member, the AFL-CIO became a major factor at election time. Challenged by this, some corporate leaders, who had been funding candidates for decades without any real restraint, began to argue for regulation of campaign expenditures in the 1960s.

After the downfall of Richard M. Nixon and the revelations of the doings of the Committee to Reelect the President, known as CREEP, Congress responded with legislation that limited campaign donations from individuals and defined PACs as vehicles for organizational contributions. Businesses and unions thus were forced to separate the money that they spent on elections from their other accounts. Some PACs grew quickly, with about four thousand by 1988. The number has dropped slightly in the years since, as some groups have decided that meeting the extensive bookkeeping requirements of the Federal Election Commission (FEC) is not a priority for their organization.

THE MODERN SCENE

The FEC enforces the laws on PACs, and its records show that the vast majority of PACs—almost sixteen hundred in 2009—belong to corporations, with about a thousand additional PACs labeled "trade organizations." In 2011, labor unions accounted for fewer than three hundred of the more than three thousand PACs, or less than 10 percent. Union PACs, however, have many more individual contributors at smaller levels and, thus, are among the largest in terms of total dollars.

For women's organizations, election reform forced a decision on whether or not to create a PAC officially separate from the main body. Some did, with the most noted being NOW/PAC, the campaign arm of the National Organization for Women. Many women also joined PACs related to their occupations, and by the 1990s PACs with large proportions of female members—such as the National Education Association and the American Federation of State, County, and Municipal Employees (AFSCME)—were among the nation's largest.

Most women's PACs were small by comparison, partly because women continue to focus on their issue-advocacy organizations that began prior to PAC legislation (see Chapter 17: Interest Groups). Organizations of and by women that defined themselves as PACs from their beginning pursued a political agenda, endorsed candidates, and spent money to influence elections. These PACs, regulated by the Federal Election Commission, donated to candidates for federal office. Many of the groups discussed here also have state affiliates that donate to state and local elections, and their reports usually are filed with the state's division of elections.

Table 18.1 Top Thirty Federal Political Action Committees (PACs), by Expenditure, 2010

Rank	Political Action Committee	Expenditures in 2010 Election Cycle
1	ActBlue	$63,970,125.25
2	Service Employees International Union	$36,260,830.72
3	MoveOn.org	$29,851,852.10
4	EMILY's List	$27,302,780.71
5	American Federation of State, County, and Municipal Employees	$18,143,346.10
6	National Rifle Association of America Political Victory Fund	$15,460,142.09
7	DRIVE (Democrat, Republican, Independent Voter)	$14,154,525.37
8	1199 Service Employees International Union Federal Political Action Fund	$13,920,018.26
9	American Federation of Teachers	$10,692,306.11
10	National Association of Realtors Political Action Committee	$10,260,778.69
11	Senate Conservatives Fund	$9,256,133.30
12	Free and Strong America	$9,133,777.64
13	United Auto Workers	$8,809,854.40
14	International Brotherhood of Electrical Workers Political Action Committee	$7,939,929.61
15	Communications Workers of America	$7,931,288.88
16	Voice of Teachers for Education (VOTE), Committee on Political Education of New York State United Teachers	$7,786,633.48
17	Lyndon Larouche Political Action Committee	$7,781,598.90
18	United Food and Commercial Workers International Union Active Ballot	$7,297,654.67
19	Democracy for America	$7,151,688.01
20	International Union of Operating Engineers	$7,131,882.24
21	National Education Association	$6,287,311.10
22	Life and Liberty PAC	$6,254,418.13
23	American Association for Justice Political Action Committee	$6,019,376.16
24	Sarah PAC (Sarah Palin, Republican vice presidential nominee)	$5,685,213.46
25	Honeywell International Political Action Committee	$5,576,195.14
26	Committee on Letter Carriers Political Education	$5,265,113.42
27	International Union of Painters and Allied Trades	$5,232,963.54
28	International Association of Firefighters	$5,192,952.76
29	AT&T	$4,604,563.48
30	American Resort Development Association Resort Owners	$4,597,793.44

Source: Federal Election Commission, "Committee Summary, 2010 Election Cycle," Federal Election Commission's Data Catalog, http://www.fec.gov/data/, accessed June 1, 2011.

All PACs included in this chapter spent $100,000 or more during the 2010 election cycle. Two groups, the Women's Senate Fund and the Women's Campaign Fund, were intended to be temporary. They did not form as permanent associations of women, but rather were PACs to elect specific candidates, and will not necessarily be a factor in future elections.

In contrast to these relatively high-dollar but temporary PACs, several organizations such as the National Federation of Business and Professional Women's Clubs (BPW), groups that had great influence on American life, have PAC affiliates that did not reach the $100,000 federal level in 2010. Some, however, spend appreciably more than that on lobbyists who advocate for their issues. They simply expect elected officials to support their cause for its own sake, and not because the politician expects a contribution from the organization's PAC.

As party platforms increasingly differed on feminist issues during the 1990s and early 2000s, nonpartisan PACs such as that of the National Women's Political Caucus (NWPC) have lost membership and money. NWPC failed to reach the $100,000 level in the 2010 election cycle. These numbers from the Federal Election Commission also make it clear that, overall, women's political dollars are extremely small compared with those of the nation's largest PACs. More than men, women seem to resist pay-for-play politics, something that is reflected in the short histories of their PACs.

With the important exception of EMILY's List, women's PACs have not proved as effective a vehicle for obtaining their goals as have the issue-oriented organizations. Even when traditional groups have a PAC, that arm has not been nearly as successful as the main body. One example is BPW, which has been hugely successful for decades on issue advocacy. Even though its PAC is not large enough to be considered a player by political standards, thousands of women nonetheless attend BPW conventions, and tens of thousands attend monthly meetings locally. They volunteer in campaigns and make personal donations to candidates, but members seem to place less value on their PAC than on their traditional operational mechanisms.

Most women appear to value meetings. They want an opportunity to share information and opinions, as well as the advantages of networking and socializing. Again with the exception of EMILY's List, women seem to resist granting power to a small number of check writers, which is the reality of the way that PACs operate. Leaders of nonpartisan national organizations also may avoid emphasis on PACs because most elections are partisan, and endorsing a Democrat over a Republican or vice versa could cause internal organizational conflict. Instead of inviting that problem, leaders allow PAC treasuries to sit nearly empty.

EMILY's List became even more exceptional because of a significant U.S. Supreme Court decision in 2010. In

Table 18.2 Top Federal Political Action Committees Devoted to Women's Issues, by Expenditure, 2010

Political Action Committee	Expenditures in 2010 Election Cycle
EMILY's List	$27,302,780.71
National Right to Life	$2,222,354.15
Susan B. Anthony List	$579,791.99
Eagle Forum	$576,141.08
Planned Parenthood Action Fund	$454,641.96
Right to Life/Oregon	$377,479.18
Concerned Women for America	$247,404.00
Women's Political Committee	$214,026.44
The WISH List	$213,064.86
Women's Campaign Forum	$170,953.11
Value in Electing Women	$125,804.88

Source: Federal Election Commission, "Committee Summary, 2010 Election Cycle," Federal Election Commission's Data Catalog, http://www.fec.gov/data/, accessed June 1, 2011.

Note: Limited to political action committees that spent more than $100,000 in the 2010 election cycle.

Citizens United v. Federal Election Commission, the Court essentially ruled that group electioneering was equivalent to free speech, and therefore Congress could not impose spending limitations on PACs. The full name of the PAC that brought the case was Citizens United, Not Timid— with an acronym that when spelled out, demonstrated a misogyny. It was formed by Republicans to oppose Hillary Rodham Clinton's 2008 presidential candidacy.

The decision quickly changed national politics, as within weeks, super PACs arose to take advantage of the new methodology. The *Washington Post* said on September 28, 2010: "A new political weapon known as the 'super PAC' has emerged. . . . Three dozen of the new committees have been registered with the Federal Election Commission over the past two months, including such major players as the conservative Club for Growth, the Republican-allied Crossroads, and the liberal women's group EMILY's List." The newspaper reported that these new "committees spent $4 million last week alone and are registering at the rate of one a day." A spokesman for Republican nominee John McCain added, "This is pretty much the holy grail."

EMILY's List was the only women's PAC efficient enough to join this new game, raising and spending some $27 million in the 2010 election cycle. Under its new rubric of Women Vote!, EMILY's List helped turn out new voters who elected Democrat Barack Obama. It also managed to hold to its longtime image of being open and positive, a real achievement in an era when countless political attack ads are launched by innocuous-sounding PACs.

Emily's List president Ellen Malcolm introduces House Democratic leader Nancy Pelosi (right) at the Emily's List luncheon "Women's Voices Say ENOUGH" in Boston in 2004. See Chapter 6 for more background on Nancy Pelosi.

Following are profiles of major federal women's PACs that had significant expenditures during the 2010 election cycle.

Concerned Women for America

1015 15th St. NW
Washington, DC 20005
202-488-7000
www.cwfa.org

Founded by evangelical Christian Beverly LaHaye in 1980, Concerned Women for America (CWA) is not to be confused with the labor union that shares its initials. Communications Workers of America is an older and much larger labor union that began with telephone operators, most of them women. Concerned Women for America, according to its platform, promotes "Biblical values." Its Statement of Faith includes declarations such as "we believe the Bible to be the verbally inspired, inerrant word of God." Like the similar Eagle Forum founded and run by Phyllis Schlafly, CWA has had only one president, Beverly LaHaye; its treasurer is Lee LaHaye.

The goals of CWA include reversing abortion rights and even contraceptive rights. Its website frankly assumes that members are Republicans and encourages lobbying on a partisan basis. It opposed the Obama administration's health care reform law and wants to amend the 1994 Violence against Women Act, enacted during the Clinton administration, to prioritize "healing the husband."

According to the Federal Election Commission, CWA raised some $247,000 in the 2010 election cycle but disbursed about $279,000. Its website claimed chapters in "almost all 50 states."

Eagle Forum

P.O. Box 618
Alton, IL 62002
618-462-5415
www.eagleforum.org

Founded in 1972 by Phyllis Schlafly, the Eagle Forum has had no other president.[1] Calling itself "the leading pro-family movement," it was the strongest organization in the defeat of the Equal Rights Amendment during the 1970s and 1980s.

The Eagle Forum also exerts political influence in areas not directly related to women and families, especially supporting a strong military. Its website in 2011 said "the Eagle Forum supports American identity. We support establishing English as our official language." Its isolationism is further shown in a pledge to "oppose all encroachments against American sovereignty through United Nations treaties or conferences," including those that promote "feminist goals."

The Eagle Forum reflects not only social conservatism but also an economic view that is strongly pro-business and antilabor. It endorses candidates, virtually all of them Republican. Claiming eighty thousand members in 2011, the Eagle Forum maintains an office in Washington, DC, but its primary address is in Phyllis Schlafly's hometown in Illinois.

Emily's List

1120 Connecticut Avenue
Washington, DC 20036
202-326-1400
www.emilyslist.org

EMILY's List began in 1985 in the basement of ELLEN R. MALCOLM's Washington, DC, home. In response to political successes by conservatives that culminated with Republican Ronald Reagan's landslide reelection in 1984, she called about two dozen feminist friends and asked these women to bring their Rolodexes. Using this low-tech database, they developed a list of likeminded women who were asked to donate to the campaigns of progressive Democratic women. Formalized into a political action committee, the group differed from others in recruiting candidates at the earliest stage of a campaign cycle and investing heavily in those most likely to win. "EMILY" stands for "Early Money Is Like Yeast—it helps the dough rise."

[1] See Chapter 16: Political Parties and Conventions.

With that strategy, EMILY's List soon became the largest of women's PACs. Its first victory was the first year after the basement meeting, when the group was a strong factor in electing Maryland's Barbara Mikulski to the U.S. Senate. She went on to be, as of 2011, the longest-serving woman in that body. EMILY's List raised almost a million dollars in its third year, and the 1988 elections of Washington's Jolene Unsoeld and New York's Nita M. Lowey reversed a decline in the number of women in the U.S. House of Representatives.[2]

Although Malcolm traveled around the country to increase membership, EMILY's List did not aim to build local chapters or lobby on issues. Instead, it concentrated its resources on the campaigns of thoroughly vetted candidates, women with electoral experience who were viable winners. As the PAC succeeded, it expanded from Congress to endorse women for governor, mayor, and other offices—always with the requirement that its female candidates be pro-choice Democrats. EMILY's List also has trained hundred of young women to work in the campaigns of its endorsed candidates, and its Majority Council, composed of politically experienced feminists, meets annually.

Most EMILY's List members, however, never attend meetings, and in this, it differs from other women's organizations. EMILY's List appeals to busy women who read the group's research on candidates and write checks accordingly, without needing to attend forums to meet and evaluate candidates individually.

A second factor in EMILY's success is that, although the group is unequivocally Democratic, it has not allowed the national party to influence its decision making or operational structure. Republican women's PACs have seemed more willing to operate as auxiliaries of the national party. In contrast, EMILY's List sends its own political professionals to work closely with campaigns and ensure that its investment is well managed.

In the 2008 election cycle, EMILY's List created a new program called Women Vote!, which aimed to register women to vote and encouraged them to vote Democratic. This affiliated superPAC of EMILY's List raised an unprecedented $6.5 million.

At the same time, the national organization began to support state organizations working to elect progressive Democratic women to lower levels of office. These groups modeled themselves on EMILY's List and took similar names. Eleanor's List in New York is named for New Yorker Eleanor Roosevelt; Annie's List honors Ann W. Richards,

whose election as governor of Texas was an early EMILY's List victory at that level; Florida's Ruth's List is for Ruth Bryan Owen, the first female U.S. representative from the South; Harriet's List in Missouri honors Harriet Woods, whose U.S. Senate campaign motivated Malcolm to form EMILY's List; and Lillian's List reflects the legacy of Lillian Exum Clement, the first woman in the North Carolina legislature.

EMILY's List celebrated its twenty-fifth anniversary in 2010 with a large Washington event. Malcolm became chairman of the board, and her successor as president was Stephanie Schriock. EMILY's List is by far the most successful women's PAC, having raised and given away about $83 million since its 1985 founding.

Naral–Pro-Choice America

www.naral.org[3]

NARAL–Pro-Choice America has had two prior versions of its name. It began as the National Association for the Repeal of Abortion Laws in 1969. When the U.S. Supreme Court ruled in *Roe v. Wade* (1973) that states could not ban early term abortions, the group kept its initials but changed its name to the National Abortion Rights Action League. Calling itself NARAL–Pro-Choice American since 2003, it is a single-issue PAC devoted to reproductive rights.

Several hundred people, including many physicians, attended the group's first meeting in Chicago, and NARAL opened a headquarters in New York City later in 1969. The organization was especially active in New York and in Massachusetts, where even birth control remained difficult to obtain. It established a national office in Washington, DC, in 1975.

NARAL's mission remains the right to a legal and safe abortion, as well as access to contraception, including modern prescriptions such as the "morning after pill." It also promotes sex education and healthy pregnancies, but, unlike the similar Planned Parenthood, it does not operate clinics.[4]

Its longtime president was Kate Michelman, who revealed her personal motivation for the cause during congressional testimony in 1991. She was the mother of three when her husband abandoned the family in 1969. When she discovered that she was pregnant, she had to

---

[2] See Chapter 6: United States Representatives and Chapter 7: United States Senators.

[3] Because of attacks on pro-choice groups, NARAL does not publicize its address.

[4] For more information on Planned Parenthood, see Chapter 17: Interest Groups.

More than traditional debates on economic policies or international entanglements, issues related to women—and especially their bodies—have come to polarize the two major political parties. The vast majority of significant political action committees (PACs) related to women are focused around reproductive issues.

These questions were not considered to be public policy issues until late in the twentieth century. Prior to that time, reproductive matters were private and personal, and politics largely stayed out of the bedroom. After U.S. Supreme Court decisions on birth control in the 1960s and abortion in the 1970s, however, many politicians have seen these as "wedge issues," meaning that they can be used to split or wedge a citizen from his or her traditional voting patterns.

Christine Day and Charles Hadley, both professors at the University of New Orleans, wrote *Women's PACs: Abortion and Elections* (2005) as part of a series edited by Paul Harrison of the University of Maryland. In their first pages, the authors commented on PACs and wedge issues.

Political parties today generally take opposing stands on feminist issues; feminists are prominent within the Democratic party coalition, while social conservatives favoring more traditional gender roles are prominent within the Republican party coalition. But when the contemporary women's movement erupted in the 1960s, the Democratic and Republican parties were nearly indistinguishable in their stance for women's rights. Both parties had claimed for decades to champion women's rights, yet neither party made it an active priority....

As the women's movement gained momentum in the late 1960s and early 1970s, and as the Civil Rights Act of 1964 largely invalidated protectionism in employment, the debate between protectionism and equality dissolved.... In 1972, both parties promised ... equality in their national platforms, and a bipartisan coalition in Congress passed the Equal Rights Amendment....

Soon, however, debates over women's rights issues began to evolve in a way that would come to polarize the parties.... The movement for women's liberation became associated with a more general rights agenda, African-American civil rights in particular, aligning it gradually with the Democratic party. In response to the rising influence of feminism in politics, many social conservatives on the religious right became politically motivated in the 1970s by such organizations as Phyllis Schlafly's STOP ERA (which later became the Eagle Forum), the Moral Majority, and Concerned Women for America.... Thus, through a period of gradual issue evolution, the two parties were quite polarized around feminist issues by the early 1980s, and that polarization has increased over time into the twenty-first century. (Day and Hadley 2005, 15–17)

If PACs provide a way of measuring views by those who are willing to put their money where their mouths are, then, dollar for dollar, Democratic women have been winning the race for decades, as the PACs of Republican women never have come close to equality with those of Democrats. Other factors enter into voters' decisions, however, and because PACs headed by men vastly outspend either Democratic or Republican women, the amount of money in women's PACs cannot by themselves predict how elections will go.

appear before an all-male hospital board for permission to terminate. The board also required her to obtain written permission from her absent husband.

NARAL strongly supported the 1992 campaign of Democrat Bill Clinton. Michelman retired in 2004 and was succeeded by Nancy A. Keenan, who was first elected to the Montana House in 1982. Keenan launched a Heartland Tour in the Midwest, using her rural background to encourage women who had experience with difficult pregnancies to speak to lawmakers about that reality. Her point was that legislators need to hear from affected constituents more than from lobbyists.

In the 2010 election cycle, NARAL contributed more than a million dollars to its endorsed candidates. Unlike the similar EMILY's List, it endorses men, as well as pro-choice candidates of either party. In 2010, it supported eight women who won congressional races and twenty-three such men.

National Right To Life Committee

512 10th Street NW
Washington, DC 20004
202-626-8800
www.nrlc.org

The National Right to Life Committee (NRLC) is not entirely analogous to other women's political action committees because its leadership has included many men, but it nonetheless is very significant because of its electoral effect on women's lives. Its president in 2011 was Wanda Franz, a West Virginia psychologist, but the woman most identified with NRLC may be MILDRED JEFFERSON, an African American physician.

The NRLC formed in Detroit, Michigan, in 1973 in direct response to the U.S. Supreme Court's decision in *Roe v. Wade*, which declared that states could not ban

Two essays in *PACs, Lobbies, and the Republican Congress* (1999) examined political action committees (PACs) related to women issues. Political scientist Mark J. Rozell began his "WISH List: Pro-Choice Women in the Republican Congress" by saying:

After the election of a Republican majority to Congress in 1994, the Christian Coalition held a Capitol Hill press conference to unveil its Contract with the American Family. . . . The executive director of the Christian Coalition, Ralph Reed, boldly proclaimed that by electing a Republican majority the public had sent a socially conservative message. . . .

Although the public clearly associates the GOP today with support for a socially conservative agenda, the alliance between the Christian Right and the party remains controversial. Exit polls in elections show a growing gender gap among voters, in part due to Republican women defecting from their party largely because of its antiabortion rights stand.

Prominent GOP women have started two groups with the purpose of changing the party's current abortion position. The better known is Republicans for Change, founded in 1989 and directed by consultant Ann Stone. Less well known, but clearly gaining in stature, is Women in the House and Senate, or WISH List. (Biersack, Herrnson, and Wilcox 1999, 184)

Neither Republicans for Change nor the WISH List, however, attracted nearly the number of members as Democratic EMILY's List would in the next decade. The Republican

PACs also were not as successful as NARAL, an older, pro-choice organization that assiduously avoided party alignment. In "NARAL PAC: Battling for Reproductive Rights," author Sue Thomas noted:

Although NARAL's goals have remained relatively constant, its political tactics have changed in response to political events. . . . The GOP takeover of Congress in 1994 was a major defeat for NARAL and forced the organization to change its lobbying tactics. When Democrats controlled Congress, NARAL sought to pass the Freedom of Choice Act to ensure abortion rights, but Republican efforts to restrict abortion access have left NARAL primarily trying to block GOP legislation. . . .

Yet abortion was salient in many House and Senate races in 1996 because of the efforts of NARAL and other pro-choice organizations. Their concerted effort to educate the public about candidate positions on issues of reproductive freedom doubtlessly influenced some close races. (Biersack, Herrnson, and Wilcox 1999, 134 and 142)

NARAL's greater success in 1996, as opposed to 1994, largely can be attributed to the fact that 1996 was a presidential election year. Millions more voters turned out in 1996 to reelect President Bill Clinton than they had for the Republican Contract with America in 1994. The point that women on either side of this or any other issue should remember is that voting matters in every election, not just those in presidential years.

early term abortions. NRLC grew rapidly, becoming deeply involved in lawsuits challenging *Roe* and in lobbying at both the state and federal level. It was especially successful in slowing research on abortifacients, which are drugs that can be used to induce abortions. That anti-research effort was achieved by boycotting certain pharmaceutical companies, and the NRLC continues to employ the boycott tactic. It also endorses candidates and had a particularly strong influence in the 2010 congressional elections.

The arm of the PAC based in Washington, DC, took in a little more than $2 million in the 2010 election cycle but spent $2.6 million. Its debt at the end of the year was almost $400,000, more than the total of many women's PACs. State NRLC affiliates added another $1.5 million. Their totals ranged from zero in Hawaii to approximately $377,000 from the Oregon Right to Life PAC.

The NRLC opposes euthanasia and assisted suicide as well as abortion, but not capital punishment. Its long

legislative agenda focused on abortion but also included repealing the Obama administration health care reform and halting the use of embryos in biological research.

Susan B. Anthony List

1707 L Street, NW
Washington, DC 20036
202-223-8073
www.sba-list.org

The Susan B. Anthony List (SBA List) emulated the pro-choice Democratic EMILY's List and was founded in the same year as the pro-choice Republican WISH List. The Susan B. Anthony List, however, promotes pro-life candidates, both men and women.

Begun in 1992, in direct response to the victories of pro-choice Democratic women in the Year of the Woman," its leader was Washingtonian Marjorie

Dennenfelser, formerly of the conservative Heritage Foundation. It endorses candidates, primarily for Congress, and participates in their campaigns. It is not tied to the Republican Party in the visible way that WISH List is, but virtually all of its endorsed candidates have been Republicans, and it actively opposed the 2008 election of Barack Obama.

The SBA List runs a strong grassroots lobbying program and, in 2009, reported that it had generated over a million pro-life letters to members of Congress. It also produces and distributes "one-minute conversations" that air on Christian media outlets. Their purpose, according to its website, is to "dispel the myth that all women are pro-choice."

Most historians dispute the claim that Susan B. Anthony would have forced a woman to continue an unwanted pregnancy. Anthony was a Republican and earned substantial fees speaking for that party, but the thousands of pages of her writing do not indicate that she would have joined today's pro-life advocates. She never spoke for or against the new state laws on the topic that were passed in the late nineteenth century. In the most relevant case that Anthony was involved in, she testified on behalf of an unwed mother who was charged with infanticide.

In the 2010 election cycle, the Susan B. Anthony List contributed somewhat less than $200,000 to its endorsed candidates. Ten were featured on its website, seven of whom were Republican men. The most prominent of the women was Rep. Michele Bachmann, a Republican of Minnesota.

The Wish List

333 North Fairfax Street
Alexandria, VA 22314
703-778-5550
www.thewishlist.org

The WISH List began in 1992 as an attempt by pro-choice Republican women to emulate the successful Democratic political action committee EMILY's List, which had begun in 1985.

"WISH" stood for "Women in the Senate and the House," and its founder was Candy L. Straight, a New Jersey investment banker. Partnering with the mixed-gender Republican Majority for Choice, WISH List won some early congressional victories, including Washington's Jennifer Dunn, Kentucky's Deborah Pryce, and Florida's Tillie Fowler.[5] None of them, however, remained in Congress as of 2009.

Like EMILY's List, the WISH List recruited candidates and trained them to win elections. It soon expanded its recruiting beyond congressional candidates. Among its first winners in other categories was New Jersey governor Christine Todd Whitman.[6] WISH List endorsed candidates all the way down to the county level and has met its greatest success in Connecticut, Illinois, and New Jersey. Its biggest win at the congressional level may have been in Florida, where state senator Ginny Brown-Waite defeated ten-term Democrat Karen Thurman in 2002.

Because the Republican platform increasingly has reflected the view of its right-to-life faction, WISH List never has achieved its aim of being competitive with EMILY's List. WISH List has given some $3 million to candidates over its lifetime, compared with about $83 million for its Democratic counterpart. Other pro-choice Republican women, especially consultant Ann Stone, also have formed PACs, but they are even smaller, failing to meet the level of $100,000 in the 2010 election cycle.

Women's Campaign Forum

1900 L Street, NW
Washington, DC 20036
202-393-8164
www.wcfonline.org

Founded in 1974, the Women's Campaign Forum (WCF) describes itself as "the only national, non-partisan political organization supporting women at all levels of office, during the earliest stages of their political life, when that support is needed most."

Its goals were similar to those of the National Women's Political Caucus, which formed in 1971.[7] Unlike the caucus, Women's Campaign Forum had no celebrity founders. It also avoided issue advocacy to instead focus on the election of women to more offices, regardless of party. It especially aims to promote promising young women. It provides fellowships, and its Next Generation program allows those younger than thirty-five to attend forum events at little cost. "She Should Run" is another effort to encourage women to consider political careers.

According to the Federal Election Commission, the WCF donated slightly more than $170,000 in 2010, endorsing candidates in twenty-eight states. The year 2010 was not good for nonpartisanship, however, and the generally progressive women it supported had more losses

---

[5] See Chapter 6: United States Representatives.

[6] See Chapter 8: Governors and Lieutenant Governors.
[7] See Chapter 17: Interest Groups.

than wins, especially at the state and local levels. Of 101 endorsed candidates, only 36 won. The worst defeat was in races for the New York Senate. The political action committee endorsed eight women, all of whom lost.

Since 2009, the president of Women's Campaign Forum has been political activist Siobhan "Sam" Bennett of Allentown, Pennsylvania. The PAC's first endorsement for 2011 was Melina Kennedy, candidate for mayor of Indianapolis.

PROFILES OF FOUNDERS OF WOMEN'S PACS

*Democrat **Ellen R. Malcolm** founded EMILY's List, which is by far the largest women's political action committee. Republican **Mildred Jefferson**, an African American physician, made a great contribution to the founding of the National Right to Life Committee.*

ELLEN R. MALCOLM (1947–)

Born wealthy in Montclair, New Jersey, Ellen R. Malcolm could have chosen a life of leisure. Instead the founder of EMILY's List worked for progressive causes since her youth.

After her 1969 graduation from Hollins College, a respected institution for women in Virginia, she went to work for Common Cause. It was then a new organization grappling with the fallout of the turbulent 1960s. Common Cause attempted to reshape government to give greater voice to citizens.

Malcolm also worked as press secretary for the National Women's Political Caucus (NWPC), created in 1971. After Jimmy Carter was elected president in 1976, she went to the White House as an assistant to Esther Peterson, who had been Eleanor Roosevelt's aide with the Presidential Commission on the Status of Women in the Kennedy administration.[8] When Carter lost the 1980 election, Malcolm went back to school, earning a master's degree in business administration from George Washington University.

She formed EMILY's List in 1985. The new political action committee (PAC) differed from NWPC in that it endorsed only Democratic women. Malcolm was a leader in educating women on the importance of not only tying candidates to the issues that one supports, but also to a sympathetic political party. Even though a candidate may support feminist goals, if she votes to put a party in control of the U.S. House or U.S. Senate that is not supportive, she has negated her political value.

As the years went by, Malcolm was more and more clear about the differences between the agendas of the major parties and that EMILY's List supported the Democratic platform. At the same time, she worked for civility in politics and, in the early 2000s, was a leader in America Coming Together, an attempt at greater political cooperation and less congressional gridlock.

Several magazines have listed Ellen Malcolm as one of the most influential women in America, and the American Association of Political Consultants voted her Most Valuable Player. She frequently appeared on televised political news shows and in 2007 co-chaired Hillary Rodham Clinton's presidential campaign. After twenty-five successful years, she retired as president of EMILY's List in 2010 but continued in public service by accepting appointment as a director of the National Park Foundation. This fits with Malcolm's personal life, which long has included enjoyment of outdoor activity.

MILDRED JEFFERSON (1926–2010)

Physician Mildred Fay Jefferson was perhaps the greatest asset in the early leadership of the National Right to Life Committee. She also was a pioneer at Harvard University, the nation's oldest college, as her 1951 graduation from its medical school was a first for black women.

Born in Pittsburg, Texas, she was the only child of middle-class parents. Her mother was a teacher and her father was a Methodist minister, and her life was grounded in Christianity. After graduating summa cum laude from Texas College, a segregated institution in the eastern Texas town of Tyler, she moved to Massachusetts. She earned a master's degree from Tufts University, near Boston.

She then successfully applied to Harvard Medical School, which had not admitted women until the emergency of World War II. The war ended in 1945, and when Jefferson graduated in 1951, she was the medical school's first black alumnae. Briefly married and divorced, she would spend most of her career as a surgeon at Boston University Medical Center.

She had been a physician for almost twenty years in 1970 when the American Medical Association passed a resolution saying that doctors could ethically perform abortions in states where the practice was legal. Dr. Jefferson firmly opposed that resolution. Seeing all abortion as sinful, she became a founder of the National Right to Life Committee in 1973. Its president from 1975 to 1978, she also served in leadership positions with Massachusetts Right to Life. She led the organization in adopting a platform asserting that life begins at the moment of conception. It aimed to outlaw all abortion.

Dr. Jefferson developed a reputation as a great orator, but she lost political credibility with unsuccessful races for the U.S. Senate. Although Catholicism (and Catholic opposition to abortion) was a big part of Massachusetts politics, she lost elections as a Republican senatorial candidate in 1982, 1984, and 1990. The Republican Party did very little to support her. Its professionals probably deemed her a less-than-viable candidate in these campaigns against Democratic senators Edward M. Kennedy and John Kerry.

Her testimony to the Senate in 1991, when North Carolina senator Jesse Helms held hearings on abortion, has been much quoted. Largely retired after that, Dr. Mildred Jefferson—who referred to herself as Negro, not African American or black—died at her home in Cambridge, Massachusetts at age eighty-four.

REFERENCES AND FURTHER READING

Biersack, Robert, Paul S. Herrnson, and Clyde Wilcox, ed. *After the Revolution: PACs, Lobbies, and the Republican Congress.* Boston: Allyn and Bacon.

Brooks, Jackson. 1988. *Honest Graft: Big Money and the American Political Process.* New York: Knopf.

Congressional Quarterly's Federal PAC Directory. 1998– 1999. Washington, DC: Congressional Quarterly Inc.

Day, Christine, and Charles Hadley. 2005. *Women's PACs: Abortion and Elections.* Upper Saddle River, NJ: Pearson Prentice Hall.

Gaer, Joseph. 1944. *The First Round: The Story of the CIO Political Committee.* New York: Duell, Sloan, and Pearce.

Gais, Thomas. 1996. *Improper Influence: Campaign Finance Law, Political Interest Groups, and the Problem of Equality.* Ann Arbor: University of Michigan Press.

Makinson, Larry. 1994. *Open Secrets: The Encyclopedia of Congressional Money and Politics.* Washington, DC: CQ Press.

Melich, Tanya. 1996. *The Republican War against Women: An Insider's Report from behind the Lines.* New York: Bantam Books.

Rymph, Catherine E. 2006. *Republican Women: Feminism and Conservatism from Suffrage to the Rise of the New Right.* Chapel Hill: University of North Carolina Press.

Sanbonmatsu, Kira. 2002. *Democrats, Republicans, and the Politics of Women's Place.* Ann Arbor: University of Michigan Press.

Shea, Maureen. 1988. *PACs on PACs: The View from the Inside.* Washington, DC: Center for Responsive Politics.

Stern, Phillip. 1988. *The Best Congress Money Can Buy.* New York: Pantheon.

Vickers, Jill, Pauline Rankin, and Christine Appelle. 1993. *Politics As If Women Mattered.* Toronto, Canada: University of Toronto Press.

19

STATE-BY-STATE GUIDE

Each of the fifty states profiled here has a rich and unique political history. These thumbnail overviews should be considered a starting point for further research. Please consult the index for more on individuals and specific chapters for more on particular offices.

For party affiliation, (D) means Democrat; (R), Republican; and (I), Independent. National rank indicates the female representation in the state house as compared with the other states. Dates reflect when the officeholders were elected.

For more information on women in the fifty states, plus the District of Columbia and Puerto Rico, see Doris Weatherford, *A History of Women in the United States: A State-By-State Reference*, Vols. 1–4 (Danbury, CT: Grolier Academic Reference, 2004), which covers women from the native tribes in each state to women of the present.

ALABAMA

Overview

Alabama was last state to organize for women's right to vote, holding its first suffrage meeting in 1902. Another eight years passed before the state association joined the National American Woman Suffrage Association. The movement grew sufficiently that when the Nineteenth Amendment to the U.S. Constitution enfranchised them, fifteen hundred women celebrated in Birmingham with a brass band.

Voters in Selma elected Hattie Hooker Wilkins to the legislature in 1922, the earliest opportunity. In the mid-twentieth century, when most women regressed, Alabama chose an uncommon number in statewide elections. Sybil Pool, first elected as secretary of state in 1944, rotated in other offices during the 1950s and 1960s, as did Agnes Baggett, Mary Texas Hurt Garner, and others. When Lurleen B. Wallace was elected governor in 1966, three of the state's eight constitutional officers were women. Even though Wallace basically was a surrogate for her husband, her election made Alabama the third state to choose a female governor.

The three women who served brief terms as U.S. senators between 1932 and 1978 were surrogates for men and were appointed, not elected. Elizabeth Andrews, the first Alabama woman in the U.S. House in 1972, also was a placeholder.

In 1974, when Janie Shores joined the Alabama Supreme Court, she was the fifth such woman in the nation. Louphenia Thomas of Birmingham in 1977 became the state's first African American female legislator. Alabama was slow to send a white woman to its state senate. Mobile's Ann Smith Bedsole was elected in 1983, when Republicans were building strength among whites in the Deep South.

Voters in 2010 finally elected their first two women to the U.S. House who were not surrogates for men: Republican Martha Dubina Roby and Democrat Terri A. Sewell, an African American who won with 72 percent of the vote. Their victories signaled a new era for Alabama women.

Key Facts

Statehood:	1819
Capital:	Montgomery
First women's rights organization:	Equal Suffrage Association, Selma, 1910
Pioneer publication:	None
First female lawyer:	Maud McLure Kelly, 1908
Full female enfranchisement:	1920
State ratification of Nineteenth Amendment:	No
First president of League of Women Voters:	Mrs. A.J. Bowron
First woman on state supreme court:	Janie Shores, 1974
State ratification of Equal Rights Amendment:	No

Statewide Elective Officeholders

Governor:	Lurleen B. Wallace (D)	1966
Lieutenant governor:	Lucy Baxley (D)	2002
	Kay Ivey (R)	2010
Secretary of state:	Sybil Pool (D)	1944
	Mary Texas Hurt Garner (D)	1954
	Bettye Frink (D)	1958
	Mabel Amos (D)	1966
	Nancy Worley (D)	2002
	Beth Chapman (R)	2006
Treasurer:	Sybil Pool (D)	1950
	Agnes Baggett (D)	1958
	Mary Texas Hurt Garner (D)	1962
	Melba Till Allen (D)	1966
	Annie Laurie Gunter (D)	1974
	Lucy Baxley (D)	1994
	Kay Ivey (R)	2002
Auditor:	Agnes Baggett (D)	1954
	Mary Texas Hurt Garner (D)	1958
	Bettye Frink (D)	1962
	Melba Till Allen (D)	1966
	Jan Cook (D)	1982
	Patsy Duncan (D)	1994
	Susan Parkman (D)	1998
	Samantha Snow (R)	2006
Public service commissioner:	Sybil Pool (D)	1954
	Juanita McDaniel (D)	1970
	Jan Cook (D)	1990
	Lucy Baxley (D)	2008
	Twinkle Cavanaugh (R)	2010

State Legislature

Firsts

House:	Hattie Hooker Wilkins (D)	1922
Senate:	Louphenia Thomas (D)	1977
Percentage of women in 2010–2011 session (5 among 35 in senate; 14 among 105 in house):	14	

National rank: 48
Presiding Officers
   Speaker of the house: None
   Senate president: None

Federal Elective Officeholders

U.S. Senate:[1]	Willa McCormick Blake (D)	1932
	Dixie Bibb Graves (D)	1937
	Maryon Pittman Allen (D)	1978
U.S. House:	Elizabeth Andrews (D)	1972
	Martha Dubina Roby (R)	2010
	Terri A. Sewell (D)	2010

FURTHER READING

Hamilton, Virginia Van der Veer. 1997. *Alabama: A Bicentennial History.* New York: W.W. Norton and Company.

McGuire, Danielle L. 2010. *At the Dark End of the Street: Black Women, Rape, and Resistance, A New History of the Civil Rights Movement.* New York: Alfred A. Knopf.

Thomas, Mary Martha, ed. 1995. *Stepping Out of the Shadows: Alabama Women, 1819–1990.* Tuscaloosa: University of Alabama Press.

ALASKA

Overview

Alaska is the only political jurisdiction in which no woman ever lobbied for the vote. Men were so eager to attract them that the vote was granted unanimously by the territorial legislature in 1913. It was the very first act of the new body.

Alaska women were slow use their rights, though, and no woman was elected to the Alaska House until 1936. That which was later than most states, but Alaska still was a territory. Nell Scott Chadwick, a Democrat, was known as "the flying legislator" because she piloted her own plane.

The first woman in the Alaska Senate also was elected prior to statehood. Anita Garlick of Juneau won in 1948 as an Independent. The territory became a state in 1959.

In 1987, the Alaska Senate was the nation's third to have female president and, in 1995, women led both legislative chambers. But Alaskans did not elect a woman to statewide office until 1994, when Fran Ulmer won the lieutenant governorship. Previously mayor of Juneau, she ran a strong race for governor in 2002 but lost to Frank H. Murkowski.

When Murkowski resigned from the U.S. Senate to become governor early in 2003, he appointed his daughter, Lisa Murkowski, to succeed him. She went on to win in her own right in 2004. The race for her second term, in 2010, also made national headlines. She lost the Republican nomination but narrowly won the general election as a write-in candidate. Only one other U.S. senator—South Carolina's Strom Thurmond—has won by this difficult method.

Alaska never has had a woman in the U.S. House, but it has had a female governor. Sarah Palin won in 2006. After joining John McCain's failed presidential campaign in 2008, Palin resigned the governorship in the summer of 2009. Women in other state executive positions remain rare.

Key Facts

Statehood: 1959
Capital: Juneau

---

[1] All appointed; none elected.

First women's rights organization:	None	
Pioneer publication	None	
First female lawyer:	Aline Chenot Baskerville Bradley Beegler, 1921	
Full female enfranchisement:	1913	
State ratification of Nineteenth Amendment:	Not applicable	
First president of League of Women Voters:	Not applicable	
First woman on state supreme court:	Dana Fabry, 1996	
State ratification of Equal Rights Amendment:	Yes	

Statewide Elective Officeholders

Governor:	Sarah Palin (R)	2006
Lieutenant governor:	Fran Ulmer (D)	1994
Secretary of state:	Not elected	
Attorney general:	None	
Financial officer(s):	None	
School superintendent:	Not elected	

State Legislature

Firsts		
House:	Nell Scott Chadwick (D)	1936
Senate:	Anita Garlick (I)	1948
Percentage of women in 2010–2011 session		
(4 among 20 in senate; 10 among 40 in house):	23	
National rank:	25	
Presiding Officers		
Speaker of the house:	Ramona Barnes (R)	1993
	Gail Phillips (R)	1995
Senate president:	Jan Falks (R)	1987
	Drue Pearce (R)	1993

Federal Elective Officeholders

U.S. Senate:	Lisa Murkowski (R)	2003
U.S. House:	None	

FURTHER READING

Hinckley, Ted. 1972. *The Americanization of Alaska*. Palo Alto, CA: Pacific Books.

Mitchell, Donald. 1997. *Sold American: A Story of Alaska Natives and Their Land.* Hanover, NH: University Press of New England.

Pinson, Elizabeth Bernhardt. 2004. *Alaska's Daughter: An Eskimo's Memoir.* Logan: Utah State University Press.

ARIZONA

Overview

Arizona became a state in 1912, and women won the vote with a 1913 referendum, prevailing by 13,442 to 6,202. Women won elective office the next year, including the nation's third female state senator.

Arizona set the national precedent for financial offices in 1926, and Republicans nominated Lena Marks, a Russian Jew, for Speaker of the Arizona House in 1928. Legislator Polly Cutler Rosenbaum won elections for forty-six years and, in 1950, Ana Frohmiller almost won election as governor. A Democrat, she lost to the male Republican by less than 1 percent.

Lorna Lockwood was elected to the Arizona Supreme Court in 1960 and went on to be the nation's first female chief justice. In 1981, Arizona senator Sandra Day O'Connor became the first woman on the U.S. Supreme Court and, in 1989, the legislature was the nation's first to have female presiding officers in both chambers.

Democrats nominated Carolyn Warner for governor in 1986, but she narrowly lost to Evan Meecham. He was impeached in 1988, and Secretary of State Rose Mofford succeeded him. Similarly, Secretary of State Jane Dee Hull became governor in 1997 when the male Republican incumbent, Fife Symington, was forced to resign because of scandals.

At the next election, in 1998, voters chose only women for all five top offices. President Barack Obama in 2009 appointed Governor Janet Napolitano as secretary of homeland security, a cabinet-level position. With Napolitano's resignation, Secretary of State Jan Brewer became governor. She won the 2010 election, making Arizona the only state to have had four female governors.

Key Facts

Statehood:	1912
Capital:	Phoenix
First women's rights organization:	No formal name, 1891
Pioneer publication:	None
First female lawyer:	Sarah Sorin, 1912
Full female enfranchisement:	1913
State ratification of Nineteenth Amendment:	Yes
First president of League of Women Voters:	Mrs. M.T. Phelps, Phoenix, 1913
First woman on state supreme court:	Lorna Lockwood, 1960
State ratification of Equal Rights Amendment:	No

Statewide Elective Officeholders

Governor:	Rose Mofford (D)[2]	1977
	Jane Dee Hull (R)[3]	1998
	Janet Napolitano (D)	2002
	Jan Brewer (R)	2010
Lieutenant governor:	Office does not exist	
Secretary of state:	Rose Mofford (D)	1976
	Jane Dee Hull (R)	1994
	Betsey Bayless (R)	1998
	Jan Brewer (R)	2002
Attorney general:	Janet Napolitano (D)	1998
Treasurer:	Carol Springer (R)	2000
Auditor:	Ana Frohmiller (D)	1926
	Jewel Jordan (D)	1950
	Carol Springer (R)	1998
School superintendent:	Elsie Toles (D)	1920
	Sarah Folsom (R)	1964
	Carolyn Warner (D)	1974

---

[2] Assumed office in 1977; did not run for election.

[3] For both Hull and Brewer (below), this indicates the year of election, after serving as governor upon the incumbent's resignation.

	C. Diane Bishop (D)	1986
	Lisa Graham Keegan (R)	1994
Corporation commissioner	Diane McCarthy (R)	1980
	Marcia Weeks (D)	1984
	Sandra Kennedy (D)	2002
	Kristin Mayes (R)	2002

State Legislature

Firsts

House:	Rachel Emma Allen Berry (D)	1914
Senate:	Frances Willard Munds (D)	1914

Percentage of women in 2010–2011 session	
(11 among 30 in senate; 20 among 60 in house):	35
National rank:	3

Presiding Officers

Speaker of the house:	Jane Dee Hull (R)	1989
Senate president:	Brenda Burns (R)	1989

Federal Elective Officeholders

U.S. Senate:	None	
U.S. House:	Isabella Selmes Greenway (D)	1932
	Karan English (D)	1992
	Gabrielle Giffords (D)	2006
	Ann Kirkpatrick (D)	2008

FURTHER READING

Miller, Kristie. 2004. *Isabella Greenway: An Enterprising Woman.* Tucson: University of Arizona Press.

Reingold, Beth. 2000. *Representing Women: Sex, Gender, and Legislative Behavior in Arizona and California.* Chapel Hill: University of North Carolina Press.

Summerhayes, Martha. 1908. *Vanished Arizona: Recollections of My Army Life.* Philadelphia: Lippincott.

ARKANSAS

Overview

The first women's rights organization in Arkansas began in Eureka Springs in 1885, but it faded until being revived by Little Rock women in 1911. They won a significant victory in 1917, when an enfranchisement act evaded constitutional questions by allowing women to vote in party primaries only. To the majority of Arkansans, Democratic primaries were the elections that mattered most. When Congress passed the Nineteenth Amendment in 1919, Arkansas was the only Southern state with an entire congressional delegation that voted positively.

Two women won seats in the Arkansas House in 1922, the first opportunity, and two soon served simultaneously in the U.S. House. In 1932, Jonesboro's Hattie Wyatt Caraway became the first woman elected to the U.S. Senate.

When the first woman joined the Arkansas Supreme Court in 1975, only five other states had set that precedent. Little Rock had its first female mayor, Lottie H. Shackelford, in 1987.

In the same 1992 election that moved Gov. Bill Clinton and his wife, Hillary Rodham Clinton, to Washington, DC, thirty-one-year-old Blanche Lambert (later Lincoln) was elected to the U.S. House. She won a U.S. Senate seat in 1998 and had risen to chair the Senate Agriculture Committee—the first woman to do so—when she fell in the Republican tide of 2010. Like every other woman elected to Congress or to statewide office in Arkansas as of 2011, Lincoln was a Democrat.

Key Facts

Statehood:	1836
Capital:	Little Rock
First women's rights organization:	Political Equality League, 1885
Pioneer publication:	*Woman's Chronicle*, Little Rock, 1888
First female lawyer:	Phoebe Couzins, 1871
Full female enfranchisement:	1920
State ratification of Nineteenth Amendment:	Yes
First president of League of Women Voters:	Mrs. T. T. Cotnam, Little Rock
First woman on state supreme court:	Elsijane Trimble Roy, 1975
State ratification of Equal Rights Amendment:	No

Statewide Elective Officeholders

Governor:	None	
Lieutenant governor:	None	
Secretary of state:	Nancy Johnson Hall (D)[4]	1961
	Sharon Priest (D)	1994
Attorney general:	None	
Treasurer:	Nancy Johnson Hall (D)	1962
	Jimmie Lou Fisher (D)	1980
Auditor:	Julia Hughes Jones (D)	1980
	Martha Schoffner (D)	2006
School superintendent:	Not elected	

State Legislature

Firsts

House:	Frances Hunt (D)	1922
	Erle Rutherford Chambers (D)	1922
Senate:	Dorothy Allen (D)	1964

Percentage of women in 2010-2011 session
  (8 among 35 in senate; 22 among 100 in house): 22
National rank: 31
Presiding Officers
  Speaker of the house: None
  Senate president: None

Federal Elective Officeholders

U.S. Senate:	Hattie Wyatt Caraway (D)	1931[5]
	Blanche Lambert Lincoln (D)	1998
U.S. House:	Pearl Peden Oldfield (D)	1929
	Effiegene Locke Wingo (D)	1930
	Catherine Dorris Norrell (D)	1960
	Blanche Lambert (later Lincoln) (D)	1992

---

[4] Appointed.

[5] Initially appointed

FURTHER READING

Bates, Daisy. 1987. *The Long Shadow of Little Rock: A Memoir*. Fayetteville: University of Arkansas Press.
Malone, David. 1989. *Hattie and Huey: An Arkansas Tour*. Fayetteville: University of Arkansas Press.
Whayne, Jeannie M., ed. 2002. *Arkansas: A Narrative History*. Fayetteville: University of Arkansas Press.

CALIFORNIA

Overview

With leadership from Emily Pitts Stevens, a San Francisco newspaper publisher, a feminist organization formalized in California in 1869. Women, however, did not conduct their first campaign for the vote until 1896. They lost and did not try again until 1911. After a highly sophisticated campaign, the winning margin was a mere 3,587 votes out of 246,487 cast, with rural men providing that edge.

Four women were elected to the legislature in 1918, and California's first woman in Congress, Republican Mae Ella Nolan, won in 1923. She was the fourth in the nation. A woman was not elected to the California Senate until 1976. The following year, March Fong Eu was elected secretary of state, becoming the nation's first Asian American woman to serve in a statewide elective office. San Francisco in 1978 was the first mega-city to have a woman as mayor, and Democrat Dianne Feinstein went on to the U.S. Senate.

California has elected a significant number of women to Congress, but its record on statewide elective offices is less impressive. Treasurer Kathleen Brown, a Democrat whose father and brother were governors, was unsuccessful in her quest for that office in the late 1990s, and Meg Whitman, a self-made billionaire, lost her gubernatorial race against Jerry Brown in 2010, despite record spending. Although the Republican Whitman lost in California, Republicans did well in other states, especially in U.S. House races. When Democrats lost the majority, San Francisco's Nancy Pelosi, the first female Speaker of the U.S. House, had to give up that post. U.S. senator Barbara Boxer, a Democrat, survived tough competition in 2010 from Republican businesswoman Carly Fiorina. Both the gubernatorial and the senatorial races of that year seem to indicate that California voters care most about party positions on issues.

Key Facts

Statehood:	1850
Capital:	Sacramento
First women's rights organization:	California Woman Suffrage Society, 1869
Pioneer publication:	*The Yellow Ribbon*, San Francisco, 1906
First female lawyers:	Clara Shortridge Foltz and Laura de Force Gordon, 1879
Full female enfranchisement:	1911
State ratification of Nineteenth Amendment:	Yes
First president of League of Women Voters:	Not applicable[6]
First woman on state supreme court:	Rose Elizabeth Bird, 1977
State ratification of Equal Rights Amendment:	Yes

Statewide Elective Officeholders

Governor:	None	
Lieutenant governor:	None	
Secretary of state:	March Fong Eu (D)	1974
	Debra Bowen (D)	2006

---

[6]The League of Women Voters did not begin nationally until 1919. Its state equivalent was the Women's Legislative Council of California, organized in December 1912. *History of Woman Suffrage* did not record its first president.

Attorney general:	Karmala D. Harris (D)	2010
Treasurer:	Ivy Baker Priest (R)	1966
	Kathleen Brown (D)	1990
Controller:	Kathleen Connell (D)	1994
School superintendent:	Delaine Eastin (NP)[7]	1994

State Legislature

Firsts

House:	Esto Broughton (D)	1918
	Grace S. Dorris (NP)[8]	1918
	Elizabeth Hughes (R)	1918
	Anna L. Saylor (NP)	1918
Senate:	Rose Ann Vuich (D)	1976

Percentage of women in 2010–2011 session
  (12 among 40 in senate; 21 among 80 in house):   28
National rank: 16
Presiding Officers:
  Speaker of the house: Karen Bass (D)   2008
  Senate president: None

Federal Elective Officeholders

U.S. Senate:	Dianne Feinstein (D)	1992
	Barbara Boxer (D)	1992
U.S. House:	Mae Ella Nolan (R)	1923
	Florence Prag Kahn (R)	1925
	Helen Gahagan Douglas (D)	1944
	Yvonne Braithwaite Burke (D)	1972
	Shirley Neil Pettis (R)	1975
	Bobbi Fiedler (R)	1974
	Barbara Boxer (D)	1982
	Sala Galante Burton (D)	1983
	Nancy Pelosi (D)	1986
	Maxine Waters (D)	1990
	Anna Georges Eshoo (D)	1992
	Jane L. Harman (D)	1992
	Lucille Roybal-Allard (D)	1992
	Lynn Schenk (D)	1992
	Lynn Woolsey (D)	1992
	Andrea Seastrand (R)	1994
	Zoe Lofgren (D)	1994
	Juanita Millender-McDonald (D)	1996
	Loretta Sanchez (D)	1996
	Ellen O. Tauscher (D)	1996
	Mary Bono (Mack) (R)	1998
	Lois D. Capps (D)	1998
	Barbara Lee (D)	1998
	Grace Napolitano (D)	1998

---

[7] Not a partisan office.

[8] California's electoral system at this time allowed multiparty allegiances. For details, see Chapter 4: State Representatives.

Susan A. Davis (D)	2000
Hilda L. Solis (D)	2000
Diane Edith Watson (D)	2000
Linda Sanchez (D)	2002
Doris Matsui (D)	2005
Laura Richardson (D)	2007
Jackie Speier (D)	2008
Judy Chu (D)	2009
Karen Bass (D)	2010

FURTHER READING

Atherton, Gertrude Franklin Horn. 1914. *California: An Intimate History.* New York: Harper and Brothers.

Cooney, Robert. 2005. *Winning the Vote.* Santa Cruz, CA: American Graphic Press.

Gullett, Gayle Ann. 2000. *Becoming Citizens: The Emergence and Development of the California Women's Movement, 1880–1911.* Urbana: University of Illinois Press.

COLORADO

Overview

When the Rev. Mrs. Wilkes of Colorado Springs organized the first feminist meeting in Colorado in 1876, she said that women owned a third of the territory's property, yet none could vote. Women lobbied the constitutional convention for statehood that year. After that effort failed, they immediately conducted an 1877 referendum, but lost that, too. An 1893 referendum, however, was successful. By a vote of 35,798 to 29,451, Colorado men enfranchised women. It was the first such victory in the nation, as female voters in Wyoming and Utah had been were enfranchised by territorial legislatures, not by referenda to male voters.

Three women from a coalition of parties won races for the legislature the next year, and in the same 1894 election, Colorado tied with Wyoming as second in electing women to statewide office. Helen Ring Robinson became the nation's second female state senator in 1912, following only Utah's 1896 precedent. When, in 1919, Colorado ratified the Nineteenth Amendment that enfranchised women in other states, state senator Agnes Riddle introduced it in that chamber, while Dr. May Bigelow and Miss Mabel Ruth Baker did so in the House.

Colorado voters tied with Wyoming in electing the nation's second female state school superintendent in 1894, and in the next decades, that office came to be seen as so thoroughly belonging to Colorado women that no party nominated a man for it. Women were slow to run for other offices, however, and it was not until 1966 that Virginia Blue was elected treasurer. In 1972, Denver elected the state's first woman in Congress, Patricia Scott Schroeder.

Gale A. Norton became Colorado's first female attorney general in 1990 and was the controversial head of the Department of the Interior during the George W. Bush administration. In 1994, Colorado was the first state to elect a black Republican woman to an executive office: Victoria Buckley served as secretary of state until her 1999 death. Her successor, Donetta Davidson, went on to be president of the National Association of Secretaries of State in 2005.

In 2011, Colorado had just one woman in its seven-member delegation to the U.S. House. Except for governor, women had been elected to all of its statewide elective executive offices at some point in the past, but by 2011, they held none. However, the state ranked first for percentage of women in its legislature in 2011.

Key Facts

Statehood:	1876
Capital:	Denver
First women's rights organization:	Equal Suffrage Association, 1896
Pioneer publication:	None
First female lawyer:	Mary Lathrop, 1896

Full female enfranchisement:	1893
State ratification of Nineteenth Amendment:	Yes
First president of League of Women Voters:	Not available[9]
First woman on state supreme court:	Jean Dubofsky, 1979
State ratification of Equal Rights Amendment:	Yes

Statewide Elective Officeholders

Governor:	None	
Lieutenant governor:	Nancy Dick (D)	1978
	Gail Schlotter (D)	1994
	Jane Norton (R)	2002
	Barbara O'Brien (D)	2006
Secretary of state:	Mary Estil Buchanan (R)	1972
	Natalie Meyer (R)	1982
	Victoria Buckley (R)	1994
	Donetta Davidson (R)	2000
	Gigi Dennis (R)	2004
Attorney general:	Gale A. Norton (R)	1990
Treasurer:	Virginia Blue (R)	1966
	Gail Schlotter (D)	1986
	Cary Kennedy (D)	2006
School superintendent:	Antoinette J. Peavey (MPC)[10]	1894
	Helen Loring Grenfell (MPC)	1898
	Katherine M. Cook (MPC)	1908
	Helen M. Wixson (MPC)	1910
	Mary C.C. Bradford (D)	1912
	Inez Johnson Lewis (D)	1930
	Nettie S. Freed (R)	1946

State Legislature

Firsts

House:	Clara Cressingham (MPC)	1894
	Carrie Clyde Holly (MPC)	1894
	Frances S. Klock (MPC)	1894
Senate:	Helen Ring Robinson (R)	1912

Percentage of women in 2010–2011 session
   (17 among 35 in senate; 24 among 65 in house):   41

National rank: 1

Presiding Officers

Speaker of the house:	Lola Spradley (R)	2003
Senate president:	Joan Fitz-Gerald (D)	2005

Federal Elective Officeholders

U.S. Senate:	None	
U.S. House:	Patricia Scott Schroeder (D)	1972

---

[9] Colorado women began voting a quarter-century before establishment of the League of Women Voters, and records do not clearly indicate who may have been entitled to this title.

[10] MPC stands for multiparty coalition.

Diana DeGette (D)	1996
Marilyn Musgrave (R)	2002
Betsy Markey (D)	2008

FURTHER READING

Jones-Eddy, Julie. 1992. *Homesteading Women: An Oral History of Colorado.* New York: Twayne.

Mead, Rebecca J. 2004. *How the Vote Was Won: Woman Suffrage in the Western United States, 1868–1914.* New York: New York University Press.

Robertson, Janet. 1990. *The Magnificent Mountain Women: Adventures in the Colorado Rockies.* Lincoln: University of Nebraska Press.

CONNECTICUT

Overview

Sisters Abby and Julia Smith of Glastonbury became feminist icons in the 1870s. When they refused to pay their taxes because they could not vote, the town confiscated their cattle. Connecticut's longtime feminist leader was Isabella Beecher Hooker, sister of author Harriet Beecher Stowe. Katherine Houghton Hepburn, mother of the famed actor, led the state suffrage movement in the twentieth century. The legislature, however, did not ratify the Nineteenth Amendment until several months after it had been added to the U.S. Constitution.

Women nonetheless were candidates in the 1920 election, and five won in November, a record unequaled in any other state. In 1924, Connecticut elected New England's first female state senator.

The first woman won the secretary of state's office in 1938, and after she was succeeded two years later by another, the post came to seen as a "woman's job." Twelve women from both parties held it between the 1938 and 2010 elections.

Connecticut had two women serve simultaneously in the U.S. House during the war years of the 1940s. A third, Ella Tambussi Grasso, went from Capitol Hill to the statehouse in 1974. She was the nation's first female governor with a career independent of her husband.

The 2004 election of Republican M. Jodi Rell meant that Connecticut followed Texas, Kansas, and Washington in twice choosing a woman for its highest office. When Rell did not seek reelection in 2010, Connecticut's highest-ranking women were the lieutenant governor and Rep. Rosa L. DeLauro, the sole woman in its five-member delegation to the U.S. House.

Key Facts

Statehood:	1788
Capital:	Hartford
First women's rights organization:	Connecticut Woman Suffrage Association, 1869
Pioneer publication:	None
First female lawyer:	Mary Hall, 1882
Full female enfranchisement:	1920
State ratification of Nineteenth Amendment:	No
First president of League of Women Voters:	Miss Mabel C. Washburn, Hartford
First woman on state supreme court:	Ellen Ash Peters, 1978
State ratification of Equal Rights Amendment:	Yes

Statewide Elective Officeholders

Governor:	Ella Tambussi Grasso (D)	1974
	M. Jodi Rell (R)	2004

Lieutenant governor:	Eunice Goark (ACP)[II]	1990
	M. Jodi Rell (R)	1994
	Nancy Wyman (D)	2010
Secretary of state:	Sara Crawford (R)	1938
	Chase Going Woodhouse (D)	1940
	Frances Burke Redick (R)	1942
	Winifred McDonald (D)	1948
	Alice K. Leopold (R)	1950
	Ella Tambussi Grasso (D)	1958
	Gloria Shaffer (D)	1970
	Barbara Bailey Kennelly (D)	1978
	Julie H. Tashjian (D)	1982
	Pauline Kazer (R)	1990
	Susan Bysiewicz (D)	1998
	Dina Merrill (D)	2010
Attorney general:	None	
Treasurer:	Denise Nappier (D)	1998
Comptroller:	Nancy Wyman (D)	1994
School superintendent:	Not elected	

State Legislature

Firsts

House:	Emily Sophie Brown (R)	1922
	Grace I. Edwards (I)	1922
	Lillian M. S. Frink (R)	1922
	Mary M. Hooker (R)	1922
	Helen Jewett (D)	1922
Senate:	Alice Virginia Merritt (R)	1924

Percentage of women in 2010–2011 session
   (8 among 36 in senate; 46 among 151 in house):   29
National rank: 9
Presiding Officers

| Speaker of the house: | Moira Kay Lyons (D) | 2003 |
| Senate president: | None | |

Federal Elective Officeholders

U.S. Senate:	None	
U.S. House:	Clare Boothe Luce (R)	1942
	Chase Going Woodhouse (D)	1944
	Ella Tambussi Grasso (D)	1970
	Barbara Bailey Kennelly (D)	1982
	Nancy Lee Johnson (R)	1982
	Rosa L. DeLauro (D)	1990

FURTHER READING

Bucki, Cecilia. 2001. *Bridgeport's Socialist New Deal, 1915–1936.* Urbana: University of Illinois Press.

Dayton, Cornelia Hughes. 1995. *Women before the Bar: Gender, Law, and Society in Connecticut, 1639–1789.* Chapel Hill: University of North Carolina Press.

[II] ACP stands for A Connecticut Party. For detail, see Chapter 8: Governors and Lieutenant Governors.

Housley, Kathleen L. 1993. *The Letter Kills But the Spirit Gives Life: The Smiths—Abolitionists, Suffragists, Bible Translators.* Glastonbury, CT: History Society of Glastonbury.

Nichols, Carole. 1983. *Votes and More for Women: Suffrage and After in Connecticut.* New York: Haworth Press.

Wawrose, Susan C. 1996. *Griswold vs. Connecticut.* New York: Franklin Watts.

DELAWARE

Overview

Delaware was one of the last states to organize for the vote, in 1895. In 1913, women joined the Pilgrim Band that marched from New York to Washington, DC. Its men made a vital difference in the 1918 election when they replaced an anti-suffrage U.S. senator with one who favored enfranchisement, which proved the key to the passage of the Nineteenth Amendment. By the time the Delaware General Assembly took up ratification in the spring of 1920, only one more state was needed to meet the constitutionally mandated threshold. Proponents organized well, but opponents, led by prominent Emily Bissell, did the same. Even with support from the powerful du Pont family, feminists lost. Tennessee subsequently provided the necessary ratification.

Delaware was the last state to admit women to its bar, in 1923, but the next year marked a turning point, as women were elected to the legislature and to statewide office. Secretary of State Fannie Harrington was the nation's second woman in that position, following only New Mexico in 1922.

Delaware had no female state senator until 1946, and the first woman was elected as state treasurer in 1956. That remained women's sole position among executive offices until 1992, when Democrat Ruth Ann Minner won the lieutenant governorship. She moved up to governor in 2000. M. Jane Brady, a Republican, was attorney general at the same time, giving women two powerful positions.

As of 2011, Delaware remained one of four states (with Iowa, Mississippi, and Vermont) that never has sent a woman to either house of Congress.

Key Facts

Statehood:	1787
Capital:	Dover
First women's rights organization:	Delaware Equal Suffrage Association, 1895
Pioneer publication:	None
First female lawyers:	Sybil Ward and Evangelyn Barsky, 1923
Full female enfranchisement:	1920
State ratification of Nineteenth Amendment:	No
First president of League of Women Voters:	Mrs. Henry Ridgely, Dover
First woman on state supreme court:	Peggy Ableman, 2000
State ratification of Equal Rights Amendment:	Yes

Statewide Elective Officeholders

Governor:	Ruth Ann Minner (D)	2000
Lieutenant governor:	Ruth Ann Minner (D)	1992
Secretary of state:	Fannie Harrington (R)	1924
Attorney general:	M. Jane Brady (R)	1994
Treasurer:	Vera Gilbride Davis (R)	1956
	Annabelle Smith Everett (D)	1958
	Emily Womack (D)	1970
	Mary D. Jornlin (D)	1972

	Janet Rzewnicki (R)	1982
	Velda Jones-Potter (D)	2008
School superintendent:	Not elected	
Insurance commissioner:	Donna Lee Williams (R)	1992
	Karen Weldin Stuart (D)	2008

State Legislature

Firts
| House: | Florence M. Hanby (R) | 1924 |
| Senate: | Vera Gilbride Davis (R) | 1946 |

Percentage of women in 2010–2011 session
   (7 among 21 in senate; 9 among 41 in house): 26
National rank: 18
Presiding Officers
   Speaker of the house: None
   Senate president: None

Federal Elective Officeholders

U.S. Senate: None
U.S. House: None

FURTHER READING

Boyer, William W., and Edward C. Ratledge. 2009. *Delaware Politics and Government.* Lincoln: University of Nebraska Press.

Hoeffecker, Carol E. 1994. *Beneath Thy Guiding Hand: A History of Women at the University of Delaware.* Newark: University of Delaware Press.

Jones, Jacqueline. 2001. *Creek Walking: Growing Up in Delaware in the 1950s.* Newark: University of Delaware Press.

FLORIDA

Overview

Although Florida is home to the nation's oldest city, St. Augustine, settled by Spanish colonists in 1565, no organized women's movement developed in the state until the 1870s. As in other states, the movement flagged in the early twentieth century but revived in 1913, when Montana's Jeannette Rankin—soon to be the first woman elected to the U.S. Congress—spoke to the Florida Legislature. Between 1915 and 1920, as real estate boomed, twenty-three new towns in Florida enfranchised women.

Florida's legislature was in session when the U.S. Senate adopted the Nineteenth Amendment on June 4, 1919, but it would adjourn the following day. Gov. Sidney Catts asked lawmakers to ratify, but suffragists did not lobby. They feared the consequences elsewhere if the amendment was rejected by the first state to vote. Three states ratified the next week, and by the time the legislature met again in 1921, women had voted in the 1920 election.

Ruth Bryan Owen in 1928 became the first woman elected to the U.S. House from the South. Mary McLeod Bethune, a Daytona Beach African American, advised President Franklin D. Roosevelt in the 1930s. Mary Lou Baker of St. Petersburg was an exceptional representative in the 1940s, and Florida finally had its first female state senator in 1962. By coincidence, both she and the second female senator, in 1966, were named Beth Johnson.

The first African American women won legislative seats in the 1970s, and Paula Hawkins of Maitland was elected Florida's first female U.S. senator in 1980. In 1986, Education Commissioner Betty Castor of Tampa became the first woman on Florida's uncommonly powerful cabinet. In 1989, Ileana Ros-Lehtinen of Miami won a special election to the late Claude Pepper's seat, becoming the nation's first Cuban American member of the U.S. House.

Both Tampa and Orlando elected women as mayors, and the election of four women to the U.S. House in 1992 helped foster the idea that it was the Year of the Woman. President Bill Clinton named Janet Reno as the nation's first female attorney general, and Carol M. Browner—like Reno, of Miami—was selected to head the Environmental Protection Agency. Martha Barnett of Tallahassee was chosen by her peers as the second female president of the American Bar Association in 2000. In 2006, Alex Sink of Tampa became Florida's first female chief financial officer. She would barely lose the 2010 gubernatorial race.

Voters in Fort Lauderdale had chosen Debbie Wasserman Schultz in 2004 to represent them in the U.S. House, and President Barack Obama named her to head the Democratic Party in 2011. As of that year, Florida had six women in its twenty-five-member House delegation.

Key Facts

Statehood:	1845
Capital:	Tallahassee
First women's rights organization:	Florida Woman Suffrage Association, 1870
Pioneer publication:	None
First female lawyer:	Louise Rebecca Pinnell, Jacksonville, 1898
Full female enfranchisement:	1920
State ratification of Nineteenth Amendment:	No
First president of League of Women Voters:	Mrs. J. B. O'Hara
First woman on state supreme court:	Rosemary Barkett, 1985
State ratification of Equal Rights Amendment:	No

Statewide Elective Officeholders

Governor:	None	
Lieutenant governor:	Toni Jennings (R)[12]	2003
	Jennifer Carroll (R)	2010
Secretary of state:	Sandra Mortham (R)	1994
	Katherine Harris (R)	1998
Attorney general:	Pam Bondi (R)	2010
Chief financial officer:	Alex Sink (D)	2006
School superintendent:	Betty Castor (D)	1986
Railroad commissioner:	Mamie Eaton-Greene (D)	1928
Public service commissioner:	Paula Hawkins (R)	1972

State Legislature

Firsts

House:	Edna Giles Fuller (D)	1928
Senate:	Beth Johnson (D)	1962
Percentage of women in 2010–2011 session		
(13 among 40 in senate; 27 among 120 in house):	25	

---

[12] Appointed to a vacancy; never elected.

National rank:		20	
Presiding Officers			
Speaker of the house:		None	
Senate president:		Gwen Margolis (D)	1990
		Toni Jennings (R)	1996

Federal Elective Officeholders

U.S. Senate:	Paula Hawkins (R)	1980
U.S. House:	Ruth Bryan Owen (D)	1928
	Ileana Ros-Lehtinen (R)	1989
	Corrine Brown (D)	1992
	Tillie Fowler (R)	1992
	Carrie Meek (D)	1992
	Karen L. Thurman (D)	1992
	Ginny Brown-Waite (R)	2002
	Debbie Wasserman-Schultz (D)	2004
	Kathy Castor (D)	2006
	Suzanne M. Kosmas (D)	2008
	Sandy Adams (R)	2010
	Frederica Wilson (D)	2010

FURTHER READING

Davis, Jack, and Kari Frederickson, eds. 2003. *Making Waves: Female Activists in Twentieth Century Florida.* Gainesville: University of Florida Press.

Hewitt, Nancy. 2001. *Southern Discomfort: Women's Activism in Tampa, Florida, 1880s–1920s.* Urbana: University of Illinois Press.

MacManus, Susan A. 2002. *Mapping Florida's Political Landscape.* Tallahassee: Florida Institute of Government.

Roberts, Diane. 2006. *Dream State: Eight Generations of Swamp Lawyers, Conquistadors, Confederate Daughters, Banana Republicans, and Other Florida Wildlife.* Gainesville: University of Florida Press.

GEORGIA

Overview

Georgia suffragists organized in 1890, led by a mother and her three adult daughters in Columbus's Howard family. They invited the National American Woman Suffrage Association to Atlanta for the 1895 convention, the first such meeting in the South. The *Atlanta Journal* featured front-page stories, and sessions at De Give's Opera House were standing room only.

With the 1913 revival of feminism, Georgia women conducted 275 meetings in cities ranging geographically from Augusta to Decatur to Macon to Bainbridge. In Rome, they even sponsored a feminist movie, *Your Girl and Mine.* A newly elected U.S. senator from Georgia helped pass the Nineteenth Amendment, but feminists correctly predicted that the state legislature would reject it.

Georgia and Mississippi women were the only ones who could not vote in November 1920, because they had not registered six months earlier. But when an incumbent U.S. senator died shortly before the 1922 election, the governor appointed eighty-seven-year-old Rebecca Latimer Felton, a strong suffragist. It was merely a courtesy, but when Congress convened on November 21, 1922, she traveled to Washington, DC, was sworn in, and made a brief speech.

Two decades passed before Georgia had a woman in the US House who was elected in her own right. Helen Douglas Mankin, a white Atlanta lawyer who served black clients, won a special election in 1946, but she served only briefly.

The era's most significant milestone was Atlanta's choice of a woman, Ira Jarrell, as superintendent of schools in 1944. She served until retirement in 1960. Iris Faircloth Blitch won election to Congress in 1954, defeating an incumbent by running on a segregationist platform.

Atlanta voters elected the state's first African American woman to the U.S. House, Cynthia McKinney, in 1992. She lost the 2002 Democratic nomination to former supporter Denise L. Majette, but when Majette gave up the House seat to run unsuccessfully for the U.S. Senate in 2004, McKenney regained her position in the House—only to lose again in 2006. Both women were black. No white woman has been elected to Congress from Georgia since 1962.

Georgia was one of the last states to elect women to executive office—in 1994, more than a century after this precedent had been set in 1892. The 2010 election marked more reversal. Women held no statewide offices, and none was in its fifteen-member congressional delegation.

Key Facts

Statehood:	1788
Capital:	Atlanta
First women's rights organization:	Georgia Woman Suffrage Association, 1890
Pioneer publication:	None
First female lawyer:	Stella Akin, 1918
Full female enfranchisement:	1920
State ratification of Nineteenth Amendment:	No
First president of League of Women Voters:	Annie G. Wright, Augusta
First woman on state supreme court:	Leah Ward Sears, 1992
State ratification of Equal Rights Amendment:	No

Statewide Elective Officeholders

Governor:	None	
Lieutenant governor:	None	
Secretary of state:	Cathy Cox (D)	1998
	Karen Handel (R)	2006
Attorney general:	None	
Financial officer(s):	None	
School superintendent:	Linda Schrenko (R)	1994
	Kathy Cox (R)	2006
Public service commissioner:	Angela Elizabeth Speir	2002

State Legislature

Firsts		
House:	Bessie Knowles (D)	1922
	Viola Ross Napier (D)	1922
Senate:	Tassie Kelley Cannon (D)	1931[13]
Percentage of women in 2010–2011 session		
(8 among 56 in senate; 47 among 180 in house):	24	
National rank:	25	
Presiding Officers		
Speaker of the house:	None	
Senate president:	None	

---

[13] Special election.

Federal Elective Officeholders

U.S. Senate:	Rebecca Latimer Felton (D)[14]	1921
U.S. House:	Florence Reville Gibbs (D)	1940
	Helen Douglas Mankin (D)	1946
	Iris Faircloth Blitch (D)	1954
	Cynthia McKinney (D)	1992
	Denise L. Majette(D)	2002

FURTHER READING

Boatwright, Eleanor Miot. 1994. *Status of Women in Georgia, 1783–1860*. Brooklyn, NY: Carlson Publishing.

Chirhart, Ann Short, and Betty Wood. 2009. *Georgia Women: Their Lives and Times*. Athens: University of Georgia Press.

Montgomery, Rebecca S. 2006. *The Politics of Education in the New South: Women and Reform in Georgia, 1890–1930*. Baton Rogue: Louisiana State Press.

Spritzer, Lorraine Nelson. 1982. *The Belle of Ashby Street: Helen Douglas Mankin and Georgia Politics*. Athens: University of Georgia Press.

HAWAII

Overview

Hawaii, the newest state, has been progressive on issues. It was the first state to ratify the Equal Rights Amendment, and it adopted universal health insurance in 1974.

Feminists in the Hawaii Territory organized in 1912, but, unlike the Alaska Territory, the legislature did not grant the vote. Women won that with the Nineteenth Amendment to the U.S. Constitution in 1920. The first woman in the Territorial House was elected in 1924; the first female senator, in 1932.

Betty Farrington became Hawaii's delegate to Congress in 1954. She was a white woman who was a strong advocate of statehood, which was achieved in 1959 over objections from congressional conservatives who were dubious about Hawaii's mixed-race population. Five years later, in 1964, Patsy Takemoto Mink became the first Asian American woman elected to the U.S. House. She held other offices, too, and was Hawaii's most important female politician until her 2002 death.

Democrat Mazie K. Hirono of Honolulu became lieutenant governor in 1994, but partly because of internal party conflict, she lost the 2002 race for governor to Republican Linda Lingle of Maui. Hirono went on to win a congressional seat in 2006. When Lingle's two terms ended, women held no state executive offices, but they composed more than a third of the 2011 legislature. Hawaii could boast an all-female delegation to the U.S. House: Its two representatives were Hirono and fellow Democrat Colleen Hanabusa. Because both of Hawaii's U.S. senators were men, women composed half of the state's congressional delegation.

Key Facts

Statehood:	1959
Capital:	Honolulu
First women's rights organization:	No formal name, 1912
Pioneer publication:	None
First female lawyer:	Almeda Eliza Hitchcock, 1888
Full female enfranchisement:	1920
State ratification of Nineteenth Amendment:	Not applicable

---

[14]Appointed not elected.

First president of League of Women Voters: Not available
First woman on state supreme court: Paula A. Nakayama, 1993
State ratification of Equal Rights Amendment: Yes

Statewide Elective Officeholders

Governor:	Linda Lingle (R)	2002
Lieutenant governor:	Jean Sadako King (D)	1978
	Mazie K. Hirono (D)	1994
Secretary of state:	Not elected	
Attorney general:	None	
Financial officer(s):	Not elected	
School superintendent	Not elected	

State Legislature

Firsts

House:	Rosalie Keli'inoi (D)	1924
Senate:	Elsie H. Wilcox (R)	1932

Percentage of women in 2010–2011 session
  (9 among 25 in senate; 17 among 51 in house):   34
National rank: 4
Presiding Officers
  Speaker of the house: None
  Senate president: Colleen Hanabusa (D)   2006

Federal Elective Officeholders

U.S. Senate:	None	
U.S. House:	Mary Elizabeth Pruett Farrington (R)	1954
	Patsy Takemoto Mink (D)	1964
	Patricia Fukuda Saiki (R)	1986
	Mazie K. Hirono (D)	2006
	Colleen Habanbusa (D)	2010

FURTHER READING

Chinen, Joyce N., Kathleen O. Kane, and Ida M. Yoshinaga. 1997. *Women in Hawaii: Sites, Identities, and Voices.* Honolulu: University of Hawaii Press.

Kadama-Nishimoto, Michi, Warren Nichimoto, and Cynthia Oshiro. 2009. Talking Hawaii's Story: Oral History of an Island People. Honolulu: University of Hawaii.

Matsuda, Mari J., ed. 1992. *Called from Within: Early Women Lawyers of Hawai'i.* Honolulu: University of Hawaii Press.

Zwiep, Mary. 1991. *Pilgrim Path: The First Company of Women Missionaries to Hawaii.* Madison: University of Wisconsin Press.

IDAHO

Overview

Suffragists in Idaho organized in a Hagerman schoolhouse in 1893 and just three years later, in 1896, won the vote. National organizer Emma Smith DeVoe led the campaign, and sixty-two of the state's sixty-five newspapers endorsed enfranchisement. The referendum carried 12,126 to 6,282, making Idaho the third state to enfranchise women.

Conservatives went to court to have the voters' decision overturned, arguing that the measure required a majority of all registered voters, not simply those who voted in the election. Women's enfranchisement in nearby Washington had been canceled in a similar case, but Idaho's courts ruled favorably for the suffragists.

The 1898 election year was remarkable. A woman won statewide office, three women won seats in the legislature, fifteen were elected county school superintendents, and four became county treasurers. By 1900, three women served as deputy sheriffs, an unusual position for a woman to hold.

When the Nineteenth Amendment, which would enfranchise all American women in 1920, went to the states for ratification, Rep. Emma Drake introduced it in the Idaho House, which voted unanimously in favor. Six senators voted negatively, despite the fact that their female constituents had been enfranchised for more than two decades.

The tradition of electing women as superintendent of public instruction, which began in 1898, ended in 1932. Voters nonetheless elected a woman as state treasurer that year, and women held that position through the century. Idaho's first female state senator was not elected until 1938, a half-century after the state's women began voting. Its first female U.S. representative, Gracie Bowers Pfost, won in 1952. She ran unsuccessfully for the U.S. Senate in 1960.

As Idaho became more conservative, its attorney general went all the way to the U.S. Supreme Court to defend state law that gave any male family member preference to any female member as executor of an estate. In *Reed v. Reed* (1971), the highest court struck it down.

Democrats nominated Linda Pall, a city council member in the university town of Moscow, for the U.S. Senate in 2000, but she lost. As of 2011, Idaho had no women in its four-member delegation to Congress and just one in its six statewide executive offices.

Key Facts

Statehood:	1890
Capital:	Boise
First women's rights organization:	No formal name, 1893
Pioneer publication:	None
First female lawyer:	Helen Louise Young, 1895
Full female enfranchisement:	1896
State ratification of Nineteenth Amendment:	Yes
First president of League of Women Voters:	Dr. Emma F. A. Drake
First woman on state supreme court:	Linda Copple Trout, 1992
State ratification of Equal Rights Amendment:	Yes in 1972; rescinded in 1977

Statewide Elective Officeholders

Governor:	None	
Lieutenant governor:	None	
Secretary of state:	None	
Attorney general:	None	
Treasurer:	Myrtle R. Davis (D)	1932
	Ruth G. Moon (D)	1944
	Lela D. Painter (R)	1946
	Margaret Gilbert (R)	1952
	Marjorie Ruth Moon (D)	1962
	Lydia Justice Edwards (R)	1986
Controller:	Donna M. Jones (R)	2006
School superintendent:	Permeal J. French (D)	1898
	Mae L. Scott (R)	1902
	S. Belle Chamberlain (R)	1906
	Grace M. Shepherd (R)	1910
	Bernice McCoy (R)	1914

Ethel E. Redfield (R)	1916
Elizabeth Russum (R)	1922
Mabelle M. Lyman (R)	1926
Myrtle R. Davis (R)	1928
Anne C. Fox (R)	1994
Marilyn Howard (D)	1998

State Legislature

Firsts
House:

Clara Permilla Little Campbell (R)	1898
Hattie Luckett Noble (D)	1898
Mary Allen Wright (Populist)	1898

Senate: Martha E. Olsen (R) 1938

Percentage of women in 2010–2011 Session
   (9 among 35 in senate; 20 among 70 in house): 28
National Rank: 15
Presiding Officers
   Speaker of the House: None
   Senate President: None

Federal Elective Officeholders

U.S. Senate: None
U.S. House: Gracie Bowers Pfost (D) 1952
   Helen P. Chenoweth (R) 1994

FURTHER READING

Carlson, Laurie M. 1998. *On Sidesaddles to Heaven: The Women of the Rocky Mountain Mission.* Caldwell, ID: Caxton Press.

Easum, Dick D. 1981. *Dowager of Discipline: The Life of Dean of Women Permeal French.* Moscow: University of Idaho Press.

Keller, Charles L. 2001. *The Lady in the Ore Bucket: A History of Settlement and Industry in the Tri-Canyon Area of the Wasatch Mountains.* Salt Lake City: University of Utah.

Penson-Ward, Betty. 1991. *Idaho Women in History: Big and Little Biographies and Other Gender Stories.* Boise: Legendary Publishing.

ILLINOIS

Overview

Illinois's first women's rights society began in 1855, with Susan Hoxie Richardson, a cousin of Susan B. Anthony, calling a meeting in Earlville. It formalized in Chicago's Library Hall in 1868.

Catherine Waite tested the gender-neutral language of the Fifteenth Amendment by attempting to vote in Hyde Park in 1871. Two years later, ten women who could not vote for themselves won the position of county superintendent of schools. Bertha Honore Palmer led what may be the greatest networking event in feminist history: under her leadership, during one week in May 1893, 330 speakers from around the globe addressed women's issues at the Chicago World's Fair.

Teacher Mary Murphy won a significant decision in 1901, when the courts ruled that she could not be fired merely because she married—something that was routine everywhere. In the same era, Chicago's Margaret Haley founded the American Federation of Teachers, and Ella Flagg Young became the first female superintendent of an urban school system.

In 1913, the legislature passed a complex bill that allowed women to vote in all elections not named in the state constitution. Conservatives sued, but women won in court. Legislatures in other states adopted the model for presidential races, and it proved crucial to ratification of the Nineteenth Amendment, which enfranchised all American women in 1920.

Illinois followed only Montana and Oklahoma in electing a woman to Congress, in 1922, and the first woman also joined the Illinois House that year. The first female senator won in 1924, but when Senator Florence Fifer Bohrer visited a state mental hospital, her claim of being a lawmaker was taken as insanity.

Chicago's Marie C. Brehm was the Prohibition Party's 1924 nominee for vice president, and in 1926 Violette Neatly Anderson was the first black woman to argue before the U.S. Supreme Court. Illinois became the first state to twice elect women to the U.S. House when Ruth Hanna McCormick won her 1928 race. She lost her 1930 bid for a seat in the U.S. Senate.

Republican Jessie Sumner and Democrat Emily Taft Douglas were political opposites at mid-century, as Illinois continued to send women to the U.S. House. Chicagoans elected Jane Byrne as mayor in 1979, and the Rockford area sent Republican Lynn Martin to Congress in 1980. After losing a 1990 race for the U.S. Senate, she headed the Department of Labor.

Illinois women were represented fairly well in Washington, DC, but not in the state capital of Springfield. Not until 1990 did voters finally elect their first woman to a statewide executive office. The Year of the Woman, 1992, was called that partly because of Illinois's choice of the first African American woman to serve in the U.S. Senate, Chicago's Carol Moseley-Braun. During most of the time that she was in the Senate, however Illinois had the largest House delegation that included no women.

The numbers of women in statewide positions improved in the next years, and as of 2011, Illinois had three women in its six executive offices. But just two women were in its twenty-one-member congressional delegation.

Key Facts

Statehood:	1818
Capital:	Springfield
First women's rights organization:	Illinois Equal Suffrage Association, 1868
Pioneer publications:	*New Era*, Elizabeth Boynton Harbert, editor, 1885
	Suffragist, late nineteenth century
First female lawyer:	Ada (or Adah) H. Kepsey, Effingham, 1870
Full female enfranchisement:	1920
State ratification of Nineteenth Amendment:	Yes
First president of League of Women Voters:	Mrs. H. W. Cheney of Chicago
First woman on state supreme court:	Mary Ann G. McMorrow, 1992
State ratification of Equal Rights Amendment:	No

Statewide Elective Officeholders

Governor:	None	
Lieutenant governor:	Corrine Wood (R)	1998
	Sheila Simon (D)	2010
Secretary of state:	None	
Attorney general:	Lisa Madigan (D)	2002
Comptroller:	Dawn Clark Netsch (D)	1990
	Loleta Didrickson (R)	1994
Treasurer:	Judy Baar Topinka (R)	2010
School superintendent:	Not elected	

State Legislature

Firsts

House:	Lottie Holman O'Neill (R)	1922
Senate:	Florence Fifer Bohrer (R)	1924

Percentage of women in 2010–2011 session
  (16 among 59 in senate; 37 among 118 in house):   30
National rank: 8
Presiding Officers
  Speaker of the house: None
  Senate president: None

Federal Elective Officeholders

U.S. Senate:	Carol Moseley-Braun (D)	1992
U.S. House:	Winnifred Sprague Mason Huck (R)	1922
	Ruth Hanna McCormick (R)	1928
	Jessie Sumner (R)	1938
	Emily Taft Douglas (D)	1944
	Marguerite Stitt Church (R)	1950
	Edna Oakes Simpson (R)	1958
	Charlotte Thompson Reid (R)	1962
	Lynn Morley Martin (R)	1980
	Judy Biggert (R)	1998
	Jan Schkowsky (D)	1998
	Melissa Bean (D)	2004
	Debbie Halvorson (D)	2008

FURTHER READING

Byrne, Jane. 1992. *My Chicago.* New York: W.W. Norton.

Corn, Wanda M. 2011. *Women Building History: Public Art at the 1893 Columbian Exposition.* Berkeley: University of California.

Friedman, Jane M. 1993. *America's First Woman Lawyer: The Biography of Myra Bradwell.* Buffalo, NY: Prometheus Books.

Materson, Lisa G. 2009. *For the Freedom of Her Race: Black Women and Electoral Politics in Illinois.* Chapel Hill: University of North Carolina.

Stebner, Eleanor J. 1997. *The Women of Hull House: A Study in Spirituality, Vocation, and Friendship.* Albany: State University Press of New York.

Weimann, Jeanne Madeline. 1981. *The [Chicago World's] Fair Women.* Chicago: Academy Press.

INDIANA

Overview

Women in the college town of Bloomington in 1841 formed a study club, the first of many such groups for women who were barred from higher education. The Wayne County town of Dublin held a women's rights convention in 1851, just three years after the very first in Seneca Falls, New York. Amanda Way of Indianapolis was the state's feminist leader, and more than a thousand people signed an 1859 petition for property rights. The existing law was egregiously unfair to widows.

Indiana appears to have been unique in allowing women whose husbands were gone during the Civil War to vote in school elections. They lost that right when the war ended. Suffragists held annual meetings in the 1870s and 1880s in towns ranging alphabetically from Anderson to Warsaw.

In 1881, legislators enfranchised women for presidential elections. Indiana was one of many states that required such laws to be passed by two consecutive sessions, however, and lawmakers in 1883 rejected this partial enfranchisement. The idea was not revived until 1913, in Illinois.

The state's most important woman at the turn of the century was May Wright Sewall of Indianapolis, longtime leader of the International Council of Women. Her work was more global than local, however, and Helen M. Gougar led

Indiana feminists. In 1917, they won the vote for offices not named in the state constitution—or thought that they had. Anti-suffragists sued, and courts canceled women's right to vote before they could use it.

Feminists then worked for the Nineteenth Amendment, which the legislature ratified. Seven women filed for the Indiana House in the 1920 election, but just one prevailed. Indiana had a major national milestone in 1926, when it was the first state to elect a woman as treasurer. Its first female U.S. representative was elected in 1932, but the first female state senator was not picked until 1946, more than a quarter-century after women won the vote.

Gary voters sent Katie Beatrice Hall to the U.S. House in a special election in 1982. Indiana's third woman in Congress and its first African American, she sponsored the bill to make the Rev. Dr. Martin Luther King Jr.'s birthday a national holiday.

In 1992, Indiana elected its first woman as state superintendent of public instruction, a hundred years after the nation's first, in 1892. Esperanza Zendejas overcame prejudices against Hispanics and women when she became the first female superintendent of Indianapolis schools in 1995.

In 2011, the lieutenant governor was the sole woman among Indiana's seven elected executives, and no women were among in its eleven-member congressional delegation.

Key Facts

Statehood:	1816
Capital:	Indianapolis
First women's rights organization:	No formal name, 1851
Pioneer publications:	*Ladies Tribune*, Amanda Way and Sarah Underhill, editors, 1859
	Ladies Own Magazine, Mary Haggart and Cora Bland, editors, 1870s
	Our Herald, Helen M. Gougar, editor, 1881
First female lawyer:	Elizabeth Jane Eaglesfield, 1885
Full female enfranchisement:	1920
State ratification of Nineteenth Amendment:	Yes
First president of League of Women Voters:	Mrs. A. H. Beardsley of Elkhart
First woman on state supreme court:	Myra C. Selby, 1995
State ratification of Equal Rights Amendment:	Yes

Statewide Elective Officeholders

Governor:	None	
Lieutenant governor:	Katherine Davis (D)	2004
	Becky Skillman (R)	2008
Secretary of state:	Sue Ann Gilroy (R)	1994
Attorney general:	Pamela Carter (D)	1992
Treasurer:	Grace B. Urbahns (D)	1926
	Marjorie O'Laughlin (R)	1986
	Joyce Brinkman (R)	1994
Auditor:	Dorothy Haberstroth Gardner (R)	1960
	Trudy Slaby Etherton (R)	1968
	Mary Atkins Currie (D)	1970
	Ann G. DeVore (R)	1986
	Connie Nass (R)	1998
School superintendent:	Suellen Reed (R)	1992

State Legislature

Firsts

House:	Julia Reynolds Nelson (R)	1920
Senate:	Dorothy Haberstroth Gardner (R)	1946

Percentage of women in 2010–2011 session
    (11 among 50 in senate; 21 among 100 in house):   21
National rank: 32
Presiding Officers
    Speaker of the house: None
    Senate president: None

Federal Elective Officeholders

U.S. Senate:	None	
U.S. House:	Virginia Ellis Jenckes (D)	1932
	Cecil Murray Harden (R)	1948
	Katie Beatrice Hall (D)	1982
	Jill L. Long (D)	1990
	Julia M. Carson (D)	1996

FURTHER READING

Bell, Janet Cheatham. 2007. *The Time and Place That Gave Me Life.* Bloomington: Indiana University Press.

Hine, Darlene Clark. 1981. *When the Truth Is Told: A History of Black Women's Culture and Community in Indiana, 1875–1950.* Indianapolis: National Council of Negro Women.

Martin, Theodora Penny. 1987. *The Sound of Our Own Voices: Women's Study Clubs.* Boston: Beacon Press.

Sewall, May Wright. 1920. *Neither Dead Nor Sleeping.* Indianapolis: Bobbs-Merrill.

IOWA

Overview

Amelia Bloomer, who moved to Council Bluffs, Iowa, from Seneca Falls, New York, was Iowa's pioneer feminist. The 1866 legislature considered women's right to vote at the request of Phoebe Palmer, a Clinton County Quaker. Iowa licensed Arabella Mansfield of Burlington as the nation's first female attorney in 1869. In the same year, Julia C. Addington was elected school superintendent in Mitchell County. The right of men to elect women was confirmed in 1875, when the Iowa Supreme Court ruled in favor of Warren County's Elizabeth S. Cooke.

Iowa's suffrage association formalized in Dubuque, and by the mid-1870s, chapters were established in towns ranging alphabetically from Algona to West Liberty. Among the leaders were three female attorneys, including the valedictorian of the University of Iowa's 1875 law school class. Mrs. A.M. Swain of Fort Dodge tested the gender-neutral language of the Fifteenth Amendment.

In the early 1880s, Des Moines became the first city to have women in its top educational posts. Mary A. Work was president of the school board, and Mrs. Lou M. Wilson was school superintendent. Other superintendents followed, including young Carrie Lane in Mason City, who later became internationally known as Carrie Chapman Catt.

The suffrage question was on the 1916 ballot but lost with 173,024 against and 162,683 in favor. Feminists continued to educate their lawmakers, and when Congress adopted the Nineteenth Amendment, only one of Iowa's thirteen members voted against it.

Iowans elected their first woman to statewide office in 1922. The state was unique in having the same woman, Carolyn Campbell Pendray, as both its first female state representative and state senator. She was not particularly a pioneer, though, because when Pendray won her 1928 election to the Iowa House, only Louisiana, South Carolina, and the Alaska Territory had yet to send a woman to their legislatures. Iowa's political women regressed further in the next decades but rebounded to some extent in the 1980s.

Mary Louise Smith began her national rise in the Republican Party, and Democrats nominated Roxanne Conlin for governor in 1982. In 1990, when Bonnie Campbell became attorney general, only two other states had set that precedent. Only North Dakota preceded Iowa the election of a woman as agriculture secretary.

As of 2011, however, there was just one woman among Iowa's seven elected state offices. No Iowa woman ever has been in Congress, a record the state shares with Delaware, Mississippi, and Vermont.

Key Facts

Statehood:	1846
Capital:	Des Moines
First women's rights organization:	Iowa Equal Suffrage Association, 1869
Pioneer publications:	*The Lily*, Amelia Bloomer, editor, 1850s
	Woman's Standard, Mary J. Coggeshall, editor, Des Moines, 1880s
First female lawyer:	Arabella Mansfield, 1869
Full female enfranchisement:	1920
State ratification of Nineteenth Amendment:	Yes
First president of League of Women Voters:	Miss Flora Dunlap, 1920
First woman on state supreme court:	Linda Neuman, 1986
State ratification of Equal Rights Amendment:	Yes

Statewide Elective Officeholders

Governor:	None	
Lieutenant governor:	Jo Ann Zimmerman (D)	1986
	Joy Corning (R)	1990
	Sally Pederson (D)	1998
	Patty Judge (D)	2006
	Kim Reynolds (R)	2010
Secretary of state:	Ola Miller (D)	1932
	Mary Jane Odell (R)	1980
	Elaine Baxter (D)	1986
Attorney general:	Bonnie Campbell (D)	1990
Financial officer(s):	None	
Superintendent of public instruction:		
	May E. Francis (R)	1922
	Agnes Samuelson (no party)	1928
	Jessie M. Parker (no party)	1938
Secretary of agriculture	Patty Judge (D)	1998

State Legislature

Firsts		
House:	Carolyn Campbell Pendray (R)	1928
Senate:	Carolyn Campbell Pendray (R)	1932
Percentage of women in 2010–2011 session		
(8 among 50 in senate; 24 among 100 in house):	21	
National rank:	32	
Presiding Officers		
Speaker of the house:	None	
Senate president:	Mary Kramer (R)	1996

Federal Elective Officeholders

U.S. Senate: None
U.S. House: None

FURTHER READING

Conlin, Roxanne Barton. 1976. *The Legal Status of Homemakers in Iowa*. Washington, DC: U.S. Government Printing Office.

Hull, Christopher. 2008. *Grassroot Rules: How the Iowa Caucuses Help Elect American Presidents*. Stanford, CA: Stanford Law and Politics.

Noun, Louise Rosenfeld. 1969. *Strong-Minded Women: The Emergence of the Woman Suffrage Movement in Iowa*. Ames: Iowa State University Press.

Schenken, Suzanne O'Dea. 1995. *Legislators and Politicians: Iowa's Women Lawmakers*. Ames: Iowa State University Press.

KANSAS

Overview

Women were among the abolitionists who rushed to Kansas in the 1850s to prevent the expansion of slavery. Because the antislavery movement had close ties to the women's movement, Kansas became a demonstration model for feminism.

Former Vermonter Clarina Howard Nichols led lobbying during the 1860 constitutional convention, but even these progressive men would not support full enfranchisement. Women settled for liberalized property rights, educational access, and the right to vote in school elections—a world first.

Kansas held the world's first referendum on full enfranchisement in 1867, with strong participation from easterners, including Lucy Stone and her husband, Henry Blackwell. It was the movement's first campaign, though, and optimism dissipated as they began to understand political reality. Only 9,070 of some 30,000 male voters voted in favor.

Many Kansas women nevertheless won school elections, and the 1881 appointment of a woman as a university regent was a national first. Men also chose women for non-school county offices in which women could not vote for themselves.

In 1886, national organizer Laura Johns ran a successful campaign for the right to vote in municipal elections, and the town of Argonia chose Susanna Salter as the nation's first female mayor. By the turn of the twentieth century, women had been elected as mayors in at least twenty-five towns, and some served with all-female boards of "aldermen."

The question of full enfranchisement went on the 1894 ballot. Full rights were different from partial rights in some male minds, and despite a strong campaign, the referendum lost: 95,302 men said yes, 130,139 said no.

As it did nationally, feminism revived in Kansas around 1910, and Kansas women ran a third and successful campaign in 1912. Six western states had fully enfranchised women, and more than a half-century after the first referendum, Kansas women won, 175,246 to 159,197. It was the easternmost state with full enfranchisement.

Voter loyalty to Republicans faded because of the Great Depression, and Kansas's first female U.S. representative was a Democrat. Banker Georgia Neese Clark became the first woman to hold the position of United States treasurer under President Harry S. Truman, but Kansas women, like most, regressed in the mid-twentieth century.

Several Kansas women won elections in the 1970s, with the decade's zenith in 1978, when Nancy Landon Kassebaum won her U.S. Senate race. Joan Finney became the nation's first woman to defeat an incumbent governor in 1990. Kansas was the first state to have women in these top two positions simultaneously.

When Kathleen Sebelius was elected the state's second female governor in 2002, Kansas tied with Arizona and followed Texas as one of three states that had twice elected women as governor. President Barack Obama appointed Sebelius to his cabinet in 2009. Like Governor Finney, she is a Democrat—a notable fact in a state that political scientists deem reliably Republican.

Her departure marked a decline from the 1990s. As of 2011, Kansas had only one woman in its six-member congressional delegation and one among seven state executive offices.

Key Facts

Statehood:	1861
Capital:	Topeka
First women's rights organization:	Kansas Women's Rights Association, 1859
Pioneer publication:	*Suffrage Reveille*, Kate R. Addison, editor, 1895
First female lawyer:	Phoebe Couzins, 1872
Full female enfranchisement:	1912
State ratification of Nineteenth Amendment:	Yes
First president of League of Women Voters:	Cora W. Brooks, 1919
First woman on state supreme court:	Kay McFarland, 1977
State ratification of Equal Rights Amendment:	Yes

Statewide Elective Officeholders

Governor:	Joan Finney (D)	1990
	Kathleen Sebelius (D)	2000
Lieutenant governor:	Sheila Frahm (R)	1994
Secretary of state:	Elwill M. Shanahan (R)	1966
Attorney general:	Carla Stovall (R)	1994
Treasurer:	Joan Finney (D)	1974
	Sally Thompson (D)	1990
	Lynn Jenkins (R)	2002
Insurance commissioner:	Kathleen Sebelius (D)	1994
	Sally Prager (R)	2002
School superintendent:	Lorraine Elizabeth "Lizzie" Wooster (R)	1918

State Legislature

Firsts

House:	Minnie Tamar Johnson Grinstead (R)	1918
Senate:	Patricia Nichols Solander (R)	1928

Percentage of women in 2010–2011 session
   (12 among 40 in senate; 33 among 125 in house): 27

National rank: 17

Presiding Officers
   Speaker of the house: None
   Senate president: None

Federal Elective Officeholders

U.S. Senate:	Nancy Landon Kassebaum (R)	1978
U.S. House:	Kathryn O'Laughlin McCarthy (D)	1932
	Martha Elizabeth Keys (D)	1974
	Jan Myers (R)	1984
	Nancy Boyda (D)	2006
	Lynn Jenkins (R)	2008

FURTHER READING

Frank, Thomas. 2005. *What's the Matter with Kansas? How Conservatives Won the Heart of America.* New York: Metropolitan Books.

Goldberg, Michael L. 1997. *An Army of Women: Gender and Politics in Gilded Age Kansas.* Baltimore: Johns Hopkins University Press.

Oertel, Kristen Tegtmeier. 2009. *Bleeding Borders: Race, Gender, and Violence in Pre–Civil War Kansas.* Baton Rogue: Louisiana State University Press.

KENTUCKY

Overview

The Kentucky frontier welcomed people with radical ideas, including Scottish feminist Frances Wright. When she spoke to a large crowd in Louisville in 1828, her comments on birth control and world government were well received. Things had changed almost thirty years later: When Lucy Stone spoke there in 1853, she was greeted with rotten eggs.

Kentucky granted an unusual form of enfranchisement in 1838. Widows with children enrolled in rural schools could vote in elections pertaining to those schools.

The first women's rights society began in 1867 in the Hardin County town of Glendale. It faded until 1881, when Laura Clay and her sisters, Anne, Mary, and Sally, founded the Kentucky Equal Rights Association. Called the ERA, it was intended to focus on property rights—something that women had obtained in most states—instead of on the more radical right to vote.

The Breckinridges were another powerful Kentucky family, and in 1901, Sophonisba Breckinridge was the world's first woman to earn a doctorate in political science. Yet, as the twentieth century began, Kentucky law granted all custody rights to the father, who even had the right to appoint someone other than the mother as guardian for an unborn child. The legal age for a girl to marry was twelve.

Madeline "Madge" McDowell Breckinridge led a 1912 feminist revival, and the organization grew from fewer than two thousand members to more than ten thousand within a year. They concentrated on the federal constitutional amendment that would enfranchise all women. Lawmakers turned out to be much more willing to join other states under the federal umbrella than to enact their own liberalization, and with Breckinridge's effective leadership, Kentucky's ratification of the Nineteenth Amendment was surprisingly smooth. Former suffragist Laura Clay disappointed many longtime friends by lobbying against it, insisting on states rights over federalism.

Kentucky holds elections for statewide offices in odd-numbered years, and in 1925, Emma Guy Cromwell became secretary of state. She was the third in the nation, following only New Mexico and Delaware. Federal elections always are in even-numbered years, and voters chose Katherine Gudger Langley as Kentucky's first female member of Congress in 1926. Her husband ran against her in 1930, and both lost. (See Chapter Six: U.S. Representatives.)

Perhaps Kentucky's most notable political woman in the 1930s and 1940s was Georgia Madden Martin. A married white woman who called herself "George," she headed the Association of Southern Women for the Prevention of Lynching.

When most American women regressed in the 1950s, Kentuckians elected women to financial offices. Thelma L. Stovall became the nation's third female lieutenant governor in 1975. She tried to push the Equal Rights Amendment as acting governor but lost a 1979 race for governor.

Martha Layne Collins succeeded Stovall as lieutenant governor and went on to be the nation's sixth female governor in 1983. That was Kentucky's banner year, as three other women won races for statewide offices. All were Democrats in an era when most of the nation was voting Republican. No other state would elect so many women simultaneously until 1998, when Arizona chose five.

That 1983 election would be the acme, as Kentucky's political women regressed. By 2011, only one held a statewide office, and the eight-member delegation to Congress included none.

Key Facts

Statehood:	1792
Capital:	Frankfort
First women's rights organization:	No formal name, 1867
Pioneer publication:	None
First female lawyer:	Sophonisba Breckinridge, 1895
Full female enfranchisement:	1920
State ratification of Nineteenth Amendment:	Yes
First president of League of Women Voters:	Mary Bronaugh, Hopkinsville
First woman on state supreme court:	Janet Stumbo, 1993
State ratification of Equal Rights Amendment:	Ratified 1972; rescinded 1978

Statewide Elective Officeholders

Governor:	Martha Layne Collins (D)	1983
Lieutenant governor:	Thelma L. Stovall (D)	1975
	Martha Layne Collins (D)	1979
Secretary of state:	Emma Guy Cromwell (D)	1925
	Ella Lewis (D)	1929
	Sara W. Mahon (D)	1933
	Thelma L. Stovall (D)	1955
	Leila Feltner Begley (D)	1969
	Frances Jones Mills (D)	1975
	Elaine Walker (D)	2011
Attorney general:	None	
Treasurer:	Emma Guy Cromwell (D)	1929
	Pearl Frances Runyon (D)	1955
	Thelma L. Stovall (D)	1959
	Frances Mills Jones (D)	1975
Auditor:	Mary Louise Foust (D)	1955
	Mary Ann Tobin (D)	1983
	Crit Luallen (D)	2003
School superintendent:	Alice McDonald (D)	1983

State Legislature

Firsts

House:	Mary Elliott Flanery (D)	1922
Senate:	Carolyn C. Moore (D)	1949

Percentage of women in 2010–2011 session
(6 among 38 in senate; 19 among 100 in house): 18

National rank: 41

Presiding Officers
Speaker of the house: None
Senate president: None

Federal Elective Officeholders

U.S. Senate:	None	
U.S. House:	Katherine Gudger Langley (R)	1926
	Anne Meagher Northup (R)	1996

FURTHER READING

Apple, Lindsey. 1997. *Cautious Rebel: A Biography of Susan Clay Sawitzky*. Kent, OH: Kent State University Press.
Asher Brad. 2011. *Cecilia and Fanny: The Remarkable Friendship Between an Escaped Slave and Her Former Mistress*.
    Lexington: University of Kentucky.
Goodman, Clavia. 1946. *Bitter Harvest: Laura Clay's Suffrage Work*. Lexington: Bur Press.
Irwin, Helen Deiss. 1979. *Women in Kentucky*. Lexington: University of Kentucky Press.

LOUISIANA

Overview

Feminist Frances Dana Gage of Ohio spoke in New Orleans in 1854, but it was Louisiana's old Napoleonic Code that first motivated women to organize. In 1878, a New Orleans woman made a substantial bequest to St. Anne's Asylum, and the board of ladies managers witnessed the will. Soon after the woman died, St. Anne's women discovered that they would not get the money because no woman could witness a legal document.

Elizabeth Lyle Saxon led an 1879 petition drive, but the next decades were more conservative. When a suffrage association finally began in 1896, women were so cautious that they avoided the terms "rights" or even "suffrage" in their name. Instead they called themselves "the Era Club," disguising the phrase Equal Rights Association.

Kate Gordon and her sister Jean longed dominated Louisiana feminists. They won a partial success in 1899, when female taxpayers in New Orleans were granted the vote for tax referenda. As it turned out, city fathers used women as pawns to pass a bond issue for a much-needed sewage system, and after it passed, their enfranchisement was repealed.

The National American Woman Suffrage Association held its 1903 convention in New Orleans, but feminism did not grow until 1913, when the Louisiana Woman Suffrage Party (WSP) began as a quiet revolt against the Gordons. Its leaders—Mrs. Edgar Cahn and Mrs. John Meehan—were Jewish and Irish, and they reached out beyond New Orleans.

Like the National Woman's Party, the WSP did not concentrate on its conservative home state but instead worked for an amendment to the U.S. Constitution. The Era Club, however, remained committed to states' rights and managed to get the enfranchisement question on the 1918 ballot. National leaders advised against this, and as they predicted, the Louisiana referendum failed. The Gordons were so committed to a state approach that they then lobbied against the federal amendment in other Southern states.

A decade passed before a woman held significant office, and even then, they were surrogates for men. When the U.S. Supreme Court overruled the exclusion of women from juries in *Taylor v. Louisiana* (1975), it was the last state that completely barred women as jurors.

Corinne Claiborne "Lindy" Boggs ushered in the modern age with her outstanding service in the U.S. House, which began in 1973. She was joined in 1985 by Catherine Small Long, who differed from the rest of that powerful family. Long was the first female U.S. representative to be a Navy veteran, having served in the World War II WAVES (Women Accepted for Volunteer Emergency Service). She defeated four others to win the seat of her recently deceased husband, but served only briefly. She was too liberal for the Long family, and they would not fund her.

Mary L. Landrieu also hails from a powerful Louisiana family, but she preserved in her independent course and was elected to the U.S. Senate in 1996. When Kathleen Babineaux Blanco won the governorship in the 2003 election, Louisiana had women in two of its three highest posts. Most states have yet to equal this record.

Blanco, a Democrat, never lost an election in a two-decade career, but when Hurricane Katrina overwhelmed Louisiana, she opted not to complicate recovery by seeking reelection in 2007. Against "expert" expectations, voters reelected Landrieu to the U.S. Senate in 2010. Yet, in 2011, Senator Landrieu was the only woman in Louisiana's nine-member congressional delegation. There was none its seven elected executive positions.

Key Facts

Statehood:	1812
Capital:	Baton Rogue
First women's rights organization:	No formal name, 1879
Pioneer publication:	None
First female lawyer:	Betty Runnels, 1898
Full female enfranchisement:	1920
State ratification of Nineteenth Amendment:	No
First president of League of Women Voters:	Mrs. Phillip Weirlein
First woman on state supreme court:	Catherine "Kitty" Kimball, 1992
State ratification of Equal Rights Amendment:	No

Statewide Elective Officeholders

Governor:	Kathleen Babineaux Blanco (D)	2003
Lieutenant governor:	Melinda Schwegmann (D)	1991
	Kathleen Babineaux Blanco (D)	1995
Secretary of state:	None	
Attorney general:	None	
Treasurer:	Mary Evelyn Parker (D)	1967
	Mary L. Landrieu (D)	1987
School superintendent:	Not elected	
Commission of elections:	Suzanne Haik Terrell (R)	2000
Registrar of deeds:	Lucille May Grace (D)	1931
	Ellen Bryan Moore (D)	1951

State Legislature

Firsts

House:	Doris Lindsey Holland (D)	1939
	Beatrice Hawthorne Moore (D)	1939
Senate:	Doris Lindsey Holland (D)	1936

Percentage of women in 2010–2011 session
(8 among 39 in senate; 15 among 105 in house): 16

National rank: 44

Presiding Officers
Speaker of the house: None
Senate president: None

Federal Elective Officeholders

U.S. Senate:	Rose McConnell Long (D)	1936
	Elaine S. Edwards (D)	1972
	Mary Landrieu (D)	1996
U.S. House:	Corinne Claiborne "Lindy" Boggs (D)	1973
	Catherine Small Long (D)	1985

FURTHER READING

Landig, Carmen. 1986. *The Path from the Parlor: Louisiana Women, 1879–1920.* Lafayette: Center for Louisiana Studies.

Moore, Diane M. 1984. *Their Adventurous Will: Profiles of Memorable Louisiana Women.* Lafayette, LA: Acadiana Press.

Schafer, Judith Kelleher. 2009. *Brothels, Depravity, and Abandoned Women: Illegal Sex in Antebellum New Orleans.* Baton Rogue: Louisiana State University Press.

Tyler, Pamela. 1996. *Silk Stockings and Ballot Boxes: Women and Politics in New Orleans, 1920–1963.* Athens: University of Georgia Press.

MAINE

Overview

At the 1856 Women's Rights Convention in New York City, Lucy Stone cited Maine as a model for other states. A woman there could transact business and go to court, and her earnings were her own and could not be claimed by her husband's creditors.

Bates College in Lewiston admitted women in 1863, during the Civil War which was the first higher education access for women on the East Coast. Maine also was the first East Coast state to admit a woman to the practice of law, in 1872. An Equal Rights Association formed in Rockland in 1868. The town of Searsport had elected a woman as school superintendent by 1872, and several held school offices by 1875. More than a thousand people attended the 1873 suffrage association's annual convention, but it was not until 1891 that a woman, Hannah J. Bailey, was elected as its president.

The Portland Equal Franchise League began to compete with the older suffrage association in 1913. Using techniques such as movie ads and speaking on street corners, women conducted a 1918 referendum. It lost, with 38,838 men voting negatively and 20,681 positively.

Legislators again put the question on the 1920 ballot. But the Nineteenth Amendment had been ratified that August, which meant that Maine women went to the polls on their own right to vote in November. The moot amendment passed, with 88,080 positive votes and 30,462 still opposed to what now was federal law.

The first woman in the legislature won in 1924; the first female state senator, in 1926. Nationally known feminist Gail Laughlin became a senator in her home state in 1937.

Maine is unique in that it elects no state executives beyond governor. Instead of state offices, women won federal positions. The first was Margaret Chase Smith, who began her congressional career in 1940. Smith's 1960 reelection to the U.S. Senate marked a first, as Democrats nominated Lucia Cormier. In the nation's first major race between two women, Smith, a Republican, prevailed.

Olympia Snowe emulated Smith, beginning her congressional service by winning a 1978 race for the U.S. House. She moved up to the U. S. Senate with the 1994 election. In the next cycle, Susan Collins, another liberal Republican, joined Snowe. With this milestone, Maine became the second state (following California in 1992) to have elected women to both of its Senate seats.

Maine had just two U.S. House seats, and Chellie Pingree won one in 2008. When Democrats won the majority in that year's state legislative elections, her daughter, Hannah Pingree, became Speaker of the Maine House. Both legislative chambers have had an uncommon number of women as presiding officers. In the 2005 legislative session, Senate president Beverly Daggett was the first in the nation to pass the gavel to another female senate president.

As of 2011, three-fourths of Maine's four-member congressional delegation was female. However, because the state elects no offices other than governor and no woman has been governor, it is the only state that never has elected a woman to a statewide executive post.

Key Facts

Statehood:	1820
Capital:	Augusta
First women's rights organization:	No formal name, 1868
Pioneer publication:	None
First female lawyer:	Clara Hapgood Nash, 1872
Full female enfranchisement:	1920
State ratification of Nineteenth Amendment:	Yes
First president of League of Women Voters:	Miss Mabel Connor
First woman on state supreme court:	Caroline Duby Glassman, 1983
State ratification of Equal Rights Amendment:	Yes

Statewide Elective Officeholders

Governor:	None
Lieutenant governor:	Not elected

Secretary of state:	Not elected
Attorney general:	Not elected
Financial officer(s):	Not elected
School superintendent:	Not elected

State Legislature

Firsts

House:	Dora Pinkham(R)	1922
Senate:	Dora Pinkham (R)	1926
	Katharine C. Allen (R)	1926

Percentage of women in 2010–2011 session
(7 among 35 in senate; 46 among 151 in house): 29
National rank: 11
Presiding Officers

Speaker of the house:	Elizabeth H. Mitchell (D)	1996
	Hannah Pingree (D)	2008
Senate president:	Beverly Daggett (D)	2002
	Beth Edmonds (D)	2004
	Elizabeth H. Mitchell (D)	2008

Federal Elective Officeholders

U.S. Senate:	Margaret Chase Smith (R)	1948
	Olympia Jean Snowe (R)	1994
	Susan Margaret Collins (R)	1996
U.S. House:	Margaret Chase Smith (R)	1940
	Olympia Jean Snowe (R)	1978
	(Rochelle) Chellie Pingree (D)	2008

FURTHER READING

Potter, Judy R., and Gail Marshall. 1977. *The Legal Rights of Maine Women.* Augusta: Maine Commission for Women.
Sudlow, Lynda L. 2000. *A Vast Army of Women: Maine's Uncounted Forces in the American Civil War.* Gettysburg, PA: Thomas Publications.
Weiner, Marli F. 2005. *Of Place and Gender: Women in Maine History.* Orono: University of Maine Press.

MARYLAND

Overview

The Maryland Equal Rights Society, founded in 1867, included men and women, blacks and whites. Three Baltimore women tested the gender-neutral language of the Fifteenth Amendment by attempting to vote in 1870. This liberalism ended with the end of Reconstruction government, and even though the National Woman Suffrage Association held its annual conventions in nearby Washington, DC, Maryland's Equal Rights Society died.

Caroline Hallowell Miller revived the issue in 1889, and six women in Baltimore unsuccessfully attempted to vote in 1896. Annapolis women were able to cast ballots on a bond issue in 1900. The legislature briefly enfranchised them because city fathers wanted women's votes to pay for a sewage system.

As the twentieth century began, fathers in Maryland had absolute custody of children, women were banned from some types of employment, and they lost their ability to be notaries public when the Maryland Supreme Court ruled against that. Because thousands of legal documents that had been notarized by women were jeopardized, the 1902 legislature amended the law.

Mary Bentley Thomas was president of the suffrage association in 1902, when women opened a state headquarters. With sponsorship from millionaire feminist Mary Elizabeth Garrett, Maryland hosted the convention of the National American Woman Suffrage Association in 1906. About six hundred Baltimore men and women took a chartered train to the capital of Annapolis in 1910, carrying some 173,000 petition signatures for the limited right to vote in municipal elections, but the legislature did not pass their bill. As in other states, younger woman formed a new organization, but Maryland's group—the State Equal Franchise League, led by Elisabeth King Ellicott—did not engage in destructive rivalry with the older suffrage association. After enfranchisement bills were voted down in 1912, 1914, and 1916, feminists gave up on their state strategy and concentrated on amending the U.S. Constitution.

No legislature was more obdurate than Maryland's on ratification of the Nineteenth Amendment. Lawmakers not only rejected it, but also funded anti-ratification efforts in other states. After it was adopted in 1920, wealthy women in the Maryland Association Opposed to Woman Suffrage filed suit. The U.S. Supreme Court in February 1922 ruled in their case, *Leser v. Garnett,* that the Nineteenth Amendment was established constitutionally. The decision came well after Maryland women had joined others in participating in the November 1920 election.

Maryland sent Mary E. W. Risteau to the House of Delegates in 1922. She also was the first female state senator and chaired committees in both chambers. The first female U.S. representative was Katharine Edgar Byron, elected in 1941.

Decades passed before the revived feminism of the 1970s, but Maryland sent a woman to Congress in each election cycle of that decade. Among the winners was Beverly Barton Butcher Bryon, daughter-in-law of the state's first woman in Congress. As a result of the 1978 election, Maryland became the first state to have a truly representative delegation to the U.S. House of Representatives, with its eight seats occupied by four women and four men.

Barbara Mikulski defeated Linda Chavez for the U.S. Senate in 1986, and as of 2011, Mikulski was the longest-serving woman in the Senate. Maryland's record on statewide offices, however, has been poor. The only woman holding such an office was Kathleen Kennedy Townsend, of the presidential Kennedy family, who became lieutenant governor in 1994 and lost her 2002 campaign for governor.

Key Facts

Statehood:	1788
Capital:	Annapolis
First women's rights organization:	Maryland Equal Rights Society, 1869
Pioneer publication:	*New Voter*, Anne Wagner, editor, 1911
First female lawyer:	Etta Maddox, 1902
Full female enfranchisement:	1920
State ratification of Nineteenth Amendment:	No
First president of League of Women Voters:	Emma Maddox Funck
First woman on state supreme court:	Rita Charmatz Davidson, 1979
State ratification of Equal Rights Amendment:	Yes

Statewide Elective Officeholders

Governor:	None	
Lieutenant governor:	Kathleen Kennedy Townsend (D)	1994
Secretary of state:	None	
Attorney general:	None	
Financial officer(s):	None	
School superintendent:	Not elected	

State Legislature

Firsts		
House:	Mary E. W. Risteau (D)	1922

Senate:	Mary E. W. Risteau (D)	1934

Percentage of women in 2010–2011 session
  (11 among 47 in senate; 47 among 141 in house):   31
National rank: 7
Presiding Officers
  Speaker of the house: None
  Senate president: None

Federal Elective Officeholders

U.S. Senate:	Barbara Ann Milkulski (D)	1986
U.S. House:	Katharine Edgar Byron (D)	1941
	Marjorie Sewell Holt (R)	1972
	Gladys Noon Spellman (D)	1974
	Barbara Ann Milkulski (D)	1976
	Beverly Barton Butcher Bryon (D)	1978
	Helen Delich Bentley (R)	1984
	Constance A. Morella (R)	1986
	Donna Edwards (D)	2008

FURTHER READING

Helmes, Winifred Gertrude, ed. 1977. *Notable Maryland Women.* Cambridge, MD: Tidewater Publishers.

Mikulski, Barbara, et al. 2001. *Nine and Counting: The Women of the Senate.* New York: Perennial.

Sander, Kathleen Waters. 2008. *Mary Elizabeth Garrett: Society and Philanthropy in the Gilded Age.* Baltimore, MD: Johns Hopkins University Press.

MASSACHUSETTS

Overview

The first national feminist convention was in October 1850 in Worcester. Representatives of nine states, as well as Lucy Stone and Sojourner Truth, attended that historic meeting. Salem's Mary Upton Ferrin collected petitions to reform property rights, and a model law was adopted in 1854. Sarah E. Wall protested against taxation without representation in Worcester, as did Boston physician Harriot K. Hunt. The influential New England Women's Club began in 1868—the same year the antifeminist movement began in Lancaster.

With Julia Ward Howe, Harriet Beecher Stowe, Louisa May Alcott, and others, Lucy Stone founded the American Woman Suffrage Association in Boston in 1869. It published *Woman's Journal*, the most prestigious feminist magazine for nearly a half-century. Mary Livermore, who moved from Illinois, was its initial editor. Abolitionists Sarah Grimke and Angelina Grimke Weld vainly led forty women to the Hyde Park polls in 1870.

Men elected four women to the Boston School Committee in 1873. Incumbents refused to seat them, but the legislature mandated that they do so. Six women won at the next election. In 1879, women were allowed to vote in school elections.

Enfranchisement bills nonetheless became almost an annual rite of filing and expecting defeat. The most creative exception was in 1895, when the legislature authorized a "mock referendum." It clearly showed that the majority of women wanted the vote: 22,204 women voted yes, while just 861 said no. This was better than proponents had expected, but they lacked the political skill to follow through.

Younger women, especially Maud Wood Park, revived the movement around the turn of the century. When they were forbidden to speak on the beach at Nantask (too easily confused with the more famous Nantuck) they spoke from the water. By 1915, Massachusetts had about two hundred suffrage societies, and the legislature put the question of women's voting rights on the ballot. Advocates ran a strong campaign for more than a year and used several smart strategies, but lost with 295,489 opposed and 163,406 in favor.

Massachusetts's U.S. senators Republicans Henry Cabot Lodge and John Weeks were very powerful opponents in Congress, and even without the vote, suffragists managed to unseat Weeks in his 1918 reelection. The Women's Trade Union League was especially important in persuading working-class men to successfully elect pro-suffrage David Walsh. Lodge still did everything he could to kill the Nineteenth Amendment, but Massachusetts legislators ratified within weeks.

Two women won legislative races in 1922. One of them, M. Sylvia Donaldson of Brockton, was unusual in being age seventy-three, but she went on to win two reelections. Massachusetts did not have a female state senator until 1936—decades after that precedent was set—but Edith Nourse Rogers, who was first elected to the U.S. House in 1925, had a long and distinguished career.

Margaret M. Heckler was the state's second female U.S. representative. A liberal Republican, she represented southeastern Massachusetts from 1966 until losing to a Democratic man in 1982. Voters finally elected their first woman to statewide office in 1986—a precedent set by North Dakota in 1892.

Jane Swift became acting governor in 2001. She set a precedent by being pregnant with twins while in office, but she was not popular enough to be nominated by her Republican in 2002. Democrat Shannon O'Brien won the 2002 Democratic nomination for governor, but she lost the general election to Republican Mitt Romney. Democrat Martha Coakley also lost a 2010 special election for the U.S. Senate.

For most of the time between Heckler's 1982 loss and Nikki Tsongas's 2007 victory, Massachusetts was the largest state with an all-male congressional delegation. In 2011, there was one woman among its twelve members. The state never has elected a female U.S. senator or governor, and Boston never has had a woman as mayor.

Key Facts

Statehood:	1788
Capital:	Boston
First women's rights organization:	Massachusetts Women's Rights Society, 1850
First female lawyer:	Lelia J. Robinson, 1892
Full female enfranchisement:	1920
State ratification of Nineteenth Amendment:	Yes
First president of League of Women Voters:	Not available
First woman on state supreme court:	Ruth Abrams, 1977
State ratification of Equal Rights Amendment:	Yes

Statewide Elective Officeholders

Governor:	Jane Swift (R)[15]	2001
Lieutenant governor:	Evelyn Murphy (D)	1986
	Jane Swift (R)	1998
	Kerry Murphy Healey (R)	2004
Secretary of state:	None	
Attorney general:	Martha Coakley (D)	2006
Treasurer:	Shannon O'Brien (D)	1998
Auditor:	Suzanne Bump (D)	2010
School superintendent:	Not elected	

State Legislature

Firsts

House:	M. Sylvia Donaldson (R)	1922
	Nancy Flavin (D)	1922

---

[15] Never elected; became governor when the incumbent resigned.

Senate:	Sybil H. Holmes (R)	1936
Percentage of women in 2010–2011 session		
(11 among 40 in senate; 36 among 160 in house):	24	
National rank:	22	
Presiding Officers		
Speaker of the house:	None	
Senate president:	Therese Murray (D)	2007

Federal Elective Officeholders

U.S. Senate:	None	
U.S. House:	Edith Nourse Rogers (R)	1925
	Margaret M. Heckler (R)	1966
	Louise Day Hicks (D)	1970
	Nikki Tsongas (D)	2007

FURTHER READING

Deutsch, Sarah. 2000. *Women and the City: Gender, Space, and Power in Boston, 1870–1940.* New York: Oxford University Press.

Hansen, Deborah Gold. 1993. *Strained Sisterhood: Gender and Class in the Boston Female Anti-Slavery Society.* Amherst: University of Massachusetts Press.

Power, Susan L., ed. 1996. *Women of the Commonwealth: Work, Family, and Social Change in Nineteenth-Century Massachusetts.* Amherst: University of Massachusetts Press.

Taymor, Betty. 2000. *Running against the Wind: The Struggle of Women in Massachusetts Politics.* Boston: Northeastern University Press.

MICHIGAN

Overview

Lenawee County women petitioned for the vote in 1849. In the 1850s, young women who later became national activists protested the University of Michigan's unwillingness to admit women. In 1868, 120 women in the town of Sturgis attempted to vote. The suffrage society began in Battle Creek in 1870, with Adele Hazlett of Hillsdate as president.

Catherine Stebbins and Nannette Gardener attempted to vote in Detroit in 1870. The registrar rejected Stebbins because she was married, but he accepted Gardener, a property-owning widow. No one objected when unmarried property owner Mary Wilson, accompanied by her lawyer, voted in Battle Creek. Sojourner Truth, the famed African American orator, owned a Battle Creek home but was turned away when she tried to vote in 1872.

Michigan lawmakers put the question of enfranchisement on the 1874 ballot. It was the third such referendum in the country, and the first east of the Mississippi River. It failed, and as in other states, the movement languished.

Women may have won Michigan's second suffrage referendum in 1912. With much evidence of fraud, the governor impounded ballot boxes. After officials spent three weeks counting, the decision was that it had lost by 762 votes out of 495,508 cast. They did win in 1918. With financial support from women such as Clara Shortridge Ford and Delphine Dodge Asbaugh, both members of automotive families, women prevailed 229,790 to 195,284.

The first female state senator came at the first opportunity, in 1920, and Eva M. Hamilton was the nation's fifth. The first female state representative, elected in 1924, was notable because, despite her Anglo names, Cora Belle Reynolds Anderson was an Ojibway. She was the nation's first female Native American legislator.

Martha Griffiths of Detroit went to Congress with the 1954 election and was the leading champion for women in an era when there were few. From the 1960s onwards, Michigan's Elly Peterson was a leading figure for Republicans nationally. Republicans recruited Lenore Romney, wife of former governor George Romney, to run for the U.S. Senate in 1970; she lost.

Michigan had no women in any top office during the late 1980s, but two African American women won U.S. House seats in the 1990s. Another member of the Romney family, Ronna Romney, ran for the U.S. Senate but lost the 1994 Republican primary.

Lynn Rivers of Ann Arbor was one of very few Democrats who won a congressional seat in 1994. At the next election, Debbie Stabenow of Lansing joined Rivers in Congress, defeating a wealthy incumbent. She again astonished experts in 2000, when she defeated the incumbent U.S. senator. When Jennifer M. Granholm was elected governor in 2002, Michigan followed Texas as the second large-population state to elect a female governor. The state has regressed, though, as with Granholm's 2011 retirement, Michigan had only one woman in its four elective statewide posts and one in a seventeen-member congressional delegation.

Key Facts

Statehood:	1837
Capital:	Lansing
First women's rights organization:	No formal name, 1849
Pioneer publication:	*Michigan Suffragist*, 1914
First female lawyer:	Sarah Kilgore, 1871
Full female enfranchisement:	1918
State ratification of Nineteenth Amendment:	Yes
First president of League of Women Voters:	Florence Belle Brotherton
First woman on state supreme court:	Mary Stallings Coleman, 1972
State ratification of Equal Rights Amendment:	Yes

Statewide Elective Officeholders

Governor:	Jennifer M. Granholm (D)	2002
Lieutenant governor:	Matilda D. Wilson (R)[16]	1940
	Martha Wright Griffiths (D)	1982
	Connie Binsfield (R)	1990
Secretary of state:	Candice S. Miller (R)	1994
	Terri Lynn Land (R)	2002
	Ruth Johnson (R)	2010
Attorney general:	Jennifer M. Granholm (D)	1998
Financial officer(s):	Not elected	
School superintendent:	Not elected	

State Legislature

Firsts

House:	Cora Belle Reynolds Anderson (R)	1924
Senate:	Eva Marie McCall Hamilton (R)	1920

Percentage of women in 2010–2011 session
(4 among 38 in senate; 27 among 110 in house): 21
National rank: 36
Presiding Officers

---

[16] Appointed, not elected.

| Speaker of the house: | None |
| Senate president: | None |

Federal Elective Officeholders

U.S. Senate:	Deborah Ann "Debbie" Stabenow (D)	2000
U.S. House:	Martha Wright Griffiths (D)	1950
	Ruth Thompson (R)	1950
	Barbara-Rose Collins (D)	1990
	Lynn Rivers (D)	1994
	Carolyn Cheeks Kilpatrick (D)	1996
	Deborah Ann "Debbie" Stabenow (D)	1996
	Candice S. Miller (R)	2002

FURTHER READING

Bordin, Ruth. 1999. *Women at Michigan: "The Dangerous Experiment."* Ann Arbor: University of Michigan Press.

Crathern, Alice Tarbell. 1953. *In Detroit Courage Was the Fashion: The Contribution of Women to the Development of Detroit from 1701 to 1951.* Detroit: Wayne State University Press.

Ftizgerald, Sarah. 2011. *Elly Peterson: Mother of the Moderates.* Ann Arbor: University of Michigan Press.

Thompson, Heather Ann. 2001. *Whose Detroit? Politics, Labor, and Race.* Ithaca, NY: Cornell University Press.

MINNESOTA

Overview

The women's movement in Minnesota began with a speech by Mary Colburn on July 4, 1866. In 1875, women mounted a quiet campaign to vote in school elections only. The legislature put the issue on the ballot, and it passed 24,340 to 19,468. Minnesota first lady Mrs. John Pillsbury spoke in favor of women on school boards, and hundreds soon served. More than seventy women had been superintendent of schools in twenty-two counties by 1883. Feminist pioneer Sarah Stearns chaired the school board in Duluth, as did Jennie Crays in Minneapolis.

With Minneapolis physician Martha Ripley as president, the state suffrage association hosted a tent at the state fair. This practice continued from 1883 to 1920. Nonetheless, bills for various forms of the vote failed, with one exception: Women were enfranchised for library boards in 1898.

Because their state constitution was difficult to amend, Minnesota suffragists were among the first to work for an amendment to the U.S. Constitution. Clara Ueland became the suffrage association president in 1914 and hired Anna Gjertson to work with Scandinavians. Black women organized under Mrs. W.T. Francis, and Mother Seraphine Ireland, the archbishop's sister, quietly made it known that she supported the vote. Both Minnesota senators voted yes on the Nineteenth Amendment, and legislators proved eager to ratify it.

In 1922, four women won elections for the Minnesota House—a record exceeded only by Pennsylvania. Democrats nominated Anna Dickie Oleson for the U.S. Senate in 1922, a milestone that Minnesota shared only with West Virginia.

Progress in the next decades was slow, however, and the first woman in statewide office was not elected until 1952. Neighboring North Dakota, in contrast, set that precedent in 1892. The first woman sent to the U.S. House from Minnesota was Coya Gjesdal Knutson, but Republicans conducted a malicious campaign to defeat her in 1958.

No women held major state offices for more than a decade, but, as with the Nineteenth Amendment, Minnesota legislators were quick to ratify the proposed Equal Rights Amendment. Their 1975 reform of rape laws became a model for other states.

Minneapolis, a largely white city, elected African American Sharon Sayles as mayor in 1993, and President Bill Clinton appointed Hazel R. O'Leary, also an African American, to head the Department of Energy.

Voters chose Minneapolis prosecutor Amy Klobuchar, a Democrat, for the U.S. Senate in 2006, and in 2011, Michele Bachmann, Republican of St. Cloud, was a candidate for president. Although Minnesotans had yet to elect a female governor, women held three of the state's five executive posts.

Key Facts

Statehood:	1858
Capital:	St. Paul
First women's rights organization:	No formal name, 1866
Pioneer publications:	*St. Cloud Visitor*, Jane Grey Swisshelm, editor, 1857
	The Bulletin, Dr. Ethel Hurd, editor, 1909
First female lawyer:	Martha Angle Dorsett, 1877
Full female enfranchisement:	1920
State ratification of Nineteenth Amendment:	Yes
First president of League of Women Voters:	Marguerite Wells
First woman on state supreme court:	Rosalie Wahl, 1977
State ratification of Equal Rights Amendment:	Yes

Statewide Elective Officeholders

Governor:	None	
Lieutenant governor:	Marlene Johnson (R)	1982
	Joanell Dyrstad (R)	1990
	Joanne Benson (R)	1994
	Mae Schunk (Reform)[17]	1998
	Carol Molnau (R)	2002
	Yvonne Prettner Solon (D)	2010
Secretary of state:	Virginia Holm (R)	1952
	Jean Anderson Growe (D)	1976
	Mary Kiffmeyer (R)	1998
Attorney general:	Lori Swanson (D)	2008
Treasurer:	Carol Johnson (D)	1998
Auditor:	Judi Dutcher (D)	1994
	Patricia Anderson (R)	2002
	Rebecca Otto (R)	2006
School superintendent:	Not elected	

State Legislature

Firsts

House:[18]	Mabel Cain	1922
	Sue Metzger Dickey Hugh	1922
	Hannah Jensen Kempfer	1922
	Mabeth Hurd Paige	1922
Senate:	Laura Johnson Naplin	1927

Percentage of women in 2010–2011 session (21 among 67 in senate; 44 among 134 in house):	32
National rank:	5

Presiding Officers

---

[17] The Reform Party was a brief-lived libertarian group that managed to elect former wrestler Jesse Ventura as governor; Schunk was his running mate.

[18] Elections for state representative were nonpartisan at the time.

Speaker of the house:	Dee Long (D)	2003
	Margaret Anderson Kelliher (D)	2007
Senate president:	None	

Federal Elective Officeholders

U.S. Senate:	Muriel Buck Humphrey (D)[19]	1978
	Amy Klobuchar (D)	2006
U.S. House:	Coya Gjesdal Knutson (D)	1954
	Betty McCollum (D)	2000
	Michele Bachmann (R)	2006

FURTHER READING

Bauer, Heidi, ed. 1999. *The Privilege for Which We Struggled: Leaders of the Woman Suffrage Movement in Minnesota.* St. Paul, MN: Upper Midwest Women's History Center.

Delton, Jennifer Alice. 2002. *Making Minnesota Liberal: Civil Rights and the Transformation of the Democratic Party.* Minneapolis: University of Minnesota Press.

Faue, Elizabeth. 1991. *Community of Suffering and Struggle: Women, Men, and the Labor Movement in Minneapolis.* Chapel Hill: University of North Carolina Press.

Stuhler, Barbara. 1995. *Gentle Warrior: Clara Ueland and the Minnesota Struggle for Woman Suffrage.* St. Paul, MN: Minnesota Historical Society.

MISSISSIPPI

Overview

The Women's Christian Temperance Union (WCTU) was founded in Oxford in 1881, and it was through the WCTU that Mississippi women saw their greatest political activism. Because of their lobbying, women who paid property taxes could vote in tax referenda and in school elections sooner than in many states considered more liberal.

Mississippi's suffrage association formalized in 1898 and had two outstanding leaders in Nellie Nugent Somerville and Belle Kearney, who never used her formal first name, Carrie. The first state convention was held in Greenville, with Hala Hammon Butt as president. The political acme came in 1916, when the Mississippi Senate tied on suffrage, 21–21. The House, however, refused to take up the issue.

When Congress passed the Nineteenth Amendment in 1919, suffragists optimistically opened a headquarters in Jackson. Women from Lauderdale County arrived with two thousand petition signatures they had collected in a few hours, and both the incoming the outgoing governors advocated ratification.

But the Southern Women's Rejection League also lobbied, and the House rejected the Nineteenth Amendment, 94–25. Senators, who had tied in 1916, did so again in 1920. Mississippi women got the vote because of other states, and feminists were chagrined when anti-suffrage leader Lizzie George Henderson was one of the first to register. State law required voters to be registered four months prior to an election, so Mississippi women joined those in Georgia as nonvoters in 1920.

In the next election, Greenville voters sent Nellie Nugent Somerville to the legislature. Less than a decade later, her daughter, attorney Lucy Somerville Howorth, would be elected. Belle Kearney audaciously ran for the U.S. Senate in 1922, but did not come close to winning the crucial Democratic nomination. In 1924, she, won the lesser race for state senator.

Mississippi native Burnita Shelton Matthews was appointed by President Harry S. Truman in 1950 as the first woman on a federal district court. Until the end of the twentieth century, Mississippi's statewide record of electing women could be summed up in one name: Evelyn E. Gandy. She held four offices between 1959 and 1980, and when she retired, the state had no women in any top position. In 2011, Mississippi ranked with Delaware, Iowa, and Vermont in never having elected a woman to Congress, but Delaware and Vermont each have had a woman as governor.

---

[19] Appointed; never elected.

Key Facts

Statehood:	1817
Capital:	Jackson
First women's rights organization:	Mississippi Woman Suffrage Association, 1898
Pioneer publication:	*Purple and White*, Janie Linfield, editor, 1913
First female lawyer:	Lucy H. Greaves, 1914
Full female enfranchisement:	1920
State ratification of Nineteenth Amendment:	No
First president of League of Women Voters:	Blanche Rogers
First woman on state supreme court:	Leonore L. Prather, 1982
State ratification of Equal Rights Amendment:	No

Statewide Elective Officeholders

Governor:	None	
Lieutenant governor:	Evelyn E. Gandy (D)	1975
	Amy Tuck (R)	1999
Secretary of state:	None	
Attorney general:	None	
Treasurer:[20]	Evelyn E. Gandy (D)	1959
Insurance commissioner	Evelyn E. Gandy (D)	1971
School superintendent:	Not elected	

State Legislature

Firsts		
House:	Nellie Nugent Somerville (D)	1922
Senate:	Belle Kearney (D)	1924
Percentage of women in 2010–2011 session		
(5 among 52 in senate; 21 among 122 in house):	15	
National rank:	47	
Presiding Officers		
Speaker of the house:	None	
Senate president:	None	

Federal Elective Officeholders

U.S. Senate:	None
U.S. House:	None

FURTHER READING

Curry, Constance, et al. 2000. *Deep in Our Hearts: Nine White Women in the Freedom Movement.* Athens: University of Georgia Press.

Mills, Kay. 1993. *This Little Light of Mine: The Life of Fannie Lou Hamer.* New York: Dutton.

Swain, Martha. 1995. *Ellen S. Woodward: New Deal Advocate for Women.* Jackson: University of Mississippi Press.

---

[20] Mississippi also elects an auditor, but no woman has held the office.

MISSOURI

Overview

The Missouri Woman Suffrage Association began in 1867. Soon after, Virginia Minor of St. Louis sued the local elections official for refusing to register her. The U.S. Supreme Court in her case, *Minor v. Happersett* (1875), essentially ruled that the language of the Fifteenth Amendment, while gender-neutral, did not apply to women.

The movement faded and did not revive until 1911. Under Helen Guthrie Miller, the St. Louis Equal Suffrage League soon had hundreds of members. By 1913, there were twenty-eight branches around the state. Armed with fourteen thousand petition signatures, women went to the capital of Jefferson City, and the legislature put the enfranchisement issue on the 1914 ballot. It failed, with 182,257 in favor and 322,463 opposed.

Feminists achieved visibility at the 1916 National Democratic Convention in St. Louis with "the golden lane" of women with yellow umbrellas that stretched for ten blocks, forcing male delegates to pay attention. Helen Miller moved to Washington, DC, that year and became an effective lobbyist, holding much sway with House Speaker Champ Clark of Missouri.

When the U.S. House passed the Nineteenth Amendment in 1919, every one of Missouri's sixteen House members voted for it—except for the St. Louis representative. The Missouri House ratified the amendment by 125–4, and only three of thirty-two senators voted negatively. One of the strongest suffragists, Emily Newell Blair, became vice chairman of the Democratic National Committee in 1922.

Leonor Kretzer Sullivan was Missouri's first female U.S. representative. She was elected in 1952, long after the first in the nation, in 1916. Sullivan is considered the creator of the food stamp program and author of the 1968 Consumer Credit Protection Act, which made credit more accessible to women.

Voters were slow to elect women to statewide offices, with the first in 1984—compared with North Dakota's 1892 precedent. Harriet Woods won the lieutenant governorship. She ran a strong 1986 campaign for the U.S. Senate but lost. That race was the inspiration for EMILY's List, which has gone on to become the country's largest women's political action committee. Jean Carnahan and Claire McCaskill won U.S. Senate races in 2000 and 2006, respectively, but Carnahan lost in 2002.

As of 2011, Missouri's eleven-member congressional delegation included three women, but there was just one in its six elected statewide offices. She was Robin Carnahan, the daughter of the former senator, and she lost a Senate race in 2010.

Key Facts

Statehood:	1821
Capital:	Jefferson City
First women's rights organization:	Missouri Woman Suffrage Association, 1867
Pioneer publication:	*Missouri Woman*, Emily B. Newall and Mary Semple Scott, editors, 1915
First female lawyer:	Helena "Lemma" Barkaloo, 1871
Full female enfranchisement:	1920
State ratification of Nineteenth Amendment:	Yes
First president of League of Women Voters:	Mrs. George Gellhorn, St. Louis
First woman on state supreme court:	Ann K. Covington, 1987
State ratification of Equal Rights Amendment:	No

Statewide Elective Officeholders

Governor:	None	
Lieutenant governor:	Harriet Woods (D)	1984
Secretary of state:	Judith K. Moriarty (D)	1992
	Rebecca M. Cook (D)	1994
	Robin Carnahan (D)	2004

Attorney general:	None	
Treasurer:	Nancy Farmer (D)	2000
	Sarah Steelman (R)	2004
Auditor:	Margaret Kelly (R)	1984
	Claire McCaskill (D)	1998
	Susan Montee (D)	2006
School superintendent:	Not elected	

State Legislature

Firsts		
House:	Mellcene Thurman Smith (D)	1922
	Sarah Lucille Underwood (D)	1922
Senate:	Mary L. Gant (D)	1972
Percentage of women in 2010–2011 session		
(6 among 34 in senate; 40 among 163 in house):	23	
National Rank:	24	
Presiding Officers		
Speaker of the House:	Catherine Hanaway (R)	2003
Senate President:	None	

Federal Elective Officeholders

U.S. Senate:	Jean Carnahan (D)	2000
	Claire McCaskill (D)	2006
U.S. House:	Leonor Kretzer Sullivan (D)	1952
	Joan Kelly Horn (D)	1990
	Pat Danner (D)	1992
	Karen McCarthy (D)	1994
	Jo Ann Emerson (R)	1996
	Vicky Hartzler (R)	2010

FURTHER READING

Corbett, Katharine T. 1999. *In Her Place: A Guide to St. Louis Women's History.* St. Louis: Missouri Historical Society.

Blair, Emily Newell. 1999. *Bridging Two Eras: The Autobiography of Emily Newell Blair, 1877–1951.* Columbia: University of Missouri Press.

Whites, LeeAnn, Mary C. Neth, and Gary R. Kremer, eds. 2004. *Women in Missouri History: In Search of Power and Influence.* Columbia: University of Missouri Press.

MONTANA

Overview

More than women in most states, female Montanans were involved in party politics early on, without needing to organize a significant feminist movement. The Populist Party even nominated Ella Knowles as its candidate for attorney general in 1892. The turn of the century was regressive, however. For example, a 1901 ruling declared that women could not be notaries public, thus questioning the legality of male voters electing them. In response, the governor recommended enfranchisement to the 1903 legislature.

CHAPTER NINETEEN

480

Legislators rejected it that year and in 1905, and not until 1911 did a revived movement, led by young Jeannette Rankin, succeed in getting the question on the 1914 ballot. With a headquarters in Butte, feminists organized a strong campaign. National anti-suffragists sent women funded by liquor interests to oppose it, but the referendum carried 41,302 to 37,588.

Their goal accomplished, suffrage associations remade themselves into Good Government Clubs, which were Montana's forerunner to the League of Women Voters. Jeannette Rankin won election to Congress in 1916, while two feminist women won seats in the Montana House. In 1918, May Trumper became Montana's first female state superintendent of public instruction. Female representatives introduced the Nineteenth Amendment to the 1919 Montana House, which ratified it unanimously, and in the next legislative session, Margaret Smith Hathaway, known as "Maggie," became the nation's first female minority floor leader.

Following their 1918 precedent, voters continued to elect an unusual number of women to statewide executive positions, but it was 1944 before Montanans had their first female state senator.

Democrats nominated longtime state representative Dorothy Bradley of Bozeman for governor in 1992. Although she ran a strong campaign in this Year of the Woman, Bradley lost. The party tried again in 1996, nominating state senator Judy Jacobson of Butte for governor, but she lost by a greater margin. In that year, Republican Judy Martz won the lieutenant governorship, and she went on to be elected governor in 2000.

The 2008 election was revolutionary, as voters chose four women for six statewide offices. In 2011, women held more than half of Montana's six statewide offices, but, except for Jeanette Rankin, Montanans never have sent a woman to represent them in Washington, DC.

Key Facts

Statehood:	1889
Capital:	Helena
First women's rights organization:	Montana Woman Suffrage Association, 1895
Pioneer publication:	None
First female lawyer:	Ella Knowles (later Haskell), 1890
Full female enfranchisement:	1914
State ratification of Nineteenth Amendment:	Yes
First president of League of Women Voters:	Mrs. Edwin L. Norris
First woman on state supreme court:	Diane G. Barz, 1989
State ratification of Equal Rights Amendment:	Yes

Statewide Elective Officeholders

Governor:	Judy Martz (R)	2000
Lieutenant governor:	Judy Martz (R)	1996
Secretary of state:	Linda McCullough (D)	2008
Attorney general:	None	
Treasurer:	Alta E. Fisher (R)	1948
	Edna Hinman (R)	1954
	Hollis Conners (R)	1972
	Andrea Hemstead Bennett (R)	1984
Auditor:	Monica Lindeen (D)	2008
School superintendent:	May Trumper (R)	1918
	Elizabeth Ireland (R)	1932
	Mary Condon (D)	1948
	Harriet Miller (R)	1956
	Delores Colburg (D)	1968
	Georgia Ruth Rice (D)	1976
	Nancy A. Keenan (D)	1988
	Denise Juneau (D)	2008

State Legislature

Firsts

House:	Margaret Smith Hathaway (R)	1916
	Emma S. Ingalls (R)	1916
Senate:	Ellenore Bridenstine, (R)	1944

Percentage of women in 2010–2011 session

(7 among 50 in senate; 28 among 100 in house):   23

National rank: 25

Presiding Officers

Speaker of the house: None

Senate president: None

Federal Elective Officeholders

U.S. Senate:	None	
U.S. House:	Jeannette Rankin (R)	1916
	Jeannette Rankin (R)	1940

FURTHER READING

Bell, Margaret. 2005. *When Montana and I Were Young.* Lincoln: University of Nebraska Press.

Lopach, James L., and Jean Lawkowski. 2005. *Jeannette Rankin: A Political Woman.* Boulder: University of Colorado Press.

Murphy, Mary. 1997. *Mixing Cultures: Men, Women, and Leisure in Bozeman, 1914–1941.* Urbana: University of Illinois Press.

NEBRASKA

Overview

Amelia Bloomer, a pioneer feminist originally from Seneca Falls, New York, was invited to address Nebraska's territorial legislature in 1855. In December of that year, the Nebraska House passed a bill for full enfranchisement, but the upper chamber adjourned without voting. Had it emulated the House, the Nebraska Territory, not Wyoming, would have been first to grant the vote.

Women won the vote for school elections in 1869 but lost it in 1875. In 1871, they conducted the nation's second referendum for full rights. They lost, but suffragists eventually regrouped. At an 1879 meting in Hebron, they established a headquarters in the capital of Lincoln. The American Woman Suffrage Association held its 1881 national convention in Omaha, and Nebraska women conducted a second referendum in 1882. With much evidence of fraud, officials reported 50,693 negative votes and 25,756 positive ones.

Clara Bewick Colby was the state's leading feminist at the turn of the century, and Ada Bittenbender was a candidate for the Nebraska Supreme Court. Laura Gregg led a third enfranchisement campaign in 1914. Again women lost but more narrowly than earlier, with 90,738 in favor and 100,842 opposed.

The 1917 legislature granted partial suffrage, but when anti-suffragists ran a petition drive against it, nineteen suffragists sued for the right to inspect what they believed were fraudulent petitions. The attorney general argued that, as nonvoters, they lacked the right to sue. However, after more hearings, the court became convinced that petitions were fraudulent, and anti-suffragists had to pay the court costs.

Nebraska women ultimately won the vote via the Nineteenth Amendment, which its legislature quickly ratified. It was the only state in which women were not previously enfranchised that voted unanimously.

Women were extremely slow to vote for themselves, though, and none won statewide office until 1982, when Republican Kay A. Orr was elected treasurer. When she ran for governor in 1986, Democrats nominated Lincoln mayor Helen Boosalis, and the nation had its first gubernatorial race between two women. Orr won, becoming the eighth female governor and the first Republican.

Virginia Dodd Smith had been elected to the U.S. House in 1976 and was reelected until announcing her retirement with the 1990 election. Since then, Nebraska has had no female representation in Congress. In 2011, a woman held only one of its six statewide offices, the comparatively lowly post of public service commissioner.

Key Facts

Statehood:	1867
Capital:	Lincoln
First women's rights organization:	No formal name, 1869
Pioneer publication:	*Woman's Tribune*, Clara Bewick Colby, editor, 1883
	Woman's Weekly, Mary Fairbrother, editor, c.1890
	Headquarters Message, Laura Gregg, editor, 1902
First female lawyer:	Ada M. Bittenbender, 1882
Full female enfranchisement:	1920
State ratification of Nineteenth Amendment:	Yes
First president of League of Women Voters:	Mrs. Charles Dietrich
First woman on state supreme court:	Lindsey Miller-Lerman, 1998
State ratification of Equal Rights Amendment:	Yes

Statewide Elective Officeholders

Governor:	Kay A. Orr (R)	1986
Lieutenant governor:	Maxine B. Moul (D)	1990
	Kim Roback (D)	1994
Secretary of state:	Elected by the state legislature	
Attorney general:	None	
Treasurer:	Kay A. Orr (R)	1982
	Dawn E. Rockey (D)	1990
	Lorelee Bird (R)	2000
Auditor:	Kathleen Witek (R)	1998
School superintendent:	Not elected	
Public service commissioner:	Ann Boyle (D)	1998

State Legislature

Firsts

House:	Clara C. Humphrey (R)	1924
Senate:	Kathleen Foote (R)	1954
Percentage of women in 2010–2011 session (11 among 49 in senate):[21]	22	
National rank:	29	

Presiding Officers

Speaker of the house:	None
Senate president:	None

---

[21] Nebraska has had a unicameral legislature since 1934.

Federal Elective Officeholders

| U.S. Senate: | Hazel Hempel Abel (R)[22] | 1954 |
| U.S. House: | Virginia Dodd Smith (R) | 1976 |

FURTHER READING

Berens, Charlyne. 2005. *One House: The Unicameral's Progressive Vision for Nebraska.* Lincoln: University of Nebraska Press.

Fink, Deborah. 1992. *Agrarian Women: Wives and Mothers in Rural Nebraska, 1880–1940.* Chapel Hill: University of North Carolina Press.

Nebraska Commission on the Status of Women. 1967. *Nebraska Women through the Years, 1867–1967.* Lincoln: Johnsen Publishing.

Tong, Bensen. 1999. *Susan La Flesche Picotte, MD: Omaha Indian Leader and Reformer.* Norman: University of Oklahoma Press.

NEVADA

Overview

Hannah K. Clapp, who had founded Nevada's first coeducational institution, led other women in an 1883 lobbying attempt for the vote. In the same era, Sarah Winnemucca led lobbying in Washington, DC, on behalf of Nevada's natives. A state suffrage association began in 1894, under Frances Williamson. Within two years, when the group met at Reno, every county was represented, and Elda A. Orr became president.

Just a decade later, in 1914, Anne Martin led the successful referendum for enfranchisement. She was affiliated with the National Woman's Party, and these younger women even went down into mines to speak with male voters. The referendum passed with a 3,679 margin of 18,193 ballots cast, even though female anti-suffragists launched a well-organized opposition.

The first woman in the Nevada House was elected in 1918, before most American women could vote. Then, however, progress slowed. The first female state senator was not elected until 1966, almost a half-century later.

Unlike nearby California, New Mexico, and Oregon, Nevadans never have elected a woman to the U.S. Senate or as governor. They also did not set other nineteenth-century precedents in the election of women to statewide office or in the judiciary, as bordering Idaho or Utah did. In the mid-twentieth century, Nevada's primary importance for women was that one could obtain a divorce there much more easily than in any other state.

More Nevada women won political offices around the millennium, and Las Vegas had female mayors. As of 2011, women held three of its six statewide executive positions, and one woman was in its five-member congressional delegation. Its most notable achievement as of 2011 was that Nevada is the only state that has twice elected women as attorney general.

Key Facts

Statehood:	1864
Capital:	Carson City
First women's rights organization:	Lucy Stone Non-Partisan League, 1894
Pioneer publication:	*Nevada Citizen,* Laura Williamson, editor, 1896
First female lawyer:	Laura May Tilden, 1893
Full female enfranchisement:	1914
State ratification of Nineteenth Amendment:	Yes
First president of League of Women Voters:	Mrs. S.W. Belford
First woman on state supreme court:	Miriam Shering, 1995
State ratification of Equal Rights Amendment:	No

---

[22] Appointed, not elected

Statewide Elective Officeholders

Governor:	None	
Lieutenant governor:	Sue Wagner (R)	1990
Secretary of state:	Frankie Sue Del Papa (D)	1986
	Cheryl Lau (R)	1990
Attorney general:	Frankie Sue Del Papa (D)	1990
	Catherine Cortez Masto (D)	2006
Treasurer:	Patty Cafferata (R)	1982
	Kate Marshall (D)	2006
Auditor:	Kathy Augustine (R)	1998
Controller:	Kim Wallin (D)	2006
School superintendent:	Mildred Bray (D)	1938

State Legislature

Firsts		
House:	Sadie Dotson Hurst (D)	1918
Senate:	Helen Kolb Herr (D)	1966
Percentage of women in 2010–2011 session		
(6 among 21 in senate; 12 among 42 in house):	29	
National rank:	30	
Presiding Officers		
Speaker of the house:	Barbara E. Buckley (D)	2006
Senate president:	None	

Federal Elective Officeholders

U.S. Senate:	None	
U.S. House:	Barbara Farrell Vucanovich (R)[23]	1982
	Shelley Berkley (D)	1998
	Dina Titus (D)	2008

FURTHER READING

Denton, Sally, and Roger Morris. 2001. *The Money and the Power: The Making of Las Vegas and Its Hold on America, 1947–2000.* New York: Knopf.

Watson, Anita Ernest. 2000. *Into Their Own: Nevada Women Emerging into Public Life.* Reno: Nevada Humanities Commission.

Zanjani, Sally. 2000. *Sarah Winnemucca.* Lincoln: University of Nebraska Press.

NEW HAMPSHIRE

Overview

The earliest women's rights conventions in the 1850s were attended by residents of New Hampshire. In 1858, Mary Harrington, an unmarried property owner in Claremont, unsuccessfully attempted to vote, and Dover's Marilla Ricker did the same in 1870. A suffrage association was founded in 1868 but languished until the new century, when Armenia White

---

[23]Mother of Treasurer Patty Cafferata; mother and daughter won in the same 1982 election cycle.

revived it. Feminists persuaded the legislature to put the question of enfranchisement on the 1904 ballot. It was only the second referendum on the issue in the East, at a time when women had won the vote in four western states. Male voters rejected it with 14,162 in favor and 21,788 opposed.

Attitudes changed by 1920, and the New Hampshire legislature unanimously ratified the Nineteenth Amendment to the U.S. Constitution, which granted the vote to women in every state. That was in August, 1920, and several women managed to file for the November election. Two won legislative seats, but conservatives argued that the right to vote did not necessarily imply the right to hold office. Legislators called a special referendum for March 21, 1921, to solve the problem by amending the state constitution, but the amendment garnered less than the required two-thirds majority. Faced with this conundrum, legislators simply ignored the legalistic problem and seated the women.

New Hampshire elects few statewide executives, but it has an extraordinarily large legislature. Hundreds of women have served in it. The state was singular in 2011 in having had five women as presiding officers of the two chambers, with some serving simultaneously.

The state also is singular in having had a woman, Jeanne Shaheen, as both governor and U.S. senator. When Kelly Ayotte joined her in the Senate after the 2010 election, New Hampshire became the fourth state (following California, Maine, and Washington) with women in both of its U.S. Senate seats. With Carol Shea-Porter in the House, it was the only state that has an entirely female congressional delegation.

Key Facts

Statehood:	1788
Capital:	Concord
First women's rights organization:	New Hampshire Woman Suffrage Association, 1868
Pioneer publication:	None
First female lawyer:	Marilla Ricker, 1890
Full female enfranchisement:	1920
State ratification of Nineteenth Amendment:	Yes
First president of League of Women Voters:	Martha S. Kimbell
First woman on state supreme court:	Linda Stewart Dalianis, 2000
State ratification of Equal Rights Amendment:	Yes

Statewide Elective Officeholders

Governor:	Jeanne Shaheen	1996
Lieutenant governor:	Office does not exist	
Secretary of state:	Elected by the legislature	
Attorney general:	None	
Financial officer(s):	Elected by the legislature	
School superintendent:	Office does not exist	

State Legislature

Firsts		
House:	Dr. Mary L. R. Farnum (D)	1920
	Jessie Doe (R)	1920
Senate:	E. Maude Ferguson (R)	1930
Percentage of women in 2010–2011 session		
(11 among 30 in senate; 58 among 150 in house):	39	
National rank:	2	
Presiding Officers		
Speaker of the house:	Donna Sytek	1996

	Terie Norelli	2006
Senate president:	Vesta Roy (R)[24]	1982
	Beverly Hollingworth	1998
	Sylvia Larsen	2006

Federal Elective Officeholders

U.S. Senate:	Jeanne Shaheen (D)	2008
	Kelly Ayotte (R)	2010
U.S. House:	Carol Shea-Porter (D)	2008

FURTHER READING

Anderson, Leon W. 1971. *New Hampshire Women Legislators, 1921–1971*. Concord: New Hampshire Savings Bank.

Moran, William. 2002. *The Belles of New England: The Women of the Textile Mills and the Families Whose Wealth They Wove*. New York: St. Martin's.

Robertson, Stacey M. 2000. *Parker Pillsbury: Radical Abolitionist, Male Feminist*. Ithaca: Cornell University Press.

NEW JERSEY

Overview

New Jersey was the only one of the thirteen original colonies that granted women the right to vote after the American Revolution, but the right was rescinded in 1807.

Lucy Stone moved to Orange soon after her 1855 marriage to Henry Blackwell and founded the state's first suffrage society in 1867. The following year she and her mother-in-law, Hannah Blackwell, attempted unsuccessfully to vote. Also that year, 172 women in Vineland marched to the polls and cast ballots that they correctly assumed would not be counted. Women in Landis Township tried to vote in an 1873 municipal election.

Mary F. Davis became the primary suffrage leader when Stone moved to Boston. Davis and Rev. Phebe Hanaford addressed the legislature in 1871. Rahway's Ann H. Connelly lobbied successfully for a bill that granted mothers equal custody, and male voters could elect women to school offices in 1873. By 1887, about fifty women who could not vote for themselves served on school boards. Later progress was slow, though, and in 1917 New Jersey became the last state in the nation to open a college that admitted female students.

As elsewhere, the suffrage movement revived around 1912, and by 1915, New Jersey had affiliates of four national associations, the largest of which had fifty thousand members in 215 state chapters. The most prominent leaders were Rev. Florence Randolph of the National Association of Colored Women's Clubs, Mina Van Winkle of the Equality League for Self-Supporting Women, Alice Paul of the National Woman's Party, and Florence Howe Hall, daughter of Julia Ward Howe, as head of the oldest group.

The legislature put the issue of enfranchisement on the 1915 ballot. Women conducted some forty-five hundred meetings and spent $80,000 on advertising, but lost with 133,281 for and 184,391 against. Alice Paul and many of her supporters, meanwhile, set their sights on Washington, DC, where they picketed the White House.

When other states made congressional passage of the Nineteenth Amendment possible, New Jersey women presented 140,000 petition signatures to the state legislature. Senators quickly ratified, as did the House—but by only by 34–24 and after a midnight filibuster.

New Jersey held off-year elections, and women won legislative seats in 1921. Newark's Mary T. Norton was elected to the U. S House in 1924 and proved to be one of the most important women in Congress of all time. Deemed the mother of women in the military, she chaired the House Labor Committee during World War II.

---

[24]This position led to Roy briefly serving as acting governor at the end of 1982.

Florence Price Dwyer successfully sponsored a state law banning pay discrimination in 1952 and also went on to Congress. East Orange voters elected Madeline Worth Williams as New Jersey's first African American female state legislator in 1958, earlier than in most states, and New Jersey was the third state to have a female Speaker of the house. On the other hand, no woman was a state senator until 1965, much later than in most states.

Millicent Hammond Fenwick, elected to the Congress in 1974, was the model for the U.S. representative in the comic strip *Doonesbury*. A liberal Republican, she lost a 1982 U.S. Senate race to a Democratic man. Two other female U.S. representatives from New Jersey also had good careers, but no new woman has won a place in Washington since 1980.

Few state offices are elective, and New Jersey's first woman to win a statewide race was not until 1993, when Christine Todd Whitman won the contest for governor. Since then, the only post won by a woman was the lieutenant governorship in 2009. As of 2011, no women were part of New Jersey's fifteen-member congressional delegation.

Key Facts

Statehood:	1787
Capital:	Trenton
First women's rights organization:	No formal name, 1867
Pioneer publication:	None
First female lawyer:	Mary Philbrook, 1894
Full female enfranchisement:	1920
State ratification of Nineteenth Amendment:	Yes
First president of League of Women Voters:	Mrs. John Schermerhorn
First woman on state supreme court:	Marie Garibaldi, 1982
State ratification of Equal Rights Amendment:	Yes

Statewide Elective Officeholders

Governor:	Christine Todd Whitman (R)	1993
Lieutenant governor:	Kim Guadagno (D)	2009
Secretary of state:	Appointed by governor	
Attorney general:	None	
Financial officer(s):	Appointed by governor	
School superintendent:	Not elected	

State Legislature

Firsts

House:	Margaret B. Laird (R)	1921
	Jennie C. Van Ness (R)	1921
Senate:	Mildred Barry Hughes (R)	1965

Percentage of women in 2010–2011 session
(10 among 40 in senate; 23 among 80 in house): 28
National rank: 15
Presiding Officers

Speaker of the house:	Marion West Higgins	1965
	Sheila Oliver	2010
Senate president:	None	

Federal Elective Officeholders

U.S. Senate:	None	
U.S. House:	Mary T. Rogers (D)	1924
	Florence Price Dwyer (R)	1956
	Helen Stevenson Meyner (D)	1974

Millicent Hammond Fenwick (R)   1974
Margaret Scafati Roukema (R)   1980

FURTHER READING

Adams, Katherine H. 2008. *Alice Paul and the American Suffrage Movement.* Urbana: University of Illinois Press.
Beard, Patricia. 1996. *Growing Up Republican: Christie Whitman.* New York: HarperCollins.
Burstyn, Joan N. 1996. *Past and Promise: Lives of New Jersey Women.* Syracuse, NY: Syracuse University.
Gordon, Felice D. 1986. *After Winning: The Legacy of the New Jersey Suffragists, 1920–1947.* New Brunswick, NJ: Rutgers University.

NEW MEXICO

Overview

Hispanic women in New Mexico were more socially free than most Anglos. They could drink, smoke, gamble, and dance without disapproval, but they were much less likely to be educated and to have political rights. When the territory became part of the Union in 1912, it was the only western state—and one of relatively few states anywhere—in which women lacked all voting rights, even for school elections.

Feminists had lobbied the constitutional convention in 1910 but won nothing. Because the new state constitution was difficult to amend, starting from their 1912 organizational meeting in Las Cruces, they concentrated on a federal amendment instead. Under the leadership of Nina Otero–Warren and Deane Lindsey, whose husband soon would be governor, women exhibited at the state fair, distributed leaflets in Spanish and English, and lobbied congressional candidates. New Mexico's congressional delegation voted unanimously for the Nineteenth Amendment. Gov. Octaviano Larrazolo was not enthusiastic about ratification, but lawmakers nonetheless ratified by 36–10 in the state house and 17–5 in the state senate.

After ratification, New Mexico's record of electing women was more progressive than most older states, and in 1922, it was the it was first to elect more than one woman to statewide office. Isabel Eckles became state superintendent of schools with the 1922 election, but that precedent had been set in North Dakota in 1892. The big 1922 milestone was the victory of Soledad Chávez Chacón, who was the nation's first female secretary of state. Eighteen women followed her in that office. Georgia Lee Lusk, who became school superintendent in 1930, went on to Congress. She won in 1946, an era when women generally regressed.

New Mexico has elected a total of twenty-nine women to state or congressional positions, and until Republican Heather A. Wilson won a U.S. House seat in 1998, all were Democrats. Attorney General Patricia Madrid, a Democrat, ran an extremely close race to unseat Wilson in 2006. Wilson then ran for the U.S. Senate in 2008, but Republicans did not nominate her. The 2010 election for governor also was between two women, and Democrat Diane Denish lost narrowly to Republican Susana Martinez.

Key Facts

Statehood:	1912
Capital:	Santa Fe
First women's rights organization:	No formal name, 1910
Pioneer publication:	None
First female lawyer:	Henrietta Hume Pettijohn Buck,[25] 1892
Full female enfranchisement:	1920
State ratification of Nineteenth Amendment:	Yes
First president of League of Women Voters:	Mrs. Gerald Cassidy
First woman on state supreme court:	Mary Coon Walters, 1984
State ratification of Equal Rights Amendment:	Yes

---

[25] Daughter Carrie Hume Buck had a distinguished career in California and Hawaii.

Statewide Elective Officeholders

Governor:	Susana Martinez (R)	2010
Lieutenant governor:	Diane Denish (D)	2002
Secretary of state:	Soledad Chávez Chacón (D)	1922
	Jennie Fortune (D)	1926
	E. A. Perrault (D)	1928
	Margaret Baca (D)	1930
	Elizabeth F. Gonzales (D)	1934
	Jessie M. Gonzales (D)	1938
	Cecilia Cleveland (D)	1942
	Alice Romero (D)	1946
	Beatrice Roach (D)	1950
	Natalie S. Buck (D)	1954
	Betty Fironia (D)	1958
	Alberta Miller (D)	1962
	Ernestine Evans (D)	1966
	Shirley Hooper (D)	1978
	Clara P. Jones (D)	1982
	Rebecca Vigil-Giron (D)	1986
	Stephanie Gonzalez (D)	1990
	Mary Herrera (D)	2006
	Diana Duran (R)	2010
Attorney general:	Patricia Madrid (D)	1998
Financial officer(s):	None	
School superintendent:	Isabel Eckles (D)	1922
	Georgia Lee Lusk (D)	1930
	Grace Corrigan (D)	1938
Corporation commissioner:	Gloria Tristani (D)	1994
Public regulation commissioner:	Lynda Lovejoy (D)	1998
	Carol Sloan (D)	2006

State Legislature

Firsts		
House:	Bertha Paxton (D)	1922
Senate:	Louise Holland Coe (D)	1924
Percentage of women in 2010–2011 session		
(10 among 42 in senate; 20 among 70 in house):	27	
National rank:	17	
Presiding Officers		
Speaker of the house:	None	
Senate president:	None	

Federal Elective Officeholders

U.S. Senate:	None	
U.S. House:	Georgia Lee Lusk (D)	1946
	Heather A. Wilson (R)	1998

FURTHER READING

Gonzalez, Deena J. 1999. *Refusing the Favor: The Spanish-Mexican Women of Santa Fe, 1820–1880.* New York: Oxford University Press.

Mitchell, Pablo. 2005. *Coyote Nation: Sexuality, Race, and Conquest in Modernizing New Mexico, 1880-1920.* Chicago: University of Chicago Press.

Schackel, Sandra. 1992. *Social Housekeepers: Women Shaping Public Policy in New Mexico, 1920–1940.* Albuquerque: University of New Mexico Press.

Whaley, Charlotte. 1994. *Nina Otero-Warren of Santa Fe.* Albuquerque: University of New Mexico Press.

NEW YORK

Overview

The world's women's movement originated in 1848 in Seneca Falls, New York, where Elizabeth Cady Stanton then lived. Abigail Bush presided at a Rochester meeting two weeks later, but after Rochester's Susan B. Anthony joined the cause in 1852, she became the star. With Matilda Joslyn Gage of Fayetteville, Stanton and Anthony wrote a three-volume history of the cause, which was published between 1881 and 1886.

Opposition arose from the beginning. An 1853 meeting at the Broadway Tabernacle was known as the "mob convention," due to the audience response, but Sojourner Truth rebutted hecklers. New York reformed its property laws in 1854, but women later lost some rights. For example, not until 1902 did mothers have equal custody of their children.

Women in Fayetteville and Nyack attempted to vote in 1871, and fifteen Rochester women, including Anthony, followed in 1872. That year, Victoria Woodhull of New York City audaciously ran for president. Suffragists finally won their first legislative victory in 1880, when women in rural areas were allowed to vote in school elections.

Many New York feminists were more inclined to lecture in western states, where women were meeting much more success, than they were to lobby their own legislature in Albany. The state's suffrage society achieved no significant victories until working women energized the movement in the early twentieth century.

Harriot Stanton Blatch, daughter of Elizabeth Cady Stanton, formed the Equality League of Self-Supporting Women in 1907. After a 1910 strike in the garment industry, New Yorkers formed an uncommon coalition of working and wealthy women, with Alva Belmont Vanderbilt especially providing funding. Young suffragists hiked from New York City to Albany in 1911, and in 1913, they preached equality while walking all the way to Washington, DC.

The legislature put the enfranchisement question on the 1915 ballot, but suffragists lost, with 238,098 in favor and 320,853 opposed. They tried again in 1917, spending more than $1 million in advertising, and won by about 100,000 votes.

New York was thus the first eastern state to enfranchise women—at a time when every western state except New Mexico had done so. The National Association Opposed to Woman Suffrage was based in New York City, and its Minnie J. Bronson was the most prominent lobbyist against ratification of the Nineteenth Amendment in other states.

Democrats nominated Harriet May Mills for secretary of state in 1918. She did not win, but set a precedent as the first female nominee in a major state. The first women were elected as state representatives that year, too, but the first female state senator would wait until 1934.

That set a pattern of New York women doing much better as candidates for federal office in Washington than as state candidates in Albany. Only four women have been elected to statewide executive posts. Three were lieutenant governors, while the fourth was secretary of state back in 1924.

In contrast, the first female U.S. representative from New York was elected in 1928, and twenty-three have won since. Some, especially Geraldine Ferraro, Shirley Chisholm, and Bella Abzug, became nationally prominent. The state's first female U.S. senator, Hillary Rodham Clinton, was elected in 2000. After Clinton joined the Obama administration, Kirsten Gillibrand won the seat in her own right in 2010.

The state, however, never has had a woman who ran a close race for governor; none has presided over either chamber of its legislature; and none has been mayor of New York City.

Key Facts

Statehood:	1788
Capital:	Albany
First women's rights organization:	No formal name, 1848
Pioneer publications:	*The Lily,* Amelia Bloomer, editor, 1849
	Sybil, Lydia Sayer Hasbrouck, editor, Middletown, 1864
	The Revolution, Susan B. Anthony and Elizabeth Cady Stanton, editors, 1869
	National Citizen and Ballot Box, Matilda Joslyn Gage, editor, 1878
First female lawyer:	Kate Stoneman, 1888
Full female enfranchisement:	1917
State ratification of Nineteenth Amendment:	Yes
First president of League of Women Voters:	Mrs. Frank Vanderlip
First woman on state supreme court:	Judith S. Kaye, 1993
State ratification of Equal Rights Amendment:	Yes

Statewide Elective Officeholders

Governor:	None	
Lieutenant governor:	Mary Ann Krupsak (D)	1974
	Elizabeth McCaughey Ross (R)[26]	1994
	Mary O. Donahue (R)	1998
Secretary of state:	Florence E. S. Knapp (R)	1924
Attorney general:	None	
Auditor:	None	
Comptroller:	None	
School superintendent:	Not elected	

State Legislature

Firsts

House:	Mary Lilly (D)	1918
	Ida Sammis (R)	1918
Senate:	Rhoda Fox Graves (R)	1934

Percentage of women in 2010–2011 session (11 among 62 in senate; 34 among 150 in house):	21
National rank:	31

Presiding Officers

Speaker of the house:	None
Senate president:	None

Federal Elective Officeholders

U.S. Senate:	Hillary Rodham Clinton (D)	2000
	Kirsten Gillibrand (D)	2010[27]
U.S. House:	Ruth Sears Baker Pratt (R)	1928
	Marian Williams Clarke (R)	1933

---

[26] Became a Democrat while still in office.

[27] Initially appointed in 2009.

Caroline Love Goodwin O'Day (D)	1934
Winifred Claire Stanley (R)	1942
Katherine Price Collier St. George (R)	1946
Edna Flannery Kelly (D)	1949
Jessica McCullough Weis (R)	1958
Shirley Anita Chisholm (D)	1968
Bella Savitzky Abzug (D)	1970
Elizabeth Holtzman (D)	1972
Geraldine A. Ferraro (D)	1978
Louise McIntosh Slaughter (D)	1986
Nita M. Lowey (D)	1988
Susan Molinari (R)	1990
Carolyn B. Maloney (D)	1992
Nydia M. Velázquez (D)	1992
Sue W. Kelly (R)	1994
Carolyn McCarthy (D)	1996
Yvette Clarke (D)	2006
Kirsten Gillibrand (D)	2006
Nan Hayworth (R)	2010
Ann Marie Buerkle (R)	2010
Kathy Hochul (D)	2010

FURTHER READING

Abzug, Bella. 1972. *Bella! Ms. Abzug Goes to Washington.* New York: Saturday Review Press.

Brammer, Leila R. 2000. *Excluded From Suffrage History: Matilda Joslyn Gage, Nineteenth Century Feminist.* Westport, CT: Greenwood Press.

Chisholm, Shirley. 1973. *The Good Fight.* New York: Harper and Row.

DuBois, Ellen. 1997. *Harriot Stanton Blatch and the Winning of Woman Suffrage.* New Haven, CT: Yale University Press.

Ferraro, Geraldine. 1985. *Ferraro: My Story.* New York: Bantam Books.

Grinzberg, Lori D. 2005. *Untidy Origins: A Story of Women's Rights in Antebellum New York.* Chapel Hill: University of North Carolina Press.

NORTH CAROLINA

Overview

North Carolina's first feminist organization was founded in Asheville in 1894. Not daring to ask for full rights, the women aimed merely to be eligible for school offices but did not even win that. As the twentieth century began, the only initiative they had won was to eliminate the use of female prisoners on chain gangs.

As elsewhere, the movement revived around 1913. New groups developed in Charlotte and Greenville, and the Equal Suffrage League formalized in 1913. State senators came close to passing partial enfranchisement in 1917, failing 20–24. Just one North Carolina U.S. representative voted for the Nineteenth Amendment. When it went to the states for ratification, suffragists viewed the fact that North Carolina senators debated it for five hours as something of a victory. They voted to postpone a decision until the 1921 regular session. By then, enough other states had voted to ratify and it had been added to the U.S. Constitution—and North Carolinians had elected a woman as a state senator.

She was Lillian Exum Clement, and her fellow attorneys respected her so much that they persuaded her to run even though her candidacy did not meet filing deadlines. Republicans nominated Mary Settle Sharp for school superintendent that year, but the party was such a minority that she had no chance of winning. Democrats already had reached out to women by electing Mary O. Graham to their national committee, and Mrs. James Cowan became mayor of Wilmington in 1924.

North Carolina set judicial precedents earlier than most states, with the first woman admitted to the bar in 1878 and the first on the North Carolina Supreme Court in 1962. It was not until the late twentieth century, though, that women truly developed political viability. In 1992, Eva Clayton, an African American from coastal North Carolina, was the first woman from the state elected to a full term as U.S. representative. In 1996, Elaine Marshall won the 1996 race for as secretary of state and became North Carolina's first woman in statewide office since 1921.

Women have done well since then, winning elections for every statewide executive office except attorney general, as well as for the U.S. Senate and for governor. In 2011, the fifteen-member congressional delegation included four women, and Governor Bev Perdue ran the state along with women who held six of ten elected positions.

Key Facts

Statehood:	1789
Capital:	Raleigh
First women's rights organization:	No formal name, 1894
Pioneer publication:	*Southern Woman*, Mary Bayard Clarke, editor, New Berne, c.1890
First female lawyer:	Tabitha Holton, 1878
Full female enfranchisement:	1920
State ratification of Nineteenth Amendment:	No
First president of League of Women Voters:	Gertrude Weil
First woman on state supreme court:	Susie Marshall Sharp, 1962
State ratification of Equal Rights Amendment:	No

Statewide Elective Officeholders

Governor:	Bev Perdue (D)	2008
Lieutenant governor:	Bev Perdue (D)	2000
Secretary of state:	Elaine Marshall (D)	1996
Attorney general:	None	
Treasurer:	Janet Cowell (D)	2008
Auditor:	Beth Wood (D)	2008
School superintendent:	June Atkinson (D)	2004
Commissioner of public welfare:	Lucy Kate Burr Johnson (D)	1921
Agriculture commissioner:	Meg Scott Phipps (D)	2000
Labor commissioner:	Cherie Berry (R)	2000

State Legislature

Firsts		
House:	Julia M. Alexander (D)	1924
Senate:	Lillian Exum Clement (D)	1920
Percentage of women in 2010–2011 session		
(6 among 50 in senate; 32 among 120 in house):	22	
National rank:	29	
Presiding Officers		
Speaker of the house:	None	
Senate president:	None	

Federal Elective Officeholders

U.S. Senate:	Elizabeth Dole (R)	2000
	Kay Hagan (D)	2008

U.S. House:	Eliza Jane Pratt (D)	1946
	Eva Clayton (D)	1992
	Sue Myrick (R)	1994
	Virginia Foxx (R)	2004
	Renee Ellmers (R)	2010

FURTHER READING

Fischer, Kirsten. 2002. *Suspect Relations: Sex, Race, and Resistance in Colonial North Carolina.* Ithaca, NY: Cornell University Press.

Greene, Christina. 2006. *Women and the Black Freedom Movement in North Carolina.* Chapel Hill: University of North Carolina Press.

Smith, Margaret Supple, and Emily Herring Wilson. 1999. *North Carolina Women: Making History.* Chapel Hill: University of North Carolina Press.

NORTH DAKOTA

Overview

North Dakota can claim four significant precedents: It was first to elect a woman to statewide office, first to have a woman as Speaker of a state house of representatives, and first to have a female agriculture commissioner. A North Dakota woman also holds the record for female legislative longevity.

Women came within one vote of being enfranchised when the first territorial convention met in 1872. North Dakota still was a territory in 1879, when women won the vote for school elections. They lost some of those rights in a complicated 1883 act, but regained them with the new state's constitution in 1889. That was a factor in North Dakota's election of the first American woman to hold statewide office, as Laura Eisenhuth became state superintendent of schools in 1892. Heartened by her victory, feminists lobbied the legislature for expanded rights, but the turn of the century proved conservative on women's issues. North Dakota's suffrage society faded and did not revive until 1910, when Fargo's Mary Darrow became president of the organization, called State Votes for Women.

The legislature put the enfranchisement question on the ballot for 1914, and women won, yet lost. They had a majority of the tally, with 49,348 more men voting for it than against it, but the state constitution required a majority of all votes cast in the election, not merely a majority of those cast on the issue. Feminists fell 151 votes short of that goal.

Darrow died in April 1915 and was succeeded by Grace Clendening of Wimbledon. The 1917 legislature passed three supportive bills, but for legalistic reasons, none became effective. Two years later, all of North Dakota's members of the U.S. Congress voted for the Nineteenth Amendment, which granted voting rights to women, and the legislature ratified overwhelmingly it: 102–6 in the House; 41–4 in the Senate.

Women won election to the legislature at the first opportunity, in 1922, including Minnie Davenport Craig, who would become the nation's first female Speaker of a state house, in 1933. Berta E. Baker, elected state treasurer in 1928, was the second such woman in the nation, following only Indiana. Brynhild Haugland, Democrat of Minot, won her legislative seat in 1938 and went on to set the national longevity record. She served for a half-century, never losing an election between 1938 and her 1988 retirement.

In contrast to these early milestones, no woman won election to the North Dakota Senate until 1950. Even after the national women's movement revived in the 1970s, North Dakotans failed to choose women for Congress or to state offices. That began to change in 1988, when voters elected the nation's first female agriculture commissioner, Democrat Sarah Vogel. North Dakota's 1992 election of a female attorney general, Democrat Heidi Heitkamp, was earlier than most states. As of 2011, however, neither precedent has been repeated.

Despite its early milestones, North was the nation's last state to add a woman to its highest court, in 2002. As of 2011, North Dakotans still had not elected any woman to represent them in Washington, DC, or to be governor. The state treasurer was the only woman among its sixteen elected executives.

Key Facts

Statehood:	1889
Capital:	Bismarck
First women's rights organization:	No formal name, 1889
Pioneer publication:	*White Ribbon Bulletin*, 1899
First female lawyer:	Helen Hamilton, 1905
Full female enfranchisement:	1920
State ratification of Nineteenth Amendment:	Yes
First president of League of Women Voters:	Mrs. Kate S. Wilder, Fargo
First woman on state supreme court:	Judith Meierhenry, 2002
State ratification of Equal Rights Amendment:	Yes

Statewide Elective Officeholders

Governor:	None	
Lieutenant governor:	Ruth Meiers (D)	1984
Secretary of state:	None	
Attorney general:	Heidi Heitkamp (D)	1992
Treasurer:	Berta E. Baker (R)	1928
	Bernice Asbridge (R)	1968
	Kathi Gilmore (D)	1992
	Kelly Schmidt (R)	2004
Auditor:	Berta E. Baker (R)	1932
School superintendent:	Laura J. Eisenhuth (D)	1892
	Emma Bates (R)	1894
	Minnie Nielson (R)	1918
	Bertha Palmer (R)	1926
Agriculture commissioner:	Sarah Vogel (D)	1988
Tax commissioner:	Heidi Heitkamp (D)	1988
Public service commissioner:	Susan Wefald (R)	1992

State Legislature

Firsts

House:	Minnie Davenport Craig (NPL)[28]	1922
	Nellie Dougherty (D)	1922
Senate:	Agnes Kjorlie Geelan (R)	1950

Percentage of women in 2010–2011 session
(6 among 47 in senate; 15 among 94 in house): 15
National rank: 46

Presiding Officers

Speaker of the house:	Minnie Davenport Craig	1933
	Janet Wentz	2003
Senate president:	None	

Federal Elective Officeholders

U.S. Senate:	Jocelyn Birch Burdick (D)[29]	1992
U.S. House:	None	

---

[28] NPL stands for Non-Partisan League.

[29] Appointed, not elected

FURTHER READING

Hudson, Lois Phillips. 1964. *Reapers of the Dust: A Prairie Chronicle.* Boston: Little, Brown.

Fothergill, Alice. 2004. *Heads Above Water: Gender, Class, and Family in the Grand Forks Flood.* Albany: State University of New York Press.

Lindgren, H. Elaine. 1996. *Land in Her Own Name: Women as Homesteaders in North Dakota.* Norman: University of Oklahoma Press.

Raaen, Aagot. 1950. *Grass of the Earth: Immigrant Life in the Dakota Territory.* Northfield, MN: Norwegian-American Historical Association.

OHIO

Overview

Ohio's Oberlin College, founded in 1833, was the world's first to admit women, and in 1849, Oberlin roommates Lucy Stone and Antoinette Brown (later Blackwell) spoke on women's rights throughout the state. Ohio hosted the second women's rights convention in 1850 in Salem, where feminist Mariana Johnson lived. Betsey Mix Cowles was elected president. Sojourner Truth made her famous "Ain't I a Woman" speech at the 1852 convention in Akron. Frances Dana Gage, a nationally known newspaper columnist, also was a founder of Ohio feminism. The 1853 legislature reformed women's property rights, and senators tied 44–44 on full enfranchisement.

The Freedman's Bureau, which assisted former slaves after the Civil War, owed a great deal to Ohio's Josephine Griffing, and after moving to Washington, DC, she led the first suffrage society there. The Cincinnati Equal Rights Association formed in 1868, as the state's feminists regrouped under Hannah Tracy Cutler, author of *Woman as She Was, Is, and Should Be* (1846). Women in South Newbury attempted to vote in the 1870s, but more than a hundred signed a petition against voting. Enfranchised for school elections in 1894, women collected some forty thousand petitions in 1898 when threatened with repeal.

Ohio feminists followed the national trend and reenergized in 1912, when they conducted a referendum for full enfranchisement. They spent $40,000, but liquor interests spent $170,000, and suffragists were defeated. Undaunted, they collected 130,000 signatures to run a 1914 referendum but again lost, with 853,685 opposed and 518,295 in favor.

The 1917 legislature enfranchised women for presidential elections only, something that had been done in Illinois and elsewhere. Anti-suffragists went to court, and feminists had to pay the costs of defending the legislative act. They lost. The repeal went on that autumn's ballot, and Ohio men voted to take away even this limited right.

Feminists then concentrated on lobbying their members of Congress for the proposed Nineteenth Amendment to the U.S. Constitution. They did such an effective job that, after the 1918 elections, just two of Ohio's twenty-two U.S. House members voted negatively. The 1919 legislature was one of the first to ratify, but opponents again sued. In *Hawke v. Smith*, the U.S. Supreme Court ruled that opponents had no valid case. The decision came down in June 1920 and was key to the final ratification in August.

The town of Fairport Harbor elected Amy Kankonen as mayor in 1921, and Florence Allen won election to the Ohio Supreme Court in 1922. Five women won seats in the two legislative chambers that year. No other state replicated this, but, as elsewhere, Ohio women regressed in the next decades. No future year would be comparable to 1922.

Ohio's most outstanding woman in Congress was Cleveland's Frances Payne Bolton. She promoted legislation for nurses during World War II and, after the war, worked on African independence. Toledo's "Marcy" Kaptur exceeded Bolton's long tenure. She defeated an incumbent in 1982, and in 2011, had been in Congress longer than any other living woman.

Ohio has elected four women to financial offices, beginning in 1970. In 2006, it was the second-to-last state to set the precedent of a female secretary of state. Women have been mayors of major Ohio cities, but the state never has elected a woman to the U.S. Senate or as governor.

Key Facts

Statehood:	1803
Capital:	Columbus
First women's rights organization:	Ohio Woman's Rights Association, 1850

| Pioneer publications: | *The Ballot Box*, Sarah Langdon Williams, editor, 1876 |
| | *Suffrage Bulletin*, c.1912 |

First female lawyer:	Annette W. Cronise (later Lutes), 1873
Full female enfranchisement:	1920
State ratification of Nineteenth Amendment:	Yes
First president of League of Women Voters:	Miss Amy G. Maher
First woman on state supreme court:	Florence Allen, 1922
State ratification of Equal Rights Amendment:	Yes

Statewide Elective Officeholders

Governor:	None	
Lieutenant governor:	Nancy Putnam Hollister (R)	1994
	Maureen O'Connor (R)	1998
	Mary Taylor (R)	2010
Secretary of state:	Jennifer Brunner (D)	2006
Attorney general:	None	
Treasurer:	Gertrude Donahey (D)	1970
	Jennette Bradley (R)	2004
Auditor:	Betty Montgomery (R)	2002
	Mary Taylor (R)	2006
School superintendent:	Not elected	

State Legislature

Firsts
House:	Nettie M. Clapp (R)	1922
	Lulu T. Gleason (D)	1922
	Adelaide Ott (R)	1922
Senate:	Nettie B. Loughead (R)	1922
	Maude C. Waitt (R)	1922

Percentage of women in 2010–2011 session	
(9 among 33 in senate; 21 among 99 in house):	23
National rank:	28

Presiding Officers
| Speaker of the house: | Jo Ann Davidson | 1995 |
| Senate president: | None | |

Federal Elective Officeholders

U.S. Senate:	None	
U.S. House:	Frances Payne Bolton (R)	1940
	Mary Rose Oakar (D)	1976
	Jean Spencer Ashbrook (R)	1982[30]
	Marcia Carolyn "Marcy" Kaptur (D)	1982
	Deborah Pryce (R)	1992
	Stephanie Tubbs Jones (D)	1998
	Jean Schmidt (R)	2005[31]

---

[30] Special election; brief tenure.

[31] Special election; subsequently reelected.

Betty Sutton (D)	2006
Marcia L. Fudge (D)	2008
Mary Jo Kilroy (D)	2008

FURTHER READING

Booth, Stephane. 2001. *Buckeye Women: The History of Ohio's Daughters*. Athens: Ohio University Press.
McGovern, Frances. 2002. *Fun, Cheap, and Easy: My Life in Ohio Politics, 1949–1964*. Akron, OH: University of Akron Press.
Morton, Marian J. 1995. *Women in Cleveland: An Illustrated History*. Bloomington: Indiana University Press.

OKLAHOMA

Overview

Except for missionaries, whites were not allowed to settle in what was called the Indian Territory until 1889. The first suffrage society formed in 1890 at Guthrie, and the legislature of the Oklahoma Territory granted the vote for school elections. Full enfranchisement failed in the territorial house by only three votes.

It passed a full enfranchisement bill in 1897, but the measure failed in the upper chamber by one vote—with anti-suffragists from Albany, New York, speaking against it. Feminists formed the Twin Territories Suffrage Association and held their 1905 meeting in Indian Territory, at Chickasha. With headquarters in Guthrie, suffragists campaigned hard for their rights to be included in the 1907 constitution for statehood, but they failed.

Feminists conducted a 1910 referendum and also lost, with 88,808 affirmative votes and 128,928 negative. They tried again in 1918 and were successful, despite having to overcome an extremely high barrier—all unmarked ballots were counted as voting against. Despite this clear victory, conservatives tried, without success, to prevent certification of the election. Women had to run still another difficult campaign to ratify the Nineteenth Amendment in 1920, and Katherine Pierce, who chaired the campaign, died after a strenuous debate.

It was particularly ironic, then, that later in 1920 Oklahomans elected anti-suffragist Alice Mary Robertson as the nation's second woman in Congress. On the positive side, two progressive women won seats in the legislature that year. Two Oklahoma tribes also had female chiefs in the 1920s. Lucy Tayish Eads headed the Kaw, or Kansa, and Alice Brown Davis was chief of the Oklahoma Seminoles.

Oklahoma City elected Hannah Atkins, an African American, to the legislature in 1968 and, in 1971, chose Patience Letting as mayor. LaDonna Harris was nationally known as the founder of Americans for Indian Opportunity, and Wilma Mankiller became Cherokee chief in 1985.

Oklahoma did not do well at electing women to top state positions. None won a statewide race until 1980, and the post, corporation commissioner, does not exist in most states. Mary Fallon became the exception during the next decade and attained the governor's office with the 2010 election. Her departure from Congress meant that no women were in the state's seven-member delegation.

Key Facts

Statehood:	1907
Capital:	Oklahoma City
First women's rights organization:	No formal name, 1889
Pioneer publication:	None
First female lawyer:	Laura Lykins, 1898
Full female enfranchisement:	1918
State ratification of Nineteenth Amendment:	Yes
First president of League of Women Voters:	Miss Aloysius Larch-Miller
First woman on state supreme court:	Alma Bell Wilson, 1982
State ratification of Equal Rights Amendment:	No

Statewide Elective Officeholders

Governor:	Mary Fallin (R)	2010
Lieutenant governor:	Mary Fallin (R)	1994
Secretary of state:	Appointed by governor	
Attorney general:	None	
Treasurer:	Claudette Henry (R)	1990
School superintendent:	Sandy Garrett (D)	1990
Commissioner of charities and corrections:		
	Kate Bernard	1907
Corporation commissioner:	Norma Eagleton (D)	1980
	Denise Bode (R)	1996
	Dana Murphy (R)	2008
Insurance commissioner:	Kim Holland (D)	2004
Labor commissioner:	Brenda Reneau Wynn (R)	1994

State Legislature

Firsts

House:	Bessie S. Colgin (R)	1918
Senate:	Mirabeau Lamar Cole Looney (D)	1920

Percentage of women in 2010–2011 session
   (4 among 48 in senate; 15 among 101 in house):   13
National rank: 49
Presiding Officers
  Speaker of the house: None
  Senate president: None

Federal Elective Officeholders

U.S. Senate:	None	
U.S. House:	Alice Mary Robertson (R)	1920
	Mary Fallin (R)	2006

FURTHER READING

Harris, LaDonna. 2000. *LaDonna Harris: A Comanche Life.* Lincoln: University of Nebraska Press.
Mankiller, Wilma Pearl. 2000. *A Chief and Her People.* New York: St. Martin's.
Reese, Linda Williams. 1997. *Women of Oklahoma, 1890–1920.* Norman: University of Oklahoma Press.

OREGON

Overview

More than most states, Oregon's movement for the vote is identified with one woman: Portland's Abigail Scott Duniway. She led about a dozen people who met in the capital of Salem in 1870. Three physicians, Bethenia Owens-Adair, Mary P. Sawtelle, and Mary A. Thompson, also were leaders. They won school enfranchisement in 1876, but in 1896 the Oregon Supreme Court struck down women's right to serve on school boards.

Feminists conducted losing referenda for full rights in 1884 and 1900 but were energized in 1905, when National American Woman Suffrage Association met in Portland. A 1906 referendum nonetheless lost, as did one in 1908. Younger feminists openly opposed the 1910 effort, which would have enfranchised taxpaying women only. That failed, too, but new leadership with more modern ideas finally won the 1912 campaign. This victory came just a year after suffragists' big win in California in 1911, and Duniway's image of losing elections must be countered by the fact that she ran more enfranchisement campaigns than anyone else. No other state equaled Oregon's six referenda.

The first woman was elected to the Oregon House in 1914, and the first female senator followed the next year. In 1920, when Oregon ratified the Nineteenth Amendment, Mrs. Alexander Thompson introduced it to her colleagues in the House. Helen Ekin Starrett was honored as the only woman still alive who had attended the first meeting a half-century earlier.

Nan Wood Honeyman won election to Congress in 1936, and Portland elected Dorothy McCullough Lee as mayor in 1948. Edith Starrett Green defeated an incumbent for Congress in 1954 and played a strong role in passage of the 1963 Equal Pay Act. Maurine Brown Neuberger won a U.S. Senate seat in 1960, an era when few women ran.

Oregonians were slow to send women to Salem and statewide office, as the first was not until 1978. After that, women surged ahead, and Barbara Roberts was elected governor in 1990. Oregon thus became one of a handful of states that have elected women both as governor and U.S. senator.

The 2000s were less progressive, and in 2011 Oregon had no women in its seven-member congressional delegation. Just two held state executive offices, and they were relatively lowly positions.

Key Facts

Statehood:	1859
Capital:	Salem
First women's rights organization:	No formal name, 1870
Pioneer publication:	*New Northwest*, Abigail Scott Duniway, editor, 1857
First female lawyer:	Mary A. Leonard, 1886
Full female enfranchisement:	1912
State ratification of Nineteenth Amendment:	Yes
First president of League of Women Voters:	Mrs. Charles E. Curry
First woman on state supreme court:	Betty Roberts, 1982
State ratification of Equal Rights Amendment:	Yes

Statewide Elective Officeholders

Governor:	Barbara Roberts (D)	1990
Lieutenant governor:	Office does not exist	
Secretary of state:	Norma Paulus (R)	1976
	Barbara Roberts (D)	1984
	Kate Brown (D)	2008
Attorney general:	None	
Financial officer(s):	None	
School superintendent:[32]	Norma Paulus	1990
	Susan Castillo	2002
Labor commissioner:	Mary Wendy Roberts (D)	1978

State Legislature

Firsts

House:	Marian B. Towne (D)	1914

---

[32] Office is nonpartisan.

Senate:	Kathryn Clarke (R)	1915[33]
Percentage of women in 2010–2011 session		
(9 among 30 in senate; 16 among 60 in house):	16	
National rank:	27	
Presiding Officers		
Speaker of the house:	Vera Katz	1985
	Beverly Clarno	1995
	Lynn Snodgrass	1999
	Karen Minnus	2003
Senate president:	None	

Federal Elective Officeholders

U.S. Senate:	Maurine Brown Neuberger (D)	1960
U.S. House:	Nan Wood Honeyman (D)	1936
	Edith Starrett Green (D)	1954
	Elizabeth Furse (D)	1992
	Darlene Hooley (D)	1998

FURTHER READING

Duniway, Abigail Scott. 1914. *Path Breaking: An Autobiographical History of the Equal Suffrage Movement in Pacific Coast States.* Portland, OR: James, Kerns, and Abbott Co. Reprint, New York: Schoken, 1971.

Edwards, G. Thomas. 1990. *Sowing Good Seeds: The Northwest Suffrage Campaigns of Susan B. Anthony.* Portland: Oregon Historical Society.

Lansing, Jewell Beck. 2003. *Portland: People, Politics, and Power, 1851–2001.* Corvallis: Oregon State University Press.

Leasher, Evelyn M. 1981. *Oregon Women: A Bio-Bibliography.* Corvallis: Oregon State University Press.

PENNSYLVANIA

Overview

Philadelphia's Lucretia Mott was the primary motivator for the world's first women's rights meeting. It occurred because she visited her sister near Seneca Falls, New York, in 1848. Elizabeth Cady Stanton lived there, and Mott had greatly influenced young Stanton when the two met at the World Anti-Slavery Convention in London in 1840.

Feminists garnered favorable attention at the 1876 celebration of the nation's one-hundredth birthday in Philadelphia, but state law was such that they had to wait for Susan B. Anthony's arrival to rent their headquarters. She was the only unmarried woman among them, and married women could not sign a contract in Pennsylvania.

Rachel Foster Avery was the most active suffragist in the next decades, but she worked more in other states than in her own. The fact that Pennsylvania's capital, Harrisburg, was far from its major population centers probably was a negative factor in suffragist failure to lobby. However, lawmakers might have been more receptive than expected. Without any real lobbying effort, the 1883 legislature passed a resolution calling on Congress to adopt a federal amendment enfranchising women.

Pennsylvania feminists conducted their only referendum for the vote in 1915 and lost with 441,034 opposed and 385,348 in favor. The state constitution did not permit another referendum for five years, and by then, the federal amendment had been adopted.

Eight women won election to the legislature in 1922—more than in any other state. Philadelphia's Crystal Bird Fauset became the first African American woman in a state legislature in 1938. Women regressed in the next decades, though, and Pennsylvania elected none to statewide office until 1954—a precedent set elsewhere in 1892.

---

[33] Special election.

Women did not win future elections in the numbers that could have been expected in so large a state: for decades, Pennsylvania was the most populous state with no women in its congressional delegation. The first three women in the U.S. House from Pennsylvania succeeded their husbands in the 1950s, and no women won in the 1970s and 1980s, when other states elected many women to Congress. In 2011, the state had just one woman among its nineteen U.S. House members, and no woman ever has been a U.S. senator or Pennsylvania governor.

Key Facts

Statehood:	1787
Capital:	Harrisburg
First women's rights organization:	No formal name, 1866
Pioneer publication:	None
First female lawyer:	Carrie S. Burnham (later Kilgore), 1884
Full female enfranchisement:	1920
State ratification of Nineteenth Amendment:	Yes
First president of League of Women Voters:	Mrs. Harriet L. Hubbs
First woman on state supreme court:	Sandra Schultz Newman, 1996
State ratification of Equal Rights Amendment:	Yes

Statewide Elective Officeholders

Governor:	None	
Lieutenant governor:	Catherine Baker Knoll (D)	2000
Secretary of state:	Genevieve Blatt (D)	1954
Attorney general:	Linda L. Kelly (R)	2010
Treasurer:	Grace McCalmont (D)	1960
	Catherine Baker Knoll (D)	1988
	Barbara H. Hafer (R)[34]	1998
	Robin Weissman (D)	2006
Auditor:	Grace McCalmont (D)	1964
	Barbara H. Hafer (R)	1988
School superintendent:	Not elected	

State Legislature

Firsts

House:	Alice M. Bentley (R)	1922
	Rosa S. De Young (R)	1922
	Sarah McCune Gallagher (R)	1922
	Helen Grimes (R)	1922
	Sarah Gertrude MacKinney (R)	1922
	Lillie H. Pitts (R)	1922
	Martha G. Speiser (R)	1922
	Martha G. Thomas (R)	1922
Senate:	Flora M. Vare (R)	1924

Percentage of women in 2010–2011 session
   (11 among 50 in senate; 33 among 203 in house):   17

National rank: 42

Presiding Officers

---

[34] Became a Democrat in 2004.

Speaker of the house:	None
Senate president:	None

Federal Elective Officeholders

U.S. Senate:	None	
U.S. House:	Veronica Grace Boland[35]	1942
	Vera Daerr Buchanan	1950
	Kathryn Elizabeth Granahan (D)	1956
	Marjorie Margolies-Mezvinsky (D)	1992
	Melissa A. Hart (R)	2000
	Allyson Y. Schwartz (D)	2004
	Kathleen "Kathy" Dahlkemper (D)	2008

FURTHER READING

Bacon, Margaret Hope. 1999. *Valiant Friend: The Life of Lucretia Mott.* Philadelphia: Friends General Conference.

Branson, Susan. 2001. *These Fiery Frenchified Dames: Women and Political Culture in Early National Philadelphia.* Philadelphia: University of Pennsylvania Press.

Katzenstein, Caroline. 1955. *Lifting the Curtain: The State and National Woman Suffrage Campaigns in Pennsylvania as I Saw Them.* Philadelphia, Dorrance.

Levinstein, Lisa. 2009. *A Movement Without Marches: African American Women and the Politics of Poverty in Postwar Philadelphia.* Chapel Hill: University of North Carolina Press.

RHODE ISLAND

Overview

Rhode Island saw the nation's first property rights reform in 1841 and, unlike in most states, married women there could conduct business as though unmarried. The state's leading feminist was Paulina Kellogg Wright Davis, who planned the first national women's rights convention. Because of its proximity for activists, the meeting was held in the central Massachusetts town of Worcester, but Davis organized the speakers and agenda from her home in Providence.

A generation later, in 1887, Sarah Doyle and Elizabeth Buffum Chace were the major leaders when Rhode Island conducted the first enfranchisement referendum in the East. Supporters worked hard but failed overwhelmingly: 21,957 men voted negatively, while just 6,889 were positive. From 1889 onward, they lobbied for the vote for presidential elections only—something that legislators could grant without a referendum—but almost twenty years passed before the bill even made it out of committee.

Funded by Alva Vanderbilt Belmont, younger women opened a summer headquarters in Newport in 1912. Rev. Anna Garlin Spencer was a major leader, and the legislature enfranchised women for presidential elections in 1917. That made the state's congressional delegation much more aware of women's potential political impact, and in 1919 they joined those in Maine as the only delegations in the Northeast to vote unanimously for the Nineteenth Amendment. The legislature ratified in January 1920, and that fall Democrats nominated suffrage president Elizabeth Upham Yates for lieutenant governor.

She did not win, and Rhode Island remained basically conservative on feminist issues. When it finally had its first female lawyer in 1920, for instance, only Delaware and the Alaska Territory had not set that precedent. Providence voters did elect a woman to the legislature at the first 1922 opportunity, but none won statewide office until 1982, sixty years after Rhode Island women began voting.

Rhode Islanders set a major precedent in 1986, when they elected the nation's first female attorney general. The state has had just one woman in the U.S. House, however, and as of 2011 no women were in its four-member congressional delegation. None has been either U.S. senator or governor.

---

[35] Two-month term.

Key Facts

Statehood:	1790
Capital:	Providence
First women's rights organization:	Rhode Island Woman Suffrage Association, 1868
Pioneer publication:	*Pioneer and Woman's Advocate*, Anna W. Spencer, editor, 1852
	The Amendment, Lillie B. Chace Wyman, editor, 1887
	The Woman Citizen, Jeannette French, editor, 1905
First female lawyer:	Ada L. Sawyer, 1920
Full female enfranchisement:	1920
State ratification of Nineteenth Amendment:	Yes
First president of League of Women Voters:	Miss Mary B. Anthony
First woman on state supreme court:	Florence Kerins Murray, 1979
State ratification of Equal Rights Amendment:	Yes

Statewide Elective Officeholders

Governor:	None	
Lieutenant governor:	Elizabeth H. Roberts (D)	2006
Secretary of state:	Susan L. Farmer (R)	1982
	Kathleen S. Connell (D)	1986
	Barbara A. Leonard (R)	1992
Attorney general:	Arlene Violet (R)	1984
Treasurer:	Nancy J. Mayer (R)	1992
	Gina Raimondo (D)	2010
School superintendent:	Not elected	

State Legislature

Firsts		
House:	Isabella Ahearn O'Neill (D)	1922
Senate:	Lulu M. Schlesinger (R)	1928
Percentage of women in 2010–2011 session (10 among 38 in senate; 19 among 75 in house):	26	
National rank:	19	
Presiding Officers		
Speaker of the house:	None	
Senate president:	M. Teresa Paiva-Weed	2009

Federal Elective Officeholders

U.S. Senate:	None	
U.S. House:	Claudine Cmarada Schneider (R)	1980

FURTHER READING

Salitan, Lucille, and Eve Lewis Perera, eds. 1994. *Virtuous Lives: Four Quaker Sisters Remember Family Life, Abolitionism, and Women's Suffrage.* New York: Continuum.

Sterne, Eleanor S. 2003. *Ballots and Bibles: Ethnic Politics and the Catholic Church in Providence.* Ithaca, NY: Cornell University Press.

Stevens, Elizabeth C. 2003. *Elizabeth Buffum Chace and Lillie Chace Wyman: A Century of Abolitionist, Suffragist, and Workers' Rights Activism.* Jefferson, NC: McFarland.

SOUTH CAROLINA

Overview

The state's first feminist society, formed in 1870, was of Civil War victors. Its leadership was largely male, and the most prominent females were three sisters in the Rollins family. The Rollins were Charleston natives of mixed-race heritage, viewed as the city's most wealthy African Americans. Protected by federal troops, some black women voted until 1877, when the occupation soldiers were withdrawn. Whites returned to control of state government then, and South Carolina's future suffragists were white.

Virginia Durant Young, feminist editor of the *Fairfax Enterprise*, organized a second association in 1890. When she spoke to the legislature, it was the first time that a woman had done so—a precedent set elsewhere a half-century earlier. She recruited some 250 members, but the group faded with her 1906 death. Columbia's Dr. Jane Bruce Guignard joined with national organizer Lavinia Engle to regroup for a third time in 1914. Women demonstrated some radicalism with a 1915 parade, and the South Carolina Equal Suffrage League soon had more than fifteen hundred members in eight locations.

With Dr. Love Rosa Hirschmann Gannt leading the lobbying, senators debated the enfranchisement issue for three days in 1917. In 1918, Mrs. W. C. Cathcart of Columbia won a coveted position on the Democratic National Committee, and a South Carolina pro-suffragist defeated an anti-suffragist for the U.S. Senate that year. Nevertheless, the legislature did not ratify the Nineteenth Amendment.

Voters elected a woman to the South Carolina Senate in 1928. But, in a reversal of the usual order, none was sent to the lower chamber until a special election in January 1945 when Harriet Catherine Frazier Johnson was the last woman in the nation to be the first in her state house. That was during World War II, when South Carolina became known for its longtime total ban on divorce. It also barred women from juries until a 1975 U.S. Supreme Court ruling.

The state was unique in having had two women serve in the U.S. House before it had two female state representatives. Moreover, a special congressional election in 1962 was between two women: Corrine Boyd Riley defeated Martha T. Fitzgerald, a twenty-two-year veteran of the South Caroline House. The special election was to fill a brief vacancy, and Riley did not run for a full congressional term.

South Carolina did set something of a precedent in 1978, when Nancy Stevenson became the nation's third female lieutenant governor. She was South Carolina's first woman in statewide office, a precedent set elsewhere in 1892. In 1986, South Carolina had its first woman elected to the U.S. House in her own right. Elizabeth J. Patterson, a progressive Democrat, lost her reelection in 1992, ironically the Year of the Woman.

In 2010, however, South Carolina defied expectations and elected a female governor. Nikki Haley, whose parents emigrated from India, was the state's second Republican woman to win a statewide election. She was the only woman among eight statewide elective offices, most of which never have been held by a woman. The 2011 legislature ranked last in the nation for its percentage of women, and the South Carolina Senate was singular in having none among its forty-six members. No women have been part of any of the state's eight-member congressional delegation since 1992.

Key Facts

Statehood:	1788
Capital:	Columbia
First women's rights organization:	No formal name, 1870
Pioneer publication:	None
First female lawyer:	Claudia J. Sullivan, 1918
Full female enfranchisement:	1920
State ratification of Nineteenth Amendment:	No
First president of League of Women Voters:	Mrs. Bertha Munsell
First woman on state supreme court:	Jean Hoefer Toal, 1988
State ratification of Equal Rights Amendment:	No

Statewide Elective Officeholders

Governor:	Nikki Haley (R)	2010
Lieutenant governor:	Nancy Stevenson (D)	1978
Secretary of state:	None	
Attorney general:	None	
Financial officer(s):	None	
School superintendent:	Barbara Nielsen (R)	1990
	Inez Tenenbaum (D)	1998

State Legislature

Firsts

House:	Harriet Catherine Frazier Johnson (D)	1945
Senate:	Mary Gordon Ellis (D)	1928

Percentage of women in 2010–2011 session
  (0 among 46 in senate; 16 among 124 in house):   9
National rank: 50

Presiding Officers
  Speaker of the house: None
  Senate president: None

Federal Elective Officeholders

U.S. Senate:	None	
U.S. House:	Elizabeth Hawley Gasque (D)[36]	1938
	Clara Gooding Macmillan (D)[34]	1939
	Willa Lybrand Fulmer (D)[34]	1944
	Elizabeth J. Patterson (D)	1986

FURTHER READING

Mack, Kibibi Voloria C. 1999. *Parlor Ladies and Ebony Drudges: African American Women, Class, and Work in a South Carolina Community.* Knoxville: University of Tennessee Press.

McCurry, Stephanie. 1995. *Masters of Small Worlds: Yeoman Households, Gender Relations, and the Political Culture of the Antebellum South Carolina Low Country.* New York: Oxford University Press.

Spruill, Marjorie, with Valinda Littlefield and Joan Marie Johnson, eds. 2009–2012. *South Carolina Women: Their Lives and Times.* Volumes 1–3. Athens: University of Georgia Press.

SOUTH DAKOTA

Overview

The Dakota Territorial Legislature came within one vote of enfranchising women in 1872, which would have emulated the Wyoming Territory and Utah Territory in 1869 and 1870, respectively. Marietta Bones of Day County was the leading feminist. She had support from nationally known feminist Matilda Joslyn Gage, who visited her adult children in Aberdeen in 1883. They lobbied the legislature, which passed a bill for full rights in 1885, but the territorial governor (who

---

[36] Special election; served less than a full term.

himself was appointed, not elected) vetoed it. South Dakota and North Dakota became states in 1889, and in both, women had the right to vote in school elections only.

An organization for full voting rights began that same year, and women ran the first of five campaigns. South Dakota's 1890 referendum was only the seventh in the nation, and national leaders came to help. Despite more than sixteen hundred speeches throughout the rural state, they lost with 45,862 opposed and 23,790 in favor. Fewer outsiders were involved in the 1894 and 1898 campaigns, and women came close to victory in 1898.

As elsewhere, the movement lagged at the turn of the century, and the enfranchisement issue did not return to the ballot for more than a decade. Mamie Shields Pyle led the campaigns in 1914 and 1916, and women finally won in 1918. South Dakota's five referenda were more than in any other state except Oregon which required six for victory. When the Nineteenth Amendment to the U.S. Constitution came to South Dakota in 1919, legislators ratified unanimously.

Mamie Shield Pyle's daughter, Gladys Pyle, became the state's most significant political woman. The first female legislator, she also was the first to win statewide office. Nationally, she was the first unmarried woman to launch a serious campaign for governor. She lost the 1930 race but briefly served in the U.S. Senate in 1938.

A long string of women followed Pyle as secretary of state, but no woman won another executive office until 1956. The first on the Public Utilities Commission was in 1974, earlier than most states. The first as lieutenant governor was in 1994. In between, in 1987, legislators elected Debra Anderson of Sioux Falls as Speaker of the state house, making South Dakota the sixth state for this precedent. In contrast to this early milestone, the 2002 addition of a woman to the South Dakota Supreme Court was the nation's last.

National attention focused on the 2004 special election of Stephanie Herseth for Congress. In a hard-fought race, she narrowly defeated the Republican incumbent. She married and had a baby while in office and was Stephanie Herseth Sandlin in 2010, when she lost to Republican Kristi Noem. As of 2011, Noem was the only woman in South Dakota's three-member congressional delegation, while no women held any of ten elected state offices.

Key Facts

Statehood:	1889
Capital:	Pierre
First women's rights organization:	No formal name, 1870
Pioneer publication:	*South Dakota Messenger*, Ruth B. Hipple, editor, c.1914
First female lawyer:	Nellie Douglas, 1893
Full female enfranchisement:	1918
State ratification of Nineteenth Amendment:	Yes
First president of League of Women Voters:	Not available
First woman on state supreme court:	Judith Meierhenry, 2002
State ratification of Equal Rights Amendment:	No

Statewide Elective Officeholders

Governor:	None	
Lieutenant governor:	Carole Hillard (R)	1994
Secretary of state:	Gladys Pyle (R)	1926
	Elizabeth Coyle (R)	1930
	Myrtle Morrison (D)	1932
	Goldie Wells (D)	1936
	Olive Ringsrud (R)	1938
	L. M. Larsen (R)	1942
	Annamae Riff (R)	1946
	Geraldine Ostroot (R)	1950
	Clara Halls (R)	1956
	Selma Sandness (D)	1958
	Essie Wiedenman (R)	1960
	Alma Larson (R)	1964

	Lorna Herseth (R)[37]	1972
	Alice Kundert (R)	1978
	Joyce Hazeltine (R)	1988
Attorney general:	None	
Treasurer:	None	
Auditor:	Fay Albee (R)	1956
	Harriet Horning (D)	1958
	Betty Lou Casey (R)	1960
	Alice Kundert (R)	1968
School superintendent:	None	
Public utilities commissioner:	Norma Kinkel (D)	1974
	Char Fischer (R)	1978
	Laska Schoenfelder (R)	1988
	Pam Nelson (D)	1998

State Legislature

Firsts

| House: | Gladys Pyle (R) | 1922 |
| Senate: | Jessie E. Sanders (R) | 1936 |

Percentage of women in 2010–2011 session
    (7 among 35 in senate; 14 among 70 in house):   20
National rank: 37
Presiding Officers

| Speaker of the house: | Debra Anderson | 1987 |
| Senate president: | None | |

Federal Elective Officeholders

U.S. Senate:	Gladys Pyle (R)[38]	1938
	Vera C. Bushfield (R)[39]	1948
U.S. House:	Stephanie Herseth Sandlin (D)	1994
	Kristi Noem (R)	201

FURTHER READING

Petrillo, Larissa. 2007. *Being Lakota: Identity and Tradition on the Pine Ridge Reservation.* Lincoln: University of Nebraska.

South Dakota Commission on the Status of Women. 1975. *South Dakota Women, 1850–1919: A Bio-Bibliography.* Pierre: South Dakota Commission on the Status of Women.

Wagner, Sally Roesch, ed. 1989–1994. *Daughters of Dakota.* Volumes 1–3. Yankton, SD: Daughters of Dakota.

TENNESSEE

Overview

Tennessee always will have a special place in the political history of women because it provided the last crucial ratification of the Nineteenth Amendment, which ensured women the right to vote in every state.

---

[37] Grandmother of U.S. representative Stephanie Herseth Sandlin.

[38] Elected to a two-month term.

[39] Appointed, not elected.

Its pioneer feminist was Elizabeth "Lide" Avery Meriwether of Memphis in the 1870s, but no statewide organization truly formed until 1900. At that late date, a Tennessee mother could not even legally name a guardian for her own children, and her husband was entitled to her wages. The Tennessee Supreme Court barred women from the practice of law until 1901—Iowa had set that precedent in 1869.

The turning point finally came in 1914, when the National American Woman Suffrage Association held its convention at Nashville's famed Ryman Auditorium. Membership grew, and in 1919, the legislature granted women voting rights for presidential and municipal elections. Thousands of women registered to vote, but anti-suffragists sued. A lower court agreed with opponents, but the Tennessee Supreme Court ruled in favor. The next year, under the leadership of Margaret Ford, lawmakers provided the vital ratification of the federal amendment that ensured full enfranchisement in every state. The two-week fight on the issue was dramatic, with some legislators going to Alabama to prevent a quorum.

Just months later, in January 1921, a woman won a special election for state senator, and another won a U.S. House seat at the next general election. However, Tennessee's constitution elects fewer offices than most Southern states, and other than the lowly post of public service commissioner, no woman has been elected to any of six executive positions.

The state elected its first female U.S. representative who was not preceded by a husband in 1974, and none followed her until the 2000s. As of 2011, Tennessee had two women in its eleven-member congressional delegation, and no woman ever has been a U.S. senator or governor.

Key Facts

Statehood:	1796
Capital:	Nashville
First women's rights organization:	No formal name, 1870
Pioneer publication:	None
First female lawyer:	Marion Scudder Griffin, 1907
Full female enfranchisement:	1920
State ratification of Nineteenth Amendment:	Yes
First president of League of Women Voters:	Mrs. George Fort Milton
First woman on state supreme court:	Holly M. Kirby, 1995
State ratification of Equal Rights Amendment:	No

Statewide Elective Officeholders

Governor:	None	
Lieutenant governor:	Office does not exist	
Secretary of state:	Chosen by legislature	
Attorney general:	None	
Financial officer(s):	Chosen by legislature	
School superintendent:	Not elected	
Public service commission:	Jane Eskind (D)	1980
	Sara Kyle (D)	1994

State Legislature

Firsts		
House:	Marion Scudder Griffin (D)	1922
Senate:	Anna Lee Keys Worley (D)	1921
Percentage of women in 2010–2011 session		
(7 among 33 in senate; 17 among 99 in house):	18	
National rank:	40	
Presiding Officers		
Speaker of the house:	None	
Senate president:	None	

Federal Elective Officeholders

U.S. Senate:	None	
U.S. House:	Willa McCord Blake Eslick (D)[40]	1932
	Louise Goff Reece (R)[38]	1961
	Irene Bailey Baker (R)[38]	1964
	Marilyn Laird Lloyd (D)	1974
	Marsha Blackburn	2002
	Diane Black (R)	2010

FURTHER READING

Little, Kimberly K. 2009. *You Must Be From the North: Southern White Women in the Memphis Civil Rights Movement*. Jackson: University Press of Mississippi.

Spruill, Marjorie, ed. 1995. *Votes for Women! The Woman Suffrage Movement in Tennessee, the South, and the Nation*. Knoxville: University of Tennessee Press.

Ramsey, Sonya Yvette. 2008. *Reading, Writing, and Segregation: A Century of Black Women Teachers in Nashville*. Urbana: University of Illinois Press.

Taylor, A. Elizabeth. 1957. *The Woman Suffrage Movement in Tennessee*. New York: Bookman Associates.

Wells-Barnett, Ida. 1995. *The Memphis Diary of Ida B. Wells*. Edited by Miriam DeCosta-Willis. Boston: Beacon Press.

TEXAS

Overview

Sarah W. Hiatt drafted an enfranchisement bill for the state of Texas in 1875, but feminists did not organize until 1893. Hortense Moore, the first woman admitted to the state bar in 1910, was an active suffragist, and Jovita Idar formed the Mexican Feminist League in south Texas in 1911. In 1918, the legislature granted the vote for party primaries—a legalism that excluded black women. Annie Webb Blanton, an active feminist, was elected superintendent of schools that fall.

Legislators also put a full-rights referendum on the ballot for May 1919, and led by Minnie Fisher Cunningham, women ran a strong campaign but lost with 141,773 in favor and 166,893 opposed. The next month Congress passed the Nineteenth Amendment that ensured voting rights for all women, and Texas lawmakers were quick to ratify.

Young Dallas attorney Edith E. Therrel Wilmans defeated an incumbent legislator in 1922, and in 1924, Miriam "Ma" Ferguson won the governorship. Although Ferguson was controversial, Texans again elected her in 1932. In 2011, she remains the only female governor to have won nonconsecutive terms. In the same era, Georgetown's Jessie Daniel Ames, a white woman, worked nationally to end lynching.

The next decades were regressive, but in 1953, President Dwight D. Eisenhower appointed Houston's Oveta Culp Hobby as the second woman in the cabinet. Lera Millard Thomas became the state's first woman elected to the U.S. House in 1966.

San Antonio elected Lila Banks Cockrell as mayor in 1975. After her 1977 election as Austin's mayor and additional marriages, Carole Keeton McClellan Rylander Strayhorn would hold two statewide offices. Annette Strauss followed as mayor of Dallas in 1987, and Fort Worth elected Kay Granger in 1991.

Houston representative Barbara Jordan became a household name in the 1970s, and in 1990, Texas became the first state to have had two female governors, when Democrat Ann Richards won. In 1998, Texas tied with Iowa and followed only North Dakota in electing a woman as agriculture commissioner. Its lieutenant governorship, however, is unusually powerful, and no woman has held it.

After losing the Republican gubernatorial nomination in 2010, U.S. senator Kay Bailey Hutchison announced her intention not to run in the 2012 election. The state's thirty-two-member delegation to the U.S. House in 2011 included just three women: Kay Granger, a white Republican, as well as black Democrats Eddie Bernice Johnson and Sheila Jackson-Lee. Women held just two of nine statewide executive offices: comptroller and railroad commissioner.

---

[40] Special election; served only briefly.

Key Facts

Statehood:	1845
Capital:	Austin
First women's rights organization:	Texas Woman Suffrage Association, 1893
Pioneer publication:	None
First female lawyer:	Hortense Moore, 1910
Full female enfranchisement:	1920
State ratification of Nineteenth Amendment:	Yes
First president of League of Women Voters:	Jessie Daniel Ames
First woman on state supreme court:	Rose Spector, 1992
State ratification of Equal Rights Amendment:	Yes

Statewide Elective Officeholders

Governor:	Miriam "Ma" Ferguson (D)	1924
	Miriam "Ma" Ferguson (D)	1932
	Ann W. Richards (D)	1990
Lieutenant governor:	None	
Secretary of state:	Not elected	
Attorney general:	None	
Treasurer:	Ann W. Richards (D)	1982
	Kay Bailey Hutchison (R)	1990
	Martha Whitehead (D)	1994
Comptroller:	Carole Keeton McClellan Rylander Strayhorn (R)[41]	1998
	Susan Combs (R)	2006
School superintendent:	Annie Webb Blanton (D)	1918
Railroad commissioner:	Carole Keeton McClellan Rylander Strayhorn (R)	1994
	Elizabeth Ames Jones (R)	2004
Agriculture commissioner:	Susan Combs (R)	1998

State Legislature

Firsts

House:	Edith E. Therrel Wilmans (D)	1922
Senate:	Margie Neal (D)	1926
Percentage of women in 2010–2011 session (61 among 31 in senate; 32 among 150 in house):	21	
National rank:	35	

Presiding Officers

Speaker of the house:	None
Senate president:	None

Federal Elective Officeholders

U.S. Senate:	Kay Bailey Hutchison (R)	1993
U.S. House:	Lera Millard Thomas (D)	1966

---

[41] Previously was a Democrat.

Barbara Charline Jordan (D)	1972
Eddie Bernice Johnson (D)	1992
Sheila Jackson-Lee (D)	1994
Kay Granger (R)	1996
Shelley S. Gibbs (R)[42]	2006

FURTHER READING

Ivins, Molly. 2004. *Who Let the Dogs In? Incredible Political Animals I Have Known.* Random House.

Jones, Nancy Baker. 2000. *Capitol Women: Texas Female Legislators, 1923–1999.* Austin: University of Texas Press.

Jordan, Barbara. 1979. *Barbara Jordan, A Self Portrait.* Garden City, NY: Doubleday.

Richards, Ann. 1989. *Straight from the Heart.* New York: Simon and Schuster.

UTAH

Overview

Settled in 1847 by the Church of Latter-day Saints (LDS), or Mormons, the territory originally was a theocracy that promoted polygamy. As non–Mormon men moved into Utah and threatened to out-vote Mormons, the territorial legislature granted women the vote in January 1870. Utah women were the first to cast ballots, as Utah's election was held prior to one in Wyoming, which had enfranchised women just weeks earlier.

Women voted for seventeen years, until 1887, when Congress outlawed polygamy and repealed women's enfranchisement. Emmeline B. Wells led lobbying in Congress, and in January 1896, Utah was admitted as a state with the women's vote restored. Later that year, Dr. Martha Hughes Cannon became the nation's first female state senator.

The Women's Relief Society, which formed before the Mormons left Illinois, published *Women's Exponent* from 1872 to 1914. Its message was feminist, especially in promoting economic independence, and Mormon women worked for the vote in other states. At the Democratic National Convention in 1900, Elizabeth M. Cohen, who had been appointed Utah commissioner of pensions, seconded the nomination of William Jennings Bryan, becoming the first woman so honored. By 1920, when most women got the vote, Utah had elected some two dozen female legislators.

U.S. representative Reva Beck Bosone, elected in 1948, was a strong feminist, but Utah became much more conservative as the century lengthened. In contrast to its support of the Nineteenth Amendment that ensured the vote, the LDS sponsored much of the successful opposition to the Equal Rights Amendment in the 1970s, and feminist Sonia Johnson was ex-communicated.

The Year of the Woman, 1992, was revolutionary in Utah, as the state's voters surprised the nation by electing three Democratic women. Salt Lake City chose Deedee Corradini as mayor and sent Democrat Karen Shepherd to Congress. Led by Georgia Rep. Newt Gingrich, Republicans targeted Shepherd in 1994, and in that party's successful sweep, she lost to Enid Greene. After her victory, Greene married Republican activist Joseph Waldholtz, who had managed her campaign. When evidence of corruption surfaced, she did not run in 1996, and Utah's congressional delegation reverted to all male. The third Democratic woman who won in 1992 marked another milestone, as Democrat Jan Graham became attorney general. She was Utah's first woman in statewide office, a century after North Dakota set this precedent in 1892.

Republican Olene Walker won the lieutenant governorship in 2000. Very well qualified, Walker rose to chair the National Conference of Lieutenant Governors in 2003 and later became acting governor. She set a national precedent by appointing another woman, Gayle McKeachnie, as lieutenant governor, but Republicans did not nominate either in 2004. Voters did not repeat these precedents, and as of 2011, Utah had no women in congressional or statewide office.

Key Facts

| Statehood: | 1896 |
| Capital: | Salt Lake City |

---

[42] Special election; served less than a year.

First women's rights organization:	Women's Relief Society, 1842[43]
Pioneer publication:	*Woman's Exponent*, Emmeline B. Wells, editor, 1872
First female lawyer:	Phoebe Couzins, 1872
Full female enfranchisement:	Won in1870, lost in 1887, re-won in 1896
State ratification of Nineteenth Amendment:	Yes
First president of League of Women Voters:	Antoinette B. Kinney
First woman on state supreme court:	Christine Durham, 1982
State ratification of Equal Rights Amendment:	No

Statewide Elective Officeholders

Governor:	Olene Walker (R), acting governor	2003
Lieutenant governor:	Olene Walker (R)	2000
	Gayle McKeachinie, (R)[44]	2003
Secretary of state:	Not elected	
Attorney general:	Jan Graham (D)	1992
Financial officer(s):	None	
School superintendent:	Not elected	

State Legislature

Firsts

House:	Sarah Elizabeth Nelson Anderson (D)	1896
	Eurithe K. LaBarthe (D)	1896
Senate:	Martha Hughes Cannon (D)	1896

Percentage of women in 2010–2011 session

(5 among 29 in senate; 15 among 75 in house):	19
National rank:	39

Presiding Officers

Speaker of the house:	None
Senate president:	None

Federal Elective Officeholders

U.S. Senate:	None	
U.S. House:	Reva Beck Bosone (D)	1948
	Karen Shepherd (D)	1992
	Enid Greene Waldholtz (R)	1994

FURTHER READING

Abbott, Delia M. 1976. *Women Legislators of Utah, 1896–1976.* Salt Lake City: Utah Chapter of National Order of Women Legislators.

Beecher, Maureen U., ed. 2000. *The Personal Writings of Eliza Roxey Snow.* Logan: Utah State University Press.

Clopton, Beverly B. 1980. *Her Honor, The Judge: The Story of Reva Beck Bosone.* Ames: Iowa State University Press.

Lieber, Constance L., and John Sillito. 1989. *Letters from Exile: The Correspondence of Martha Hughes Cannon and Angus M. Cannon, 1886–1888.* Salt Lake City: Signature Books.

Madsen, Carol Cornwall. 2006. *An Advocate for Women: The Public Life of Emmeline B. Wells, 1870-1920.* Provo, Utah: Bingham Young University Press.

---

[43]The society begun in 1842 in Nauvoo, Illinois, which was the Mormon headquarters until the 1847 move to Utah.

[44]Appointed by Acting Governor Walker.

VERMONT

Overview

An African American woman, Lucy Terry Prince of Sunderland, successfully argued a property rights case before a representative of the U.S. Supreme Court in 1797. Vermont pioneered feminism in the 1850s, but the state arguably became more conservative as many of its liberals moved west, where they had a progressive effect in newer states. Clarina Howard Nichols is an example. She spoke to the 1852 Vermont legislature but moved on to activism in Kansas and California. Vermont's women's movement disappeared with the Civil War, and when it regrouped in 1883, the vast majority of the officers were men.

The legislature granted the vote for school elections in 1880, and by 1883, women held thirty-three educational offices. Suffragists had affiliates in some seventy towns by the turn of the century, but progress was slow, and suffragists did not win their goal of municipal suffrage until 1917. In 1919, two of Vermont's three U.S. representatives supported the Nineteenth Amendment granting full voting rights to women, but Republican governor Percival Clement refused to call the legislature for ratification. Vermont women won the vote in 1920 because of other states.

Orange County voters elected Edna Beard to the Vermont House just two months later in 1920, and in the 1922, election, she became the first female state senator. The next big milestone waited until 1953, when Consuelo Northrop Bailey became Speaker of the state house. When she was elected lieutenant governor the next year, she automatically won the right to preside over the Vermont Senate. An exceptional politician in an era of feminist regression, she was the nation's first woman to hold such power.

Vermont was the seventh state to elect a woman, Madeleine M. Kunin, as governor. She was a Democrat, and although Vermont long was known as Republican, the majority of women elected to statewide office have been Democrats.

The state is proud of its "citizen legislature," which has a large membership and offers little compensation. The result is that it has more women than most legislatures. In 2011, they made up 39 percent, a tie with neighboring New Hampshire, which also has a large legislature, and following only Colorado at 41 percent. But no women held any executive office in Montpelier or a congressional seat in Washington, DC. Vermont is one of four states that never has sent a woman to Congress—the others are Delaware, Iowa, and Mississippi.

Key Facts

Statehood:	1791
Capital:	Montpelier
First women's rights organization:	Vermont Women's Rights Society, 1852
Pioneer publication:	None
First female lawyer:	Jessie D. Bigwood, 1902
Full female enfranchisement:	1920
State ratification of Nineteenth Amendment:	No
First president of League of Women Voters:	Lilian Olzendam
First woman on state supreme court:	Denise R. Johnson, 1990
State ratification of Equal Rights Amendment:	Yes

Statewide Elective Officeholders

Governor:	Madeleine M. Kunin (D)	1984
Lieutenant governor:	Consuelo Northrop Bailey (R)	1954
	Madeleine M. Kunin (D)	1978
	Barbara Snelling (R)	1992
Secretary of state:	Deborah Marowitz (D)	1998
Attorney general:	None	
Treasurer:	Stella B. Hackel (D)	1974
Auditor:	Elizabeth M. Ready (D)	2000
School superintendent:	Not elected	

State Legislature

Firsts
House:	Edna Beard (R)	1920
Senate:	Edna Beard (R)	1922

Percentage of women in 2010–2011 session
(11 among 30 in senate; 59 among 150 in house):   39
National rank: 2

Presiding Officers
Speaker of the house:	Consuelo Northrop Bailey	1953
	Gaye Simington	2005
Senate president:	Consuelo Northrop Bailey	1955

Federal Elective Officeholders

U.S. Senate:	None
U.S. House:	None

FURTHER READING

Garzina, Gretchen Holbrook. 2008. *Mr. and Mrs. Prince: How an Extraordinary Eighteenth-Century Family Moved Out of Slavery and Into Legend.* New York: Armistad.

Kunin, Madeleine. 1994. *Living a Political Life.* New York: Knopf.

Smith, Jean K. *Those Indomitable Women of Vermont.* 1999. Washington, DC: American Association of University Women.

Sussman, Susan M. 1998. *The Legal Rights of Women in Vermont.* Montpelier, VT: Governor's Commission on Women.

VIRGINIA

Overview

Virginia women played leading roles in colonial settlement, the American Revolution, and the Civil War, but they were slow to assert themselves in local politics. Long the most populous state without any female representation in Congress, Virginia has elected only one woman to statewide office.

The first feminist organization did not reflect typical Virginians. Instead, Union victors in the Civil War, including many men, led its January 1870 formation. President Anna Whitehead Bodeker unsuccessfully tested her right to vote. After federal troops withdrew from the South in 1877, the organization collapsed.

Not until 1909 did the Equal Suffrage League of Virginia revitalize the cause. Supporters included Lady Astor, the first woman in the British Parliament, who was born in Virginia as Nancy Langhorne. Some feminists, especially novelists Ellen Glasgow and Mary Johnston, campaigned to greater success in other states, but their own legislators rejected the Nineteenth Amendment that enfranchised Virginia women in 1920.

State elections were in odd-numbered years, and in 1923, two women won seats in the House of Delegates. Helen Ruth Henderson would be the first woman followed in office by her daughter, as Helen Timmons Henderson won her mother's former seat in 1927. Six women, all Democrats and former teachers, won Virginia House seats during the 1920s, but the next decades were regressive, and no woman joined the Virginia Senate until the 1979 election.

Richmond was earlier than most cities to have a woman as mayor, but the first woman in statewide office was not until 1985, more than a century after North Dakota set that precedent. On the other hand, Democrat Mary Sue Terry was the nation's second female attorney general, following only Rhode Island. Voters failed to promote Terry, however, when she later ran for governor.

When the Alexandria area elected Democrat Leslie Byrne as Virginia's first female U.S. representative, in 1992, Virginia was by the far the most populous state that never had sent a woman to the nearby national capital. Two more women have been elected since, but none served longer than six years. In 2011, Virginia again was the largest state to have no women in top offices. None held an executive office in Richmond, and none was in the state's thirteen-member congressional delegation.

Key Facts

Statehood:	1788
Capital:	Richmond
First women's rights organization:	Virginia State Woman Suffrage Association, 1870
Pioneer publication:	*Virginia Suffrage News*, Alice Overbey Taylor, editor, 1914
First female lawyer:	Belva Lockwood, 1879[45]
Full female enfranchisement:	1920
State ratification of Nineteenth Amendment:	No
First president of League of Women Voters:	Adele Clark
First woman on state supreme court:	Cynthia Dinah Fannon Kinser, 1997
State ratification of Equal Rights Amendment:	No

Statewide Elective Officeholders

Governor:	None
Lieutenant governor:	None
Secretary of state:	Not elected
Attorney general:	Mary Sue Terry (D)
Financial officer(s):	None
School superintendent:	Not elected

State Legislature

Firsts		
House:	Sarah Lee Fain (D)	1923
	Helen Ruth Henderson (D)	1923
Senate:	Eva Mae Scott (R)	1979
Percentage of women in 2010–2011 session (8 among 40 in senate; 19 among 100 in house):	19	
National rank:	38	
Presiding Officers		
Speaker of the house:	None	
Senate president:	None	

Federal Elective Officeholders

U.S. Senate:	None	
U.S. House:	Leslie L. Byrne (D)	1992
	Jo Ann Davis (R)	2000
	Thelma Drake (R)	2004

FURTHER READING

Brown, Kathleen M. 1996. *Good Wives, Nasty Wenches, and Anxious Patriarchs: Gender, Race, and Power in Colonial Virginia.* Chapel Hill: University of North Carolina Press.

Holloway, Pippa. 2006. *Sexuality, Politics, and Social Control in Virginia, 1920–1945.* Chapel Hill: University of North Carolina.

Lebsock, Suzanne. 1999. *Virginia Women, 1600–1945: "A Share of Honor."* New York: W.W. Norton.

Varon, Elizabeth R. 1998. *We Mean to Be Counted: White Women and Politics in Antebellum Virginia.* Chapel Hill: University of North Carolina Press.

---

[45] Lockwood practiced in nearby Washington, DC, but was admitted to the Virginia bar for a probate case.

WASHINGTON

Overview

Washington was the third territory to enfranchise women, and Seattle was the first major city to elect a woman as mayor. In 2011, Washington was the only state that had women in its top three positions—as governor and as U.S. senators.

Mary Olney Brown led other women in testing the right to vote in the 1870s, and the territorial legislature enfranchised women in 1883. However, the vote was lost in *Harlan v. Washington* (1887). Mary A. Leonard became an attorney in 1885, after being acquitted of murdering her husband.

The vote was not restored until 1910, and Emma Smith DeVoe of Tacoma was the skilled leader of that victory. She also led enfranchisement campaigns in other states. At the request of Idaho's governor, where women also voted, Washington feminists joined the National Council of Women Voters in 1911.

At the first opportunity in 1912, two women won races for the legislature. One of them, Frances C. Axtell, was a feminist who later won an appointment from President Woodrow Wilson. Voters also elected a woman as state superintendent of schools in 1912. A little more than a decade later, Bertha Knight Landes became mayor of Seattle; she was the nation's first female mayor of a sizeable city. The first woman in a statewide office other than school superintendent was in 1938, and Washington's first woman in Congress was in 1958, both eras when women generally regressed.

Washington elected Democrat Dixy Lee Ray as governor in 1976, and when Democrat Christine Gregoire followed in 2004, it followed only three states that twice had chosen a woman as governor. Contrastingly, Washington never has had a female lieutenant governor nor elected a woman to a financial office.

The state has sent an appreciable number of women to Congress and, after the 2004 election, when Democrat Maria Cantwell joined Democrat Patty Murray in the U.S. Senate, Washington followed only Maine and California in having women in both of its U.S. Senate seats. In 2011, Cathy McMorris Rogers and Jaime Herrera Beutler, both moderate Republicans, represented Washington in the U.S. House. In another case of female mentorship, Buetler previously was Rogers's aide. They were, however, the only women in the state's nine-member House delegation.

Key Facts

Statehood:	1889
Capital:	Olympia
First women's rights organization:	Washington Territorial Woman Suffrage Association, 1871
Pioneer publication:	*Washington Votes for Women*, Mrs. M.T.N. Hanna, editor, 1909
First female lawyer:	Mary A. Leonard, 1885
Full female enfranchisement:	Won in 1883, lost in 1887, re-won in 1910
State ratification of Nineteenth Amendment:	Yes
First president of League of Women Voters:	Emma Smith DeVoe, 1911
First woman on state supreme court:	Carolyn Reaber Dimmick, 1981
State ratification of Equal Rights Amendment:	Yes

Statewide Elective Officeholders

Governor:	Dixy Lee Ray (D)	1976
	Christine Gregoire (D)	2004
Lieutenant governor:	None	
Secretary of state:	Belle C. Reaves (D)	1938
Attorney general:	Christine Gregoire (D)	1992
Financial officer(s):	None	
School superintendent:[46]	Josephine C. Preston	1912
	Pearl A. Wanamaker	1940

---

[46] Office is nonpartisan.

| | Judith Billings | 1988 |
| | Theresa Bergeson | 1996 |

Miscellaneous Offices
Commissioner of lands: Jennifer Belcher (D)   1992
Insurance commissioner: Deborah Senn (D)   1992

State Legislature

Firsts
House: Frances C. Axtell (R)   1912
     Nena Jolidon Croake (Prohibition)   1912
Senate: Reba J. Hurn (R)   1922
Percentage of women in 2010–2011 session
     (17 among 49 in senate; 29 among 98 in house):   31
National rank: 6
Presiding Officers
     Speaker of the house: None
     Senate president: None

Federal Elective Officeholders

U.S. Senate:	Patty Murray (D)	1992
	Maria Cantwell (D)	2004
U.S. House:	Catherine Dean May (R)	1958
	Julia Butler Hansen (D)	1960
	Jolene Unsoeld (D)	1988
	Maria Cantwell (D)	1992
	Jennifer Dunn (R)	1992
	Linda Ann Smith (R)	1994
	Cathy McMorris Rogers (R)	2004
	Jaime Herrera Beutler (R)	2010

FURTHER READING

Andrews, Mildred Tanner. 1994. *Woman's Place: A Guide to Seattle and King County*. Seattle, WA: Gemil Press.
Guzzo, Louis R. 1980. *Is It True What They Say About Dixy? A Biography of Dixy Lee Ray*. Mercer Island, WA: Writing Works.
Haarsager, Sandra. 1994. *Bertha Knight Landes of Seattle: Big-City Mayor*. Norman: University of Oklahoma Press.
Ross-Nazzall, Jennifer. 2011. *Winning the West for Women: The Life of Suffragist Emma Smith DeVoe*. Seattle: University of Washington.

WEST VIRGINIA

Overview

West Virginia was the second-to-last state to ratify the Nineteenth Amendment, which enfranchised women. The story of that successful fight was dramatic, involving a tense cross-country journey by Sen. Jesse Bloch to vote. Women had been slow to organize for enfranchisement, and its suffrage association, begun in 1895, was one of the last in the nation. They held their only referendum on the issue in 1917 and, despite professional publicists and a large investment from national organizations, lost with 63,540 in favor and 162,607 opposed.

Voters nonetheless elected two women to the legislature, Democrat Anna Johnson Gates and Republican Elizabeth A. Davis, in 1922, the first opportunity. Although appointed, not elected, Minnie Buckingham Harper became the nation's first African American woman in a legislature, in 1928. Izetta Jewel Brown was a nationally known Democrat who ran credible campaigns for the U.S. Senate in 1922 and 1924. West Virginia's delegation to the 1924 Democratic convention even placed her name in nomination for vice president.

Despite this hopeful beginning, the state proved slow to elect women to higher positions. From 1933 onward, governors appointed women to the West Virginia Senate, but the first was not elected until 1964. By then, West Virginians had had a female U.S. representative, as Democrat Maude Elizabeth Kee was elected in 1950. The legislature ratified the Equal Rights Amendment of the 1970s, and West Virginia had a woman on its highest court in 1988, earlier than many states. In 2000, Republican Shelley Moore Capito became the state's second woman in Congress. As of 2011, West Virginia had six statewide executive positions, but women never had held any other than secretary of state.

Key Facts

Statehood:	1863
Capital:	Charleston
First women's rights organization:	West Virginia Equal Suffrage Association, 1895
Pioneer publication:	None
First female lawyer:	Agnes J. Morrison, 1896
Full female enfranchisement:	1920
State ratification of Nineteenth Amendment:	Yes
First president of League of Women Voters:	Mrs. John Ruhl
First woman on state supreme court:	Margaret L. Workman, 1988
State ratification of Equal Rights Amendment:	Yes

Statewide Elective Officeholders

Governor:	None	
Lieutenant governor:	None	
Secretary of state:	Elizabeth "Betty" Ireland (R)	2004
	Natalie Tennant (D)	2008
Attorney general:	None	
Financial officer(s):	None	
School superintendent:	Not elected	

State Legislature

Firsts

House:	Elizabeth A. Davis (R)	1924
	Anna Johnson Gates (D)	1924
Senate:	Bettie H. Baker (D)	1964

Percentage of women in 2010–2011 session

(2 among 34 in senate; 20 among 100 in house):	16
National rank:	43

Presiding Officers

Speaker of the house:	None
Senate President:	None

Federal Elective Officeholders

U.S. Senate:	None	
U.S. House:	Maude Elizabeth Kee (D)	1950
	Shelley Moore Capito (R)	2000

FURTHER READING

Brisbin, Richard A., Jr. 2008. *West Virginia Politics and Government*. Lincoln: University of Nebraska Press.

Loeb, Penny. 2007. *Moving Mountains: How One Woman and Her Community Won Justice From Big Coal*. Lexington: University of Kentucky.

Mason, Carol. 2009. *Reading Appalachia from Left to Right: Conservatives and the 1974 Kanawha County Textbook Controversy*. Ithaca, NY: Cornell University Press.

West Virginia Women's Commission. 1983. *Missing Chapters: West Virginia Women in History*. Charleston: West Virginia Women's Commission.

WISCONSIN

Overview

Immigrants, especially Germans and Scandinavians who came in the mid-nineteenth century, greatly influenced Wisconsin. Mathilde Anneke, who fled Europe after participating in its 1848 revolutions, was a leading Milwaukee feminist. The first suffrage association formed in 1869, when women met in Janesville and elected Rev. Augusta Chapin as president. The legislature passed a bill allowing women to be elected to school offices in 1870, and within two decades, as many as eighteen counties had female school superintendents simultaneously.

Full voting rights were delayed for decades, but the legislature put the issue on the 1912 ballot. Women ran a strong campaign, including advertising via airplane. Male voters rejected it, 125,736 in favor and 227,054 opposed, with most of the opposition coming from the beer industry and German Catholics. After that, feminists concentrated on the proposed Nineteenth Amendment to the U.S. Constitution, and, on June 10, 1919, it was the first state to ratify.

Although the state does not have a large African American population, Wisconsin voters were the first in the nation to elect a black woman, Velvalea Rodgers Phillips, to statewide office, in 1978. Milwaukee's Gwen Moore, the second Wisconsin woman elected to Congress, also is African American.

A long gap occurred between the first women in the Wisconsin House, three of whom won in 1924, and the first state senator, elected in 1976. Near the end of the twentieth century, Wisconsin was the largest state that had never elected a woman to Congress. When Madison voters finally selected a woman to represent them in the U.S. House, they chose Tammy Baldwin, who was the nation's the first openly lesbian member. Wisconsin also became one of a minority of states that have elected a female attorney general, in 2001, but it never has had a woman in its highest posts, governor and U.S. senator.

Finally, University of Wisconsin professor Gerda Lerner is considered the chief pioneer of American women's history, and Kathryn Clarenbach was a key founder of the National Organization for Women.

Key Facts

Statehood:	1848
Capital:	Madison
First women's rights organization:	Wisconsin Woman Suffrage Association, 1869
Pioneer publication:	*Wisconsin Citizen*, Martha Parker Dingee and other editors, 1887
First female lawyer:	Lavinia Jane Goodell, 1875
Full female enfranchisement:	1920
State ratification of Nineteenth Amendment:	Yes
First president of League of Women Voters:	Jessie Jack Hooper
First woman on state supreme court:	Shirley S. Abrahamson, 1976
State ratification of Equal Rights Amendment:	Yes

Statewide Elective Officeholders

Governor:	None	
Lieutenant governor:	Barbara Lawton (D)	2002

	Rebecca Kleefisch (R)	2010
Secretary of state:	Velvalea Rodgers Phillips (D)	1978
Attorney general:	Peg Lautenschlager (D)	2002
Treasurer:	Dena A. Smith (R)	1960
	Cathy S. Zeuske (R)	1990
School superintendent:[47]	Barbara S. Thompson	1972
	Elizabeth Burmaster	2000

State Legislature

Firsts
House:	Mildred Barber (R)	1924
	Hellen M. Brooks (R)	1924
	Helen Thompson (R)	1924
Senate:	Michele G. Radosevich (R)	1976

Percentage of women in 2010–2011 session
(8 among 33 in senate; 23 among 99 in house): 24
National rank: 23
Presiding Officers
 Speaker of the house: None
 Senate president: None

Federal Elective Officeholders

U.S. Senate:	None	
U.S. House:	Tammy Baldwin (D)	1998
	Gwen Moore (D)	2004

FURTHER READING

Berger, Meta Schlichting. 2001. *A Milwaukee Woman's Life on the Left*. Madison: State Historical Society of Wisconsin.
Freeman, Lucy. 1986. *Belle: The Biography of Belle Case La Follette*. New York: Beaufort Books.
McBride, Genevieve G. 1993. *Wisconsin Women: Working for Their Rights from Settlement to Suffrage*. Madison: University of Wisconsin Press.
Schier, Mary Lahr. 2001. *Strong-Minded Woman: The Story of Lavinia Goodell, Wisconsin's First Female Lawyer*. Northfield, MN: Midwest History Press.

WYOMING

Overview

The Wyoming Territory was the world's first jurisdiction to grant women full voting rights, on December 10, 1869. In 1870, it had the nation's first female law enforcement officer, Esther Morris, as well as the first female jurors.

Julia Bright, wife of the territorial governor, led enfranchisement. Because Wyoming men wanted to attract women to their frontier, they also passed the world's first equal pay law. When some members of the U.S. Congress objected to allowing female voters to join the Union, Wyoming men refused to consider statehood without women as full citizens.

---

[47] Office is nonpartisan.

Theresa Jenkins was the nation's first woman to be a delegate to a national political convention, that of the Republicans in 1892. In 1894, Wyoming tied with Colorado for election of nation's second female superintendent of public instruction. Estelle Reel also pioneered federal educational office.

Laramie voters sent Mary Bellamy to the Wyoming House with the 1910 election. In 1912, legislators Anna Miller and Nettie Traux provided examples of female variety: Traux was unmarried; Miller, the mother of six. Nellie Tayloe Ross became the nation's first female governor, elected in 1924.

More than most states, Wyoming voters elected women to executive offices, including financial ones, during the first half of the twentieth century. The Wyoming House had two women as Speakers in the 1960s, which was an extremely unusual.

Later history was less liberal. In 2000, it was the very last state to put a woman on its highest court. Wyoming has sent only two women to Congress, and the first Republican Barbara L. Cubin, elected in 1994, made a point of disassociating herself from women who worked for equal rights.

Key Facts

Statehood:	1890
Capital:	Cheyenne
First women's rights organization:	No formal name, 1869
Pioneer publication:	None
First female lawyer:	Grace Raymond Hebard, 1899
Full female enfranchisement:	1869
State ratification of Nineteenth Amendment:	Yes
First president of League of Women Voters:	Mrs. Cyrus Beard
First woman on state supreme court:	Marilyn S. Kite, 2000
State ratification of Equal Rights Amendment:	Yes

Statewide Elective Officeholders

Governor:	Nellie Tayloe Ross (D)	1924
Lieutenant governor:	Office does not exist	
Secretary of state:	Thyra Thompson (R)	1962
	Kathleen Karpan (D)	1986
	Diana J. Ohman (R)	1994
Attorney general:	None	
Treasurer:	Minnie Mitchell (R)	1950
	Shirley Wittier (R)	1978
	Cynthia M. Lummis (R)	1998
Auditor:	Minnie Mitchell (R)	1954
	Rita Meyer (R)	2008
	Cynthia Cloud (R)	2010
School superintendent:	Estelle Reel (R)	1894
	Rose A. Bird Maley (D)	1912
	Edith K. O. Clark (R)	1914
	Katherine A. Morton (R)	1918
	Esther L. Anderson (R)	1938
	Edna B. Stolt (R)	1946
	Velma Linford (D)	1954
	Lynn Simons (D)	1978
	Diana Ohman (R)	1990
	Judy Catchpole (R)	1994
	Cindy H. Hill (R)	2010

State Legislature

Firsts

House:	Mary Godat Bellamy (D)	1911
Senate:	Dora McGrath (R)	1933

Percentage of women in 2010–2011 session
  (1 among 30 in senate; 13 among 60 in house):   16

National rank: 45

Presiding Officers

Speaker of the house:	Edness Kimbell Wilkins (D)	1966
	Verda I. James (R)	1969
Senate president:	April Brimmer-Kunz (R)	2003

Federal Elective Officeholders

U.S. Senate:	None	
U.S. House:	Barbara L. Cubin (R)	1994
	Cynthia M. Lummis (R)	2008

FURTHER READING

Scheer, Teva J. 2005. *Governor Lady: The Life and Times of Nellie Tayloe Ross.* Columbia: University of Missouri Press.

Garceau, Dee. 1997. *The Important Things of Life: Women, Work, and Family in Sweetwater County, Wyoming.* Lincoln: University of Nebraska Press.

Hebard, Grace Raymond. 1940. *How Woman Suffrage Came to Wyoming.* New York: W.D. Embree.

INDEXES

NAMES INDEX

Italicized page numbers indicate illustrations, photos, or tables.

A

Aaron, Leila, *24*
Abbott, Anna, 26
Abbott, Edith, 50
Abbott, Grace, 293
Abbott, Julia, 26
Abbott, Merrie Hoover, *39*, 46, 354
Abbott, Mrs. Lyman, 29
Abel, Hazel Hempel, *189*, 194, *206*, 484
Ableman, Peggy L., 360, 361
Abraham, Spencer, 203, 378
Abrahamson, Shirley S., 360, 361, 366, 521
Abrams, Ruth, 360, 361, 364, 472
Abzug, Bella Savitzky, 157, *157*, 197, *405*, 414, 491, 493
Achtenberg, Roberta, 306
Adams, Abigail, 3
Adams, Annette, 354
Adams, Gerry, 336
Adams, Irene, *25*
Adams, Mrs. Jewett, 29
Adams, John Quincy, 2, 3, 4, 296, 320, 383
Adams, Mary N., *25*
Adams, Sandy, *177*, 451
Adams, Mrs. Thomas B., 29
Addams, Jane, *25*, 38, 52, 290, 316, 328, 353, *384*, 389, 390, *405*, 417, 418
Addington, Julia C., 41, 460
Agnew, Frances A., *27*
Agnew, Spiro T., 104, *272*, 275, 277, 396
Ahler, Annette B., *27*
Aiken, George D., 274
Airey, Grace Stratton, *28*, *89*
Akers, Dolly Lucille Smith Cusker, 99
Akin, Stella, 347, 452
Albee, Fay, *64*, 509
Albright, Joseph Medill Patterson, 313
Albright, Madeleine K., *291*, 294, 305, 306, 308, 312–313, 318, 337

Alcott, Louisa May, 11, 26, 36, 269, 471
Aldrich, Ann, *371*
Aldrich, Anna E., *27*
Alexander, Bill, 202
Alexander, Caroline B., 26
Alexander, Jane, 305
Alexander, Julia M., 96, *98*, 494
Algeo, Sara M., *27*
Alger, Mary Donlan, *370*, *371*
Alito, Samuel A., Jr., 377, 381
Allen, Beverly, 26
Allen, Corrine Tucker, *27*, 367
Allen, Mrs. D. M., *25*
Allen, Daisy, *89*
Allen, Dorothy McDonald, *115*, *117*, 125, 441
Allen, Ethan, 367
Allen, Florence Ellinwood, *27*, 55, 360, 361, 362, *362*, 363, 365, 366, 367, *370*, *371*, 372, 379–380, 497
Allen, George, 361
Allen, Mrs. J. D., *28*
Allen, James B., 196, 197
Allen, Katharine C., *115*, *117*, 120, 469
Allen, Maryon Pittman, *189*, *206*, *437*
Allen, Melba Till, *63*, 66, *436*
Allen, Mildred P., *59*
Allen, Nancy R., *25*
Allen, Mrs. S. L. Ober, *25*
Allen, Sophia Ober, *27*
Allen, Virginia, 407
Allison, Angeline, *25*
Alming, Ludwig, 74
Almy, Martha R., *27*
Altgeld, John Peter, 46, 50
Alvarez, Aida, *293*, 304
Ames, Jessie Daniel, 394, 512
Ames, Mary, *29*
Amory, Cleveland, 272
Amos, Mabel, *59*, 66, *436*

Anaya, Toney, 361
Anderson, Carla, 315
Anderson, Cora Belle Reynolds, 96, *98*, 473, 474
Anderson, Debra, *108*, 508, 509
Anderson, Elizabeth Preston, *27*
Anderson, Esther L., *57*, 523
Anderson, Eugenie, 329–330, 400
Anderson, Frances B., *25*
Anderson, Helen Eugenie Moore, 273, 327
Anderson, John B., 400
Anderson, Mary, 50, *292*, 293–294, 406
Anderson, Patricia, *64*, 476
Anderson, Sarah A., *39*, 82
Anderson, Sarah Elizabeth Nelson, *28*, *80*, 81, *83*, 189, 514
Anderson, Violette Neatly, 354, 381, 457
Andrews, Elizabeth Bullock, *140*, *157*, 158, 435, 437
Andrews, Leila P., *27*
Andrews, Thomas H., 201
Andrus, Anna, *25*
Andrus, Cecil D., 361
Angell, Mary M., *27*
Anneke, Mathilde, *6*, 521
Annenberg, Leonore "Lee," 333
Annunzio, Frank, 166
Anthony, Almira W., 26
Anthony, Katherine, 408
Anthony, Lucy, 34
Anthony, Mary, *27*, 505
Anthony, Susan B., *6*, 8, 9, 10, 11, 12, 13, *14*, 14–15, *16*, *27*, 30, 31, 32, 33, 34, 35, 49, 267, 269, 271, 349, 356, *384*, 386, 387, 388, 389, 401, 405, *405*, 408, 415, 420, 421, 423, 431, 432, 456, 491, 492, 502
Aponte, Mari Carmen, 338
Aquino, Corazon, *268*
Archer, Mrs. E. O., *25*

Binkley, Kate, *25*
Binsfield, Connie, 474
Bird, Benjamin, 109
Bird, Lorelee, 483
Bird, Portia, 109
Bird, Rose Elizabeth, 361, 364, 366, 442
Bird, Susie, *28*
Birdsall, Mary B., *25*
Bishop, C. Diane, 56, *440*
Bishop, Jim, 272
Bissell, Emily P., *29*, 448
Bissell, Hannah S., *27*
Bittenbender, Ada, 347, 353, 482, 483
Black, Diane, *177*, *182*, 511
Black, Hugo L., 192–193
Black, Shirley Temple, 331, 333–334
Black, Susan H., *371*, 376
Blackburn, Marsha, *177*, *178*, 511
Blackman, Eva, *40*, 43
Blackwell, Alice Stone, 10, 13, 26, 36, 421
Blackwell, Antoinette Brown, 26
Blackwell, Elizabeth, *27*
Blackwell, Emily, *27*
Blackwell, Emma L., 26
Blackwell, Hannah, 26, 487
Blackwell, Henry, 11, 13, 17, 36, 462, 487
Blaine, James G., *384*, 387–388
Blair, Emily Newell, 26, 391, 392, 479
Blair, Henry William, 322
Blake, Lillie Devereux, *27*, *384*, 389
Blake, Mary J. S., *39*, 42
Blake, Willa McCormick, *437*
Blakely, Delora W., *89*
Blanco, Kathleen Babineaux, *214*, *215*, 221, *225*, *226*, 466, 467
Bland, Cora, *28*, 459
Blaney, Maude L., 58
Blankenbaker, Virginia, 174
Blankenburg, Lucretia L., *27*
Blanton, Annie Webb, *39*, 55, *57*, 511, 512
Blatch, Harriot Stanton, 13, 19, *27*, 36, 491
Blatt, Genevieve, *55*, *59*, 60, 503
Blinn, Leola May, 360
Blitch, Iris Faircloth, *152*, 153, 452, 453
Bloch, Jesse, 23, 519
Bloch, Julia Chang, 334
Blood, "Colonel" James, 287
Blood, Thomas, 306
Bloomer, Amelia, 7, *25*, 27, 35, 460, 461, 482, 492
Bloomer, Mrs. Nevada, *28*
Blue, Virginia, *63*, 444, 445
Bobodilla, Isabel, 213
Bode, Denise, *71*, 500
Bode, Mary Jane, 112
Bodeker, Anna Whitehead, 9, 516
Boggs, Corinne Clairborne "Lindy", *140*, *141*, *157*, 160, 184, 337, *385*, 397, 466, 467
Boggs, Hale, 160, 184
Bohrer, Florence Fifer, *115*, *117*, 119–120, 457

Boies, James, 41
Boies, Martha, *40*, 41
Boland, Veronica Grace, *140*, *147*, 148, 504
Bolton, Frances Payne, *140*, *141*, *147*, 183, 208, 274, 497, 498
Bolton, John R., 338
Bolton, Sarah Knowles, *27*
Bondi, Pam, *69*, 450
Bones, Marietta, 507
Bono, Mary, *167*, 174, 443, *443*
Bono, Sonny, 174
Boosalis, Helen, 218, 483
Boozman, John, 202
Bosone, Joseph P., 99
Bosone, Reva Beck, *80*, 99, 112, *140*, 150, 169, 513, 514
Boswell, N. K., 41
Botensek, Elsie B., 347
Bottsford, Harriette, *25*
Bouchles, Olympia, 201. *See also*, Snowe, Olympia Jean
Bowen, Debra, *59*, 442, *442*
Bowers, Cynthia Jeanne, 236. *See also* Shaheen, Jeanne
Bowles, Erskine, 204
Bowman, Annette, *25*
Bowring, Eva Kelly, *189*, 194, *206*
Bowron, Mrs. A. J., *436*
Boxer, Barbara Levy, 163, *163*, 168, *189*, *199*, 200, 205, *206*, *207*, 309, 442, 443, *443*
Boyce, Etta Estey, *28*
Boyd, Annie Caldwell, *28*
Boyd, Mary A., 26
Boyda, Nancy, 177, 180, 181, 463
Boyer, Ida Porter, *27*
Boyle, Ann, *70*, 483
Boyle, Patricia Jean E.P., *370*
Boynton, Elizabeth, *25*
Bozeman, Dorothy Bradley, 481
Brackenridge, Eleanor, *28*
Bradford, Mary Carol Craig, 13, *39*, 44, 50, *56*, 445
Bradley, Bill, 219
Bradley, Jennette, *64*, 497
Bradwell, James, 355
Bradwell, Myra Colby, *25*, 42, 348, 349, 350, 355–356
Brady, M. Jane, 68, *69*, 448
Brandenburg, Margaret J., *27*
Branstad, Terry E., 231, 361
Brassington, Mary Clare, *24*
Braun, Michael A., 210
Bray, Mildred, *55*, *56*, 485
Brayton, Alice I., 26
Brazile, Donna, *386*, 398
Brazill, Ruth, 362
Brazille, Donna, 184
Breckinridge, Madeline "Madge" McDowell, *25*, 464
Breckinridge, Sophonisba, 347, 353–354, 418, 464, 465

Breese, Mrs. Yarde, *29*
Brehm, Marie C., 60, 271, 393, 457
Bremer, Frederika, 6
Brennan, Joseph E., 361
Brent, Margaret, 213, 346
Brevard, Caroline, *25*
Brewer, Jan, *59*, *214*, *215*, 223, *225*, *226*, 227, *228*, 308, 439, *439*
Brewer, John, 223
Bridenstine, Ellenore, *115*, *117*, 123, 482
Briggs, Emily Edson, *28*
Bright, Betty, 9–10
Bright, Julia, *28*, 51, 522
Bright, William, 51
Brimmer-Kunz, April, *131*, 524
Brinker, Nancy Goodman, 337
Brinkman, Joyce, *63*, 459
Britton, John Bayard, 416
Brizzolara, Stella, *24*
Brock, Mrs. Horace, *29*
Brokaw, Ann Clare, 342
Brokaw, George, 342
Bronaugh, Mary, 465
Bronson, Minnie J., *29*, 491
Brooke, Edward V., 188
Brooke, Edward W., 281
Brooks, Bryant, 49, 215
Brooks, Cora W., 463
Brooks, Elizabeth Carter, 411
Brooks, Harriet S., 26
Brooks, Hellen M., 95, *98*, 522
Brooks, Jean Willard, *40*, 49, 215
Brooks, Mary Burt, *24*
Brotherton, Florence Belle, 26, 474
Brown, Adella Maxwell, *25*
Brown, Antoinette, 6, 7, 36, 497
Brown, Corrine, *167*, 169, *171*, 451
Brown, Emily Sophie, 90, 447
Brown, Hallie Q. Brown, *384*
Brown, Izetta Jewell, 60, 190–191, 273, *384*, 392, 393
Brown, Janice Rogers, 377
Brown, Jerry, 361, 442
Brown, Kate, *59*, 501
Brown, Kathleen, *63*, 67, 442, 443, *443*
Brown, Linda, 380
Brown, Mary Olney, 8, 518
Brown, Olympia, 26, *28*, 390
Brown, Sarah A., 44
Brown, Scott P., *69*, 205, 310
Brown, Sophie Brown, *97*
Brown, Virginia Mae, *292*, 298
Brown, Willie, 276
Brownback, Sam, 338
Browner, Carol M., *292*, 305, 313, 450
Brown-Waite, Ginny, 169, 177, *177*, 178, 432, 451
Brundtland, Gro, *268*
Brunner, Jennifer, *59*, 497
Bryan, Mary Baird, 17, 21, 343, 392

Cordray, Richard, 310
Corman, James C., 162
Cormier, Lucia, 194, 195, 198, 211
Corner, Mary T., *28*
Corning, Joy, 461
Corradini, Deedee, 513
Corrigan, Grace J., *56*, 490
Cosu, Mrs., 17
Cotnam, Mrs. T. T., *24*, 441
Coues, Lucy L., 45
Coulter, Mary Geigus, *28*, *39*, *80*, *89*
Courche, Belle, *28*
Courville, Cindy, 337
Couzins, Phoebe, 26, 43, 347, 349, 350, 353, *384*, 441, *441*, 463, 514
Covington, Ann K., 360, 361, 479
Cowan, Mrs. James, 493
Cowell, Janet, *64*, 494
Cowles, Betsey Mix, *6*, 497
Cowles, Edith Clark, *28*
Cox, Cathy, *59*, 452
Cox, Elizabeth M., 84
Cox, George "Boss," 383
Cox, James M., *384*, 392, 393
Cox, Kathy, *56*, 452
Cox, Lenore Hanna, *25*
Coyle, Elizabeth, 508
Coyne, Elizabeth, *59*
Coyne, Jeanne, 375
Crabb, Barbara Brandriff, *370*
Craig, Cola Barr, *29*
Craig, Edward, 92
Craig, Katherine L., *56*
Craig, Mary Carol, 50. *See also* Bradford, Mary Carol Craig
Craig, Maybelle, *24*
Craig, Minnie Davenport, *80*, 91, 92, *98*, 99, *108*, *108*, 112, 133, 495
Crane, Philip M., 179
Cranston, Alan, 199, 200
Cranston, Martha S., *24*
Crawford, Helen, *27*
Crawford, Mrs. S. K., 26
Crawford, Sara B., *55*, *59*, 447
Crays, Jennie, 475
Cressingham, Clara, *39*, 80, *80*, 81, *83*, 445
Croake, Nena Jolidon, 85, *89*, 519
Crocker, Lucretia, 41, 43
Crockett, Mrs. A. P., *27*
Crofoot, Mrs. L. F., *29*
Croley, David, 421
Croly, Jane Cunningham "Jennie June," 13, *405*, 406, 409, 420–421
Cromwell, Emma Guy, *55*, *59*, 62, *64*, 76, 464, 465
Cronise, Annette W. "Nettie," 347, 350, 497
Cronise, Florence, 351
Crosby, Robert, 194
Cross, Ermine, *25*
Crowley, Mrs. Fred, *25*
Cubin, Barbara L., *140*, *167*, 173, 181, 523, 524

Culp, Oveta, 316. *See also* Hobby, Oveta Culp
Cunningham, Catherine Campbell, *24*
Cunningham, Mildred, *25*
Cunningham, Minnie Fisher, *28*, 191, 511
Cuomo, Mario M., 165, 280, 360, 361
Currie, Mary Atkins, *63*, 459
Curry, Mrs. Charles E., 501
Curtis, Elizabeth Burill, *27*
Cushing, Mrs. George, *27*
Cutler, Hannah Tracy, *27*, 497

D

Daggett, Beverly, *131*, 132, 468, 469
Dahlgren, Madeleine, *29*
Dahlkemper, Dan, 182
Dahlkemper, Kathleen "Kathy," *177*, 182, 504
Dalianis, Linda Stewart, 360, 361, 365–366, 486
Dall, Caroline Healey, 26
Dalton, Martha, *27*
D'Amato, Alfonse M., 160, 197, 285
Danforth, John C., 197
Daniel, Alice, *25*
Daniels, Mrs. Josephus, *27*, 28
Daniels, Lou J. C., *28*
Danner, Pat, *167*, 170, 480
Darrow, Mary, *27*, 495
Darwin, Mary A. P., *25*
Davenport, Lacey, 160
Davenport, Mattie Griffith, *25*
Davenport, Minnie, 92
Davidson, Donetta, *59*, 444, 445
Davidson, Jo Ann, *108*, 498
Davidson, Rita Charmatz, 360, 361, 470
Davis, Elizabeth A., 93, 519, 520
Davis, Gray, 200
Davis, Jo Ann, 176, *177*, 517
Davis, John W., 60, 191, *384*, 393
Davis, Katherine, 459
Davis, Mary F., 487
Davis, Myrtle R., *56*, 455
Davis, Paulina Kellogg Wright, 6, *27*, 504
Davis, Ruth A., 337
Davis, Susan A., 176, *177*, 444
Davis, Vera Gilbride, *63*, *115*, *117*, 123, 448, 449
Day, Christine, 430
Day, Dorothy, 17
Day, Mrs. Francis, *29*
Day, Sharon, 398
Day, Stephen, *149*
Dayton, Anna, *29*
Dean, Howard, 281, 282
Debs, Eugene V., 389, 392
DeCrow, Karen, 414
Deering, Mabel Craft, *24*
DeGette, Diana, *167*, 174, 446
DeLauro, Rosa L., 166, *167*, 168, 446, 447
DeLee, Debra, 398
Dellums, Ronald V., 175, 287
Del Papa, Frankie Sue, *59*, 68, *69*, 485

Denish, Diane, 223, *229*, 489, 491
Dennenfelser, Marjorie, 431–432
Dennett, Mary Ware, 26, *405*, 415
Dennis, Gigi, *59*, 445
Denny, Ida L., 26
Des Georges, J. A., 58
DeVoe, Emma Smith, *14*, *28*, 109, 185, 454, 518
DeVore, Ann G., *63*, 459
DeVos, Dick, 227
De Vou, Mary R., *24*
Dewey, John, 52
Dewey, Thomas E., 110, *149*, 154, *385*, 394
Dewing, Ardelia Cooke, *27*
Dewson, Mary Williams "Molly," 95, 295, *385*, 391, 394, 397, 399
De Young, Rosa, 91, *98*
Dick, Nancy, *229*, 445
Dickens, Charles, 406, 421
Dickerson, Mahala Ashley, 412
Dickinson, Anna, 8, 40
Didrickson, Loleta, *63*, 457
Dietrich, Mrs. Charles, 483
Digby, Pamela, 336–337. *See also* Harriman, Pamela Churchill
Diggs, Annie L., 47
Dilley, Cameron, 227
Dimmick, Carolyn Reaber, 360, 361, 364, 518
Dingee, Martha Parker, 521
Dingell, John D., 172
Dingley, Anna, 26
Disney, Roy, 125
Divine, J. M., 74
Dixon, Alan J., 200
Dixon, Sharon Pratt, 315
Docking, Jill, 219
Dodge, Mrs. Arthur M., *29*
Dodge, Mrs. Charles, *29*
Dodge, Mary Abigail, *384*, 388
Doe, Jessie, 90, *97*, 486
Dole, Elizabeth Hanford, *189*, 198, *199*, 204, 205, *206*, 223, *268*, 280, 281, *291*, *294*, 301, 302, 303, 307, 312, 313–314, *386*, 398, 494
Dole, Robert "Bob," 173, 202, 209, 220, *272*, 280, 301, 302, 309, 314, *386*, 398
Donahey, Gertrude, *64*, 66, 497
Donahue, Mary O., 492
Donaldson, M. Sylvia, *80*, 91, *98*, 472
Donelson, Bettie, *28*
Donnan, Mary Fant, 73
Donovan, Eileen R., 330
Dorman, Marjorie, *29*
Dormer, Cecil, 326
Dornan, Robert K., 174
Dorris, Grace S., *80*, 87, *89*, 443, *443*
Dorsett, Mrs. John W., *25*
Dorsett, Martha Angle, 26, 347, 351, 476
Dorsey, Sarah A., 26
Dougherty, Nellie, 91, *98*, 495
Douglas, Emily Taft, *149*, 457, 458

Hauser, Elizabeth, *27*, 389
Hawkins, Gene, 208
Hawkins, Paula Fickes, *70*, 71–72, *189*, 197, 206, *206*, 208–209, 450, 451
Hay, Mary Garrett, *27*, 392
Hayes, Rebecca Henry, *28*
Hayes, Rutherford B., *384*, 387
Hayward, Elizabeth, *21*, *89*
Hayward, Mary Smith, 26
Hayworth, Nan, *177*, 493
Hazard, Rebecca N., 26
Hazard, Mrs. Roland, *29*
Hazeltine, Joyce, *59*, 60, 509
Hazlett, Adele, 26, 473
Head, Mrs. J. D., *24*
Heale, J. M., 123
Healey, Kerry Murphy, 472
Healy, Bernadine P., *292*, 303
Hearnes, Betty, 218
Hearst, Phoebe Apperson, *40*, 47
Hearst, William Randolph, 47
Heartz, Evangeline, *39*, 80, 81, *83*
Heath, Sarah Louise. *See* Palin, Sarah
Hebard, Grace Raymond, *28*, 47, 347, 523
Hebert, F. Edward, 287
Heckler, John, 300
Heckler, Margaret M. "Peggy," *141*, *155*, 156, 159, 180, *291*, 300, 303, 304, 333, 472, 473
Height, Dorothy I., *405*, 413
Heitkamp, Heidi, 68, *71*, 495
Helmer, Bessie Bradwell, 356
Helms, Jesse, 204, 306, 434
Heltkamp, Heidi, *69*
Henderson, Mrs. Archibald, *27*
Henderson, Helen Ruth, *80*, 94, 95, 516, 517
Henderson, Helen Timmons, 94, 95, *98*, 516
Henderson, Mrs. John, *29*
Henderson, Julia C., *25*
Henderson, Karen, 376
Henderson, Lizzie George, 477
Henry, Claudette, *64*, 500
Henry, Mrs. J. M., *25*
Henry, Mrs. Thomas, 26
Hepburn, Katherine Houghton, *24*, 446
Hericourt, Jeanne de, 328
Herman, Alexis M., *291*, 305, 307
Hernandez, Aileen, 414
Heron, Mrs. John B., *29*
Herr, Helen Kolb, *115*, *117*, 127, 485
Herrera, Mary, *59*, 490
Herron, Mrs. I., *25*
Herschensohn, Bruce, 200
Herseth, Lorna, *59*, 60, 62, 509
Herseth, Stephanie, 62, *140*, *177*, 178, 508
Hershiser, Nettie P., 26
Hewitt, Emily C., 378
Hiatt, Sarah W., *28*, 511
Hickey, Margaret, *405*, 406
Hicks, Louise Day, *157*, 157–158, 473
Higgins, Marion West, *108*, 488

Higginson, Ella, 109
Hill, Anita F., 168, 210
Hill, Cindy H., *57*, 523
Hill, Lister, 193
Hill, Mrs. W. B., *25*
Hillard, Carole, *229*, 508
Hillerman, Abby, *27*
Hilles, Florence Bayard, *24*
Hills, Carla Anderson, *291*, *294*, 298, 299, 312, 315. *See also* Anderson, Carla
Hills, Roderick, 315
Hincks, Mrs. William T., *24*
Hindman, Matilda, *27*
Hinkle, James F., 73
Hinman, Edna, *64*, 481
Hinton, Mary Hilliard, *29*
Hipple, Ruth, *28*, 508
Hirono, Mazie K., *171*, *177*, 180, 221, 222, *229*, 453, 454
Hitchcock, Almeda Eliza, 347, 353, 453
Hitler, Adolf, *148*, *149*, 326, 330
Hoar, George F., 352
Hobart, Mrs. Garret A., *29*
Hobby, Oveta Culp, *291*, *294*, 296, 297, 299, 312, 316, 511. *See also* Culp, Oveta
Hobby, William P., 316
Hobson, Anne, *24*
Hochul, Kathy, *177*, 182, 493
Hodes, Paul W., 205
Hoeven, John, 361
Hoffa, Jimmy, 380
Holcomb, Marcus H., 24
Holder, Janice, 366
Holla, Blanche R., 325
Holland, Doris Lindsey, 96, *98*, *115*, *117*, 123, 467
Holland, Kim, *71*, 500
Hollingworth, Beverly, *131*, 131–132, 487
Hollister, Nancy Putnam, *214*, 227, *228*, *229*, 497
Holly, Carrie Clyde, *39*, 80, 81, *83*, 445
Holm, Virginia, *55*, *59*, 476
Holmes, Genta Hawkins, 337
Holmes, Julia Archibald, *28*, 43
Holmes, Lydia Wickcliffe, *25*
Holmes, Mary E., 45
Holmes, Sybil H., *115*, *117*, 123, 473
Holt, Marjorie Sewell, *157*, 158, 471
Holton, Tabitha, 347, 353, 494
Holtzman, Elizabeth, *141*, 151, *157*, 158, 159, 197, 285, 493
Honegger, Barbara, 301
Honeyman, Nan Wood, *140*, *145*, *146*, 501, 502
Hooker, Isabella Beecher, 24, *24*, 352, *384*, 446
Hooker, Mary M., 90, 97, 447
Hooley, Darlene, *167*, 175, 502
Hooper, Ben W., *14*
Hooper, Jessie Jack, 190, 521
Hooper, Shirley, *59*, 490

Hoover, Herbert, 65, 120, 121, *144*, 294, 322, 369, *385*, 393, 394
Hoover, J. Edgar, 157
Hoover, Lou Henry, 394
Hopkins, Frances, 360
Hopkins, Mary, 184. *See also* Norton, Mary Teresa
Hoppin, Louise, *29*
Horn, Joan Kelly, *167*, 480
Horne, Alice Merrill, *39*, 82, *83*
Horning, Harriet, *64*, 509
Horowitz, Roberta Frances, 162
Hoskins, Annie, 26
Hosmer, Katherine Tipton, 44
Hospers, John, 275
Hough, Sue, 91
Houghton, Agnes, 26
Houston, Elizabeth Good, *28*
Houston, Margaret W., *24*
Howard, Katherine, 395
Howard, Marilyn, *56*, 57, 456
Howe, J. H., 42
Howe, Julia Ward, 11, *16*, 26, 42, 269, *405*, 406, 408, 471, 487
Howell, Mary Seymour, *27*
Howland, Emily, *14*, *27*
Howorth, Joe, 94
Howorth, Lucy Somerville, 94–95, 477
Hubbard, Mrs. S. M., *25*
Hubbs, Mrs. Harriet L., 503
Huber, Mrs. J. C., *25*
Huck, Winnifred Sprague Mason, *140*, *142*, 458
Huffington, Adrianna, 200
Huffington, Michael, 200
Hufstedler, Shirley, *291*, *294*, 298, 299, 308, 370, 372
Hugh, Sue Metzger Dickey, *98*, 476
Hughes, Charles Evans, 18–19, *384*
Hughes, Elizabeth, *39*, 87, *89*, 443, *443*
Hughes, George, 372
Hughes, James, *24*
Hughes, Josephine, *24*
Hughes, Kate, *25*
Hughes, Martha "Mattie." *See* Cannon, Martha "Mattie" Hughes
Hughes, Mildred Barry, 488
Hughes, Sarah Tilghman, *370*
Hulett, Alta, *25*, 348, 349, 351
Hull, Cordell, 325, 344
Hull, Jane Dee, *59*, *108*, *214*, 215, 220, 221, 223, *225*, 227, *228*, 308, 439, *439*, *440*
Humphrey, Clara C., 95, *98*, 483
Humphrey, Hubert H., 156, 196–197, 276, *385*, 396
Humphrey, Muriel Buck, *189*, 196, *206*, 477
Hundley, Mrs. O. R., *24*
Hunin, Madeleine M., *225*
Hunstein, Carol W., 366
Hunt, Elizabeth, 26
Hunt, Frances, 93, *98*, 441, *441*

Kemp, Jack F., 280

Kempfer, Hannah Jensen, 91, *98*, 476

Kendrick, Ella B., *24*

Kenelly, Barbara Bailey, *59*

Kennan, Nancy A., *56*

Kennedy, Anthony M., 375

Kennedy, Cary, *63*, 445

Kennedy, Cornelia Groefsema, *370*, 372–373

Kennedy, Edward M., 69, 205, 209, 277, *385*, 397, 434

Kennedy, Jacqueline, 314

Kennedy, John F., 60, *61*, 101, 111, 125, 133, 134, 153, 154, 155, 156, 194, 195, 210, 211, 222, 273, 275, 277, 297, 298, 309, *311*, 313, 314, 329, 330, 331, 341, 363, 368, *370*, 372, *385*, 395, 399, 407, 408, 413, 433

Kennedy, Melina, 433

Kennedy, Robert F., 154, 156, 222, 277, 284, 314, 396

Kennedy, Sandra, *70*, *440*

Kennelly, Barbara Bailey, *141*, 163, *163*, 280, 447

Kenny, Mrs. John, *28*

Kent, Patience, *24*

Kepsey, Ada (or Adah) H., 347, 348, 457

Kerry, John, 178, 281, *386*, 398, 434

Keys, Martha Elizabeth, *141*, *157*, 160–161, 463

Kezer, Pauline R., *59*

Kicklin, Mrs. F. T., *28*

Kiffmeyer, Mary, *59*, 476

Kilbreth, Mary G., *29*

Kilgore, Carrie S. Burham, *27*

Kilgore, Sarah, 26, 347, 474

Kilpatrick, Carolyn Cheeks, 166, *167*, 174, 475

Kilroy, Mary Jo, *177*, 181, 499

Kimball, Catherine "Kitty," 360, 361, 365, 366, 467

Kimball, Martha S., 486

Kimbell, Sarah M., *28*

Kimborough, Mrs. D. T., *28*

King, Angie J., 351

King, Ann Holden, *89*

King, Carolyn Dineen, *371*

King, Jean Sadako, *55*, 454

King, Martin Luther, Jr., 75, 154, 156, 164, 354, 396, 459

Kingman, J. W., 42

Kingsbury, Fannie, *24*

Kinkel, Norma, 509

Kinney, Antoinette B., 514

Kinney, Mary Strong, 86, *89*

Kinser, Cynthia Dinah Fannon, 360, 361, 517

Kirby, Holly M., 360, 361, 510

Kirchner, Cristina Fernandez de, *268*

Kirkpatrick, Ann, *177*, 181, *440*

Kirkpatrick, Evron "Kirk," 341

Kirkpatrick, Jeane Duane Jordan, 333, 334, 339, 341–342

Kite, Marilyn S., 360, 361, 366, 523

Klatschken, Martha, 26

Kleefisch, Rebecca, 522

Kleven, Victor, 112

Klink, Ron, 203

Klinkel, Norma, *71*

Klobuchar, Amy, *189*, 204–205, *206*, 476, 477

Klock, Frances S., *39*, 80, 81, *83*, 445

Klou, *207*

Knapp, Florence E. S., 492

Knaue, Virginia, 298

Knoll, Catherine Baker, *64*, *229*, 503

Knowles, Bessie, 91, *98*, 452

Knowles, Ella, 46, 347, 353, 480, 481

Knowles, Tony, 204, 361

Knox, Henry, 290

Knox, Janette Hill, *27*

Knutson, Andy, 110

Knutson, Coya Gjesdal, 101, 109, 110–111, *140*, *152*, 153, 475, 477

Kodzoff, Anita. *See* Garnick, Anita

Kong, March. *See* Eu, March Fong

Kong, Yuen, 74

Koon, Larry, 224

Korbel, Josef, 312, 318

Korbelova, Marie Jana "Madlenka." *See* Albright, Madeleine K.

Kosmas, Suzanne M., *177*, 182, 451

Kramer, Mary, *131*, 461

Kravitch, Phyllis A., *370*, 373

Kreglo, Laura, *25*

Kreps, Clifton, 299

Kreps, Juanita, *291*, *294*, 298–299, 300, 303

Krueger, Bob, 201

Krupsak, Mary Ann, *55*, *229*, 231, 492

Kumaratunga, Chandrika, *268*

Kundert, Alice, *59*, *65*, 509

Kunin, Arthur, 234

Kunin, Madeleine M., *214*, *215*, 218, 226, *226*, *229*, 230, 232, 233, 234, 334, 361, 365, 515

Kurtz, Howard, 282

Kyle, Sara, *71*, 510

L

LaBarthe, Eurithe K., *39*, *80*, 81, 82, *83*, 189, 514

Lachance, Janice, 305

Laddey, Clara S., 26

LaDuke, Winona, *268*, 280, 281

LaFeber, Walter, 333

La Follette, Belle, *28*, 190, 390

La Follette, Robert M., 95, 190, 390

LaHaye, Beverly, 428

Laird, Margaret B., 90–91, *97*, 488

Laise, Carol C., 330, 331

Lake, Celinda, 397

Lakey, Alice, 26

Lamar, Mirabeau, *115*

Lamar, Mrs. Walter D., *29*

Lambert, Blanche, *167*, 170, 202, 440, 441, *441*

Lamm, Carolyn, 355

Lamm, Richard D., 361

Land, Mrs. L. K., *24*

Land, Terri Lynn, *59*, 474

Landes, Bertha Knight, 518

Landon, Alfred M. "Alf," 197, 327, *385*, 394, 399

Landon, Nancy, 209

Landrieu, Mary, *64*, 67n, *189*, 202, 205, *206*, *207*, 466, 467, 6666

Lane, Carrie, 460

Langley, John Wesley, *144*

Langley, Katherine Gudger, *140*, *141*, *142*, *143*, *144*, 464, 466

Larch-Miller, Aloysius, *27*, 499

Larouche, Lyndon, 426

Larrazolo, Octaviano, 489

Larsen, L. M., *59*, 508

Larsen, Sylvia, *131*, 132, 487

Larson, Alma, *59*, 508

Larson, T. A., 121

Lathrop, Julia Clifford, *40*, 49, 50–51, 290–291, *292*, 293, 347

Lathrop, Mary, 444

Lau, Cheryl, *59*

Laughlin, Gail, 26, 93, 109, 111, 468

Lautenberg, Frank R., 160

Lautenschlager, Peg, 69, *69*, 522

Lavelle, Rita, 300

Lawrence, Regina G., 282

Lawson, Mrs. Eugene, *27*

Lawton, Barbara, *229*, 521

Lazio, Rick A., 203

Leach, Antoinette, *25*

Leary, Eliza Ferry, *29*

Lease, Mary Ellen, 388

Leavitt, Michael O., 228

Le Barthe, Eurithe K., 82

Lee, Barbara, *167*, *171*, 175, 443, *443*

Lee, Blair, 361

Lee, Dorothy McCullough, 501

Lee, Frances, *39*, 80, *83*, 84

Lee, Mrs. Frank M., *29*

Lee, Mrs. M. H., *24*

Lee, Richard Henry, 3

Lehtinen, Dexter, 166

Leisner, Susan, 72

Lendrecie, Helen de, *27*

Lent, Mary E., 26

Leonard, Barbara, *59*, 505

Leonard, Daniel, 353

Leonard, Mary A., 347, 353, 501, 518

Leonard, Mrs. R. H., *25*

Leopold, Alice K., *59*, 447

Lerner, Gerda, 105, 413

Letcher, Marion, 322

Letting, Patience, 499

Levine, Beryl J., 360, 361, 365

Levitt, William Homer, 343

Lewis, Ann, 300, 306, 397

Lewis, Anthony, 303–304

Ordway, Evelyn W., *25*
O'Reilly, Leonora, 49, *405*, 418
Orr, Elda A., 26, 67n, 484
Orr, Kay A., *55*, *64*, 66, *214*, *215*, 218, 219, 224, *225*, 230, 483
Ortega, Daniel, 333
Ortega, Katherine D., *311*, *386*
Ortiz y Pino, Concha de, *80*, 100, 109, 111–112
Ortiz y Pino, Dona Josefa, 111
Ortiz y Pino, José, 111
Orwig, Maria, *25*
Osborne, Mabel V., *24*
Osgood, Samuel, 290
Oshkosh, Cora Hurtz, 351
Ostrander, Nancy, 332
Ostroot, Geraldine, *59*, 508
O'Sullivan, Mary Kenny, *405*, 418
Otero-Warren, Nina, 27, 58, 489
O'Toole, Mary, 362
Ott, Adelaide, 91, *98*, 498
Otto, Rebecca, *64*, 476
Owen, Mary Robinson, *25*
Owen, Priscilla, 377–378
Owen, Reginald, 343
Owen, Ruth Bryan, *140*, *141*, *142*, *143*, *145*, 166, 296, 322–325, 327, 328, 339, 343–344, 353, 389, 429, 449, 451
Owens, Mary Meade, *25*
Owens, Meade, *25*
Owens-Adair, Bethenia, 500

P
Packard, Elizabeth Parsons, 349
Page, Alice Nelson, *27*
Pague, Lydia Beckley, 360
Paige, Mabeth Hurd, 91, *98*, 476
Paige, Rod, 308
Painter, Lela D., *63*, *65*, 455
Paist, Harriet W., *27*
Paiva-Weed, M. Teresa, *131*, 505
Palin, Sarah, 204, *214*, *215*, 220, 223, *225*, 226, *226*, *268*, 272, 282, 286, *386*, *398*, 401, 437, *438*
Palin, Todd, 286
Pall, Linda, 455
Palmer, Bertha Honore, *25*, 387, 389, 456
Palmer, Bertha R., *56*, 495
Palmer, Fanny Purdy, *27*
Palmer, Phoebe, 460
Pankhurst, Emmeline, *14*, 16
Papa, Sue Del, 60
Park, Charles, 421
Park, Maud Wood, 10, 18, 19, 23, 26, *405*, 410, 421–422, 471
Parker, Alton B., *384*, 389
Parker, Jessie M., *56*, 461
Parker, Mary Evelyn, *64*, *65*, 467
Parker, Sarah, 366
Parker, Susan, *63*
Parks, Rosa, 275

Parmalee, Annette W., *28*
Parnell, Harvey, 191
Parsons, Sophronia O. C., *39*, 44
Partridge, Mary, *24*
Patel, Marilyn Hall, *371*
Paterson, David A., 180, 205
Patil, Pratibha, *268*
Patterson, Anne W., 337–338
Patterson, Elizabeth J., *163*, 165, 506, 507
Patterson, Hannah, *27*
Patton, Grace Espy, *39*, *56*
Paul, Alice, *14*, 16, 17, 26, 30, 32, 33–34, 271, 392, 407, 421, 487
Paulus, Norma, *55*, *56*, *59*, 501
Paxman, Acsha, *28*
Paxton, Bertha, 93, *98*, 490
Peabody, Lucia M., *39*, 42
Pearce, Drue, 131, *131*, *438*
Pearson, Benita Y., 378
Pearson, James B., 209
Pearson, Josephine, *29*
Peavey, Antoinette J., *39*, 44, *55*, *56*, 445
Peckham, Rhoda A. F., *27*
Pederson, Sally, 461
Pedro, Leonar Bint, 213
Pell, Claiborne, 163
Pelosi, Nancy Patricia D'Alesandro, *141*, *163*, 165, 166, 179, 180, 181, 182, 183, 185, 280, *386*, 398, *428*, 442, 443, *443*
Pelosi, Paul, 185
Pendray, Carolyn Campbell, 96, *98*, *115*, *117*, 123, 460, 461
Penn, Hannah, 213
Penn, William, 213
Pennewell, Mrs. J. W., *24*
Pepper, Claude, 166
Peraza, Dona Ines, 213
Perdue, Bev, *214*, *215*, 223, *225*, *225*, *226*, *229*, 494
Perkins, Frances, 185, *291*, *294*, 294–295, 296, 297, 302, 303, 311, 312, 316–317, 391, 399, 406
Perkins, Kate, *27*
Peron, Isabel "Evita," *268*
Peron, Juan, 342
Perpich, Rudy, 361
Perrault, E. A., *59*, 490
Perry, Rick, 201
Peters, Ellen Ash, 361, 364, 446
Peters, Laura, *28*
Peters, Mary E., *291*, 308
Peterson, Elly, 396
Peterson, Esther, 298, *405*
Pettigrew, Nina, *28*
Pettis, Shirley Neil, *157*, 161, 443, *443*
Pfaelzer, Mariana, *370*
Pfost, Gracie Bowers ("Hell's Belle"), *140*, 151, 152, *152*, 154, 196, 455, 456
Phelps, Almira Lincoln, *29*
Phelps, Mrs. M. T., *439*
Philbrook, Mary, 347, 488

Phillips, Gail, *108*, 438
Phillips, Mrs. George, *29*
Phillips, Lena Madesen, *405*, 406
Phillips, May Price, *24*
Phillips, Velvalea Rodgers, *59*, 60, *61*, 73, 75, 521, 522
Phipps, Meg Scott, *70*, 72–73, 494
Pickler, Alice, *28*, 46
Pierce, Julia, *28*
Pierce, Katherine, *27*
Pierson, Alice, *24*
Pike, Martha, *28*
Pillsbury, Mrs. John, 475
Pinckard, Mrs. James S., *29*
Pingree, Chellie, *177*, 181, 198, 201, 468, 469
Pingree, Hannah, *108*, 468
Pinkham, Dora, 93, *98*, *115*, *117*, 120, 469
Pinnell, Louise Rebecca, 347, 354, 450
Pinny, Eva, *27*
Pinochet, Mrs. Gifford, *27*
Pittman, Maryon, 196
Pitts, Lillie H., 91, *98*, 503
Platt, Mrs. Malcolm, *27*
Pleasant, Mrs. Ruffin G., *29*
Plischke, Elmer, 322, 328, 334, 337
Polk, James K., 321
Pollak, Mrs. Ignatius, *24*
Pool, Sybil, *55*, 58, *63*, *65*, 66, *70*, 71, 435, *436*
Pope, Mrs. Gustavas, 26
Porter, Mary, 399
Post, Amalia, *28*
Post, Amy, 5, *6*, *27*
Potter, Elizabeth Herndon, *28*
Pou, Mrs. John Dozier, *25*
Powell, Colin L., 308
Powell, Katherine, *28*
Powell, Nancy Jo, 337
Powell, Sallie B., *24*
Powers, Anne F., 65
Praeger, Sandy, *70*
Prager, Sally, 463
Prather, Lenore L., 360, 361, 478
Pratt, Eliza Jane, *140*, *149*, 495
Pratt, John, *144*
Pratt, Ruth Sears Baker, *140*, *142*, *144*, 492
Preston, Ann, *27*
Preston, Josephine C., *39*, 49, *55*, *57*, 518
Preston, Mrs. Thomas J., *29*
Priest, Ivy Baker, *55*, *63*, *65*–66, 150, 311, *311*, 395, 443, *443*
Priest, Sharon, *59*, 441, *441*
Prince, Lucy Terry, 346, 515
Printz, Armegot, 213
Pruyn, Mrs. John V. L., *29*
Pryce, Deborah, *167*, 172, 181, 432, 498
Pryor, David, 361
Putnam, Mrs. William, *29*
Pyle, Gladys, *55*, 58, *59*, 67, 73, 75–76, 95, *98*, *189*, 193, *206*, 224, 508, 509
Pyle, John L., 75–76
Pyle, Mamie Shields, *28*, 75–76, 508

Q

Quayle, Dan, 166, *386*
Quayle, Marilyn, *386*
Quimby, Mary E., 26
Quinby, Annie Laurie, *27*

R

Radosevich, Michele G., *115*, *117*, 128, 522
Raimondo, Gina, 505
Rambo, Sylvia H., *370*
Ramo, Roberta Cooper, 354, 412
Randall, Delia, 26
Randolph, Edmund, 290
Randolph, Florence, 26, 487
Rankin, Jeannette, 19, 26, *39*, 50, 65, 86, 139, *140*, *141*, *142*, 182, 185, 208, 418, 449, 481, 482
Raoul, Eleanore, *25*
Rawls, Nancy V., 331
Ray, Charlotte, 347, 350, 353
Ray, Marguerite "Dixy Lee," 73, *214*, *215*, 217, 218, 221, 222, 225, *225*, 233, 234–235, *292*, 298, 361, 364, 518
Ray, Mrs. Robert, *27*
Rayburn, Sam, *148*
Read, Edyth E., *89*
Read, Lizzie Bunnel, *25*
Read, Robin, 130
Ready, Elizabeth M., 65, 515
Reagan, Nancy, 105, 397
Reagan, Ronald, 66, 105, 128, 136, 159, 162, 163, 164, 197, 209, 217, *272*, 277, 279, *294*, 298, 299, 300, 303, 304, 306, 307, *311*, 314, 315, 332–333, 342, 343, 369, 372, 374, 378, 381, *385*, *386*, 397, 408, 428
Reaves, Belle C., 518
Redd, Anabel, *25*
Redick, Frances Burke, *59*, 447
Redfearn, Mrs. D. H., *25*
Redfield, Ethel E., *56*, 456
Reece, Louise Goff, *155*, 156, 511
Reed, Anna B., *27*
Reed, Ralph, 431
Reed, Suellen, *56*, 459
Reel, Estelle, *39*, *40*, 44, 46, 50, 51–52, *55*, *57*, 290, *292*, 523
Reeves, Belle C., *59*
Rehnquist, William H., 375, 377
Reibman, Jeanette, 130
Reich, Robert B., 303
Reid, Charlotte Thompson, *155*, 458
Reid, Harry, 201
Reinhardt, Mrs. David J., *29*
Rell, M. Jodi, 130, *214*, *215*, 220, 222, *225*, *226*, *228*, 446, 447
Reman, Mrs. Paul, *28*
Remond, Sarah, *6*, 10
Reno, Itta K., *28*
Reno, Janet, 68, *291*, *294*, 304, 305, 312, 317–318, 354, 450

Reynolds, Mrs. Fred, *29*
Reynolds, Mrs. J. H., *24*
Reynolds, Kim, 461
Reynolds, Minnie J., 26
Reynoso, Cruz, 364
Rhodes, Margaret Olive, *27*
Rice, Carrie Shaw, *40*, 46
Rice, Condoleezza, *291*, *293*, 308–309, 312, 318–319, 337, 338, *386*
Rice, Georgia Ruth, *56*, 481
Rice, Rebecca, *27*
Rice, Susan, 338
Richards, Ann W., 65, 66, 112, 201, *214*, *215*, 218, 220, 224, 225, *225*, *226*, 230, 233, 235, *386*, 397, 429, 511
Richards, David, 235
Richards, Ed, 99
Richards, Emma L., 26
Richards, Mrs. J. H., *25*
Richardson, Laura, *171*, *177*, 181, 444
Richardson, Margaret, *292*, 305
Richardson, Susan Hoxie, *25*, 456
Richey, Clara M., *25*
Richey, Mary Anne, 373
Ricker, John, 357
Ricker, Marilla Young, 9, 26, *28*, 322, 347, 353, 355, 357, 485, 486
Riddle, Agnes, 444
Ridgely, Mrs. Henry, 448
Ridgway, Rozanne "Roz," 332, 339
Riff, Annamae, *59*, 508
Riley, Corrine Boyd, *155*, 506
Riley, Louise M., 26
Riley, Mary Ann, *370*
Ringsrud, Olive A., *59*, 508
Riojas, Alma Morales, *405*
Riordan, Daniel, 19
Rios, Rosa Gumataotao, *311*
Ripley, Martha, 26, 475
Risch, Jim, 338
Risteau, Mary E. W., 93, *98*, *115*, *117*, 123, 470, 471
Rivers, Lynn, *167*, 172, 474, 475
Rivers, Mendel, *147*
Rivlin, Alice M., 305
Roach, Beatrice, 490
Roback, Kim, 483
Roberts, Albert, 28–30, 218
Roberts, Barbara, *59*, 60, *214*, *215*, 219, 220, *225*, 501
Roberts, Betty, 359, 360, 361, 501
Roberts, Dennis, 77
Roberts, Elizabeth H., *229*, 505
Roberts, Jack, 359
Roberts, John G., Jr., 377
Roberts, Margaret S., *25*
Roberts, Mary Wendy, *71*, 73, 501
Roberts, Patricia, 314–315. *See also* Harris, Patricia Roberts
Robertson, Alice Mary, *29*, 43, *140*, *141*, *142*, 180, 191, 499, 500

Robertson, Nellie Gray, 362
Robertson, Mrs. U. O., *25*
Robin, Mrs. Albert, *24*
Robins, Margaret Drier, 418
Robinson, Elizabeth G., *24*
Robinson, Harriet Hanson, 26, *386*
Robinson, Helen Ring, *39*, 114, *115*, *117*, 132, 136–137, 444, 445
Robinson, Joseph T., 192, 216
Robinson, Lelia J., 347, 353, 472
Robinson, Mary Lou, *268*, 336, *370*
Roby, Martha, *177*, 182, 435, *437*
Rockefeller, John D., Jr., 340, 389
Rockefeller, Nelson A., 274
Rockey, Mrs. A. E., *29*
Rockey, Dawn E., *64*, 483
Rodham, Dorothy, 284
Rodham, Hugh, 284
Roessing, Mrs. Frank M., *27*
Rogers, Blanche, 478
Rogers, Cathy McMorris, 518, 519
Rogers, Edith Nourse, *140*, *141*, *142*, *143*, *145*, *146*, 164, 183, 208, 472, 473
Rogers, Mary T., 488
Rogers, Rebecca, *25*
Rohde, Borge, 325, 344
Rohde, Ruth Bryan, 326, 344. *See also* Owen, Ruth Bryan
Roland, Mrs. W. P., *25*
Rolfe, Mary Louise. *See* Farnum, Mary L.
Romer, Christina Duckworth, 305, 310
Romero, Alice, 490
Romero, Alicia Valdez, *59*
Romney, George, 474
Romney, Lenore, 474
Romney, Mitt, 472
Romney, Ronna, 474
Roosevelt, Eleanor, 92, 100, 110, *146*, *147*, *148*, 195, 202, 211, 216, 275, 282, 296, 298, 323, *327*, 328, 340, *385*, 391, 394, 395, 399, *405*, 406, 407, 419, 429, 433
Roosevelt, Franklin D., 10, 32, 50, 65, 76, 87, 93, 95, 110, 121, 123, *145*, *146*, *148*, *149*, 150, 158, 191, 208, 211, 233, 235–236, 273, 275, 293, 294, *294*, 295, 296, 297, 312, *312*, 316, 317, 322, 325, 326, 327, 328, 340, 341, 344, 354, 367, *370*, *371*, 373, 376, *385*, 394, 395, 399, 419, 449
Roosevelt, Theodore, 16, 46, 88, 123, 290, *384*, 389, 390, 391, 401
Ropes, Hannah, *25*
Rose, Ernestine, *6*, *6*, 7, *27*
Rose, Melody, 282
Rosebaum, Ann R., 26
Roseborough, Mrs. Lee, 26
Rosenbaum, Edwynne C. Polly, 101
Rosenbaum, Polly Cutler, 439
Rosenberg, Anna, 151, *292*, 295, 296, 311
Ros-Lehtinen, Ileana, *163*, 166, *171*, 450, 451
Ross, Elizabeth McCaughey, 492

Ross, Nellie Tayloe, 54, *214*, 215, *215*, 216, *225*, *226*, 233, 235–236, *292*, 312, *312*, 523
Ross, William, 235
Rossi, Dino, 222
Rostenkowski, Dan, 166
Roth, Jane Richards, 376
Rothstein, Barbara Jacobs, *370*
Roukema, Margaret "Marge" Scafati, 162, *163*, 166, 488
Rouseff, Dilma, *268*
Rovner, Ilana Diamond, 376
Rowe, Audrey, 231
Rowe, Charlotte, *29*
Rowland, John G., 222
Roy, Elsijane Trimble, 357, 360, 361, *370*, 373, 441, *441*
Roy, Vesta, 131, *131*, *214*, 227, *228*, 487
Roybal-Allard, Lucille, *167*, 168, *171*, 176, 443, *443*
Rozell, Mark J., 431
Rubin, Robert E., 315
Ruble, Alice M., *89*
Rudd, Helen, 343
Ruffin, Josephine St. Pierre, 10, 411
Ruhl, Mrs. John, 520
Ruhn, Mrs. L. S., *24*
Runbeck, Linda, 176
Runnels, Betty, 347, 467
Runyon, Laura, 26
Runyon, Pearl Frances, *64*, 465
Ruschenberger, Mrs. Charles W., *27*
Russell, Mrs. Hardee, *27*
Russell, Julia, *29*
Russell, Sarah A., *27*
Russert, Tim, 282
Russum, Elizabeth, *56*, 456
Rutherford, Mildred, *29*
Ruthsdotter, Mary, 420
Ruutz-Rees, Caroline, *24*
Ryan, C. J., 351
Rylander, Carole Keeton, *65*, 71
Rymer, Pamela Ann, 376
Rymph, Catherine E., 396, 397
Rzewnicki, Janet, *63*, 449

S

Sacagawea, *14*
Safford, Mary Augusta, *25*
Saiki, Patricia Fukuda, *163*, 165, *171*, 199, 454
St. George, Katharine Price Collier, 150
St. Hill, Shirley Anita, 183–184. *See also* Chisholm, Shirley Anita
Saiz, Porfirra Hidalgo, 97–99
Salk, Jonas, 297
Salley, Mrs. Julian B., *28*
Salter, Susanna, *39*, 44, 462
Sammis, Ida, 87, *89*, 492
Samuelson, Agnes, *56*, 461
Sanchez, Linda, *171*, *177*, 178, 444
Sanchez, Loretta, *167*, *171*, 174, 178, 443, *443*

Sanders, Harriet B., 26
Sanders, Jessie E., *115*, *117*, 123, 130, 509
Sandlin, Stephanie Herseth, 178, 182, 508, 509
Sandness, Selma, *59*, 508
Sanford, Terry, 361, 363
Sanger, Margaret, *405*, 414, 415
Santorum, Rick, 203
Sargent, Aaron A., 12, 49, 352
Sargent, Ellen Clark, 12, 49
Sauerbrey, Ellen, 164
Saufley, Leigh Ingalls, 366
Saulsbury, Willard, Jr., 20
Savery, Annie C., *25*
Sawtelle, Mary P., 500
Sawyer, Ada L., 347, 505
Sawyer, Sarah Hardin, *25*
Saxon, Elizabeth Lyle, *25*, 466
Saylor, Anna L., *80*, 87, *89*, 443, *443*
Scalia, Antonin, 375
Schakowsky, Jan, *167*, 175
Scheck, Rosemary, *27*
Scheer, Teva J., 216
Schenk, Lynn, 167, *167*, 176, 443, *443*
Schermerhorn, Mrs. John, 488
Schkowsky, Jan, 458
Schlafly, John, Jr., 401
Schlafly, Phyllis McAlpin Stewart, 396, 399, 401–402, 428, 430
Schlesinger, Lulu Mowry, *115*, *117*, 121, 505
Schlotter, Gail, 445
Schmidt, Jean, *177*, 179, 180, 498
Schmidt, Kelly, *64*, 495
Schneider, Claudine Cmarada, *140*, 162–163, *163*, 164, 505
Schneiderman, Rose, *405*, 419
Schoelen, Mary J., 377
Schoenfelder, Laska, *71*, 509
Schoettler, Gail S., *63*
Schoffner, Martha, 441, *441*
Schrenko, Linda, 55, *56*, 452
Schriock, Stephanie, 429
Schroeder, Harriet, *28*
Schroeder, Jamie, 286
Schroeder, Jim, 279, 286
Schroeder, Mary M., *371*, 374
Schroeder, Patricia "Pat" Nell Scott, *141*, *157*, 158, 159, *268*, 279, 280, 286–287, 445
Schroeder, Scott, 286
Schuler, Nettie Rogers, 22, *27*
Schultz, Debbie Wasserman, *177*, 178–179, 398
Schunk, Mae, 476
Schuyler, Lorraine Gates, 119, 135
Schwab, Susan C., 308
Schwartz, Allyson Y., *177*, 203, 504
Schwegmann, Melinda, *229*, 467
Schwimmer, Rosika, 408
Scott, Anne Firor, 135
Scott, Eva Mae, *115*, *117*, 129, 517
Scott, Mrs. Henry P., *29*

Scott, Mae L., *56*, 455
Scott, Mary Semple, 479
Scott, Nell Chadwick, 96, *98*
Scott, Rick, 223
Scott, Mrs. William Force, *29*
Scott-Heide, Wilma, *405*, 414
Scowcroft, Brent, 318
Sears, Belle, 26
Sears, Leah Ward, 360, 361, 365, 452
Sears, William, 343–344
Seastrand, Andrea, *167*, 172, 175, 443, *443*
Sebelius, K. Gary, 221
Sebelius, Kathleen, 72, 180, *214*, 215, 221, *225*, *226*, 230, *291*, 310, 462, 463
Sekula-Gibbs, Shelley, *177*, 179
Selby, Myra C., 360, 361, 459
Sellers, Kathryn, *28*, 360
Selmes, Isabella, *146*
Senn, Deborah, *71*, 203, 519
Severance, Caroline, *16*, 24, 26
Sevier, Julia, *25*
Sewall, Eunice D., *24*
Sewall, May Wright, *14*, *16*, *25*, 31, 408, 458
Sewell, Terri A., *171*, *177*, 182, 435, *437*
Sexton, Minola Graham, 26
Seymour, Horatio, *384*
Seymour, John, 200
Seymour, Stephanie Kulp, *371*, 374
Shackelford, Lottie H., 440
Shadegg, Stephen, 329
Shaffer, Gloria, *59*, 447
Shaheen, Bill, 236
Shaheen, Jeanne, *189*, *199*, 205, *207*, *214*, 215, 220, *225*, *226*, 233, 236, 361, 365, 486, 487
Shalala, Donna E., *291*, 304, 306, 310
Shanahan, Elwill M., *59*, 463
Shapiro, Mary, *293*, 305–306, 311
Shapiro, Norma Levy, *370*
Sharp, John, 399
Sharp, Mary Settle, 493
Sharp, Susie Marshall, 360, 361, 363, 366, 494
Sharpton, Al, 281
Shaw, Anna Howard, *14*, 15, 19, 26, 30, 32, 33, 34, 35, 49, 294, *384*, 388, 390, 408, 421
Shaw, Leslie M., 47
Shaw, Pauline, 421
Shaw, Samantha, *63*
Sheaheen, Jeanne, *206*
Shea-Porter, Carol, *140*, *177*, 180, 486, 487
Shee Shiu, 74
Sheetz, Mrs. M. M., *24*
Sheheen, Vincent, 224
Shelton, Sally A., 332
Shepherd, Grace M., *56*, 455
Shepherd, Karen, *167*, 169, 513, 514
Shepherd, Matthew, 178
Shering, Miriam, 360, 361, 484
Sherman, Janann, 195
Sherwood, Grace, *28*

Stumbo, Janet, 360, 361, 465
Sturgeon, Mrs. T. H., *29*
Suchocka, Hanna, *268*
Sukarnoputri, Megawati, *268*
Sullivan, Claudia J., 347, 506
Sullivan, John B., 152
Sullivan, Leonor Kretzer, *140*, 152, 479, 480
Sumner, Jessie, *145*, *146–147*, 457, 458
Sundquist, Don, 361
Sununu, John E., 205, 236
Sutton, Betty, *177*, 180, 499
Swain, Mrs. A. M., 460
Swain, Eliza, *28*
Swank, Emma B., *25*
Swanson, Lori, 69, *69*, 476
Swetman, Emily Pierson, *24*
Swift, Frances Cater, *25*
Swift, Jane, *214*, 227–228, *228*, 472
Swift, Mrs. Lucius B., *29*
Swift, Mary Wood, *24*
Swisshelm, Jane Grey, 26, 27
Sykes, Diane Schwerm, 377
Symington, Fife, 220, 439
Symington, Gaye, *108*
Symons, John, 41
Symons, Martha, 41
Symons, Mrs. Theodore, *29*
Sytek, Donna, *108*, 486

T

Tabor, Elizabeth "Baby Doe," *24*
Taft, Emily, *149*. *See also* Douglas, Emily Taft
Taft, William Howard, *14*, 16, 49, 50, 88, 290, *384*, 390, 422
Takemoto, Patsy, 136. *See also* Mink, Patsy Takemoto
Talent, Jim, 203, 204
Tashjian, Julie H., *59*, 447
Tator, Nettie C., 350, 352
Tauscher, Ellen O., *167*, 174, 443, *443*
Tayloe, George, 216
Tayloe, Nellie, 235. *See also* Ross, Nellie Tayloe
Taylor, Alice Overbey, 517
Taylor, Anna, *25*, *370*
Taylor, Mrs. Issac, *27*
Taylor, Mary, *64*, 497
Taylor, Nellie, 26
Taylor, Zachary, *294*
Teeters, Nancy H., *292*, 300
Tenenbaum, Inez, *57*, 507
Tennant, Natalie, *59*, 520
Terrell, Mary Church "Molly," 10, *28*, *405*, 411, 418, 422–423
Terrell, Phyllis, 422
Terrell, Robert, 422
Terrell, Suzanne Haik, *70*, 202, 467
Territt, Amelia, *28*
Terry, Mrs. D. D., *24*
Terry, Mary Sue, *55*, 68, 69, *69*, 516, 517
Thatcher, Margaret, *268*

Thaw, Mrs. William, Jr., *27*
Thomas, Albert, 156
Thomas, Clarence, 168, 199, 210
Thomas, Gertrude C., *25*
Thomas, Lera Millard, *140*, *155*, 156, 173, 511, 512
Thomas, Louphenia, 435, *436*
Thomas, Martha Carey, *14*, 26, 27
Thomas, Martha G., 91, *98*, 503
Thomas, Mary Bentley, 470
Thomas, Mary F., 7, *25*
Thompson, Mrs. Alexander, *21*, 501
Thompson, Anne Elise, *370*
Thompson, Barbara S., *57*, 522
Thompson, Helen, 95, *98*, 522
Thompson, Mrs. Henry B., *29*
Thompson, Jill Long, 166, 224
Thompson, Lilly Wilkinson, 26
Thompson, Mary, *25*, 27
Thompson, Mary A., 500
Thompson, Ruth, *140*, *141*, 151, *152*, 475
Thompson, Sally, *64*, 463
Thompson, Thyra, 523
Thompson, Zenas, 26
Thomson, Thyra, *59*
Thorning-Schmidt, Helle, *268*
Thurman, Karen, *167*, 169, 177, 432, 451
Thurmond, Strom, 204, 437
Tibbetts, Margaret, 330, 332
Tilden, Laura May, 347, 484
Tilden, Samuel, 43, *384*, 387
Tillman, Benjamin, 47
Tilton, Lib, 269
Tilton, Theodore, 269
Timberlake, Clare H., 329
Tingley, Rowena P. B., *27*
Titus, Dina, *177*, 181, 485
Toal, Jean Hoefer, 360, 361, 365, 506
Tobin, Mary Ann, *64*, 465
Todd, Chuck, 282
Toles, Elsie, *39*, *55*, 56, *439*
Toliver, Mrs. T. S., 216
Topinka, Judy Baar, *63*, 457
Topping, Lucille Dyas, 26
Tousend, Grace, *24*
Towne, Marian, *80*, 86, 88, 89, 501
Townsend, Kathleen Kennedy, *55*, 222, *229*, 470
Train, George Francis, 11
Traux, Nettie, 523
Travell, Janet, 298
Tristani, Gloria, *70*, 490
Trout, Grace Wilbur, *25*
Trout, Linda Copple, 360, 361, 455
Truax, Nettie, 85, *89*
Truman, Bess, 327, 395
Truman, Harry S., 110, *149*, 150, 185, 235, 273, 275, 295, 296, 297, 311, *311*, 317, 327, 328, 329, 340, 344, *370*, *371*, 372, 379, *385*, 394, 395, 400, 407, 462, 477
Trumper, May, *39*, *55*, 56, 481

Truth, Sojourner, 5, 6, *6*, 7, 9, 10, 26, 411, 471, 473, 491
Tsongas, Nikki, *177*, 180, 472, 473
Tsongas, Paul E., 180
Tubbs Jones, Stephanie, 175–176
Tubman, Harriet, 327, 411
Tubman, William, 327
Tuck, Amy, *229*, 478
Tuck, Annabelle, 359
Turner, Sarah Lucille, 91, 93, *98*
Tweed, William "Boss," 383
Tyler, Louise M., *24*
Tyson, Laura D'Andrea, *292*, 305

U

Udall, Morris K., 104
Ueland, Clara, 26, 475
Ulmer, Fran, 222, *229*, 437, *438*
Underhill, Sarah, *25*, 459
Underwood, Sarah Lucille, 480
Unsoeld, Jolene, *163*, 165–166, 173, 198, 429, 519
Upton, Harriet Taylor, *14*, 15, *27*, 46, 389, 392
Urbahns, Grace B., *55*, 62, *63*, 459
Uren, Martha, 41

V

Valentine, Lila Meade, *28*
Vanderbilt, Alva Belmont, 491
Vanderbilt, Cornelius, 267, 287–288
Vanderlip, Mrs. Frank, 492
Van Kleeck, Mary, 49–50, 293
Van Lew, Elizabeth, *40*, 41
Van Ness, Jennie, 90–91, *97*, 488
Van Rensselaer, Maria, 213
Van Sant, Samuel R., *14*
Van Winkle, Mina, 26, 27, 487
Van Wye, May M., 91, *98*
Vardaman, James K., 135
Vare, Edwin H., 119
Vare, Flora, *115*, *117*, 119–120, 130, 503
Vazquez, Martha, 376
Velázquez, Nydia M., *167*, 169, *171*, 493
Veneman, Ann M., *291*, *294*, 307
Ventura, Jesse, 476n
Vernon, Mabel, *24*
Verveer, Melanne, 338
Vezin, Clara A., *29*
Vigil-Girón, Rebecca, *59*, 490
Vike-Feiberga, Vaira, *268*
Villalpando, Catalina Vasquez, *311*
Villard, Fanny Garrison, *27*
Violet, Arlene, 68, *69*, 73, 76–77, 505
Vogel, Sarah, *70*, 72, 495
Voinovich, George V., 378
Von Bülow, Claus, 77
Von Bülow, Sonny, 77
von Damm, Helene A., 332–333
von Suttner, Bertha, *14*
Voss, Tarquinia, *25*
Vou, Mary R., 23

SUBJECT INDEX

Boxes, figures, and tables are indicated with b, f, and t following the page number. Illustrations and photos are indicated with italicized page numbers.

BPW. *See* National Federation of Business and Professional Women's Clubs

Bradwell v. Illinois (1873), 348

Branch Davidian cult, 304

Brown v. Topeka Board of Education (1954), 153

Bush (G.H.W.) administration
  ambassadors under, 338
  cabinet positions, 300–303
  federal court appointments, 376

Bush (G.W.) administration
  ambassadors under, 337
  cabinet positions, 306–309
  secretary of State, 308–309

Business and Professional Women. *See* National Federation of Business and Professional Women's Clubs

C

Cabinet and subcabinet, 290–319. *See also specific departments*
  1933 and 1953, 294–297
  1955–1980, 297–300
  1981–1993, 300–303
  1992–2000, 303–306
  2000s, 306–311
  African Americans, 295, 299, 300, 304–305
  Asian Americans, 307
  attorneys general, 303–304, 354
  Bush (G.H.W.) administration, 300–303
  Bush (G.W.) administration, 306–309
  Children's Bureau, 290, 293
  Clinton administration, 303–306
  female U.S. treasurers, by appointment year, 311*t*
  first women cabinet-level positions, by year of department creation, 294*t*
  Hispanics, 305, 309–310
  lower levels, 290–294
  Native American schools, 290, 297
  notable appointments below cabinet level, by year, 292–293*t*
  Obama administration, 308, 309–311
  press secretaries, 305
  profiles, 312–319
  Reagan administration, 300–303
  Secretary of State, 305, 306*b*, 308–309, 337, 338
  women in, by year, 291*t*

Cable Act of 1922, 410

California
  enfranchisement, 86, 442
  federal elective officeholders, 443–444
  key facts, 442
  lieutenant governors, 229
  overview, 442
  state legislature, 443
  state representatives, 86–87
  statewide elective officeholders, 442–443
  U.S. senators, 199–200

Campaign accountability, 425

Campaign finance, 279

Carrie Chapman Catt Center, 405

Cash for Clunkers program of 2009, 180

CEA. *See* Council of Economic Advisors

Center for American Women and Politics, 405

Central Intelligence Agency (CIA), 163, 333

CFTC (Commodity Futures Trading Commission), 305

Charter Party, 248

Child labor, 293, 295

Children's Bureau, 290, 293

The Church of Jesus Christ of Latter-day Saints. *See* Latter-day Saints

CIA. *See* Central Intelligence Agency

CIO. *See* Congress of Industrial Organizations

Citizens Party, 278

Citizens United v. Federal Election Commission (2010), 223, 427

Civilian Conservation Corps, 295

Civil rights. *See also* Women's rights
  African Americans, 196
  early colonial, 1–2
  lynching, 10*b*, 193, 394, 411, 413, 419
  slavery, 322, 386
  Wyoming, 41

Civil Rights Act of 1964, 274, 406

Civil Rights Commission, 300, 301

Civil Rights Restoration Act of 1988, 163

Civil Service Commission, U.S., 86, 294, 296*b*

Civil War, 8, 348, 403, 419

Clinton administration
  cabinet positions, 303–306
  federal courts, 376–378
  national education policy, 57
  Secretary of State, 306*b*, 337
  Violence Against Women Act, 175

Colorado
  enfranchisement, 80, 444
  federal elective officeholders, 445–446
  key facts, 444–445
  overview, 444
  Republican Party, 1894, 80
  state legislature, 445
  state representatives, 80–81, 81*b*
  statewide officeholders, 445

Commerce Department, 298–299, 303

Commission on the Status of Women, 104, 153, 298, 407–409

Committee to Reelect the President (CREEP), 426

Commodity Futures Trading Commission (CFTC), 305

Concerned Women for America (CWA), 428

Congress, U.S. *See also* House of Representatives, U.S.; Senate, U.S.
  creation of, 79, 188
  defined, 139
  feminism in, 197
  women of 75th Congress, *146*

Congressional Black Caucus, 158

Congressional Caucus for Women's Issues, 156, 159

Congressional districts, reapportionment, 104, 139

Congressional Global Health Caucus, 176

Congressional Union Party, 392

Congress of Industrial Organizations (CIO), 295, 425

Connecticut
  federal elective officeholders, 447
  key facts, 446
  overview, 446
  state legislature, 447
  statewide elective officeholders, 446–447

Consent, age of, 415*b*, 416*t*, 417

Constitution, U.S.
  Fourteenth Amendment, 8–11
  Fifteenth Amendment, 8–11, 267, 270*b*, 277
  Sixteenth Amendment, 13–14
  Seventeenth Amendment, 14, 182, 188–189
  Eighteenth Amendment, 19, 21, 88, 242, 417
  Nineteenth Amendment, *84*
    background, 19
    effect of, 190
    other state action on, 22*t*
    state ratification, 21*t*, 23, 30, 88
  Congress, creation of, 79, 188
  courts, creation of, 369
  equal protection, 8–11
  federal judges, 369
  Supreme Court, creation of, 369

Constitutional Union Party, 383

Consumer Credit Protection Act of 1968, 152

Consumer Financial Protection Bureau, 310

Consumer Product Safety Commission, 298, 303

Contraception. *See* Reproductive rights

Contract with America (1994), 164, 165, 431*b*

Corruption, 243, 352*b*

Council of Economic Advisors (CEA), 305, 310

Courts. *See also* Judiciary and law practice
  appellate courts, 359
  Constitution, U.S., 369
  federal courts, 369–382. *See also* Federal courts
  jurisdiction, state courts, 359
  state courts, 359–368. *See also* State courts
  Supreme Court. *See* Supreme Court, U.S.

CREEP (Committee to Reelect the President), 426

CWA (Concerned Women for America), 428

D

Daughters of the American Revolution, 140

Dawes Act of 1887, 43

Dayton Accords, 337

Declaration of Conscience (1950), 193*b*, 194

Declaration of Sentiments (1848), 4*b*, 5

Deepwater Horizon oil spill of 2010, 179, 202

Defense Department, 296

Defense Education Act of 1958, 153

Delaware
  federal elective officeholders, 449
  key facts, 448
  overview, 448

Arizona, 227
colonial governors, 213–215
female governors
  by region, 225t
  by state, 215t
  by year, 214t
Kansas, 218–219
lieutenant governors, 228–232
  California, 229
  election variations, 230–231
  first woman elected as in each state, by
    year, 229t
  job variations, 229–230
  party affiliation, 231
  region, 231–232
  South Carolina, 232b
  Texas, 229
marriage and motherhood, 225–226
New Jersey, 219, 220b
Oregon, 219
population and, 225, 226t
powers, 213
preparation for, 230b
profiles, 233–236
regional analysis, 224–225
religion and, 226
Texas, 201, 218
unelected governors, 226–228, 228t
Wyoming, 216b
Great Depression
  child labor, 293, 295
  elections during, 58
  employment, effect on, 419
  federal activism, 297
  financial offices, 62
  political decline for women, 97, 243
  socialism, 99
  state senators, 121–124
  U.S. representatives, 144–147
  U.S. senators, 192
Great Recession, 309b, 310, 311
Greenback Party, 44, 387
Greenhouse gases, 310
Green Party, 280, 281
Gun control, 200

H
Harvard Medical School, 6
Hawaii
  federal elective officers, 454
  key facts, 453–454
  overview, 453
  state legislature, 454
  statewide elective officeholders, 454
Hawke v. Smith (1920), 24, 28
Health, Education, and Welfare Department
    (HEW), 296–297, 299, 300
Health and Human Services Department
    (HHS), 299, 300–301, 304, 310
Health care, 297, 410, 428, 431
Hispanics
  cabinet positions, 305, 309–310
  MANA, 410–411
  as U.S. treasurer, 311

History of Woman Suffrage, Volume IV
    (Anthony & Harper), 82, 322
History of Woman Suffrage, Volume VI (Harper),
    44, 85
HIV. *See* AIDS/HIV
Homeland Security Department, 310
House of Representatives, U.S., 139–187
  1920s, 141–144
    1922 and 1923, 142
    1924, 142–143
    1926-1929, 143–144
    women elected to House, 1916–1929,
      142t
  1930s, 144–147
    1930, 145
    1932 and 1933, 145–146
    1934, 146
    1936, 146
    1938 and 1939, 146–147
    women elected in, 145t
    women of 75th Congress, *146*
  1940s, 147–151
    1940, 147–148
    1941 and 1942, 148
    1944, 148–149
    1946, 149–150
    1948 and 1949, 150–151
    women elected in, 147t
  1950s, 151–154
    1950, 151
    1952, 151–152
    1954, 152–153
    1956, 153–154
    1958, 154
    pornography, 153–154
    race and racism, 152–153
    women elected in, 152t
  1960s, 154–157
    1960, 154–155
    1961 and 1962, 155
    1964, 156
    1966, 156
    1968, 156–157
    globalization, 155
    women elected in, 155t
  1970s, 157–162
    1970, 157–158
    1972, 158–160
    1973 and 1974, 160–161
    1975 and 1976, 161
    1978, 161–162
    women elected in, 157t
  1980s, 162–166
    1980, 162–163
    1982 and 1983, 163–164
    1984 and 1985, 164–165
    1986, 165
    1988 and 1989, 165–166
    women elected in, 163t
  1990s, 166–176
    1990, 166–167
    1992, 167–170
    1994, 170–173
    1996, 173–174

1998, 174–176
    women elected in, 167t
  2000s, 176–182
    2000 and 2001, 176
    2002, 176–178
    2004, 178–179
    2005 and 2006, 179–180
    2007 and 2008, 180–182
    2009 and 2010, 182
    party realignment, 182
    women elected in, 177t
  Armed Services Committee, 159b
  Black Caucus, 170
  first female House members by year of
    election, 140t
  Great Depression, 144–147
  minority women elected, by year, 171t
  before Nineteenth Amendment, 139–141
  notable women, milestones and
    achievements by year, 141t
  NOW, 157
  NWPC, 157
  profiles, 182–186
  Senate compared to, 188
  Speaker of the House, 139
  United Nations representatives from, 149
Housewife to Heretic (Johnson, S.), 278
Housing and Urban Development
    Department (HUD), 298, 299
Hoyt v. Florida (1961), 354
Humor and humorists, 272b
Hurricane Katrina, 202, 222
Hyde Amendment of 1976, 415–416

I
Idaho
  federal elective officeholders, 456
  key facts, 455
  overview, 454–455
  state legislature, 456
  state representatives, 82–83
  statewide elective officeholders, 455–456
Illinois
  federal elective officeholders, 458
  key facts, 457
  overview, 456–457
  state legislature, 457–458
  statewide elective officeholders, 457
Illinois Equal Suffrage Association, 45
Illinois Republican Women's Club, 142
Immigration and Naturalization Service, 305
Immigration Quota Act of 1924, 195
Indiana
  federal elective officeholders, 460
  key facts, 459
  overview, 458–459
  state legislature, 459–460
  statewide elective officeholders, 459
Insanity, adjudication of, 349b
Interest groups, 403–424. *See also* Political
    action committees; *specific groups*
  conservatives, 404
  establishment of major groups, by year of
    founding, 405t

ILLUSTRATION CREDITS